WORLD CENTRED ON DELHI

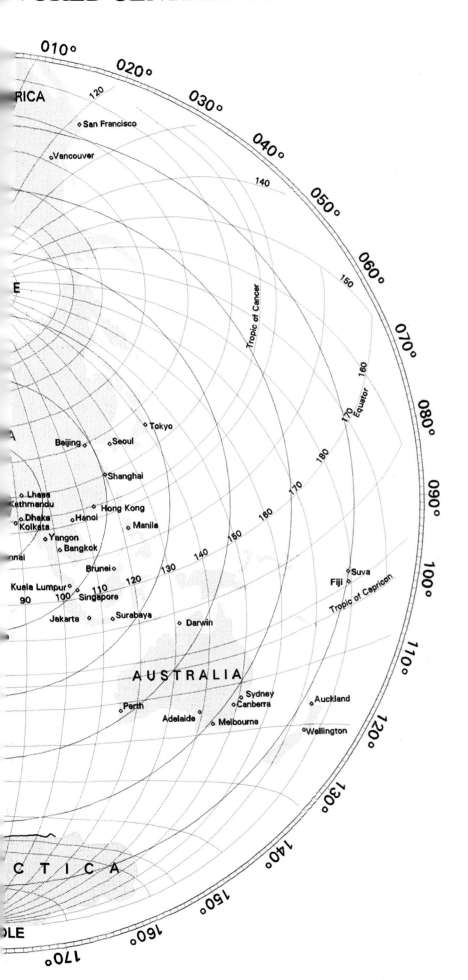

Read off the value on the graduated circle to get the true bearing to the nearest degree, of well known places radially from Delhi.

Examples :- True bearings from Delhi to San Francisco, Tokyo, Cape Town and Moscow are 015°, 065°, 226°, and 325°, respectively.

Transition
to
Eminence

The Indian Navy 1976-1990

Transition
to
Eminence

The Indian Navy 1976-1990

Vice Admiral
GM Hiranandani
PVSM, AVSM, NM, Ph D (Retd)

Published by

Principal Director of Administration
Integrated Headquarters
Ministry of Defence (Navy)
Naval Headquarters, New Delhi

in association with
Lancer Publishers

First published in India by
Lancer Publishers & Distributors
K - 36A (FF) Green Park Main, New Delhi-110016
lancerindia@vsnl.net

ISBN 81 7062 266 2

"The heights by great men reached and kept,
Were not attained by sudden flight;
But they, while their companions slept,
Were toiling upwards in the night".

This volume is dedicated to all those great men and women, in India and
abroad, who helped India's Navy to achieve what it did
as much as it is dedicated to the not-so-great, but nevertheless very
industrious, innovative and loyal officers, sailors and civilians of the Navy who
too never desisted from toiling in the night whenever the occasion demanded

एडमिरल अरूण प्रकाश
पी वी एस एम, ए वी एस एम, वीर चक्र, वी एस एम, ए डी सी

नौसेनाध्यक्ष

Admiral Arun Prakash
PVSM, AVSM, VrC, VSM, ADC

Chief of the Naval Staff

★★★★

रक्षा मंत्रालय
एकीकृत मुख्यालय
नई दिल्ली-110011
Integrated Headquarters
Ministry of Defence (Navy)
New Delhi-110011

Foreword

In keeping with the endeavour to preserve our naval tradition for posterity, Naval Headquarters are pleased to bring out the fourth volume in a series that document the Indian Navy's history. This one entitled, most appropriately, "Transition to Eminence" covers the period 1976-1990, which saw our Service emerge as a navy of substance.

The term "eminence" has been used in the title by the author with deliberation. In addition to significant deployment of India's maritime power in Sri Lanka and Maldives, this period was epochal, due as much to a series of remarkable innovations by our ship designers and builders, as to a far-sighted submarine, aircraft and ship acquisition programme. All of these were to have a significant impact on the regional balance of power.

Nothing symbolises this era better than the "Time" magazine issue dated 3rd April 1989, which carried on its cover, the caption "Super India". The purport of this hyperbolic declaration was that the world had begun to take note of India as an emerging power. Such is the symbolism of maritime power, that to substantiate this statement, the cover was illustrated with an imposing photograph of the indigenous but hybrid INS Godavari, bristling with SSM launchers!

In VAdm GM Hiranandani, the author of this volume, we are extremely fortunate to have an indefatigable researcher, who has taken great pains to unearth and record with diligence, historical facts in minute detail. While giving us the benefit of his incisive analysis, he has avoided being judgmental, and in the best tradition of historians, left the reader to largely draw his own conclusion. We are indeed indebted to him for his labours.

Certain measures have been initiated by NHQ to institutionalise historical record-keeping, and it is my earnest hope that this volume and its predecessors will now become part of a continuum of the Indian Navy's recorded history.

(Arun Prakash)
Admiral
Chief of the Naval Staff

4 December 2004
New Delhi

Acknowledgements

During the years of research that have led up to this volume, I have incurred many debts of gratitude.

Much of this volume is based on interactive interviews with personages who were directly involved with the events between 1976 and 1990. I am grateful to all the senior officers, service and civilian, and friends and colleagues who spared time to interact and share their insights.

I am indebted to the many libraries in India and abroad for extending their facilities and also to the authors, their publishers and other institutions from whose works I have quoted excerpts to present overviews of events. Credits have been given in the footnotes. Every effort has been made to contact copyright holders. The author and the publishers will be grateful for misquotes, errors and omissions to be brought to their attention.

The maps have been prepared by the National Hydrographic Office. I am grateful to the Chief Hydrographer, Rear Admiral KR Srinivasan (recently retired), and to Commander Suryajit S Kandal to whom this task was assigned and to his team of cartographers for preparing the maps so meticulously.

The photographs have been culled from naval archives and the personal collection of Commander Srikant Sharma of NHQ's Directorate of Personal Services. I am indebted to him for his support and advice on the technical as well as photographic aspects.

The staffs of the Naval History Cell and the Naval History Project put in considerable effort to help sort and compile source material. Petty Officer Writers Mangal Singh and K Vijayan, the Leading Writers and the civilian stenographers worked tirelessly to transcribe interview tapes and to prepare the manuscript of this volume. I am grateful to them all. I am particularly grateful to Naval Headquarters for providing all assistance very graciously and to the Directorates of Administration and Personal Services.

Many, many more who have not been mentioned individually, have helped. My grateful and heartfelt thanks to all of them.

My special thanks go to my wife, son, daughter and brother-in-law – to my son Manik for his support during my research in Europe and the US; to my wife Susheel, daughter Meera and my retired naval brother-in-law Captain Vijay Ramchandani for their advice on how to make the text understandable for both the lay reader and the naval scholar; and most of all to my wife for tolerating so patiently the long hours that the writing of history entails. The full extent of what I owe to my wife is immeasurable.

Preface

Preamble

The history of the Indian Navy covering the period 1976 to 1990 is fascinating for several reasons. This period laid the foundation for its emergence as the eminent Navy of the South Asian region.

The international competition to 'sell arms' presented the Navy with the opportunity to acquire the latest technology from both the Soviet Union and the West, indigenise through transfer of technology and increase self reliance. New technologies drove innovation in indigenous shipbuilding concepts, in tactical doctrines, in personnel policies and in maintenance, refit and logistic procedures.

In the preceding decade, the transition had been from British acquisitions to Russian acquisitions, from guns to missiles, from steam propulsion to gas turbines and from analogue to digital electronics.

Between 1976 and 1990, the transition was qualitatively different. A whole generation of ingenious middle rank officers had developed the skills to probe suppliers as to the whys and wherefores of what was being offered. There was effervescence in tactical and technical thought. There was sharper focus on how effectively the new systems would meet operational requirements and how they would perform in tropical conditions.

Specialist teams mushroomed – Weapon Testing and Tuning Teams, Sonar Evaluation Teams, Harbour Acceptance Trials, Sea Acceptance Trials, Workup Teams, Weapon Analysis Units, Tactical Committees, Tactical Evaluation Groups, Machinery Testing and Tuning Teams, Diesel Testing and Tuning Teams, Gas Turbine Testing and Tuning Teams, Ship Maintenance Authority – the list was endless. Every working level strove to obtain and sustain peak performance.

This pressure to keep abreast of technological change generated stresses. It besieged the time-tested importance of leadership and shifted the priority to technical ability. Except for a few who had the insight to sense what was happening and 'manage' the change, the remainder sailed on dutifully, doing their best to cope with technology.

It became habitual to theorise about the peripheral relevance of naval traditions when compared to mastering technology, to complain about the inadequate quality of intake, to bemoan the slump in discipline, to criticise the tempo of acquisitions and to attribute the adverse effects on morale to all these external factors.

Junior officers started losing touch with their senior officers. Senior sailors started losing touch with their junior officers. Junior sailors started losing touch with their senior sailors. The edifice of leadership and man management came under strain. The expectation that seminars, lectures and management nostrums would relieve the strain turned out to be a mirage. Overall, there was a rise in cynicism.

The Navy owes a great deal to that handful of senior officers who were able to rise above this state of affairs. By their upright stand on contentious issues and their deft management of slender naval budgets, they were able to lay strong foundations for the future Navy.

To give the reader a quick overview, the key sections of this volume have been summarised below. This will allow the reader to choose areas of interest at will, while saving the rest for more leisurely reading.

Towards Eminence

Eminence is contextual. This section provides an overview of the growth of the Navy between 1976 and 1990. It provides also a perspective of why, since the 14th century, more than one foreign power has sought to dominate the Indian Ocean and how motives and manipulations have remained unchanged over the centuries.

Overview of the Growth of the Navy 1976 to 1990

During this period, the Navy's growth was affected by three crises, each of which delayed the import of naval equipment and the implementation of approved projects.

The first crisis followed the 1973 Arab-Israel war when the price of oil rose very sharply. The second crisis from 1987 onwards originated from the failure of the monsoon in 1986 and the prolonged drought and financial austerity that ensued.

Many of the Navy's ships, submarines and aircraft were of Soviet origin. The third crisis started in the late 1980s when the Soviet Union started re-structuring its economy, freeing its industry from centralised control, requiring factories to become financially self sustaining by charging international prices and requiring payment in dollars. The deliveries of Soviet equipment and spares were disrupted. It took some years to restore normalcy, partly because India herself was going through a financial crisis.

Viewed in retrospect, these crises were, for the Navy, a blessing in disguise. Though they were a cause for concern at the time, they compelled the Navy to innovate, to develop indigenous substitutes and to make better use of its resources.

External Naval Presence in the Indian Ocean

Over the past 600 years, naval power has invariably come from outside the Indian Ocean – the Chinese in the 15th century, the Portuguese in the 16th century, the Dutch, the English and the French in the 17th and 18th centuries. The British predominance in the 19th century lasted until the middle of the 20th century after which the United States took over.

Neither motives nor manipulations have changed for non-regional countries to maintain their naval presence in the Indian Ocean. In the earlier centuries, the Europeans needed oriental aromatics, textiles and spices. In the 21st century, the world needs Persian Gulf oil.

The Europeans did not enter the Indian Ocean to acquire territory. They were in search of a cheaper sea route to carry oriental commodities to Europe.[1] Since monopoly increased profits, the early Europeans were monopolists. They were not imperialists. Empire came later, as a safeguard for monopoly.

The long sailing expeditions from Europe to the Indian Ocean had to be financed by what is known today as 'venture capital' and were expected to provide a 'return on investment'. Whilst the Portuguese expeditions were partly a royal monopoly and partly financed by merchants, the 'East India Companies' set up by the Dutch, the English and the French were private trading companies, started and financed by rich merchants under 'charters' granted by their governments.

In their competition to secure monopoly rights in the highly profitable, well established intra-Indian Ocean textile and spice trade, these mercantile trading companies found that by selectively taking sides in internecine feuds between local Asian rulers, they could progressively acquire exclusive trading rights in territories which could be supported from the sea.[2] Soon, it became worthwhile for them to set up private local armies and arm their ships to assist the success of their protégés.

Almost every war in Europe bred a contest between the armed merchantmen of the 'East India Companies', supported whenever necessary by their national navies. These naval contests were essentially to safeguard economic well-being. The profit of their company underlay each nation's geo-economic interest in the Indian Ocean and determined foreign policy.

Today, the rationale is no different. American and European oil companies have extensive investments in Persian Gulf oil whose importance for their economy compels the deployment of their navies in the Indian Ocean.

Over the centuries, in almost all cases, the greed of Company employees defrauded Company profits. This led to the taking over of each Company by its Government and the conversion of the territory over which it exercised trade monopoly into a colony. The colony gradually became the source of raw materials for the factories being spawned in Europe's 18th century Industrial Revolution. In turn, the colony became a cosseted market for the products of its colonial ruler's factories. The responsibility for the security of distant colonies passed from each Company's armed merchantmen to each nation's Navy. Mutually expedient political and naval alliances between the colonising powers safeguarded their maritime trade from disproportionate depletion.

After Europe's Napoleonic wars ended with the Congress of Vienna in 1815, Britain became the world's predominant naval power. By the middle of the 19th century, India became the hub and the centre-piece of British power in Asia.[3]

To cope with threats to India from landward, Afghanistan and Tibet were crafted into buffer states between Tsarist Russia and Manchu China.

India's first war of independence in 1857 compelled Britain to formally take over the governance of India and disestablish its East India Company.

Britain's Navy assumed strategic responsibility for the Indian Ocean. It developed naval bases where its warships could refuel (initially with coal and later with oil), replenish fresh water and provisions, carry out essential maintenance and be docked without having to return all the way to Britain.

---

1. Caravan transportation by the Central Asian 'Silk Route' had become expensive because of the tolls imposed by the Ottoman Turks who straddled these routes.

2. Internecine feuding and squabbling is a universal facet of human nature. It led to the endless wars for empire between the dynasties of Europe. It led also to the colonisation of Asia, Africa and the Americas.

3. See Reference Note No 2, page 410.

The base in:	controlled:
Simonstown (South Africa)	the choke point around the Cape of Good Hope.
Aden	the choke point at the southern entrance to the Red Sea and traffic through the Suez Canal.
Bahrain	the sea lane through the Persian Gulf.
Trincomalee (Ceylon)	the sea lane across the North Indian Ocean.
Singapore	the choke point at the southern entrance to the Straits of Malacca.

The core of British naval strategy was to prevent rival powers from establishing a naval base in the Indian Ocean – without access to a friendly base, no hostile warship could operate in this oceanic expanse for any length of time.

During the 1914-18 World War, raids by the German cruiser *Emden* sank merchant ships and generally paralysed shipping in the North Indian Ocean.[4]

During the 1939-45 World War, Japan occupied India's Andaman and Nicobar Islands in the Bay of Bengal. Japanese air power, both shore based and aircraft carrier based, inflicted heavy losses on British warships off Singapore, Colombo and Trincomalee and forced the British Fleet to withdraw to Madagascar off the east coast of Africa.[5]

After each of these two 'World Wars' of the 20th century, earlier empires dissolved. The victors created new nation-states.. After the second of these wars, colonies obtained independence and two powers emerged to contest for global ideological dominance – the United States of America and the Union of Soviet Socialist Republics.[6]

During the Cold War that lasted from 1947 (immediately after the 1939-45 War ended) until 1991 (when the Soviet Union fragmented), new conglomerations were shaped under the headship of these two powers. In the mid 1960s, Britain announced its decision to gradually withdraw from the Indian Ocean, in step with the United States taking over.

In the background of the Cold War and to safeguard against interruptions in the flow of Persian Gulf oil, the United States leased the island of Diego Garcia from Britain.[7] The Soviet Union countered by deploying ships to the Indian Ocean. With the winding down of the Cold War in the end 1980s, the Soviet Navy withdrew, leaving the US Navy as the predominant naval power which it remains to this day.

In the 1990s, two economically resurgent nations emerged in the Orient – India in the South Asian region and China in the East Asian region. Despite their differing profiles, the Navies of both nations have come to be regarded with respect.

Today, global interest in the Indian Ocean centres on the oil and gas resources of the Persian Gulf. Nations whose economies are critically dependant on the uninterrupted flow of this oil have a strong interest in ensuring that this region does not fall under the sway of states potentially hostile to their well-being. There is basis also for unease, particularly where international straits are located. The Straits of Hormuz, of Bab el Mandeb, of Malacca, and the Mozambique Channel are zones where the seaways narrow to an extent that makes it easy for amorphous 'non-state' entities to dislocate the movement of tankers carrying petroleum products and ships carrying high value cargo.

India's geo-strategic significance is evident from the Equidistant Map of the World Centred on Delhi. India encounters Russia and China in the north, the Persian Gulf in the west and Southeast Asia in the east. In the North Indian Ocean extending from the coast of Africa to the coast of Malaysia, India is the largest, stable, respected, multi-ethnic democracy. It does not have any overseas territorial interests. It has a modern efficient Army, Navy and Air Force. It is accepted as a rising world power having the potential for a larger regional role in the years ahead.[8]

Today, bilateral agreements foresee cooperation in protecting the sea lines of communication. Navies of the United States, Russia, France, Britain, Southeast Asian and Indian Ocean countries look forward, just much as the Indian Navy does, to holding joint exercises and building bridges of friendship.

---

4. See Reference Note No 3, page 411.

5. See Reference Note No 5, page 413.

6. In the 19th century, 'liberalist' European concern for the welfare of the underclass of 'workers' and 'peasants' had led to the emergence of the ideologies of 'Socialism' and 'Communism', which advocated 'class war' between the 'exploiting capitalist class' and the 'exploited working class'. This set the stage for the 20th century's global ideological confrontation between 'the rich, imperialist, capitalist, colonising, exploiting classes' and the 'exploited worker/peasant and poor/colonised classes'.

7. Located in the middle of the Indian Ocean, Diego Garcia's huge protected anchorage gave it the potential of a ship, submarine and air base. The island's sparse plantation labour was relocated to Mauritius and thereby removed all possibility of political agitation.

8. "The US increasingly regards India as the focus of its interests in South Asia. Over the longer term, India is regarded as a more stable and regional partner". (Excerpt from the *Strategic Survey 2001-2002* by the International Institute for Strategic Studies, London)

Towards Self Reliance

Eminence is relative. Between 1976 and 1990, India's Navy grew to be the largest and strongest in South Asia. The acquisitions from abroad synergised with innovations in warship design and production.

Innovation in Warship Design and Indigenous R & D

The period 1976-90 was lively and exciting, both for innovation in design and for self reliance.

New ships entered service at a brisk pace, along with their new sonars, radars, electronic warfare systems, missiles, torpedoes, propulsion and power generation systems. Few navies could have been so fortunate as to acquire at the same time such a wide variety of technologically modern equipment. The Navy's gifted young officers grasped the opportunity. The results, in the areas of 'Warship Design and Production' and of 'Research & Development', were beyond expectations.

By bold improvisations, Russian, European and indigenous systems and equipment were successfully integrated and installed in Indian hulls. This process started in 1976, when the entire missile and close-range gun system of a 200-tonne Russian missile boat was disconnected and re-installed in a 15-year old British anti submarine frigate along with the latest Italian electronic warfare systems, thereby giving the Fleet an ocean-going, missile-warfare-capable frigate.

A few years later, it was decided to fit the entire missile and gun system, identical to that of the latest 800-tonne Russian rocket boats[9] then being acquired, along with indigenous and European equipment, in a hull design evolved from the preceding Leander class frigates. The outcome was the three Godavari class frigates of the 1980s.

Once the intricacies had been mastered of interfacing electrical and electronic equipment, regardless of their origin, voltage and frequency, there was no looking back.

Appreciative of the success of Indian innovation, the Russians offered their latest weapon systems for the series of ships that followed – the 1500-tonne missile corvettes of the Khukri class, the 6500-tonne missile destroyers of the Delhi class and the 4000-tonne missile frigates of the Brahmaputra class.

Side by side with these innovations in warship design, the Naval R & D laboratories developed sensors, weapons and systems better suited to India's tropical climate conditions and maximising indigenous content.

The outstanding naval R & D project of this period was the APSOH sonar, specially designed for hot and humid tropical conditions and proved at sea in Indian waters for a full year during extensive trials. Its derivatives continue to be fitted in the Navy's latest ships, twenty years after it was first developed. Less spectacular, but equally important R & D developments for the Navy were the ongoing development, and improvement, of the sensors, weapons systems and munitions already in service.

The Air Arm

There were numerous developments in the Naval Air Arm during the fifteen years between 1976 and 1990.

A second aircraft carrier, *Viraat*, and a wide variety of aircraft and helicopters equipped with the latest sensors and weapons were acquired.

Vikrant underwent two modernisations, in preparation for embarking the new Sea Harrier fighter aircraft and the new Mk 42 B Seaking ASW helicopters.

The 'maritime reconnaissance' role was transferred from the Air Force to the Navy in 1976 with the taking over of the Air Force Super Constellations. The acquisition in 1977 of the MRASW Ilyushin (IL) 38s from the Soviet Union marked the rebirth of the shore-based arm of naval aviation.[10] In due course, the longer range and better equipped Long Range Maritime Patrol Tupolev (TU) 142s replaced the Super Connies.

The combat capability of the Air Arm leapfrogged from the technology of the 1950s to that of the 1980s:

- The new sensors were the dunking sonars and sonobuoys in the Russian Kamov and British Seaking helicopters, and the Russian IL and TU maritime aircraft, the Magnetic Anomaly Detectors in the Russian ILs and Kamovs, the electronic warfare systems in the British Mk 42 B Seakings and Sea Harriers and the Russian ILs and TUs, and the modern radars in all these aircraft and helicopters.

- The new weapons were the French air to air missiles in the Sea Harriers, the British anti ship Sea Eagle missiles in the Sea Harriers and Mk 42 B Seakings, the Italian A 244 and the Russian anti submarine homing torpedoes in the helicopters and the anti submarine depth bombs in the Kamovs.

---

9. Known in Western naval parlance as 'Nanuchkas'.

10. The amphibious Sealand aircraft had phased out in the 1960s.

- New naval air stations were commissioned. They made more complete the sea areas covered by naval reconnaissance. At the older air stations, the runways were lengthened and strengthened to operate the new aircraft and the naval air station facilities were modernised.

- Training syllabi were updated and training facilities were expanded. Simulators were acquired for training Sea Harrier pilots, TU ASW teams and Seaking Mk 42 B maintenance personnel.

- New aircraft maintenance workshops were established at the air stations where the squadrons were based.

The Submarine Arm

There were equally significant developments in Navy's Submarine Arm.

In the early 1970s, evaluation had commenced of European submarines to decide which of these best met the Navy's requirements for commencing submarine construction in India. This evaluation culminated in the late 1970s with the short-listing of the German HDW 1500 submarine and the Swedish Kockums 45 B submarine. The German HDW 1500 was selected after prolonged technical evaluations and competitive commercial negotiations. Contracts were signed in December 1981 for two submarines to be built in Germany followed by two to be built in Mazagon Docks, with an option clause for two more to be built in India.

To learn all aspects of submarine design, construction, overseeing, factory acceptance and sea trials and to facilitate transfer of technology, personnel from the Navy and from Mazagon Docks were deputed to Germany whilst the first two submarines were being constructed in Germany. These two submarines arrived from Germany in 1987.

The 3rd and 4th submarines built in Mazagon Docks commissioned in 1992 and 1994.

Negotiations for the 5th and 6th submarines were discontinued in 1987 due to a combination of cost escalation and resource constraints.

The performance of the HDW submarines fully met the Navy's operational requirements. This was as much a tribute to Indian learning skills and meticulous insistence on quality as to the thoroughness of German training and transfer of technology.

During this period, the studies that had commenced in the 1960s on nuclear propulsion were continued. To better understand the technology, it was decided in the early 1980s to lease a nuclear propelled submarine from the Soviet Union for three years. The crew underwent training in Russia. *INS Chakra* operated in Indian waters from 1988 to 1991. During these three years, valuable understanding was acquired of nuclear submarine culture, the practical aspects of handling nuclear power plants afloat and anti submarine operations against nuclear propelled submarines.

The Submarine Arm had started with eight submarines from Russia – four Kalvari class in 1968-69 and four Vela class in 1973-74. Due to the increased corrosion experienced in warm saline tropical waters and the deferment of 6-yearly refits because the repair facilities in Visakhapatnam Dockyard were not ready, the deterioration in the material state of the first four submarines was tackled on two fronts:

- Submarines started being sent back to Russia for 6-yearly repairs. Concurrently, 6-yearly repairs were commenced in Visakhapatnam with Russian assistance, using whatever limited facilities were available. It took some years for the situation to stabilise. Between 1975 and 1992, five submarines underwent 6-yearly repairs in Russia and six submarines underwent 6-yearly repairs in Visakhapatnam.

- Discussions were initiated with the Soviet side for successors to the earlier eight submarines. These culminated in the acquisition of the eight 877 EKM submarines between 1986 and 1990.[11]

Submarine Arm projects were not restricted to Europe and Russia. A landmark deal was the VLF transaction, with an American firm. When submerged, submarines can only receive wireless messages on Very Low Frequency (VLF). The discussions that had been in progress with the Soviet Union and the United States culminated in 1984 with the selection of an American company, in collaboration with an Indian company, to design, manufacture, install and commission the VLF transmitting station; it was commissioned in 1990.

The Indo-Russian Naval Interaction

The naval acquisitions from the Soviet Union had started in 1965 when the Navy's traditional supplier, the British Navy, because of its own constraints, was unable to meet the Navy's requirements for more powerful destroyers and the latest conventionally propelled submarines.

---

11. Known in Western naval parlance as the 'Kilo' class.

The initial acquisitions of ships and submarines from Russia had been designed for the Russian Navy, which operated in a cold and dry climate and in cold, low salinity seas. They had not been designed to operate in the hot humid climate and the warm, saline and highly corrosive seas typical of the tropics. As the Navy gained experience of operating Russian vessels in tropical conditions, it identified the essential alterations and additions required to 'tropicalise' the Russian designs.

Each vessel was covered by a twelve-month guarantee period during which the Russian 'guarantee specialists', deputed to India by the respective 'Original Equipment Manufacturers' (OEM) factories, rectified all shortcomings and replenished all the spare parts consumed. The feed back by these specialists to their respective factories in Russia reinforced Naval Headquarters' projections to the Russian side of the essential improvements. As a result, each successor series of Russian acquisitions gradually became better than their predecessors.

The Inter Governmental Agreements for the supply of ships, submarines and aircraft catered also for their associated infrastructure. These encompassed facilities for the maintenance, repair and refit of equipment, the storage, maintenance and preparation of weapons, the training of crews in schools fitted with identical equipment and simulators on which the crews could practice operating procedures and tactics.

The Navy's successful operations during the 1971 Indo-Pakistan War led to two positive developments:

● The 1973 and 1975 Defence Reviews recommended, and approval was accorded, for the Navy's proposals for acquiring modern Russian ships, submarines and aircraft.

● The Soviet side responded positively to the Navy's requests for better equipment in future Russian acquisitions and for the installation of Russian weapons in Indian-built hulls, interfaced with European and indigenous equipment.

'Hybridisation' began with the fitment in the 1960 vintage, British anti submarine frigate, *Talwar*, of a surface to surface missile systems removed *en bloc* from a Russian missile boat. Talwar's installation was completed in 1975. The next step was the installation of Russian radar and missile systems in the Godavari class missile frigates of Project 16. The next step, again in consultation with the Russian Ministry of Shipbuilding and its Design Bureaus, was the installation of the latest Soviet systems in the Khukri class missile corvettes of Project 25, the Delhi class missile destroyers of Project 15 and the Brahmaputra class missile frigates of Project 16 A.

Concurrently licensed production commenced of the gas-turbined missile boats of Project 1241 RE.

By 1987, this wide scope of cooperation in warship building required monitoring at high levels. Agreements had to be signed at the right time, to ensure that deliveries were effected to the warship building yards – Mazagon Docks in Bombay, Garden Reach in Calcutta and Goa Shipyard – at the right time to avoid delays in their construction schedules. A Joint Indo-Soviet Working Group on Shipbuilding was set up to smooth the way and clear problems in the licensed production of 1241 REs and the design assistance for the fitment of Soviet weapon systems in indigenous warships. It was chaired jointly by the Deputy Minister of Shipbuilding of the USSR and India's Secretary of Defence Production.

There were some issues that figured repeatedly in the naval interaction between the Indian and Russian sides between 1976 and 1990. Some were well resolved. Others could not be resolved.

● The Indian Navy's projections for better and better sensors, weapons and equipment, all suitably modified for Indian conditions, to be fitted in successive acquisitions of ships, submarines and aircraft.

The maximum headway was made in this regard.

● Repair Facilities for the Soviet Acquisitions.

The crux of the problem was how best to keep the Russian-supplied ships, submarines and aircraft properly maintained and repaired until the requisite refit facilities ashore were fully established at the respective home-ports.

Some headway was made on this issue. By the 1980s, the essential repair and maintenance facilities were set up at the respective naval ports and air stations from where these ships, submarines and aircraft actually operated. With increased foreknowledge of the equipment and weapons being inducted, it became possible to augment the facilities that had already been created instead of setting up new facilities.

In the case of submarines, where 'safety when dived' was paramount, the Soviet side helped by undertaking their 6-yearly Medium Repairs in the Soviet Union, whenever this became inescapable.

● Participation in the Soviet State Committee Trials Prior to the Delivery Acceptance Trials of Ships and Submarines Constructed for the Indian Navy.

Based on the experience gained over the years in successive Delivery Acceptance Trials, the Indian side considered it essential that Indian naval specialist officers participate in the initial Soviet State Committee Acceptance Trials. This would avoid dissension on performance parameters during the subsequent Delivery Acceptance Trials. It would also enable the Indian specialists to learn and understand how, in later years, to restore peak performance after equipment had been overhauled during major refits.

No headway could be made on this issue. Under the constitutional law of the Soviet Union, it was not permissible for foreign naval personnel to be allowed into Soviet warship building yards where warships were also being constructed for the Soviet Navy. Similar considerations limited the Indian side's requests for Naval Dockyard civilian workers and supervisors to be allowed access into Soviet equipment factories for being given in depth, on-the-job, hands-on, deep-repair training.

Instead, the Soviet side did permit Naval and civilian specialists to see and learn how Indian submarines were refitted in their Vladivostok yard. Special arrangements were also made for Indian personnel to be trained in the deep repair/overhaul of major equipment like gas turbines, the major repairs of a Rajput class ship, etc in Special Training Centres set up for the Indian Navy.

● Model Contract.

In accordance with the Soviet procedure, a separate contract had to be processed for ships and separate contracts for their infrastructure. The Indian side felt it preferable to formulate a 'Model Contract' which, in a comprehensive document for each acquisition, would dovetail the timeframes for the delivery of the vessels and their exploitation documentation in the English language, with the timely delivery of equipment for their refit facilities and for the timely availability of the entire spectrum of refit spares, refit documentation etc. This would help to eliminate the difficulties resulting from separate un-synchronised contracts.

No headway could be made on this issue. The insurmountable problem was that too many ministries were involved and under Soviet procedure, each ministry had to draw up its own contract in terms of financial clauses, delivery dates, documentation, guarantee specialists etc.

● Timely Indenting and Delivery of Spares.

From the logistics point of view, problems were serious enough to require attention at very high levels. The Soviet Union's centralised, state-controlled, industrial system required meticulous compliance with Russian codification and nomenclature when preparing indents for spares in the Russian language.

On the one hand, the Russian side considered it imperative that requirements be precisely forecast and indents forwarded in good time to mesh with the Soviet Union's annual and five-year production plans.

On the other hand, India's rigorous scrutiny of the financial aspects of every indent invariably took time because it required item-wise costing and this was not readily available from the Russian factories.

Apart from the language barrier (very few in the Indian Navy knew or spoke Russian), the fact that in every organization, everywhere, logistics is considered so mundane an activity as to be delegated to somebody else, the Indo-Russian naval interaction in the field of logistics tended to be prickly, though without any *malafides* on either side.

From the mid 1980s onwards, the Soviet Union's economic restructuring started freeing their factories from central control and required them to become self-sufficient for resources. This resulted in an unforeseen interruption in the supply of the spares earlier indented. It took some time for new arrangements to be concluded with individual 'original equipment manufacturers/factories. In some cases, Russian production lines had closed down, leaving the Indian Navy with the difficult choice whether to indigenise obsolescent spares or to cannibalise. In other cases, allegations of excessive indenting at prices inflated by OEMs and middlemen led to suspension of approvals for indents until Boards of Enquiry could recommend how loopholes should be closed.

The chapter on the Russian Acquisitions discusses how the basic goodwill that has been the foundation of Indo-Russian naval cooperation surmounted these difficulties and fostered an embargo-free naval relationship.

Operations

The induction of new ships, submarines, aircraft and helicopters from 1976 onwards and the evaluation in Indian waters of their capabilities enabled the Navy to evolve and prove at sea, the tactics appropriate for its unique mix of platforms, sensors and weapons.

Carefully structured exercises helped to pin down inadequacies and provide feedback to the R & D laboratories.

The two significant operations were Operations Pawan and Cactus.

Operation Pawan in Support of the IPKF in Sri Lanka – 1987 to 1990

Sri Lanka's location astride the main shipping routes of the Indian Ocean and its proximity to the Indian mainland has strategic significance for the security of India's southern seaboard. The political situation is complex – it has entailed the Navy's involvement for over 30 years.

Operation Pawan started with the induction of the IPKF on 30 July 1987. The de-induction started in August 1989 and by October 1989, the bulk of the IPKF had withdrawn. Operation Pawan terminated on 24 March 1990, when the final contingent of the IPKF sailed out of Trincomalee on board ships of the Eastern Fleet. When the last elements withdrew, there still had been no solution of the political problem that had necessitated the induction, nor indeed has a solution emerged till the date of publication.

In round figures, over 1200 deaths and 3500 wounded was the price that the officers and men of India's Peacekeeping Force paid to help a neighbour in distress.

Though often criticised, Operation Pawan achieved the objectives that had been listed by India's Prime Minister Rajiv Gandhi in his letter to Sri Lanka's President Jayawardene when the Indo-Sri Lankan Accord was signed on 29 July 1987:

"You had, during the course of our discussions, agreed to meet some of India's concerns as follows:

- Your Excellency and myself will reach an early understanding about the relevance and employment of foreign military and intelligence personnel with a view to ensure that such presence will not prejudice Indo-Sri Lankan relations.

- Trincomalee or any other ports in Sri Lanka will not be made available for military use by any country in a manner prejudicial to India's interests.

- The work of restoring and operating the Trincomalee oil tank farm will be undertaken as a joint venture between India and Sri Lanka.

- Sri Lanka's agreement with foreign broadcasting organisations will be reviewed to ensure that any facilities set up by them in Sri Lanka are used solely as public broadcasting facilities and not for any military or intelligence purposes."

During Operation Pawan, the wear and tear on naval ships was substantial. The usage of ships exceeded stipulated norms by 50%. Despite the heavy toll that it took in terms of wear and tear, it was invaluable for its experience of low intensity conflict and inducting troops over uncharted beaches.

Personnel stood up well to the multifarious tasks of providing operational and logistic support for the IPKF, maintaining round the clock ship and air patrols in the Palk Strait and along Sri Lanka's eastern seaboard and transhipping refugees, many of whom had to be given medical attention at sea.

Immediately after the last contingent of the IPKF had been de-inducted from Sri Lanka, ships and aircraft of India's Navy and Coast Guard were deployed for Operation Tasha to patrol the Palk Strait to minimise the movement of militants and their material between Sri Lanka and India. Operation Tasha started in April 1990 and continues to this day.

In the years after 1990, India has abstained from further direct involvement and has encouraged every peace-making effort for reconciliation between the Sri Lankan Government and the LTTE.

The lessons of Operation Pawan are instructive for future missions of a humanitarian but political nature, which the Navy will be called upon to undertake, or assist, as it grows in eminence.

Operation Cactus in Support of the Maldivian Government 1988

Whilst Operation Pawan was in full swing, a crisis erupted in Male, the capital of the Maldive Islands. On the night of 2/3 November 1988, between 300 and 500 armed, Tamil / Sinhala-speaking mercenaries landed in Male harbour by boats from a mother ship and captured key locations. During this attempted coup, President Gayoom went into hiding and, in the early hours of 3 November, sought India's help and immediate intervention.

During the next 24 hours, the nearest naval ships were diverted to Male at maximum speed, naval reconnaissance aircraft established surveillance over the Maldive Islands. On the night of 3rd /4th, Air Force aircraft landed troops on Male's airport on Hulule Island. On learning that these troops were headed for Male, the mercenaries hijacked the merchant vessel 'Progress Light', taking Maldivian VIP hostages with them, and set course for Sri Lanka. In Male, law and order was restored as soon as Indian troops arrived on the morning of the 4th.

INS Godavari was diverted towards Colombo to embark, by helicopter, the team of negotiators that had been flown from Male to Colombo.

Reconnaissance aircraft shadowed all moving contacts during the night of 3rd /4th. At first light on the morning of the 4th, the aircraft confirmed the detection of *Progress*

Light and homed *INS Betwa* as soon as it arrived on the night of 4th /5th. *INS Godavari* who had by then embarked the negotiators from Colombo arrived by midday on the 5th.

Negotiations for the release of the hostages made no progress. The mercenary leader insisted that the *Progress Light* would proceed only to Colombo and demanded intervention by an international team. The Sri Lankan Government intimated that the rebel ship would not be allowed to enter Sri Lankan waters. The Maldivian Government desired that the Progress Light should not be allowed to proceed to Colombo.

Throughout the 5th, the negotiators were unable to dissuade *Progress Light* from steaming towards Colombo. On the 6th morning, when *Progress Light* was 60 miles from Colombo, pressure commenced with small arms fire, followed by air-dropped depth charges ahead of the ship, followed by a gun broadside across the bows. When, despite a final warning, *Progress Light* still refused to stop, a broadside was fired on the forward cargo section. The ship stopped immediately.

Naval teams boarded the ship and rescued the hostages. Godavari's helicopter evacuated the injured hostages to the Military Hospital at Trivandrum. The mercenaries were handed over to the authorities at Male. *Progress Light*, already listing and flooding, capsized on the 7th morning, 56 miles southwest of Colombo.

Assistance Rendered by the Navy in Peacetime

Integral to the Navy's day to day operations are the myriad facets of the assistance that the Navy provides in peacetime at sea and in the island territories. Together with the Army and the Air Force, the Navy assists in disaster relief operations, particularly in the calamitous cyclones that devastate the coastal areas every year.

Personnel

A number of problem areas coalesced to compel introspection and reform. On the one hand, the scope of innovation and reform in personnel management policies was circumscribed by inter service equivalence and statutory regulations. On the other hand, the urgency of providing the manpower to man the new acquisitions generated resistance to change.

The crux of the problem was:

Having started to replace its ageing ships, submarines and aircraft with technologically better Russian, European and indigenous equivalents, the need increased for the Navy to have technically educated manpower in larger numbers and for them to build up and conserve expertise.

The prevalent recruitment, training and promotion process was not yielding quality personnel in the numbers that the Navy needed.

In the job market, service in the Armed Forces was no longer considered attractive. Emoluments, frequent transfers and career prospects were seen to be inferior to those in the civil sector.

Conserving expertise on hi-tech equipment was a knotty problem especially in warships and to a lesser extent in the Air and Submarine Arms. The need was to arrive at the right balance between two incompatible requirements, each of which was logical but whose consequence was sub-optimal:

- The promotion regulations stipulated that promotion depended on demonstrated proficiency at sea. This required that every officer and sailor be appointed to a ship for 'sea time' in successive ranks and be given the opportunity for his fitness to be assessed for promotion. The consequence was a continuous movement of personnel between shore and ship assignments in short tenures.

- Hi-tech naval equipment required expert handling. Expertise on equipment was best developed by continued and repetitive association. Continuous movement of personnel in and out of ships had two adverse effects –it conflicted with the need for continued association and it resulted in personnel of inadequate experience repeatedly 'learning on the job' to the detriment of operational equipment.

The 'sea time vs expertise' dilemma first became crucial in the mid 1960s when the Navy began to acquire ships from Russia. In these ships, the number of bunks was less than what was required to accommodate the Indian Navy's trades / specialisations. Every possible measure was tried to resolve the problem:

- Categorising personnel as 'seagoing' and 'non-seagoing'. This was resented by those categorised as 'non-seagoing'.

- Channelising personnel into British and Russian equipment 'streams'. This helped for a few years but could not arrest the dilution of expertise.

- Lengthening tenures at sea. This conflicted with the need to give 'timely sea time' to avoid demotivating personnel on account of delayed promotions.

- Installing complete systems in training schools every time new equipment entered service. This became prohibitively expensive.

- Imparting 'Pre-Commissioning Training' (PCT) just prior to joining a ship. This required that sufficient manpower be available to assemble an incoming crew to undergo PCT before relieving the outgoing crew. In an expanding Navy, there just wasn't enough manpower.

These difficulties in conserving expertise led to the unwanted ripple effects that have been discussed in the chapters on Manning, Training, Maintenance and Logistics.

Some reforms like 'Fixed Commissions' and 'Operator-Maintainer' could only make limited headway. Shortages in manpower constrained adoption of 'Fixed Commissions'. Resistance to change constrained 'Operator-Maintainer'.

It took time to strike the right balance. Pay Commissions improved emoluments. Cadre Reviews improved career prospects. The Navy detached itself from the Army's recruitment organisation and soon better educated and better quality manpower began to join the sailor cadre. Innovative schemes for officer and artificer entry helped to attract volunteers of the required calibre in sufficient numbers. Training was revitalised. The decision to train each man for his next job at sea eliminated deadwood in syllabi. Increased availability of family accommodation and schooling facilities and longer tenures in shore billets helped to induce experienced personnel to stay on in service.

Challenges of Change

While the previous sections deal with the effervescence in tactical and technical thought that led the Indian Navy to eminence in South Asia, this section addresses some of the challenges that accompanied this change.

The urge to keep abreast of technological change strained the traditional edifice of leadership and man management. It besieged the time-tested importance of leadership and shifted the priority to technical ability.

There were many examples of institutions wearing down, with undesirable consequences:

- The decay of well established, and statutory, procedures that underpinned naval leadership – the Divisional System, Evening Quarters, Divisions and Rounds.

- The neglect of drab chores like hull maintenance on the reasoning that within the working hours available, the Navy's over-riding priority had to be technical proficiency.

- The resistance to grapple with difficult issues like Operator-Maintainer or Maintainer-Operator, ostensibly on the grounds that the change would be too difficult to manage, which led to the over-manning of ships.

- The inability, in the field of anti submarine warfare, to compel the fraternities in the surface ships, the submarines and the naval air arm to interact constructively and evolve the best way of detecting and killing hostile submarines. Instead, each fraternity succumbed to the temptation of one-upmanship and, during exercises at sea, exaggerated their claims of effectiveness.

Apart from such operational and leadership issues, there were events that attracted adverse public attention:

- The allegations in 1987 of kickbacks in the choice of submarine in the SSK Submarine Project.

- The senior officers alleged to have courted politicians for personal advancement and key appointments.

- The disinclination to stand by an officer, imprisoned for alleged treason, who subsequently was cleared by the Supreme Court.

- The marked increase in the number of cases where senior service officers started seeking the intervention of the Courts to redress the injustice that they felt had been done to them.

Being in the public domain, these events have been addressed to the extent that information is reliable and not *sub-judice*.

There has been much soul searching amongst Senior Officers of the Armed Forces as to the causes that have led to this situation.

It is perhaps wise to view this in the context of the changes sweeping across the socio-cultural framework of India as a whole. The Navy could not remain unaffected by the societal churning that was transforming a medieval, splintered, colonial India into a modern, unified, democratic nation-state.

In the 1970s and 80s many incoming personnel held values which were markedly more 'self-centred' than centred on 'Navy' or 'nation'. Weaknesses ingrained in the fabric of a feudal society emerging from colonial rule showed up as flattery and sycophancy, a desire to please those in power and putting self interest above the larger naval interest.

'Careerism' was contaminating substantial segments of Indian society.

"The careerist officer believes that he has a job to perform within a corporate bureaucracy, that the true measure of success is how far and how fast he can climb to what he perceives as the ladder of success. His credo is risk avoidance and promotion of self, his loyalty is entirely

personal, his ethics situational. If he manages to manoeuvre himself into a command position, he uses subordinates to advance his career, showing little understanding or appreciation of his role as a leader, a teacher and example to his subordinates. This tragedy of the careerist is that he is self replicating, for which he drives off many of the very type of officer that the country needs".

These psychological compulsions of self preservation, self glorification and enhancing personal image by denigrating predecessors, all combined to enfeeble the 'good judgment' that is the underpinning of naval leadership. Several well-meant but populist changes were introduced on the reasoning of 'what is wrong with change', only to be reversed a short while later.

It was not unusual to hear an officer boasting to his younger officers of how necessary it was to play golf and how he left it to others who 'worked too hard'. Loners were suspect. Thinkers who stood firmly by their views were sidelined and weeded out. The egalitarian, anti-elitist, anti-excellence spirit of the time insisted that all points of view had equal value.

The trends discussed in the chapter on the Erosion of Leadership Values, led directly, in the 1980s, to the breakdown of faith in an essentially sound system of naval administration. The increasing number of 'redressal of grievance' petitions and the resort to the courts to obtain 'justice' tarnished the image of the Navy as 'the silent service'.

Also addressed in this section are issues relating to Defence Procurement and the Checks and Balances in the relationship between Naval Headquarters and the Ministry of Defence.

There are certain endemic professional problems that affect combat effectiveness and are relevant to future contingencies. They have been discussed to help future generations to find solutions pertinent to their time.

In the case of the Indian Navy during the period 1976 to 1990, each of these problems was more multifaceted than usual because of the interaction of several basic decisions taken by a navy trying to be modern on an austere budget. Each decision was logical. The cumulative outcome was sub-optimal.

It has been the Navy's overriding priority to be as contemporary as possible in technology. Until indigenous production can meet the Navy's needs, shortfalls will continue to be imported. The ships, submarines, naval aircraft and helicopters that have been acquired have invariably been the latest available and, except for the two aircraft carriers, have entered the Indian Navy at nearly the same time as they have entered the Navy of the supplier country. Inevitably, this determination to 'acquire the latest' has resulted in the Navy having to 'debug' the acquisition and suffer delays until a realistic ranging and scaling of spares can be arrived at. A worrisome aspect is that during crises, imports from the West have been vulnerable to embargos.

The relationship between Indigenisation and Logistics poses a dilemma. On the one hand there is the national priority to be self-reliant and achieve transfer of technology and indigenisation to the maximum cost-effective extent. On the other hand is the reluctance of Indian industry to develop what the Navy needs unless it finds it profitable to do so. This requires that the Navy's 'order quantity' be large enough and there be assurance of 'repeat orders' to justify the development costs incurred by Industry. The Navy, being small, cannot make its 'order quantity' large enough to permit economies of scale. The assurance of 'repeat orders' is governed by the system of 'lowest tender' whenever a repeat order is to be placed. Indigenisation in hi-tech has taken longer than expected. In low-tech areas, the enthusiasm for indigenisation has tended to erode every time an indigenous substitute fails at sea.[13,14]

One topic that has not been touched upon in this volume is the Advanced Technology Vessel (ATV) Project. Apart from its being classified, the anecdotal fragments in the public domain are insufficient for meaningful history. It would suffice to say that nuclear propulsion for ships was considered as early as 1964 by Dr Homi Bhabha and pursued by his successors.

The preceding volume, '*Transition to Triumph*', had taken as its start point the year 1939 when the 1939-1945 World War started. It presented an overview of the events concerning the Indian Navy between 1965 and 1975. It analysed the developments that preceded the two wars of 1965 and 1971, and the developments that followed them. This volume has, in certain chapters, covered a wider canvas.

By combining source material in the public domain and memoirs and recollections of participants, it presents a reconstruction of events that is as accurate and authentic

---

13. Known in Western naval parlance as the "Kashins".

14. Naval-Air Force mutual understanding blossomed in 2003 when the Air Force and Navy jointly interacted with the Russian side during the Navy's negotiations for the MiG 29 K aircraft that would operate from the aircraft carrier Gorshkov.

as the information available. Contentious topics have been candidly discussed without mentioning personalities and without trying to vindicate or criticise. My aim is to place before the serious and thoughtful reader, carefully researched facts and overviews of events that can help him to arrive at his own conclusion.

As in the preceding volume, this volume too has been structured for publication in two versions:

- The abridged volume is for the general reader and naval officers.

- The unabridged volume contains more information. It provides naval scholars with a datum for further research as more information emerges in the public domain.

To save the reader the tedium of having to refer back to the preceding volume, most chapters in this volume present an overview of the events prior to 1975, discuss the developments, achievements and shortfalls during the period 1976 to 1990 and end with a summary of developments after 1990.

Viewed in perspective, the growth of the Navy between 1976 and 1990 was extraordinary. Everyone in India, and all those abroad, who helped in meeting the Navy's needs can rightly feel gratified with their individual and collective contribution.

This growth would not have been absorbable without the natural genius and ability of Indians in all walks of life to swiftly adopt new technology, to constantly innovate, to improvise when faced with difficulties and to persevere in keeping equipment going.

Despite being accorded lesser priority than the Army and the Air Force in the allocation of resources, the Navy was able not only to stay abreast of other navies in naval propulsion, weapon, sensor and computer technology, but also to achieve a respectable measure of self reliance.

This volume discusses how well and how much was achieved in certain areas and how much that remained had to await tackling in the 1990s.

A great strength of the Navy has been the candour with which it analyses the reasons for the problems that it experiences. It is my hope that in maintaining the Navy's tradition of candour, this volume will help the reader to create the future rather than just grasp the present and the past.

Although this volume of the history has been sponsored by the Indian Navy, the views and the interpretation of facts are entirely my own. They do not reflect the views either of the Indian Navy or the Government.

New Delhi
15 October 2004

(G M Hiranandani)
Vice Admiral (Retired)

Glossary

Unless otherwise stated, a 'mile' in the text refers to a 'nautical mile', which is equal to 1.85 kilometres. One knot is a naval unit of speed equal to one nautical mile per hour.

A

As & As	Alterations and Additions
AA	Anti Aircraft
AAM	Air to Air (Anti Aircraft) Missile
a/c	Aircraft
ACC	Appointments Committee of the Cabinet
ABER	Anticipated Beyond Economical Repair (categorisation of ships' equipment when pre-planning refits/modernisations)
ACR	Annual Confidential Report
Adm	Abbreviation for 'Admiral'
ADS	Air Defence Ship
AEW	Airborne Early Warning (aircraft/helicopter)
AIO	Action Information Organisation
AIRCATS	Air Crew Categorisation and Standardisation Board (naval)
A&N	Andaman and Nicobar Islands (in the Bay of Bengal)
ALH	Advanced Light Helicopter
AMD	Anti Missile Defence
APSOH	Advanced Panoramic Sonar Hull-mounted
ARD	Annual Review Demands (for stores and spares)
ASM	Air to Surface (anti-ship) Missile
AST	Afloat Support Team
ASV	Anti Surface Vessel (role for a helicopter)
ASW	Anti Submarine Warfare
ATAS	Active Towed Array Sonar (see also TAS=passive Towed Array Sonar)
ATC	Air Traffic Control (tower)
ATE	Avionic Test Equipment (for aircraft)
AVSM	Ati Vishisht Seva Medal (award for distinguished service of an exceptional order)

B

B & D	Basic & Divisional (initial training imparted to officers)
B & D	Base & Depot (refers to ships' spares stocked ashore)
BEC	Basic Engineering Course (in INS Shivaji)
BEL	Bharat Electronics Ltd (at Bangalore)
BHEL	Bharat Heavy Electricals Ltd
BMF	Base Maintenance Facility (for Russian aircraft)
BMU	Base Maintenance Unit (for ships)
BOMS	Basic Operator-Maintainer School
BPT	Battle Practice Target (for surface firing practices)
BRO	Base Repair Organisation
BT	Bathythermograph
BTE	Boys Training Establishment

BVR	Beyond Visual Range (air-to-air missile)

C

CABS	Commodore Bureau of Sailors
Cactus	The name of the 1988 naval operation in the Maldives
CAP	Combat Air Patrol (aircraft)
Capt	Captain (naval rank. Also Commanding Officer of a ship)
CAS	Chief of the Air Staff
CASEX	Combined Anti Submarine Exercise
CBI	Central Bureau of Investigation (the Central Government's investigation arm)
CCPA	Cabinet Committee of Political Affairs
Cdo	Commando
Cdr	Commander (naval rank)
CDS	Combined Defence Services (entrance examination)
CDT	Clearance Diving Team (CCDT=Command Clearance Diving Team)
CED	Central Equipment Depot
CENTCOM	Central Command (United States)
CFL	Cease Fire Line (in Jammu and Kashmir)
CG	Coast Guard
Chennai	New name of Madras
CIA	Central Intelligence Agency (foreign intelligence arm of the United States)
CinC/CINC	Commander in Chief
CKD	Completely Knocked Down (equipment/assemblies for reassembly at destination)
CLCS	(United Nations) Commission on the Limits of the Continental Shelf
CLS	Controller of Logistic Support (naval)
CMD	Chairman & Managing Director (of naval warship building yards)
Cmde	Commodore (naval rank)
CMP	Controller of Material Planning (naval logistics)
CMS	Coastal Minesweeper
CNW	College of Naval Warfare (at Bombay)
CNS	Chief of the Naval Staff
CO	Commanding Officer
COAS	Chief of the Army Staff
CODOG	Combined Diesel or Gas (propulsion system designed for using diesel engines for cruising at economical speed or using gas turbines for dashing at high speed)
COL	Chief of Logistics (naval)
COM	Chief of Material (naval)

COP	Chief of Personnel (naval)
CPO	Chief Petty Officer (naval)
CPRO	Controller of Procurement (naval logistics)
Crore	Ten million rupees (=one hundred lakhs)
CRs	Current Repairs (three yearly refits of Russian ships and submarines)
CSL/KSL	Cochin/Kochi Shipyard Limited (in Cochin renamed Kochi)
CTS	Cadet Training Ship
CTS	Controller of Technical Services (naval logistics)
CW	Commission Worthy (sailor candidate considered suitable for becoming an officer)
CWH	Controller of Warehousing (naval logistics)
CWPA	Controller of Warship Production & Acquisition (in Naval Headquarters)

D

D & M	Divisional & Management (successor course to B & D)
db	decibel (a logarithmic unit of acoustic (sound) measurement)
DCNS	Deputy Chief of the Naval Staff
DCPT	Director of Combat Policy and Tactics (now DSR)
DF	Direction Finding
DG	Director General
D/G	Degaussing (reducing the underwater magnetic influence of ships to avoid triggering magnetic mines)
DGND	Director General Naval Design
DGNP	Director General Naval Project (B)-Bombay, (V)-Visakhapatnam
DGS&D	Director General Supplies and Disposals (Central Govt)
DLRL	Defence Electronics Research Laboratory
DM	Defence Minister (see also RM)
DPRO	Director of Procurement (naval logistics)
DPS	Defence Planning Staff
DRDL	Defence Research & Development Laboratory
DRDO	Defence Research and Development Organisation
DSR	Director of Staff Requirements (formerly DCPT)
DSRV	Deep Submergence Rescue Vessel
DSSC	Defence Services Staff College
Dunking Sonar	Equivalent of VDS but fitted in helicopters (during hover, the sonar is lowered deep into the sea to detect submarines)

E

EinC	Engineer in Chief
EAP	Electrical Artificer Power/Control System/Weapon
EAR	Electrical Artificer Radio/Radar/Sonar
ECDIS	Electronic Chart Display Information System
ECM	Electronic Counter Measures (electronic warfare)
ECCM	Electronic Counter Counter Measures (electronic warfare)
EEZ	Exclusive Economic Zone
EKM	Project designation of Russian submarine (NATO designation Kilo class)
ELF	Extremely Low Radio Frequency (below 10 khz)

ELINT	Electronic Intelligence (electronic warfare)
EMI/EMC	Electro Magnetic Interference/Electro Magnetic Compatibility (refers to the mutual interference/ compatibility of radar, communication and EW equipment/antenna fitted in a warship and its masts)
EOD	Explosive Ordnance Disposal
ER	Extended Refit (western ships)
ERA	Engine Room Artificer
ESM	Electronic Sensing Measures (electronic warfare)
EW	Electronic Warfare

F

FADS	Financial Adviser Defence Services
FDN	Floating Dock Naval
ffe	free foreign exchange (essential for paying for import of naval equipment)
FOCEF	Flag Officer Commanding Eastern Fleet
FOCIF	Flag Officer Commanding Indian Fleet (predecessor of FOCWF and FOCEF when India had only one Fleet)
FOCINC	Flag Officer Commanding in Chief
FOCWF	Flag Officer Commanding Western Fleet
FODA	Fleet Operational Demand to be Air-freighted (for very critical items, as against LPO for critical items. FODAs are raised for both foreign and local items)
FODAG	Flag-officer Offshore Defence Advisory Group
FOGA	Flag Officer Goa Area
FOMA	Flag Officer Maharashtra Area
FONA	Flag Officer Naval Aviation
FORTAN	Fortress Commander Andaman and Nicobar Islands (predecessor of CINCAN)
FOSM	Flag Officer Submarines
FOST	Flag Officer Sea Training
Foxtrot class	NATO nomenclature of Russian submarines (Indian Kalvari & Vela class)
FXP	Fleet Exercise Programme

G

GEBCO	General Bathymetric Chart of the Oceans
GED	General Engineering Department (of the erstwhile Soviet GKES) (dealt with the delivery and exploitation of ships, submarines and aircraft)
Gen	General (Army)
GMDSS	Global Maritime Distress Safety and Rescue Services Scheme
GKES	State Committee for Foreign Economic Relations (the apex approving body of the erstwhile Soviet Union for meeting Indian naval requirements)
GPS	Global Positioning System (Global satellite-based navigation position fixing system)
GOCINC	General Officer Commanding in Chief (Army)
GRSE	Garden Reach Shipbuilding and Engineering (in Calcutta)
GRT	Gross Registered Tons (ship size)
GRW	Garden Reach Workshops (in Calcutta renamed GRSE)
GSE	Ground Support Equipment (for aircraft)
GSL	Goa Shipyard Limited (in Goa)

GTD	General Technical Department (of the erstwhile Soviet GKES) (dealt with shore infrastructure and interface with Soviet factories of items supplied by the GED)	IPV	Inshore Patrol Vessel (Coast Guard)
		ISI	Indian Standards Institution (now called BIS-Bureau of Indian Standards)
		ISRO	Indian Space Research Organisation
GTs	Gas Turbines	ITTE	Integrated Type Training Establishment

H

hz	hertz (unit of frequency)		
HAL	Hindustan Aircraft Limited	J&K	Jammu and Kashmir
HATs	Harbour Acceptance Trials	JCOs	Junior Commissioned Officers (Army counterparts of naval MCPOs and CPOs)
HDL	Hooghly Docking Ltd (in Calcutta)		
HDW	Howal Deutsch Werke (German Submarine Construction firm)	JISWOG	Joint Indo Soviet Working Group on Shipbuilding (now JIRWOG)
HF	High Frequency (long distance communications)		

J

K

HSL	Hindustan Shipyard Limited (in Visakhapatnam)	KA	Prefix for Russian helicopters manufactured by Kamov
HUK	Hunter Killer (anti submarine operation)		
HUMVAD	Hull Mounted and Variable Depth sonar	Kilo Class	NATO nomenclature of Russian submarine (see EKM)

I

		Kms	Kilometres
IAF	Indian Air Force	Knot	unit of ship speed - one nautical mile per hour
IB	Intelligence Bureau (India's internal intelligence agency)	Kochi	New name of Cochin
		Kolkata	New name of Calcutta
IBL	International Boundary Line	KV	Kendriya Vidyalaya (Central School)
ICCP	Impressed Cathodic Current Protection (electric system activated in harbour to minimise underwater hull corrosion and prolong hull life)		

L

		Lakh	One hundred thousand
IDSA	Institute of Defence Studies and Analysis (think tank)	LAPADS	Lightweight Airborne Passive Acoustic Detection System
IEDs	Improvised Explosive Devices	LCA	Light Combat Aircraft
IFF	Identification Friend or Foe (radar-associated interrogator facility to identify friendly contacts appearing on radar. Lack of response is classified as foe)	LCU	Landing Craft Utility
		LOC	Line of Control/Communication
		LOFAR	Low Frequency Acoustic Ranging
		LOGREQ	Logistic Requirement (signal)
IFTU	Intensive Flying Training Unit (evaluates naval aircraft on induction)	LPO	Local Purchase Order for critical items. (Can be raised for both foreign and local items). (Soviet demand procedure for meeting operationally required spares for ships/submarines/aircraft)
IGA	Inter Governmental Agreement (umbrella agreement for acquisition of Soviet/Russian military supplies)		
IIT	Indian Institute of Technology (the five IITs at Bombay (Pawai), Delhi, Kanpur, Roorkee and Madras (Chennai) along with the venerated Indian Institute of Science at Bangalore are the "Ivy League" of India's technological higher studies)	LRMP	Long Range Maritime Patrol (aircraft)
		LST	Landing Ship Tank (M)-Medium, (L)-Large
		LTA	Light Transport Aircraft
		Lt	Lieutenant (naval rank)
		Lt Cdr	Lieutenant Commander (naval rank)
IKL	Ingeneer Kontor Lubeck (German Submarine Designing firm)	LTTE	Liberation Tigers of Tamil Eelam (Secessionist elements in Sri Lanka)
IL	Prefix for type of Russian aircraft manufactured by Ilyushin		

M

ILMS	Integrated Logistic Management System (naval)		
IMS	Inshore Minesweeper	MAD	Magnetic Anomaly Detector (sensor in naval aircraft/helicopters for detecting submarines)
IMSF	Indian Marine Special Force		
IN	Indian Navy	MARCOS	Marine Commandos
INAS	Indian Naval Air Squadron	Maritime	Relating to navigation or commerce on and in the sea (See also Naval)
INS	Indian Naval Ship/Submarine		
IPC	Initial Provisioning Committee (constituted for every new type of ship/submarine/aircraft to recommend the range and scale of spares to be ordered for each fitted equipment for stocking 'On Board' and in the 'Base & Depot' spares).	MARS	Marine Acoustic Research Ship
		MAT	Manning and Training (series of committees for working out the complements of Russian origin ships and the training of their commissioning crews)
IPKF	Indian Peace Keeping Force (in Sri Lanka 1987 to 1990)	MATCH	Multi-role Anti Submarine Torpedo Carrying Helicopter

MCF	Marine Commando Force	NHQ	Naval Headquarters
MCM	Mine Countermeasures	NIETT	Naval Institute of Education Teaching and Training
MCPO	Master Chief Petty Officer (I/II=First/Second Class)	NIO	National Institute of Oceanography
MDL	Mazagon Docks Limited (in Bombay)	NIOHC	North Indian Ocean Hydrographic Commission
MEA	Ministry of External Affairs	nm	nautical mile of 2000 yards (vis a vis terrestrial mile of 1760 yards)
MERs	Matric (10th standard) Entry Recruits (Sailors)		
MES	Military Engineering Services (Inter-service organisation for all defence building construction and maintenance)	NM	Nao Sena Medal (awarded for gallantry in the face of the enemy. Also awarded for sustained operational proficiency not considered as gallantry)
Met	Meteorology	NMERs	Non-Matric (below matric) Entry Recruits (Sailors)
MHQ	Maritime Headquarters	NMS	New Management Strategy (naval)
MI	Prefix for Russian helicopters manufactured by Mikoyan	NODPAC	Naval Oceanographic Data Processing and Analysis Centre
MIS	Management Information System	NOIC	Naval Officer in Charge
Mk	Mark (British codification to indicate the vintage of equipment)	NPOL	Naval Physical and Oceanography Laboratory
MO	Medical Officer (naval). Also Material Organisation (naval logistics)	NRs	Navigation Repairs (Russian ships)/Normal Refits (other ships)
MOD/MoD	Ministry of Defence	NSB	Naval Selection Board
MOR	Maritime Operations Room	NSD	Naval Store Depot
MOU	Memorandum of Understanding (between two Governments spelling out the scope of cooperation)	NSRY	Naval Ship Repair Yard
		NSTL	Naval Science and Technology Laboratory

O

MPA	Maritime Patrol Aircraft	OEM	Original Equipment Manufacturer.
MRASW	Maritime Reconnaissance and Anti Submarine Warfare (naval aircraft)	OJT	On Job Training
		ONGC	Oil and Natural Gas Commission
MR	Medium Range (guns), Maritime Reconnaissance (aircraft)	OOD/ OOW	Officer of the Day/ Officer of the Watch
		OPDEF	Operational Defect (report made by ships)
MRs	Medium Repairs (six-yearly refits of Russian ships and submarines)	OPSTATE	Operational State (report made by ships and submarines)
MRSOW	Maintenance Reserve and Strike-Off Wastage (for aircraft and helicopters)	OPV	Offshore Patrol Vessel
		ORI	Operational Readiness Inspection
MS	Material Superintendent (naval logistics)	OTC	Officer in Tactical Command
Mumbai	New name of Bombay	OTIs	Operating and Tactical Instructions (Ships, submarines and aircraft)
MVC	Maha Vir Chakra (award for gallantry of a very high order in the face of the enemy)		

P

N

		Pawan	The name of the Inter-Service Operation in Sri Lanka (1987-1990)
NA	Naval Attaché / Naval Adviser (in embassies)		
NAD	Naval Armament Depot	PCT	Pre Commissioning Training
NAI	Naval Armament Inspection	PM	Prime Minister/Pradhan Mantri
NAIS	Naval Aircraft Inspection Service	PNC	Price Negotiating Committee
NARO	Naval Aircraft Repair Organisation	PO	Petty Officer
NAS	Naval Air Station	POL	Petrol, Oil and Lubricants
NATS	Naval Air Technical School	PPM	Planned Preventive Maintenance
NAVAC	Naval Academy	PR	Photo Reconnaissance
Naval	Relating to ships or shipping. (See also Maritime)	psi	pounds per square inch (pressure)
NAY	Naval Aircraft Yard	PSO	Principal Staff Officer (in Service Headquarters)
NBCD	Nuclear, Biological, Chemical and Damage Control	PSU	Public Sector Undertaking (government owned undertaking as opposed to private owned)
NCML	Naval Chemical and Metallurgical Laboratory		
ND	Navigation (and aircraft) Direction (specialisation)	PTA	Pilotless Target Aircraft (for anti aircraft firing practices)
NDA	National Defence Academy		
NDC	National Defence College	PVC	Param Vir Chakra (award for gallantry of the highest order in the face of the enemy)
NDES	Naval Dockyard Expansion Scheme		
NGRI	National Geographical Research Institute	PVSM	Param Vishisht Seva Medal (award for distinguished service of the highest order)
NGS	Naval Gunfire Support (bombardment by gunfire from the sea to support army operations on land)		

Q

NHO	National/Naval Hydrographic Office	QRF	Quick Reaction Force

R

R Adm	Rear Admiral
R & AW	Research and Analysis Wing (India's external intelligence agency)
R & D	Research and Development
R & R	Rest and Recreation (visits of warships from distant countries to friendly ports in between long periods of deployment at sea)
R/T	Radio Telephony
R/V	Rendez Vous (meeting point at sea)
Radar	Radio Detection and Ranging device (above the sea)
RCC	Recompression Chamber (divers)
Recce	Reconnaissance
Retd	Retired
RM	Raksha Mantri (Defence Minister)
RRM	Rajya Raksha Mantri (Minister of State for Defence)
RN	Royal Navy (British)
RO	Reverse Osmosis (technology/plant to convert sea/brackish water to potable water)
RTD	Repair Technical Documentation (Russian)
Rupee	Indian currency

S

SA	Scientific Adviser (to the Defence Minister/CNS). Also Supplementary Agreement (to procure items from Russia)
S Lt	Sub Lieutenant (naval rank)
S/M	Submarine
SAM	Surface to Air (guided) Missile
SAR	Search and Rescue (by ships, aircraft and helicopters at sea)
SATs	Sea Acceptance Trials
SBS	Special Boat Section (commandos)
SD	Special Duties (cadre of officers promoted from sailor cadre)
SDB	Seaward Defence Boat
SEAL	Sea, Air & Land (US Navy acronym for their Marine Commandos)
Seabird	Project designation of the new naval base at Karwar (in Karnataka)
SFNA	School for Naval Airmen
SITREP	Situation Report (a report which summarises the present situation)
SLMS	Ship Logistics Management System
SLOCs	Sea Lines of Communication
SMA	Ship Maintenance Authority
SMP	Self Maintenance Period (a period, normally in harbour, when a ships company carries out maintenance without outside assistance)
SMU	Ship Maintenance Unit
SOC	Senior Officers Conference
SOMC	Stabilised Operational and Manning Cycle
Sonar	Sound Navigation and Ranging (underwater)
SOP	Standard Operating Procedure
SRV	Submarine Rescue Vessel
SSB	Services Selection Board
SSG	Special Services Group (commandos)

SSK	(Submarine Search and Kill) (conventional diesel/electric-powered, quiet, Hunter Killer submarines). Project Designation of the German HDW 1500 submarines built in India
SSM	Surface to Surface (anti ship) Missile
STE	Sailors Training Establishment (INS Chilka in Orissa)
STEALTH	Technology of designing warships and aircraft to minimise their detection by adversary radars/sensors
STOL	Short Take Off and Land (as applicable to Sea Harrier aircraft)
STOVL	Short Take Off and Vertical Land (as applicable to Sea Harrier aircraft)
STS	Sail Training Ship
SWA	Shipwright Artificer

T

TAS	Torpedo Anti Submarine (officer specialisation). Also Towed Array Sonar
TOT	Transfer of Technology
TOTED	Towed Torpedo Decoy
TU	Prefix for Russian aircraft manufactured by Tupolev

U

UHF	Ultra High Radio Frequency (for short distance communications) (300,000 to 3,000,000 khz)
UK	United Kingdom (Britain)
UN	United Nations
UNCLOS	United Nations Conference on the Law of the Sea
URR	Urgent Refit/Repair Requirement (Demand procedure for equipment/spares urgently required to complete the refit/repair of a Soviet/Russian origin ship/submarine/aircraft/equipment)
US / USA	United States / United States of America
USS	United States Ship
USSR	Union of Soviet Socialist Republics (Soviet Union till 1991, thereafter Russia)

V

V Adm	Vice Admiral
VCNS	Vice Chief of the Naval Staff
VDS	Variable Depth Sonar (fitted in ships enables the sonar of a fast moving ship to be lowered on a cable, deep into the sea to detect submarines)
VHF	Very High Radio Frequency (for communications) (30,000 to 300,000 khz)
VIP	Very Important Person
Visakhapatnam	New spelling for Vizagapatam/Vishakapatnam
Vizag	Naval parlance for Vizagapatam /Visakhapatnam
VLCC	Very Large Crude-oil Carrier
VLF	Very Low Frequency (communication with submerged submarines) (10 to 30 khz)
VrC	Vir Chakra (award for gallantry of a high order in the face of the enemy)
VSM	Vishisht Seva Medal (award for distinguished service)
VTOL	Vertical Take Off and Land (as applicable to Sea Harrier aircraft)

W

WATT	Warship Acceptance Trials Team
W/T	Wireless Telegraphy
WECORS	Weapon Control and Repair Shop (at Bombay)
WED	Weapon Equipment Depot
WESEE	Weapon & Electronic Systems Engineering Establishment (successor of WESO)
WOT	Warship Overseeing Team
WPS	Warship Production Superintendent
WW I	1914-1918 World War
WW II	1939-1945 World War

X

XO	Executive Officer (2nd in command of a ship/naval establishment)

Contents

List of Maps

1

External Naval Presence In The Indian Ocean

Features of the Indian Ocean

Smallest of the world's oceans, the Indian Ocean encompasses one fifth of the world's sea area. It washes the shores of 34 littoral states and 11 hinterland states. It contains half the world's seabed minerals. By 2020, two thirds of the world's trade is likely to be passing through it.

Three features distinguish this Ocean. Unlike any other ocean, it is capped by a huge land mass. It lies in the middle of two great oceans, the Atlantic and the Pacific, and forms the connecting link between the two. Its shores are occupied by developing countries to a greater extent than the other oceans.

It has a maximum west-east extent of 4200 nautical miles and a maximum north-south extent of 3700 nautical miles. Geographically, the Indian peninsula is the predominant feature of the northern Indian Ocean.[1]

The western region has twenty seven littoral countries compared with seven bounding the eastern region. Also in the western zone are all the territories still owned by the erstwhile European colonial powers or in special association with them. France owns the Mayotte and Esparses islands in the Mozambique Channel, as well as Tromelin, Reunion, Amsterdam, St Paul, Crozet and Kerguelen. In addition, Djibouti and Mayotte are in special relationships with France. Britain's possessions are now restricted to the islands comprising the Chagos Archipelago, of which the island of Diego Garcia, has been leased to the USA.

The ensuing historical overview summarises the motives that have driven developments in and around the Indian Ocean and the inevitability of their continuance.

Historical Overview of Naval Presence until the 19th Century [2]

The causes that led to the arrival of external naval presence are linked to the pattern of trade between China, India, Southeast Asia and Europe over the centuries.

For millennia, the sailing vessels of China, India and Arabia availed of seasonal monsoon winds to carry commodities between the *entrêpots* of their era to barter the prized products of their time and trans-ship them to destinations in the west and the east.[3] Segments of these voyages were vulnerable to piracy. Neither cargo owners nor cargo carriers armed their ships for protection from pirates. For safe passage, it was cheaper to pay the local pirate chieftains, who controlled the choke points and the vulnerable coastal segments, than to maintain armed ships.

In the centuries BC, Chinese silk and Indian cotton travelled to Greece and Rome. As the Chinese empire expanded and China's Han dynasty made Central Asia safe for east-west caravans, a network of overland trade routes developed from China and India to Syria and Asia Minor. By 100 BC, the 6000-kilometre Silk Route was well established. Because of the distance, traders concentrated on luxury items high in value but low in weight. These were traded on through intermediaries rather than remaining with a single merchant. Bulkier items continued to be transported in ships of the coastal trade rather than on camel-back.[4]

In the 13th and 14th centuries, the Mongols derived substantial revenues from their colonies in the Caucasus, Persia, Central Asia and northern India that straddled the Silk Route. In the 14th and 15th centuries, the Ottoman

---

1. Sub continental India has a coastline of 6300 km, with the island territories adding another 1100 km.

   The coastline has 11 major, 20 intermediate and 100 minor ports. India has an Exclusive Economic Zone of 2.2 million square kms. By 2010, over 70% of India's energy needs will come from abroad, nearly one third of which will be consigned to northwest India alone.

2. For details prior to the 19th century, see Reference Note No 1, page 403.

3. There is no historical basis for the notion that until the arrival of the Europeans, there was no intra-regional maritime trade in the Indian Ocean.

4. After the opening of the sea route between Europe and Asia in the 16th century, trade on these land routes decreased in favour of ocean-borne trade.

Turks conquered Asia Minor. They increased their customs duties on the Silk Route goods that transited through their territory. This raised the prices of oriental merchandise in European markets.

By the 15th century, a stable pattern had evolved of India's overseas trade:

- The eastern trade was largely in the hands of Surat's merchants.[5] Their vessels plied between India's west coast and Malacca, where Indian, Chinese and Javanese ships met to exchange their wares.[6] Apart from the Muslim merchants from Surat, Hindu merchants from the east coast and Bengal also visited Malacca.

- To the west, the carrying trade in the Arabian Sea was mainly in the hands of Arab ship owners and flowed along two well established maritime routes:

  – Through the Red Sea, overland to Cairo and Alexandria from where Venetian ships carried the cargoes to Europe.

  – Through the Persian Gulf, up through Basra and Baghdad to join up with the Silk Route to Lebanon and ports in the eastern Mediterranean.

The Arabs, who were successful as merchant mariners, were mainly commercial navigators. They were not instruments of any national policy nor had they the support of any organised government.

The urge of European merchants to finance sea voyages to outflank the Ottoman stranglehold on the land route coincided with the voyages of exploration that were taking place in the 15th century.[7]

At that time, the Portuguese were among the few European nations seeking navigational knowledge of the west coast of Africa, having developed the capability for long sea voyages in sturdy ships fitted with cannons. From 1434 onwards, Portuguese influence spread down the west coast of Africa towards the southern tip of Africa.

External naval power appeared in the Indian Ocean for the first time in the 15th century.

Oddly enough, the first 'exploratory fleet' came not from the west but from the east. The Chinese Ming Dynasty's Admiral Cheng Ho (Zheng He) made seven voyages between 1405 and 1434 visiting ports as far as the coast of Africa.

In 1488, fifty four years after the Chinese voyages ceased, the first Portuguese ship entered the Indian Ocean from the west when the Portuguese mariner Bartholomeu Dias rounded the southern tip of Africa that came to be called the Cape of Good Hope. A decade later, he was followed by Vasco da Gama's ships which reached the Malabar coast (now part of the Indian state known as Kerala) in southwest India in 1498. What Vasco da Gama and his successors introduced into Indian maritime history was the claim to an 'exclusive control of the seas', a conception wholly at variance with what had been accepted as the 'natural law' both in Europe and in Asia.

The sailing expeditions from Europe to the Indian Ocean had to be financed. Whilst the Portuguese expeditions were partly financed by the monarchy and partly by merchants, the East India Companies set up later by the Dutch, the French and the English were private trading companies, financed wholly by wealthy merchants. These companies were granted charters by their respective governments, authorising them to acquire territory wherever they could and to exercise in the acquired territory various functions of government, including legislation, the issue of currency, the negotiation of treaties, the waging of war, and the administration of justice.

The companies found that they could gain exclusive trading rights by siding with one side or the other in local feuds. It became worthwhile for them to have troops and arm their merchantmen to help the success of their protégés and be rewarded by trading privileges in wider territories. Successful companies became substantial contributors to their national economies back in Europe. Their continued profitability became a 'national interest' in their Government's foreign policy. Over time, however, avarice tempted company employees to become covert private entrepreneurs and line their own pockets. Decrease in company profits and mismanagement led each home Government to take over its company, convert the territory into a 'colony' and provide for its seaward defence by its Navy.

In recent times, it has become comfortable for some to voice the view that "the European invasion of India that started from the sea in the 15th century was successful because India had neglected its seaward defences. Indian rulers are to be blamed for pre-occupation with invasions from Central Asia and pre-occupation with internecine

---

5. Surat's ancient prosperity was founded on the export of inexpensive white cottons that were an article of mass consumption in the Arab lands.

6. Merchants from Arabia and Persia journeyed to Surat to embark ships bound for Malacca.

7. There was also the lure of the Orient, whose fabulous wealth had become legendary. Christopher Columbus set out westward from Spain in 1492 in quest of the riches of the Indies. The entry in his ship's log on 10 October 1492 states "...I had started out to find the Indies and would continue until I had accomplished that mission". When he made landfall on the island he named San Salvadore, he believed he had arrived in Asian waters.

wars within India." The historical record admits of a more pragmatic view.

Firstly, the Europeans did not enter the Indian Ocean to invade India or to acquire territory. They were in search of a cheaper sea route to carry exotic oriental textiles, aromatics and spices to Europe because transportation by the Central Asian Silk Route had become increasingly expensive.

Secondly, in the 16th and 17th centuries, the coastal kingdoms were willing partners in seaborne trade. When disputes led to hostilities, ships of the coastal trading kingdoms on the west coast of India did successfully harry European ships, despite the superiority of European shipborne firepower. Ships of the Zamorin of Calicut's fleet often defeated the Portuguese. Ships of Maratha Chatrapati Shivaji and his successors bested British ships in many skirmishes.

Thirdly, when the wars in Europe spilled over into the Indian Ocean, Indian kingdoms who were perpetually struggling for supremacy had no hesitation in manipulating the competing companies to their own advantage for short term gains. It was only when India became an independent, integrated nation in 1947 that one could talk of a 'national navy'.

The uncomfortable reality is that the feuds between local chieftains and kingdoms facilitated the piecemeal subjugation by the European powers of the coastal sections of India. Whenever local rulers were weak and naïve, the Europeans successfully manipulated circumstances to their own advantage.[8] On the other hand, when faced with strong rulers, manipulative subjugation was rarely successful.

There is some substance in the view that the European trading companies would have done better for themselves if they had resisted the temptation to meddle in local squabbles.[9]

British Predominance in the 19th Century

During the Napoleonic Wars, Britain had captured the Cape of Good Hope in 1806, seized Mauritius (France's last Indian Ocean harbour) in 1810 and seized Java and Batavia (Holland's main base in the East Indies) in 1813. The 1815 Congress of Vienna which established the 'European order' after the defeat of France recognised, *de facto*, Britain's global naval supremacy:

- Britain retained the Cape of Good Hope, Mauritius and Ceylon.
- Java was returned to Holland but Britain acquired a foothold is Singapore in 1819.

With India as the pivot of British presence, possession of these bases made the north Indian Ocean a 'closed sea'.

With its central situation in the Indian Ocean, India became a supplier of vast military manpower and resources. The defence of India and of the regional sea lines of imperial communication became a major consideration in Britain's expansion in Asia. India became 'the keystone in the arch of Imperial defence'.

The occupation of Aden in 1839, the opening of the Suez Canal in 1869, the laying of undersea telegraph cables from Britain to her Indian Ocean bases in the 1870s, the advent of steam-propelled, propeller-driven warships, the establishment of coaling stations, dry docks and armament depots in the naval bases all combined to underpin Britain's Indian Ocean strategy.[10] The core of this strategy was:

- To maintain the strongest ships of her fleet in British waters and deploy smaller-older-weaker squadrons in distant bases. As soon as a threat was reported to Britain's sea lines of communication, warships of the appropriate power and speed would be directed by telegraph to converge on the threat. In the event of a prolonged confrontation, reinforcements would be moved in from elsewhere.
- To prevent rival powers from establishing a naval base in the Indian Ocean. Without access to a friendly base, no hostile warship could operate in this oceanic expanse for any length of time.

At the beginning of the 20th century, the location of Britain's naval bases and the segments of the Indian Ocean sea-lanes that they controlled were:

---

8. Internecine feuds and squabbles led to the endless wars for empire between the rulers of European nations. They led to the colonisation of Asia, Africa and the Americas. They continue to this day, as do their manipulations by vested interests.

9. Thomas Saunders,® a perceptive employee of the English East India Company, wrote to his directors in London from his governor's seat at Fort St David in 1751:

   "We must recognise that if the Europeans had not interfered in their affairs and had left India's princes to resolve their own quarrels that might have been infinitely more beneficial to the trade."

10. Reference Note No 2 elaborates this strategy. (page 410)

The base in:	Controlled the sea-lane:
Simonstown (South Africa)	around the Cape of Good Hope
Aden	through the Red Sea
Bahrain	through the Persian Gulf
Trincomalee (Ceylon)	across the North Indian Ocean
Singapore	through the Straits of Malacca

The Emergence of Oil as a Strategic National Interest

Coal combustion had led to coal-fuelled steam-propelled warships. The discovery of oil[11] led to oil-fuelled steam-propelled warships.

As oil replaced coal as the primary source of energy, America, Britain, Russia, Germany and Japan, all realised the importance of oil for the sustenance of their industrialised economies in peace and the mobility of their armies and navies in war.

The discovery of oil in Persia raised the importance of the Persian Gulf region. Britain, which already had major stakes in this region because of its proximity to its arch imperial rival Russia, now had increased interest because of oil. Territories which had originally been brought under British rule or influence to secure India's maritime flanks now came to acquire a strategic importance in their own right.

The 1914-1918 World War

In the First World War of 1914-1918, Britain, France and Japan fought against Germany and Russia.

At the outbreak of the war in 1914, the world's leading oil producers were the United States, Russia and Mexico. New oilfields were being discovered in Persia and Mesopotamia and exploratory drilling had begun. Both Britain and Russia were seriously concerned about their respective oil supplies from the Gulf and from Baku, on the borders of the Caspian Sea, in view of the threat to these areas posed by the Ottoman Turkish Army.

By the end of this war, the central place of petroleum in world strategy had become obvious. British and French dependence on the United States for oil proved to be one of the most critical logistic crises of the war. At one point, Britain was on the verge of ending hostilities because of the effectiveness of the German U-boat campaign against the oil and food sea lines of communication (SLOCs) across the Atlantic. The thirst for oil for military and naval operations led to fears that there might be a global oil shortage.

The United States entered the war in 1917[12]. Its massive contribution in men and material to the defeat of Germany marked the first step in the world's acceptance of the US as a global power. Its role in the Peace Treaty of Versailles and the founding of the League of Nations confirmed this position.

During this war, new forms of warfare made their debut and changed the nature of war:

- Naval air power in the form of aircraft carriers.
- Unrestricted submarine warfare.
- Land based air power in the form of fighter, bomber aircraft and aerial reconnaissance.
- Fast, tracked, armoured vehicles like tanks and personnel carriers.
- Chemical warfare.

All these forms of warfare were dependent on oil fuel and its derivatives.

Between the Wars

In the 'new world order' after 1918, the Austro-Hungarian and Ottoman empires were carved up into numerous small states. America and Britain quickly created protégé kingdoms (Saudi Arabia, Iraq, Syria, Jordan) and sheikhdoms (Kuwait, Bahrain, Qatar, Oman, the Trucial States) in the oil rich areas around the Persian Gulf. In these states and sheikhdoms, they established their proprietary oil producing companies. In the late 1920s, when the first Iraqi well was drilled, 200 wells were producing in Iran. In 1931, the first well was drilled in Bahrain. Care was taken to ensure that all Gulf oil production remained firmly under Anglo-American control.

In the 1930s, all the major world powers started rearming. Russia already had oilfields in the Caspian Sea and knew that there was plenty of oil in nearby Iran. Germany and Japan, having no assured access to oil in case of war, planned to stockpile enough oil to sustain their campaigns until they secured the nearest oilfields. In its contingency

---

11. The first oil well was drilled at Titusville in Pennsylvania in the USA in 1859. The US became the pioneer in the commercial production of oil. As the imperatives of the Industrial Revolution exerted their pressures, the demand for oil grew. Geologists quickly recognised that the conditions existing in the USA had to be duplicated in other parts of the world. The search for new petroleum fields, employing American-pioneered exploratory drilling, spread around the globe and reached the Persian Gulf. In 1911, Persia (now Iran) became the first country in the Persian Gulf to produce petroleum in commercial quantities.

12. In his address to Congress on 2 April 1917, US President Wilson declared, "The present German submarine warfare against commerce is warfare against mankind. It is a war against all nations".

plans, Germany, in addition to developing an oil substitute, planned to first capture the oilfields in Romania and later in the Caspian Sea; Japan planned to capture the oilfields in the Dutch East Indies (Indonesia).

The 1939-1945 World War – Indian Ocean Aspects

When the Second World War broke out in 1939, it was a European conflict between Germany and an Anglo-French-Polish coalition. No immediate threat was perceived to Britain's naval supremacy in the Indian Ocean. Until mid 1941, the British Joint Planning Staff in India were preoccupied with sustaining the Anglo-German land battles in Egypt.

America's relations with Japan had deteriorated over several years. In September 1940, Japan coerced German-occupied France into giving up northern Indochina. America retaliated by prohibiting the export to Japan of steel, scrap iron, and aviation fuel.

In April 1941, Japan signed a neutrality treaty with the Soviet Union as insurance against a Soviet attack in case conflict erupted with Britain or America whilst Japan started occupying Southeast Asia. When Germany attacked the Soviet Union in June 1941, Japan considered terminating its treaty with the Soviet Union and attack it from the east. It chose instead to concentrate on Southeast Asia.

On 23 July 1941 Japan occupied southern Indochina. Two days later, America and Britain froze Japanese assets. The effect was to prevent Japan from purchasing oil and strategic metals, which would help cripple its army, navy and air force. Japan had only six months oil reserves. It decided to secure the resources of Southeast Asia before it was too late.

On 7 December 1941, the Japanese Navy attacked Pearl Harbour in the middle of the Pacific Ocean and inflicted severe damage on the battleships of the US Pacific Fleet. On the same day, Japanese forces struck the American bases in the Philippine Islands and the British bases in Hong Kong, Siam and Malaya. On the 8th December, America declared war on Japan. On the 10th December, Japanese torpedo bombers operating from Saigon in southern Indochina sank the two British battleships that had arrived to defend Singapore. On 11th December, Germany and Italy declared war on America. The Soviet Union had already entered the War after Germany invaded it on 22 June 1941.

For the next four years, the 'Allied Powers' – the United States, the Soviet Union, Britain and France were ranged against the 'Axis Powers'[13] - Germany, Italy and Japan.

In Southeast Asia, Japan's Navy had within a few days successfully crippled British and American naval and maritime power. By the end of March 1942, Japanese armies had occupied the Dutch East Indies and their oilfields, Singapore, Malaya and Burma and started advancing towards India.

Japanese naval forces captured the Andaman and Nicobar Islands in the Bay of Bengal, bombed Visakhapatnam on the east coast of India and attacked and paralysed merchant shipping in the Bay of Bengal. A pincer attack was being planned – overland into northeast India toward the oilfields of Assam and over the sea to capture Ceylon. This invasion could not take place. The Indian Army blocked the landward advance into northeast India

In April, a Japanese fleet entered the Indian Ocean and sank British naval ships off Colombo and Trincomalee.[14]

To avoid further losses and regroup, the remnants of the British Navy in the Indian Ocean withdrew westwards to the coast of Africa and attacked the French naval base at Diego Suarez on the northern tip of Madagascar.[15]

The closure of the Suez Canal had resulted in all shipping to and from the Indian Ocean having to go around the southern tip of Africa. This concentration of shipping attracted the attention of German submarines. By mid 1943, German U boat operations had extended around the Cape of Good Hope and northwards into the Mozambique Channel, which was a focal area for shipping proceeding to and from the Red Sea and the Persian Gulf. Several U boats penetrated the Persian Gulf in 1944.

Japanese submarines also operated in the Indian Ocean and sank shipping as far west as the Mozambique Channel.

These distant submarine deployments entailed replenishment of fuel and food and rest and repair bases between missions. Three rest and repair bases were established in Japanese occupied ports:

- Penang, off the west coast of Malaya, was the main submarine base. The first German U boat entered in July 1943.

---

13. Treaties between Germany, Italy and Japan in 1936-1937 brought into being the Berlin-Rome-Tokyo Axis. The Axis Powers thereafter became the collective term for these countries and their allies.

14. See Reference Note 4, page 411.

15. See Reference Note 5, page 413.

- Batavia (Jakarta) in the Dutch East Indies was the second base.
- Singapore's repair base was operational from mid 1944 until it was recaptured in 1945.

Throughout 1943 and 1944, German U boats were deployed on offensive operations in the Indian Ocean, replenishing from tankers and proceeding to Penang for rest and repairs.

The recapture of the Andaman Islands was delayed by three years. The British Navy could not control the Bay of Bengal until the Japanese Fleets had been overpowered. This was achieved by the United States Navy after the major Pacific Ocean battles in the Coral Sea on 7th and 8th May 1942 and off Midway in June 1942.

In 1943, the British Navy returned to Trincomalee. In June 1944, ships from the British squadron at Trincomalee carried out the first bombardment of the Andaman Islands. A year later, after more battleships had been assembled, bombardment of the islands led to the surrender of the Japanese garrison.[16]

British Strategic Perceptions Regarding India in 1946

As the 1939-1945 World War neared its end, it was clear that the world order based on the British Empire had come to an end. The United States and the Soviet Union had emerged as the contestants for global dominion.

In 1980, Her Majesty's Stationery Office published "The Transfer of Power 1942 to 1947". These volumes contained the Top Secret and Secret correspondence between the Viceroys and Commanders in Chief in India and their counterparts in the British Government in London in the years prior to 1947 regarding the strategic implications of India becoming independent.

These documents reveal three consistent strands of strategic anxiety:
- The threat of Russia invading India after the British left.
- The serious implications for Imperial Defence if an independent India opted out of the British Commonwealth and became susceptible to Russian influence.
- The feasibility of propping up an independent Pakistan against threats from Russia and India.

These documents also reveal the basis for developments in the Indian Ocean during the second half of the 20th century and the Anglo-American mindsets during this period.

Of particular interest are the 1946 assessments of India and her potential by the General Headquarters of the Commander in Chief India.[17]

Strategically, the British were extremely apprehensive of what the Soviet Union would do, particularly in the context of the Great Game that Britain and Russia had played in Central Asia for nearly a hundred years to counter each other's expansion.[18]

The crux of the British fears was:
- When they evacuated India, the Russians would penetrate and there would be no effective defence of India against external dangers.
- If India became dominated by the Russians, communications with Australia and New Zealand would be cut off.
- The position of the British Commonwealth would be seriously injured because India would cease to be a participant in the British Commonwealth Defence System.[19]

The British Joint Planning Staff Memorandum of 1947 for the India-Burma Committee on 'Strategic Requirements in India' therefore started positioning Pakistan as a possible ally in the event that a 'hostile' India emerged. This document stated that:

"The area of Pakistan is strategically the most important in the continent of India and the majority of our strategic requirements could be met, though with considerably greater difficulty, by an agreement with Pakistan alone."

In hindsight, it is clear that a pro-Pakistan mindset not only governed British policy when Pakistan invaded Jammu and Kashmir in October 1947; it was also conveyed to the US when the British told them that with the end of the British Empire looming, Britain would hand over the baton to the US.

Even though the 1939-1945 War had greatly impoverished Britain, she still enjoyed the prestige of a great power. She saw herself as a true partner of the

---

16. See Reference Note 6, page 413.

17. See Reference Note 7, page 413.

18. See Reference Note 8, page 416.

19. To hedge against this contingency, the British Government in London was promising the British Indian Government in India as early as 1944 that the Royal Indian Navy would be given modern ships after the war ended.

United States – equal in status and influence if no longer in actual power. She still ruled over a vast empire and her American ally continued to defer to her the leading role in South Asia and the Middle East. At the time of India's independence, America was content to follow the British lead in the region.

American Indian Ocean & Persian Gulf Policy During the Cold War – 1947 to 1991

In the years after the war, additional discoveries of oil in Saudi Arabia, Qatar, Abu Dhabi and Dubai made the Persian Gulf the world's major source of liquid energy. The Soviet Union, having surplus oil, could assure its availability to its protégés. For the United States, it was vital to ensure the security of oil supplies from the Persian Gulf to the 'non-communist world.'

In 1946, a dispute erupted between Iran and the Soviet Union regarding Iran's northern border with the Soviet state of Azerbaijan.[20] The Soviet Union took a rigid stand. The Soviet Union's immediate proximity to the oilfields of the Persian Gulf loomed as a threat to US oil supplies. Fearing that pro-Soviet groups might eventually topple the fragile regimes in Iran, Greece and Turkey and send them into the Soviet bloc, America declared the Truman Doctrine in 1947.

The gist of the 1946 Truman Doctrine was that 'the US must support free people who are resisting attempted subjugation by armed minorities or outside powers.' It declared the US commitment to preserve the pro-West orientation of states in the Persian Gulf bordering the Soviet Union to preclude the Soviet Union from gaining control of the region.[21]

The US secured military facilities in Dhahran (Saudi Arabia) in 1947 and port facilities in Bahrain for US Navy ships in 1949. Today Bahrain is the base for the US Navy's Fifth Fleet.

America started providing substantial economic and military assistance to these and other countries bordering the Soviet Union to preserve their pro-US orientation and from 1947 onwards, US policy had two priorities:

- To maintain uninterrupted, the flow of oil from the Persian Gulf, at a reasonable price, to the capitalist industrialised nations of the world (most of whom became its allies in the Cold War against Communism).

- To counter the political and military influence in the region which the Soviet Union enjoyed because of its contiguous border with Iran along the Caspian Sea.

This was to be achieved through a series of alliances and arms supply relationships. It signified the beginning of the US decision to globally counter Soviet interests and started the Cold War that was to last until 1990.

After the Suez crisis and the Arab Israeli war in 1956, the credibility of Britain and France in peacekeeping in the Middle East evaporated. The US Administration concluded that 'the existing vacuum in the Middle East must be filled by the United States before it is filled by Russia.' The US assumed this responsibility and codified it in the Eisenhower Doctrine.[22]

The Nixon Administration fashioned what came to be known as the Nixon Doctrine.[23] The US would draw back militarily from selected areas of the world and rely on local allies to make the primary contribution to self-defence and local security.

In the Persian Gulf, this was supplemented by its 'Twin Pillars' policy wherein the US sought to promote Saudi-Iranian cooperation in maintaining stability. This policy fitted neatly into the plans of the Shah of Iran to acquire the armed muscle necessary to protect the Iranian oil lifeline running the length of the Persian Gulf. It was strengthened by the Saudi decision to embark on a similar programme to arm itself. The US played the major role in helping

---

20. See Reference Note 9, page 417.

21. The Truman Administration had in any case decided that any further progress of Communism would adversely affect American interests. The Truman Doctrine of extending American economic and military aid to European countries (known as the Marshall Plan) to contain the Soviet Union's expansion in Europe was the first step in America's global strategy to contain the Soviet Union's expansion in Europe.

22. The Eisenhower Doctrine enunciated in January 1957 sought to contain and reduce the growth and spread of Arab nationalism and radical forces, which were perceived as a sign of increasing Soviet influence in the region. The doctrine premised that the US must be prepared to use its armed forces "to secure and safeguard the territorial integrity and political independence of such states, requesting any aid against overt armed attack and aggression from any country controlled and directed by international Communism." The doctrine declared a very strong commitment to eliminate Soviet influence in the Gulf region.

23. The Nixon doctrine sought to avoid repetition of the Vietnam experience by using regional surrogate states, instead of direct involvement, to protect US interests. The doctrine's emphasis was to build and militarily strengthen American allies in the region who saw their interests tied to US interests and objectives in the area. Countries threatened by communist aggression must take the primary responsibility for their defence. This did not mean that US forces had no military role; what it did mean was that threatened countries had to be willing to bear the primary burden of supplying the manpower. It undertook to provide arms and money to nations in the path of direct or indirect aggression, if they could provide the men.

Saudi Arabia to procure modern weaponry and training for its armed forces believing that cooperation between Iran and Saudi Arabia would ultimately protect US security interests.

In 1968, Great Britain announced a total withdrawal of its remaining military forces east of Suez. This was immediately followed by the first deployments of Soviet naval ships in the Indian Ocean. The Soviet Navy's deployments to the northern Indian Ocean in 1967-68 stemmed from two developments:

- To fill the vacuum following Britain's 1964 decision to withdraw from 'east of Suez'.

- The threat to the southern Soviet Union posed by the 4000-kilometre Polaris missiles that could arise if the US decided to deploy its nuclear-powered ballistic missile equipped submarines to the Arabian Sea. The US' development of facilities in Diego Garcia[24] and in Australia added to this apprehension.

To minimise the need for base facilities in the Indian Ocean littoral, the Soviet Navy relied on floating anchorages having ships with repair facilities in international waters.

During the 1973 Arab-Israel war, the Organisations of Arab Petroleum Exporting Countries clamped a complete embargo on oil exports to the US because it supported Israel. To exert further pressure on the US, the Organisation instituted a series of cutbacks in oil production that reduced the availability of oil worldwide, created an acute shortage of oil and caused the price of oil to skyrocket.

By the mid 1970s, the US realised that a permanent naval presence would be necessary for rapid deployment in the Gulf. It planned to further develop Diego Garcia as a basing facility for a US task force in the Indian Ocean.

One of the first actions by the Carter Administration in 1977 was to initiate negotiations with the Soviet Union leading toward a demilitarisation of the Indian Ocean. That effort was suspended as a result of Soviet and Cuban intervention in the Horn of Africa.

In 1978, the US increased the flow of arms and advisers to Iran to bolster the Shah of Iran's efforts to counter growing domestic dissidence against 'westernisation'. In response to Soviet concern over US attempts to influence developments in Iran, the US stated that whilst they would not interfere in Iran's internal affairs, the US firmly supported the Shah in his efforts to restore tranquility in

Iran and would maintain relations with Iran in foreign policy, economics and security. In the end of 1978, a conservative Islamic revolution, inspired by Ayatollah Khomeini, took over and forced the Shah to abdicate.

The US Administration was now faced with progressive instability in the strategic 'Northern Tier' of the Middle East that had been designed in the Eisenhower era to block the Soviet Union's southward expansion – Turkey, Iran, Afghanistan and Pakistan were all becoming unstable. This led to the temporary deployment to the Indian Ocean of aircraft carriers from America's Pacific Ocean Fleet and the crystallisation of longer-range plans for the Indian Ocean - a Rapid Deployment Force (RDF) and the expansion of the facilities in Diego Garcia.

America therefore now turned to a new ally Saddam Hussein in Iraq.[25]

By 1980, with Soviet help, Iraq had built up its military strength to become the most powerful state in the Gulf. The US Administration started improving relations with Iraq. Militarily, Iraq was the Gulf's most important state and, after Saudi Arabia, the Gulf's most important oil producing state. After its Revolution, Iran had become America's new enemy.

Iraq seized the opportunity of the Revolution in Iran to settle old territorial disputes. It invaded Khuzistan, where Iran's oil fields were located. During the war, the US Administration facilitated arms sales to Iraq not so much to support Mr Saddam Hussein, but out of antipathy toward Iran's Ayatollah Khomeini. The Iran-Iraq war lasted from 1980 to 1988.[26] Iran recovered its territory at an enormous cost in lives. When Iraq resorted to chemical warfare, Iran sued for peace.

After Iraq won that devastating war, Mr Saddam Hussein continued to pursue independent economic development rather than letting transnational corporations reap profit from his country's oil resources. He worked to form the Arab Cooperation Council to join Iraq with Jordan, Egypt, and Yemen in a regional trading bloc.

The Reagan Administration reiterated the re-imposition of the Carter Doctrine, with the aims and intentions of the Truman Doctrine, which represented 'an unequivocal commitment to respond, in whatever fashion necessary, to any strategic effort to gain a geopolitical presence in the Gulf.'

---

24. See Reference Note 10, page 418.

25. See Reference Note 11, page 419.

26. See Reference Note 12, page 420.

MAJOR AND MINOR PORTS OF INDIA

INDEX
● MAJOR PORTS
○ Minor Ports

INDIA

ARABIAN

SEA

BAY

OF

BENGAL

Jakhau
Mundra KANDLA
Navlakhi
Rozi
Okha Sikka
Salaya
Porbandar
Navibandar
Mangrol
Veraval Diu Simar
Bhavnagar Dehaj
Magdalla
Pipavav
Jafarabad
Daman

MUMBAI
Revadanda
Murud - Janjira
Srivardhan Bankot
Harnai
Dabhol
Jaigarh
Pavas Ratnagiri
Devgarh Vijayadurg
Malvan
Vengurla
Redi
MORMUGAO
Betul
Karwar
Belikeri
Honavar
Bhatkal
Coondapoor
Malpe
NEW MANGALORE
Mangalore
Kasaragod
Azhikal
Cannanore
Chetlet Tellicherry
Kiltan Badagara
Kadmat Beypore
Amini Ponnani
Kalpitti Androth Chetwai
Kavaratti Azhikkal
Kalpeni KOCHI
Alleppy Mandapam
Quilon Veppalodai
Kolachel TUTICORIN
Vilinjam
Minicoy

LAKSHADWEEP

KOLKATA
HALDIA
Baleshwar
Dhamra
PARADIP
Gopalpur
Bavanapadu
Kalingapatnam
Bhimunipatnam
VISHAKHAPATNAM
Kakinada
Machilipatnam
Nizampatnam
Vadarevu
Ramaypatnam
Krishnapatnam
Ennore
CHENNAI
Mahabalipuram
Pondicherry
Cuddalore
Porto Novo
Nagapattinam

SRI
LANKA

Landfall I
Temple Sound Port Cornwallis
Stewart Sound
ANDAMAN Maya Bandar
Rangat
Port Anson Elphinston Hr
Port Meedows Laccam Hr
ISLANDS Fusilier Chan
Port Blair
Jackson Cr Dugong Cr
Hut Bay

Sawai Bay
Mus Anch Car Nicobar
Batti Malv

Castle Bay
NICOBAR Nancowry
Katchal
East B
ISLANDS Pulo Milow Laful B
St. Georges Ch Campbell
South B

MALDIVE

ISLANDS

INDIAN OCEAN

N
NW NE
W E
SW SE
S

By the end 1980s, when it became clear from the Soviet Union's reforms to dismantle its centralised economic structure that the Cold War was nearing its end, there was a significant shift in US policy.

Mr John Lehman, the Secretary of the Navy said in his report for Fiscal year 1987 to the US Congress that:

"We no longer depend on West Asia and the Gulf for our vital energy needs. Oil from this area now forms less than 5% of our total oil imports. Today the United States has an Indian Ocean orientation at least equal to our involvement with Europe in war. We plan to deploy two Carrier Battle Groups and one Battle Ship Group to operate in the Indian Ocean".

Later, in the same report, the US Chief of Naval Operations, Admiral Watkins stated:

"The scope of US world wide interests focus on the developing world and not necessarily as parts of a strategy to counter the Soviets in global war..."

In 1990, Iraq invaded Kuwait to settle several disputes—territorial and financial. It led to the US led Gulf War of 1991 that forced Iraq to withdraw from Kuwait.[27] The Administration of President Bush (Senior) described the Persian Gulf region as a 'nerve centre' of the industrialised and developed Western economies. In the US view, it was a "stark struggle against Iraq for domination and control of oil resources of the region – these oil resources were not only the life-blood of modern developed countries but also a vital element of military power."

After the end of the Cold War in 1991, the dissolution of the Soviet Union and the Warsaw Pact meant that the US no longer had a global superpower to confront, except for China, which was seen as a long-term future rival. Consideration began of how the US should recast its Gulf policy and transform the roles of its Armed Forces.

This bird's eye view of American policy in the Persian Gulf makes it clear that the successive 'Doctrines' announced by the US are links of a constantly evolving policy to maintain control of the energy resources of the Persian Gulf.

India's Transition to South Asian Maritime Eminence

For the first time in the history of the Indian Ocean, India, a littoral country, has emerged in the region extending from the coast of Africa to Malaysia as the largest, most stable, democratic, populous, multi-ethnic nation, whose modern Navy is being looked at for its potential to contribute to maritime stability.

Certain facets of geo-strategy are, and will continue to be relevant:

- The continuity in American Indian Ocean and Persian Gulf naval policy.
- The continuing presence of western navies.
- The trend towards entrusting to regional navies the safeguarding of their respective segments of the Indian Ocean SLOCs.
- The expectation that in the years ahead the Indian Navy could and should play a stabilising role in the northern half of the Indian Ocean.

India has neither territorial claims nor any clash of maritime interests. For over 30 years, it has steadfastly supported the United Nations resolution for this Ocean to be a zone of peace. It also has an efficient Army, Navy and Air Force to defend its interests. India's contribution to regional stability will therefore be invaluable.

India's bilateral strategic and cooperative relationships with the US, Russia and with other countries in the region will need to reconcile, and be comfortable, with the reality that:

- The US has made heavy investments over decades to safeguard its interests in the Indian Ocean and the Persian Gulf. Its forces are not going to leave soon. The Fifth Fleet will remain in the Persian Gulf, as will pre-positioned intervention capability and its facilities in Diego Garcia.
- Regardless of anti-American hostility in the Persian Gulf, to which America has become accustomed over the decades, US policies will, as in the past, adroitly manage regional disputes.

India has little to lose from this reality. Continued US presence will help ensure that Persian Gulf oil is available at affordable prices without interruption. The US effort to politically stabilise India's neighborhood is in India's interest.

The Indian Navy's transition to eminence has been timely and essential to secure India's growing role as an economic powerhouse and to contribute towards a secure and prosperous region.

It is against this background that the development of the Indian Navy during the period 1976 to 1990 is best viewed.

---

27. See Reference Note 13, page 420.

2

Diego Garcia, Addoo Atoll And Gan

Diego Garcia

Historical Background

The semicircular Chagos Archipelago, a group of islands and coral atolls, is located in the central Indian Ocean, about 1,000 miles (1,600 km) from the southern tip of India. It has an area of 44 sq km encircling a V-shaped, 24 km long, 11 km wide lagoon that is open at the north end.

Diego Garcia is the largest of the fifty-two islands that comprise the archipelago. It was discovered by the Portuguese in the early 1500s. In 1715, the island was claimed by the French and governed from Mauritius. After the English captured Mauritius in 1810, France formally ceded possession in 1814.

In the past, under both French and English rule, the island was used primarily for coconut plantations. During French rule, the plantations flourished under individual ownership. After France lost the area to England, the plantations were sold to private companies based in Mauritius, Seychelles and England. A coaling station and a phosphate mine were set up in the 19th century.

During World War I, the German commerce-raiding cruiser *Emden* put into Diego Garcia for some time. During World War II, Indian troops manned the coast battery guns and the seaplane base at East Point. Until the early 1950s, the island was used as a coaling station for ships travelling between Australia, New Zealand and Indonesia to and from the Seychelles and Mauritius.

In 1964, Britain decided to start withdrawing its forces from 'East of Suez' and pass on the strategic responsibility for the Indian Ocean to the USA. The Chagos Archipelago was strategically situated at the centre of the Indian Ocean, it lay out of the path of cyclonic storms and there was no likelihood of any local political opposition. At the time, it was the best available choice for a naval base.

On 8 November 1965, before granting independence to Mauritius, Britain created a new colony called the British Indian Ocean Territory (BIOT),* by amalgamating the Aldabra Islands and the Farquhar and Desroches islands (all of which were purchased from the Seychelles, a British Colony) with the Chagos Archipelago (which was formerly a dependency of Mauritius).

Under a bi-lateral agreement in 1966, the islands of the BIOT were earmarked for defence purposes. Britain leased Diego Garcia to the US for an initial period of 50 years, under dual British and US control, as part of their worldwide communication network.

After 1966, most of Diego Garcia's transient population was relocated to Mauritius and the Seychelles. In 1968, Britain announced the withdrawal of its remaining military forces east of Suez. This was immediately followed by the first deployments of Soviet naval ships in the Indian Ocean.

Until 1970, the production of copra from coconut palms was the only economic activity. About 350 people, most of them from Seychelles, were employed at the East Point plantation. They picked and processed about 100 tonnes of coconut per month for export to India via the Seychelles.

Britain finally withdrew its forces from east of Suez on 30 November 1971. In 1971, when the US commenced construction activity, only one plantation remained in operation and the last of the plantation workers and their families were moved to Mauritius.

From the outset, the littoral and island states of the Indian Ocean protested against the development of Diego Garcia. They wanted to preserve the 'zone of peace', non-militarised status of the Indian Ocean as embodied in United Nations resolutions, but to no avail.

In June 1976, the islands purchased from the Seychelles were returned to the newly independent Republic of Seychelles. After that date, the BIOT comprised only the islands of the Chagos Archipelago.

From 1965 to 1976, the administrative headquarters of the BIOT were at Victoria in the Seychelles. After 1976,

---

* See Reference Note 10, page 418.

DIEGO GARCIA

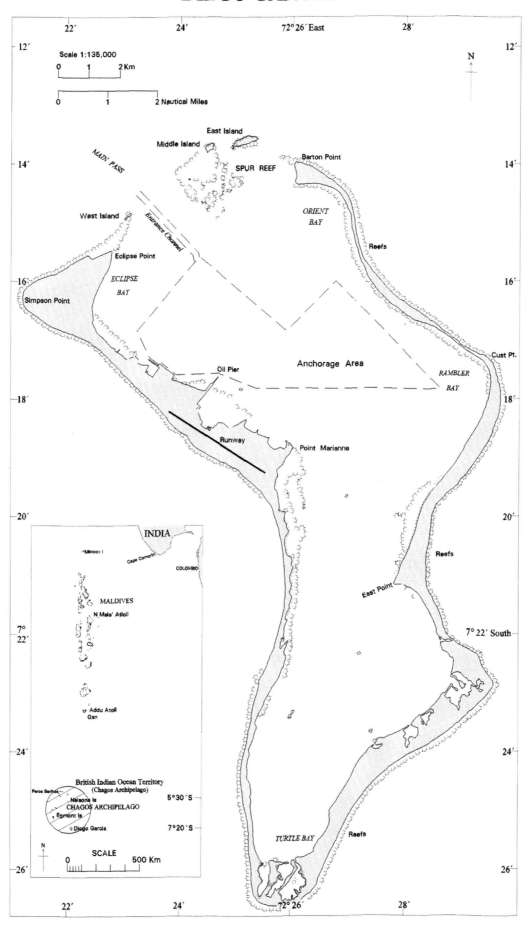

Scale 1:135,000

0   1   2 Km

0   1   2 Nautical Miles

N

MAIN PASS

East Island

Middle Island

SPUR REEF

Barton Point

West Island

Entrance Channel

ORIENT BAY

Eclipse Point

Reefs

ECLIPSE BAY

Simpson Point

Cust Pt.

Anchorage Area

RAMBLER BAY

Oil Pier

Runway

Point Marianne

Reefs

East Point

7° 22' South

INDIA

Minicoy I

Cape Comorin

COLOMBO

MALDIVES

N Male' Atoll

7° 22'

Addu Atoll
Gan

British Indian Ocean Territory
(Chagos Archipelago)

Peros Banhos

Nelsons Is

CHAGOS ARCHIPELAGO

Egmont Is

Diego Garcia

5° 30' S

7° 20' S

N

SCALE

0   500 Km

TURTLE BAY

Reefs

72° 26'

they were at the Foreign and Commonwealth Office in London.

The Development of US Facilities in Diego Garcia

Construction commenced in March 1971. A naval communications facility and an 8,000-foot runway were commissioned in 1973. By 1974, a ship channel and turning basin was dredged in the lagoon, the original 8,000-foot runway was extended to 12,000 feet, new hangars, taxiways and accommodation were constructed and all support facilities augmented.

During the 1973 Arab-Israel war, the Organisations of Arab Petroleum Exporting Countries clamped a complete embargo on oil exports to the US because it supported Israel. To exert further pressure on the US, the Organisation instituted a series of cutbacks in oil production that reduced the availability of oil worldwide, created an acute shortage of oil and caused the price of oil to skyrocket.

By the mid 1970s, the US concluded that the security of oil supplies necessitated a permanent US naval presence for rapid deployment in the Persian Gulf. It planned to further develop Diego Garcia as a basing facility for a US task force in the Indian Ocean.

In 1976, the US Senate opposed this expansion until the President reported to Congress his Administration's efforts to negotiate with the Soviets on de-militarisation and naval arms limitations in the Indian Ocean. The Ford Administration turned down the suggestion on the grounds that negotiations on such matters were not in the US interest while the Soviet Union and its Cuban surrogate were actively engaged in support of revolution in Africa, especially in Angola.

In 1975 and 1976, Diego Garcia's facilities were expanded to provide logistic support for US Navy task groups operating in the Indian Ocean. Additional projects were undertaken in 1978.

In the end of 1978, a conservative Islamic revolution, inspired by Ayatollah Khomeini from France, took over and forced the Shah of Iran to abdicate.

The toppling of the Shah of Iran, the success of the anti-American Iranian Revolution and the Soviet intervention in Afghanistan in December 1979[1] combined to sharpen US concern about the security of the oilfields in Iran.

The US Administration was now faced with progressive instability in the entire strategic 'Northern Tier' of the Middle East that had been designed in the Eisenhower era to block the Soviet Union's southward expansion – Turkey, Iran, Afghanistan and Pakistan were all becoming unstable.

The US Administration decided to deter any direct intervention in Iran that the Soviet Union might be tempted to contemplate. This led to the 1980 Carter Doctrine.[2] It created the Rapid Deployment Force (RDF) in February 1980, which led to the temporary deployment to the Indian Ocean of aircraft carriers from America's Pacific Ocean Fleet and the expansion of the facilities in Diego Garcia.

The new US defence posture in the Indian Ocean area posited the need for pre-positioned materials to support the rapid deployment force and a more active US presence in the area. It was decided to further expand the facilities at Diego Garcia in order to provide support for several pre-positioned ships, loaded with critical war supplies. By the end of 1980, the Naval Facilities Engineering Command had advertised a $100 million contract for initial dredging at Diego Garcia to expand the berthing facilities.

In January 1983, the Rapid Deployment Force transformed into the Central Command (CENTCOM), whose Headquarters were in the United States. For all practical purposes, the Gulf Region came under the direct control and protection of the United States. Diego Garcia saw the most dramatic build-up of any US location since the Vietnam War.

In 1986, on completion of a $500 million construction programme, Diego Garcia became fully operational as a Naval Support Facility. Thus, what began simply as a communication station on a remote atoll became a major fleet and US armed forces support base by the 1980s.

The 1990 Iraqi invasion of Kuwait marked the most intense operational period in Diego Garcia's history. From 1 August 1990 to 28 February 1991, NAVSUPPFAC Diego Garcia provided levels of support, which outstripped all contingency planning. The base population doubled almost overnight, with the deployment of a Strategic Air Command Bombardment Wing and other aviation detachments. Diego Garcia became the only US Navy base that launched offensive air operations during Operation Desert Storm.

---

1. President Carter's Secretary of State, Zbigniew Brzezinski, is reported to have publicly stated that the United States funded the Afghanistan Mujahedeen six months before the Soviet Union intervened in 1979 in an attempt to provoke the Soviets into an 'un-winnable' war.

2. The Carter Doctrine stated, "Any attempt by any outside force to gain control of the Persian Gulf Region will be regarded as an assault on the vital interests of the US and such an assault will be repelled by any means necessary, including military force."

There is no permanent civilian population in Diego Garcia. In the mid-1990s, about 3,500 US and British military and contract civilian personnel were stationed there.

Addoo Atoll

In 1940, the British East Indies Fleet became seriously concerned about a foray by the more powerful Japanese Navy into the Bay of Bengal. Knowing that its naval bases in Colombo and Trincomalee were weakly defended, it secretly built up fuelling and replenishment facilities at Addoo Atoll in the Maldive Islands.

In February and March 1942, the Japanese captured Singapore and Rangoon. Their next target was expected to be Ceylon. Except for the forces deployed to defend Colombo and Trincomalee, all other British warships in the Indian Ocean were assembled at Addoo Atoll.

In April, the Japanese Navy entered the Bay of Bengal. The details of the naval operations that followed are summarised in the Reference Notes.

By 1944, the Japanese naval threat had ceased to exist. Addoo Atoll was no longer required. The British Fleet returned to Trincomalee from where it launched its operations to recapture the Andaman and Nicobar Islands.

Gan

Gan is a small island in the Addoo atoll, the southernmost atoll of the Maldives Islands. In round figures, it is 700 miles from Sri Lanka, 350 miles from the southern tip of India, 700 miles from Cochin and 380 miles from Diego Garcia.

In 1956, Britain entered into an agreement with the Maldives for the establishment of a British Air Force staging post at Gan and a radio station on the nearby island of Hitadu.

In 1960, the agreement was revised and Gan was leased to Britain for 30 years beginning 1956 against an immediate grant of 100,000 pounds and a further payment of 750,000 pounds spread over an unspecified period as 'project aid'. In 1969, Britain agreed to provide an additional 500,000 pounds for 'developmental projects'. The essential features of the agreement were that the facilities could be used only for Commonwealth defence and for exclusive use by Britain.

In 1974, Britain decided to close down Gan and eventually withdrew in 1976. The Maldives then advertised in leading papers in Hong Kong, Singapore and London inviting tenders for leasing Gan and the facilities thereon for any purpose considered reasonable. Apparently, the decision to advertise was taken because bilateral efforts to interest the US, Germany and France had not evoked any positive response.

In 1976, Gan had the following facilities:
- A 9,000-foot Class A airfield.
- Air surveillance radars, radio communication and satellite tracking facilities.
- A naval anchorage and refuelling and watering facilities.
- Living accommodation for a battalion.
- Base facilities for 60 officers, 500 other ranks and local manpower.

India's position was, and remains, that it is committed to the consensus that as a 'zone of peace', the Indian Ocean should be free from military bases. Since Gan is within striking distance of India's southern coast, it would be not be in its strategic interest if Gan's facilities were made available for military use by an inimical power.

Operation Cactus in 1988 reinforced the close and friendly relations between India and the Maldives. These continue to this day.

ADDOO ATOLL

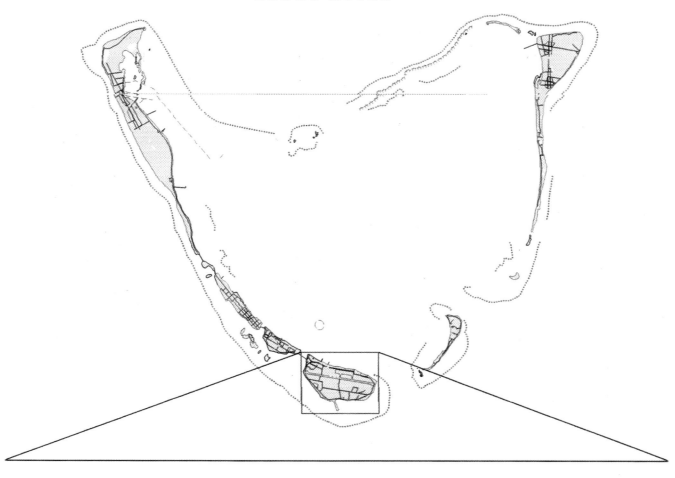

GAN

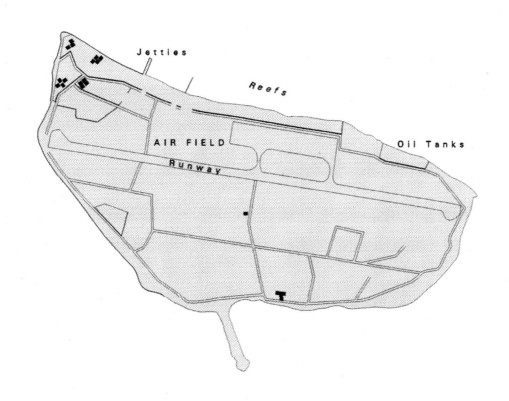

3

The Development Of The Navy Till 1975

Overview

When India attained Independence from Britain in 1947, she had no overseas national interests. The role of the Navy was straightforward – to defend India from seaward aggression.

Independent India's overriding priority was the removal of economic and social backwardness to bring India's millions into the mainstream. Her foreign policy was one of friendship with all, with particular empathy towards countries that were attaining independence after colonial rule. Territorial border disputes with neighbouring countries that were a legacy of de-colonisation were to be resolved bilaterally or in the forum of the British Commonwealth or in the United Nations.

The difficulty started in 1947 with Pakistan's position on Kashmir. The situation became complex with the contest for global supremacy between the United States and the Soviet Union, with both sides forging alliances and arming their Cold War allies. For India, the problem aggravated in the 1950s when India declined the US invitation to participate in the Cold War and Pakistan accepted the invitation. Pakistan received generous military and economic aid as a CENTO and SEATO ally. The aid was meant to counter communism. Everyone knew that Pakistan intended to use it against India. The anti-communism facade faded when Pakistan seized the opportunity to cultivate ties with Communist China after the 1962 India-China border dispute.

Against this brief backdrop, a bird's eye view of the thirty odd years of the Indian Navy's development from 1947 to 1975 shows three peaks:

- 1957 to 1959 when the Navy took measures to cope with United States aid to the Pakistan Navy.
- 1963 to 1965 when, after China's intrusion in 1962, the 1964-69 Defence Plan was formulated to counter

threats from Pakistan and China and the Navy turned to Russia for its acquisitions after the US and Britain had declined naval assistance.

- 1973 to 1975 when, after the 1971 Indo-Pakistan War, the 1974-79 Defence Plan was formulated and Indo-Russian naval cooperation moved to a higher threshold.

Both the 1964-69 and the 1974-79 Defence Plans were approved after consideration of the threats, the inter service priorities, the scarcity of foreign exchange, the scope for self reliance, the likelihood of soft credit being available for the requirements that had to be imported and the capabilities and limitations of Defence R&D and Defence Production.

Developments Between 1947 and 1965

The Acquisition of Ships from Britain

Even though the allocations to the Navy after Independence in 1947 were not high, a modest force was gradually built up. India had chosen to remain a member of the British Commonwealth. As part of the "Commonwealth's defence against the Soviet Union", Britain provided warships to India, as it did to the other members of the Commonwealth. India paid Britain from the sterling balances that had accumulated for the services provided by India to Britain during the 1939-45 World War. In sum, India was able to obtain its immediate defence requirements; Britain was able to dispose of its war surpluses and at the same time run down the war debt represented by the sterling balances.

Despite the Government disinclination to increase defence expenditure and even after meeting the pressing needs of the Army and Air Force, the Navy's percentage share of the defence budget rose from 4% in 1950/51 to 9% in 1956/57 and 12% in 1959/60. From 1961 onwards, the Navy's allocation steadily declined to a low of 4% in 1964/65, because of the pressing need to expand and modernise the Army and the Air Force to cope with China.[1]

Reaction to the US Build-up of the Pakistan Navy

By 1956, Pakistan had joined the US-led anti-Communist CENTO and SEATO alliances and had been promised substantial naval assistance. The US committed to directly supply two destroyers and eight minesweepers and pay Britain for refurbishing and supplying a cruiser and four destroyers. To cope with this development, the Indian Navy obtained approval for the acquisition of destroyers from Britain and decided to retain the existing aging ships in commission. Together with the eight new frigates under construction in Britain, the expectation was that the increased number of ships in the Fleet would balance the increased size of the Pakistan Navy.

Since the Bombay Dockyard would not have been able to berth the increasing number of ships, approval was accorded in 1958 for setting up a major naval base at Vishakhapatnam and the immediate construction there of a jetty and a base workshop.

As an immediate measure to relieve the congestion of ships at Bombay and to ease the growing workload on the Navy's only Dockyard in Bombay, the Navy re-based some ships at Cochin, Vishakhapatnam and Calcutta.

China's Intrusion in 1962 and the 1963-64 Defence Review

The Chinese intrusion in the northern and northeastern land borders in 1962 inflicted serious and humiliating military reverses. It led to a comprehensive review of national security and of the pressing requirements of the Army, Air Force and Navy. This 1963 reappraisal was based on the premise of continuing hostility from both Pakistan and China.

To enable the Army to concentrate its attention on the land borders with Pakistan and China, the Navy took over the coastal defence batteries and the responsibility for coastal defence. The Army also handed over to the Navy the garrisoning and defence of the Andaman and Nicobar Islands; this would help to cope with Indonesia's naval build up that had commenced in 1958 with Soviet assistance.

The 1963 review recommended that the Navy should have a Fleet in the Arabian Sea and a Fleet in the Bay of Bengal, together with the requisite base and logistic support facilities. The Government accepted the acquisition during the 1964-69 Defence Plan of additional ships, submarines and aircraft. These requirements were projected to the United States, the Soviet Union and Britain. In 1964, high-level Inter Service Defence Delegations visited these countries. Only the Soviet Union was willing and able to meet the Navy's requirements.

The Leander Frigate Project

Discussions and negotiations had been in progress with Britain since 1960 for the construction in India of frigates. In October 1964, an agreement was concluded for Mazagon Docks in Bombay to collaborate with Britain to build three Leander class frigates. The first Indian frigate would be built to be in step with its latest counterpart being built in Britain for the British Navy. This would enable the personnel deputed from India to acquire hands-on training and facilitate step-by-step transfer of technology.

The Changeover to Russian Naval Acquisitions

In 1965, a succession of events precipitated the decision to acquire the ships and submarines that the Soviet Union had offered in 1964, the acceptance of which had been deferred:[2]

- In April, Pakistan intruded into Indian territory in Kutch[3]

- In May, Britain informed India that due to its financial difficulties, after having extended credit for the Leander Frigate Project, it was unable to extend credit for a submarine to be built in a British shipyard.[4]

---

1. The 'sterling balances' had exhausted by 1957. By then the new frigates, the second cruiser and the aircraft carrier had been ordered. Overall, the acquisitions from Britain during this period included second hand warships (an aircraft carrier, two cruisers, six destroyers, and a landing ship), followed later by eight new postwar frigates and six new minesweepers.

2. The Navy had been diffident, and reluctant, to sever its traditional connection with Britain's Navy and wanted to await Britain's final response regarding financial assistance for constructing in Britain an Oberon class submarine similar to those being built for the British Navy.

3. Prima facie, the intrusion was to resolve a border claim. Subsequent revelations in Pakistani memoirs revealed that it was a rehearsal for a more aggressive operation planned for taking over Kashmir in August-September of that year.

4. Subsequent revelations indicated that a segment of Britain's Naval hierarchy considered it unwise of India to start a Submarine Arm with an advanced submarine like the Oberon. At another level, there was opposition to the release of this latest technology in view of India's developing defence relationship with the Soviet Union. In November 1965, after India had signed the naval agreement with the Soviet Union, Admiral Mountbatten was to write "I have been instrumental in getting almost all of the requirements of the Indian Navy met by the British Government, including the two cruisers, the aircraft carrier, the destroyers, the organisations for building the frigates at Bombay etc. I had even managed to get more favourable terms for the construction of a British submarine but alas it all took so long that this particular transaction fell through" (quoted in Rear Admiral Sridharan's 'Maritime History of India' page 429.)

- In June, Indonesian intrusions increased in the Nicobar Islands.[5] The Navy recommended to the Government an immediate increase in the naval presence in the Bay of Bengal to deter such intrusions.

- Britain's inability to extend credit to build a submarine (and its earlier expressed inability to meet the Navy's requirements for ships) and the need for increased naval presence in the Andaman and Nicobar (A&N) Islands precipitated the Government's decision to accept the offer of ships and submarines that the Soviet Union had made in September 1964.

- In September 1965, an agreement was concluded for the acquisition from Russia of four submarines, a submarine depot ship, five Petya class submarine chasers, two Landing Ships Tank Medium and five patrol boats, all for deployment in the Bay of Bengal and the A&N Islands.

The 1965 War [6]

Pakistan launched its Operation Gibraltar on 5th August. Sixty companies of Pakistani personnel in disguise, armed with modern weapons and explosives, infiltrated across the cease-fire line over a 700-kilometre front from Kargil to Chhamb. Their task was to blow up bridges and disrupt movement, to raid supply dumps, to kill VIPs and to cause arson. The Indians as well as the local Kashmiris were taken by surprise.

On 5th August itself, some infiltrators were apprehended.[7]

"It was only on 8 August 1965 that more detailed information about extensive infiltration by armed men from Pakistan was provided to India's Prime Minister, Shastri. The Prime Minister asked the Chief of the Army Staff to take whatever action he considered necessary to prevent new infiltrations.

"On 9th August, as per its pre-arranged plan, Pakistan announced a rebellion in Kashmir and the heroic exploits of the freedom fighters who were helping them. It also reported receiving a broadcast, by a secret radio station calling itself as the 'Voice of Kashmir', of the setting up of a Revolutionary Council to take over all authority in Kashmir. Within days, however, it became clear to the world that this was a propaganda hoax. Soon, even Pakistani newspapers ceased further propaganda. By 11th August, the Pakistan Army realised that Operation Gibraltar had flopped. From 15th August onwards, the Pakistan Army stepped up its violation of the cease-fire line on the Srinagar-Leh road".[8]

"The firm decision that the Army should cross the Cease-Fire Line to root out the infiltrators' bases and, in case Pakistan regular forces intervened, our forces should be free to retaliate at any suitable place of their choice was taken on the night of 13th August by the Prime Minister, when the Defence Minister and certain officials, including the Chief of the Army Staff, were present. These decisions were taken on the request of the Chief of the Army Staff that to check infiltration, the infiltrators' bases should be destroyed and in any fight between regular forces, the Services should not be restricted. Shri Lal Bahadur Shastri was anxious to avoid any extension of the conflict but was determined that measures to liquidate infiltrators should be pursued vigorously. The Prime Minister gave expression publicly to the decision taken at his speech from the Red Fort on 15th August, when he declared, "Resort to the sword will be met with the sword". And even as the speech was being made, our troops occupied certain posts across the Cease-Fire Line near Kargil and, in the following days, occupied various places across the Cease-Fire Line, including Haji Pir and destroyed the infiltrators' hideouts." [9]

When Pakistan Army Headquarters found that the tide was turning against them, pressure mounted to retrieve the situation by launching the third phase – Operation Grand Slam – to capture Akhnoor and Amritsar. This operation would require the Pakistan Army to move across the international frontier. On 1st September, a column of seventy tanks and two brigades of troops drove towards

---

5. Aceh, the turbulent province in the northern tip of Indonesia's island of Sumatra is separated from the southern tip of India's island of Great Nicobar by a mere 90 miles.

6. The details of the events leading up to, and the naval operations during the 1965 War have been discussed in the preceding volume titled 'Transition to Triumph – History of the Indian Navy 1965 -1975.' In this volume, this war has been dealt with as briefly as possible so that the reader can co-relate the pattern of events with that in the 1971 War and again in the end 1990s.

7. In his foreword to Air Marshal Asghar Khan's book 'The First Round', Mr Altaf Gauhar, then Pakistan's Secretary of Information and Broadcasting states: (Page xii).

"The truth is that the first four volunteers who were captured by the Indians described the whole plan in a broadcast on All India Radio on 8 August 1965, nearly a month before India crossed the international boundary." On hearing these broadcasts, Pakistan realised that its secret plan was now open knowledge.

8. Mr CP Srivastava, the Private Secretary to Prime Minister Shastri in 1965, in his memoirs 'Lal Bahadur Shastri,' Page 208.

9. Mr PVR Rao, the Defence Secretary in 1965, in his 1972 Lecture to the United Services Institution of India.

Akhnoor Bridge to cut off the supply line from the Punjab to Kashmir.

Intense air battles took place over the next few days. The Pakistan Army achieved initial surprise at Chhamb. By 5th September, when they were only 20 miles from Jammu, on their way to the crucial Akhnoor Bridge over the River Chenab, the Air Force halted the Pakistani columns at Jaurian.

"When the conflict started in the Jammu area of Kashmir and their tanks came into our territory where our tanks could not easily go because the bridges were not strong enough, there was a real dilemma. It was still being thought of as a local battle. But we realised that the terrain where we were fighting was one where we were much more vulnerable and communication depended on a couple of bridges – if they were blown up, we just would be completely cut off. And, therefore, thought turned to using the plan, which had been earlier evolved, for marching into Lahore. But even then, it was a very firm decision that we would not allow things to escalate into a full-scale war – I mean war in the legal sense – between India and Pakistan.

"Admiral Soman (India's Chief of the Naval Staff) had in the meantime – ever since the involvement of the Air Force (on 1st September) – been straining at the leash saying, 'Look, let me go into action.' But again the same consideration, which was acting as a restraint – on using the Air Force or going into Lahore – prevailed. It was felt that if we now opened up another front off Karachi, it would become a major engagement and would no longer be a matter of localised conflict. So the decision was taken that the operation to march into Lahore would be launched but that the Navy would not be involved.

"The Indian Army crossed the international border at Wagah on the morning of 6th December and headed for Lahore. President Ayub (of Pakistan) went on the air. It was a very, very strong and angry broadcast. Admiral Soman thought that the opening of the Lahore front meant that a no-holds-barred situation had come and he, I think, issued a signal that we were at war with Pakistan. This signal had to be countermanded, because we did not want to go to that stage so soon. But still we realised that the Navy had the capability and if the events so necessitated, I don't think there would have

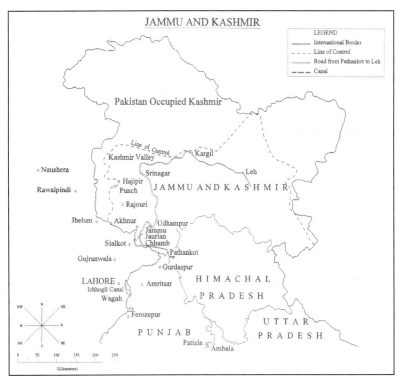

been too long a hesitation to use it. But the feeling was strong that if we could contain the Pakistani forces and hold them on land, then perhaps it would be wiser not to get the Navy involved. I knew that the Navy was not happy with this decision because they were very anxious to go into action."[10]

At Naval Headquarters in New Delhi, the situation was quite vexed. After the Chinese intrusion in 1962, the Army had handed over the garrisoning and defence of the A&N Islands to the Navy. Between 1962 and 1965, close relations had developed between Indonesia and Pakistan. Pursuant to Indonesia's intrusions into the islands in 1964, the best the Navy could do was to show a strong presence in the region with whatever ships were available. In August 1965, when Pakistan launched Operation Gibraltar, all the operational ships of the Indian Fleet were in the Bay of Bengal. When Pakistan's intrusions started in August and the Navy considered bringing the Fleet back to Bombay from the east, it was told not to get involved. When the Pakistan Army crossed the international border on 1st September, the Fleet was recalled to Bombay – ships arrived a week later in ones and twos because of their disparate speeds.

"On 6th September, the Pakistan Flotilla received the news that the Indian Army had attacked across the

---

10. Mr LK Jha, the Principal Secretary to the Prime Minister, in "Blueprint to Bluewater" Pages 460 et seq.

international border in the Lahore area and ships sailed for their pre-assigned war stations.

"On the afternoon of 7th September, Pakistan Naval Headquarters directed a task group, comprising the cruiser, five destroyers and a frigate, to bombard Dwarka the same night and added that one or two enemy frigates may be encountered in the area in addition to enemy air threat. The task group refuelled from their tanker and arrived off Dwarka at midnight. Dwarka was blacked out and could only be identified on radar… After a four-minute bombardment, the task group withdrew at full speed."[11]

The attack on Dwarka outraged India and humiliated the Navy.[12] There were questions in Parliament as to where the Navy was and what it was doing. The fact was that the ships of the Fleet had just trickled into Bombay and were replenishing prior to sortying out on 10th September.

Until the cease-fire on 23rd September, the Fleet patrolled off the coast of Saurashtra. No contact occurred with any units of the Pakistan Navy.

Viewed in retrospect, the Navy's development between 1947 and 1965 was steady:

- Eight new frigates from Britain had augmented the old ships of the 1939-45 World War.

- The indigenous construction of a modern frigate, as also minor war vessels, had been taken in hand.

- Agreements had been signed for the induction of Russian ships and submarines.

- Useful operational lessons had been learnt in the 1965 War.

Developments Between 1965 and 1975

The Russian Acquisitions

From 1968 onwards, the Russian ships and submarines, contracted for in 1965, started arriving in India. The 1960s technology in these Russian acquisitions was more advanced than the 1950s technology that had entered service between 1958 and 1961 in the new British frigates. On the other hand, these Russian vessels and their machinery and equipment had been designed for the Soviet Navy – for colder temperatures, for colder and less corrosive seas, for Russian dietary requirements, for Russian naval norms of fresh water consumption / capacity, etc. The number of bunks conformed to Russian officer and sailor branches and specialisations. The maintenance,

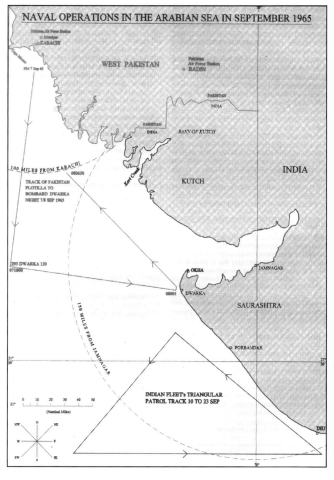

NAVAL OPERATIONS IN THE ARABIAN SEA IN SEPTEMBER 1965

refit and logistics procedures conformed to practices in the Soviet Union. And so on.

Almost as soon as the ships and submarines commissioned, the Indian side started suggesting modifications. Interaction between the Navies and with the designers and shipyards in the Soviet Union enabled some modifications to be incorporated before delivery. This positive interaction resulted in the Navy placing orders in end 1971 for five more Petya class submarine chasers and four more submarines.

The Submarines and the Build-up of Anti Submarine Proficiency

The arrival of the submarines from 1968 onwards gave the anti submarine frigates and the aircraft carrier's anti submarine Alize aircraft their long awaited 'exercise time' with submarines. The increase in anti submarine effectiveness was, however, short of expectations. There were several reasons:

---

11. The Story of the Pakistan Navy, pages 216 et seq.

12. Revenge for this outrage was to manifest itself in the 1971 Indo-Pakistan War in wanting the Indian Fleet to bombard ports on Pakistan's Makran Coast.

- For the first time, the Navy came to grips with the unusual hydrological conditions in Indian waters. These conditions favoured the submarines – they could lurk in shadow zones beneath layers of sea temperature. Sonars mounted on ships' hulls could not penetrate these layers – their sound waves got refracted. This highlighted the urgent need for ships and helicopters to have sonars that could be lowered to depths at which submarines could be detected.[13]

- The submariners were eager not only to demonstrate their offensive potential in pro-sub exercises but also to work out their capabilities and limitations for operational patrols during war. Submarine time had, therefore, to be shared between anti submarine work-up exercises, pro-sub exercises and training more submarine personnel to enable the fledgling Submarine Arm to grow.

- The annual rotation of ships crews meant that personnel who had acquired anti submarine proficiency had to be replaced by others who needed to acquire this proficiency. This retarded the overall build up of anti submarine expertise.

- The time lag in the setting up of specialised workshops and test facilities resulted in ships' sonars not being in top condition.

The Seaking Anti Submarine Helicopters

In 1964, the US had loaned the Pakistan Navy its first submarine, the Ghazi. After the 1965 War, the Pakistan Navy's programme for acquiring French Daphne class submarines with longer-range torpedoes made it clear that it intended to concentrate its offensive potential in submarines and deploy its surface flotilla defensively.

At this time, the US Navy was developing anti submarine helicopters equipped with 'dunking' sonar that could be lowered into the sea while hovering and armed with an air-dropped, anti submarine homing torpedo. This innovative combination overcame the hazards that surface ships faced when combating a submarine. Firstly, being airborne, the helicopter could not be hit by a submarine torpedo. Secondly, by having a sonar device, whose depth under the surface could be raised and lowered to obtain maximum detection range, the helicopter could overcome adverse hydrology and deprive the submarine of its ability to evade detection by lurking below the temperature layers

of the sea. Britain was developing equivalent Seaking helicopters for its Navy.[14]

In 1969, approval was accorded for the Navy to acquire from Britain six Seakings and their homing torpedoes. In 1970, an order was placed for their delivery in 1971. The Seakings arrived a few months before the Indo Pakistan War broke out in December 1971.

The Advent of Anti Ship Missiles

After the Pakistan Navy's bombardment of Dwarka in the 1965 War, Naval Headquarters had been deliberating measures for the defence of the Kutch and the Saurashtra coast against Pakistani hit and run raids.

In the early 1960s, the Soviet Union had supplied small, fast, thin-skinned boats armed with surface-to-surface missiles to the Indonesian and Egyptian navies. These boats had also been offered to the Indian delegation that had visited Russia in 1964, but their acquisition had been accorded lesser priority because their effectiveness had yet to be proved in war.

In the 1967 Arab-Israel war, anti ship missiles fired from an Egyptian boat deployed for harbour defence, summarily sank, within minutes, an approaching Israeli frigate at a range well beyond the latter's guns. It heralded the eclipse of gun battles between warships and the transition to swift missile engagements beyond visual range.

In 1968, the Navy obtained approval to acquire missile boats from Russia, primarily to deter Pakistani ships from bombarding the Kutch and Saurashtra coast. In 1969, an agreement was concluded with Russia for the supply of missile boats. Eight of these boats arrived in early 1971.

The Russian Acquisitions

By 1971, four submarines, a submarine depot ship, a submarine rescue vessel, two landing ships, five submarine chasers, and five patrol boats had arrived and were based in Vishakhapatnam. Though they had been acquired for the Bay of Bengal and the A&N Islands, they had started exercising in the Arabian Sea as well. The eight missile boats were based in Bombay.

To support these acquisitions, work had commenced in Vishakhapatnam on the construction of a new Dockyard, of submarine support facilities, of torpedo preparation facilities and of training facilities. The construction of the

---

13. In ships, these sonars were called variable depth sonars. In helicopters, they were called 'dunking sonars'.

14. The Seaking gearboxes were of US origin. When the US imposed sanctions after India's nuclear tests in 1998, some Seaking gearboxes were in the US for overhaul and came within the purview of the sanctions. It took several years for these gearboxes to be returned even after the sanctions were lifted. The Chapter on Defence Procurement discusses the nuances of such vexatious embargos.

new workshops was retarded, however, by the sinking of their floors, due to the inability of the local marshy soil to bear their heavy weight. These delays in setting up maintenance and refit facilities seriously afflicted the operational state of Russian equipment.

The Leander Frigate Project

The construction of the first two frigates had commenced but was behind schedule due to the teething problems of start up, the changeover from British analogue electronics to Dutch digital electronics in radars, fire control systems and AIO from the second frigate onwards and the problems of indigenising major items like the propulsion and auxiliary machinery systems.

Aircraft for Vikrant

The only aircraft that could replace the aircraft carrier's ageing Seahawks were the US Navy's A4 Skyhawks. Efforts to acquire the A4s had not been successful. It was decided, therefore, to avail of the opportunity to acquire the Seahawks being disposed of by the German Navy. These aircraft arrived in 1968 and were to prove useful in 1971.

The 1971 War[15]

During the months preceding the outbreak of war in December 1971, there were developments connected with the two latest acquisitions – the Russian missile boats and the British anti submarine helicopters. The first was the working through of the innovative concept of Fleet ships towing the tiny, limited-range but fast and powerful, missile boats into the Arabian Sea from where they could be detached, under escort, to carry out a missile attack and to be taken back in tow after the attack. The second was to maximise the effectiveness, in tropical hydrological conditions, of the new Seakings against Pakistan's newly acquired Daphne class submarines. The missile boat innovation was successful. The Seakings were not fully exploited.

There was a sharp contrast between the type of operations in the Bay of Bengal (Eastern Naval Command) and those in the Arabian Sea (Western Naval Command).

In the Bay of Bengal, there was no surface threat. At the very beginning of the war, the submarine threat vanished after the US-loaned, Pakistan submarine, *Ghazi*, exploded at the entrance to Vishakhapatnam harbour whilst laying mines. There was no air threat after Indian Air Force attacks grounded aircraft in East Pakistan.

Carrier borne aircraft avoided attacking neutral merchant shipping at sea. They concentrated on immobilising Pakistani vessels and cratering all airstrips, which Pakistani forces in East Pakistan might use to escape capture. Ships of the Eastern Fleet enforced contraband control until tasked with an amphibious landing to cut off escape routes into Burma.

Pakistan's forces in the east laid down their arms after a short, sharp campaign of thirteen days. The new nation of Bangladesh came into being.

The situation in the Arabian Sea was altogether different. The submarine, surface and air threats were higher. There were differences in the assessment of these threats between Naval Headquarters and Headquarters Western Naval Command. These were serious enough for FOCINCWEST to voice his concern.

The first missile boat attack on Karachi, launched from Saurashtra along the coast, was a success – it sank a Pakistani destroyer and a coastal minesweeper. In Naval Headquarters and Headquarters Western Naval Command, however, there was restlessness at the Western Fleet's diversion southward to shake off Pakistani reconnaissance aircraft because this diversion delayed the second missile boat attack that was to be launched by the Fleet from seaward. After the Fleet regrouped, it detached ships to attack Karachi and the Makran ports on night 6/7 December. On the afternoon of 6th December, Naval Headquarters intervened to cancel the Fleet's attack on Karachi.[16]

Unknown to the Indian side, the Pakistan Flotilla had prudently withdrawn into Karachi harbour:

"After the missile attack, the position of the surface ships at sea became almost untenable, as they had no defence against missiles. On 7th December, the Flag Officer Commanding the Flotilla, after consulting his sea going commanders, met the C-in-C. He acquainted him with the prevailing situation and suggested a withdrawal of the ships inside the harbour in order to escape a missile attack, which was most likely to occur. The ships would of course be more susceptible to air attack there, but could also provide a powerful anti aircraft threat, particularly against a low flying attack.

---

15. The details of the events leading up to, and all the naval operations during the 1971 War have been discussed in the preceding volume titled "Transition to Triumph – History of the Indian Navy 1965 - 1975.'

16. That very morning a Pakistan Air Force aircraft had mistakenly attacked a Pakistan Navy frigate on patrol off Karachi. India's Chief of Naval Staff assessed that the state of alertness off Karachi signified by this incident warranted a postponement of the missile boat attack speeding to strike Karachi that night.

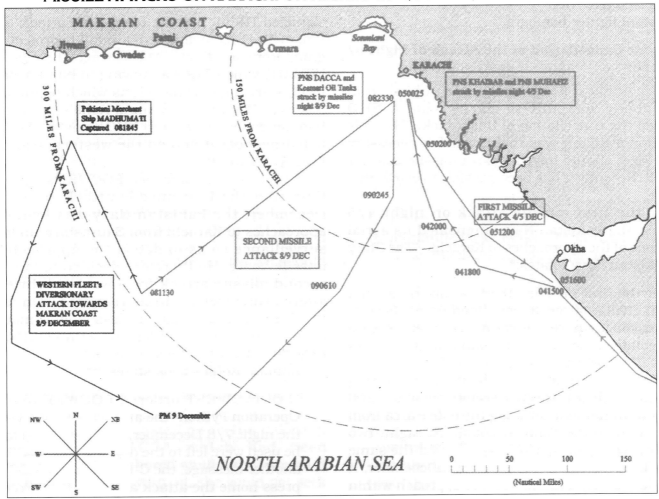

It was, therefore, decided to withdraw all ships to the harbour on 8th December, except for the fleet oil tanker, which was fully loaded. It had to stay out because of the fire hazard within the harbour by its presence and also since its deep draught restricted entry into port. The oil tanker *Dacca* was, therefore, ordered to anchor with the other merchant ships away from the port."[17]

The Indian Fleet planned its next attack for night 8/9 December – a missile boat attack on Karachi and gun bombardment of Jiwani on the Makran coast to divert attention from the missile boat group. The bombardment group, under the cruiser *Mysore*, apprehended Pakistani merchant ship *Madhumati* south of Jiwani after she had transmitted an SOS to Karachi. After *Madhumati* had been boarded, FOCWEF called off the gun bombardment of Jiwani as he considered the merchant ship's SOS to Karachi a sufficient distraction for the missile attack group

racing towards Karachi. Once again, the missile attack achieved surprise. Fortuitously, a missile set Karachi's fuel storage tanks aflame and another hit *Dacca,* the Pakistan Navy's tanker, at the anchorage.

These two missile attacks on Karachi resulted in international shipping seeking from the Government of India in New Delhi an assurance for safe passage out of Karachi. The Western Fleet had achieved dominance of the sea approaches to Karachi.

However, once again, there was restlessness in Naval Headquarters and Headquarters Western Naval Command at the *Mysore* Group not bombarding Makran to avenge the 1965 bombardment of Dwarka.

On 7th December, Naval Headquarters prodded FOCINCWEST to do something about the Pakistani submarine that had been reliably D/F'd off Bombay. On

---

17. Excerpt from "Pakistan's Crisis in Leadership" by Maj Gen Fazal Muqeem Khan published in Pakistan in 1972, soon after the war.

8th December, two frigates, *Khukri* and *Kirpan,* were sailed from Bombay to 'flush' this submarine away from the Saurashtra coast where ships were assembling for the next missile attack on Karachi.

On the evening of 9th December, the Pakistani submarine *Hangor* successfully torpedoed and sank the *Khukri*.[18] A sustained anti submarine operation over the next four days was unable to prevent the *Hangor's* return to Karachi.[19]

On the evening of 10th December, an Alize aircraft was sent to probe suspicious activity near the Indo-Pakistan naval border off Jakhau. It ended in a fatal chance encounter. The Alize fell prey to a Sidewinder missile fired by a homeward-bound Pakistani fighter aircraft.

The war ended on 17th December when Pakistan accepted India's offer of a cease-fire.

In Retrospect

- In the West, the Fleet's rigorous work up and preparation for war validated the maxim that flexibility in battle is gained only through long and arduous preparation. The loss of the *Khukri* was the result of the contentious notion: "How can we have an enemy submarine sitting outside Bombay and do nothing about it." Had the new Seaking anti submarine helicopters acquired from Britain been as rigorously worked up for anti submarine operations against Daphne class submarines as the missile boats had been worked up by the Fleet for missile action at sea, the outcome may well have been different. The lethality of the Daphne's long-range torpedoes was known. Khukri's deliberate decision to search at slow speed so as to increase the chances of her sonar detecting the submarine at longer range sealed her fate.

- In both Fleets, the material state of ships was poor despite a pre war preparation period of seven months. The fact that they achieved what they did was a tribute to the perseverance and ingenuity of the Dockyards and the sheer grit of the ships at sea.

- The Indian Air Force attacks on the installations at Karachi were both precise and timely. The maritime reconnaissance effort by the over-aged Super Connies was as earnest as it could be but totally inadequate to cope with modern submarines like the Daphnes.

The lessons learnt in the war were invaluable. Two basic conclusions shaped the Navy's planning for its future warships.

The first conclusion was that large-calibre gun engagements between warships were no longer likely. Anti ship missiles would dominate future surface warfare. Small calibre guns would be essential for defence against incoming missiles. This led to the decision that future ships should be equipped with surface-to-surface missiles and high rate-of-fire small calibre guns. To start with, a squadron of eight longer-range missile boats was acquired from Russia. The next step was to graft a complete Russian missile boat system on to the British-built frigate *Talwar* and into a missile coast battery at Bombay. From 1976 onwards, all the new ships like the 800-tonne ocean going Durg class rocket boats, the Rajput class destroyers, the Godavari class frigates, the Khukri class corvettes, and their successors, were equipped with missiles, rapid fire guns and active / passive means of electronic warfare. In due course, the new improved Seakings and the new Sea Harriers were equipped with anti ship missiles.

The second conclusion was that defence against a modern conventional submarine required a three-dimensional anti submarine capability:

- *In the air* – MRASW aircraft and anti submarine helicopters with better weapons.

- *In ships* – improving the effectiveness of existing sonars, fitting better sonars and anti submarine weapons in new ships and improving the prediction of hydrological conditions.

- *Under the sea* – acquiring Hunter-Killer (SSK) submarines.

The Post War Defence Reviews

In 1973, the Government constituted an Apex Committee, headed by the Deputy Chairman of the Planning Commission. Its task was to examine the immediate requirements of the three services based on a re-assessment of the threat and to dovetail its recommendations with the resources likely to be available in the 5th Five Year Plan 1974-79.

The general economic conditions and financial perspectives within which the Committee conducted its deliberations were:

- After China's attack in 1962, Government spending had increased and the years between 1963 and 1967 had experienced rapid inflation.

- Between 1965 and 1967, there had been an extended drought and development outlays had to be cut back.

- The economy improved from 1968 onwards. Between

---

18. This was the first occasion after the 1939-45 World War that a submarine torpedoed and sank a major warship.

19. This setback was to drive the Navy's efforts in ensuing years to improve anti submarine capability.

1970 and 1973, the harvests had been good, there was price stability and development outlays had been increased.

- The only cloud on the horizon was the steadily increasing burden of repayments to Russia. India had started to borrow from Russia for development purposes in 1955. The first defence credit became available in 1965. By the early 1970s, more than 50% of the value of exports from India to Russia under the Trade Plan was being used for payment of interest and repayment of loans. Of this, two thirds was on defence account and one third was on development account. This increasingly required the diversion of India's traditional exports like tea, jute and leather to balance the rupee-rouble trade. Nevertheless, in view of the acute shortage of free foreign exchange, which restricted imports from the West, imports from Russia and the Eastern bloc countries like Poland remained preferable because of their softer terms.

The Committee recommended special consideration for naval development and cleared the Navy's proposals for replacing old ships and the development of support facilities. The Navy progressed discussions with Russia to crystallise the next series of naval acquisitions within the framework of the Committee's recommendations.

The Arab Israel War of October 1973 was followed by a sharp rise in the international prices of oil. This dislocated India's national budgeting and decelerated all defence projects. By 1975, the debilitating impact of spiralling inflation on defence projects made it necessary to appoint another high-level committee.

The tasks of this second committee were to review the needs of the three services in the light of:

- The compulsions of the economic situation and the rise in oil prices.
- The latest weapon systems that had been fielded in the Arab Israel War.
- The need to improve fighting capacity as cost effectively as possible.

It recommended enhanced allocation of funds to support core naval projects.

Between 1972 and 1975, the following had been inducted:

- *Ships:* Five Russian Petya class submarine chasers, eight Russian missile boats, the first two indigenous Leander class frigates (*Nilgiri* in 1972 and *Himgiri* in 1974) and four Polish LSTs.
- *Submarines:* Four Russian submarines.
- *Aircraft:* Six Seakings from Britain. The aircraft carrier *Vikrant* underwent a refit from 1972 to 1975 during which facilities were installed for operating Seaking helicopters.

Overview of Naval Acquisitions from 1947 to 1975

MDL	–	Mazagon Docks Ltd, Mumbai	GSL	–	Goa Shipyard
GRW	–	Garden Reach Workshops, Kolkata	HDL	–	Hooghly Docking Ltd
HSL	–	Hindustan Shipyard Vishakhapatnam	WW	–	Second Hand Ships ex 1939-45 World War

Acquisition	Standard Displacement (Tonnes)	Name	Vintage	Year Ordered	Year Delivered	Supplier
Light Cruiser	7000	DELHI	WW		1948	Britain
Light Destroyers	1700	RAJPUT RANJIT RANA	WW		1949	Britain
Landing Ship Tank	2200	MAGAR	WW		1949	Britain
Escort Destroyers	1000	GODAVARI GOMATI GANGA	WW		1953	Britain
Light Tanker	3500	SHAKTI	WW		1953	Italy
Inshore Mine - sweepers	120	BASSEIN BIMLIPATAM	NEW	1952	1954	Britain

Coastal Mine-sweepers	360	KARWAR CANNANORE CUDDALORE KAKINADA	NEW	1952	1956	Britain
Light Cruiser	8700	MYSORE	WW		1957	Britain
Anti Aircraft Frigates	2250	BRAHMAPUTRA BEAS BETWA	NEW	1955	1958 1958 1960	Britain
Surface Escorts	2150	TRISHUL TALWAR	NEW	1955	1959	Britain
Anti Submarine Frigates	1200	KHUKRI KIRPAN KUTHAR	NEW	1955	1958 1959 1959	Britain
Seaward Defence Boats (for Central Board of Revenue)	63	SUBHADRA SUVARNA SHARAYU SAVITRI	NEW		1957 1958	Italy
Seaward Defence Boats	86	SHARADA, SUKANYA	NEW		1959	Yugoslavia
Repair and Store Ship	4600	DHARINI	Second Hand		1959	Italy
Seaward Defence Boats Mk I	120	AJAY ABHAY AKSHAY	New Indigenous		1960 1961 1962	GRW and HDL
Light Aircraft Carrier	18000	VIKRANT	WW	1957	1961	Britain
Survey Ship	2800	DARSHAK	New Indeginous	1954	1964	Hindustan Shipyard
Landing Ships Tank (Medium)	730	GHARIAL, GULDAR	New	1965	1966	Russia
Patrol Boats	80	PAMBAN PANVEL PANAJI PURI PULICAT	New	1965	1967	Russia
Fleet Tanker	22,600	DEEPAK	New	1964	1967	Germany
Inshore Minesweepers	170	BHATKAL BULSAR	New Indigenous	1961	1968 1970	MDL
Submarines	1975	KALVARI KHANDERI KARANJ KURSURA	New	1965	1967-69	Russia
Submarine Depot Ship	5900	AMBA	New	1965	1968	Russia
Anti Submarine Vessels	1000	KAMORTA KADMATT KILTAN KATCHALL KAVARATTI	New	1965	1968-69	Russia

Seaward Defence Boats Mk I	150	AMAR AJIT ATUL	New Indigenous	1963	1969	GRW
Missile Boats	180	VINASH VIDYUT VIJETA VEER NIRGHAT NIRBHIK NASHAK NIPAT	New	1969	1971	Russia
Submarine Rescue Vessel	800	NISTAR	Reserve Stock	1969	1971	Russia
Leander Class Frigate	2960	NILGIRI	New Indigenous	1966	1972	MDL
Anti Submarine Vessels	1000	ARNALA ANDROTH ANJADIP	1968/69 from Reserve Stock	1971	1972	Russia
Fleet Tug	700	GAJ	New Indigenous	1968	1973	GRW
Anti Submarine Vessels	1000	ANDAMAN AMINI	New Improved	1971	1973-74	Russia
Submarines	1975	VELA VAGIR VAGLI VAGSHEER	New Improved	1971	1973-74	Russia
Leander Class Frigate	2960	HIMGIRI	New Improved	1968	1974	MDL
Landing Ships Tank (Medium)	1120	GHORPAD KESARI SHARDUL SHARABH	New Improved	1972	1975-76	Poland

4

The Growth Of The Navy
1976 – 1990

Preamble

Two major Defence Reviews had marked the closing years of the decade 1965 to 1975. In 1973, the high level APEX Committee recommended special consideration for the Navy's development and cleared the Navy's proposals for replacing old ships and the development of support facilities. Before any agreements could be negotiated, the Arab Israel war erupted in October 1973. As a reaction to America having rushed military aid to Israel, the Arab oil producing nations sharply increased the international price of oil. Since India imported much of her oil from the Persian Gulf, the unavoidable increase in the outflow of foreign exchange seriously dislocated national budgeting and decelerated defence projects. The Navy, nevertheless, continued its ongoing discussions with Russia, so that when times became better, ideas would be clearer about the next series of Russian acquisitions.

The debilitating impact of spiraling inflation in 1974 made it necessary to appoint another high level Apex Committee to review defence needs in the light of strategic developments and economic compulsions. This Committee recommended enhanced allocation of funds to support core naval schemes which otherwise would have languished.

The Government's acceptance of these recommendations underpinned the major acquisitions in 1975.

The failure of the monsoon in 1986 and the resultant drought led to a serious resource crisis from 1987 onwards. To cope, the Navy had to:

- Curtail administrative expenses.
- Reduce inventory levels.
- Reduce fuel consumption.
- Consider preservation of ships and submarines.
- Upgrade the seven Offshore Patrol Vessels (OPVs) to give them a limited combat role.

Some recommendations of the 4th Pay Commission remained un-implemented even in 1990.

Two compulsions had a bearing on the Navy's development. In many ways, they were a blessing in disguise:

- The priority accorded to Army and Air Force requirements to counter land-ward threats limited the Navy to a ship replacement programme. The slowed pace of replacement by indigenous construction and acquisition from Russia helped successive inductions to be technologically superior to their predecessors
- The scarcity of foreign exchange for importing the latest technologies compelled the Navy to innovate and indigenise.

The austerity that resulted from these compulsions kept the Navy lean and agile.

Overview of Ship Acquisitions 1976 - 1990

Acquisitions

- **From Britain:** Second-hand aircraft carrier *Viraat*.
- **From Russia:** Guided missile destroyers, ocean going rocket boats, extended range missile boats, gas turbine propelled missile boats, anti submarine patrol vessels, coastal minesweepers, inshore minesweepers.
- **From Poland:** Landing Ships Tank.
- **From Germany:** Fleet Tanker.
- **From Korea:** Offshore Patrol Vessels.

Indigenous Construction

- 3rd and 4th Leander frigates.
- Improved 5th and 6th Leander frigates.
- Missile frigates of the Godavari class.
- Missile corvettes of the Khukri class.
- Offshore Patrol Vessels.
- Landing Ship Tank Large, Cadet Training Ship, Survey

ships, Fleet Tug, Seaward Defence Boats, Survey Craft, Torpedo Recovery Vessels, Landing craft.

- Diving Support Vessel as Interim Submarine Rescue Vessel.

Modernisations

- *Talwar* and *Trishul* were fitted with Russian missiles.
- *Vikrant* was fitted with a ski jump, new radars, AIO and other facilities to operate the Sea Harrier aircraft and Seaking helicopters

Conversions

- The late 1950s-vintage anti aircraft frigates *Brahmaputra*, *Betwa* and *Beas* were converted to the 'training role' to replace the early 1940s- vintage *Cauvery*, *Krishna* and *Tir*.

Overview of Submarine Acquisitions

Acquisitions

- From **Russia**: - 877 EKM submarines.
  - Nuclear-propelled submarine, *Chakra*, on lease for 3 years.
- From **Germany** - HDW 1500 submarines.

Modernisations

- The improvements effected in the VELA class submarines were retrofitted in the earlier submarines.

Overview of Aircraft and Helicopter Acquisitions

Aircraft Acquisitions

- From **Britain**: - Sea Harriers to replace the Seahawks.
  - Islander aircraft.
- From **Russia**: - TU 142 LRMP and IL 38 MRASW aircraft.
- From **USA**: - Pilotless Target Aircraft.
- **Indigenous** - Transfer from the Air Force of Super Constellation MR aircraft.
  - HJT 16 and Kiran Jet Trainer Aircraft.
- **Modernisations** - Refurbishment of Alizes.

Helicopter Acquisitions

- From **Britain** - ASW and Commando Seakings.
- From **Russia** - ASW Kamovs.
- **Indigenous** - MATCH and SAR helicopters.

Highlights of Developments Between 1976 and 1990

The details of the major developments during the period covered by this volume have been discussed in the respective chapters on:

- The Russian Acquisitions.
- Indigenous Warship Construction.
- The Submarine Arm and the SSK Submarine Project.
- The Air Arm.
- The Revitalisation of Training.

The priorities which the Navy was able to fulfill in large measure were:

- Hybridising Russian, European and indigenous systems in indigenously built ships.
- Induction of the new Sea Harriers, new ASW / ASV helicopters and the aircraft carrier *Viraat*.
- Induction of new submarines and commencing submarine construction in India.
- Anti ship missiles in ships, aircraft, helicopters and coastal defence batteries.
- Improved sonar and sonobuoy systems, and anti submarine weapons in ships, submarines, helicopters, and MRASW and LRMP aircraft.
- Evolving and validating tactical doctrines for the Navy's unique mix of weapons platforms and weapons.
- Creation and upgrading of all maintenance and refit facilities for ships, submarines and aircraft.
- Revitalising Naval Training.
- Building up facilities in the Andaman and Nicobar Islands.
- Synergising Naval R&D.
- Introducing computer culture in all areas of naval activity.

Ships and Submarines Acquired Between 1976 and 1990
Abbreviations used in the table

MDL	–	Mazagon Docks Ltd, Mumbai
GRSE	–	Garden Reach Shipbuilders and Engineers, Calcutta
HSL	–	Hindustan Shipyard Ltd, Visakhapatnam
GSL	–	Goa Shipyard Ltd, Goa
HDL	–	Hoogly Docking and Engineering Works Ltd, Calcutta

Acquisition	Standard Displacement (Tons)	Name	Vintage	Year Ordered	Year Delivered	Supplier
Missile Boats	255	PRALAYA PRATAP PRABAL PRACHAND CHATAK CHAMAK CHAPAL CHARAG	New	1973	1976-77	Russia
Leander Class Frigate	2995	UDAYGIRI DUNAGIRI	New	1967 1970	1976 1977	MDL
Fleet Tanker	22580	SHAKTI	New	1974	1976	Germany
Ocean-going Rocket Boats	675	VIJAYDURG SINDHUDURG HOSDURG	New	1975	1976 1977 1978	Russia
Coastal Minesweepers	800	PONDICHERRY PORBANDAR BHAVNAGAR BEDI ALLEPPEY RATNAGIRI	New	1975	1977 1978 1979 1979 1980 1980	Russia
Seaward Defence Boats MK II	210	T 51 T 52 T 53 T 54 T 55	New	1972 1972 1972 1980 1980	1978 1977 1978 1982 1983	GRSE
Guided Missile Destroyers	4890	RAJPUT RANA RANJIT	New	1975	1980 1982 1983	Russia
Landing Craft Utility Mk I	560	L 31 L 32	New	1974	1978 1981	HDL
Landing Craft Utility Mk II	560	L 33 L 34 L 35	New	1975	1980 1983 1983	GSL
Improved Leander Class Frigates	3040	TARAGIRI VINDHYAGIRI	New	1970	1980 1981	MDL
Survey Ships	1930	SANDHAYAK NIRDESHAK NIRUPAK INVESTIGATOR	New	1973 1976 1976 1986	1981 1983 1985 1990	GRSE
Torpedo Recovery Vessels	160	TRV A 71 TRV A 72	New	1978	1982 1983	GSL
Ocean Going Tug	1630	MATANGA	New	1973	1983	GRSE
Inshore Minesweepers	100	MALVAN MANGROL MAHE MULKI MAGDALA MALPE	New	1981	1983 1983 1983 1984 1984 1984	Russia

GODAVARI Class Frigates	3610	GODAVARI GANGA GOMATI	New	1978	1983 1985 1988	MDL
Survey Craft (SDB Hulls)	200	MAKAR MITHUN MEEN MESH	New	1979	1984 1984 1984 1984	GSL
Seaward Defence Boats Mk II	210	T 56 T 57 T 58 T 59 T60 T 61	New	1980	1984 1985 1985 1985 1985 1986	GRSE GSL GRSE GSL GRSE GSL
Torpedo Trials Vessel	160	ASTRAVAHINI	New	1980	1984	HSL
Landing Ship Tank(Medium)	1410	CHEETAH MAHISH GULDAR KUMBHIR	New	1982	1984 1985 1985 1986	Poland
Submarines (SSK)	1655	SHISHUMAR SHANKUSH	New	1981	1986 1986	Germany
Cadet Training Ship	2650	TIR	New	1982	1986	MDL
Submarines (EKM)	2890	SINDHUGHOSH SINDHUDHVAJ SINDHURAJ SINDHUVIR SINDHURATNA SINDHUKESARI SINDHUKIRTI SINDHUVIJAY	New	1983 1987 1988	1986 1987 1987 1988 1988 1988 1989 1990	Russia
Coastal Minesweepers	880	KARWAR KAKINADA CUDDALORE CANNANORE KONKAN KOZHIKODE	New	1983	1986 1986 1987 1987 1988 1988	Russia
Landing Craft Utility Mk III	560	L 36 L 37 L 38 L 39	New	1982	1986 1986 1986 1987	GSL
Guided Missile Destroyers	5055	RANVIR RANVIJAY	New	1981	1986 1987	Russia
Landing Ship Tank (Large)	5655	MAGAR	New	1981	1987	GRSE
Aircraft Carrier	28,500	VIRAAT	Second Hand	1985	1987	Britain
Fast Missile Attack Craft	500	VEER NIRBHIK NIPAT NISHANK NIRGHAT	New	1984	1987 1987 1988 1989 1989	Russia

Diving Support Vessel	2160	NIREEKSHAK	Second Hand	-	1988	MDL
Offshore Patrol Vessels	1890	SUKANYA SUVARNA SUBHADRA SAVITRI SARAYU SARADA SUJATA	New	1987 1987	1989 1990 1990 1990 1991 1992 1993	Korea Korea Korea HSL HSL HSL HSL
Anti Submarine Patrol Vessel	485	ABHAY AJAY AKSHAY AGRAY	New	1986	1989 1990 1990 1991	Russia
Missile Armed Corvettes (Project 25)	1350	KHUKRI KUTHAR KIRPAN KHANJAR	New	1986 1987	1989 1990 1990 1991	MDL MDL GRSE GRSE

Retrospect

The growth of the Navy during the period 1976 to 1990 was the outcome of several serendipitous factors:

- The growth between 1976 and 1983 was the result of the Defence Reviews carried out by the Apex Committees in 1973 and 1975. Their recommendations led to the acquisition of Russian guided missile destroyers, ocean going rocket boats, minesweepers MRASW aircraft and ASW helicopters.

- These Russian acquisitions coincided with the redesigning then in progress of the frigates that would follow the sixth and last of the Leanders. It led to the Project 16 Godavari class frigates redesigned to fit the Russian weapon systems, retaining the steam propulsion of the earlier Leanders and installing as many as possible indigenous systems of proven performance.

- The growth between 1984 and 1987 stemmed from the unprecedented harmonious relationship between the Navy and the Ministry of Defence. A similar harmony prevailed between the three service chiefs themselves. It led to the swift acceptance of the British offer in 1985 to sell their aircraft carrier *Hermes*. The need to replace the ageing earlier Russian acquisitions led to the acquisition of better submarines, fast missile attack craft, anti submarine patrol vessels, landing ships and maritime reconnaissance aircraft.

- The success of implanting Russian weapon systems in the Godavari class frigates synergised with the

momentum that had built up in the indigenous warship-building programme. Confidence had grown in the capability of the Navy's Design Organisation. The warship building yards (Mazagon Docks, Garden Reach and Goa Shipyard) had begun to press the Ministry of Defence Production for long term orders to keep their workforce gainfully employed. Russia continued to offer to India its latest weapons for installation in Indian built hulls. There was willingness from the Russian side to assist indigenous warship production.

- All these factors culminated in the sanctions for the indigenous production of guided missile destroyers (Project 15) and frigates (Project 16 A), missile corvettes (Project 25A), gas turbine propelled missile boats (Project 1241 RE), landing ships, survey ships, tankers and diverse smaller ships.

The failure of the monsoon in 1986 led to the drought of 1987 and financial stringency until 1990. The financial crisis of 1991 prolonged the period of austere naval budgets. Fortunately, Naval Headquarters' systematic and swift staff work in 1985 and 1986 had obtained sanctions for all naval priority projects and it was possible to keep these projects moving albeit at a slower pace, until the economy started recovering from 1994 onwards.

The outcome of the 1971 war had given the Navy triumph. The reforms, the consolidation and the shipbuilding achievements between 1976 and 1990 gave the Navy regional eminence.

5

Indian Ocean Deep Seabed Mining

The Mineral Potential

Polymetallic nodules, found in abundance on the floor of the world's oceans, are a rich source of metals. These potato-shaped, porous nodules are found between depths of 3,500 metres and 6,000 metres. Besides manganese and iron, they contain nickel, copper, cobalt, lead, molybdenum, cadmium, vanadium and titanium, many of which are of strategic industrial importance.

In the Indian Ocean, polymetallic nodules lie outside India's Exclusive Economic Zone. The area covered by these nodules is 10 to 18 million square kilometres. The total estimated reserves in the Indian Ocean are 0.15 trillion tonnes.

Successful exploitation depends on:

- Technological development.
- Geological and environmental factors.
- Metallurgical factors.
- Legal and political factors.

The International Seabed Area

In 1970, drafters of the Laws of the Sea Convention had proposed that the deep-sea areas beyond national jurisdiction be held in trust of the United Nations as the 'Common Heritage of Mankind' and the resources be developed by a United Nations' enterprise. This idea was not accepted by most nations. A compromise was, therefore, made with respect to deep-sea mining with certain concessions to nations that had already made an investment in exploration.

India's interest in deep seabed mining evolved from its long-term requirements for manganese, nickel, cobalt and copper. In the early 1970s, a systematic study of the ocean floor revealed that about 15 million square kilometres, deep in the middle of the Indian Ocean, had mineral nodules, mainly manganese, of different size and quality.

The Allocation of the Seabed Mining Site

The 1982 UN Convention on the Law of the Sea prescribed a regime for the International Seabed Area and granted India, France, Japan and the Soviet Union 'pioneer status' for seabed mining. The conditions for qualifying as a pioneer investor were that the nation should have spent $ 30 million on deep-sea mining. India qualified by proving her capability to extract nodules from the seabed.[1]

In August 1987, on the basis of the delineation of a prospective area covering 3,00,000 square kilometres, the Preparatory Commission for the International Sea Bed Authority (ISBA) allotted to the Department of Ocean Development (DOD) a 150,000 square kilometre area in the central Indian Ocean Basin to carry out seabed exploitation activities for the recovery of polymetallic nodules. India became the first state to be registered as a 'pioneer investor'. Half of the allotted area was to have been surrendered to the International Seabed Authority by 2002 for its technical arm named 'Enterprise'.[2]

The area is located 1,080 nautical miles south of Cape Comorin, the southern tip of India, and within 1,000 kilometres of the US naval base at Diego Garcia.

Survey of the Site

India surveyed and mapped the area. The richest area in the site had a density of up to 30 kilograms of nodules per square metre.

The survey for mapping and detailed bathymetry of the pioneer area was subsequently strengthened by the use of a multi-beam swath bathymetric system (hydrosweep) on the DOD's Oceanic Research Vessel (ORV) *Sagar Kanya*. Environmental data, baseline oceanographic data on physical, chemical and biological map parameters was also collected.

Detailed sampling was carried out at 2,500 locations. Over 250 tonnes of nodules were collected and supplied to

---

1. Department of Ocean Development's 'Vision 2015'.

2. Ibid.

INDIA'S SEABED MINING SITE

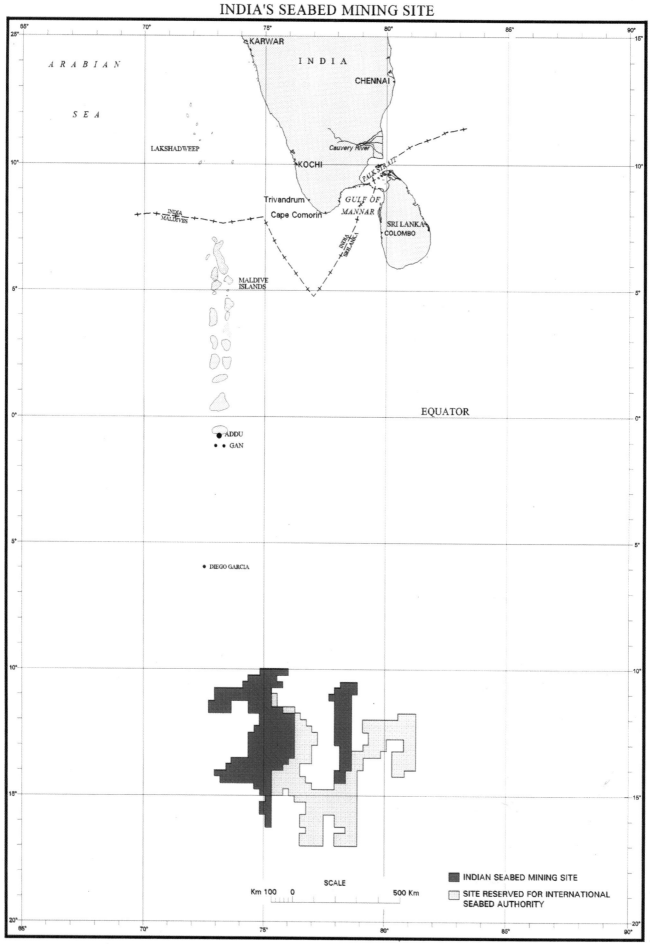

SCALE
Km 100   0   500 Km

█ INDIAN SEABED MINING SITE
☐ SITE RESERVED FOR INTERNATIONAL
  SEABED AUTHORITY

various laboratories for extractive metallurgy programmes. In the area allotted to India, resources translated into 607 million metric tonnes of manganese, copper, cobalt and nickel nodules.[3]

Development of Seabed Mining Technology

Research & Development on the design concepts of seabed mining technology has been entrusted to the National Institute of Ocean Technology (NIOT) in Chennai and organisations in the public and private sectors.

Five pilot plant campaigns were completed at the National Metallurgical Laboratory, Jamshedpur and the Regional Research Laboratory, Bhubaneswar for obtaining material and energy balance under the Extractive Metallurgy Project. A joint workshop has also been held with the United Nations Industrial Development Organisation (UNIDO) on Marine Industrial Technology for developing marine non-living resources.

At the time of writing, India has developed expertise in metallurgical processes and has established at Hindustan Zinc Limited at Udaipur a pilot plant for extracting metals from nodules. A nucleus has been established for developing a test mining system.

India's potential capabilities in deep seabed mining have been recognised. Norway, Finland and Japan have offered assistance for jointly developing a test mining system.

India's Department of Ocean Development is the nodal agency for implementing the deep seabed-mining programme. It has drawn up a long-term plan to fulfil its obligations as Pioneer Investor, and reach the stage for seeking production authorisation as quickly as possible.

---

3. In-situ resources of Polymetallic Nodules in the Pioneer Area in million metric tonnes (MMT):

Wet Nodules	759 MMT
Dry Nodules	607 MMT
Manganese	144 MMT
Cobalt	0.85 MMT
Nickel	7.00 MMT
Copper	6.5 MMT
Total Metal	14.0 MMT

(*Source:* Department of Ocean Development)

6

Training Of Foreign Naval Personnel

Region	Country	Years in which Naval Personnel Attended Courses in India	Total Trained since 1956
INDIAN OCEAN	Maldives Mauritius Seychelles	1984, 1988, 1989, 1990 to 1993, 1996 to 2003 1974, 1975, 1982, 1983, 1985 to 2003 1989, 1991, 1992 to 2001	82 264 49
SOUTH ASIAN SEABOARD	Bangladesh Myanmar Sri Lanka	1973 to 1979, 1982 to 2003 1973, 1996 to 2000 1965 to 1986, 1988 to 2003	290 13 1862
SOUTH EAST ASIAN SEABOARD	Cambodia Fiji Indonesia Malaysia Philippines Singapore Thailand Tonga Vietnam	1974 to 1980, 2001, 2002 1981 1969-71, 1974-75, 1978-80, 1989-92, 1997 to 2001 1965 to 1971, 1973 to 1986, 1988 to 2001, 2003 1979, 1996, 1997 1973 to 1976, 1978 to 1982, 1984, 1995, 1996 1974 to 1986 1984, 1985 2002, 2003	15 1 39 144 2 21 8 2 3
SOUTH WEST ASIAN SEABOARD	Aden Iran Iraq Kuwait Oman Qatar UAE Yemen	1969, 1970 1974, 1982 to 1988, 1992, 1998 to 1999 1968 to 1979 2003 1989, 1991 to 1998, 2000, 2001 1988 1991, 1996 to 1999 1969	2 52 106 10 30 7 4 1
EAST AFRICAN SEABOARD	Ethiopia Kenya South Africa Sudan Tanzania Uganda Zanzibar	1967 to 1971, 1972, 1986 to 1990 1974 to 1987, 1989 to 2000 1999 1970, 1973 to 1983, 1986, 1987 1973 to 1987, 1998 to 2001 1981, 2002 1980 to 1982, 1985 to 1988	6 27 4 49 87 11 6
WEST AFRICAN SEABOARD	Benin Gambia Ghana Namibia Nigeria Sierra Leone	1982 1996 1967 to 1984, 1987-88, 1993 to 2003 2000, 2001 1965 to 1989, 1994-95, 1997 to 2003 1978	8 1 333 3 1483 3
OTHER	Malta	1981, 1982	2

7

Visits By Foreign Naval Ships
1976 To 1990

Nationality	Name of Warship/s	Port/s Visited	Dates
France	Jeanne D'Arc, Forbin	Bombay	9-15 Feb 76
Malaysia	Perdana, Serang Ganas, Ganyang	Madras	16-21 Feb 76
Sri Lanka	Gajabahu	Cochin	23-26 Feb 76
USSR	F Bellinsgausen	Bombay	25-27 Jun 76
USSR	Kallisto	Bombay	22-25 Jul 76
USSR	Vasily Golovin	Bombay	29 Jul-2 Aug 76
Australia	Hobart	Cochin	14-16 Aug 76
France	Protet, La Dieppoise	Cochin	20-25 Sep 76
USSR	Destroyer 143, Patrol Sloop No.835	Cochin	12-15 Dec 76
France	Commandant Bourdais, Commandant Kersant	Bombay	18-22 Dec 76
Iran	Rostam, Bushehr	Bombay	6-10 Jan 77
Sweden	Alvanabben	Bombay	1-5 Feb 77
USSR	Admiral Vladimirsky, F Bellinsgausen	Bombay	11-15 Feb 77
Thailand	Prasae, Maeklong, Pinklao	Andaman & Nicobar Islands	7 Mar 77
USSR	Peter Libodev, Soruy Vasilov	Bombay	18-21 Mar 77
Sri Lanka	Samudra Devi Ranakamie, Balawatha	Cochin	4-8 Apr 77
France	Bouvet, Tourville	Bombay	31 May-6 Jun 77
USSR	Dauria	Bombay	7-14 Jun 77
USSR	Professor Vaze	Bombay	14-18 Jun 77
USSR	Priliv, Privoy, Ockjan, Academik Shirshov	Bombay	22-25 Jun 77
Italy	San Giorgio	Bombay, Cochin	29 Jul-9 Aug 77
Australia	Melbourne, Brisbane	Bombay	27 Jul-29 Aug 77
Italy	San Giorgio	Madras	2-5 Sep 77
Japan	Katori, Takatsuki	Bombay	2-6 Oct 77
Korea	Jun Duck, Kyong Nam	Bombay	2-5 Nov 77
France	Doudart De Lagree	Cochin	8-14 Dec 77
USSR	Destroyer 239, Patrol Sloop 215	Bombay	16-21 Dec 77

Nationality	Name of Warship/s	Port/s Visited	Dates
New Zealand	Monowai	Bombay	30 Dec 77-1 Jan 78
Britain	Hydra, Hecate	Bombay	10-27 Feb 78
France	Ouragan, Tartu	Bombay	17-21 Feb 78
Germany	Deutschland	Bombay	27 Feb-3 Mar 78
France	Commandant De Pimodan	Cochin	21-25 Mar 78
Britain	Tiger, Rhyl, Mohawk, RFA Grey Rover	Bombay	22-27 Mar 78
France	Jeanne D'Arc, Forbin	Madras	24-27 Mar 78
USSR	Borodino	Bombay	21-25 Apr 78
Indonesia	Martadinata, Monginsidi	Bombay	2-5 May 78
Sri Lanka	Sooraya, Weeraya	Madras	27-29 Jun 78
Sri Lanka	Dakshay, Sooraya	Madras	5-7 Jul 78
Iran	Milanian, Kahna Muie	Bombay	20-23 Sep 78
Iran	Artemiz, Palang, Fara Marz, Larak	Bombay	20-24 Sep 78
Iran	Milanian, Kahna Muie	Cochin	25-28 Sep 78
Sri Lanka	Korawakka	Rameshwaram	3-4 Oct 78
France	La Galissonniere, Victor Schoelcher	Cochin	17-23 Oct 78
USSR	Ocean	Bombay	1-5 Nov 78
Belgium	Westdiep	Bombay	4-7 Nov 78
Britain	Fox, Hydra, Heraid, Pawn	Bombay Bombay Bombay	13-29 Jan 79
France	Doudart De Lagree, Duquesne	Bombay	30 Jan-5 Feb 79
Norway	Veermar	Calcutta Visakhapatnam	3-4 Feb 79
Australia	Vampire, Perth	Madras	10-14 Feb 79
Portugal	Sagres	Goa Bombay	24-27 Feb 79 1-5 Mar 79
USSR	Borodino	Madras	23-27 Mar 79
Netherlands	Tromp, Foolster, Kortenaer, Drenthe	Bombay	12-16 Apr 79
USSR	Liman	Bombay	20-25 Apr 79
Malaysia	Hang Tuah	Bombay Cochin	11-15 Jun 79 18-20 Jun 79
Italy	Lupo, Ardito	Bombay	13-16 Aug 79
Singapore	Resolution	Cochin	10-14 Sep 79
France	La Combattante	Cochin	27-30 Sep 79
Malaysia	Handalan, Pendekar, Perkasa, Gempita	Goa	14-17 Oct 79
Britain	Norfolk, Arrow, Dido and Fort Grange	Cochin	9-13 Nov 79
USSR	Sevastopol, Victoria,	Bombay	27 Feb-3 Mar 80
Thailand	Racharit, Udomdet, Withayakhon	Madras	8-10 May 80
Germany	Luetjens, Hessen, Coburg, Spessart	Bombay	10-14 Jun 80
Australia	Perth	Madras	4-8 Oct 80
Britain	Coventry	Bombay	6-10 Nov 80

Nationality	Name of Warship/s	Port/s Visited	Dates
Australia	Brisbane	Bombay	19-21 May 81
USSR	Borodino	Madras	7-11 Oct 81
USSR	Yamal, Apsheron	Madras	15-21 May 82
Britain	Aurora	Bombay	16 to 20 Aug 82
Thailand	Maeklong & Prasae	Madras	11-14 Mar 83
Thailand	Chon Buri	Bombay	10-13 May 83
Britain	Avenger	Madras	12-16 May 83
Thailand	Songkhla	Bombay	17-20 Aug 83
Britain	Invincible Aurora Rothesay Andromeda, Achilles	Bombay Goa Cochin	10-14 Oct 83 11-15 Oct 83 12-18 Oct 83
USSR	Stvor & Cheleken Admiral Vladimirsky, F Bellinsgausen	Bombay Bombay	18-22 Nov 83 22-26 Nov 83
France	Jacques Cartier	Cochin	28 Nov-1 Dec 83
Thailand	Phuket	Bombay	12-16 Dec 83
France	Eridan, Var	Bombay	12-16 Dec 83
Portugal	Sagres	Goa	28-31 Jan 84
USSR	Novorossiysk, Nikolaev Poryvisti, Boris Butoma	Madras	5-10 Feb 84
USA	Whipple	Cochin	16-18 Feb 84
Britain	Glamorgan, RFA Blue Rover	Cochin	20-25 Feb 84
Iran	Hangam, Bandar Abbas	Goa	21-25 Feb 84
Iran	Bandar Abbas, Hengam	Madras	10-14 Mar 84
Britain	Glasgow	Goa	3-7 May 84
USA	Lewis B Puller	Bombay	21-25 May 84
Malaysia	Mahawangse	Bombay	15-17 Jun 84
Germany	Niedersachsen, Lubeck, Qucksburg	Cochin	21-24 Sep 84
Britain	Peacock, Plover	Goa	25-27 Oct 84
Oman	Shabah	Goa Cochin	30 Oct-2 Nov 84 5-8 Nov 84
USSR	Razumny, Revnostny	Bombay	15-19 Nov 84
Singapore	Endurance(LST L 201)	Cochin	21-24 Jan 85
Sweden	Carlskrona	Bombay	14-18 Feb 85
Iran	Larak Bushehr	Bombay Goa	15-19 Feb 85 9-13 Mar 85
Oman	Al-Said	Bombay (For Repairs)	20 Feb-20 Mar 85
USA	Downes	Goa	28 Feb-3 Mar 85
Australia	Adelaide, Sydney	Bombay	22-25 May 85
USSR	Gordelivey	Bombay	1-5 Jun 85
Indonesia	Martha, Kristina Tiya Hahu	Bombay	13-14 Jul 85

Nationality	Name of Warship/s	Port/s Visited	Dates
Japan	Katori, Makigmo	Bombay	22-26 Sep 85
Malaysia	Hng Tuah, Mutiara	Madras	24-30 Oct 85
USSR	Boris Butoma	Bombay	17-22 Nov 85
Oman	Shabab	Cochin Bombay	12-17 Oct 85 22-27 Oct 85
Malaysia	Nangtuah	Madras	26-28 Oct 85
USSR	Boris Butoma	Bombay	17-22 Nov 85
Iran	Bandar Abbas, Hangem	Cochin	23-28 Feb 86
Italy	Scirocco	Bombay	2-4 Mar 86
Italy	Grecale	Goa	5-7 Mar 86
Thailand	Pinklao	Bombay	11-15 Mar 86
Malaysia	Mahamir, Jeral, Ledang, Kinabalu	Bombay	17-20 Mar 86
Britain	Broadsword	Bombay	7-9 Apr 86
USA	Rathburne	Cochin	12 May 86
Indonesia	Hasanudin	Bombay	23-26 Jun 86
USSR	Training Ship 126	Madras	21-25 Aug 86
USA	Marvin Shield	Bombay	6-10 Oct 86
France	Victor Schoelcher, Var	Bombay	16-21 Oct 86
Britain	Illustrious	Bombay	14-16 Nov 86
USSR	Donuslav, Deresan, Naval Tug MB- 105	Bombay	23-26 Nov 86
USSR	F Bellensgausen, V Golovnin	Bombay	8-12 Dec 86
USA	Robison, Goldsborough	Cochin	12-14 Jan 87
Iran	Tonb, Kharg	Cochin	8-10 Mar 87
Egypt	Al Nasser	Bombay	29 Mar-1 Apr 87
USSR	Boris Butoma	Bombay	9 Apr-12 Apr 87
USSR	Akademik Nikolayandrev	Madras	27 Apr-30 Apr 87
USSR	Irkut	Bombay	18 May-22 May 87
Germany	Deutschland	Madras	21 May-25 May 87
USSR	C 522 (Rescue Tug)	Bombay	27 May-1 Jun 87
USA	Worden, Crommelin	Bombay	3-7 Jun 87
France	Commandant Bory	Bombay	8-12 Jun 87
USSR	N-905 & N-737	Bombay	25-29 Jul 87
France	La Gracieure, La Railloure Jeanne D'Arc, La Motte Picquet	Madras Bombay	17-21 Aug 87 31 Aug-3 Sep 87
Thailand	Bang Rachan	Bombay	7-11 Sep 87
Britain	Edinburgh	Bombay	14-17 Oct 87
USA	Harold E Halt, Curt & Perry	Cochin	5-8 Nov 87
USSR	Marshal Shaposhnikov, Admiral Zakarov, Boevoy	Bombay	29 Nov-3 Dec 87
France	Clemenceau, Suffren	Bombay	30 Dec 87-3 Jan 88
USSR	Stovr, F Bellensgausen	Cochin	5-9 Jan 88

Nationality	Name of Warship/s	Port/s Visited	Dates
France	Jeanne D'Arc Commandant Bourdais	Cochin	11-15 Jan 88
Indonesia	YDS Sudarso	Bombay	12-14 Jan 88
USA	Reasoner	Madras	24-28 Feb 88
Iran	Lavan, Kharg	Bombay	9-12 Mar 88
Singapore	Excellance	Goa	10-14 Mar 88
USSR	Marshal Vasilevsky (N-645)	Bombay	16-19 Mar 88
France	Jeanne D'Arc & Commandant Bourdais	Madras Pondicherry	14-17 Apr 88 18 Apr 88
Thailand	NCM4 Sarai	Bombay	18-22 Apr 88
USSR	472 & 381	Bombay	6-10 May 88
New Zealand	Manawanui	Cochin	14-16 May 88
Britain	Britannia	Cochin	4 Jun 88
Greece	Aris	Bombay	27-29 Jul 88
USA	Fanning	Madras	28 Jul-1 Aug 88
USSR	Marshal Shaposhnikov	Bombay	5-10 Aug 88
Italy	Caio Duilio	Bombay	12-17 Aug 88
Netherlands	Vitte De with Kortenaer Jan Van Bra Kel, Juldenkruis	Bombay	24-29 Aug 88
USSR	Marshal Shaposhinikov Poryvisty 626	Bombay	26-30 Sep 88
Indonesia	Multatuli, Pulau Rengat & Pulau Rupat	Bombay	11-13 Oct 88
Britain	Ark Royal, RFA Fort Grange	Bombay	15-19 Nov 88
USSR	N 695	Bombay	16-19 Nov 88
USA	Barbey	Bombay	27 Nov-1 Dec 88
USSR	Vassily Golovin (R V)	Bombay	1-5 Dec 88
Indonesia	Oswald Siahan	Cochin	27-29 Jan 89
France	Marve, Protet, De Grasse	Bombay	2-7 Feb 89
USSR	Profenor Shotoman	Goa	15-17 Feb 89
USA	Leftwich	Cochin	17-21 Feb 89
Thailand	Sichang, Pinklao, Tachin	Bombay	9-12 Mar 89
USSR	N 541K	Goa	11-15 Mar 89
France	Marve, Protet	Cochin	13-17 Mar 89
Australia	Derwent, Stuart	Madras	13-17 Mar 89
USSR	Profenor	Madras	17 Mar 89
Bangladesh	Abu Bakr, Umar Farooq	Cochin	23-25 Mar 89
Britain	Billiant	Bombay	7-11 Apr 89
USSR	Iskatel-4	Goa	20-25 Apr 89
USSR	Radm Perchin, MV-99	Goa	29 Apr-2 May 89
USSR	Profenor Shotoman	Goa	8-10 May 89
USSR	Borodino	Goa	14-18 May 89
Australia	Oxley	Cochin	9-14 Jun 89
France	Garonne, Psyche	Cochin	29 Jun-3 Jul 89

Nationality	Name of Warship/s	Port/s Visited	Dates
Brazil	Ne Brasil	Bombay	17-20 Jul 89
USSR	Yurka 702	Madras	24-27 Jul 89
USSR	Boevoy	Madras	7-11 Aug 89
USA	Lawrence, Joseph Hewes	Goa	10-13 Aug 89
Indonesia	Nanggala	Cochin	21-23 Aug 89
USSR	Yakor	Madras	26-31 Aug 89
USSR	Adm Spridonov	Cochin	6-9 Sep 89
USA	USS Leahy	Cochin	18-19 Sep 89
USSR	PM 92	Goa	18-21 Sep 89
USA	Ford	Cochin	27-28 Sep 89
Oman	Al Mubrukah	Cochin	6-9 Oct 89
USA	Gary, McClusky	Bombay	24-26 Oct 89
Oman	Zinat al Bahaar	Goa Bombay	28 Oct-3 Nov 89 4-10 Nov 89
Korea	Chungnam, Kyungbuk	Bombay	2-5 Nov 89
USSR	VFA	Visakhapatnam	3-4 Nov 89
Sweden	Carlskrona	Bombay	20-24 Nov 89
Malaysia	Kasturi, Mahawangsa	Goa	21-23 Nov 89
USSR	Zaryad	Goa	5-8 Dec 89
Indonesia	Baruna Jaya II	Cochin	10-12 Dec 89
USA	Stein	Madras	14-17 Dec 89
Britain	Beaver	Goa	29 Jan-2 Feb 90
USSR	Vasily Golovnin	Goa	6-9 Feb 90
Britain	Minerva, Bristol	Cochin	19-22 Feb 90
USSR	Borodino	Cochin	26 Feb-2 Mar 90
Iran	Kharg	Cochin	3-6 Mar 90
USSR	Admiral Vladimirsky	Cochin	8-12 Mar 90
Indonesia	Baruna Jaya III	Cochin	13-15 Mar 90
France	Jeanne D'Arc, Commandant Bory, Commandant Bourdais	Bombay	13-17 Mar 90
Britain	Charybdis	Madras	3-6 Apr 90
USSR	Izumrud	Bombay	18-21 Apr 90
Indonesia	Abdul Halim Perdanakusumah	Cochin	5-7 May 90
Italy	Libeccio	Bombay	7-10 May 90
Turkey	Turgutreis (F-241)	Madras	11-13 May 90
France	Marne, Doudart De Lagree	Bombay	28 May-1 Jun 90
Oman	Nasr Al Bahr	Goa	29 May-1 Jun 90
Australia	Oxley	Cochin	9-14 Jun 90
Mexico	Cuauhtemoc	Bombay	9-12 Aug 90
USSR	Admiral Tribuz	Goa	12-16 Sep 90
Oman	Al Maubrukah	Goa	3-6 Oct 90

Nationality	Name of Warship/s	Port/s Visited	Dates
USSR	Kedrov	Goa	11-15 Oct 90
USSR	Akedemic Nikolay Andreyev	Bombay	18-21 Nov 90
Portugal	Macau	Cochin Goa	25-30 Nov 90 2-9 Dec 90
Portugal	Macau	Daman Bombay Cochin	11-13 Dec 90 14-19 Dec 90 22-26 Dec 90
Oman	Fulk al Salamah	Madras	19-24 Dec 90

8

Warship Design And Production

Preamble

Warship design and construction during the period 1976 to 1990 covered a wide field of activity. Separate chapters deal with the Leander Frigate Project, the Project 16 Godavari class frigates, the Project 25 Khukri class missile corvettes and the SSK Submarine Project.

This chapter deals the generic and chronological aspects of warship design and construction and the other ships designed and constructed during this period.

Overview of Warship Design and Construction

Delivered up to 1975

- Leander Class Frigates: *Nilgiri, Himgiri*
- Survey ship *Darshak* (French design, built at Hindustan Shipyard)
- Seaward Defence Boats (SDBs) Mk I: *Ajay, Abhay, Akshay, Amar, Ajit* and *Atul*
- Fleet Tug: *Gaj*
- Inshore Minesweepers: *Bhatkal* and *Bulsar*
- Yard craft (harbour tugs, grab dredgers, bucket dredgers, hopper barges, oilers, HSD tankers, Avcat tankers, ammunition barges, water barges, victualling barges, ferry craft, diving boats, water boats, berthing pontoons, boat pontoons etc.)

Delivered 1976 to 1990

Frigates

- Leander Class: *Udaygiri and Dunagiri*
- Improved Leander Class: *Taragiri* and *Vindhyagiri*
- Project 16 Godavari Class: *Godavari, Ganga* and *Gomati*

Missile Corvettes

- Project 25 Khukri Class: *Khukri, Kuthar*

General

- Landing Ship Tank-Large (LST-L): *Magar*

- Offshore Patrol Vessel: *Savitri*
- Cadet Training Ship: *Tir*

Survey Flotilla

Survey Ships

- Sandhayak Class: *Sandhayak, Nirdeshak, Nirupak*
- Improved Sandhayak Class: *Investigator*

Survey Craft

- *Makar, Mithun, Meen* and *Mesh*

Minor War Vessels

- Seaward Defence Boats Mk II: T 51 to T 55
- Seaward Defence Boats Mk III: T 56 to T 61
- Landing Craft Utility (LCUs) Mk I: L 31 and L 32
- Landing Craft Utility (LCUs) Mk II: L 33 to L 35
- Landing Craft Utility (LCUs) Mk III: L 36 to L 39

Auxiliaries

- Ocean Going Tug: *Matanga*
- Torpedo Recovery Vessels (TRVs): A 71 and A 72
- Torpedo Launch and Recovery Vessel (TLRV): *Astravahini*

Delivered After 1990

Destroyers

- Project 15 Delhi Class: *Delhi, Mysore* and *Mumbai*

Frigates

- Project 16 A Improved Godavari Class: *Brahmaputra* and *Betwa*

SSK Submarines

- *Shalki* and *Shankul*

Missile Corvettes

- Project 25 Khukri Class: *Kirpan* and *Khanjar*
- Project 25 A Improved Khukri Class: *Kora, Kirch, Kulish* and *Karmuk*

General

- Fleet Tanker: *Aditya*
- Landing Ship Tank-Large (LST-L): *Gharial*
- Offshore Patrol Vessels: *Saryu, Sharda* and *Sujata*

Survey Ships

- Improved Sandhayak Class: *Jamuna* and *Sutlej*
- New Darshak Class: *Darshak* and *Sarvekshak*

Minor War Vessels

- Fast 400-tonne Missile Craft: *Vibhuti, Vipul, Vinash, Nashak, Vidyut, Prahar, Prabal* and *Pralaya*
- Fast Attack Craft: *Trinkat, Tillanchang, Tarasa* and *Tarmugli*
- Extra Fast Attack Craft: T 80 to T 83

Auxiliaries

- Ocean Going Tug: *Gaj*
- Marine Acoustic Research Ship (MARS): *Sagardhwani*
- Sail Training Ship (STS): *Tarangini*

Under Construction in 2004

Destroyers

- Project 15 A: Improved Delhi class

Frigates

- Project 16 A Improved Brahmaputra class
- Project 17 Shivalik class

Shipbuilding

Historical Background of Warship Building Yards

In the 17th, 18th and 19th centuries, Indian-built wooden-hulled sailing ships, built of Malabar teak, were renowned for their sea-worthiness and survivability in the East India Company's (and later England's) contests for empire.[1]

The English East India Company set up its first trading post at Surat in 1613. In 1661, the Company moved its headquarters from Surat to Bombay.[2] In 1735, at the invitation of the Company, a talented young shipbuilder, Lovji Nusserwanji Wadia, moved from Surat to Bombay to start building ships in a new shipyard.[3]

The dock at Mazagon was completed in 1774. It was built primarily to cater to ships of the East India Company, all of which could not be taken into the Naval Dockyard due to overcrowding. Ships started being built there in 1801. Mazagon's first dry dock was built in 1839 and the second in 1865.

Between 1735 and 1884, a succession of master shipbuilders of the Wadia family built, both in Mazagon and in the Bombay Dockyard, a total of 300 ships for the Company, for the English Navy and for private owners. One of these warships, still afloat, is the *Trincomalee* launched in Mazagon and fitted out in the Bombay Dockyard between 1814 and 1817.[4]

In the second half of the 19th century, several developments took place. Two major English shipping companies, Peninsular and Orient (P&O) and British India Steam Navigation Company (BISN) established a monopoly of all sea-borne passenger traffic and sea-mail delivery 'East of Suez'. In 1860, the P&O acquired Mazagon Docks at Bombay to build, maintain and repair its ships operating in the Arabian Sea and westward and southward. BISN acquired the Garden Reach Workshops in Calcutta to repair and maintain its ships operating in the Bay of Bengal and eastward and southward.

The Suez Canal opened in 1869 and traffic increased manifold. Steel hulls gradually replaced wooden hulls. Steam-driven ships gradually replaced sail driven ships. In Mazagon Docks, ship repair skills overtook shipbuilding skills. In every British war east of Suez, ships of both these companies were converted in their dockyards at Bombay

---

1. The 5,000-year old Malabar teak beams found in the ruins of Ur in Babylon testify to the antiquity of Indian ships built of teak.

2. The Portuguese had handed over Bombay to the English in 1655. In 1658, the East India Company had assumed responsibility for Bombay.

3. This shipyard was the forbear of today's Naval Dockyard at Bombay that celebrated its 250th Anniversary in 1985. In 1750, it had Asia's first contemporary dry dock. Its predecessor – the dock at Lothal, located at the northern tip of the Gulf of Cambay – was built circa 2,500 BC.

4. *Trincomalee* was constructed by Indian craftsmen using Indian materials under the direction of Jamsetjee Bomanjee Wadia. When she arrived in England in 1819, the Napoleonic Wars had ended. She spent the next 25 years in reserve and became obsolete. In the 1840s, she was converted into a corvette – 24 large cannons replaced her 44 smaller cannons. For the next 12 years, she sailed the oceans of the world on anti slavery patrols, fishery protection, disaster relief, coastal surveys and Arctic exploration. By the late 1850s, sailing warships had become obsolete. In 1857, she was converted into an afloat training ship for reserve sailors. (Her Bombay built sister, the 84-gun battleship Ganges, was converted into an afloat training ship for serving sailors.) In the mid 1890s, she was acquired by a philanthropic ship preserver and renamed *Foudroyant*. In the 1990s, she underwent an extensive restoration. In 2002, she was renamed *Trincomalee* and was opened to the public as the last classic frigate of the sailing era. (Source: *Trincomalee: the last of Nelson's Frigates* by Andrew Lambert, Chatham Publishing House, 2002).

and Calcutta to ferry thousands of Indian troops to and from the battle zones.

On the eve of the 1914-18 World War, P&O merged with the BISN and became the British Empire's largest shipping cartel – the 'P&O Group'. It also became the main operator for India's coastal passenger traffic. Its services linked India with the Persian Gulf, the Far East and East and South Africa. The Mazagon Dock Company was formed in 1915. The Group improved the facilities at Mazagon Docks and Garden Reach Workshops to sustain their ships. The Group also held a controlling interest in the Mogul Line in Bombay. Until the first half of the 20th century, the Group successfully edged out every Indian-owned company that tried to penetrate their monopoly, with one exception – the Scindia Steam Navigation Company

Acquisition of Hindustan Shipyard Limited

During the 1939-1945 World War, an urgent need arose to build merchant ships in India to replace Britain's wartime losses. In 1941, the Scindia Steam Navigation Company was given a site at Vishakhapatnam on the east coast of India. It launched its first merchant ship in 1948. In due course, this shipyard was taken over by the Government and renamed Hindustan Shipyard Limited (HSL).

Acquisition of Mazagon Docks Limited and Garden Reach Workshops[5]

By the mid 1950s, mail was being delivered by air and there was a slump in world shipping. In 1956, the P&O Group offered to sell Mazagon Dock Limited (MDL) to the Government of India. The reaction to this offer was that "the demand for ships of 4,000 GRT and below, especially for new ships, and the demand for odd harbour craft are so small that it would not be advantageous for Government to consider taking over Mazagon Docks merely for the construction of smaller vessels"[6]

In 1957, Mr VK Krishna Menon became India's Defence Minister. He was an ardent pioneer of self-reliance in defence, particularly for core requirements of warships, tanks and aircraft. HSL was fully occupied building merchant ships. The choice for building warships lay between MDL and Garden Reach Workshops (GRW). He appointed a committee to look into MDL's capabilities for building frigate-sized warships.

After protracted negotiations, the Government purchased MDL and GRW in a package deal for 12.1 million pounds (approximately Rs. 3.85 crore at that time) on 19 April 1960. The deal provided for part of the payment to be adjusted towards repairs of P&O Group ships after take over.

Acquisition of Goa Shipyard Limited

In the 1950s, Japan started rebuilding its industries after the devastation it had suffered during the 1939-45 World War. It evinced interest in importing iron and manganese ore from Goa, which at that time was still a Portuguese enclave. Development commenced of the mines in the hills upstream of the Rivers Zuari and Mandovi. The ore was to be transported in barges down these rivers to bulk-ore-carrying merchant ships at anchor off Marmogoa.

In 1957, the Portuguese established, at the mouth of the River Zuari, a small shipyard named 'Estaleiro Navais de Goa' to construct and repair ore carrying barges, provide assistance to maintain and refit merchant ships and assist visiting Portuguese warships. By 1960, this yard could repair barges. By 1961, the yard had set up rudimentary facilities to construct barges.

Operation Vijay (17 to 20 December 1961) liberated Goa from 450 years of Portuguese rule and marked the formation of Goa as a Union Territory. The Naval Officer in Charge Goa was appointed as the custodian of the shipyard. A few months later, the yard was entrusted to MDL Bombay on lease and renamed as Mazagon Dock Goa Branch.

From 1962 onwards, yard infrastructure was expanded to help maintain and repair the ore barges. From 1964 onwards, the yard started constructing barges.

In 1967, the lease agreement with MDL ended. The yard became an autonomous subsidiary of MDL and renamed itself as Goa Shipyard Ltd (GSL). Under this subsidiary arrangement, MDL provided GSL with technical know-how for shipbuilding and ship repair, assistance in securing orders and purchase of materials, and transferring, at book value, machinery from MDL's yard at Bombay.

GSL's 15-year plan commenced with setting up fabrication and joiner shops and slipways. The existing workshops were expanded. New ICE, Fitting Out and Machine Workshops were set up. This enabled GSL, under the Norwegian aid scheme, to construct deep-sea fishing trawlers.

In 1970, GSL started taking naval orders. Between 1975 and 1977, the building berths were extended, new slipways

---

5. Garden Reach Workshops (GRW) was later renamed as Garden Reach Shipbuilding and Engineering (GRSE).

6. *History of Mazagon Docks Ltd* by Rear Admiral K Sridharan.

and a fitting out jetty built, overhead cranes installed, etc. This enabled GSL to construct, between 1980 and 1987, minor war vessels like Landing Craft Utility, Torpedo Recovery Vessels, survey craft and Seaward Defence Boats.

From 1990 onwards, GSL started constructing larger ships like offshore patrol vessels and survey ships and participate in the licensed production of Russian 400-tonne missile boats.

The Navy's Constructor Cadre

The Navy's design capability started literally from scratch. At the time of independence in 1947, there was no indigenous in-house design capability.

Rear Admiral SM Misra, who retired in 1990 as Chairman and Managing Director of Garden Reach Shipbuilding and Engineering (GRSE) recalls:

"In 1951, Naval Headquarters recruited three civilian naval architects. Mr Paramanandhan had been trained in Britain and was working in the Bombay Port Trust. Mr Dhotiwala had been trained in Britain. Mr Dhumal had been trained in the Massachusetts Institute of Technology in the US. All three were designated as Technical Assistants (Construction) – two were appointed to the Naval Dockyard Bombay and one to NHQ.

"At that time, 'naval construction' was in the domain of the Engineering Branch. To build up a cadre of naval constructors, Indian naval cadets undergoing engineering training in Britain were invited in 1952 to convert to 'naval constructors'. This entailed a further four years training in naval architecture followed by practical training under British naval architects. Only one volunteered. In 1955, 1956 and 1957 two cadets volunteered every year – all had qualified as marine engineers before commencing training as constructors.[7]

"The Navy, however, needed marine engineers and was reluctant to spare them for the constructor cadre. From 1958 onwards, naval architects who had qualified from the IIT Kharagpur started joining the Navy's constructor cadre. In 1962, it was arranged that the IIT Kharagpur would increase its course by 18 months for those naval architects who were being recruited for the Navy. This helped to dispense with the initial four years' training in Britain. Most of them were sent to Britain for a two-year 'Long Naval Architecture Course' and attachment with the British Navy.

"From the mid 1960s onwards, the faculty and the officers undergoing training as naval architects at IIT Kharagpur started feeling that naval architecture training would be better done in Delhi, closer to Naval Headquarters, where warships were being designed and where experienced naval architects could give them lectures. From the mid 1970s onwards, the IIT Delhi started the training of naval architects.

"In the 1970s, when Russian equipment started being fitted into indigenous ships, naval constructors started being sent to the Soviet Union as well as to Britain for the 'Long Architecture Course'. Today the strength of the Constructor Cadre is well over 200 naval architects."

A separate Constructor Cadre was sanctioned in 1974. In 1977, the venue of training of naval constructor officers was shifted from IIT Kharagpur to IIT Delhi. A Constructors' Training Office was set up in the Naval Dockyard Vishakhapatnam to impart practical training to precede professional training.

In 1987, it was decided to augment the intake of Naval Constructors through the 10+2 Technical Cadet Entry Scheme. Sanction was obtained for the attachment of 8 Technical Cadets per year with the Department of Ship Technology, Cochin University for the regular B Tech (Naval Architecture) Course.

From then onwards, the Navy has had three sources from which naval constructors enter service – the IIT Delhi, the Cochin University and the IIT Kharagpur.

Mr Paramanandhan joined in 1952 and retired in 1983 as the Director General of Naval Design and became the doyen of the Navy's warship designers. He recalls:

"In 1952, the total number of naval architects available was three civilians, Mr Dhotiwalla, Mr Dhumal and myself. Whatever leisure we had was spent with the draftsmen who were ex general apprentices. With these resources, we managed to convert not only *Shakti* and *Dharini,* but also two sloops, one into the cadet training ship, *Tir* and the other into the survey vessel, *Investigator.* Even though certain decisions could be taken on board, but the drawings had to be generated with whatever facilities we had. I suppose we had a lot more stamina in those days than now.

"Much of NHQ's organisation and working was based on the British Admiralty Pattern. One British naval constructor Captain came on deputation and by that

---

7. The first to volunteer was VP Garg, in whose memory a lecture is held at the IIT Delhi every year. The late AN Thukral and SM Misra volunteered in 1955, D Dean and KK Lohana volunteered in 1956, Prakash and Kapoor volunteered in 1957. From IIT Kharagpur, Damodaran and Kamath joined in 1958, Mohan Ram and M Mukherjee joined in 1959 and so on. Warship design, construction, overseeing and modernisation during the period up to 1990 were done by these officers and some of their younger colleagues.

time we had decided to form the Corps of Constructors. The first plans for the formation of the Corps with 18 officers was prepared under the guidance of then COM, Capt Daya Shankar. It was in his own handwriting and is a part of the historical record in the Directorate. The initial graduate training at IIT Kharagpur was to be followed by post graduation training in Britain.

"When the plans paper for the training of constructors was put up, the Government was very reluctant to approve their post graduate training in Britain. They asked a simple question, 'Does it mean that the training in India would not be as good?' The straight answer for that was 'Because there are no R&D facilities to upgrade our technology in the area of naval architecture, we have no other option.' When I explained what happens to a naval architect who studies abroad as an undergraduate and comes back, and the low level at which his technology will be after 10 years, the Government agreed. I firmly believe that whenever we put our problems fairly and tell the Government 'This will be the end result and it is up to you to take a decision', they tend to take the right decision.

"So the Navy decided to form its own Design Organisation. There was a bid from Mazagon Dock and from the Ministry of Defence Production to take over the Design Organisation. Some senior naval officers asked me, 'Wouldn't you feel more comfortable working in a Public Sector Enterprise?' My answer was simple, 'If the Navy is not directly involved in ship design, its building and its commissioning, we will meet the same fate as a Defence Production Unit, where the hardware is made and the Services are not accepting it, because the Services are not deeply involved right from day one. The Navy's involvement should be right from the Staff Requirement, which should be refined by the Material Branch as regards our own capability. The Staff Branch and the Material Branch should work hand in hand till the design is frozen and then it can be given for production'.

"The second advantage is that the design period may be four years. Till the design is frozen, the shipyard does not know what to do. We can overlap the three-year design period plus the production at every stage and ensure that we get the best out of the ship at the time of commissioning. This proved to be correct in the Project 16 frigates which we designed later."

The Navy's Design Organisation

The Directorate of Naval Construction (DNC), when first established in the 1950s, was responsible for all aspects of naval construction – policy, planning and hull maintenance. As the sole repository of expertise, not only was it responsible for the design and construction of ships but it was also the nodal agency at Naval Headquarters for the acquisition and induction of all ships from abroad.

In 1965, the overseeing of the construction of the frigates being built at Mazagon Docks was entrusted to the DNC and Mr Dhumal became the first Officer in Charge of the Warship Overseeing Team in Bombay.

In 1968, the management of the Russian acquisition programme was hived off from DNC and entrusted to a new Directorate of Acquisition Project (DAP).

In 1969, the Frigate Cell of DNC was hived off to become the Directorate of the Leander Project (DLP). In due course, DLP became today's Directorate of Naval Ship Production (DNSP).

A major objective of the 1969-74 Defence Plan was self-reliance in the field of warship design and warship production. Accordingly, the indigenous construction of frigates, patrol craft, submarines, minor war vessels and auxiliaries had been accepted in this plan.

In 1969, there was an acute shortage of naval architects and specialist constructer officers. The Navy did not have either adequate experience or capacity to undertake indigenous design of the range of ships and craft envisaged in the plan. In its proposal to Government for a full-fledged Directorate of Naval Design (DND), Naval Headquarters envisaged induction of foreign warship designers on loan with assurance of back up from their parent organisations.

In 1970, the Design Cell of DNC hived off to become the Directorate of Naval Design (DND). It started off with designs for new classes of Seaward Defence Boats (SDBs Mk II), Survey Vessels and a Landing Ship Tank (LST). From the outset, DND was conceived and created as an integral part of Naval Headquarters. This ensured close interaction with all the professional directorates in NHQ at all levels, while functioning under the scrutiny of the Naval Staff. In later years, DND was upgraded to become the Directorate General of Naval Design (DGND).

Negotiations with Britain for the deputation of warship designers on loan did not bear fruit. In 1973, a team of warship designers from the Soviet Union visited India to suggest the organisation to design, *de novo*, frigates and submarines. They quantified the requirement to be at least 170 specialists for the *ab initio* design of a 'new' frigate and, likewise, at least another 170 specialists for the *ab initio* design of a new submarine. This magnitude of manpower was just not available. The only alternative was to do the best that could be done until the cadre of naval constructors gradually built up.

In 1985, the Directorate of Naval Construction (DNC) was renamed Directorate of Naval Architecture (DNA).

Vessels Designed and Constructed

Seaward Defence Boats

Captain (then Lieutenant) J Subbiah recalls:

"My first assignment in DND was the design of fast Seaward Defence Boats (SDBs). The Staff Requirements, as originally formulated, envisaged a six-in-one design. In pure naval architecture terms, it was a more challenging assignment than even the later Godavari class frigate. The SDBs Mk I then in service were operating at a speed of less than 15 knots. The staff requirements for the new SDBs called for a sprint speed of around 30 knots. This involved the development of an entirely new hull form.

"We developed the hull form successfully and carried out the model tests at (the then) National Physical Laboratories, Feltham, England in 1972. The SDB Mk II version was powered by two 3,500 horsepower British Deltic engines with an integral gearbox. We were able to pack this power within the same 37.5 metre hull length of the earlier SDBs.

"This design was later modified in the SDBs Mk III to fit the German MTU engines. Since the MTU engines were larger and since a separate gearbox had to be accommodated, the length was increased.

"These SDBs did not sport any impressive weapon package. Had the Staff wanted one, the hull form could have accommodated it. In fact, a study was made to fit the then popular French Exocet surface-to-surface missiles, but was not pursued due to policy constraints on the choice of weapons. This ability to fit weapon packages of different origin blossomed later in the Godavari class frigates.

"On the whole, as a first design from the Directorate of Naval Design, it was a professionally satisfying and successful project. The concept of 6-in-1 design was substantially fulfilled. This design was built in four versions – SDBs Mk II and III, Torpedo Recovery Vessels, Survey Craft and Customs Craft."

Eventually, five SDBs Mk II, six SDBs Mk III, four Survey Craft, two Torpedo Recovery vessels were delivered to the Navy and a number of SDBs were delivered to the Coast Guard, all built either at Garden Reach Calcutta or at Goa Shipyard.

Landing Craft Utility

Between 1978 and 1987, a total of 9 LCUs were delivered. The first two Landing Craft Utility (LCUs) Mk I were built at Hooghly Docking Calcutta. Three LCUs Mk II and four LCUs Mk III were built at Goa Shipyard.

The design did not prove entirely suitable and no further LCUs of that design were ordered.

Landing Ship Tank – Large

The Landing Ship Tank-Large (LST-L) design evolved from 1973 onwards. Staff requirements were steadily updated to enable it to embark troops, tanks, heavy vehicles, jeeps, assault landing craft and two Seaking Mk 42 C large troop-carrying helicopters.

In 1980, the order for its construction was given to Mazagon Docks. The following year, the order was transferred to GRSE. At that time, its displacement of 5,500 tonnes made it the largest vessel to have been designed (and built) indigenously.

The first (LST-L), *Magar*, commissioned in 1987 and the second, *Gharial*, in 1997. The third was launched in 2004.

Survey Ships

The new design of a survey ship crystallised by 1974 and the order for the first ship was placed on GRW in 1975. In 1976, two more ships were ordered from GRW. *Sandhayak, Nirdeshak* and *Nirupak* commissioned between 1981 and 1983. This new class of survey ships was fitted with the latest survey equipment available at that time – Hifix, Trisponder, satellite navigation receivers, side scan sonar etc.

The *Sandhayak* design and its survey equipment were improved upon and the first ship of the improved Sandhayak class, *Investigator,* commissioned in 1990. It was followed by two more survey ships of the same class, *Jamuna* and *Sutlej* in 1991 and 1993.

The design and the survey equipment were further improved upon in the new Darshak class survey ships, *Darshak* and *Sarvekshak*, which commissioned in 2001 and 2002 respectively.

Ocean-Going Tug *Matanga*

The order for the ocean-going tug was placed with GRSE Calcutta in 1973. Due to the prolonged difficulties that GRSE was experiencing, *Matanga* could only be commissioned in 1983.

Cadet Training Ship *Tir*

In 1978, the Design Directorate commenced the design of a Cadet Training Ship having a displacement of 2,400 tonnes, a maximum speed of 18 knots, a complement of 354 including 120 cadets and a helicopter deck but no hangar. To keep the cost low, it was decided that the ship would be built to American Bureau of Ship (ABS) Standards i.e. merchant ship standards rather than warship standards. It was intended that three such ships would be built by Mazagon Docks to replace the ageing Brahmaputra class ships that had been converted earlier to the training role.

Construction commenced in 1982, the ship was launched in 1983 and commissioned as *Tir* in 1986. In the intervening years, it was decided not to build the other two cadet training ships. *Tir* remained the only ship of her class.

Fleet Tanker *Aditya*

The order for the fleet tanker was placed with GRSE in 1985. Due to the prolonged difficulties that GRSE was experiencing, the tanker could only be commissioned in 2000.

Project 15 Delhi Class Destroyers (*Delhi, Mysore and Mumbai***)**

Design development of the '10th, 11th and 12th frigates' commenced in 1980. At the initial stage, these ships were to be designed as 'follow-ons' to the 7th, 8th and 9th frigates of Project 16 that were to be commissioned in the 1980s as the Godavari class.

Commander (later Rear Admiral and DGND) NP Gupta was associated with the design of Project 15 from the design stage till production commenced in end 1987. He recalls:

"In July 1980, I was shifted to DGND and was asked to work on the design of Project 15 frigates. Work commenced with very brief Staff Requirements in the form of a note from the then DCPT. A new ship design was to be made, based on a mix of Soviet and Western weapon package similar to the Godavari class with the addition of Russian RBU 6000 anti submarine rockets. Gas turbine propulsion was specified.

"A very small design team developed the hull form in four months. This design of about 3,500 tonnes displacement and 124 meters LBP (a few metres longer than Godavari) was presented to the Naval Staff as well as the Material Branch, but could not be taken for model tests as the decision with respect to the weapon package and propulsion package was not finalised.

"In September 1980, a request was made to the Soviet Union for an updated weapon package of Godavari plus RBU 6000.

"During 1981, there was debate within Naval Headquarters on the selection of the Gas Turbine propulsion package. The contenders were the General Electric LM 2500 and the British Rolls Royce SM 1 A. Two separate design studies were carried out in 1981 to integrate the SM 1 A and the LM 2500 in the designed hull. The SM 1 A did not find favour because of its development status and low power output.

"During 1982, examination continued of a Western anti missile defence option and of propulsion and weapon configurations.

"In 1983, the Soviets offered a modern weapon package and also a propulsion package of a reversible gas turbine that made us completely change the platform design. The earlier hull form, of about 3,500 tonnes, just could not take the finally selected weapon and propulsion package. The redesign resulted in a ship 161 meters long and about 6,300 tonnes displacement. It was no longer a frigate. It became a destroyer.

"But even to arrive at that size of the ship, we virtually had no data. Our experience till then in warship design was very limited. Experienced designers like Capt Mohan Ram and Capt Subbiah who were the mainstay of the design team of Godavari class were not available when the Project 15 design commenced. However, even though our team members were all inexperienced, there was a lot of enthusiasm in the multi-disciplinary design team for the project.

"Success or failure of a warship design largely depends on initial estimates of displacement and stability, which depend heavily on the available data of ships similar in size. These two parameters are very important for the success of any warship design. While the Godavari was only 20% bigger than a Leander, Project 15 was 75% to 80% bigger than the Godavari. We were on a very difficult wicket on this. Certain additional margins to displacement and stability were added purely on professional judgment, as these could not be supported by any calculations.

"The hull form and the ship design started in mid 1984 when the Russian team came and data on the propulsion and weapon packages started coming to us. Within nine months we were ready with the new larger platform design for model testing.

"Model tests were carried out at SSPA, Sweden in the latter half of 1985. They were surprised to see a large 6,300 tonne warship design coming from India. When the actual model tests were going on, the then Chief of the Naval Staff, Admiral Tahiliani, visited Sweden. He also visited SSPA and witnessed the model going through the sea keeping tests in the Ship Dynamic Laboratory. He asked the SSPA about the quality of the hull form and was informed that Project 15 would be a good ship. When the results of the measurements were analysed, SSPA declared that the ship would be an excellent weapons platform. This was demonstrated when the first ship faced extremely rare storm conditions for several hours in 1999.

"We had also decided to carry out parallel model tests at Krylov Institute in the Soviet Union. These were carried out in 1986. The results from SSPA and Krylov were similar and within the limits of normal accuracy of such tests.

"While designing Project 15, it was realised that sharply raked bows which were the feature of most Soviet designs in particular the Rajput class gave a fierce look, befitting a warship. It would also improve sea-keeping qualities. We adopted this feature in our design.

"Since a ship is designed around the weapon and propulsion packages, the required data / inputs were provided by specialists from the Soviet Design Bureau. The leader of the Design Bureau team made it clear that the ship's design was the responsibility of the Indian side. The hull form, the displacement, the main dimensions etc were finalised by us independently. The overall design responsibility was with us and Soviets ensured that all information pertaining to the weapon and propulsion package and their integration was provided to us.

"As regards EMI and EMC, in the mid and late 1980s, when Project 15 was on the drawing board, we were still in the process of planning and setting up our NEC. Though initially we had planned to off load a study to a suitable western agency to carry out copper model studies, this was not done for security reasons. Since the weapon / sensor package was predominantly Soviet, the Soviet side developed and supplied the mutual interface suppression system to ensure that these sensors performed satisfactorily. The Indian designers for the first time separated the communication transmitters and receivers and solved the associated design problems. This was a challenge but was handled satisfactorily. Further, general EMI / EMC guidelines in the layout of cables/equipment as per the normal shipbuilding practices were followed.

"We faced an interesting challenge in the integration of the Variable Depth Sonar (VDS). Our initial calculations showed that the VDS could be used up to sea state 4. We were keen to push it up to sea state 5, at par with the other weapons on board. Considerable time was spent in thinking of how to do this. We also studied the stern design of the Rajput class where we found a very complex diamond shape on the bottom of the stern. We could not figure out how it had been done and whether or not it had any relation with the operation of VDS.

"So we devised our own simple method of increasing the stability of the VDS by providing a mini cut-up just below the VDS gear. Even though it looked very simple, it was difficult to implement the scheme structurally. When we were doing model tests at SSPA, we devised a test procedure to model this phenomenon and then confirmed that it was really possible to operate the VDS in sea state 5.

"When Project 15 was on the drawing board, there were several other projects including Project 25 corvettes, the Landing Ship Tank, the Cadet Training Ship etc. at various stages of design. The Submarine Design Group was also being set up and required a large number of Naval architects to be deputed for training. This affected the availability of suitable Naval architects for Project 15. Lieutenant Commander Sainath (Later Commander Sainath) and Lieutenant Commander Ram Mohan (now Commander) joined the team in 1985/86 on return from training in Russia, but by then the basic design had already been completed. Commander Sequeira (now Commodore) also joined in late 1985 and made significant contributions in detailing the design.

"Crucial decisions taken and leadership provided by certain individuals went a long way in ensuring the success of the Project 15 design. In the early 1980s, when the search for weapons was on, the pragmatic approach of JDNP Captain (later Vice Admiral) RB Suri and JDCPT Captain (later Rear Admiral) RB Vohra in recommending acceptance of the Soviet integrated weapon and Gas Turbine propulsion packages was crucial to the project, despite opposition from certain quarters.

"Embarking on a design of such complexity without even a discussion was an equally bold decision reflecting the confidence reposed by the Naval Staff in their ship designers. Internally, the DGND Captain KK Lohana and Rear Admiral Damodaran gave tremendous support and freedom to the design team to take technical decisions. They were always there when the design team required them. But for the break-up of the Soviet Union and the delays in the arrival of the contracted weapon and propulsion packages, the first ship of Project 15 would have commissioned in 1994 instead of 1997".[8]

---

8. Eventually, *Delhi* commissioned in 1997, *Mysore* in 1999 and *Mumbai* in 2001.

Offshore Patrol Vessels

In 1986, sanction was accorded for seven helicopter-capable ships for patrolling the offshore assets in the Bombay High region. Three of these offshore patrol vessels (OPVs) *Sukanya*, *Subhadra* and *Suvarna* were built in Korea in 1989-90. The remaining four, *Savitri*, *Saryu*, *Sharda* and *Sujata*, were built at Hindustan Shipyard to the Korean design and delivered between 1990 and 1993.

Licensed Production of Project 1241 RE Gas-turbined Missile Craft

The development of 400-tonne missile boats was first mentioned by the Soviet side in 1972 – their production was expected to commence in 1976. Since the Navy required more missile boats earlier, eight 200-ton 'extended range' missile boats with better missiles were ordered in 1973. These were delivered in 1976-77.

The development of the 400-tonne missile boats took longer than anticipated. In 1981, they were formally offered to the Navy and shown to a naval delegation as Project 1241 RE.

The Navy had assessed its requirements as twenty boats by 1990. Accordingly:

- Five boats were ordered for delivery in the period 1986-90.

- Discussions were held with the Soviet side in 1982 and 1983 for the licensed production of the remaining fifteen boats in Indian shipyards, with the weapon and propulsion packages being supplied by the Soviet side as was being envisaged for Projects 16, 25 and 15. These discussions concluded that it would not be possible for all fifteen boats to be produced by 1990. The plan for licensed production was scaled down to six boats by 1990 and the remaining nine by 1995.

- Indigenous production was to be shared between Mazagon Docks and Goa Shipyard.

  – Five boats were commissioned in the Soviet Union between 1987 and 1989.

  – MDL delivered a total of three boats (1991, 1992 and 1994).

  – GSL delivered a total of five boats (one each in 1993, 1995, 1997 and two in 2002.

In the 1990s, due to financial stringency and rise in costs, the Navy decided not to build any more 1241 REs after 2002. Of the fifteen boats originally envisaged for indigenous construction, only eight were eventually built.

System Integration by WESO 1978 to 1984 & WESEE from 1985

Until the advent of the Project 16 Godavari class frigates, system integration was not a major problem since European equipment in the Leanders was mutually compatible.

In the Godavari class, however, in view of the hybrid of Russian and European systems, there arose a requirement to interface inputs and outputs in varying forms. It was also necessary to ensure that in view of the 'Cold War' between the West and the Soviet Union, the sensitive parameters of Soviet and Western equipment were protected from each other. This was resolved by the Weapons and Electronic Systems Organisation (WESO) designing microprocessor-based interface boxes that fulfilled the above functions. To minimise degradation of reliability, the number of interface boxes needed to be minimised. This was achieved by persuading as many suppliers as possible to accept changes in the input / output specifications of their respective equipment. The success of the interface boxes in the Godavari class led to their adoption in all subsequent new construction ships.

Rear Admiral (then Commander) A Ganesh, who was in WESO from 1979 onwards recalls:

"In 1978, when the go-ahead was given for the design of the Godavari class frigate to be a hybrid of Russian weapon systems and numerous other European and indigenous equipments, the question arose as to who would be responsible for eventually handing over a fully integrated ship to the Navy?

"MDL stated that it did not have the expertise but was willing to fund a separate organisation from the Frigate Project budget. This led to the creation in 1978 for a period of six years of an ad hoc Project Management Group that soon became an autonomous organisation, WESO, under the Ministry of Defence. WESO was headed by Commander (L) JJ Baxi who was also the member secretary of the WESO Steering Committee headed by the Scientific Adviser to the Defence Minister and whose other members were the Chief of Material and the Assistant Chief of Naval Staff (Policy and Plans).

"In 1978, WESO's primary task was to interface the Russian weapon systems into the Godavari frigate design and assist the Department of Electronics to develop and install the Computer Aided Action Information System (CAAIS) system for *Godavari*.

"Before the six-year sanction expired in 1984, the case was taken up to convert WESO into a permanent systems establishment, Weapons and Electronics Systems Engineering Establishment (WESEE), to handle the numerous other projects, which had crystallized after 1978".

Naval Interaction with the Department of Electronics

In the early 1970s, the Electronics Commission had been set up on the same lines as the Atomic Energy Commission. The Department of Electronics (DOE) was a department under the Electronics Commission. Its charter was to undertake market surveys for electronic products, set up Electronic R&D Centres adjacent to the electronic production centres and help entrepreneurs to set up electronic product factories.[9]

In the 1970s, DOE's role progressively expanded into that of a regulatory body. It had the authority to decide what could be produced in India. All proposals for import of anything electronic had to be cleared by DOE. During the decade 1975-1985, the Navy had to entrust several projects to the DOE, like ASW computer for the 5th and 6th Leander class frigates, Computer Aided Action Information System (CAAIS) for the aircraft carrier *Vikrant* and the Godavari class frigates and Data Highway System for the Godavari class frigates.

In each of these cases, the DOE decided that it could be designed and produced indigenously by DOE itself and therefore vetoed import.

CAAIS for Godavari Class Frigates

In the case of the CAAIS, little progress was made until 1981 when only two years were left before Godavari commissioned. DOE then decided to clear the import of a CAAIS system. Dutch, Italian and British suppliers were short-listed. Despite the Navy's preference for the Dutch CAAIS system, DOE cleared the import of the Italian CAAIS system. When *Godavari* commissioned in 1983, she had no CAAIS. Eventually, the Italian IPN 10 system was installed in the third frigate, *Gomati*, in 1989.

Electronic Data Highway for Godavari Class Frigates

In 1979, it had been decided that the Godavari class frigates would be fitted with an electronic data highway system to integrate the disparate weapon, sensor and CAIO systems. This would dispense with complex and dense direct cabling. Until 1985, DOE could not decide on which system to import – American or Norwegian. Eventually, DOE's veto was over-ruled and it cleared the import of the American system. As a result of the delay in the clearance to import, each of the three ships had to be fitted with direct cabling. Eventually, when the data buses arrived, they could only be retrofitted during major refits.

Since removal of the now redundant direct cabling would entail ripping open the entire ship, it had to be retained.

Disengagement of DOE from Naval Projects

These and other such delays had led to the constitution of a Committee to monitor the progress of the Navy's projects being handled by the DOE. Since the requirements pending with DOE had eventually to be imported, the Committee discreetly closed the earlier projects and no further projects were entrusted to DOE.

Indo-Soviet Interaction in Indigenous Warship Design and Production

The first decade of Indo-Russian naval interaction, 1965 onwards, had focused entirely on the acquisition of Russian produced ships and submarines. From 1974 onwards, in addition to acquiring better ships, submarines, aircraft, helicopters and weapons from Russia, there was increasing interaction on the acquisition of Russian weapons and systems for installation in Indian built hulls, interfaced with Western and indigenous equipment.

This 'hybridisation' began with the fitment in the 1960 vintage, British anti submarine frigate, *Talwar*, of the surface to surface missile system removed *en bloc* from a Russian missile boat. *Talwar's* installation was completed in 1975. This has been discussed in the chapter on 'Warship Modernisations and Half Life Refits'.

The next step was to decide the weapon package for the three ships that had been sanctioned to follow the six Leanders built at Mazagon Docks. In 1976, particulars became available of the 5,000-tonne frigates of the Rajput class and 800-tonne ocean going rocket boat of the Durg class, the contract for which had been signed in 1975. In consultation with the Soviet Ship Design Bureau, consideration began of the installation of the Rajput's radar and the Durg's surface to surface and surface to air missile systems in a new hull design. The outcome has been discussed in the chapter on 'Project 16 – The Godavari Class Frigates'.

The next step, again in consultation with the Russian Ministry of Shipbuilding and their Ship Design Bureau, was the installation of more modern systems in the new Corvettes of Project 25, the new Destroyers of Project 15 and of Project 16A, the successors of the earlier Godavari class frigates. In due course, similar consultations took place for the follow-on Corvettes of Project 25A and the follow-on Destroyers of Project 15A.

Concurrently the first step in 'licensed production' was

---

9. This led to the setting up of KELTRON in Kerala and MELTRON in Maharashtra, both of which in later years produced equipment for the Navy.

taken in the new 400-tonne, gas-turbined missile boats of Project 1241 RE.

By 1987, it became clear to both the Soviet and the Indian sides that the expanding scope of cooperation in shipbuilding required monitoring at high levels to ensure that agreements and protocols were signed at the right time, to ensure that orders were placed and deliveries effected to Mazagon Docks, Goa Shipyard and Garden Reach at the right time to avoid delays in construction.

The Joint Indo Soviet Working Group on Shipbuilding (JISWOG) was set up to smooth the way and clear such problems. It was chaired jointly by the Deputy Minister of Shipbuilding of the USSR and India's Secretary of Defence Production to deal with licensed production of 1241 REs, the design assistance for the fitment of Soviet systems in the indigenous hulls of Projects 25, 15, 25A, 16A etc.

The first meeting of the JISWOG was held in New Delhi in March 1988. Thereafter meetings were held every six months, alternately in Russia and India, in which the Chairmen of the Defence shipyards also participated. In due course, the JISWOG's terms of reference were expanded to include discussion of product support problems for ships and equipment that had already been supplied.

Indigenous Warship Design and Production in Retrospect

The success of 'hybridisation' depended on electronic integration and interfacing. Commander JJ Baxi's team of bright young WESO officers laid the foundation in 1979 when designing the Godavari class frigates for integrating the diverse electronics of Russian, European and indigenous systems. Their success led to similar integration in the ships that followed.

Rear Admiral Baxi, the first Director of WESO and in later years the Chairman and Managing Director of Bharat Electronics, recalls:

"There were several organic elements which contributed to the success of the Navy's projects:

– First and foremost, amongst the three services, the Indian Navy has shown the greatest determination to be self sufficient and self-reliant. And this was by a genre of people over generations, not merely by one individual.

– Secondly, by creating the Directorate General of Naval Design within Naval Headquarters, we got an agency, manned by officers on deputation, responsible for indigenisation, under the direct control of Naval Headquarters, which slowly started to build up complete design and project management skills in-house, within the Navy.

– Thirdly, the Navy started inducting naval constructors in uniform. These uniformed constructors became a highly specialised cadre, capable of handling all aspects of naval architecture, ship design and ship construction.

"On the Mazagon Docks side, the Navy sent some of their best officers and best brains to go into shipbuilding. The best naval technical officers were placed at the disposal of Mazagon Docks to be able to build the ships.

"This total involvement of Naval Headquarters in ship design, ship construction, development, inspection and testing, whereby NHQ was itself the vendor and was also the customer, led to a pragmatic approach by NHQ whenever confronted with compromises in the design process.

"Unfortunately, in the Army and the Air Force, exactly the reverse happened. Because there was the Defence Research Development Organisation and there was the Directorate General of Inspection, most of the time they treated these two organisations as if they were the vendors and the Army Headquarters or the Air Headquarters were the customers. Because they themselves did not have any design or construction responsibility, they tended to treat the designer or Indian industry at that stage at par with their corresponding designer in the world market. In that mindset, if I get a MiG 21 from the world market, I want a MiG 21 from HAL. This was never possible and never feasible. And because there was no involvement on the part of the service, they were not able to succeed.

"Whereas in our case, first of all, progressive indigenisation was done. The goal and ambition were limited. The first Leander was made totally from sub systems imported from Britain. The second Leander had partial indigenisation, in the sense that whatever systems were available within the country or could be developed were utilised. The remaining systems were imported. And so on.

"Then naturally the next corollary was that we re-designed the fifth Leander, the *Taragiri*, with one Seaking helicopter. Then we went on to the seventh frigate, the *Godavari* that again was designed by naval officers, with two Seaking helicopters. The Directorate of Combat Policy and Tactics, was the one who actually did the concept designing and asked why can't we have two Seaking helicopters on board? Right from top-level decision makers like DCPT and DNP, down to a Lieutenant in the naval architecture branch, everybody learnt to take technological and professional decisions. A complete, integral, decision-making process built up within the confines of NHQ.

"This is the one and only reason why, other than the Atomic Energy Commission and later on the Space Organisation, Naval Headquarters is the only service in this country which had truly succeeded in indigenisation. If you see the ingredients of Space and Atomic Energy, it is exactly the same story as Naval Headquarters. Space and Atomic Energy had nobody to fall back upon. They were the designers, they were the ones who formulated the concepts, they were the ones who did the designs, they ultimately had to see that their rocket fired and so a large amount of in-house work had to be done in developing systems, sub-systems and concepts in design. These are the three services you can be proud of, who have done true indigenisation namely Naval Headquarters, ISRO, and the Department of Atomic Energy. In my opinion, this is the crux of the matter.

"I have always maintained that nothing succeeds like success. The indigenisation of the propulsion system, the main machinery, the auxiliaries, the switchboards, the cables, the fire control systems, including those that were manufactured by Bharat Electronics under license from Holland, all gave NHQ a lot of confidence. This confidence, of having succeeded with a concept and the feeling that we can do it, led to the design of the *Taragiri* and the subsequent design of *Godavari* and then of Project 25 (Khukri class corvettes), Project 16 Alpha (Brahmaputra class frigates) and Project 15 (Delhi class destroyers) and the Navy has never looked back. The ingredients of why NHQ succeeded, which NHQ actually implemented, are not being replicated by many organisations in this country."

Captain S Prabhala, later Chairman and Managing Director of Bharat Electronics Ltd, recalls:

"This commitment to indigenisation, the willingness to experiment and the willingness to suffer the consequences by way of delays, by way of equipment still undergoing trials, even though the ship is complete is a tremendous plus point with the Navy. Of all the three services, the Navy had this risk taking ability, it had the internal organisational mechanisms to initiate major indigenous programmes, and it had the ability to coax, persuade and control the indigenous manufacturers to also rise to the occasion. It was a tremendous experience.

"There was only one occasion when, to my mind, the Navy erred. That was in their impatience to go in for more and more indigenisation and feeling that Bharat Electronics was not responding fast enough, the Department of Electronics came forward and said that they could develop the CAAIS. The Navy, without realising that an equipment or a system for shipboard use is not something that can come out of a Government office or a laboratory, placed too much faith in that Department. It took some time for the Navy to extricate itself from that."

Captain NS Mohan Ram recalls:

"It is essential that the time taken for the delivery of the vehicle be minimised to reduce the level of obsolescence. This requires appropriate organisational structures, systems and procedures, which facilitate speedy decision-making and implementation.

"The Navy's surface ship programme has been singularly successful. Series of frigates, corvettes, offshore patrol vessels, landing ships, training ships and a number of other smaller vessels have been indigenously developed and are in active service. Undoubtedly there have been some delays in these projects but still the ships have come out and are in service.

"The most important reason for this superior track record is the setting up of organisations within the Navy responsible for design and induction of the first of class ships and for repeat orders. Co-location of the designers and project managers of the ships, under one roof and single point accountability for the end result, has been the common factor in the success of these programmes.

"This aspect of single point accountability becomes more and more important as project complexity increases. Sub-system responsibility can be entrusted to different specialist organisations but there has to be one set up accountable for the overall result.

"Distance impedes communication and results in distortions. The Naval Design Directorate and Directorate of Ship Production have overcome the problem by co-locating the specialists together under one roof. The Naval Constructors have taken on the role of total vehicle system responsibility. Their location in Naval Headquarters has facilitated constant interaction with the Naval Staff.

"It will be fair to say that the real credit belongs to the Senior Naval Officers who took decisions in the 1960s and 1970s on organisational structures, which is paying us good dividends today."

Captain J Subbiah was associated with the design and construction of the Godavari class frigates, the Khukri class corvettes and the Delhi class destroyers. He recalls:

"Both in Britain and the USA, the concept has been in vogue, for several years, of developing detailed design drawings and processes for the first ship in a shipyard designated as a 'lead yard', and later to transfer the know-how to other yards designated as 'follow-on yards'. This concept provides for orderly transfer of services and ensures that the follow-on yards need not 're-invent the wheel'.

"In India, partly due to the smaller number of ships programmed to be built and due to the need for the injection of large amounts of capital to develop the shipyards, this concept was not practiced up to the early 1980s.

"However, during the second half of the 1980s, when the build programme of the Navy increased substantially, Mazagon Docks Limited (MDL) alone could not cope up with the load. It was around 1986 that the Navy and the Coast Guard decided to put this concept into practice.

"The contract for the first three Project 16 ships was awarded to Mazagon Docks and the contract for the second lot, designated Project 16A was awarded to Garden Reach Shipbuilding and Engineering (GRSE). MDL's Design Department was asked to ensure the transfer of technology to GRSE.

"Similarly, the second lot of Project 25 was also awarded to GRSE and the process was repeated.

"In the case of Goa Shipyard Limited (GSL), MDL acted as the lead yard for the Offshore Patrol Vessels and the 1241 REs. The design drawings and processes were transferred to GSL to build the follow-on ships.

"Successful implementation of this concept improved the flexibility of the Navy and the Coast Guard in managing the build programme and also injected an element of competitiveness.

"As General Manager of the Design Department, I was responsible for implementing this concept of Technology Transfer and in retrospect, it was a success.

"Having been associated with the development of concept and basic designs of Project 16 and Project 25 ships and the detailed designs of several projects, I was inevitably part of the concept of 'telescoping of design into production to reduce the total time of Concept to Delivery'. The concept certainly reduced the total time in the case of Project 16. However in later years, the degree of 'telescoping' was increased to perhaps an unacceptable level and it had its fall-outs.

"In fact, this resulted in a controversy, which led to the appointment of (late) Mr Lovraj Kumar to study the concept and submit a report on its suitability. I spent several sessions with Mr Lovraj Kumar explaining the concept and going through the case studies, both the successful and the not so successful ones. As in any concept of this nature, there is no 'black and white' answer. If practiced in moderation, the concept will yield certain benefits in the form of reduced lead-time.

"The reason for delving into this subject is to lay the foundation to discuss the cost-plus and fixed price contracts. When the design is fully completed, there is no reason for going for a cost-plus contract since all elements are known. Even in this case, most capital goods contracts like shipbuilding cater for increase in contract price due to 'change orders' from the 'owners'. Even in a fully developed design, in the first ship of a class, there are bound to be a large number of change orders and the inevitable haggling in the price. This would, of course, reduce in the subsequent ships of a series.

"Resource-constrained Navies have a problem. Very seldom do we build a large number of ships to the same design. Even in the Leander programme, no two ships were built to the same design in terms of weapon package and the associated internal layout. This imposes a tremendous strain in going through the fixed price contract. In fact, the time spent in the negotiation of the contract price variation may be disproportionately larger than the time spent in settling the technical aspects of the design changes, if fixed price contracts were to be practiced in such cases.

"Having spent almost 20 years in the development of basic designs and detailed designs for warships, most of them with Soviet weapon packages, I was associated with several delegations of Soviet Designers who had come to India to work on the projects. I had also visited the erstwhile Soviet Union."

Viewed overall, the Navy's achievements in the field of warship design and production were amazing. In the twenty five years between 1965 and 1990, a tiny 'ship design cell' that was designing yard craft had blossomed into the Directorate General of Naval Design that was designing an aircraft carrier, submarines, destroyers and numerous types of large auxiliary and minor war vessels.

The Soviet Shipbuilding Ministry, its Warship Design Bureaus and Weapon Supply organisations were unstinting in their help. The regular interaction that had started in the 1970s at high levels regarding the developments of future Russian systems enabled planners in the Naval Staff to arrive at cost effective Russian weapon packages to achieve standardisation in systems and economy in inventories.

Enormous synergy was generated by the interchange of talented young naval architects between ship design assignments in the Directorate General of Naval Design and assignments as naval overseers in the warship building yards to oversee the construction of the ships that they had helped to design. This synergy helped Mazagon Docks, Garden Reach and Goa Shipyard to acquire the confidence in the 'hybridising' that was to become standard practice in Indian naval warship building.

9

The Leander Frigate Project

Preamble

In November 1960, soon after Mazagon Docks was taken over, Government approved the construction of three Leander class frigates. MDL held discussions in Britain with shipbuilding firms and the Admiralty. After receiving MDL's report on its requirements for additional facilities, the British firm of Sir Alexander Gibbs and Partners (who were also consultants for the Expansion Scheme of the Bombay Naval Dockyard) were retained to advise and prepare plans for expanding MDL's facilities, both for ship repair and ship construction.

In 1964, agreements were concluded for the construction of the latest design Leander class frigate, in step with the construction of a similar frigate in Britain to be commissioned in 1969. This would enable the personnel deputed by the Navy and MDL to undergo training, to see and learn at first hand how a modern frigate was built and inspected at every step and subjected to rigorous harbour and sea trials before acceptance into service.

The First Frigate Nilgiri

Nilgiri's keel was laid on 15 October 1966. She was commissioned on 3 June 1972. The problems encountered and overcome, and the delays experienced, have been recounted in the previous volume of this series *"Transition to Triumph – The History of the Indian Navy 1965-1975"*.

Changeover From Analog to Digital Electronic Systems

Initially, the Government had ordered only one frigate. There was delay in placing the order for the second and third frigates because India was going through a foreign exchange crisis. Eventually in 1967, an order was placed on MDL to build two more frigates. Naval Headquarters took advantage of this delay to upgrade the radars, fire control systems and the Action Information Organisation (AIO) of the Operations Room.

Lieutenant Commander (L) (later Captain) S Prabhala was in the first team which went to Britain for training in early 1964. Later he was in the Directorate of the Leander Project and later still he was Chairman and Managing Director of Bharat Electronics. He recalls:

"We found that the company SIGNAAL in Holland, which supplied the fire control equipment and the radars for the Dutch Navy's Leanders, had superior equipment, superior in the sense they were already using digital electronics as opposed to the analog electronics of the British systems. The Navy, therefore, felt that if we went in for the indigenous manufacture of the analog systems, we would be stuck with them for the next several years. Why should we make outdated analog systems when digital electronics were already coming into vogue? If we were going to make anything indigenously, we should start with something technologically more up to date than the obsolescent analog British systems then available.

"Then we found that if we were to fit the Signaal equipment, the ship would require some modifications in the hull and in the structure, related only to these equipments and not to a wholesale change of design. Therefore, we needed somebody to supply us the modified shipbuilding drawings to enable us to fit the Dutch Signaal radars and fire control in a broad beam Leander and for that we tied up with NEVESBU, the Dutch Warship Design Bureau. The Dutch fire control and radar equipment were then licensed for manufacture to Bharat Electronics, which was the only Indian company at that time that had some experience of manufacturing radars and electronic equipment for the Defence Services."

Eventually, *Himgiri*, and the subsequent Leanders, were fitted with the following Dutch SIGNAAL equipment:

- The VM 45 fire control system for the 4.5-inch gun.

- Two VM 44 fire control systems for two, sided, Seacat anti aircraft guided missile launchers.

- Long range Air Warning Radar LW 04, Surface Warning Radar DA 05 and Navigation Radar ZW 06.

- DS 22 Display Systems in the Operations Room. This

system was still under development by Signaal and the Indian Navy was the first customer for it.

Since a better, modified British Sonar 184 M was being offered, it replaced the earlier Sonar 184.

The Second Frigate Himgiri

Himgiri's keel was laid on 4 November 1968. She was launched on 6 May 1970. MDL had been able to reduce the time between keel laying and launch from 25 months to 18 months. The fitting-out, however, was considerably delayed due to the late arrival of major items, both from abroad and within India.

The machinery installation was completed in December 1973, Basin Trials were successfully completed in January 1974 and the Contractor's Sea Trials commenced on 6 April 1974. At the preliminary full power trials, the temperature of the gearbox bearings was found to be rising above acceptable limits. The gearbox was the first to have been made in India to the Swiss MAAG design. In consultation with the Swiss designers, it was decided to modify the bearings and check the alignment of the turbines. The Repeat Contractor's Sea Trials in September 1974 were successful, and *Himgiri* commissioned on 23 November 1974.

On the plus side, *Himgiri* got better radars, sonars, AIO and fire control equipment and two Seacat guided missile launchers instead of one. Design changes were also made in the communication systems and the layout of mess decks to improve habitability in tropical conditions.

The Third Frigate Udaygiri

Since orders for the second and third frigates had been received together, MDL was able to build them faster than the first frigate. The fabrication work on the third frigate, scheduled to commence in January 1970, started in April 1970 due to late receipt of steel from Hindustan Steel Ltd.

In 1969-70, there had been an acute shortage of steel. MDL had been able to carry on production without serious dislocation because its earlier orders for steel had materialised. By 1970-71, however, the fall in steel production adversely affected MDL's work. The interval between keel laying and launching increased to 25 months. The main machinery that should have arrived at the time for the ship's launching in October 1972 was actually received in May 1974, thereby further delaying the ship's commissioning till 18 February 1976.

The Fourth Frigate Dunagiri

Orders for the next three frigates were placed in July 1970. The fourth Leander was launched on 9 March 1974. She was on the slipway for only 14 months as compared to 18 to 25 months for the second and third frigates respectively. Fitting out was affected by delays in receipt of indigenous as well as imported equipment. The main engines and gearboxes were received in May 1975. Basin trials were carried out in October 1976 and sea trials completed satisfactorily in November / December 1976. The final inspection of hull, weapons, radio compartments and systems was completed in early 1977. *Dunagiri* commissioned on 5 May 1977.

The time between keel laying and launching had been reduced to 14 months. The time from launching to delivery had been reduced to 38 months – the shortest period yet achieved. Nevertheless, the total of 58 months from start of production was still too long by world standards. On the other hand, the range of equipment being indigenously produced for the first time by Indian industry was impressive – main boilers, main turbines, main gearing, main circulators, turbines for turbo alternators, diesel alternators, stern tube bushes, heat exchangers, radar and fire control equipment, data processing computers, air conditioning and refrigeration machinery, broadcast equipment, telephone and teleprinter equipment, main and auxiliary switch boards, complex system valves, fire detection sensors and a host of other minor equipment.

By the time the fourth Leander had been built, considerable confidence had built up at all levels.

Improvements in Anti Submarine Capability in the Fifth and Sixth Leanders

In 1972 and 1973, operating experience started building up on the newly commissioned first Leander, the *Nilgiri*, and the recently acquired Seaking anti submarine, dunking sonar helicopters. In view of the continuing acquisition by Pakistan of modern submarines from France, it was clear that future Leanders would require greater anti submarine capability.

In early 1973, Naval Headquarters initiated studies to improve the anti submarine capability of the 5th and 6th Leanders. These changes crystallised in mid 1973. The major changes envisaged embarking the heavy Seaking helicopter (instead of the smaller MATCH role helicopter) and improving the anti submarine sonars and weapons.

Seaking Helicopter

In 1966, the Canadian Navy had pioneered the operation of a Seaking helicopter from the deck of a frigate. This entailed designing a 'Bear Trap' Haul-down and Traversing system for moving the heavy helicopter on the small flight deck, providing a large hangar and strengthening the flight deck to bear the weight of a heavy helicopter. All these changes would affect the ship's overall design, stability and sea-keeping qualities.

To meet the conflicting requirement of a large hangar and a long clear flight deck, the hangar would have to be telescopic. Extra flight deck space aft could only be made available by removing the anti submarine Mortar and the Variable Depth Sonar wells.

Lieutenant Commander (later Rear Admiral and Chairman) JJ Baxi recalls:

"When I came back to NHQ in 1973, NHQ had decided that the design of the fifth frigate would be given to the Director (ate) of Naval Design (DND) and not to the Director (ate) of the Leander Project (DLP). As DDLP, I realised that we really did not have much to do, because if the design was being done by DND, what was going to be DLP's role? In those days, DND had come up with a design for a new weapon package.

"In the meanwhile, I went into the technical feasibility of DND's design to see whether a large anti submarine helicopter like a Seaking could operate from a Leander. I distinctly remember we consulted some Admiralty Fleet Orders and then invited the DND, who had earlier given an opinion that this was not feasible, to discussions with DLP. When I went into it, it was on a limited presumption that the anti submarine Mortar Mark 10 fitted at the rear end of the ship was required and that it could never be removed. Then we came up with the idea that if the mortar well was covered up, the overhead space would be just enough for a Seaking to operate from there. The anti submarine mortar could be replaced by another type of forward throwing rocket launcher like the Swedish Bofors SR 375. Then I worked day and night so that no one else would come to know what we were doing. Between Constructor Captain Choudhary who was in the Directorate of Leander Project and myself, we did all the initial design work, showing the new flight deck, showing the new helicopter and showing the new weapon package that was involved. This was the most creative time of my life as a designer.

"We actually came up with a new design concept. We gave a presentation to the Chief of the Naval Staff and he accepted our design. Dr Roy Choudhary was the Scientific Adviser to the Defence Minister and he also accepted that our design would work. Even Mr Paramanandhan, who had by then become the Director General of Naval Design, was gracious enough to accept that operating a Seaking helicopter from a frigate was

feasible. Finally, the design was accepted. That is how we in DLP came back into the design of the 5th frigate, the *Taragiri*."

Anti Submarine Sonars and Weapons

The design modifications and changes were discussed with individual equipment suppliers in Canada, Sweden, Britain and Italy in 1974. By 1975, the changes had been finalised:

- The British Mortar Mk 10 anti submarine ahead throwing weapon fitted aft would be replaced by the Swedish Bofors SR 375 Twin Rocket Launcher with its integral magazine and hoist, all fitted in the bows forward of the gun mounting.

- Two, sided Torpedo Tube Launchers would be fitted to fire the latest Italian A-244 homing torpedoes being acquired as successors to the obsolescent British Mk 44 torpedoes.

- British Graseby's 184 SS (solid state) search sonar would be fitted in lieu of the earlier valve version Sonar 184 M in the preceding Leanders.

- French Thomson-CSF solid state, search and attack sonar Diodon would be fitted in lieu of the earlier valve version attack Sonar 170 M in the preceding Leanders.

- British Graseby's Sonar GI 738 Underwater Telephone would be fitted in lieu of the earlier Sonar 182.

- India's Department of Electronics would produce the ASW fire control computer to control the new SR 375 Rocket Launcher and the deck launched A 244 torpedoes.

- The latest available Italian electronic warfare equipment would be fitted.

The Fifth Frigate Taragiri

The design work for these extensive modifications was, for the first time, undertaken by the Naval Design Organisation.

These design changes delayed the commencement of construction, which should have started immediately after the launching of the fourth frigate. Production could commence only in April 1975. The keel was laid six months later and the ship was launched on 25 October 1976. Thereafter there was a major setback in fitting-out because of a delay of one year in receipt of the main engines. This created its own chain of delays. Contractor's Sea Trials commenced in April 1979. During trials, vibrations were observed in the main turbines. The defects were rectified, repeat sea trials were satisfactorily completed in December and *Taragiri* commissioned on 16 May 1980. Whilst the time from keel laying to launch had been only 12 months, the least period so far, the time taken from launching to commissioning was 43 months, much more than the time taken for any of its predecessors.

The Sixth Frigate Vindhyagiri

Vindhyagiri was the first Leander to have the steam-atomised Dieso-burning system to mitigate the boiler refractory problems that had been experienced in the earlier Leanders.

In other respects, she was identical with *Taragiri*. Construction commenced on 5 July 1976. Her keel was laid on 5 November 1976, and she was launched on 12 November 1977 after a period of 12 months, the same time as was taken for the *Taragiri*. She commissioned on 8 July 1981, having taken 44 months from launch to delivery.

Conversion from Furnace Fuel Oil (FFO) to Steam-Atomised Dieso-Burning System

In 1967, the British Navy commenced trials to changeover from FFO to Diesel fuel in its Leander class frigates. Vice Admiral (then Lieutenant) L Lowe was deputed to Britain to participate in these trials. He recalls:

"My deputation to the Admiralty Marine Engineering Establishment, Haslar was to associate with the trials team formed by the Royal Navy for converting their boilers from FFO to Diesel. The Royal Navy found it expedient to go in for a single fuel at that point of time, because of the induction of gas turbines into their Navy. Having FFO burning Leanders and follow on steam ships would create logistic problems for them, and therefore, they thought it wise to go in for a 'single fuel Navy'.

"Added to this, they had problems while operating steam ships and steam boilers in that some of their ships had experienced a number of furnace failures and explosions. It was with this in mind that they thought they would overcome the problem by changing over from FFO to diesel.

"The Indian Navy got a place for one Engineering officer to participate in these trials, which were really of a Research and Development nature and buttressed by actual trials on a Y-160 boiler at Haslar. Trials were done in a most methodical and professional manner, where frequent inspections of the furnace from inside were backed by a lot of effort from their labs in UK. A number of burners were experimented with until they arrived at the most optimum geometry for these burners, which gave the most optimised atomiser for the burning tips. Although trials were not hundred percent complete, my deputation period ended on a satisfactory note of not having any major problems with the burning of diesel. Trials did continue after I returned.

"We went into it by the year 1976, when Naval Headquarters decided to implement it. We could not implement it until 1979 because even the Royal Navy required a large number of conversion kits for their own ships."

The Minutes of the Commanders' Conference 1981 state:

"*Vindhyagiri*, the sixth Leander and the last of series was commissioned on 8 July 1981. This is the first Leander with the steam atomised Dieso burning system, which should reduce the boiler refractory problems that have plagued earlier Leanders. All Leanders are to be converted to this system during their planned refits."

Overview of Construction Timelines						
MDL Yard No.	228	248	274	298	308	318
Ship's Name	Nilgiri	Himgiri	Udaygiri	Dunagiri	Taragiri	Vindhyagiri
Order Placed on MDL	Jul 65	Sep 67	Sep 67	Jul 70	Jul 70	Jul 70
Fabrication Commenced	May 66	Jul 68	Apr 70	Sep 72	Apr 75	Jul 76
Keel Laid	Oct 66	Nov 68	Aug 70	Jan 73	Oct 75	Nov 76
Launched	Oct 68	May 70	Oct 72	Mar 74	Oct 76	Nov 77
Commissioned	Jun 72	Nov 74	Feb 76	May 77	May 80	Jul 81

Overview of Improvements in Combat Capability

This table shows the improvement in sensors and weapons between the first and the sixth Leander. Equally significant improvements were effected in the engineering and electrical machinery.

	NILGIRI (First Leander)	HIMGIRI, UDAYGIRI DUNAGIRI (2nd, 3rd and 4th Leanders)	TARAGIRI VINDHYAGIRI (5th and 6th Leanders)
Surface to Air Missile Fire Control	British	Dutch	Dutch
Gun Mounting Fire Control	British	Dutch	Dutch
Ship Launched Torpedoes	-	-	Italian
Anti Submarine Weapon	British	British	Swedish
Anti Submarine Helicopter	French Alouette with British Torpedoes	Indian Alouette with British Torpedoes	British Seaking with Italian Torpedoes
Close Range AA Guns	20 mm Oerlikon (ex stock)	20 mm Oerlikon (ex stock)	20 mm Oerlikon (ex stock)
Chaff	-	-	-
Radars	British	Dutch	Dutch
Sonars	British	British	British and French
Action Information System	British	Dutch	Dutch
Electronic Warfare System	British	British	Italian

The Leander Project in Retrospect

The Leander Frigate Project, which commenced with the construction of the *Nilgiri* on 23 October 1966, completed with the commissioning of the *Vindhyagiri* on 8 July 1981. During these fifteen years, six frigates were delivered, an average of 30 months per ship. By the time of the 6th Leander, the indigenous content of bought out equipment had risen to 70%. The 5th and 6th ships had an imported content of only 27% as against 70% in the case of the first frigate.

Vice Admiral BA Samson was the Chairman and Managing Director of MDL when the first few frigates were being built. He recalls:

"The specifications, the very fine tolerances, the performance ratios and the fact that all equipment had to be shock-proof, were parameters which Indian Industry, by and large, were totally unaware of and had never experienced. Thanks to the inspiration of Mr Krishna Menon, indigenisation was progressed relentlessly. He had always maintained that unless India was self-sufficient in major items of defence equipment, we would never be totally free and that, further if we were dependent on the West or on anyone else, we would be badly let down, in time of war when the 'crunch' came. And indeed this was proved time and again, in the conflicts with Pakistan in 1948 and 1965, when both Britain and the USA imposed embargos.

"Today looking back, it is quite extraordinary the degree to which indigenisation was achieved. For instance, we are now accepting, without demur, the Main Gearing being manufactured by Walchand Nagar in collaboration with MAAG of Switzerland. And yet in 1966, when this was first suggested, there was horror. The very idea of a highly sophisticated piece of equipment like the main gearing being manufactured, way out in the middle of nowhere, some 60 to 70 miles outside Poona, in what was originally a sugar factory in a little village, was unbelievable to most. And yet it did succeed.

"There were numerous problems, aggravated to some

extent by doubts and lack of confidence, but we won through. What is important is that it created the kind of confidence and experience, both in the Service and specially in Indian Industry who, having succeeded in producing equipment of such high specifications for the Navy, were emboldened to go in for higher technology."

Captain NS Mohan Ram, a naval constructor, recalls:

"The Directorate of Leander Project in 1969/1970 was very exciting. I had excellent colleagues. On the electrical side there were Commanders Baxi and Ganesh, on the engineering side there was Commander Bose. We did the very first composite layouts of compartments like the galley, the electronic warfare office, the electronic warfare equipment room etc. We did the complete air conditioning of the *Nilgiri*.

"I also did the collapsible hangar, which the Royal Navy did not have. We needed a hangar that could collapse like an accordion, so that when the helicopter was landing, the hangar would be closed and when the helicopter was parked, the hangar would be open. Nobody had done this in a ship of *Nilgiri's* size. We got a company called Dominion Aluminum Fabricating Company of Canada to do the collapsible hangar.

"It was a very interesting time because we were learning on the job. And stupid mistakes used to happen also. I went to Mazagon Docks for an inspection of the helicopter landing deck. The Alouette is a three-wheeled helicopter, the front wheel is in the middle. The helicopter guide platforms were welded as per the original British design for the British Westland Wasp, which was a four-wheeled helicopter. When I went and asked the Naval Air Staff. 'Why didn't you tell us earlier'? I got no reply. To rectify that mistake, we had to change the whole insulation and the wiring. We did a lot of foolish things. But we were learning all the time.

"In those four or five years, Mazagon Docks and the Navy learnt so much. I think the future of the Navy was laid in the Leander Frigate Project. For the first time, we were getting into the nitty gritty of building warships and this really culminated when the Navy put the big Seaking helicopter in *Taragiri* with a bigger extendable hangar. It was something quite phenomenal, something to be proud of."

Commodore (then Commander) SC Bose, an engineer officer, recalls:

"We had the Department of Defence Production, Ministry of Defence, working hand in hand with Naval Headquarters and Mazagon Docks towards indigenisation. In retrospect, I would say this was the best and most systematic indigenisation effort the Navy ever had. And taking the totality into account, it was possibly the best in the country at that time.

"While the main engines of the first ship were imported, the second ship's set of main engines were made by BHEL in Bhopal, using the same English Electric drawings made in Foot Pound System by converting the measurements to the Metric System, which had been adopted in India and in which Bhopal's machines were set. We also developed an indigenous version of Allen's steam auxiliaries with Jyoti of Baroda and BHEL Bhopal. A steam test rig was set up in Bhopal, financed by the Navy, to give these machines a test run under steam before accepting the machinery for installation on board.

"Special weld-able steel, known as Ship Building Quality Steel or Lloyd's grade A/B is used in shipbuilding. These steels were not manufactured in India till then. We had the blessings of the Ministry of Steel to undertake the project at Rourkela Steel Plant and they did a fairly successful job, though it did not meet the specification to 100%. This steel was considered acceptable under deviation and used in constructing the second Leander. Subsequently, of course, it was found that imported steel was of quicker delivery and cheaper, and was used. Having established an indigenous source of manufacture of shipbuilding quality steel, we could always revert to it whenever necessary.

"The boilers of the first Leander were erected in the Naval Dockyard Bombay. A new Boiler Shop was created and the boilers, with drums, tubes, mountings etc from the British firm Babcock and Wilcox were erected. Being very heavy and bulky, these boilers were put on trailers in the Naval Dockyard Bombay and transported to Mazagon Dock for installation on board.

"The development of the main shafting was attempted at the Heavy Engineering Corporation (HEC) Ranchi. But HEC was experiencing serious administrative problems. As such the project did not finally succeed. They met the specifications in only 50% of the items. They could have had 100% success had they carefully followed our instructions of cropping the ends of the forgings before rolling the shafts. In order to achieve good quality forgings for turbine rotors for the Navy and for Power Houses, HEC had initiated action for procurement and installation of a Vacuum Degassing Plant and a 6,000-tonne press. Unfortunately, after installation, these valuable plants were lying idle due to lack of initiative, and rotor forgings were being imported by BHEL and other turbine manufacturers.

"The main gear cases, a very critical piece of machinery, were also indigenised. In the first Leander, we used imported David Brown gearing but for the second Leander we went in for ones to be produced at Walchand Nagar near Pune, under collaboration with MAAG Gearwheel Co of Zurich.[1] Here again we faced many problems in conversion of metric CGS into Foot Pound Systems, as the terminals had to be in the FPS system to match with the turbines and shafting while the internals imported from MAAG were in CGS system. I must say that the Directorate of Leander Project (DLP), the Directorate of Marine Engineering (DME) and the Directorate of Warship Projects (DWP) under the Ministry of Defence Production burnt midnight candles in Walchand Nagar, checking every dimension and manufacturing tolerance, meeting both FPS and CGS system of the terminal components. It was a success in one shot.

"We had set up a Test Rig using a redundant cruising turbine of a Khukri class frigate for back-to-back test under actual steam and give both the gear wheels overspeed and overload runs of the kind it would experience in a ship for maximum exploitation. We were told that such trials were done only in Canada and in Switzerland. We ran continuous trials for 72 hours. The trial runs went as scheduled except for one incident when one set of bearings failed. We immediately knew what it was due to. The representative of MAAG Gearwheel, a renowned designer, was present at the trials. We all agreed with the corrective actions and continued with the trials. I don't think such a bold step would be taken anywhere, to introduce into service a gear case, which was never tried earlier. We were very lucky that the propulsion system with the changed component gave no problem of noise or vibration in any mode.

"We developed all the gun-metal valves and fittings indigenously. Similar indigenous substitutes were found for electrical fittings, items of domestic and hotel services nature, etc."

Captain Prabhala recalls:

"The success of the indigenisation effort in building the Leanders and the machinery that came into existence with it, the organisation of the Directorate of Warship Projects initially and the organisation of the Directorate of Production and Inspection Navy later, gave us the confidence that we can go ahead more boldly with procurement of equipment from indigenous resources.[2] For instance, the communication equipment, ICS 3, for the Leanders was imported from the UK but we were able to get Bharat Electronics to develop it – whether it was the UHF transreceiver or the CCS equipment and the Versatile Console System – to a degree which the other two services did not indigenise. The naval constructors also rose to the occasion and came out with improved designs of the Leanders like the *Taragiri* and the Project 16 Godavari class frigates."

Overall, the Leander Frigate Project was, for its time, a significant achievement. The boldness of the naval decision makers, the enthusiasm, perseverance and dedication of the implementers in Mazagon Docks, in the Ministry of Defence Production and in the Navy, the assistance by the British Admiralty, by the British shipbuilding collaborators, Vickers and Yarrow, by the Dutch Design Bureau NEVESBU, the assistance of the diverse suppliers – all these contributed to the success of the project.

Particularly valuable was the close and informal interaction, between personages as high as the Secretary Defence Production, HC Sarin, his Additional Secretary (and later Secretary) MM Sen and their teams in the Ministry of Defence, Defence Production and Defence Finance, and the bright young naval officers of the Leander Project. Within the Navy, the elders trusted the youngsters to do what they thought best. The success of indigenisation was a direct result of the Indigenisation Study Group's free, frank and helpful interaction with Indian Industry through DWP and DPI (N).

The self-confidence gained in this project by the Navy's weapon planners, the naval architects and the shipbuilder laid the basis for the success of the series of warships that followed.

---

1. Since 1966, Swiss MAAG gearing had already been fitted and was working satisfactorily in Canadian Navy frigates that were similar to our Leanders.

2. The Directorate of Warship Projects (DWP) looked after the engineering items. The Directorate of Production and Inspection, DPI (Navy), looked after the common user Naval Store items, Electrical and Electronic items and machinery spares.

10

Project 16 - The Godavari Class Frigates

Evolution of the Design

Project 16 was the designation given to the three frigates that followed the six ships of the Leander Project. The staff requirements for this new design were formulated in 1972 before *Nilgiri,* the first Leander, had even been commissioned.[1] They incorporated the lessons learnt in the recently concluded 1971 Indo-Pakistan War.

Discussions in 1973 and 1974 made it clear that the Navy did not have, and was not likely to have, naval architects and warship designers in the numbers required to undertake a *de novo* frigate design. During these two years, detailed discussions had been going on with the Soviet side for the next series of Russian acquisitions, which included Kashin class guided missile destroyers and Nanuchka class ocean-going rocket boats. Progress was also being made in the development of indigenous systems.

In 1974, the Directorate of Combat Policy and Tactics (DCPT)[2] suggested that the Project 16 frigates should have:

- The Russian surface-to-surface missile, surface to air missile and gun systems of the Nanuchka class rocket boats and the surface warning cum height finding radar of the Kashin class.

- Two Seaking anti submarine helicopters (instead of the one that Vindhyagiri had) so as to ensure that at least one serviceable helicopter would always be available.[3]

- The latest Indian APSOH sonar designed for Indian waters, instead of British sonar.

- A mix of Soviet and Indian radars and Italian CAAIS and EW systems.

The Directorate of Marine Engineering suggested that steam propulsion be replaced by gas turbine propulsion.

Since constraints[4] precluded a totally *de novo* design with gas turbine propulsion, the Naval Staff approved this hybrid weapon package but retained the indigenous propulsion machinery and other equipment developed for earlier Leanders. Approval was also accorded for having two Seakings embarked, along with a system that would assist the recovery and movement of these heavy 10-tonne helicopters on a heaving deck. In end 1975, the Naval Staff and the Government accepted this design. Detailed drawing and design work started in 1976.

The design was entrusted to a project team headed by Commander (later Captain) NS Mohan Ram, a naval architect, trained in Britain and who had worked in the British Leander Design Section. Lt Cdr (later Captain) J Subbiah was the second member of the team.

Captain J Subbiah recalls:

"Initially, the proposal to upgrade the Leander weapon package was being handled by the Directorate of Leander Project. The project was later moved to Directorate of Naval Design because:

– Apart from upgrading the package, the staff requirements called for augmentation and a mixed origin of weapons.

– From an essentially anti-submarine project, the project called for the addition of surface-to-surface missiles, more powerful anti aircraft weapons and ability to carry two large helicopters.

---

1. It takes ten years from the time the 'staff requirement' is formulated till the time a frigate is commissioned. During this ten-year period, many developments can and do occur – changes in threat assessments, availability of new and better weapons and systems, successful development of indigenous systems etc. The 'staff requirement' foresees these as best as possible to avoid subsequent piecemeal modifications in design that would delay the completion of construction.

2. Now known as the Directorate of Staff Requirements. The author was DCPT at the time.

3. A Naval Headquarters Technical Team visited Canada in 1974 and saw a Canadian 4,100-tonne Destroyer that had two Seakings embarked.

4. There were neither enough trained draughtsmen nor junior designers. Expertise had to be developed in-house. Organisational capability had to be built up concurrently with the design.

"Neither of these requirements could be achieved in the existing platform. It was decided, therefore, to develop a new design.

"Before taking up the design of Project 16, we carried out an experiment of fitting Soviet missiles in an existing hull, much against the advice of the Soviet experts. We cannibalised the surface-to-surface missiles from a missile boat and fitted three missiles abreast on the foc'sle[5] of a British Type 12 frigate – *Talwar*. Although we made some mistakes in the finer aspects of the design, the concept proved to be successful in the final weapon trials. This gave us substantial confidence in taking up the Project 16 design with the mixed weapon package.

"The work on the design of Project 16 commenced in 1974, the preliminary design was completed by 1975 and work then commenced on the detailed design in 1976.

"In end 1980, in keeping with the policy of assigning the designers of a ship to the task of building the ship, I was sent to the Warship Production Superintendent organisation in Bombay. For the next three years, my main assignment, as the Naval Overseer, was to ensure completion of the first ship of Project 16".

Captain NS Mohan Ram recalls:

"My team consisted of just six officers, two each of construction, engineering and electrical and weapons disciplines. Our draftsmen were inexperienced and were mostly non-matriculate apprentices trained by us in-house. We had a few experienced civilian design specialists who had also come up from the ranks. No other navy in the world would have dared to embark on a project of that magnitude with such meagre resources and inexperienced personnel.

"When we started the design, we had no data on Soviet weapons and systems. I started the deck layout scaling up dimensions from the small photographs of Soviet frigates and missile ships from the well-known military publication *Jane's Fighting Ships*! From a photo of about six inches or so length, we had to scale up space requirements and clearances for sophisticated missiles and guns.

"The next issue was the power plant to get the higher speed in a bigger ship. The Leanders displaced about 3,000 tonnes and had a top speed of about 28 knots. The Naval Staff wanted a minimum one knot extra from this ship, which was estimated to displace about 3,600 tonnes and be about 12 to 13 metres (40 feet) longer.

The Leander was propelled by two steam turbines of 15,000 shaft horsepower each. The first assumption was that the larger ship would need about 40,000 horsepower total and would need major changes to the power plant. The marine engineers of the Navy wanted to fit gas turbines, which we had never done before. We had some experience with operating gas turbines in ships acquired from the Soviets but designing a ship for gas turbine propulsion was a very complex affair.

"I was keen to minimise changes from known aggregates and to resort to fresh design effort only where essential. In any case, we had to design the ship to house new weapons and fire control systems. The hull had to be larger resulting in totally new hull systems. If we changed the power plant also, it would involve total redesign of the ship and the problem became even more intractable. I was, therefore, keen to continue using the steam turbines, which were manufactured under license in India by Bharat Heavy Electricals Limited.

"I asked myself 'What would happen, if I powered the new ship with the same power plant – two turbines of fifteen thousand horsepower each, without any change. How much would the speed drop? Was there any chance of convincing the naval staff that a small sacrifice in top speed would make the ship more economical and easier to construct?' I did a quick back-of-the envelope calculation to estimate the speed loss. To my utter surprise, the answer came out that the ship did not lose speed at all. On the contrary, it would go a full knot faster, at 29 knots, which the naval staff wanted!

"No one believed me at first. I was greeted with a stony silence and most of my colleagues, thought that I had gone out of my head. I could not blame them, as my findings were totally counter-intuitive. I then asked my colleague, Lieutenant Commander Subbiah, a brilliant designer, to check the power requirements and speed independently. He also arrived at the same answer. Our boss, the Director General, Mr Paramanandhan, did not believe me at first. But when both Subbiah and I, two of his brightest officers had come to the same answer, he realised that I might have stumbled on to something extraordinary. He still insisted that another officer should check the numbers. Lo and behold, the answer was the same. We realised that we could preserve the power plant of the Leander class frigates and meet the Naval Staff's requirement for higher speed.

"We had to find the reason for this windfall benefit. A detailed analysis showed that below twenty-two knots

---

5. In naval terminology, the front part of a ship is called the forecastle or 'foc'sle' for short, the middle part is called 'midships' and the rear part is called 'quarterdeck'.

speed, the larger ship required more power for the same speed as the Leander. At around twenty-two knots, both ships required the same power but above 22 knots, the bigger ship required less power. Again, above 31 knots, the bigger vessel was again at a disadvantage compared to the Leander class ships. But happily, at 29 knots plus, the larger ship needed only the same power as the Leander's 30,000 HP. A happy combination of the laws of hydrodynamics was working to our advantage.

"Further analysis revealed that at lower speeds, the resistance to ships' motion was primarily due to friction, in which the larger ship with about 20% greater wetted surface area (area exposed to the water) was at a disadvantage. Above 22 knots, the resistance to motion from wave making due to the ship cleaving through the sea became more prominent than friction. If the interference between the waves created by the bow (front) of the ship and the stern (rear) of the ship were positive, resulting in a crest at the rear end, resistance due to wave-making would be lower. If the interference between the bow and stern wave systems resulted in a trough at the stern, the resistance due to wave-making would be higher. The interference is a function of a factor called Froude Number, which relates the square of the speed of the ship to the length of the ship.

"In the case of the Leander at 28 knots, the interference caused a trough at the stern increasing the wave-making resistance. But in the new longer ship, the interference resulted in a crest. This resulted in a lower wave resistance in the bigger ship, which more than compensated the increased drag due to greater area. Overall, this led to the bigger ship going faster. Once we had done this detailed analysis, the picture became a lot clearer.

"We also found that the same principle was being adopted in 'jumboising' super tankers by adding a new mid section, making the ships longer to carry more crude without losing speed.

"While we could reach the top speed comfortably with the same engines, at the normal cruising speeds the ship consumed twenty per cent more fuel than the Leander. We had to increase the fuel tank capacity of the ship.

"Using the same power plant, gearing, transmission and even propeller as the Leander in the new ship enabled us to save immense design effort and cost. Moreover, Mazagon Docks experience of constructing six Leander class ships with the same power plant would make engine-related erection easier.

"When we announced our findings to the Naval Staff, the Marine Engineering Directorate questioned the validity of our calculations. Many meetings ensued, but we prevailed.

"A peculiar problem arose due to the mixture of Soviet and Western weapon systems. Soviet ships use 380 volts, 3 phase, 50 cycles main power supply while Western ships use 440 volts, 3 phase, 60 cycles power supply. This required that the ship should operate two distinct electrical systems. Enquiries with auxiliary machinery suppliers revealed that changeover of power systems to 380 volts from 440 volts and from 60 to 50 cycles would result in major changes in dimensions and geometry of the machinery, which would in turn cause major changes to the engine room and boiler room arrangements. So we decided to keep the main power generation from diesel and turbo alternators as per the Leanders' 440 volts, 3 phase and 60 cycles.

"For Soviet weapons and systems, we decided to install two motor alternators of 350 kW each, converting the supplies to 380 volt and 50 cycles. This solution of having two distinct power supplies in one warship was unorthodox and was one of the many departures from convention in the design of the ship.

"By physically locating all machinery spaces, diesel alternator rooms, boiler room, engine room, stern compartments and propeller shaft supports and the propeller supporting bracket at the same relative locations and distances as in the original Leanders, substantial engineering redesign was averted.

"The evolution of the new design involved calculated risk-taking, innovation and extrapolation of available knowledge. The decision to go ahead was a bold act of faith on the part of the Navy. It reflected the confidence the Navy had in its young designers and the growing capability of Mazagon Docks.

"The go-ahead was given in 1975. The keel was laid in 1977. *Godavari* commissioned in December 1983. She fully met the specifications and exceeded all major performance requirements".[6]

Mr S Paramanandhan headed the Design Directorate. He recalls:

"The Navy was looking around for a cost effective option where surface to surface, air to surface and anti-air capabilities would be available from a single ship. This naturally required the ship to have helicopter launched air to surface missiles, surface to surface missiles, surface to air missiles, a large stock of anti submarine

---

6. In recognition of his contribution, Commander Mohan Ram was awarded the Vishist Seva Medal.

INS *TARAGIRI*, the fifth indigenously-built Leander class frigate, having improved sonars and anti submarine weapons and hangar for one Seaking anti submarine helicopter (1980s)

INS *GANGA*, the ninth indigenously-built frigate of Project 16, having surface-to-surface and surface-to-air missiles, modern electronic warfare and anti missile systems and hangar for two Seaking anti submarine helicopters (1980s)

INS *KHUKRI* (top) and INS *KUTHAR* (below) indigenously-built corvettes of Project 25, having surface-to-surface missiles, anti missile systems and capable of operating a Chetak helicopter (1980s)

INS *DELHI* - the first indigenously-built missile destroyer of Project 15 with hangar for two Seaking Mk 42 B helicopters

Newly-designed, helicopter-capable Survey Ship of the 1980s

INS *SUKANYA* helicopter-capable Offshore Patrol Vessel (1980s)

Indigenously-built Landing Craft Utility - LCU (1980s)

Russian Project 61 ME Missile Destroyer (1980s) with hangar for one Kamov helicopter

Russian INS *RAJPUT* (left) and indigenous INS *GODAVARI* (right)

Polish Landing Ship Tank capable of landing five main battle tanks
during amphibious operations

INS *VEER* - Russian Project 1241 RE Fast Missile Attack Craft

INS *ABHAY* - Russian Project 1241 PE Anti Submarine Patrol Craft (1980s)

INS *PORBANDAR* - Russian Project 266 ME Coastal Minesweeper (1970s)

Russian Project 205 Extended Range Missile Boat firing an anti ship missile (1970s)

torpedoes and two Seaking helicopters, so that at any one time you could keep one helicopter in the air, be it for an anti submarine mission or an anti ship mission. The Staff definitely wanted two Seakings. They were not happy with only one. With surface-to-surface missiles, surface-to-air missiles and two Seakings, it appeared to be a cost effective ship. Certainly the Leander hull was in no position to take it.

"The second problem that came up was the economics of it. We had invested more than Rs 150 crore in the indigenous development of the steam machinery. This led to a clear decision that the propulsion package would remain the same, but the ship must have the weapon package, which meant both the L Band and the S Band radars and, to accommodate the Soviet design philosophy and their weapons, dedicated radar for each weapon. This was too much to go into a Leander design. This naturally meant that a new frigate had to be designed from scratch, except for the propulsion package, which should not change.

"Our initial check indicated that we might lose around 2 knots of speed but could provide 20% longer range, 150% more aviation fuel, all weapon packages and additional complement to man the weapons and the helo included. The Naval Staff were willing to accept the 2-knot penalty.

"From there, we proceeded to do a serious design. Halfway through, we realised the ship was getting longer and thinner and if we adopted the same propulsion package, the length advantage might give an edge and we might be able to do just about half a knot less than the Leander. From that proposition, we went for a model test. Of course, we changed the fore part of the ship because the Leander fore part would have posed a lot of obstruction, both for the missile, the gun and the surface-to-air missile. Starting from that point, there was very little commonality between the Leander and Project 16.

"There was another technical fineness in ship propulsion and ship model test. When, at maximum speed, the cut-up under the stern of a ship happens to be in the trough of the bow wave, the ship loses speed. If the cut-up happens to be on the crest of the bow wave, the ship gains speed. When Mohan Ram, Subbiah and I had a look at the model test results, we found that the ship was comfortably sitting on the crest and we were overwhelmed. It seemed possible that the ship might go even faster than the Leander at full power. This was amply proved during sea trials. Till 60%, 70%, 75% of

full power, she was one and a half knot slower than the Leander. But the moment she reached 85% to 90% of full power, her acceleration was higher and she could overtake the Leander.

"We had a group of engineer and electrical officers working with us. Mazagon Dock wanted them to help build the ship. I gladly agreed to let them go. When the ship went out for trials, there were Soviet experts on board. They had their own misgivings about the ship's speed but when they observed she was doing 29 knots, 29.5 knots and even up to 30 knots, they were surprised and equally, we were surprised. The ship was keeping up with the gas turbine propelled *Rajput*.[7]

"When both ships were asked to do a zigzag manoeuvre, the *Godavari* could do better than the *Rajput*. The wake of the Project 16 was classic, whereas the *Rajput* was churning the ocean. Any commanding officer would like to have a ship that has no wake at all, or at least a partially suppressed wake.

"I do not claim any credit for me or for any of my design officers. It's one of those things where fortune favours those who are willing to take the risk. And *Godavari* happened to have ended well."

Captain KK Lohana succeeded Mr Paramanandhan as DGND. He recalls:

"I had one other small part to play when we were doing the upper deck layout. When the missile containers were put on either side of the super structure, which was protruding out towards the forward end from the main superstructure, there was not enough space for people to walk past the containers, after allowing for the minimum distance between the containers. My main contribution in this area was suggesting that there should be sponsons on either side of the weather deck to locally create more width to allow for the extra space required. This proved to be a successful and distinctive feature of the ship.

"After this project was finally approved for construction, Mazagon Dock wanted the Navy to send somebody who would help the shipyard in translating the Navy's design into workshop drawings. I was asked to go to Mazagon Dock as the Head of the Warship Design Section and entrusted with the task of doing that. It was a great opportunity. As the work progressed, there was constant interaction between the production side on one hand and the Naval Headquarters design organisation on the other. It was tight rope walking between the two, which we managed to do successfully.

7. *Rajput* was the first of the 5,000-tonne Soviet Kashin class guided missile destroyers. It arrived in India in 1981 and, at the time of *Godavari's* sea trials in 1982, was the Navy's latest and best ship of that size. Hence the elation of the designers at *Godavari's* comparative performance.

"At the same time, the colleague who was in charge of the Merchant Ship Drawing Office also resigned and left, so I had the opportunity of heading the entire design organisation of the Mazagon Docks. And by the time I was called back to Naval Headquarters as DGND, the *Godavari*, the first ship of the class, had almost proceeded to completion. I attended her commissioning ceremony."

Rear Admiral (then Cdr) JJ Baxi[8] was associated initially with the design and later headed the new Weapon and Electronic Systems Organisation, WESO, which was created to resolve the electronic integration between the Russian, European and indigenous systems. He recalls:

"After *Taragiri*, (the 5th Leander class frigate), there was a very healthy competition between the Directorate of Naval Design and the Directorate of Leander Project. Commander (later Captain) Mohan Ram and Lieutenant Commander (later Captain) Subbiah, who were the two best young naval constructors that the Navy had, joined the Directorate of Naval Design. They said, "If an electrical officer like Baxi can meet the staff requirement for a frigate with one Seaking helicopter, why can't we come up with a larger and better hull which can meet the staff requirement for two Seaking helicopters?

"By that time, the Directorate of Combat Policy and Tactics had suggested that Soviet weapon systems be integrated into the next design. Not only were they cheaper and more cost effective but would also enable standardisation of missile inventory.

"I distinctly remember that I was opposed to that idea, thinking that we would not be able to carry out the interfaces. But ultimately, history proved that this was the right decision and we became the first Navy in the world to succeed in designing a hybrid ship, the *Godavari* of Project 16, having a mix of Soviet and Western sensors and weapon systems.

"We found that putting Soviet systems in an Indian hull, which also had Western systems was not only feasible but also realistic. The only thing that we did not know was how to interface the various Western electrical inputs and outputs with those coming out of the Soviet weapon systems to make it suitable for whichever

protocols were available in the Western world at that time. This is where the idea of WESO came in.

"The WESO idea was not really mine. It came originally from Captain PR Sen. He had taken the idea from a Japanese Naval Review on how the Japanese do system engineering on their warships. The Japanese had created an organisation like WESO to avoid invoking the embargo of the Americans. That paper was followed up by Commodore Mudholkar.[9] Then it was followed up by Captain Prabhala,[10] then he handed it over to the Directorate of Weapons and Equipment, Commander Venkatesh[11] and finally it came to Directorate of Electrical Engineering to Commander Ravi Kohli.[12] It is at that point of time that Naval Headquarters decided to create the WESO.

"In 1977, there was a discussion in Naval Headquarters between the Chief of the Naval Staff and the Scientific Adviser to the Defence Minister to decide the person who would be able to handle this and who had weapon system background. Although I was a Commander, I was appointed as the Director of the Organisation in 1977. That is when from 1978 to 1984, we actually designed the interfaces that finally made the ship successful.

"As regards availability of Soviet system data, we had Commander Pradeep Kar and Lieutenant Commander Avadhanulu on the staff of WESO. In my opinion, they were amongst the brainiest naval officers our country has produced in terms of technology. These two started going into the Soviet system of documentation.

"There was a general belief in the Navy that Soviet documentation did not give enough data. That proved to be wrong, because very detailed information was available. The problem only arose when we needed a specific electrical design characteristic. Naturally, no user handbook had this kind of information. It is at that point that there were a lot of 'doubting Thomases' in Naval Headquarters.

"That is the point of time when we wrote to you in

---

8. Rear Admiral JJ Baxi (then Commander) was the first Director of WESO, the organisation that interfaced and integrated the electronics of the Russian and European sensor and weapon systems. In later years, he rose to become Chairman and Managing Director of Bharat Electronics after Captain S Prabhala.

9. Commodore BG Mudholkar was the Director Naval Research and Development. He had undergone electrical training with the British Navy and at Cambridge. He rose to become the Chief Controller of Research and Development in the Defence Research and Development Organisation.

10. Captain S Prabhala later joined India's premier public sector electronics firm Bharat Electronics where he played a sterling role in indigenising and productionising naval radars and sonars. He rose to become Chairman and Managing Director of Bharat Electronics.

11. Commodore R Venkatesh rose to become Chairman and Managing Director of Goa Shipyard.

12. Later as a Vice Admiral, Ravi Kohli was the Director of Naval Research and Development.

Russia and requested you to send us the data.[13] We had no other option, since we had been given the charter to get the data.

"Having got the data, we started doing the interface. Once the Soviet specialists from the Design Bureau came to know that I had what I wanted, they become helpful. Commodore Mudholkar used to take measurements on existing Soviets ships and a Russian expert would stand behind him with an avometer to help him because they also began to realise the importance of our requirement.

"The Russians realised the importance of interfacing with Western systems so as to have greater universal marketability of Soviet systems. They had not been thinking like that earlier. For the first time, they realised that there could be a better sensor or a better fire control system or a better missile by taking indigenous systems or weapons of other countries and yet maximise the importance of Soviet systems. Once we had broken the ice, we never had any difficulty. Hundred percent data came through the formal and official sources.

"WESO was the first organisation to come up in an under-developed country to take on the major exercise of weapon system engineering. The Soviets gave us the data for the first time, some of which you yourself had sent. We had all the Western interfaces available to us. Fortunately, the Indian designers, and particularly naval officers, had already understood the power of computers. And although we used older computers, which are now out of date, but for the purpose of converting Soviet data into Western data and vice versa, the power of these computers was adequate.

"The only contribution which I think I made as a technical manager was in bringing together brilliant people of diverse background like Ajay Sharma, A Ganesh, Pradeep Kar, Avadhanulu and Muthangi. Each of them was brilliant in his own right. But I had to make sure that they worked together as a team and produced the requisite output.

"It was really three people Kar, Avadhanulu and Muthangi who first thought of the idea of having a computer box with requisite processing power and memory and having outputs which interface directly either with a western weapon or an indigenous system. This modular design, which could act as an interface device between Soviet and Western weapons was the primary reason for success. This kind of success that we had, both with hardware and software development,

has given a tremendous boost to the weapon system engineering ability of the Indian Navy today.

"The Navy also realised at that time that this kind of weapon system engineering could not succeed unless the Executive Branch themselves had a strong professional group which looked into the application level software. So we had a Rule Writing Group. This group has now come of age and they are giving a lot of inputs to WESO which later on was renamed WESEE - Weapons and Electronic Systems Engineering Establishment.

"WESEE has given the Indian Navy system engineering expertise, which only the more advanced countries have. The most important thing is that this expertise is within Naval Headquarters and not in industry. Today everybody in the other two services realises that they have a lacuna in this area and are considering seriously whether to replicate WESEE."

Problem Areas

Computer Aided Action Information System (CAAIS)

The Godavari class frigates were to be fitted with a wide variety of equipment: Russian radars, missiles, guns, anti submarine rockets and their associated fire control systems, indigenous radars and sonar, German gyros, French logs, etc, all of which had to be electronically interfaced.

DOE decided to produce the Command and Control CAAIS system. Little progress was made until 1981. Only two years were left before *Godavari* commissioned. MDL voiced serious concern that the Rs 200 crore being invested in these frigates were being held up by a lack of decision on 4 crore worth of CAAIS. It was then decided to clear the import of the CAAIS system. Dutch, Italian and British suppliers were short-listed. Despite the Navy's preference for the Dutch CAAIS system, DOE cleared the import of the Italian CAAIS system. Due to this delay, when *Godavari* commissioned, she had only two DS 22 displays as in the earlier Leanders.

Eventually, when the Italian IPN 10 system was installed in the third frigate, *Gomati* in 1989, it required extensive de-bugging as had been anticipated during evaluation.

Electronic Data Highway

In 1979, it had been decided that these frigates would be fitted with an electronic data highway system to integrate the disparate weapon, sensor and CAAIS systems. This would dispense with complex and dense direct cabling.

---

13. The author was in the Soviet Union as the Commanding Officer designate of the first Project 61 ME destroyer that later commissioned as the *Rajput*. The young electrical officers of the commissioning crew, whilst undergoing training, obtained the required design characteristics from their Soviet naval instructors. The data was sent back to Commander Baxi and his team. This direct interaction eliminated procedural delays.

Until 1985, DOE could not decide on which system to import – American or Norwegian. Eventually, the Ministry intervened and cleared the import of the American system. As a result of this delayed decision, however, each of the three ships had to be fitted with direct cabling. Eventually, when the data buses arrived, they could only be retrofitted during major refits. Since removal of the now redundant direct cabling would entail ripping open the entire ship, it had to be retained.

Retrospect

Godavari was launched in May 1980 and commissioned in 1983. *Ganga* was launched in 1982 and commissioned in 1985. *Gomati* was launched in 1984 and commissioned in 1988.

In each of the three ships fitting out was delayed due to the late supply of items of machinery and equipment from various manufacturers.

Rear Admiral (L) (then Commander) A Ganesh headed the WESEE from 1984 onwards, after Commander Baxi. He recalls:

"Where else would one find Indian radars RAWL/RAWS feeding information through an American data bus to an Italian command and control system (IPN 10) to control Russian fire control and weapon systems? The

Rule Writing Group (RWG) under Commander (later Commodore) Man Singh wrote the rules for IPN 10 so well that they have become standard for subsequent programmes.

"I recall an industrialist, who had participated in several indigenous ventures, telling me:

"The Navy has been a very tough customer. We quickly realised that they did not believe in a traditional customer- contractor relationship; they were more our collaborators and consultants in design, production, quality control, inspection and even in some aspects of management. They were very inconvenient, asking too many questions along the way and were stubborn about relaxation of standards.

"Despite some flutters, we did not lose monetarily with the one-off, high tech production activity, but we did not make very high profits either. But our true gains have been in the realisation that concepts such as TQM, ISO standards of documentation etc have been a way of life with the Navy and the execution of your orders has given us so much confidence and recognition in other markets that we are easily able to satisfy the toughest customers and yet be competitive even against global bidders. Thank you, Indian Navy; you have made us come of age."

The Progression from the *Nilgiri* of 1972 to the *Godavari* of 1983

The last column of this table shows how the improvements achieved in the first six frigates
followed on into the next three frigates of the Godavari class in the 1980s.

Year	1972	1974 to 1977	1980-81	1983 to 1988
: :	*Nilgiri* (First Leander)	*Himgiri, Udaygiri Dunagiri* 2nd, 3rd and 4th Leanders)	*Taragiri Vindhyagiri* (5th and 6th Leanders)	Project 16 *Godavari, Ganga, Gomati* (7th, 8th & 9th Frigates)
Anti Ship Missiles	–	–	–	**Russian SSMs**
Surface to Air Missiles				
a) Launchers b) Fire Control	One Seacat British	Two Seacats Dutch	Two Seacats Dutch	Russian SAM Russian
Gun Mounting Fire Control	Twin 4.5-inch British	Twin 4.5-inch Dutch	Twin 4.5-inch Dutch	Twin Russian 57 mm Russian
Ship Launched Anti-Submarine Torpedoes Anti Submarine Weapon	British Mortar Range 1000 Yards	As for *Nilgiri*	Sided launchers for Italian torpedoes Swedish rocket Range 3,750 metres	Sided launchers for Italian torpedoes. Range 8,000 metres Russian Range 6000 metres
ASW Computer	British	As for *Nilgiri*	Indigenous	Indigenous
Anti Submarine Helicopter	French Alouette with British torpedoes	Indian Chetak with British torpedoes	British Seaking with Italian torpedoes	Two Seakings with Italian torpedoes
Close Range				
Guns	20 mm Oerlikon	20 mm Oerlikon	20 mm Oerlikon	Four twin automatic Russian 30 mm Mountings
Close Range Fire Control System				**Russian**
Chaff				**British:**
Radars	British	Dutch	Dutch	Russian & Dutch
Search Sonar **Attack Sonar**	British British	British British	British French	Indigenous
AIO	British	Dutch	Dutch	Italian
Electronic Warfare	British	British	Italian	Italian
Communications **HF**	British	British	British	Indigenous
VHF	British	British	Indigenous	Indigenous
UHF	British	Indigenous	Indigenous	Indigenous

11

Project 25 Khukri Class Corvettes

In the mid 1960s, Government had accepted the Navy's requirements for 500-tonne patrol craft. In subsequent years, various options were considered – building them in Bombay in the Gun Carriage Basin near *INS Kunjali*, building them in the new Naval Dockyard at Vishakhapatnam etc.

By the early 1970s, two schools of thought had emerged. One view was that with the cost of ships steadily increasing, the Navy had no option but to go in for small, fast, missile armed corvettes. The other view was that all the staff requirements could not be met in a 500-tonne patrol craft.

The Petya class submarine chasers that had been acquired from the Soviet Union in the late 1960s would also need to start being replaced in the end 1980s. The outcome was that the 500-tonne patrol craft got renamed as the Corvette Project, to be built in two versions – anti aircraft and anti submarine. International tenders were called for and various weapon packages were considered.

The rise in oil prices after the 1973 Arab-Israel War led to a serious shortage of foreign exchange. Naval Headquarters then decided that the corvettes would be designed and built indigenously for the defence of the island territories and offshore oilrigs.

Design work commenced in 1976, which eventually culminated in the Khukri class corvettes of Project 25.

Captain J Subbiah was the leader of the Corvette Project Team. He recalls:

"The corvettes had an interesting background. The 1,500-tonne, Khukri class, Type 14 frigates, acquired from Britain had very little armament.

"In the late 1960s, the Navy acquired the 1,200-tonne Petyas from the Soviet Union. These were lighter, faster and more heavily armed. The anti submarine capabilities, in particular, were considered far superior to the Type 14. The Petyas, however, had one weakness - inability to carry a helicopter.

"During the late 1960s and the first half of the 1970s, the Navy examined the possibility of acquiring corvettes from other countries. None met the requirements of the Naval Staff. The problem was the same as that encountered in Project 16 – the need for a heavier punch and a mixed package, in addition to the need for a helicopter in a ship of the same size as a Petya.

"Eventually, the project was assigned to the Directorate of Naval Design and the work on this commenced in 1976. We were able to meet the Staff Requirement in full. The highlights were:

– A new hull form was developed. This was later tested in the SSPA tank in Sweden and they declared that the hull form was at least 10% better than the contemporary international hull forms available at that time.

– The sea keeping qualities were also found to be far better and met the needs for helicopter operation from such a small platform.

– The anti surface and anti air weapons were of Soviet origin and the sonar was ours.

– We could accommodate a helicopter, which was a major plus point as compared to the Petyas.

– The design was completed in 1978 and presented to the Naval Staff. We were able to demonstrate that we could pack a much heavier weapon load than in the Leanders at less than half the displacement.

"However, the project suffered a delay of two years on account of the choice of propulsion package. The original design was based on a Pielstick engine. Later, the Directorate of Marine Engineering desired to replace it with a MTU engine. Several studies were carried out. It was found that the MTU engine could not be accommodated without a major redesign exercise, which would have involved a much longer and heavier hull and increased cost. After two years of discussions, the design was eventually cleared with the original propulsion package of the Pielstick engine.

"Later, the project suffered some more delays on account of clearance for the weapon package from the Soviet Union.

"Eventually the detailed designs were developed at Mazagon Docks and the corvettes were built with very little change to the original concept design."

Mr Paramanandhan was the Director General of Naval Design at that time. He recalls:

"The Corvette Project had been going up and down, with French collaboration, with international tenders and with British private companies putting in a bid. All that took very nearly three years. But nothing came out of the series of discussions we had, either with the French or with the British. The Naval staff then took a decision to go ahead and start work on a design and construct a Corvette to our own specification, which would accommodate a helo plus four Soviet surface-to-surface missiles and a Soviet gun mounting. After this decision was taken, the normal process of model testing, powering and general layout were all finalised as a preliminary design.

"There were a lot of discussions whether for anti missile defence we should go in for the Soviet 30 mm gun mountings or the Bofors 40/70 gun mountings. That took about six to seven months. Ultimately, a clear decision was given that we should have four surface-to-surface missiles plus the Soviet guns. It was also decided to fit some of the Leanders' radars, sonar, communication equipment etc.

"The point where the decision got delayed was the propulsion package. There was discussion as regards a single engine room or two engine rooms, two engines per shaft or one engine per shaft etc. The gearing of two diesel engines to one shaft posed problems. Would it be better to have a single robust engine rather than two, in a small ship of this size? Should we have a fixed pitch propeller or a CPP?

"To settle these issues, Naval Headquarters constituted a group of officers to write a service paper. The then Chief of Material and the Director of Marine Engineering produced a paper based on which the design proceeded

and the final powering calculation was completed. The choice of propeller was also settled and it was decided to go in for a controllable pitch propeller (CPP). However, that resulted in a slightly heavier tail shaft and propeller and a higher trim aft. The discussions on engines, and the mid course correction which some people wanted that it should not be a single engine per shaft or two engines per shaft, did push the project back by about 18 months.

"When you are working on a Naval Staff Requirement and when the total project starts sliding back 18 months, everybody gets fresh ideas. Fresh weapons, fresh helicopters, fresh radars, fresh sonar and everyone wants to pitch in. That has a very deleterious effect.

"By the time I left NHQ, the ship had been ordered, the design had been frozen and the model tests had been completed. But I believe the Soviets insisted that the bridge structure should go further aft. And it got shifted. I would not have permitted that to happen. It caused some trim problem which had to be adjusted by other means. In my opinion, Project 25 was a fairly well thought out design, it had a well thought out weapon package which I believe is giving good service."

Orders for the first two corvettes were placed on Mazagon Docks in 1986. *Khukri*, launched in December 1986, was delivered in 1989. *Kuthar* was launched in January 1988 and delivered in 1990.

Mazagon Docks then acted as the lead yard and provided all drawings and shipbuilding material inputs to Garden Reach for building the next two corvettes. *Kirpan* was delivered in 1990 and *Khanjar* in 1991.

Except for the Russian weapon systems, all four corvettes were fitted with indigenous equipment to the maximum extent possible.

Later in the 1990s, orders were placed on Garden Reach for four more corvettes of Project 25 A.

12

Indigenous Submarine Construction
The SSK Project

Preamble

In the 1960s, the conventional wisdom, based primarily on Western naval journals, was that "Russian submarines were noisy and that Western submarines were quieter". In the deadly game of hunter-killer-submarine-warfare, where one submarine stalks another submarine deep under the sea, the quieter submarine has the advantage of being able to detect earlier, the noisier submarine.

As early as 1960s, the Navy started considering the construction in India of smaller SSK[1] submarines specifically for submarine versus submarine operations.

By 1969, ideas crystallized to build small SSK submarines in India in collaboration with a European firm, on lines similar to what was being done for surface ships in the Leander Frigate Project. Discussions had been initiated with Dr Gabler, the reputed and experienced designer of German submarines during World War II.

What started as a project to build small submarines gradually ballooned into a larger coastal submarine. By the time Dr Gabler's design met the Navy's staff requirements, its cost had overshot the resources available. These discussions however, helped the Navy to understand the complexities of submarine design and the trade-offs that had to be made in the 'staff requirements'.

Since foreign exchange was always a constraint on acquiring ships, submarines or aircraft from European sources, enquiries were initiated with the Soviet Union. Their response was that they did not have any submarines of the size and characteristics that the Navy wanted, but they could design one.

After the 1971 Indo-Pakistan War, the project for indigenous submarine construction resumed momentum. In response to enquiries for constructing SSK submarines in India, proposals were received from the reputed submarine manufacturers of Europe.

Evaluation of these proposals helped to update the staff requirements for a SSK submarine of about 1,500 tonnes.

A delegation visited Sweden in 1973 to discuss the feasibility of collaborating with Kockums for building submarines in India.

The steep rise in oil prices after the 1973 Arab-Israel War perpetuated the shortage of foreign exchange and the SSK project had to be deferred. Comparative evaluation continued of the various proposals.

A study was also carried out as to which of the shipbuilding yards – Mazagon Docks in Bombay or Garden Reach in Calcutta or Hindustan Shipyard in Vizag – should undertake the SSK project. Submarine fabrication required specialised heavy-duty machines. For fabricating the hull, the shipyard had to have a Plate Bending Machine to bend the ring frames made of special, 35 mm thick, steel plate. The shipyard had to have Plater and Assembly Shops for profile cutting and edge preparation of these thick steel plates prior to welding. Highly specialised welding skills were required to weld these ring frames together to form a circular pressure hull, which would withstand the crushing pressure of the sea at deep depth.

Mazagon Docks in Bombay had some of these machines in its yard where oilrigs were being fabricated for the Bombay High Offshore oilfield. And Mazagon Docks was near to the engineering sub-contractors in the Bombay industrial area to whom the machining and fabrication of non-critical jigs and fixtures could be entrusted. It was decided that Mazagon Docks was best suited for collaboration in the building of SSK submarines. MDL started preparing for this project.

Also by 1979, the Navy was able to evaluate in great detail the pros and cons of the German HDW Type 1500 and Kockums Type 45, both of which were still on the drawing

---

1. SSK was the US Navy acronym for Submarine Search and Kill.

board. Kockums shipyard, despite being highly automated (all designing was done by computer, without the help of a scale model) and having excellent infrastructure, had not exported any submarines and their experience was limited to building submarines of 1,400 tons for the Swedish Navy. On the other hand, the HDW shipyard had built 130 submarines for the German Navy, had exported 60 submarines. It was building submarines for numerous countries and was backed by the design organisation IKL at Lubeck. IKL had an efficient design facility founded by Dr Gabler and fully backed the HDW shipyard in submarine design.

The Considerations That Led to the Selection of HDW

In 1975, the Apex Defence Review Committee supported the Navy's proposal for constructing submarines. The Soviet Union had already indicated that it did not have submarines of the size that the Navy was looking for. In 1977, Government accepted the requirement for looking at alternate sources for building submarines.

The May 1977 Delegation to Evaluate European Submarine Building Yards

The delegation was led by Rear Admiral NP Datta and comprised three submariners – Commanders (X) VS Shekhawat, (L) Thukral and (E) Chaudhury.

Rear Admiral (later Vice Admiral) NP Datta recalls:

"As DCNS, I was part of the delegation which went in 1977 to five European countries – France, Germany (two shipyards in Germany), Holland and Sweden to evaluate the various types of submarines offered to us. We short-listed two possible sources of cooperation. These were the two German shipyards and the Swedish Kockum shipyard.

"We ruled out the French Agosta primarily because it was too small for our requirement, it was not fully tropicalised and they had no great advantage in sensors and weapon systems over the Russian submarines that we had."

Commander (later Admiral) VS Shekhawat (who had commanded submarines) recalls:

"I accompanied Admiral Datta to Europe in the early part of 1977. We visited shipyards in Germany, Sweden, Holland and France to see what they had to offer which could be compared with the earlier Swedish offer, both in technological terms as well as in financial terms, transfer of technology, support, documentation, etc.

"The visit to France was disappointing. They were reluctant to even show us their Agosta class submarine. After some pressure had been exercised, they agreed to take us to see an Agosta that was building in Cherbourg.

"As far as the Dutch submarine was concerned, it was too small for our requirement though they showed us two submarines of a very interesting design.

"Germany's HDW seemed well positioned to build submarines for us. They had already supplied a number of submarines to other countries. They had the background and experience of the German Submarine Fleets during the First and Second World War – a considerable body of experience and data available from what were extensive sea-going operations. And German Industry, both pre-war and post-war, had a reputation for engineering skills and thoroughness.

"Having studied the Kockums submarine theoretically and having had a glimpse of the HDW facilities and visited a submarine being built for a South American country, my own views were that eventually it did not very much matter which of these two submarines we went in for because the idea was that we should develop the capacity to design and build for ourselves."

Captain M Kondath was the Director of the Submarine Arm and dealt with the SSK Project from 1977 until the contract was signed in 1981. He recalls:

"In the Directorate of the Submarine Arm, we analysed the report of this 1977 delegation. When it was put up the Government, the Ministry suggested that every submarine building shipyard, including Russian, should be invited to offer their proposals. Britain did not respond except for offering their wire-guided torpedoes.

"Formal proposals were received from:

– Howal Deutsch Werke (HDW) of Kiel, Germany for their Type 209-1.

– Thyssen Nord See Werke (TNSW) of Emden, Germany for their Thyssen 1500/1700.

– Italcantieri of Italy for their 'Sauro' class.

– DTCN of France for their 'Super Agosta' class.

– Kockums of Sweden for their Type 45 B/Naaken.

– Nevesbu of Holland for their 'Swordfish" class.

– Vickers of Britain for the wire guided Tigerfish torpedo.

"A paper evaluation was carried out of these offers. Based on this initial evaluation, the shipyards were requested to indicate if they were prepared to modify their design or alternatively design a submarine to meet the Navy's staff requirements. Holland and France declined and withdrew from the list of contenders.

CCPA Approval in Principle

"Approval 'in principle' was accorded in February 1979 for the induction of four submarines from non-Soviet sources, two to be built abroad and two to be built in India. The total outlay estimated at that time was Rs 350 crore (including Rs 275 crore in foreign exchange). Mazagon Docks, which was to build the submarines, was to invest around Rs 10 crores on infrastructure. Approval was also accorded for setting up a Negotiating Committee."

The May 1979 Policy-Technical Delegation to Italy, Germany and Sweden

The Shipyards were informed of the points that the Indian side wanted included in an inter Government MOU:

- The foreign shipyard has the necessary authorisation of its Government to sell submarines to India.

- The shipyard is authorised to collaborate with India for constructing submarines in India under licence and with provision for incorporation of subsequent improvements and modifications.

- Assurance of the supplier Government for continued product support in all its aspects for the life cycle of the submarines or for 25 years.

- Similar assurance that no prohibitions or restrictions will be imposed by the supplier Government on the supply and services and continued flow of product support for that period.

- Authorising the shipyard for transfer of the full range of technology for the construction of submarines in India.

- Transferring from the supplier's Navy the full range of design technology for the development of submarine design capability in India.

- Government clearance for sale to India of connected weapons, armament, sensors, machinery and systems.

- Support by the supplier Navy for the training of:
  - Naval and Dockyard personnel for the operation, maintenance, repair and overhaul of submarines and the related systems.
  - Naval crew in all aspects of submarine warfare including tactical doctrines and electronic warfare, consistent with national commitments.
  - Indian personnel for the logistic support for the submarine and its systems.

- Quality control, certification, trials and acceptance of the submarine and its related systems by the supplier's Navy and supply of necessary documentation.

- Assurance by both sides regarding security of information and equipment.

- Consultations between the two Governments to resolve problems, if any, arising out of the implementation of the collaboration project.

Indo-German 'Agreement on Technical Assistance'

As a policy, the German Government avoided defence supplies that might aggravate tension. After the 1971 Indo-Pakistan War, the Indian subcontinent had been declared an area of tension. It was also reluctant to supply defence equipment to non-NATO countries because such equipment might be used against their allies.

In the end 1970s and early 1980s there was scepticism in Germany, France, Britain and Italy, that if the scope of defence cooperation with India was enhanced, India because of its close relationship with the Soviet Union may not be able to protect NATO hi-tech information from Soviet espionage.

In view of these considerations, India considered it essential, as a measure of abundant caution, that before contracts were signed, there should be agreement at the Government to Government level to safeguard Indian interests. The 1979 Delegation had already informed the European shipyards of the safeguards that the Navy would like incorporated in an Inter-Government Memorandum of Understanding (MOU).

Between June 1980 when the CCPA approved the collaboration with HDW for the SSK Project and December 1981 when the contracts were signed, there were detailed discussions to formulate the MOU. The best that could be achieved was an 'Agreement on Technical Assistance' between the German and Indian Ministries of Defence. This was signed in July 1981.

Contracts Signed on 11 December 1981

After detailed negotiations, contracts were signed in on 11 December 1981:

- To build two submarines at the HDW yard in Germany, where Indian personnel would acquire practical training in submarine construction techniques and Indian naval architects and overseers would learn how to design, understudy how to build and oversee the construction of submarines.

- To transfer technology and material packages to MDL for building two more submarines in India. MDL personnel would acquire on-job training in Germany during the period when the first two submarines were under construction.

- Giving the Indian side the option of ordering material packages for two more submarines before December

1982 at the same baseline cost as the first four submarines.

- Supply of wire-guided torpedoes.

Subsequently, in 1985, a contract was signed for the SSK Simulator for installation in the Submarine Headquarters Complex in Bombay.

Teams Deputed to Germany for Overseeing Construction and Design Technology

The teams deputed to the HDW shipyard at Kiel were:

- Overseeing and Quality Control Teams of the two submarines to be built there.
- Key personnel of the commissioning crews.
- Base and Dockyard Teams to undergo training for manning, maintaining and repairing sonar, torpedoes, shafting, main diesel, compressors, auxiliary machinery, hydraulic systems, damage control, power generation distribution and propulsion, ESM, gyro and navigation aids, refrigeration and air conditioning, etc.
- Material Management and Logistics Group and the Documentation Cell.

The Submarine Design Team was deputed to IKL at Lubeck and the Naval Armament Inspectors were deputed to Wedel to inspect and accept the torpedoes.

Submarine Construction Schedule

- 12 months for planning.
- 6 months for preparation of detailed engineering drawings.
- 6 months for part fabrication and assembly of sub-units.
- 12 months for complete fabrication.
- 6 months on the pontoon for fitting out.
- 6 months for sea trials escorted by a HDW vessel.
- Total time 48 months.

Commencement of the Type 1500 Design by IKL

IKL started work on the detailed design only after the conclusion of the contract because the weight and volume calculations could only be carried out during placement of orders.

Full Scale Submarine Model

To aid production by HDW, IKL produced a finished model of the Type 1500 submarine. All equipment, machinery, cables and pipe-fittings were modelled. Three Indian Navy shipwrights participated in the production of this model.

Transfer of Submarine Design Technology

The programme for the transfer of design technology was formulated through extensive discussion between IKL and NHQ. It was decided that the ideal method for achieving this would be in two distinct phases:

- By a combination of formal lectures and discussions with IKL experts, IKL would give to the Design Team complete details of the design of the Type 1500 submarine.
- To check whether the Design Team had fully understood the complexities of submarine design, it would, under the guidance and supervision of IKL's experts, develop *de novo* a new design according to the staff requirements specified by NHQ.

Design Training started in 1982. By mid 1984, 98% of the syllabus was completed and the Design Team became fully occupied with the *de novo* design.

Construction of SSKs 1 and 2 in Germany

Captain (later Rear Admiral) DN Thukral, an experienced submariner, was deputed to HDW as the leader of the Indian Naval Submarine Overseeing Team (INSOT) from 1982 to 1987 when the first two submarines were under construction in Germany. He recalls:

"In Germany, Professor Gabler was known as the 'Father of Submarine Design.' Ingeneer Kontor Lubeck (IKL), the design arm and Machinen Bow Gabler, the manufacturing arm, were located in contiguous premises – he looked after both of these. While we were there, he turned 75, there was a big function, and he handed over charge of both the design and the manufacturing aspect to two directors who had been with him for a number of years. It was a very professionally run organisation.

"Our submarines were designed by Professor Gabler. He was with us throughout the period when HDW was constructing our submarines. There is no doubt that his experience was unbeatable. He treated the Indian Design Team with great respect because he realised that the IQ level of the technical officers that the Navy had sent was high. He was with them not only at the senior level, but also at the junior level when they were doing the design and doing mock ups. He would saunter into the Design Room and interact with our people. He really was a 'father figure'. I have a lot of respect for him.

"There were two separate contracts – one for the submarines to be built in Germany and one for the submarines to be built by MDL. There was a dual responsibility. Firstly, to inspect the submarines being built in Germany and secondly to build the submarines in India.

"The task of building the submarines in India was that of Mazagon Docks. Their team was the first to arrive in Germany. They had been carefully selected to learn all aspects of submarine construction. MDL's team was also responsible for the inspection of the German material packages to be shipped to India for the 3rd and 4th submarines.

"Right from the initial planning stages, it was decided at Naval Headquarters that there had to be a dual presence in the shipyard at Kiel. The first was that of the Naval overseers who were directly from the Navy as the Indian Naval Submarine Overseeing Team. The second presence was of MDL who had to learn how to build the submarine, how the material package was to be dispatched to India in a phased and timely manner and to ensure that the inspectors who were from the Navy would eventually transfer their expertise to MDL.

"In the overseeing team I had two categories of people. The first lot were there for approximately a year and a half – they were supposed to learn their part of it, then go back to India and start the inspections for the first one and a half years of the MDL programme. By this time, the rest of the Kiel team would have learnt the balance part of inspections and would go back to India and take on the specialised inspections of the latter half.

"My team had technical professionals from the Engineering, the Electrical and the Hull side. We laid down our own priorities. Quality was to be Number One priority because there is nothing like a 99% safe submarine; it has to be 101% safe. The second priority was Timely Completion. Most projects had the bad reputation of having time and cost over-runs. Quality and Time were the two major aspects that we looked at, at every stage.

"I must highlight that we were concurrently learning and applying the knowledge to inspection. We were learning from the German Organisation called the BWB, which oversees quality assurance for the German Navy, as well as for a foreign Government if the foreign Government decides to use their facility. It was recommended by HDW that BWB were meant for this purpose and, for a small fee, one could use their facilities. So we had a presence of BWB in the shipyard.

"Initially, we learnt from them and finally, having picked up whatever was required, we carried out the inspection ourselves. The important thing was that our team realised that time over-runs are caused whenever there is a delay in inspection. If a certain function by the shipyard has been completed and the next step can only be taken after inspection, then it has to be done immediately. There is no question of weekends or waiting for the next morning. If a schedule was made that a certain inspection was to be done at a certain time, we were there to do so, all the time.

"Initially, in the implementation stage, we had very few hiccups in Germany. Those that did occur were absorbed well in time, because when the contract was finalised with the Germans, tremendous penalties had been stipulated for delays.

"But soon we had problems. The first problem was the rejection of a number of sections of the first submarine hull. And linked with this were 'welding technology' problems.

"There were a certain number of ring frames, which had been specially designed for automatic welding. The welding of these sections required a very carefully controlled environment – temperature wise and humidity wise – to make sure that the weld was totally defect free. Earlier, most of HDW's welding was manual. These automatic-welding stations had their teething problems and some of these problems caused permanent damage. Repairing a badly welded frame costs four times more than a new frame. The Germans initially tried to say that 'This is OK, we will get the welding institutes to have a look at it'. But I would like to compliment the support we got from Naval Headquarters who said, 'Just make sure that you do not get pressurised. Go ahead and take the assistance of anybody, whether in India, or Germany or abroad.'

"Luckily, when we approached the welding institutes and the people who were welding technology experts in Germany, they agreed with our stand. The BWB also supported us 100% and said 'Yes, you are right to reject them. There are hair line cracks and we cannot accept any kind of nonsense as far as quality is concerned.' And, therefore, some seven or eight sections had to be rejected.

"It probably cost HDW a few million marks but finally they accepted the fact. Later, after a couple of years, we read reports in various technical journals where HDW tried to tell the world that for the sake of quality they had sacrificed so many million marks. As far as we were concerned, we never allowed any aspect of submarine quality to be jeopardised. Eventually, the HDW yard realised that we were professionals.

"German Navy submarines had not experienced this kind of welding problem because all German submarines were of smaller lengths and their sections were welded manually. This was the first time that specially constructed automatic welding stations were being used by HDW. I can only say that these were teething problems.

"With a view to becoming self reliant in submarine design, Naval Headquarters had deputed a separate design team to IKL to acquire hands-on design experience under the supervision of Dr Gabler. Project X was the code name given to an indigenous design of a submarine. It was supposed to be a little larger submarine than the Type 1500. It had a dual objective. Firstly, to learn how to design a submarine. Secondly, to meet the staff requirements, which were given to the Project X team.

"The Overseeing Team was also involved in the training of the crews and the sea trials. Our crews had two elements of training. One was classroom training. We had selected experienced submariners for these submarines and very few were new, so that aspect was not difficult at all.

"For sea training, we divided the crews into two halves. One on morning shift and one on evening shift, on the same submarine, depending on the time available. Sometimes, when both our submarines were at sea, we had a little more flexibility. Let me take one submarine, one crew. Normally, the Germans did the operation of the submarine during sea trials. Because of the safety aspect and the fact that you cannot cross the figure of 40 because of the limitation of the size of the rescue sphere. These were some of the mandatory aspects that you just cannot avoid. You cannot carry 41 bodies on board. Therefore, it had to be 20 German crew and 20 of our crew Consequently, training had to be slightly lengthened to make sure that every man got his man-days or man-hours on a particular equipment or in operations or in navigation or whatever. This had been carefully planned and, therefore, the entire submarine training as far as the crew was concerned went more or less on schedule.

"Then there were other elements where the inspection teams were not involved in the full aspect, except for relevant people. For example, the sonar trials and the weapon firing trials etc were done by the HDW team teaching our people. The German Navy provided targets as and when required and the training aspect was generally handled by HDW.

"As regards sea trials, we had difficulties from time to time. Certain equipment that did not function absolutely correctly had to be either replaced or repaired. I would say that by any universal standard, it was a satisfactory period. Hitches are there in any choice and I do not think we got a larger share of problems than normal.

"The specifications of the submarines that we ordered were spelt out in tremendous detail in various volumes. Except for minor changes, which resulted on the basis of trials carried out or some technical reason, no major changes were brought about. Minor changes of adding a weight here or shifting an item from A to B were effected as necessary. Technically, the submarines are absolutely sound.

"Right from day one, the Submarine Overseeing Team found themselves in a very professionally run organisation. We realised that we had a lot to learn and to apply that learning to inspection. Therefore, the interaction with the shipyard personnel had to be very professional. This paid us dividends eventually because the quality of our submarines has been outstanding as has been borne out of the experience of the last 13 years."

The first two submarines built in Germany were commissioned as *INS Shishumar* (S 44) on 22 September 1986 and *INS Shankush* (S 45) on 20 November 1986.

MDL's Submarine Construction Facilities

MDL had started liasing with HDW immediately after the CCPA had decided on HDW in June 1980. In May 1982, a separate liaison office was started at the HDW shipyard at Kiel.

Separate and dedicated submarine construction facilities were set up in MDL's East Yard. They consisted of three large workshops and a dry dock:

- The first workshop, 50 m x 25 m, had two 20-tonne cranes for fabricating the ring frames of the pressure hull.
- The second workshop, 100 m x 30 m, had two 60-tonne cranes for fabricating pressure hull sections.

These two workshops were completed in February 1984.

The Prime Minister, Mrs Indira Gandhi, formally inaugurated the 'submarine construction facilities' on 6 May 1984.

- The third workshop, 99 m x 35 m, was for fitting out and joining the pressure hull sections to form a complete submarine. This workshop and the 90 m x 17 m dry dock, with all its services, were completed in February 1986.

A separate dedicated Pipe Shop and a Stores Complex were also built in the East Yard.

Construction of SSK 3 and 4 in Mazagon Docks

The shipping, from Germany, of the material packages, along with the first set of drawings, had commenced in 1982 and went on till 1983.

Construction of the third SSK commenced on 12 January 1984. It took five years for her to be launched on 30 September 1989 and three more years till she commissioned as *INS Shalki* (S 46) on 7 February 1992.

Construction of the fourth SSK began on 12 September 1984. She commissioned ten years later as *INS Shankul* (S 47) on 28 May 1994.

Dropping of SSKs 5 and 6 and Discontinuance of Indigenous Submarine Construction

The HDW contract contained an option clause, to be exercised by end 1982, for two more SSK submarines at the 1981 baseline price, but to which escalation would be 'addable'. For various reasons, NHQ and MoD were unable to exercise the option by 1982 and sought, and obtained, extensions from HDW to hold the baseline price.

From MDL's point of view, it was essential that the submarine production line was not interrupted. If SSKs 5 and 6 were not ordered in time, it would be forced to divert to other jobs, the manpower that was being trained for submarine construction at such high cost.

In the intervening years, NHQ had interacted with HDW on improving the operational capability of SSKs 5 and 6 and for incorporating changes like the better super-charged diesel engine, better sensors and weapons, substitution of obsolescent equipment etc.

By 1985, three options were considered for SSKs 5 and 6:

- Build both in HDW (Favoured by HDW and those who wanted to upgrade the design with the latest equipment).
- Build both in MDL (Favoured by MDL 'to keep the submarine production line going').
- Build one in HDW and one in MDL (To get the best of both options).

In October 1985, approval was accorded for the acquisition of two more HDW submarines. Negotiations were to be based on the "one by HDW and one by MDL" option.

The preliminary discussions in 1985 revealed that the prices quoted by HDW had increased steeply. These were never built / acquired.

MDL delivered SSK 3 in 1992 and SSK 4 in 1994. Their operational performance met the Navy's expectations.

13

Warship Modernisations And Half-Life Refits

Overview

The Navy's endeavours in the field of warship modernisation commenced in the mid 1960s with a study called FRAMRAJ on the 'Fleet Refit and Modernisation of Rajput' (a destroyer of 1940s vintage). By the time the study took shape, its cost effectiveness was undermined by the vastly higher level of technology that was entering service in the Soviet supplied Petyas. The study was, however, valuable for realising the intricacies of modernising aged warships.

By the early 1970s, the experience of the eight new British frigates acquired between 1958 and 1961 indicated that whereas the life of their hulls might be stretched to 20 or 25 years, the operational reliability of naval electronic equipment could not be stretched beyond 11 to 12 years.

In 1974, following the recommendations of the Subramaniam Committee, the Government laid down a life of 12½ years for electronic equipment. This enabled the Navy to pre-plan the replacement of electronic systems during 'Modernisation-cum-Half life Refits'. Together with overhaul of essential machinery and renewal of hull plates, these refits were expected to give ships' hulls and electronics an additional operational life of 11 to 12 years.

The Modernisation Half-Life Refit programme had been planned to commence in 1971-72 with the Khukri class frigates. The loss of *Khukri* in the 1971 war and the deterioration in the material state of *Kuthar* and *Kirpan* during the same war made their half-life refit non cost effective.

The arrival of the missile boats from Russia in early 1971, immediately sparked interest in fitting surface-to-surface missiles in other ships. After seeing the effectiveness of the missiles in the 1971 war, the Navy explored the fitment of these missiles in its fastest British-built ships that were nearing the half-life refit stage. These were the cruiser *Mysore* and the frigates *Talwar* and *Trishul*.

A study was carried out of what was required to modernise *Mysore*. It emerged that whereas her hull and armour plate were sound, her propulsion system was so old as to make its modernisation impractical.

The frigate *Talwar* was the first to be fitted with a complete missile system removed from a non-operational missile boat. The innovation proved successful.

It was decided to commence the Modernisation Half-life Refit programme with the modernisation of *Talwar's* sister ship, *Trishul*, in two phases. The staff requirements envisaged fitment of a mix of Russian, Italian and British systems. Phase 1 commenced in 1975 and completed in 1977. Phase 2 commenced in 1979 and completed five years later in 1984.

The long endurance of the three diesel-engined Brahmaputra class frigates made them particularly suitable for conversion into cadet training ships. From 1976 onwards, one ship at a time was taken in hand for conversion, the last of which completed in 1980.

The aircraft carrier *Vikrant* underwent modernisation in two phases – the first from 1979 to 1981 and the second from 1987 to 1989.

In the end 1970s, the study for modernising the 1960-vintage Russian Petyas showed that it would not be cost effective.

In the 1980s, the study for modernising the first, 1972-vintage, Leander class frigate, *Nilgiri*, was overtaken by the inability to obtain firm commitments for the delivery of Russian weapon systems contemporary with those being fitted in ships being acquired from Russia.

In the case of the Russian-built ships and submarines, upgradation-cum-modernisation could be implemented only to a limited extent during their major six-yearly Medium Repairs.

Framraj

In 1966, the Navy initiated its first detailed study in the field of warship modernisation. The project was named FRAMRAJ – Fleet Refit and Modernisation of the sturdy, high-speed Rajput class destroyers built during the 1939-45 World War.

Rear Admiral then Lieutenant Commander JJ Baxi was associated with the study. He recalls:

"Primarily Framraj was not pursued because it would have been cheaper at that time to buy a new ship from the Soviet Union than to spend so much money on modernising an old ship like *Rajput* where the life of the machinery and the hull system were absolutely doubtful and inadequate."

The great benefit of the Framraj study was the opportunity it provided to the planners and designers to come to grips with the difficulties, the trade-offs, the costs and the benefits of modernisation.

Fitment of Russian Missiles in British-Bulit Warships

The missile boats arrived from Russia in the first half of 1971. The Navy saw at first hand the compactness and the operational potential of this new system. Even before the missiles proved their effectiveness in the December 1971 war, the Navy requested the Soviet side to supply a set of missile launchers along with the fire control system and installation drawings and to depute Soviet specialists to help fit the system on board an ageing ship on an experimental basis.

In 1972, the Soviet side agreed to depute a group of Russian specialists to study the feasibility of fitting missiles in existing Indian ships.

In 1974, as the first step towards implementing the overall approval that had been accorded for the 'modernisation of ships', Naval Headquarters commenced design work on the modernisation of *Talwar* and *Trishul*. The staff requirements envisaged fitment of Russian missiles, Russian radar controlled 30 mm guns, improved British sonar and an Italian Electronic Warfare ESM system that would help in identifying adversary warships from their radar transmissions at ranges compatible with the range of the missiles and whose ECM would be an essential element of anti missile defence.

Fitting Missiles in *Talwar*

Since the design for modernisation would take time, it was decided to upgrade *Talwar* with whatever was readily available and complete the remainder of the modernisation later.

During the Long Refit between December 1974 and November 1975, *Talwar's* 4.5-inch mounting and its FPS 5 fire control system was removed and in its place was installed an entire missile, radar and fire control system after lifting it out of a non-operational missile boat. Since

the width of *Talwar's* fox'le did not permit the siting of four missile launchers abreast, it was decided to fit only three abreast.

The first missile firing was carried out on 11 December 1975. It scored a bull's eye on a target moored at a range of 20 miles.

Mr Paramanandhan, the then Director of Naval Design, recalls:

"The Russians were not at all in favour of putting one of the three missiles on the centre line. I did not see anything wrong in putting it there, as long as the deflectors were correct and we knew the correct distances and if the flame should strike the bulkhead, there should be no damage done. So we decided to have a forward bulkhead with an air space and also have a walkway for people in case something went wrong.

"We had a group of scientists in the first firing for which we wrote down the specifications for firing the missile. That raised the eyebrows of some officers in the Material Branch, especially in the Directorate of Weapons and Equipment. They said 'Who are these naval designer jokers in Ramakrishnapuram[1] to tell us what to do with the weapons on board?' But we were worried about an accident, nothing more than that.

"We had asked for many measurement 'gadgets'. One of these was to put a series of shoe-strings along the deck and on the bulkhead. We knew what their charring temperature was. That would immediately indicate how far the deflectors were effective and how far they were not effective.

"A salvo of three missiles was fired successfully."

Constructor Captain (then Commander and later DGND) KK Lohana recalls:

"It was a very bold step to remove the missile containers from a missile boat and fit them in Type 12 frigate. The Soviets were not particularly enthusiastic about such a proposal. It was, therefore, decided that we would do it on our own.

"Secondly, the three-missile configuration, which was planned for *Talwar's* fox'le deck to get maximum benefit out of the deck area available, was something unique. There were definitely inherent doubts and risks as to how the flight paths would be affected and what were the clearances required and what should be the interface with the rest of the equipment and so on.

"This assignment became an article of faith with Mr Paramanandhan. In the absence of clear cut

1.   The Directorate of Naval Design was located in Ramakrishnapuram, an office complex in New Delhi.

documentation and data, quite a large amount of study had to be carried out of the existing fittings in the missile boat in order to decide what equipment was to be removed in addition to the containers themselves, what was the interface, how the fire control would work and so on. And I must say that the whole exercise, in spite of certain technically inspired assumptions, was something which went off very well and the Navy could well be very proud of it."

Modernisation of *Trishul*

The *Trishul* modernisation was entrusted to Mazagon Docks and was implemented in two phases:

- In Phase 1, which commenced in 1976 and completed in 1977, surface to surface missiles and associated fire control system were fitted in the place of the gun mounting and its fire control system, as had been done earlier in *Talwar*.

- Phase 2 modernisation commenced in 1979 and though expected to complete in 1982, completed five years later in 1984. During this phase:

  - A flight deck was provided for operating a MATCH role helicopter.

  - Radars and AIO were replaced by Dutch Signaal systems as in the Leanders.

  - 90% of the hull plates were renewed and all cabling changed.

  - All propulsion machinery was either given a major overhaul or renovated.

  - The ship was fully air-conditioned.

Lessons Learnt from *Trishul's* Modernisation

Analysis of the time and cost overrun of *Trishul's* Phase 2 modernisation concluded that half-life refits and modernisation could not be afforded. Extensive renewal of hull plating and rewiring the main cabling literally meant taking the ship apart and rebuilding it. Both cost and time wise, it was found cheaper to build a new ship than to do a *Trishul*-type modernisation.

After the *Trishul* experience, such extensive modernisations of frigates were never attempted again. Only limited modernisations were contemplated and, for a variety of reasons, even these became limited to replacement of specific systems.

Conversion of *Brahmaputra, Beas* and *Betwa* for Cadets Training

When the Naval Academy was started in 1971 to increase officer intake, it became necessary also to increase the capacity afloat for training cadets and midshipmen at sea. To start with, the cruiser *Delhi* was converted to undertake this sea training. Thereafter, the three British-built frigates *Brahmaputra, Beas* and *Betwa,* which had commissioned in 1958, 1959 and 1960 were converted for undertaking the sea training of cadets. The conversion involved the removal of weapons, construction of classrooms, cadets' accommodation and mess, installation of equipment to facilitate training in astro and coastal navigation, etc.

Modernisation of Vikrant

Phase One

After the 1971 war, *Vikrant* needed a long refit to replace the boilers as they had revealed cracks. Since this was expected to be a long refit from 1979 to 1981, it was decided to concurrently undertake as much modernisation of weapons, sensors and Action Information Systems as possible.

During the Phase One modernisation refit, the major items undertaken were:

- Renewal of boilers.

- Extension of air-conditioning.

- Fitment of the Dutch Signaal LW 04, DA 05, ZW 06 radars and DS 22 Action Information system as in the Leander class frigates.

- Installation of Sea Harrier facilities, LUDS and floodlighting of the flight deck.

- Fitment of LIOD Optronic Sights and Bofors 40/70 gun mountings for anti missile defence.

- Fitment of new UHF, VHF, HF, MF communication sets.

- Installation of a towed torpedo decoy, an expendable bathythermograph and a sonic ray plotter.

- The catapult and arrestor gear were overhauled and retained for launch and recovery of the Alizes.

- The main and auxiliary machinery were refurbished to the maximum extent feasible.

Mr Paramanandhan, the then DGND recalls:

"There was a serious proposal to put the large Soviet combined surface warning – height estimating – S band radar on the ship. *Vikrant's* masts were already saturated. We were asked to find out some way of putting the antenna up there. We worked with the IIT Madras on the structural side and we gave a proposal, which was workable. But the cost factor and the time required was such that the Naval Staff decided to forego that radar.

"The second thing we spent a lot of money and a lot

of time on was that a lot of DC / AC alternators were put on board *Vikrant* to create a larger AC power capacity for dedicated services.

"There was a proposal to fit the new Bofors 40 / 70 guns and a new type of laser sensor for anti missile defence. The initial proposal was to fit the Soviet 30 mm gun mountings in lieu of the old hand-operated Bofors. If we had gone firm on that, probably we would have achieved it at a much lesser cost and much quicker. While the Soviet weapon systems had their own deficiencies, they had the advantage that they suited our culture and way of working and maintainability. Each 30 mm mounting had its own dedicated radar and its own display, which made it autonomous for operation. So if one mounting did not work, at least the other one would be available. That philosophy was not accepted half-way through. And when they changed over to the new weapon system, our Directorate was not involved any further."

Phase Two

During this phase of modernisation from 1987 to 1989, *Vikrant* was fitted with:

- A ski jump for launching Sea Harriers in the Short Take Off mode. Since the Alizes had phased out, the catapult and arrestor gear were removed.

- Facilities for operation and maintenance of the new dual role anti submarine / anti ship Seaking Mk 42 B helicopter.

- LIOD Fire Control Systems and indigenous medium range chaff launchers.

- Magazine stowage for the new weapons of the Seaking Mk 42 B helicopters like the Sea Eagle anti ship missiles, the A 244 S anti submarine torpedoes and the chaff rockets.

Installation of the Ski-Jump

Rear Admiral (then Captain) A Ganesh was the General Manager Refit in the Bombay Dockyard in 1989 when the ski jump was installed during Phase 2 of *Vikrant's* modernisation. He recalls:

"The ski jump installation in *Vikrant* was a massive exercise which virtually involved redesign of the forward one third of the ship – removal of the steam catapult, re-appropriation of a whole lot of compartments below the steam catapult, extensive structural modification of the deck, creation of new compartments under the ski jump, rendering the flight deck worthy and coating it with the new anti skid paint developed by NCML.

"*Vikrant's* ski jump was to have an exit angle of 9.75 degrees. The challenges were the precise execution of the structural design, translating it from pre-fabricated modules to be placed precisely and welded without distortions to achieve the exact exit angle with a tolerance of plus minus 10 seconds of arc. British Aerospace had specified 54 minutes of arc as the tolerance of the exit angle.

"To start with, British Aerospace said that the Navy would not be able to tackle the ski jump's structural design. We said 'we know exactly what we can do. Please pass on the drawings to us'. Then they said that 'you cannot achieve this in just 18 months time'. *Vikrant* was dry docked in the Cruiser Dock for a total period of 7 months, at the end of which the ski jump had been installed.

"When the Royal Navy Harriers arrived for the test flights, they had planned a series of 18 aircraft configurations with which the ski-jump would be tested. At the end of three test flights, they had determined that the exit angle had been achieved with accuracy of plus minus 10 minutes of arc, far below the specified minimum of 54 minutes of arc. As a result, all further test flights were deemed to be of no use except the most imbalanced configuration of a Sea Harrier having under one wing a 1,000 pound bomb (that had failed to release) and nothing under the other wing. Take off and landing with this imbalanced configuration represented the worst case. This too succeeded beyond expectation.

"At the end of it, the Chief of Naval Staff passed on to us a very nice letter from the Chief Engineer of British Aerospace, commending the quality of work of the Naval Dockyard Bombay."

After completion of modernisation in 1989, *Vikrant* was operational till her final sea outing on 23 November 1994. After that, she remained alongside until she was decommissioned on 31 January 1997.

Modernisation of the Petyas

The 6-yearly Medium Repair programme of the Petyas had been repeatedly postponed for several reasons like the delays in completion of the facilities in the new Naval Dockyard coming up in Vizag, their bunching at the time of acquisition meant bunching for Medium Repairs, the delays in getting spares from the Soviet Union, etc.

In 1979, consideration commenced on modernising the weapons and sensors of the Petyas during their 6-yearly Medium Repairs. The Navy preferred to fit sensors and weapons similar to the ships recently acquired from the Soviet Union like the RBU 6000 anti submarine rockets, 30 mm mounting with their fire control etc. Discussions with the Soviet ship designer revealed that this would entail such extensive redesign that it would not be cost effective.

Modernisation of the First Leander Class Frigate *Nilgiri*

In 1971, the British Navy started the half-life modernisation of their earlier FSA 29 Leanders. This envisaged the fitment of the French Exocet surface-to-surface missiles, the British Seawolf surface-to-air missile, the Ikara anti submarine missile, Computerised Action Information System (CAIS) in the Operations Room and the Westland Wessex WG 13 helicopter for anti submarine and anti ship roles.

In 1980, staff requirements were prepared for the modernisation of the *Nilgiri,* which had commissioned in 1972. In view of the high cost of the extensive modernisation based on the staff requirements prepared in 1980, NHQ reviewed the scope of modernisation in early 1981. It was decided to modernise *Nilgiri* only to the extent necessary to make it a viable first rate anti submarine frigate. Even this could not be achieved due to the non-availability from the Soviet Union of RBU 6000 anti submarine rocket launchers and 30 mm gun mountings and their fire control system.

14

The Naval Air Arm

The State of the Air Arm in 1975

VIKRANT and Her Air Squadrons

Vikrant and her Seahawk and Alize squadrons had commissioned in 1961.[1] In the fourteen years that had elapsed till 1975, both *Vikrant* and her aircraft had aged considerably: *Vikrant* herself was becoming due for a major refit cum modernisation.

Despite the acquisition of the German Navy's surplus Seahawks in 1966, the serviceability of the Seahawks had become unpredictable. Their replacements had been identified as the Sea Harriers, but these were still under development in Britain.

The three-year, 1975-1978 refurbishment programme to extend the life of the Alizes up to the 1980s had commenced but was being afflicted by the non-availability of critical spares, which were no longer under production in France.

The Helicopter Fleet

Seaking Anti Submarine Helicopters. The six Mk 42 Seakings that had arrived from Britain in 1971 had experienced numerous teething problems during the December 1971 Indo-Pakistan War. They underwent extensive evaluation and defect rectification in 1972 and 1973. By 1974, six new Seakings had arrived, repair and test facilities had been set up and expertise had begun to develop, all of which led to a marked improvement in availability and role worthiness.

Kamov 25 Anti Submarine Helicopters. Agreements had been signed for these helicopters to be embarked on board the Russian guided missile destroyers *Rajput, Rana* and *Ranjit* when they commissioned from 1980 onwards.

MATCH Alouettes. *Nilgiri* and *Himgiri* had each embarked a Multi-role Anti submarine Torpedo Carrying Helicopter.

The MATCH also had been ordered for the next two frigates, *Udaygiri* and *Dunagiri*. It had been decided that in the last two Leander frigates, *Taragiri* and *Vindhyagiri* the MATCH would be replaced by the much larger and heavier Seaking.

SAR Chetaks. These were the French Alouette IIIs being manufactured by HAL under license. SAR flights were operational at sea in *Vikrant* and *Deepak,* and ashore in *Hansa* and *Garuda.*

Reconnaissance Aircraft

Agreements had been signed for three Russian IL 38 MRASW aircraft to be delivered in 1977 and for the aircrew to commence training in Russia in 1976.

The Transformation in Tactical Missions

Seahawk Air-to-Air Role

When *Vikrant* was first acquired in 1961, the basic role of the Seahawks was 'fighter-ground attack'. The Seahawks were not designed to intercept other aircraft. During exercises, however, a modest capability had been built up by officers from the aircraft carrier 'directing' a Seahawk, on *Vikrant's* radar, to within visual range of an intruding aircraft, for carrying out an attack using its 20 mm guns.

Seahawk Anti Ship Role and Hawk-Alize Cooperation

For the anti-ship role, the Seahawks' armament options were bombs, rockets and 20mm guns. Since the Seahawks were not fitted with radar, they had to be homed on to a target. The basic problem was to pinpoint the target ship for the Seahawks to attack.

The Alize was fitted with radar and one of its roles was tactical reconnaissance within a hundred miles of the aircraft carrier. If, during daytime, a contact was visually

---

1. The Seahawks first saw action in the Anglo-French attack on Egypt in 1956 in the ground attack and interdiction role. In 1956, the Dutch Navy purchased 22 aircraft and the West German Navy purchased 64 aircraft. The Indian Navy ordered 9 second hand aircraft in 1956, followed in 1961 by an order for the last 14 new aircraft that were produced and the purchase of 22 more second hand aircraft. In 1966, the Navy purchased 28 second-hand aircraft from West Germany. Of the Navy's total induction of 73 Seahawks, 14 were new and 59 second hand.

identified as hostile, the Alize could call for and home a strike by Seahawks. If, at night, a radar contact behaved suspiciously, it would be shadowed until dawn and, if visually identified to be hostile, a Seahawk strike would be homed in. Since dusk and dawn were tactically critical times for a Seahawk attack to arrive over the target, Seahawk pilots had to qualify for being recovered and launched during darkness.

The procedure that had evolved for Seahawk-Alize cooperation comprised three steps:

• The Alize would search a given area to locate the adversary. As soon as a contact was identified as hostile, it would ask *Vikrant* to launch a Seahawk strike. Positioning itself between *Vikrant* and the target, the Alize would home the Seahawks towards itself, allow the Seahawks to overtake it and head towards the target.

• The Seahawks would strike the target.

• On completion of the strike, the Alize would tell the Seahawks the direction in which they should fly to reach back to *Vikrant*.

Between 1966 and 1971, Hawk-Alize cooperation improved steadily. Experience showed that identification and attack during darkness would improve if the target could be illuminated. Lepus flare bombs were imported from Sweden.

Alize's Anti Submarine Role

For the Alize's anti submarine role, the sequence of events would be:

• The Alize might detect an echo on its radar or a radar transmission on its ESM system. If the echo quickly disappeared, it was suggestive of a submarine having crash-dived.

• The Alize would proceed to the position of the radar contact / estimated position of the radar transmission and drop a pattern of passive non-directional sonobuoys. The amplitude of noise detected by the sonobuoys would be transmitted to the sonobuoy receiver in the Alize. By correlating these amplitudes, the receiver would estimate a range. Where these estimated range circles intersected, the receiver would indicate the approximate area where the submarine might be. The Alize would then drop a third sonobuoy, get a third range intersect and obtain the most probable position of the submarine.

• The Alize would track the submarine by dropping more sonobuoys. When it was confident of carrying out an accurate attack, the Alize would drop anti submarine depth charges on top of the submarine.

• Should a submarine be surprised on the surface and attempt to crash dive, the Alize would attack it with anti-submarine rockets fitted with special pressure hull-penetrating warheads, which were most effective when the submarine had not had the time to dive too deep.

From the outset, the efficacy of the Alizes in the anti submarine role fell short of expectations. The limited availability of submarines and the disappointing performance of passive non-directional sonobuoys in the waters where anti submarine exercises were carried out led the Navy to acquire, from France, the Julie system. The Julie concept was to drop a mini bomb (called bombette) near the pattern of sonobuoys, which would then record not only the explosion of the bombette but also its echo from the submarine, if there was one in the vicinity. The time interval between the two echoes was converted into a range to get a more accurate position of the submarine. The two additional Alizes acquired from France were fitted out with the Julie recording system. Julie recorders were also imported for retrofitting in the earlier Alizes.

The Indo-Pakistan War of 1971

During the 1971 war, the Seahawks attacked ground targets and ships in harbour in East Pakistan, as they were designed to do. Since there were no Pakistan Navy ships in the Bay of Bengal, there was no occasion to resort to Hawk-Alize cooperation. On the one occasion when an intruding British RAF aircraft inadvertently flew over *Vikrant*, the Seahawk was unable to catch up with and visually sight the intruder.

Whenever the wind on deck was not sufficient to launch Seahawks, Alizes were utilised to bomb ground targets, but only at night so as to reduce their vulnerability to anti aircraft fire due to their slower speed. One Alize would drop a Lepus flare to illuminate the target and a second Alize would drop the bombs. The Alizes also proved useful in stopping those merchant ships that tried to evade contraband control by dropping depth charges well ahead of them. The Alizes operating from Bombay did not obtain any worthwhile contacts of Pakistan Navy submarines on their sonobuoys.

Regretably, the capability of the newly arrived Seaking Mk 42 helicopters deployed at Bombay was not fully harnessed for combating the Pakistan Navy's newly acquired Daphne class submarines. Partly, this was due to the diffidence arising out of the technical teething problems experienced at Bombay. But mainly it was due to the differing opinions on how the Seakings should be employed. The first batch of aircrew that went to Britain to accept the first Seakings did not have the benefit of a combat workup with submarines. Plans for utilising Seakings primarily for the defence of Bombay appear to have been based on the assessment of the first batch. The second batch of aircrew underwent a full-scale work up in Britain with submarines and when they arrived in Bombay in October, they were more confident of Seaking capabilities. By this time, however, the plans for defensive utilisation had already firmed up. The tempo of events in November precluded attention on maximising the offensive potential of this latest combination of dunking sonar – air dropped torpedo anti submarine system which, being airborne was completely safe from being hit by submarine fired torpedoes.

After the War

From 1972 to 1974, *Vikrant* was under refit. Her workshops were re-equipped to enable her to operate Seakings. In 1973, three new Seakings arrived, followed by three more in 1974, enabling the commissioning of the second Seaking squadron INAS 336. Thereafter, Seaking availability and efficiency improved considerably. With a larger number of submarines having arrived from Russia and now available on both coasts, the Seakings were able to evolve and coordinate their anti submarine search and attack tactics and procedures with the latest anti submarine ships like the Russian Petya class submarine chasers and the British Leander class frigates.

Policy Regarding Helicopters in Frigates and Destroyers

The embarkation of helicopters in ships had started in the 1960s with the French Alouette IIIs in *Vikrant* (for the SAR role), in *Darshak* (for assisting survey work) and in *Deepak* (for assisting vertical replenishment) followed, in the 1970s, by the MATCH Alouettes in the first four Leander frigates. Thereafter:

- *Taragiri* and *Vindhyagiri* had one Seaking each. The Rajput class destroyers from Russia had one Kamov each. The Godavari class frigates of Project 16 had two Seakings each, as would their successors, the Delhi class destroyers of Project 15. The amphibious Landing ships, *Magar* and *Gharial*, were designed to embark the commando variant Seakings.

- All other frigate sized ships would have the lighter Chetaks – *Trishul* and *Talwar* after being fitted with surface to surface missiles, *Brahmaputra*, *Beas* and *Betwa* after conversion to the training role, the new cadet training ship *Tir*, the new survey ships and the new Khukri class corvettes of Project 25.

Developments Between 1976 and 1990

Overview

During the fifteen years between 1976 and 1990, the Naval Air Arm underwent momentous changes, many of which could not have been entirely foreseen.

Acquisitions included a second aircraft carrier and a wide variety of aircraft and helicopters equipped with the latest sensors and weapon systems.

Vikrant underwent two modernisations in preparation for embarking the new Sea Harrier Vertical/Short Take Off and Land (V/STOL) fighter aircraft and the new Seaking Mk 42 B ASW helicopters.

The transfer of the 'maritime reconnaissance' role from the Air Force to the Navy marked the rebirth of the shore-based arm of naval aviation.[2] This started with the taking over of the Air Force's Super Constellations (Super Connies) by the Navy in 1976 and the acquisition of the Maritime Reconnaissance and Anti Submarine Warfare (MRASW) Ilyushin (IL) 38s from Russia in 1977. Eleven years later, the much longer range and much better equipped Russian Long Range Maritime Patrol (LRMP) Tupolev (TU) 142s replaced the Super Connies.

The combat capability of the Air Arm leapfrogged from the technology of the 1950s to that of the 1980s:

- The new sensors were the dunking sonars in the Kamovs and the Seakings Mk 42 B, the latest sonobuoys in the Seakings Mk 42 B, the ILs and the TUs, the Magnetic Anomaly Detectors (MAD) in the ILs and Kamovs, the ESM in the Seakings Mk 42 B, the tail radar warners in the Sea Harriers, the ILs and the TUs, and the modern radars in all these aircraft and helicopters.

- The new weapons were the French Matra air to air missiles in the Sea Harriers, the British anti ship Sea Eagle missiles in the Sea Harriers and Seakings, the Italian A 244 S and Russian anti submarine homing torpedoes in the helicopters and the anti submarine depth bombs in the Kamovs.

- The tactical missions of naval aircraft changed considerably, in step with the changes in the capabilities of their sensors and weapons.

- Three new naval air stations were commissioned. They made more complete the sea areas covered by maritime reconnaissance. At the older air stations, the Air Traffic Control facilities were modernised and runways lengthened and strengthened to operate the heavier new aircraft.

---

2. The amphibious Sealands were phased out in the 1960s.

- The latest simulators were acquired for training Sea Harrier pilots, TU ASW teams and Seaking Mk 42 B maintenance personnel.

- New aircraft maintenance workshops were set up at Kochi for the Seakings, at Goa for the Sea Harriers and the Russian ILs and Kamovs and at Arakkonam for the TUs.

- Training syllabi were updated and training facilities were expanded. To facilitate the practical training of air technical personnel at HAL and with the Air Force, a site was identified at Bangalore for a spacious new Naval Air Technical School.

Aircraft Carriers

Aircraft Carrier VIKRANT

Between 1975 and 1979, flying operations aboard *Vikrant* started posing problems that compelled changes in the roles of aircraft.

Vikrant's radars had become unreliable and overdue for replacement. The tracking and marshalling of Seahawks had become stressful. Seahawk availability and the reliability of their navigation systems had become unpredictable. When the Seahawks embarked *Vikrant* for the last time in 1978, they could only carry out weapon and PR sorties.

Even though two refurbished Alizes were embarked, the inaccuracies of their navigation system degraded the effectiveness of Hawk-Alize cooperation and of anti submarine exercises using sonobuoys. The anti submarine role shifted from the Alize aircraft to the Seaking helicopters and the Alizes' main role became tactical reconnaissance.

Vikrant underwent two-modernisation refits – the first from 1979 to 1981 and the second from 1987 to 1989. During the Phase One modernisation refit, the major items undertaken were:

- Renewal of boilers.

- Extension of air-conditioning.

- Fitment of the Dutch Signaal radars, similar to those fitted in the Leander class frigates.

- Installation of Sea Harrier facilities, LUDS and flood-lighting of the flight deck.

- Fitment of L 70 guns and LIOD Sights for gun control.

- Fitment of new UHF, VHF, HF, MF communication sets.

- Installation of a towed torpedo decoy, an expendable bathythermograph and a sonic ray plotter.

- The catapult and arrestor gear were overhauled and retained for launch and recovery of the Alizes.

Between 1982 and 1986, *Vikrant* operated with Alizes in the tactical recce role and Seakings Mk 42 in the anti submarine role.

During the Phase Two modernisation from 1987 to 1989, *Vikrant* was fitted with:

- A ski jump for launching Sea Harriers in the Short Take Off mode. Since the Alizes had phased out, the catapult and arrestor gear were removed.

- Facilities for operation and maintenance of the new dual role anti submarine / anti ship Seaking Mk 42 B helicopter.

- LIOD Fire Control Systems and indigenous medium range chaff launchers.

- Magazine stowage for the new weapons of the Sea Harriers and Seaking Mk 42 B helicopters. The new weapons were the Sea Eagle anti ship missiles, the Matra air-to-air missiles, the A 244S anti submarine torpedoes and the chaff rockets.

During 1989-90, for the first time the Navy had two aircraft carriers at sea at the same time.

Aircraft Carrier VIRAAT

'Elephant' was the name intended for last of the series of the 1939-45 World War, 22,000 tonne, Centaur class, 'light fleet aircraft carriers' designed in Britain in 1943. When the war ended in 1945, construction of the Elephant was suspended. A few years later, construction was resumed, Elephant was renamed '*Hermes*' and launched in February 1953. The original design of 1943 had envisaged the operation of propeller driven aircraft. This design had to be modified extensively to cater for the operation of jet-propelled aircraft and the new weapon systems that had entered service after 1943. *Hermes* commissioned in the British Navy in November 1959.

Hermes' first deployment was as a 'strike carrier' in Southeast Asia from 1960 onwards. Britain's economic difficulties in the 1960s led to the decision that it would withdraw from 'East of Suez,' reduce the size of its Navy and transfer her naval air arm's 'strike' aircraft to its Air Force. The British Navy decommissioned a number of its aircraft carriers. *Hermes*' catapult and arrestor wires were removed and she was placed in reserve. In 1973, she was taken out of reserve and refitted as an 'Anti submarine Helicopter Carrier' to meet NATO commitments in the Atlantic Ocean.

The British Navy, however, remained reluctant to forego the tactical advantages that aircraft carriers conferred in distant naval operations that were beyond the reach of shore based Air Force aircraft. It pursued two projects:

- A new smaller class of ship called the 'Through Deck Cruiser' that would have a "ski jump" to assist V/STOL aircraft to take off from a carrier without having to be catapulted. The V/STOL capability also dispensed with the need for arrestor wires.

- The development of the naval version of the P 1127/ Harrier V/STOL aircraft that had been in service with the US Marine Corps and the British Air Force since 1970. By the mid 1970s, the Sea Harrier had taken shape.

In 1978, Sea Harrier trials were held on board *Hermes*. In 1980, *Hermes* was fitted with a 12-degree ski jump to enable it to operate Sea Harrier aircraft.

In 1981, again because of financial difficulties, Britain considered whether its Navy should be essentially an ASW force built around destroyers and frigates, whether the Through Deck Cruiser programme should be halted, whether the *Hermes* should be scrapped and whether the first through deck cruiser, *HMS Invincible,* should be sold to Australia. These considerations were overtaken by the crisis precipitated by Argentina's invasion of Britain's Falkland Islands, located in the distant South Atlantic Ocean. Argentina had decided to try and solve the longstanding dispute regarding its sovereignty over these islands.

Both *Hermes* and *Invincible,* with Sea Harrier strike aircraft and Seaking anti submarine helicopters embarked, were made operational and dispatched to the Falklands in April 1982. Both aircraft carriers returned to Britain in mid 1982, unharmed by the Argentine Air Force's Mirages and Skyhawks, but having lost a number of Sea Harrier aircraft and pilots in combat.

In 1983, Britain decided to place *Hermes* in reserve and continue the construction of 'Through Deck Cruisers'. In November 1983, *Hermes* sailed to Portsmouth for being mothballed and decommissioned. She remained idle from 1984 onwards.

In early 1985, Britain offered *Hermes* to India for outright purchase. By this time, the first batch of the Indian Navy's Sea Harriers had already been in service for over a year. The Navy had a long pending need for a second aircraft carrier to ensure that out of two carriers, at least one would be available should a sudden need arise.[3]

Admiral Tahiliani was the Chief of the Naval Staff in 1985. He recalls:

"I got a letter from my counterpart in the British Navy. I still remember the letter was dated 1 March 1985. He simply said that because they had now three newly built aircraft carriers in commission, they were going to put *Hermes* in the reserve fleet and would India be interested in getting this carrier? He said further that the price would be competitive and, if I remember rightly, even quoted the figure of 35 million pounds. He said that if I was interested, I should send out a team to look at the ship and its material state before they actually mothballed it.

"This looked like an excellent opportunity. Although we had been wanting to start building our own carrier, we hadn't got the sanction and were nowhere near ready to begin our programme so that we would have a carrier to replace *Vikrant* when she was phased out in another 8 to 10 years.

"We sent out a team led by the Deputy Chief of the Naval Staff. He came back and gave us a report that although *Hermes* had been commissioned in 1959 (which was before *Vikrant*), but because she had been periodically laid up and had had three extensive refits / modernisations, her material state was ten years younger than *Vikrant*. We took up the proposal with Government and, happily for us, everything worked out right."

The Navy thoroughly examined the material state of *Hermes*, assessed the magnitude of the refit that would be required, determined the minimum requirements of new equipment and systems that were essential for providing an all weather, day and night capability for air operations, determined the stowage and supply arrangements for the new air to surface and air to air missiles, which were entering service and negotiated how much all this would cost.

On 24 April 1986, the Government announced in Parliament that an agreement had been signed with Britain to acquire the *Hermes*. A 63 million pound sterling acquisition package was worked out that included drydocking, refit, spares, stores and services. The ship was towed to Plymouth for dry-docking and a 12-month refit that included:

- Shot blasting of the underwater hull and repair and preservation of fittings to ensure that the ship would not require docking for at least five years.

---

3. During the 1965 war, *Vikrant* was under refit. During the 1971 war, *Vikrant* was afflicted by cracks in her boilers that restricted her speed.

- Re-tubing of all boilers and overhaul / replacement of auxiliary machinery.
- Stripping and re-coating of the flight deck.
- Rectification of all pending defects and updating onboard systems.
- Alterations to weapon spaces, air department spaces and galleys.

The new equipment to be fitted included a Computerised Action Information Organisation system, modern deck landing and flight facility systems, and all the latest facilities required to operate the Sea Harriers and the new Seaking Mk 42 B helicopters.

On completion of refit, *Hermes* commissioned at Plymouth as *INS Viraat* on 12 May 1987. After sea trials off Plymouth and work up off Portland, *Viraat* sailed from Britain on 23 July 1987. She arrived off Bombay on 21 August 1987 where Prime Minister Rajiv Gandhi boarded her, much as his grandfather Prime Minister Jawaharlal Nehru had welcomed *Vikrant* twenty-six years earlier in 1961.

The Sea Harriers embarked a month later in September. They dropped their first weapons – 1,000-pound bombs and cluster bombs – on 5 November 1987.

Viraat was the quickest acquisition that the Navy had ever made of a major war vessel.

The Indigenous Air Defence Ship (ADS) Project

The project for the indigenous aircraft carrier first took shape in 1979. Since the Navy's design capacities were fully stretched in designing ships and since the Navy had no experience of designing an aircraft carrier, discussions on design collaboration were held with shipbuilders in Europe who had built aircraft carriers for their Navies. During the course of these discussions, the staff requirements crystallised.

The main consideration was the type and number of aircraft that the ADS would operate. In 1979, the Navy had opted for the V/STOL Sea Harriers to operate from *Vikrant*. With the acquisition of *Viraat* in 1987, it became certain that the Sea Harriers would still be flying in the decade after 2000, after *Vikrant* decommissioned. The ADS would, therefore, need to have a ski jump until the Sea Harriers phased out.

To avail of the benefits of self-reliance and of standardisation, the choice of aircraft narrowed down to between:

- The Short Take Off But Arrested Recovery (STOBAR)

Russian MiG 29 K that was of the same lineage as the MiG 29 acquired by the Air Force, and

- The navalised version of the Light Combat Aircraft (LCA) that was being developed indigenously for the Air Force.

At the time of writing, it has been decided to acquire MIG 29K aircraft along with the second-hand Russian aircraft carrier *Admiral Gorshkov*. The naval LCA is under development.

Fighter Aircraft

Phasing out of Seahawks

The Seahawks disembarked from *Vikrant* for the last time on 8 May 1978. Even ashore, their availability could not be sustained. By end 1978, the Seahawks phased out from service. The last Seahawk flight took place on 16 December 1983, when it escorted the first three Sea Harriers as they arrived overhead the Naval Air Station at Goa.

In 1995, as a gesture of goodwill, one of the Seahawks that had been purchased from the German Navy in 1966 was formally handed over in Goa to the Chief of German Naval Aviation for their Air Arm museum.

The Acquisition of the Sea Harriers and Their Role

V/STOL aircraft had been under development in Britain since the end 1960s for the British Air Force. The British Navy intended to acquire the naval version, the Sea Harrier. In July 1972, a Harrier had come to India and landed and taken off from *Vikrant* to establish, prima facie, that V/STOL aircraft could operate from *Vikrant's* flight deck.

The roles envisaged by the British Navy for the Sea Harrier were:

- Air Defence, with particular emphasis on the shooting down of Maritime Reconnaissance and snooper aircraft.
- Reconnaissance.
- Air Strike, particularly against missile boats and surface targets.

In the ensuing years, the Indian Navy followed the development of the Sea Harrier. In 1977, the Navy obtained approval in principle for the acquisition of the Sea Harriers as replacements for the Seahawks. The first British Navy Sea Harrier flew in 1978 and by mid 1979, the first few aircraft were undergoing intensive flying trials.

In 1979, the Indian Navy placed an order for six Sea Harriers and two Sea Harrier Trainers for delivery in 1983.

The British Navy's aircraft carrier operations against Argentina in the Falkland Islands in 1982 provided the opportunity to assess Sea Harrier performance in combat. They performed effectively in the ground attack role using 30 mm front guns and bombs. In the air-to-air role, their effectiveness remained unproven because the British aircraft carriers stayed outside the strike range of the Argentine Navy's shore based Mirage and Skyhawk strike aircraft.

The Indian Navy's tactical problem was that even if the Fleet was operating outside the range of enemy shore-based strike aircraft, there would still be the threat from a hostile maritime reconnaissance aircraft armed with anti ship missiles. Hence the need for carrier borne aircraft to shoot down the snooper before it released its missiles. Being a V/STOL aircraft, it was known that the Sea Harrier was constrained by limitations on all up weight and its airborne time had to be optimised.

The view of the Indian Air Force, who had earlier evaluated the Harrier aircraft, was that vectored thrust aircraft had no chance against contemporary high performance supersonic aircraft. Moreover, the aircraft's engine performance would de-rate in the hotter Indian climate.

When the Navy proposed the acquisition of additional Sea Harriers, it was decided that a joint Indian Navy-Indian Air Force study should be carried out of the likely effectiveness of the Sea Harrier against the threat posed by missile-armed maritime reconnaissance aircraft.[4]

The scenario was straightforward. The enemy maritime reconnaissance (MR) aircraft needed to determine, on its radar, the direction and distance from which to fire its missiles. To do so, it would have to expose itself to detection by the target ship's radar. Starting from the time that the MR aircraft was detected on ship's radar, the question was whether a Sea Harrier (either already airborne on patrol or on deck ready for immediate take off) would be able to shoot down the MR aircraft before it released its missiles or would this only be possible after it had fired its missiles?

After computer assisted analyses of numerous variables, it was jointly agreed that:

- The Sea Harrier's ability to shoot down an enemy MR aircraft before it fired its missiles would be only marginal.
- However, after the anti ship missiles had been fired, the

Sea Harrier would always be able to catch up with and shoot down the enemy MR aircraft.

- Not having Sea Harriers at all would give enemy MR aircraft total freedom to fire missiles unhindered and at leisure.
- Having Sea Harriers would unquestionably constrain enemy MR aircraft freedom of action before firing missiles and ensure certain destruction after missile release.

It was clear that in future operations, the primary role of the Sea Harrier would be the air defence of the Fleet, for which it had to have its own radar (to detect and track enemy aircraft) and air-to-air missiles (to shoot down enemy aircraft). For its role of anti ship attack, it would need an anti ship missile. For its role of ground attack, it would need front guns and bombs. An ESM pod would be valuable for specific missions.

Selection and Training of Sea Harrier Pilots

The skill and speed of response required of a pilot of an aircraft which can hover in the air, and take off and land vertically are different from, and higher than, those required of a normal fixed wing pilot. After rigorous selection and several months of intensive training on the Air Force's high performance fighter aircraft, the first three pilots went to Britain in 1982.

After nine months of conversion, they underwent eight months Operational Flying Training with the British Navy from April to November 1983 on the aircraft produced for the Indian Navy. The bulk of this training comprised radar interception work and air-to-air combat training. Deck landings were practiced on board the *Hermes*.

The first three Sea Harriers (603, 604 and 605) took off from Britain on 13th December and, after overnight halts in Malta, Egypt and Dubai, landed at Goa on 16th December. After a brief maintenance period, the first Sea Harrier landed on *Vikrant's* deck on 20 December 1983.

On 26 January 1984, Sea Harriers participated in the Republic Day Flypast. During the Beating the Retreat ceremony on 29 January 1984, an astonished audience saw a Sea Harrier flown by then Commander (now Admiral and Chief of Naval Staff) Arun Prakash fly gently into Vijay Chowk, stop in hover, turn to face the President, dip its nose in salute, turn away, point skywards and take off with its engines roaring. Everyone was enthralled – the potential of V/STOL aircraft needed no further elaboration.[5]

---

4. The author represented the Navy in this study.

5. This remarkable demonstration was accomplished despite the presence of birds. Fortunately, engine noise helped to keep them away. To avoid mishap, this demonstration was never repeated.

Three more Sea Harriers (601, 602 and 606) and the first trainer (651) arrived in 1984. With the arrival of the second trainer (652) in 1985, the delivery of the first batch of eight Sea Harriers was complete.

Lieutenant (now Rear Admiral) Shekhar Sinha was the commissioning QFI of the squadron. He recalls:

"It was a great honour to be selected as the first Qualified Flying Instructor of the yet to be commissioned Sea Harrier Squadron in April 1982 and to be nominated to accompany then Commander Arun Prakash who was nominated as the Squadron Commander. I had already obtained instructional Cat 'B' on the Kiran aircraft from the IAF and done a stint at the Air Force Academy. Learning the Harrier in the United Kingdom was not easy. The aircraft being unstable in yaw and neutrally stable in roll and pitch meant that she was not going to land / take off like a conventional aircraft. Also, it was incumbent on my part to understand the aerodynamics of it all to ensure that I taught the right thing when we got back. We went through learning basics at 233 OCU located at RAF station Wittering. Apart from the two of us (Indians), we also had two Spanish Navy pilots and four each from RAF and RN. It was indeed a unique experience flying in the UK given the vagaries of weather and dialects. On completion of basic V/STOL training, Commander Arun Prakash and I got posted to the British Aerospace Sea Harrier assembly line at Dunsfold which is in Guildford County, Surrey. We were required to maintain continuity in flying on the company's aircraft as also gain background factory experience, which would assist us in mastering the test-flying techniques. This is where we had the great opportunity to fly and interact with renowned Harrier test pilots like John Farley, Mike Snelling, Heinz Frick and Taylor Scott (who subsequently died in an accident). We utilised our insights to write the first draft of SOPs and the Sea Harrier Guide Book. We virtually saw steel being cut of the first aircraft IN 601 and subsequent ones till its acceptance. This tenure gave us very deep understanding of this wonder machine. By December 1982, we had finished with this phase.

"In January 1983, we moved to the IN detachment at Royal Naval Air Station Yeovilton (HMS Heron) for Operational Flying Training (OFT). We were joined by Commander RT Rajan and Lieutenant Commander Sanjoy Gupta (AWI designate). They had both finished their OCU phase while we were at Dunsfold. Our OFT was being conducted by INTU headed by Lieutenant Commander Mike Blisset, RN. We also had Flight Lieutenant Paul Barton (RAF) and Lieutenant Steve Thomas, RN (both decorated for gallantry during the Falkland War of 1982). During this OFT, we exploited the Sea Harrier (our own aircraft) in her various roles, which included air interception by day and night using Blue Fox radar, photo recce, air to ground and air-to-air weapon firings, instrument rating and deck landing up to DLQ stage on board the HMS Hermes (which later became INS Viraat). This training lasted for nearly 10½ months. We had the entire IN team of technical officers and sailors doing their OJT under RN supervision.

"At the end of it, I left for 233 OCU at Wittering to undergo the 'Competent to Instruct' (C to I) course on the Harrier. The RAF was saddled with a major problem. I did not have adequate flying hours on the Harrier, which was required by their system to join the Harrier QFI course. The then Naval Advisor, Commodore Santosh Gupta, MVC, NM, came down to Wittering and resolved the issue by committing that should there be a requirement to fly additional sorties to achieve the required standards of an instructor, the Government of India would provide for it. Well, at the end of the C to I course there was no additional sortie required and the RAF CFS (equivalent to our AEB/Aircats) were happy to categorise me as a Harrier QFI. That indeed was a matter of satisfaction for me and a great relief to the Navy that a Harrier QFI was born. I was fully aware that with qualifications of Fully ops, DLQ, CTOI and Green rating, I had the responsibility of training a fresh generation of Naval fighter pilots in techniques of V/STOL aviation. I am happy that for the next 10 years, I devoted myself to this task. I was extremely fortunate to have had the professional and timely guidance of Commander Arun Prakash (now Admiral) at every stage of Sea Harrier exploitation."

Lieutenant (now Rear Admiral) SK Damle completed training in Britain and was in the Sea Harrier Squadron from 1984 to 1989. He recalls:

"While operating from Vikrant, we learnt how to operate the Sea Harrier from a carrier. When Viraat came in, we progressed from these basic concepts and started operating in bad weather, taking advantage of the Sea Harrier's capabilities to land from any direction. The carrier did not have to turn into the wind.

"With the help of the Indian Air Force, we developed the air combat potential of the Sea Harriers.

"In the Seahawk days, the emphasis used to be on close formation flying and delivery of air to ground weapons. But as far as air-to-air combat was concerned, there was no radar on the Seahawks and any air-to-air radar interception capability was definitely not there during the Seahawk days.

"The Sea Harrier was a quantum jump. The aircraft was more advanced, almost state of the art technology. Secondly the aircraft could carry more all up weight, more load in terms of weapons, various kinds of weapons and, therefore, many modes of delivery. Thirdly, we had air-to-air radar and, therefore, we could do air-to-air interception.

"Air-to-air combat was something that had to be developed in our Navy after the Sea Harriers were acquired. During the Seahawk days some attempt had been made to actually do some kind of air combat, but we found that people were not very keen and it was never really done as a serious business. But in the Sea Harriers we had to take it seriously because we understood well that Sea Harriers were the air defence fighters operating from the carrier and we had to learn air combat to the same level that the Air Force's interceptors and fighters did.

"Similarly, we started flying in bad weather much more than the Sea Hawks used to do. With the inertial navigation system, we had a navigation kit available on board. We could also use our own radar for assessing clouds and for navigation. The instrumentation of the Sea Harrier was much better than that of the Seahawks. With all these advantages, we developed the art of flying in bad weather, which we never used to do in the Sea Hawks."

Lessons Learnt in the Early Years of Sea Harrier Operations

After operating from the carrier, two problems came into focus that required attention:

- A minimum of one operational aircraft and one trainer was required for training pilots ashore. This left only six aircraft available for embarkation in the aircraft carrier. Since all six could not always be serviceable, more Sea Harriers needed to be acquired.

- Air to air interception was best carried out with the Sea Harrier located below the aircraft to be intercepted. It was essential that the Sea Harrier's radar should display a clear picture when looking forward and upward. The radar fitted in the Sea Harriers displayed sea clutter when looking downwards and this made interception difficult, though an experienced pilot could still effect a successful interception. The next lot of Sea Harriers needed to have a radar free of sea clutter.

Every effort was made to acquire better radar in the next batch of Sea Harriers, but no better radar was available. Waiting for a better radar to be developed conflicted with the Navy's need to acquire additional Sea Harriers as early as possible.

The Upgradation of Sea Harrier Capability

The overall development and delivery cycles of modern high performance aircraft are never in step with the development and delivery cycles of their advanced avionics and weapon systems. This reality affected the combat capability of the batches of Sea Harriers acquired by the Navy. A total of 23 Sea Harriers and 4 Sea Harrier trainers were acquired between 1983 and 1992:

Batch	Contracted	Fighters	Trainers	Delivered
I	Nov 79	6	2	1983
II	Nov 85	10	1	1989-90
III	Oct 86	7	1	1990-92

From the 'equipment fit' point of view, they could be considered as Batch One and Batch Two.

Batch One

For the air defence role, these Sea Harriers (equivalent to the British Navy's FRS 1) had the Blue Fox radar, the French Magic Matra close range, air-to-air missile and a tail-warning receiver. For the anti ship / ground attack role, these Harriers could carry 30 mm gun pods, 68 mm rockets in pods, runway denial bombs, cluster bombs and 1,000 pound 'iron' bombs of 1939-45 World War vintage. All weapon release modes were calculated by weapon aiming computers and displayed on head-up symbology.

Batch Two

Due to the British Navy's financial constraints, its FRS 2 Sea Harriers started entering service only in the end 1980s. The replacement for the Blue Fox radar, named Blue Vixen, was still under development. The Navy had to decide whether to delay the induction of the additional Sea Harriers until the better radar was available or to accept the same standard as was fitted in the British Navy's FRS 2s, namely the same Blue Fox radar but now with two types of air-to-air missiles:

- The Beyond Visual Range (BVR) missile that had a capability of several tens of kilometres for distant combat, and

- The 'All Aspect Air to Air Missile' for close range combat that enabled attack from all aspects, rather than only from behind the target.

Admiral of the Fleet, Sir Benjamin Bathurst of the British Navy recalls:[6]

---

6. Personal correspondence

"In 1982, the Blue Fox radar was the only show in town. The Royal Navy had a very tight budget for the Sea Harrier Project and it was the only radar that could have met the In Service Date (ISD). Until early 1982, (British) aircraft carriers and the Sea Harrier force were under the sentence of death, only to be reprieved by the Falklands campaign. There was no way the Blue Vixen radar could have been fitted to meet your (the Indian Navy's) ISD, even if you had been prepared to fund the development. The issue of any security concerns about technology transfer is irrelevant. Blue Vixen did not enter service in our Sea Harrier 2s until the second half of the nineties."

In view of these considerations, the improvements in the Indian Navy's Batch Two Harriers delivered between 1989 and 1992 were:

- The Sea Eagle anti ship missile.
- The French Matra Magic Two, All Aspect, Air to Air Missile.
- Wider coverage for the tail radar-warning receiver.
- Photo-reconnaissance pod.
- Associated changes in the weapon aiming computer software.

Of the nineteen Batch Two Sea Harriers, three fighters and one trainer arrived in 1989, eight fighters (607 to 614) and one trainer (653) arrived in 1990, four fighters (616, 617, 620 and 621) arrived in 1991 and the remaining two fighters (618 and 619) arrived in 1992.

For all practical purposes, the sea clutter problem had to be overcome by rigorous training.

Weapon Capability

Though the first batch of Sea Harriers arrived in India in 1983, the ski jump first became available after *Viraat* arrived in 1987. *Vikrant*, after installation of its ski jump, became available only in 1989.

It took some years to complete, satisfactorily, the numerous trials for proving Sea Harrier weapon capability:

Trial	Completed
Indigenous ECM pods for Sea Harrier successfully tried on MIG 21	1989
Runway penetration bombs and Twin Magic Matra air-to-air missiles	Nov 1989
Reconnaissance pods	Nov 1989
Sea Eagle air to surface anti-ship missile demonstration firing	Apr 1990
Vikrant's ski jump proving trials	Apr 1990
500 lb bombs	Under trial in 1990
Chaff and flares	Under trial in 1990
Runway penetration bombs	Procurement held in abeyance due to shortage of foreign exchange

Samples of indigenously manufactured gun ammunition had to be sent to British Aerospace in Britain for EMI/EMC clearance, as had to be done with the 500 lb iron bombs of 1939-45 World War vintage.

Sea Harrier Simulator

The Sea Harrier Simulator was commissioned in the Naval Air Station at Hansa in 1984. It provided *ab initio* and re-familiarisation training, practicing of emergency procedures, tactical and mission training, accident investigation and validation of mission profiles.

The simulator was upgraded by a Bangalore firm to cater for the Batch Two Sea Harriers and re-commissioned in 1998. The upgradation provided:

- Integration of Blue Fox radar with Sea Eagle and Magic Matra missile delivery capability.
- Day and night visuals.
- Improvements of Electronic Warfare, Record/Replay and IOS features.

Ongoing Training of Sea Harrier Pilots

Until 1984, the 'basic conversion' and subsequent 'operational' training of Sea Harrier pilots was carried out in Britain. After the first trainer aircraft arrived in 1984, 'operational' training commenced in India. Basic training, however, continued to be carried out in Britain, despite its high cost, because there weren't enough aircraft.

The Batch Two and additional trainer Harriers started arriving in 1989. In 1990, the Sea Harrier Operational Flying Training Unit was formed as a separate unit within the Sea Harrier Squadron (INAS 300), with three Harriers and two trainers, to carry out both 'basic' and 'operational' training. In 1991, this unit was moved to the training squadron as INAS 551 Bravo Flight.

Since 1996, this flight has been functioning, informally, as a supplementary Sea Harrier squadron. In addition to training budding Sea Harrier pilots, the squadron imparts technical on-job-training to tradesmen of frontline and second line servicing units. When required, it augments 300 Squadron with aircraft and aircrew, afloat and ashore.

Anti Submarine Aircraft

Refurbishment of Alizes

In 1974, the Navy decided to refurbish the Alizes and extend their life into the 1980s. This decision had been based on four factors:

- The Seahawks were nearing the end of their life. The Sea Harriers were not expected to arrive until the 1980s. If the Alizes were not refurbished, there would no aircraft available to fly from *Vikrant*.

- NARO had established the capability to undertake maintenance related inspections up to 1,200 hours but not for the mandatory 2,400-hour refurbishing. It would be more economical to undertake this refurbishing in NARO than sending them to France.

- The Alizes had already gone out of production in France and out of service in the French Navy. This would be the last chance to acquire whatever Alize spares were available in France.

- The French Navy's experience in refurbishing its Alizes could be availed of.

A small team was deputed to France to undergo six weeks training. Refurbishing of the first Alize started in 1977 and completed in 1978. The refurbishment programme of the remaining nine aircraft completed in 1982. The extent of refurbishment achieved was:

- Airframe completely refurbished;

- Engine completely overhauled;

- Radar, sonobuoy monitoring system and ESM components changed;

- The navigation system could not be satisfactorily refurbished. It was no longer in production. The French Navy had phased it out. No replacements were available for the worn out mechanical parts, which perforce had to be repaired, refitted and replaced locally in India as best as possible. The Omega Navigation System was evaluated as a possible replacement but its accuracy was found to be short of the requirement.

As a result, even though the Alize airframe, engine and electronics were refurbished by 1982, the inaccuracy of its navigation system degraded the accuracy of its sonobuoy monitoring system.

It also became clear that the Julie system, acquired with great expectations, had been designed for the French Navy's deep water anti submarine operations, where echoes from the sea bottom did not clutter the sonobuoys. In the comparatively shallower waters off the coast of India where anti submarine exercises were generally carried out, the

Julie system gave such disappointing results that it went into disuse. This was compounded by the general lack of expertise on the Julie system itself.

Overall, the performance of refurbished Alize radars and ESM improved but the accuracy of the sonobuoy monitoring remained sub optimal. As a result, the Alize's ASW role died out. The last launch of Alizes from *Vikrant* took place on 2 April 1987. Thereafter they operated only from ashore.

During Operation Pawan in Sri Lanka, a detachment of two Alizes operated from Madurai from February 1988 till October 1989 and flew 1,800 hours in support of the Indian Peace Keeping Force. The aircrew won three Nao Sena Medals, four Mentioned in Despatches, four CNS commendations and twelve commendations by FOCINCEAST.

In November 1988, during Operation Cactus to assist the Government of the Maldives in suppressing an attempted coup, an Alize dropped charges ahead of the rebel's escape vessel, *MV Progress Light*, to persuade it to stop.

The Alizes stopped flying on 12 April 1991 and the Squadron was decommissioned in August 1991. Five Alizes were left of the total of 14 acquired. During the 30 years of the squadron's service, the Alizes had flown 35,912 hours and done 7,144 deck landings.

Helicopters

The British Seaking 42 Series

The Mk 42s

Twelve anti submarine Seakings Mk 42 had been acquired between 1971 and 1974, six in 1971 and six in 1974. Of these, four have been lost, leaving eight in service.

On 19 July 1979, the Seaking Flight and Tactical Simulator (FATS) commissioned in Garuda.

The Mk 42 As

Three anti-submarine Seakings Mk 42 A were acquired in 1980. These had been modified for being hauled down on to the flight decks of the 5th and 6th Leanders, *Taragiri* and *Vindhyagiri*, using the Recovery, Assist, Secure and Traverse (RAST) system.

Commodore (then Commander) V Ravindranath carried out the first landing trials. He recalls:

"The Seaking landing trials on *Taragiri* were carried out during the monsoon of 1980 and 1981. It was the first time in the world that a large helicopter of Seaking size was successfully flown off from a Leander. The object of the trials was to determine the limiting parameters of sea state, all up weight, and wind conditions on deck in which a Seaking could be operated.

"Initially we carried out the trials with the RAE Bedford doing the instrumentation of the aircraft and the ship. That was a complete failure, because the RAST equipment, which is used to hold down the helo, failed completely. In fact we had a couple of risky moments during the trials. The Royal Navy also didn't give us any data on the test. They just told us what should have been achieved in such and such conditions.

"The second time the trials were carried out, the RAE Bedford came as observers. The instrumentation was done by our ARDE Kirkee in a fantastic manner. That is why the trials were very successful. In fact, the Seakings were cleared in record time for operating from Leander class frigates."

After the Canadian Navy, the Indian Navy became the second navy in the world to have the RAST system and the first to operate a helicopter of Seaking size and capabilities from a small ship the size of a Leander.

Of the three Mk 42 As acquired in 1980, one was lost, leaving two in service.

The Selection and Induction of Seaking Mk 42 Bs

By 1981, the Seakings Mk 42 had been in service for ten years and had begun to age. Replacement ASW helicopters were required not only for *Vikrant* but also for the Godavari class frigates, each of which was designed to embark two ASW helicopters.

The Navy's staff requirements stipulated both an anti submarine (ASW) and an anti ship (ASV) role. For the anti submarine role, the requirements were for a better dunking sonar, MAD and a LOFAR system to monitor low frequency sonobuoys. For the ASV role, the requirement was for an anti ship missile.

In March 1982, approval was accorded for 20 ASW/ASV helicopters – 6 for INAS 330, 2 for INAS 336, 4 for a new squadron INAS 339, 2 each for *Godavari* and *Gomati* and 4 for MRSOW. International tenders were floated. Three contenders were identified:

- An updated version of the British Seaking;
- The Italian Agosta. It transpired that this was the Italian version of the British Seaking; it was therefore excluded from further consideration;
- The French Super Puma.

The comparative evaluation of the British Seaking and

the French Super Puma indicated that:

- The Super Puma's fuselage and rotor blades were made of the latest composite material. This was considered to be an advantage because the Seakings acquired in 1971 had to be grounded whenever their nitrogen filled rotor blades leaked. Whilst the Super Puma was not yet operational in any Navy in the ASW role, the ASW equipment being offered for fitment met the Navy's staff requirements and was operational in French MRASW aircraft and their Dauphine helicopters. However, the French could not offer the Exocet anti ship missile with the Super Puma because of a commitment they had given to the Pakistan Navy, when supplying them Exocet anti ship missiles for their Seaking helicopters. Nor were the British agreeable to let their Sea Eagle anti ship missile be released for fitment in the French Super Puma.

- The updated version of the Seaking, named 42 B, was still on the drawing board and none of the avionic systems being offered had yet been proven. On the other hand, the Indian Navy had acquired ten years experience in operating the Seakings and both infrastructure and expertise had built up. The Sea Eagle anti ship missile was available. And the Seaking AEW helicopter, then under development, appeared a promising option to meet the Navy's pressing need for an AEW platform for anti missile defence.

Whilst the choice between the Seaking and the Super Puma was still under discussion, the Navy decided to carry out, in Indian waters, comparative evaluations of the sonars being offered.

Commander (later Commodore) SV Purohit, an experienced Seaking pilot participated in these trials. He recalls:

"We evaluated, very systematically, three dunking sonars. These were the American Bendix, Plessey's modification of their British sonar 195 and the French Thomson CSF HS 12. NPOL was extensively involved in these trials, which were conducted off Cochin in the early 1980s.

"By this time we had considerably improved upon the procedures of the early 1970s for evaluating and testing helicopter sonars and had learnt the technique of making the manufacturers accept our demands that their sonars be tested in our own waters. We had realised that the hydrological conditions in their waters and overall sonar performance in their temperature were different from those in India. Equipment often gave problems because of heat and humidity and did not perform as well because of our peculiar hydrological conditions.

"For the first time, there were three Seakings fitted with these three different sonars and pinging against the same submarine in the same hydrological conditions. Their performance in identical conditions was scientifically compared."

The Bendix performed better than the HS 12 and the British 195.

There were two competing radars – the French Iguane / Varan pulse compression radars that were operational in the French Navy and the British Mel MAREC 2. The British were not agreeable to put the French radar on the Seaking nor were the French agreeable to fit the British radar in the Super Puma.

The competing sonobuoy systems were the French Lamparo and the British LAPADS, both of which were flying in their respective MRASW aircraft and both of which would require to be miniaturised for fitment in a helicopter.

In the light of the pros and cons of all these options, views became divided, both in the Air Arm and in the Navy, for and against the Seaking and the Super Puma. Eventually, when the choice was made in favour of the Seaking Mk 42 B, there was speculation that the choice had been made on extraneous considerations.

It is more likely, however, that the primary factor was to standardise on Seakings, minimise the cost of additional infrastructure and capitalise on the ten years experience of operating Seakings in India's tropical conditions.

In July 1983, agreements were signed with:
- British Westlands for the helicopters;
- British Rolls Royce for the spare engines;
- British Marconi for the Hermes ESM;
- French Thompson CSF for the HS 12 sonar;
- Italian Whitehead Motofides for the A 244 S torpedo installation.

After the Seaking Mk 42 B was chosen as the basic platform, the software had to be developed to integrate the equipment chosen by the Navy into a Tactical Mission System. Delays started being experienced in developing this software. The Indian team deputed to Britain for inspection and trials helped to develop the software and devised a number of modifications to improve the overall effectiveness of the system. Eventually, when the Seakings Mk 42 B entered service in 1988, two years later than scheduled, they were fitted with:
- Composite fuselage and rotor blades (the development of which had also delayed delivery);

- The French HS 12 dunking sonar;
- The British LAPADS sonobuoy system ;
- The British Sea Eagle anti ship missile;
- The British Hermes ESM system.

Commander Purohit was deputed to Britain as part of the team for the induction of the Seaking Mk 42 Bs. He recalls:

"The Indian Navy constituted a multi disciplinary team consisting of air engineers, air electricals and experienced Seaking aircrew. The team, which was sent to UK actually did the work of developing and defining the parameters and algorithms. This team was actually behind the development of the entire software for this helicopter and we should be proud of it. The bigger problem was of developing the software with the Tactical Mission System of the 42 Bravo. In the process we acquired the confidence to undertake the techniques of interfacing weapons with platforms.

"After the 42 Bravos started arriving in India, Naval Headquarters took the very wise decision that before these helicopters were deployed as operational units, they must be tactically evaluated and a document be promulgated for their optimum utilisation and exploitation. The UK manufacturers had given only the capabilities of the sensors. These capabilities had to be evaluated in our environment, our work culture, our operating philosophy and our ship capabilities.

"Based in Cochin, this was done by the Intensive Flying Training Unit (IFTU) in a period of ten months. Naval Headquarters, Southern Naval Command and Western Naval Command made available their best units. Whichever ship, submarine or aircraft was asked for, it was always provided. Handpicked aircrew carried out very intensive flying. We looked at maintenance practices; we tried to establish failure rates; which kind of failure we should expect; which items were more likely to fail for which more spares should be procured. We operated with every type of ship, every type of submarine, every type of aircraft and used every sensor under controlled and methodically planned conditions.

"At the end of it, we came out with a Guide Book that was prepared by the IFTU and the School of Maritime Warfare and Tactics and had been actually tested in operational conditions with inputs coming from submarines, ships and aircraft. There was complete interaction between the surface, sub-surface and airborne Navy.

"The punch and the capability that the 42 Bravo has are amongst the best in the world. We could not have had it if we had not taken the bold step of contracting

INS *VIKRANT* prior to the fitment of the ski jump

INS *VIRAAT* fitted with ski jump

Dec 1983 on *VIKRANT's* flight deck to witness Sea Harrier operations at sea. Standing (from left) CO of 300 Squadron Cdr (now Admiral) Arun Prakash; Prime Minister Mrs Indira Gandhi; (on her left) Chief of the Naval Staff Adm OS Dawson; (third from right) QFI of 300 Squadron Lt Cdr (now Rear Adm) Shekhar Sinha. Mr Rajiv Gandhi, later Prime Minister of India, can be seen behind him

Sea Harrier - Vertical/Short Takeoff & Land (V/STOL) Aircraft hovering over *VIKRANT's* Flight Deck prior to vertical landing

Sea Harrier taking off from INS *VIRAAT's* ski jump (1980s)

Aircraft Carriers *VIRAAT* (foreground) and *VIKRANT* (background) at sea in 1990

During the 'Beating Retreat' ceremony in New Delhi on 29 January 1984, an enthralled audience saw a Sea Harrier flown by Cdr (now Admiral) Arun Prakash fly slowly into Vijay Chowk, stop in hover, turn to face the President of India, dip the aircraft's nose in salute, turn away and take off skywards

Sea Harriers parked to the right of *VIKRANT's* ski jump (1989)

Anti submarine *Seaking Mk 42* helicopter in hover and lowering its sonar body into the sea.
INS *VIKRANT* in the background (1970s)

Seaking Mk 42 B armed with two Sea Eagle anti ship missiles

Russian Anti Submarine *Kamov 25* helicopter-twin contra-rotating rotors (1980s)

Commando version British *Seaking Mk 42 C* (1980s)

Russian *IL 38* - Maritime Reconnaissance & Anti Submarine Aircraft (1970s)

Russian LRMP *TU 142* and British *Sea Harrier* air defence fighter aircraft (1980s)

Maritime Patrol Aircraft (MPA) *Dornier 228*

for something which nobody had and which was still in the concept stage."

Twenty anti submarine Seakings Mk 42 B were inducted between April 1988 and 1992. These were for the Godavari class frigates and the aircraft carriers *Vikrant* and *Viraat*. In the anti ship role, the Mk 42 Bs were capable of firing Sea Eagle anti ship missiles. Of the Mk 42 Bs, three have been lost, leaving seventeen in service.

The Mk 42 Cs

Each indigenous Landing Ship Tank (Large) was designed to embark two troop-carrying helicopters. In May 1985, sanction was accorded for three Seakings Mk 42 C for the first LST (L). Sanction was also accorded for three Mk 42 Cs for the Marine Commandos defending the offshore oil platforms at Bombay High. These six Seakings Mk 42 C arrived in 1987. All six are in service.

The Russian Kamov Series

The Ka 25s

The twin-engine Kamov 25s were acquired for the first three Russian guided missile destroyers ordered in 1975. The first Ka 25 entered service with the commissioning of the guided missile destroyer *Rajput* in Russia in March 1980. On 11 December 1980, the Kamov helicopter squadron was commissioned at Hansa and designated INAS 333.

A total of seven Ka 25s were inducted starting in October 1979, of which one was lost, leaving six in service.

The Ka 28s

By 1981, when the contract was signed for the next two guided missile destroyers, the Ka 25s had gone out of production and had been replaced by the Ka 28s. A total of thirteen Ka 28s were inducted starting on 7 July 1986, of which two have been lost, leaving eleven in service.

INAS 321 – Chetak SAR Helicopter Squadron

The French Alouette III light helicopters, productionised by HAL as 'Chetaks', first entered service in 1964.

When this squadron commissioned as INAS 321 on 15 March 1969, it comprised the SAR flights of *Vikrant, Hansa, Garuda* and *Deepak*. In subsequent years, flights embarked, whenever required, in:

- The old ships – *Trishul* and *Talwar* after they had been fitted with missiles, and in *Brahmaputra*, Beas and *Betwa* after conversion to the training role.
- The new ships – cadet training ship Tir, tanker Shakti,

survey ships, LST(M)s, offshore patrol vessels (OPVs) and Khukri class corvettes of Project 25.

Since most ships were based in Bombay, embarkations were of short duration. INAS 321 relocated to *INS Kunjali* in Bombay on 1 August 1980.

In the early 1980s, HAL indicated that they were considering discontinuing the production of Chetak helicopters. Since the production of the replacement ALHs would take considerable time, HAL continued production.

A total of 85 Chetaks had been inducted into the Navy till 2002, of which 19 have been lost, leaving 66 in service.

Genesis and Development of the Advanced Light Helicopter (ALH)

In 1967, the Government had constituted the Aeronautics Committee to recommend the priorities for self-reliance. In 1969, the Committee recommended that capability should be developed for designing helicopters. In 1970, the Defence Committee of the Cabinet approved the conclusion of a Technical Assistance agreement with the French firm of SNIAS to design, develop and produce an Armed Light Helicopter for the Army, Air Force and Navy as a successor to the Cheetah and the Chetak. The Helicopter Design Bureau was established in 1970.

In 1976, financial sanction was accorded for the development of the single engine helicopter. In 1977, based on the feedback of the Vietnam War and the Arab-Israel conflict, the Air Force recommended to the Helicopter Steering Committee that the ALH should be twin-engined. In 1979, approval was accorded for the twin-engine configuration and the project was renamed as Advanced Light Helicopter.

In 1984, sanction was accorded for the development of the twin engined ALH under technical consultancy of the German firm of Messerschmitt-Bulkow-Blöhm (MBB).[7] Each of the three services had estimated its requirement at over a hundred ALHs.

The Navy's staff requirements had envisaged a medium sized helicopter that, within an all up weight of about 5,000 kg, (lighter than the 10,000 kg Seaking but heavier than the Alouette), would permit its role to be changed to carry out anti submarine (ASW), anti ship (ASV), commando carrying (Utility) or Search and Rescue (SAR) missions.

The ASW variant is planned to have sonar, sonics, EW, weather radar, a Tactical Mission System (TMS) and armed with homing torpedoes / depth charges. The ASV version

---

7. MBB's present name is Eurocopter-Deutschland.

is planned to have fire control radar, EW, TMS and armed with anti ship missiles. The Utility version is planned to have a rescue hoist and the ability for medical evacuation by stretcher, ferry up to 14 personnel, slither commandos, etc.

Commodore Purohit recalls

"After our experience in the development of the 42 Bravo, NHQ rightly placed an experienced and well chosen team of officers at the full-time disposal of HAL. We brought about significant changes, which have combined pragmatism with the requirement. We have simplified the ALH to the extent possible so as to reduce our maintenance problems, reduce inventory cost and increase the availability on any given day because we know what happens on board ship where spares are hard to come by, test equipment is hard to come by and we cannot afford to have too many spares. We have methodically used our experience of the 42s, the 42 Alphas and the 42 Bravos in ensuring that the chosen sensors are more reliable. They require less maintenance, they are more compact and they cause fewer problems."

Maritime Reconnaissance

Background

The system inherited from the British was that the Air Force operated Maritime Rreconnaissance MR aircraft for the Navy. The hostilities with Pakistan in 1965 highlighted the inadequacy of this arrangement. In 1966, the Navy recommended to the Government that responsibility for MR and the command and control of shore based MR aircraft be transferred from the Air Force to the Navy. The Air Force was not agreeable and preferred status quo. Cogent reasons were advanced for and against the Navy's proposal.

The Navy's position was that correct recognition of enemy warships at sea and the subsequent co-ordination of tactical action with cooperating surface forces required such extensive training that it was more cost effective for MR aircrews to be naval officers familiar with flying over the sea. It was for this reason that in all the major navies of the world (USA, Russia, Japan, China, France, Germany and Holland), MR aircraft were controlled and operated solely by the Navy. The only exceptions were Britain, India and Australia.

This was because in the early years of the British Air Force at the beginning of the 20th century, MR had been solely an Air Force responsibility. After the 1914-1918 World War, the Coastal Command of the Royal Air Force

had been formed from the Royal Naval Air Service and was largely manned by naval aviators who had transferred en bloc to the RAF Coastal Command at birth. Naval experience had, therefore, been available to the RAF and it was on this foundation that the RAF Coastal Command had evolved. Commonwealth countries like India and Australia had unquestioningly adopted the British model and in view of the developments in naval warfare, there was no justification for its continuance.

The Air Force position was that in the British Manual of Joint Operations, MR was a joint responsibility, that this system had stood the test of time in Britain and Australia, that there would be greater flexibility in aircraft utilisation if MR remained with the Air Force, (since the aircraft could be used for other roles as well) and that in the 1965 operations, the Air Force had done the best it could to meet the Navy's MR requirement within the inadequate resources available.

After prolonged discussions, it was decided to maintain the status quo. The Air Force was to remain responsible for MR as long as the existing Super Constellation aircraft were in service. The question of command and control of MR would be reviewed when considering the induction of new MR aircraft.

In subsequent years:

- From Pune and Bangalore, the Air Force continued to operate the vintage 1939-45 War Liberators and the Super Constellations airliners phased out by Air India.

- Every major Fleet exercise repeatedly highlighted the number of carrier-launched air strikes that were wasted at sea, time and again, because of mistaken identification. It became clear that the correct identification of ships at sea required extremely high skills of aircrews to distinguish between, and positively identify, own, enemy and neutral ships.

- The Joint Sea Air Warfare Committee evaluated the French Atlantic and the British Nimrod MRASW aircraft.

Decision for the Navy to Acquire MRASW Aircraft

During the 1971 war, a Pakistan Navy submarine sank the Indian frigate *Khukri*. After the war, the Navy pressed its requirement for a versatile MRASW aircraft having radar, sonobuoy systems, sensors like magnetic anomaly detector (MAD), and submarine diesel exhaust trail indicator (sniffer), which could rapidly search a probable submarine operating area, locate a surfaced or snorting submarine whilst recharging batteries and with its weapons attack and sink the submarine.

In anti submarine operations, MRASW aircraft, anti submarine helicopters and anti submarine ships are three elements of a mutually supporting system. The high degree of coordinated response by each of these elements to effectively counter submarine evasive action is best achieved when all three elements are naval.

In addition to its primary anti submarine role, this type of aircraft would also meet the Navy's pressing need for maritime reconnaissance.

The Navy, therefore, urged the Government for an early decision to acquire a suitable naval MRASW aircraft. The available options were the British Nimrod, the French Atlantic and the Russian IL 38.

In May 1973, the Government accepted the Navy's reasoning and approved, in principle, the acquisition of four shore-based MRASW aircraft. The rise in oil prices after the Arab-Israel war of October 1973 created a shortage of foreign exchange and ruled out the purchase of either the Atlantic or the Nimrod.

Efforts then focused on obtaining IL 38 MRASW aircraft from Russia. The IL 38 production line was closing down. The Russian Navy was reluctant to spare these aircraft. After persuasion, the Russian side agreed and in February 1975, an agreement was signed for the acquisition of three IL 38s. In June 1975, Government took the decision to vest the command, control and operation of the IL 38s with the Navy.

Shri Govind Narain was the Defence Secretary in 1976. He recalls:

"The control of the air reconnaissance system over the sea was in the hands of the Air Force. The Navy wanted this control to be transferred to it. This matter had been pending with the Government for nearly 10 years and it could not get resolved. In the 1971 war, all the three wings of the defence forces played a very significant part and all concerned could observe their respective roles. The performance of the Navy in Karachi was brilliant and the whole country was very impressed.

"Pressure continued to mount from the Naval side that they would do even better if their operators felt more confident, if the air recce system was also within their own control. On the other hand, the Air Force pleaded that they had all the airfield arrangements, they had all the know how, they knew which aircraft from which

country could be best for what purpose, they had the maintenance facilities. All these were very strong points.

"When this matter came repeatedly to the Defence Ministry, what we did was to send the whole problem to the Committee of the three Chiefs of Staff and told them to deliberate afresh on these problems. We gave them two months time to come back to the Defence Ministry with an agreed solution. Whatever agreed solution was found would be acceptable to the Defence Ministry.

"At the end of the two months, no solution was forthcoming. In individual discussions, the three Chiefs expressed their helplessness that no agreement could be reached. We gave them another two months time to reconsider this matter as it was very urgent, very important and required their considered views. But again the matter remained with them for two more months and there was no solution forthcoming. Then we discussed with the three Chiefs that if they could not reach any conclusion, would they like the Defence Ministry to consider the whole matter objectively and find a solution. All the three Chiefs agreed that this should be done.

"Thus the matter came to be considered in the Defence Ministry. We collected the necessary information from the various countries of the world, which had developed a system of maritime reconnaissance. Then we analysed our own position. We went into great details of the points of view of the Navy. We went into great details of the points of view of the Air Force. Then we in the Defence Ministry prepared an elaborate note of 20 or 25 pages, putting down all points of view and reached the conclusion that it would be more prudent if maritime reconnaissance was put under the control of the Navy but the maintenance of the aircraft could be left with the Air Force. Naturally the Navy was jubilant and the Air Force was unhappy, but this solution was accepted by the Defence Minister, by the Political Affairs Committee of the Cabinet and finally by the Prime Minister and was enforced as a Government order."[8]

Transfer of the Super Constellations to the Navy[9]

The contract for the IL 38s had been signed in 1975 for delivery in 1977. A large number of aircrew and maintenance personnel had been sent to the Soviet Union to undergo training on the IL 38. In 1976, the

---

8. This is a noteworthy example of how the Ministry of Defence resolved a contentious problem where each Service Headquarters held strongly held and persuasive professional views.

9. Some of the inter-service 'gamesmanship' that followed the IL 38 decision and led to the offer of transfer of the Super Constellations has been recounted in the Air Arm chapter of the previous volume 'Transition to Triumph'.

Air Force attempted to retrieve the situation. It offered to immediately hand over some of their old Super Constellation MR aircraft to the Navy. The offer had a caveat. Should the Navy not be able to cope with the large multi-engine Super Constellations, then the MR role, along with the Super Constellations and the IL 38s as well should revert to the Air Force.

In 1976, Rear Admiral (later Vice Admiral) NP Datta was the Deputy Chief of the Naval Staff in charge of the Naval Air Arm. He recalls:

"The most interesting episode during my tenure as DCNS was the acquisition of maritime reconnaissance capability. We had been trying for the Navy to take over maritime reconnaissance since 1965 when I happened to be in NHQ in the Personnel Branch. Admiral Soman was the Naval Chief at that time. He sent for me one day. Since I had been his Fleet Operations Officer, he used to consult me occasionally. He said, 'The question has come up of the Navy taking over maritime reconnaissance and would I prepare a note, which would be put before the Chiefs of Staff Committee'. So in 1965, we fired the first salvo why the Navy should have maritime reconnaissance aircraft. The Air Force reaction was straightforward – 'over our dead body'. Therefore, we did not make much headway at the Chiefs of Staff Committee. We approached the Ministry of Defence directly and both sides argued their cases vigorously. The Defence Minister, Sardar Swaran Singh, must have got quite fed up. He wanted the two services to settle it. He did not want to be an arbitrator between the two services.

"From our point of view, a stroke of good luck was when Air Chief Marshal Moolgavkar took over as Chief of Air Staff. He had the reputation of being an ace fighter pilot and he decided to 'go for the jugular vein'. He wrote a letter to the Defence Minister, copy to the CNS, saying that instead of creating bad blood between the two services, he had five Super Constellation aircraft that they were operating and in his opinion, the Navy did not have the expertise to operate this kind of big multi-engined aircraft, as the Air Force themselves were finding it difficult. Since the Navy was so keen on having maritime reconnaissance, he made an offer. He was prepared to hand over the five Constellations to the Navy. He was prepared to help during a transition period of six months to train our pilots and maintenance engineers. After that, he would withdraw all his people and then the Navy could operate these aircraft. If the Navy made a success of it, then the Navy could keep the MR role. On the other hand, in case the Navy had accidents and was not able to maintain them nor able to operate them and not able to get the flying hours, then the Navy should shut up forever and let the Air Force keep maritime reconnaissance.

"When this proposal came to NHQ, the CNS, Admiral Cursetji, sent for me and said, 'This is a booby trap and we should not fall into it.' I replied, 'Sir, I think, it is a booby trap all right, but not for us – it is for the Air Force. If you are challenged, you must accept.' He said, 'No, No, Moolgavkar is a very experienced man, he knows our difficulties. We are a small plane operator, single engine maintainer. The aeroplanes that they fly are twenty times the size of our aircraft. How can we maintain them, how can we operate them, how can we fly them?' I said, 'I will consult the Naval Air Staff and I will come back to you.'

"So I sent for my DNAS, Commodore Puri, and DNAM, Commodore Joginder Singh, From their professional point of view, they threw their hands up. Puri said, 'No, sir, I cannot spare the pilots.' And Joginder Singh said, 'I have not got the maintenance engineers, or the extra tools, or the bodies to maintain them. I don't think we should take them.'

"It looked like the situation was out of our hands. But the more they resisted, the more cussed I became. I said, 'Instead of saying no, go and find ways in which we can take them over. I give you a week.' They came back and said, 'There are various ways of doing it. We don't operate certain types of aircraft. We will withdraw them from service, send up some people for training with the Soviets for multi-engine aircraft, withdraw some people from training and likewise for maintenance personnel.'

"Meanwhile I had been making my own inquiries and found that maintenance was a complete bugbear. The entire maintenance of the Constellations was being done by Air India at Bombay. I went down to Bombay and asked the Air India people to show me around. They showed me around a cavernous stock room in which they had about 15 years of spares for these Constellation aircraft. They said, 'We will never use these in their life time, they will all go waste. So there is no problem. You send them to us for first line, second line and third line maintenance. We will do it for you, because we are doing it already and that's how the Air Force is operating them. They do no maintenance of their own.' That was one strong point that I explained to Joginder Singh and he said, 'Yes, that is a possibility.' As regards Puri, I think it ultimately came down to 'I will ground the Seahawk squadron', which really did not make much difference, because the aircraft carrier was going in for a long refit anyway. So we reduced the strength of the pilots on training duties at Goa and we sent them all for training all over the place.

"Slowly, within six months we were able to man these aircraft, first of all under the supervision of the Air Force and then on our own. The individual Air Force officers were very cooperative and they trained our people. But when it looked like becoming a success, the Air Force gradually withdrew them much before the six month stipulated period. So when six months were over, we were entirely on our own. And we slowly picked up the expertise for maintaining them and operating them successfully.

"As it turned out, we were able to get more flying hours out of those five ancient machines than the Air Force ever did. This experience helped us when acquiring the Russian IL 38 maritime aircraft, which we were able to fly and operate in no time. Ever since then, maritime reconnaissance has been an integral part of the Navy.

"Sometimes it pays if you are thrown into the deep end."

Five Super Constellation aircraft of the Air Force's No 6 Squadron at Pune were taken over from the Air Force on 18 November 1976 and designated INAS 312.

Four Super Connies were phased out between April 1981 and September 1983. The fifth aircraft collapsed whilst taxiing out in January 1983.

The squadron was wound down in January 1984 awaiting the arrival of replacements. In due course, the Super Connies were replaced by the Russian TU 142s, which started arriving in 1988.

Induction of IL 38s for MRASW (INAS 315)

Three IL 38s arrived in Goa in October 1977. The requirement steadily increased for these aircraft to be available for concurrent MR in the Bay of Bengal and the Arabian Sea, and for concurrent ASW exercises with the Western and Eastern Fleets.

In 1979, the Soviet side was requested to supply five more IL 38s. Their response was that the aircraft were going out of production and that the Indian side should indicate their requirements of what their replacements should have. The Navy indicated that the requirement was for longer endurance at longer range.

Since the three ILs in service fell due for major overhaul in Russia at the same time, the Soviet side was again urged to release five ILs from their Navy. Eventually, a contract was signed in May 1981 for two more IL 38s and these aircraft joined the squadron in 1983.

A total of 5 IL 38s had been inducted into the Navy, of which 2 have been lost, leaving 3 in service.

Induction of TU 142s for LRMP (INAS 312)

In 1981, in response to the Navy's requirement for MRASW aircraft having longer endurance at longer range, the Soviet side stated that they would not be able to supply new aircraft but would examine the possibility of providing refurbished TU 142 aircraft from their existing fleet.

The Navy was hesitant about the TU because its much larger size, much heavier weight and different equipment would require the runways to be upgraded and extended and maintenance facilities to be augmented. The Navy, therefore, pressed for three of the IL 38s being phased out of the Russian Navy to be refurbished. The Russian side was unable to do this. Eventually, an agreement was signed in December 1984 for the acquisition of eight TUs.

A total of 40 pilots and observers, 16 technical officers and 128 sailors underwent twelve months training in batches at Riga commencing May 1987. On completion of training, these personnel were sub-divided specialisation-wise and appointed to man the squadron, the Base Maintenance Facility at Goa and the Naval Air Technical School at Kochi. Four sets of aircrew were trained.

On 30 March 1988, the first three TU 142 M aircraft took off from Simferopol in the Crimean peninsula and arrived at Goa after a non-stop flight. Two more aircraft arrived on 13th April.

The squadron was commissioned at Hansa on 16th April and designated INAS 312. The remaining three aircraft arrived between August and October 1988.

In May 1992, the squadron relocated to the new naval air station INS Rajali at Arkonam on the east coast of India.

The Maritime Patrol Aircraft (MPA) Dornier 228s

In the early 1980s, consideration commenced of the indigenous production of a 'Light Transport Aircraft', the LTA, to meet the needs of the Air Force, the Navy, the Coast Guard and of Vayudoot, the feeder airline for Indian Airlines. The concept was to have a common airframe and a common engine and fit it with equipment to suit the needs of individual customers. Each service had given its basic staff requirements. The Navy gave its requirements in terms of endurance and sensor loads.

Four aircraft were evaluated. The British Islander, the German Dornier, the Italian Casa and the American Twin Otter. The Dornier did not meet the Air Force needs. The Navy, the Coast Guard and Vayudoot found that the Dornier best met their needs. The Dornier was chosen for production at HAL Kanpur.

The evaluation of the productionised version, called Dornier 228, was done in Germany. The Navy envisaged the Dorniers as replacements for the Alizes in INAS 310.

In 1986, sanction was accorded for the Navy to acquire 10 Dorniers (3 for observer training, 4 for surveillance and 3 as MRSOW) equipped with radar and air-to-surface missiles. Sanction was also accorded for 4 Dorniers, funded by the Ministry of Petroleum, equipped only with radar and IFF transponders (similar to the Coast Guard version) for the surveillance around the offshore oil assets of Bombay High.

The drought of 1986 led to financial stringency and for the next few years, no foreign exchange could be released to HAL for the Dornier's radars and missiles. HAL postponed the delivery of the Dorniers to 30 months after the release of foreign exchange. Eventually, orders were placed in 1990 on HAL for one 'fly-away' Naval Dornier and 4 Dorniers for Bombay High in which the radars would be retrofitted.

New Naval Air Stations

The naval air station at Port Blair was commissioned as *INS Utkrosh* on 11 May 1984.

Development of Aircraft Operating Facilities Ashore

	WEST COAST	EAST COAST
Upgradation of Existing Major Air Stations	*INS Hansa* at Goa *INS Garuda* at Cochin	
New Major Air Stations	@Kalyan near Bombay/ Enclave at Santa Cruz Bombay	*INS Dega* at Vishakhapatnam *INS Rajali* at Arakkonam
Minor Naval Air Stations	NAS Kunjali II at Bombay *Daman @Belgaum @Sulur	*INS Utkrosh* at Port Blair
Forward Operating Bases	@Mangalore *Trivandrum	@Kayattar Enclave at Meenambakkam Madras Campbell Bay in Great Nicobar @Kavaratti in Lakshadweep Diglipur in North Andaman
Advance Landing Grounds for ASW Helicopters	Okha Porbandar Diu	

By 1990, naval facilities had been established at all the locations except:
● At Daman and Trivandrum marked * where the Navy shared the facilities developed by the Coast Guard.
● At the locations marked @ where, for technical/financial reasons, it was decided not to create exclusively naval facilities.

By the early 1980s, the Navy's infrastructure development plan for shore facilities had crystallised under five broad headings.

Trainer Aircraft

Islanders (INAS 550)

In 1972, there was a sharp increase in the requirement for Observer officers. The Air Force was unable to accommodate the Navy's needs. Experience had also shown that the purely navigation oriented training being imparted by the Air Force to naval Observers had to be supplemented by sorties over the sea. A proposal was initiated to acquire a suitable aircraft for training Observer officers, for coastal reconnaissance and for Fleet requirements.[10]

After comparative evaluation of available options, the British made, piston-engined, propeller-driven Islander (BN2A) was chosen. The first two Islanders arrived in Cochin and joined INAS 550 on 18 May 1976. The remaining three arrived by end 1976.

In 1981, two Islanders of INAS 550 were based at Port Blair for the surveillance of the A&N Islands. In 1984, these were commissioned as INAS 318 when the naval air station at Port Blair was commissioned as *INS Utkrosh*. Two more Islanders were procured for INAS 550 in Kochi. In end 1996, six 2T variant Islanders were acquired for INAS 550.

In May 2000, an Islander Flight was positioned at Dega.

A total of 17 Islanders had been inducted into the Navy, of which 4 have been lost, leaving 13 in service.

Kiran Jet Training Aircraft (INAS 551)

The Vampires were phased out by 1976. In 1978, the last of the Seahawks was returned to INAS 300.

Eight Kirans Mk II (the armed version) ex HAL Bangalore joined the squadron between July 1987 and February 1988. These aircraft are used for training jet pilots for the frontline squadron, for meeting fleet requirements like anti aircraft tracking practices and for consolidation flying of staff pilots.

---

10. The Fleet Requirement Unit (FRU) had commissioned as INAS 550 on 17 June 1959. At that time it had consisted of 10 Amphibian Sealands, 10 Fireflies and 3 HT 2s.

A total of 23 Kirans had been inducted into the Navy, of which 9 have been lost, leaving 14 in service.

Sea Harrier Training Squadron (INAS 551 B)

In December 1990, INAS 551 B was established as an independent Sea Harrier Training Squadron at Goa. This unit began undertaking the *ab initio* conversion on Sea Harrier aircraft and relieved 300 Squadron of this commitment.

Personnel

Observers

By 1978, an acute shortage had built up in the Observer Cadre. Several factors had contributed to this shortage:

- The steady rise in demand. From manning only Alizes from 1961 onwards, new manning requirements had arisen for Observers to man Seakings in 1970, the Islanders in 1975, the IL 38s in 1976, and the Kamovs in 1978. Also, the increase in night flying (in Goa by IL 38s and in Cochin by the Seakings) required more Observers in the naval air stations.

- The Air Force was unable to train the additional observers required by the Navy. Islander aircraft were acquired to enable the Navy to train its observers.

- The duration of observer training had to be increased to cover specific naval requirements of practical training in ASW and maritime surveillance.

- A shortage of volunteers, caused by a perception that career prospects in the Observer cadre were not as good as in other cadres.

- Even though the strength of trainees per course was doubled from 3 to 6, the attrition during their rigorous training was 1 to 2 officers per course.

Pilots

By the early 1980s, the Navy's requirements of pilots exceeded what the Air Force was willing to train. The Navy started considering undertaking the *ab initio* training of its pilots in Cochin. The trainer aircraft evaluated were HAL's HPT 36 and the Russian MIG trainers being considered by the Air Force. It transpired that the Air Force required all the HPT 36s that HAL could produce and had dropped consideration of the MIG trainer. Without a trainer aircraft, there was no way that the Navy could train its pilots. It continued to train its pilots with the Air Force.

Aircrew Categorisation and Standardisation Board

By 1979, the diversity of aircraft and helicopters in naval service had increased substantially. Ashore, Super Constellations, IL 38s, Kirans and Islanders had entered service. On board ships, there were Seakings in *Vikrant*, Seaking Mk 42 As in *Taragiri* and *Vindhyagiri*, Kamovs in the Rajput class destroyers, MATCH in the earlier Leanders and Chetaks in a number of ships. The demand on skills of aircrew varied from aircraft to aircraft.

It was decided to establish a Board that would periodically categorise the professional knowledge of aircrew, on lines similar to what was being done by the Air Force's Aircrew Examination Board (AEB). Establishing standard procedures and yardsticks by which professional merit could be assessed and graded, would help to improve professionalism, aircrew motivation and individual career development. A naval team studied the Air Force AEB system, reoriented it towards naval operational requirements and formulated a standard syllabus, procedure and assessment system for grading each category of aircrew – pilots, observers, flight engineers, flight signallers, aircrew divers and air traffic control officers.

The Aircrew Categorisation and Standardisation Board (AIRCATS) was established in 1983 and based at Goa. Their primary duty was to carry out aircrew categorisation and standardisation and conduct Flight Safety Inspection of all units once in a year.

In subsequent years, AIRCATS fully met the objectives for which it had been set up.

Navy-Air Force-Army Pilot Exchange Programme

By the mid 1980s, the inter-service pilot exchange programme had stabilised as follows:

	Fixed Wing Aircraft	Helicopters
Navy pilots with the Air Force were flying	MIGs and Ajeets	MI 8s
Navy pilots with the Army were flying	-	Air OP Chetaks
Air Force pilots with the Navy were flying	Sea Harriers	Seakings and Chetaks
Army pilots with the Navy were flying	-	Chetaks

Developments After 1990

Aircraft Carriers

Vikrant

Vikrant underwent a short 6-month refit in 1991 and was operational for 10 months. She underwent a 14-month refit from 1992 to 1994 and was operational flying Sea Harriers, Seakings and Chetaks until her final sea outing on 23 November 1994.

In January 1995, NHQ directed that *Vikrant* be kept 'Safe to Float' and that no further refit/dry docking be planned. She was laid up until she was decommissioned on 31 January 1997.

Viraat

During her refit in Britain prior to commissioning in 1987, *Viraat's* underwater hull had been shot blasted and coated with the latest special long-life paint so that she would not require bottom cleaning for at least five years. It had also been decided that until the new graving dock was commissioned in Bombay, *Viraat* would be docked in Cochin Shipyard.

The first docking of *Viraat* in 1991 was followed by a second short docking in 1995 for repairs. She underwent refit and modernisation from 1999 to 2001. Phase I Medium Refit and Dry Docking at Cochin Shipyard lasted from May 1999 to November 2000. The modernisation Phase II at Naval Dockyard Bombay lasted till April 2001.

Except for these docking and refit periods, *Viraat* was operational throughout and participated in Fleet exercises.

Gorshkov

The 44,500 tonne, steam propelled *Gorshkov* is the second of the series of three aircraft carriers, *Minsk, Baku* (renamed *Gorshkov*) and *Ulganov* built to succeed the Kiev class carriers. Baku had commissioned in 1987, served in the Soviet Black Sea Fleet and later in Russia's Northern Fleet. She was operational until 1996.

After the Soviet Union dissolved and Russia started downsizing its Navy due to financial constraints, the Russian side offered the *Gorshkov* to India, along with MIG 29 K aircraft developed specifically for carrier borne operations.[11] The acquisition of *Gorshkov* formed part of the joint Indo-Russian Protocol on Military Technical Cooperation signed in December 1994. The financial aspects were unusual – *Gorshkov* 'as is, where is' would be free; India need only pay for the cost of refit and the aircraft.

As had been done in the case of *Viraat*, the Navy thoroughly examined *Gorshkov's* material state, assessed the magnitude of the modernisation and refit that would be required and identified the essential requirements of new equipment, weapons and systems.

The Short Take Off But Arrested Recovery (STOBAR) MiG 29 K aircraft to be acquired with the *Gorshkov* would, like the Sea Harriers, take off from a ski jump and land, like the Sea Hawks, by hooking on to arrestor wires.

In January 2004, the agreement was signed for the acquisition of the *Gorshkov* and its aircraft.[12] The ship was to undergo a four and a half year refit in which she would be extensively refitted and nearly 80% of her equipment replaced with modern equivalents. Expected to commission in 2008, she would serve the Navy for over two decades, during which period the indigenous Air Defence Ship should enter service.

Indigenous Air Defence Ship

Approval was accorded in 2000 for the Air Defence Ship (ADS) to be built in Kochi Shipyard. The acquisition of the STOBAR MIG 29 K aircraft with the *Gorshkov* removed the grey area of the type of aircraft that this ship should be designed for. Meanwhile, development is continuing of the navalised version of the Air Force's Light Combat Aircraft (LCA). The naval LCA, like the MIG 29 K would be a STOBAR aircraft. Its operation from both the Gorshkov and the ADS would enable cross-operation.

Sea Harriers

By 1992, the last of the Sea Harriers ordered in the 1980s had arrived. Thereafter, all the earlier Sea Harriers were upgraded in India to Batch 2 standard.

Further improvements were also approved. These included better indigenous radar warning receivers, self-protection jammers, Global Positioning System (GPS), etc.

Efforts continue to acquire affordable pulse doppler radars, longer range 'Beyond Visual Range' air to air missiles and 'smart' data links.

As replacements for the aircraft lost, an order was placed for two-second hand, ex British Navy, Sea Harrier trainer aircraft. These arrived in early 2003.

Maritime Reconnaissance

The IL 38s and TU 142s acquired in the 1980s continued to meet the Navy's requirements. Until replacements could be identified and acquired, it was planned to extend the life of both these types of aircraft as long as possible.

---

11. The fourth generation MiG 29 K carrier borne fighter aircraft (of the same lineage as, but different from, the Indian Air Force MiG 29) had been developed for the Russian Navy's aircraft carriers.

12. In the true spirit of inter-service cooperation, the Air Force was fully associated with the evaluation, negotiations and contractual provisions of the Navy's MiG 29 K aircraft.

The first naval Dornier from HAL joined INAS 310 on 24 August 1991. The second Dornier arrived later in 1991 and the next two in 1992. The fifth Dornier was delivered fitted with the Super Marec (maritime reconnaissance) radar. In subsequent years, the remaining Dorniers were retrofitted with this radar during their major inspections by HAL Kanpur.

For the coastal reconnaissance role, ten more Dorniers were acquired, in addition to the five acquired earlier. These Dorniers were progressively fitted with ESM, GPS and sonobuoy systems for the surveillance, ASW and EW roles.

By 2002, the Navy had acquired a fleet of 15 Dorniers.

Anti Submarine Helicopters

Seakings

The Seakings acquired in the 1970s were phased out as they reached the end of their useful life.

The Seakings MK 42 B, acquired in the 1980s continued to perform well. By 2000, the need was felt for more such helicopters and evaluations commenced for their successors.

Kamovs

The Kamov 25 continued to operate from the first three destroyers *Rajput*, *Rana* and *Ranjit*. Its successor, the Kamov 28, continued to operate in the next two destroyers *Ranvir* and *Ranvijay*. It was larger than the Kamov 25 and too big to fit into the Kamov 25 hangars.

Advanced Light Helicopters (ALH)

The ALH has emerged as a multi role helicopter in the 4.5 to 5.5 tonne weight class, designed and developed by HAL to meet the specific needs of different customers like the Army, the Navy, the Air Force, the Coast Guard and civilian organisations like ONGC, Pawan Hans etc. Its advanced technologies include the Integrated Dynamic System, Hingeless Main Rotor, Bearingless Tail Rotor, 4-axis Automatic Flight Control System, Full Authority Digital Electronic Control System and 6-axis Anti Resonant Isolation System.

The first flight of the Army / Air Force prototype flew in 1994 and that of the Navy in 1995. Series production started in 1996 and deliveries commenced in 2002.

At the time of writing, delivery to the Navy of the Utility variant ALHs has commenced. Deliveries of the ASW variant are expected to commence in 2005 and of the ASV variant in 2007.

Airborne Early Warning

With the advent of anti ship missiles in the 1970s, a clear operational need had emerged for the Navy to have airborne early warning aircraft. This would increase the reaction time required for dealing with hostile platforms before they came close enough to our own force to fire their missiles.

Large rotodome fitted aircraft, of the type the Americans and the Russians had, were neither available nor affordable. An indigenous R&D project to fit a rotodome on an Avro aircraft was unsuccessful.

The Navy pinned its hopes on acquiring AEW helicopters that were then under development. The British Seaking MK 42 D turned out to be too expensive. The Russian Kamov 31 was preferred and negotiations were concluded for their acquisition. Four KA 31s were inducted in early 2003.

New Naval Air Stations

With the increasing number of helicopters on board the ships based in Bombay, it became necessary to have a helipad area from where helicopters could continue flying when ships were alongside. In view of its proximate location, *INS Kunjali* became the Navy's helicopter base in Bombay.

For similar reasons, a naval air station was commissioned at Vishakhapatnam as *INS Dega* on 21 October 1991.

The fifth naval air station, on the east coast of India, commissioned in 1992 as *INS Rajali*.

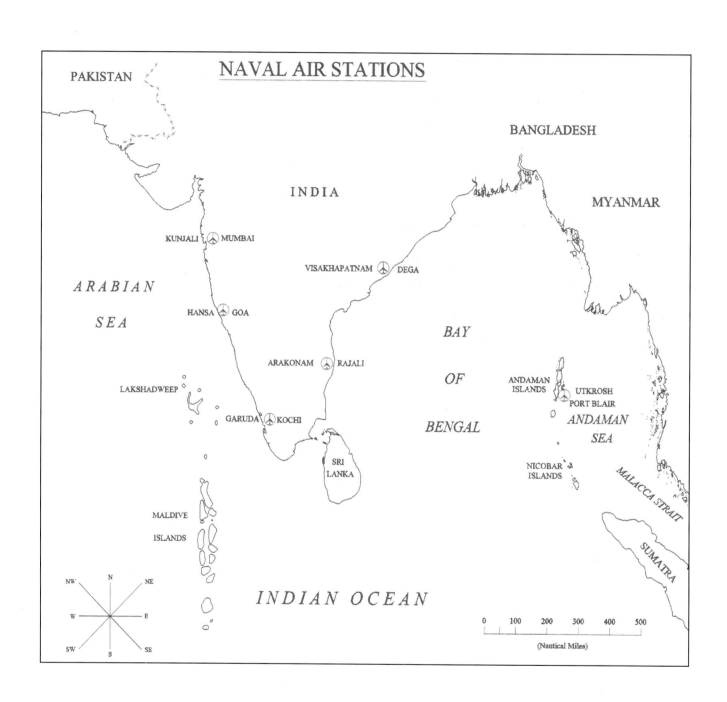

NAVAL AIR STATIONS

PAKISTAN

INDIA

BANGLADESH

MYANMAR

KUNJALI ✈ MUMBAI

VISAKHAPATNAM ✈ DEGA

ARABIAN

SEA

HANSA ✈ GOA

BAY

OF

BENGAL

ARAKONAM ✈ RAJALI

LAKSHADWEEP

ANDAMAN
ISLANDS

UTKROSH
PORT BLAIR

GARUDA ✈ KOCHI

ANDAMAN
SEA

SRI
LANKA

NICOBAR
ISLANDS

MALACCA STRAIT

MALDIVE

ISLANDS

SUMATRA

NW   N   NE

W   E

SW   S   SE

INDIAN OCEAN

0   100   200   300   400   500

(Nautical Miles)

Overview of the Growth of the Air Arm 1976-1990

Year	Carrier Borne Aviation	Ship Borne Helicopters	Maritime Surveillance	Trainers & Simulators
1975	• Seahawks, Alizes and Seakings operate from *Vikrant*	• MATCH in Udaygiri • Chetak in Shakti		
1976	• *Vikrant* operational	• MATCH in Dunagiri • Chetak in Talwar	• Five Super Connies taken over from the Air Force and based in Goa	• Five Islanders arrive and based in Cochin • Vampires phase out. • Kirans MK1 phase in
1977	• *Vikrant* operational		• Three IL 38s arrive and based in Goa	
1978	• *Vikrant* operational • Seahawks phase out	• Chetaks in Brahmaputra class training frigates		
1979 to 1981	*Vikrant's* Phase 1 Modernisation Refit	• Seaking MK 42 A in Taragiri		• Seaking FATS Simulator commissioned
1980	*Vikrant* under refit	• Kamov 25 in Rajput • Seaking MK 42 A in Vindhyagiri		
1981	*Vikrant* under refit	• Kamov 25 in Rana • Chetaks in Trishul and Sandhayak	• Two Islanders based at Port Blair	
1982	• Alizes and Seakings operate from *Vikrant*			
1983	• Sea Harriers arrive	• Kamov 25 in Ranjit • Chetaks in Godavari and Nirdeshak	• Super Connies phase out • Two more IL 38s acquired	
1984	• *Vikrant* operational • Sea Harriers embark Vikrant	• Chetak in Ganga		• Two Sea Harrier trainers arrive and based in Goa
1985	• *Vikrant* operational	• Kamov 28 in Ranvijay • Chetaks in Gomati and Nirupak		• Sea Harrier Simulator commissioned
1986	• *Vikrant* operational	• Kamov 28 in Ranvir • Chetak in Tir		
1987	• 1987 to 1989 Vikrant's Phase 2 Modernisation Refit • *Viraat* commissioned • Sea Harriers operate from Viraat • Alizes phase out	• Seakings MK 42 B arrive and replace the Chetaks in the Godavari class frigates		• Kirans MK 2 phase in
1988	• *Vikrant* under refit	• Seakings MK 42 B embark *Viraat*	• Eight TU 142s arrive and based at Goa	• Seaking MK 42 B Simulator commissioned
1989	• *Vikrant* under refit • *Viraat* operational	• Seakings MK 42 C phase in and embark Maga		
1990	• Sea Harriers and Seaking MK 42 Bs operate from *Vikrant* • *Viraat* under refit	• Chetak in Investigator		

15

The Submarine Arm

Preamble

This chapter starts with a retrospect of the international law aspects of submarine warfare.

It is followed by an overview of submarine and anti submarine tactics to help the reader to better understand the concerns that drove several inter-related naval developments during the period 1976 to 1990:

- The taking over of the Maritime Reconnaissance role from the Air Force, the induction of Russian IL 38 MRASW and TU 142 LRMP ASW aircraft and the induction of British Seaking Mk 42 B and Russian Kamov ASW helicopters. These have been dealt with in the chapter on the Air Arm.

- The selection of the German HDW 1500 design for commencing indigenous construction of SSK submarines in India. This has been dealt with in the chapter on "Indigenous Submarine Construction – The SSK Project".

- The acquisition from the Soviet Union of the latest 877 EKM (Kilo class) SSK submarines to replace the earlier Russian submarines.

- The indigenous manufacture of submarine propulsion batteries for all classes of submarines in service with their designs improved for better performance in tropical conditions.

- The leasing of a Russian nuclear propelled submarine to better understand its capabilities and limitations.

Submarine Warfare

The London Protocol of 1936 stated that submarines must conform to the rules of international law to which surface vessels are subject; and these rules included the provisions that a merchant ship's crew must, before the ship itself was destroyed, be put in a place of safety. Moreover a ship's boat is not a 'place of safety'.

An attempt to fulfil this condition was made in the case of SS Laconia in 1942 when three U boats towed boats full of survivors for several days until attacked by Allied aircraft. Admiral Donitz thereafter sent his famous "Be Harsh" signal to all U boats.

At Nürnberg, the Tribunal gave a hedged judgment:

- It recognised that both sides had conducted submarine warfare of considerable ferocity, and that there had been justification for German attacks on British shipping, particularly as that shipping was defensively armed and had orders to report submarines.

- But it found against Admiral Donitz for conducting attacks on neutral vessels without warning and for the fact that submarine crews had failed to rescue survivors.

During war, international law places submarines under stringent constraints. On the other hand, "It is universally recognised that in every war, the actions of any nation are influenced substantially by the behaviour of its opponent."[1]

The following excerpts from the memoirs of Grand Admiral Raeder, the Chief of the German Navy during the 1939-1945 World War, are pertinent.[2]

"The German Naval War Staff ensured that:

- Every precaution was taken against any violation of the rules of international law in regard to war at sea.

- No actions should be taken, no orders or directives issued, which could lead to a violation of the moral law of the sea as it is recognised by all civilised peoples.

"I knew positively that Admiral Donitz, as Commander of the Submarine forces, had on several occasions deliberately put some of our U-boats and their crews in positions of utmost danger from enemy attack in order to insure the safety of surviving crew members of torpedoed ships."

---

1. German Navy's Grand Adm Raeder's memoirs 'My Life', page 388.

2. Ibid 'Unrestricted Submarine Warfare' Pages 394 et seq.

At the 1945-46 "trials of war criminals" held in Nürnberg by the Allied International Military Tribunal, Admirals Raeder and Donitz were charged with having 'conducted naval warfare contrary to the rules of civilised warfare' with particular reference to unrestricted submarine warfare by the German Navy. To prepare the defence against this charge, their defence counsel sent questionnaires to the British and American Navies.

"From the answers of the British Admiralty, it was established, and accepted by the court, that at the very beginning of the war, the British Navy had begun arming British merchant ships in accordance with directives already laid down in 1938 in their *Handbook for the Merchant Marine*. It had   also sent ships out under armed escort. British merchant ships had orders to report all submarines sighted, and for this purpose were made part of the British Navy's reconnaissance and warning system. On 1 October 1939, the British Navy had directed British merchant ships to ram German submarines whenever possible. And on 8 May 1940, the British naval forces had received orders to sink, *without warning,* any ship encountered in the Skagerrak."

"Admiral Nimitz was equally frank and helpful in his answer to the questionnaire. Immediately upon outbreak of the war with Japan, he avouched, the US Government had declared the whole Pacific Ocean a war zone, and had ordered all-out war against Japan. In this war zone, the largest ocean area in the world, US submarines had authority to attack, without warning, all merchant ships sighted. Hospital ships, and other vessels proceeding under security protection for humanitarian purposes, were the only ships exempted from this directive.

"The crucial question in the questionnaire sent to Admiral Nimitz was this: *'Were American submarines forbidden, either by specific order or recognised practice, to take measures for rescue of the passengers and crews of ships sunk without warning if the safety of the submarines themselves were endangered by these measures?'*

The unequivocal reply of the US Admiral was: "In general practice, the US submarines did not rescue enemy survivors if such an attempt meant an unusual additional risk or if the submarine was thereby endangered in the further execution of its tasks."

"These replies proved to the Nürnberg court that the German Navy had conducted its own naval warfare in accordance with the same rules and customs that were observed by the two largest sea powers with whom it was engaged. As a result, the International Military Tribunal completely vindicated the German Navy in its methods of warfare, certifying that such warfare had been conducted in full accord with the rules of international law."

Submarine and Anti Submarine Tactics

Stealth and Snorting

Stealth is the watchword of all submarines. The modern, diesel-electric propelled SSK submarine is very stealthy, provided the utmost care has been taken to minimise its self noise.[3] Carefully handled, she can be as quiet as the grave. At low speeds, the soft hum of her electric propulsion power unit is almost un-discernable. Unlike a nuclear propelled submarine, she has no reactor requiring the support of numerous mechanical subsystems, all of which are potential noise-makers.

When dived, the submarine is propelled by a set of huge electric batteries. Depending on how much battery power is used up (the higher the speed, the quicker the battery runs down), the batteries require to be recharged regularly by diesel generators. Just as a car engine needs an intake of oxygen, so do the two internal combustion diesel generators in a submarine. The diesel engine must have air. To get air, a submarine must come up to at least periscope depth and then she becomes vulnerable to detection.

Batteries can be recharged either by being on the surface (more vulnerable) or by remaining at periscope depth and sucking in air (less vulnerable). When a diesel-electric submarine comes to periscope depth and raises her snort mast to suck in the air required to run her diesel generators to recharge her batteries, the process is known as 'snorting'.[4]

Even though a submarine hull is not visible whilst snorting, the acoustic noise of its diesel engines can be heard by another submarine if in the vicinity. Its periscope and snort masts that stick out above the water can be detected on ship and aircraft radar. The ions in the diesel exhaust can be 'sniffed' by detectors fitted in MRASW

---

3. Self noise is a critical parameter in submarine design and construction. It has to be rigorously monitored and minimised throughout a submarine's operational service. The ocean offers natural visual and electro-magnetic camouflage. By reducing the noise generated by the submarine at or below the natural noise of the sea, the submarine can effectively conceal itself in the ocean.

4. The 'snort' is a waterproof hollow tube that can be raised and lowered when at periscope depth, through which air can be sucked in for the diesel engines. Prior to the invention of the "snort", submarines had to be on the surface to recharge their batteries and when batteries were low, became very vulnerable to ramming, sudden attack, etc. In effect, the snort enables the submarine to recharge batteries with her hull below the surface and only the top of the snort being visible.

aircraft. There is little a submarine can do about these limitations, except to stop recharging and crash dive every time her ESM detects radar emissions of an approaching ASW aircraft/helicopter or her passive sonar detects the noise of approaching ships.[5]

During war, a submarine patrolling in hostile waters comes up near the surface only when she has to recharge her batteries. Even then, she will only do so at night, and for the shortest possible time, so as to minimise the chance of being detected and 'localised' for attack.[6]

Submarine and Anti Submarine Tactics

For successful attack, a submarine relies on concealment and surprise rather than concentration of force. A submarine attack is more successful because it detects the ship earlier and can deliver a high weapon density attack before being detected – this quality provides surprise.

To avoid mutual interference, submarines operate singly. When more than one submarine is deployed in the same region, each submarine is given a specific demarcated area in which to operate.[7]

A submarine stalks its prey. Its target – a warship, a merchant ship, or a convoy – seeks clues as to a submarine's presence in order to take evasive action. In anti submarine warfare, MRASW aircraft, ASW helicopters, sonar fitted warships and SSK submarines are the predators and submarines the prey.

When a submarine closes its target ship or submarine, the latter try to counterattack and evade the blow. When anti submarine forces localise a submarine, it either fights like a cornered beast or goes silent and tries to slip away.

The crux of all submarine warfare is to sink the enemy target, get away from the area and survive the anti submarine chase that is sure to follow.

Sonar Propagation

Sound is virtually the only form of energy that propagates usefully underwater, where electromagnetic waves, including light, are rapidly attenuated.

The temperature of the sea becomes cooler as depth increases. This change in temperature affects the velocity (and hence the path) of the sound waves transmitted by a sonar. Temperature layers in the sea refract sound waves much the same way that a prism refracts light.[8]

The sound velocity gradient near the sea surface is considered 'positive' if velocity increases with depth, 'negative' if velocity decreases with depth.

A positive gradient causes upward refraction of sound energy. Upward refracted rays will be reflected by the air-sea interface at the surface and surface reflection will be continued. Positive velocity gradients give rise to surface bounded ducts that can carry acoustic energy for very long distances since the spreading is two-dimensional. Long-range detection can be made under these conditions if the sonar and its target are both located in this duct.

A negative velocity gradient refracts sound waves downwards. As a result, a shadow zone is created which is not insonified. Under these conditions, by operating in this shadow zone, a submarine can, without being detected, move close to its target to within torpedo firing range.

The way to detect a submarine lurking in a shadow zone or below a temperature layer is to position the sonar in the same shadow zone or below the same temperature layer. This is achieved on board ships by lowering a large towed sonar dome (called Variable Depth Sonar – VDS) to the required depth whilst maintaining speed. Anti submarine helicopters lower their small sonar dome (called 'dunking sonar') whilst hovering.

Submarine Location, Detection and Attack

Submarines are potent weapon platforms. Their traditional task is to attack enemy warships and enemy submarines.[9] They are designed to minimise the chances of their being detected and to withstand anti submarine attacks. They are equipped with accurate and lethal weapons for attack and for self-defence.

---

5. The great advantage of a nuclear propelled submarine is that it does not need to come to the surface to recharge batteries because it does not need propulsion batteries. The nuclear reactor heats water to generate steam that runs steam turbines that drive the propeller. Its mobility and endurance when dived has none of the limitations of a diesel-electric propelled submarine.

6. Since recharging batteries exposes the diesel-electrical submarine to detection, or in other words to be 'indiscreet', the parameter 'indiscretion rate' (how often a submarine is compelled to be indiscreet) is regarded as vital as 'self noise' in submarine design and in the technology of submarine batteries.

7. For a short period in 1942-43, during the 1939-1945 World War, German U-boats operated successfully as 'wolf packs' against convoys in the Atlantic Ocean. This was possible because submarines generally operated on the surface and dived only for the attack.

8. Every sea area is subject to diurnal and season effects and also prevalent and changing currents. The combination of these effects causes different temperature patterns at different depths.

9. In recent years, submarines have attacked land targets with precision guided missiles.

A submarine's asset is its invisibility when dived. Its limitation is that its underwater mobility is constrained by the endurance of its propulsion batteries. When recharging batteries, a submarine loses its asset of invisibility.

As mentioned, when dived, a submarine is propelled by electric motors that are powered by batteries. The endurance of these batteries depends on the speed of the submarine. The faster it goes, either to get as far away from the position where it was first detected or to evade the weapons fired at it, the quicker the batteries get exhausted. The submarine then has to surface and recharge its batteries before it can dive again with its mobility restored by recharged batteries.

The crux of anti submarine warfare is to compel the submarine to remain dived by repeated and intense attacks and thereby exhaust its batteries, to reduce its mobility to evade attack and hit it with weapons to force it to surface and surrender.

In ASW tactics, the ship tries to evade or avoid a submarine probability area. It endeavours to confuse and constrain submarine tactical choices by deft combinations of speed and manoeuvre.

MRASW Aircraft

When a submarine is sighted on surface or it makes a wireless transmission that betrays its presence by giving Direction Finding (D/F) equipment an approximate position of the transmission, a maritime reconnaissance anti submarine warfare (MRASW) aircraft speeds to that position. It drops a number of sonobuoys to 'localise' the contact and if possible to attack it. The MRASW aircraft, therefore, is in the first line of submarine location, detection and attack.

The objective of an MRASW aircraft is to obtain an initial position of a submarine. For example an indication on its detector of the 'magnetic anomaly' created by the submarine's steel hull or a 'sniff' of diesel exhaust ions or a disappearing radar contact suggestive of a submarine having crash dived to evade detection. As soon as the MRASW aircraft obtains an initial position, it drops a pattern of passive sonobuoys to localise the contact.

Modern conventional submarines (and their batteries) are designed to minimise the need to snort to a few hours every few days. This time is too short for an MRASW aircraft to get an accurate enough localisation. On the one hand, an MRASW aircraft may choose not to use its radar to detect the submarine's snort mast sticking out of the water – but to do so would reveal its presence to the submarine. On the other hand, continuous patrols by MRASW aircraft operating

their radar can constrain a submarine's freedom to recharge its batteries.

In rough weather and poor sonar conditions, localisation by an MRASW aircraft could be as poor as an area of several hundred square miles, almost like looking for a needle in a haystack.

However as soon as a submarine has been localised and accurately tracked, the aircraft attacks it with its own weapons. Additional MRASW aircraft can help to maintain pressure on the submarine to remain dived.

Anti Submarine Ships and Their ASW Helicopters

As soon as the MRASW aircraft localises a contact, ships designed for anti submarine warfare and having anti submarine helicopters on board proceed to the area where the MRASW aircraft's sonobuoy patterns have been laid.

Anti submarine helicopters can search a given area quicker and, being airborne, they cannot be hit by submarine fired torpedoes. After ascertaining the progress on localisation from the MRASW aircraft, they either lay their own sonobuoys to localise the contact or use their dunking sonar to search. If the sonar search is passive, their sonars listen for tell tale noise of submarine presence.

If the sonar search is active and a submarine is present, the sonar receives an acoustic echo back from the submarine hull and the submarine can be tracked by sonar transmissions. As soon as the submarine's position and movements are accurately determined, helicopters release their anti submarine homing torpedoes. Helicopter attacks continue until the submarine is hit and sinks or the submarine surfaces and surrenders because its batteries have exhausted.

A submarine knows when it has been detected on sonar – it can hear the sonar transmissions. It knows it will come under attack. It will try to evade helicopters. When cornered, it may choose to attack the ship because a ship can be instantly sunk by submarine fired torpedoes.

The role of the anti submarine ship is to stand-off outside the range of the submarine's torpedoes and keep on re-fuelling and re-arming the helicopters until the submarine nears exhaustion. She then moves in to fire intensive barrages of anti submarine rockets.

Submarine Search and Kill (SSK) Submarines

The advantage of having submarines to search and kill enemy submarines is that both share the same undersea environment to detect and track each other, without being limited by shadow zones and temperature layers. Using active sonar would immediately betray presence. Detection by passive sonar requires high skills in picking up even the faintest noise emanating from the opposing SSK. Hence the emphasis, during SSK designs, on silent machinery and minimum noise levels.

SSKs are deployed in areas where there is likelihood of encountering only enemy submarines and no possibility whatsoever of own anti submarine forces mistaking own SSK for an enemy SSK. The contest is between two dived SSKs.

Once the opposing SSK has been detected and tracked and the fire control problem solved, wire guided torpedoes are fired in a way that the target SSK would not have time to fire its own wire guided torpedoes in self defence. In effect, this means getting as close as possible to the victim before firing – but in so doing, it also means that the victim SSK may hear you and fire its own torpedoes before you fired yours. The direction from which the retaliatory torpedoes would come is predictable – straight down the direction that the incoming torpedo's homing head starts its active sonar transmissions. At this moment, decoys can be released to seduce the incoming torpedo away.

Both submarine warfare and anti submarine warfare are driven by constantly evolving frontier technologies. With long years of peace interspersed by short sharp wars, success requires:

- The continuous intensive training of highly motivated and experienced personnel.
- Sustaining the highest standards of material readiness of the platforms (ships, submarines, aircraft and helicopters) and their sensors (sonars, radars and ESM) and their weapons (torpedoes, rockets, and depth bombs).

The State of the Submarine Arm in 1975

The First Eight Submarines

The Submarine Arm started with the acquisition from the Soviet Union of four of their latest Project i 641 K (NATO classification Foxtrot class) 2,000 tonne ocean going submarines. These arrived between 1968 and 1970. The problems experienced in operating the first of these Kalvari class submarines in tropical conditions were fed back to the design bureaus in Russia. Improvements were gradually introduced in the remaining three submarines before delivery.

Another four submarines were contracted for in 1971. These improved Vela class submarines arrived between 1973 and 1975.

By 1975, the material state of the first four submarines had deteriorated. This was a cumulative result of several factors:

- The tropical, hot and humid Indian climate, the corrosion caused by the higher salinity of tropical seas and the corrosive atmospheric pollution caused by the industrial emissions at Vishakhapatnam.
- Bunching. The induction of the first four submarines in 24 months and the next four submarines in 16 months meant that their major six-yearly refits would also have to be undertaken after six years within periods of 24 and 16 months respectively. This bunching of major refits could not have been avoided – it made no sense to order one submarine at a time when starting a Submarine Arm.
- Submarine repairs required highly skilled, experienced and deeply specialised expertise. The Navy did not have this expertise. It could only be built up slowly because officers and artificers were periodically transferred and the civilian cadres of the new Dockyard were being built up from scratch.

Six-yearly refits could not commence on time because the submarine refit workshops and facilities were still coming up in the new Dockyard. The new civilian workforce had no knowledge of submarine repair technology. Even though vertically specialised and experienced Soviet specialists in submarine repair were available, they had no Indian counterparts to whom they could transfer their technology and expertise.

All these factors were aggravated by the procedural delays in the delivery of submarine refit spares from Russia. The only solution was for submarines to be refitted in Russia.

Initially, the Indian side found it difficult to countenance sending submarines to Russia for refit. Not only might it indicate lack of self-confidence, but also because heavy investments had been made in setting up the new Dockyard for this very purpose.

The Russian side too, perhaps for security reasons and their own submarine refit workload, was reluctant to accept Indian submarines in their dockyards. After considerable interaction, both sides realised that there was no other option.

Submarine Depot Ship – *Amba*

The Submarine Depot Ship *Amba* had commissioned in 1968 and had been based in Vishakhapatnam. Between 1969 and 1971, *Amba* supported the submarines operating on the West Coast.

INS *SHISHUMAR* - German-design HDW 1500 (SSK) submarine (1980s)

INS *SHANKUL* - German-design HDW 1500 (SSK) submarine (1980s)

INS *SINDHUGHOSH* - Russian Project 877 EKM submarine (1980s)

Compartment containing the huge batteries that provide electric propulsion for a submarine when dived

Russian Project i641 (Foxtrot class) submarine (1970s)

An HDW 1500 submarine (on pontoon) and an 877 EKM submarine in dock for refit

INS *AMBA* - Submarine Depot Ship

On INS *CHAKRA*'s arrival at Visakhapatnam in January 1988, she was received by Prime Minister Rajiv Gandhi.
Also seen are Defence Minister KC Pant, Vice Admiral SC Chopra (FOC in C East) and *Chakra*'s Commanding Officer
Captain (later Vice Admiral) RN Ganesh

INS *CHAKRA* - Russian nuclear-propelled submarine leased from 1988 to 1991

Russian *Kamov 25* anti submarine helicopter (1980s)

British *Seaking Mk 42 B* anti submarine helicopter lowering its sonar dome into the sea (1980s)

Anti submarine torpedo fired from INS *RAJPUT* during a practice firing

French *Alize* - Carrier-borne Anti Submarine & Reconnaissance Aircraft (1960s)

Russian *TU 142* - Long Range Maritime Patrol & Anti Submarine Aircraft (1980s)

After it was decided to base the four new submarines of the Vela class at Bombay, *Amba* was re-based at Bombay. She provided the essential battery recharging facilities until a full-fledged battery charging facility was established ashore in 1978. In addition, she had a recompression chamber, could prepare torpedoes, recharge High Pressure air and provide comfortable accommodation for submarine crews.

Shortage of Submarine Personnel

In the short period of eight years between 1966 and 1974, the Navy had manned eight submarines as well as their technical facilities ashore. Personnel shortages began to cause concern. The 'rejection' procedure was reviewed and made more pragmatic. To induce personnel to volunteer, monetary incentives like Submarine Allowance, Submarine Pay, and Hard-lying Money at full rates were sanctioned, special benefits like Special Submarine Rations and Special Submarine Clothing were authorised, procedures were simplified and sustained recruitment drives were resorted to.

Submarine Infrastructure Facilities

The 1965 agreement with Russia covered not only the delivery of ships and submarines, but also the creation of a modern dockyard at Vishakhapatnam, along with infrastructure.

The shore infrastructure for the Submarine Arm comprised a submarine base, a submarine training establishment, submarine maintenance and repair workshops, facilities to charge submarine propulsion batteries and high-pressure air bottles and facilities for blowing the ballast tanks and preparing submarine torpedoes. Since the new Dockyard would take several years to come up, interim arrangements were made for the Base Repair Workshop in Vishakhapatnam to be expanded.

Developments Between 1976 and 1990

Six-Yearly Refits (Medium Repairs) of Kalvari and Vela Class Submarines

It was decided that the first submarine, *Kalvari* would be refitted by the Russian side in Vladivostok and that the second submarine, *Khanderi* would be refitted in Vishakhapatnam. A team from the Naval Dockyard Vishakhapatnam was deputed to participate in *Kalvari's* 18-month refit in Russia to acquire hands-on experience of a six-yearly refit and, on return to Vishakhapatnam,

to assist in carrying out *Khanderi's* refit with the help of Russian specialists.

Kalvari started her refit on 1 January 1975 and returned to Vishakhapatnam in mid 1976 with 'zero defects'. The performance of her equipment was so satisfactory that *Kalvari* provided the benchmark for the high standard that Vishakhapatnam had to achieve for *Khanderi's* refit.

When *Khanderi's* refit started in mid 1976, the position was:

- The new Naval Dockyard under construction at Vishakhapatnam was nowhere near ready to undertake such a complex refit.[10] The only facilities available were a two-and-a-half-bay, rudimentary, Base Repair Workshop, the submarine battery commissioning / charging-discharging facility called the Energy Block, and the Torpedo Preparation Workshop.

- There was neither the capability for the survey of a submarine's pressure hull nor a naval dry dock in which to dock a submarine.

- The team of Dockyard officers and civilian foremen that had been deputed to Russia to participate in *Kalvari's* refit had, to a limited extent, imbibed what needed to be done, how it was to be done and how best to improvise facilities in Vishakhapatnam until the new workshops were ready.

- The set of Refit Spares required for the mandatory, time-bound replacement / overhaul of critical equipment had not arrived.

- The Repair Technical Documents (RTDs) required for the repair and refit of equipment were incomplete. Whatever had been received was in the Russian language. There was a shortage of translators and a backlog had built up of documents awaiting translation from Russian into English.

On the plus side, the expert civilian Russian specialists from the factories that manufactured equipment could be requested for to assist and provide guidance on how to refit the equipment.

However, Russian specialisation was very narrow – each specialist from each manufacturing factory knew all about his specific equipment but not much about the other equipment.

The Indian side was reluctant to afford the high costs that would have to be incurred for the deputation of such a large number of specialists.

---

10. See chapter on "Refit, Repair and Maintenance Facilities", page 142.

The *Khanderi* refit was beset with all these problems. There was no way to overcome the inexperience of dockyard workers, their low productivity, their learning curve, their low expertise, the shortage of spares and documentation and the inadequate infrastructure.

In 1980, the Naval Expert Committee was constrained to comment:

"Over 80 Soviet specialists had been imported for facilitating *Khanderi's* medium refit. Each one of them was a specialist in repair of submarines. The Chief Shipbuilder had an experience of about 12 years in refitting submarines alone. Soviet specialists included ship builders, designers, technologists, specialists in quality control, electro-deposition and specialists on almost each important equipment and system on which they had long experience.

"Despite the Soviet specialists, the refit was taking more than twice as long and was nowhere near finishing. If the Navy had to acquire and replicate the expertise possessed by the Soviet specialists, in time to come, the following steps were unavoidable:

- Undertake most meticulous planning of work and material requirements.

- Create Bureaus of ship builders, technologists and designers as recommended by the Soviet side, consisting of 32 Technologists and 15 Designers for submarines alone.

- Create a core of supervisory staff and workers and specialise only in refit of submarine hull and its equipment. This would mean a larger requirement of manpower, but narrow specialisation to preserve the quality of work appeared to be the only answer to the problems being experienced."

Kalvari's refit in Vladivostok had lasted 18 months. *Khanderi's* refit in Vizag lasted five and a half years, from 1976 to 1981. It was, nevertheless, a significant learning experience. Considerable innovation had to be resorted to as was done for testing critical equipment like high-current-carrying propulsion battery breakers and the back-to-back testing of the overhauled main electric-propulsion motor.

In subsequent years, both expertise and productivity gradually improved. For the reasons discussed in the chapter on Logistics, the delivery of Refit Spares continued to remain untimely. Delays were inescapable in the completion of a massive project like the new Vishakhapatnam Dockyard. And because the submarines were acquired in bunches of four, there was no escape from the 'bunching' of their six-yearly refits.

Kursura was laid off for a number of years and cannibalised to keep the other submarines operational. In 1985, it was decided to make her operational. Subsequently, she sailed and dived for a full operating cycle before she was pulled up on to Vishakhapatnam beach after decommissioning in 2001 and made into a museum. In 1987, *Khanderi* was laid up for cannibalisation, as *Kursura* had been earlier.

The overall sharing of the six-yearly refits (Medium Repairs) of the first eight submarines between refit yards in Russia and Vishakhapatnam was:

- Russia:

  Kalvari (1975-76), *Karanj* (1978-79), *Vela* (1980-82), *Vagli* (1981-84), *Vaghsheer* (1983-85)

- India:

  Khanderi (1976-81), *Kursura* (1977-95), *Vagir* (1981-84), *Kalvari* (1984-88), *Vela* (1986-88), *Karanj* (1988-96), *Vela* (1993-98),*Vagli* (1997-99)

The Indigenisation of Submarine Propulsion Batteries

From the inception of the submarine acquisition programme, the Navy had decided to become self sufficient for its requirements of submarine propulsion batteries. The offers of competing Indian firms and their foreign collaborators were evaluated. Standard Batteries of Bombay were chosen in 1973 to manufacture propulsion batteries in technological collaboration with Tudor of Sweden.

The first eight submarines had commissioned with Russian propulsion batteries. Each submarine's set of batteries weighed over 300 tonnes and comprised 448 battery cells, each one metre high, and half a metre wide. The set had to be charged before loading on board. To recharge the batteries at sea, a submarine had either to come to the surface or, to be safer, come to snort depth, and use the diesel generator for recharging. The battery set had a life of 100 charge-discharge cycles or two and a half years, whichever was earlier. The Russian Navy had adjusted their submarine operating cycle such that these 100 cycles would be expended between three-yearly refits called Current Repairs. To avoid having to lay off an operational submarine during its operational cycle, the Russians always installed a set of new batteries during the three-yearly refit.

The Navy's experience with Russian batteries soon revealed that in Indian tropical conditions, the evolution of hydrogen when recharging the batteries was much greater than in the cooler Russian weather. Mixing additives to the electrolyte solved this problem partially. A basic design problem, however, was the inability of the electrolyte cooling system in the Russian battery to cope with high tropical temperatures.[11]

Standard Batteries modified the design of the Swedish Tudor battery to overcome these problems. It innovated tubular construction instead of grid construction and, instead of having cooling coils in the electrolyte, it achieved more efficient cooling through ducts in the bus bars. After the initial teething troubles had been overcome, the performance of indigenous batteries proved to be better in Indian conditions than that of imported batteries.

The German HDW submarines, which entered service in 1986, were equipped with German Hagen batteries. The design of the Hagen battery was indigenised by Chloride India, the makers of Exide batteries.

The Russian EKM submarines started entering service from 1986 onwards. The indigenisation of their batteries was once again entrusted to Standard Batteries.

In 1990, the Battery Commissioning Facility in Bombay was completed. It met the requirements of the both the EKM and HDW submarines based at Bombay and dispensed with the need for Russian submarines to go all the way round to Vizag to replace their batteries.

The indigenisation of submarine propulsion batteries was a success story. Despite setbacks and teething problems, perseverance, innovation and close interaction between submariners and the factories culminated in the production of propulsion batteries that had superior cooling power in the tropics, longer life, higher capacity, superior plate technology all of which helped to lower indiscretion rate. In later years, Russia and other countries started importing these batteries from India.

Indigenous Submarine Construction – The SSK Project

In the early 1970s, proposals were invited from reputed and well-established submarine manufacturers. Based on the technologies reflected in the offers that they sent, the Navy incorporated the desired features of each proposal and informed them of its 'revised staff requirements'.

In 1981, after prolonged evaluations, a contract was signed with HDW of Germany for four 1,500-tonne submarines – the first two to be built in Germany and the next two by Mazagon Docks, Bombay. The German-built

submarines commissioned in 1986. Due to initial start-up problems, the submarines built by MDL commissioned in 1992 and 1994.

The selection and construction of these submarines have been discussed in the chapter on "Indigenous Submarine Construction - The SSK Project".

The Induction of Russian 877 EKM (Kilo Class) Submarines

In the late 1970s, the Russian side was requested to suggest replacements for the eight Foxtrot class submarines that had been inducted in earlier years, concurrently as the case was on for building SSK submarines in India.[12] The Russian response in 1978 was that the EKM design was on the drawing board and that India should make up its mind quickly so that its requirements could be bulked. The Navy was hesitant to do so, seeing in the Russian offer, perhaps rightly, that it was to compete with the Swedish and German SSK evaluations then in progress. Years passed.[13] In February 1981, the Russian side offered the 877 EKM submarines. The Navy asked for its team to see the 877 but was asked to wait. By this time, the decision had already been taken to collaborate with HDW of Germany for the indigenous construction of submarines and final negotiations were in progress. The German HDW SSK agreement was signed in December 1981.

In 1983, an Indian team visited and evaluated the 877 and found that its design and performance as an SSK was comparable to that of the HDW SSK. In 1984, an agreement was signed for six submarines. The seventh submarine was contracted in 1987 and the eighth submarine in 1988.

These eight 877 EKM Sindhughosh class submarines (NATO classification Kilo class) were commissioned between 1986 and 1990. They were a generation ahead of the earlier i641 Foxtrot class and on par with the German HDW 1500 submarines.

The Moscow newspaper *Pravda* published the following report in 1988:

"The *Sinduratna* is an 877 EKM submarine of the Kilo class. When surfaced, she displaces 2,300 tonnes and is capable of a speed of 10 knots. Fully autonomous for 45 days, it can dive to 300 metres, carries a crew of 52 and is equipped with six 533 mm torpedo tubes. The submarine was developed at the Rubin Design Bureau in St Petersburg.

---

11. Russian batteries used grid plate technology instead of tubular plate technology.

12. The Russian side was aware of the Navy's discussions with European builders of submarines and had advised against diversifying the types of submarines in service.

13. It emerged later that during these years the prototype 877 had been undergoing sea trials.

"The 240 feet long, 3,000 tonnes dived, extremely quiet, diesel-electric Kilo class SSK can run submerged at speeds up to 17 knots.

"The battery gives the Kilo a range of some 400 miles, running slowly and silently, before she needs to recharge. She can travel 6,000 miles 'snorting' before refuelling."

Almost all the officers who underwent EKM training in Russia gathered the impression from their Russian instructors that the EKM's teardrop hull, its anechoic rubber tiling and other attributes were features of a submarine that was supposed to take a miniaturised nuclear reactor. But during development, either the reactor could not be fitted in the space available or technical problems constrained further miniaturisation and it was converted into a diesel-electric propelled boat. This helps to explain why, despite the Russian Design Bureau's experience of the Indian side's need for more air conditioning capacity when operating Russian submarines in tropical conditions, the shortfall in air conditioning could not be remedied before the submarines commissioned.

Commander (later Captain) KR Ajrekar underwent training in Russia and on return to India became Commanding Officer of the *Sindhughosh*. He recalls:

"Russian training was the best training we ever received. The best part was the training on the torpedo fire control system. The instructor was a commanding officer who had just come from an operational submarine. He had 15 years experience in operational submarines and it was absolutely invaluable. After each attack, we had to point out our own mistakes and the rest of the junior officers watched the commanding officer analyse his mistakes. I found that people did come out with their own mistakes and such mistakes were not repeated a second time."

Recalling the qualities of the EKM submarine that he commanded, he said:

"The tear-drop hull configuration, being hydro-dynamically the best underwater, the underwater management of the EKM is excellent. The EKM has auto diving control – you can steer the submarine automatically even from the fire control computer. The hydroplanes are located in the midship portion where there is no interference with the sonar. The submarine hull is covered with rubber tiles that absorb the acoustic energy of enemy sonar transmissions. The radiated noise of the submarine was very low. The sonar could pick up HE at very long ranges. Never before had I picked up those kinds of ranges. In fact, we thought that we would pick up these ranges only in Arctic waters or the Baltic Sea. However, within a month of our arrival

in India, extensive sonar trials were carried out and the ranges obtained were just slightly less than what we had obtained in the Baltic. The sonar is excellent, the underwater telephone facility is excellent, and the intercept sonar is very good. In addition there is mine hunting sonar which is very useful."

In the initial years, the EKM submarines suffered inadequacy of air conditioning in tropical conditions. This was progressively resolved by increasing the air conditioning capacity. The acute shortage of fresh water was eventually resolved by fitting reverse osmosis plants.

Personnel Shortages

The tempo at which submarines were inducted necessitated measures to increase induction of personnel into the submarine cadre. Basic submarine courses were increased from one per year to two per year and recruitment drives were intensified. But it was only after the Fifth Pay Commission in the 1990s that emoluments improved sufficiently to start attracting personnel of the desired calibre to volunteer for the Submarine Arm.

Very Low Frequency Communications with Submarines at Sea

Whereas a submarine on the surface can transmit and receive wireless messages just like a ship can, submerged submarines can only receive wireless messages on Very Low Frequency (VLF). VLF transmitters require huge antennae suspended high above the ground.

The initial discussions were solely with the Russian side, from whom the submarines had been acquired. Later enquiries with western manufacturers indicated that better technology might be available from America. Parallel discussions were, therefore, pursued both with Russia and with America.

Between 1979 and 1984, modalities were worked out for Continental Manufacturing Company of America, in collaboration with Triveni Sangam Ltd of India, to be responsible for the detailed design, manufacture, site installation and commissioning of the VLF Transmitter and the Auto Transmitting Units.

The hardware arrived by 1986. Installation of the VLF Transmitter commenced in 1987. Trials were completed in 1989.

During the same period, the Defence Research and Development Organisation undertook the design of the antennae to be fitted in submarines for receiving VLF transmissions.

On 20 October 1990, the VLF Transmitting Station was commissioned as *INS Kattaboman* in Tamil Nadu on the southern tip of India.

Command and Control of Submarine Squadrons

After the arrival from Russia of the fourth submarine in end 1969, all four submarines of the Kalvari class (Russian Project i 641, NATO designation Foxtrot class) constituted the 8th Submarine Squadron. It was based at Vishakhapatnam under *INS Virbahu*, which commissioned in 1971. CO *Virbahu* functioned as Captain SM 8 and Class Authority for all submarines.

The next four Vela class improved versions of the Kalvari class were based in Bombay. When the fourth submarine arrived in end 1974, these four submarines, under Captain SM 9, constituted the 9th Submarine Squadron. Captain SM 8 at Vishakhapatnam continued to function as the class authority for submarines.

The first submarine of the Sindhughosh class (Russian Project 877 EKM, NATO designation Kilo class) arrived in 1984. The first four submarines constituted the 11th Submarine Squadron and were based at Vishakhapatnam to facilitate the training of EKM commissioning and replacement crews. Facilities to carry out their annual repairs were taken in hand for completion by 1990.

The first two Shishumar class SSK submarines arrived in Bombay from Germany in 1987 and constituted the 10th Submarine Squadron.

The next four EKM submarines that arrived by 1990 were based in Bombay and constituted the 12th Submarine Squadron. The four ageing Vela class submarines of the 9th Submarine Squadron gradually relocated to Vishakhapatnam.

The last two, MDL-built SSK submarines joined the 10th Submarine Squadron in 1992 and 1994.

Until *INS Vajrabahu* was commissioned in Bombay in 1996, the submarines based in Bombay were administered locally and Submarine Headquarters in Vishakhapatnam dealt with technical matters.

With multiple squadrons based in Bombay and Vishakhapatnam, the Commanding Officers of *Virbahu* and *Vajrabahu* were initially designated as COMSUB East and West and later re-designated as Commodore Commanding Submarines (COMCOS) East and West respectively.

Submarines were placed under the operational and administrative control of the respective Cs-in-C, who were designated as Submarine Operating Authorities. The COMSUBs were responsible to their Cs-in-C for operational readiness and providing their submarines with 'Base' and 'Material' support.

Flag Officer Submarines (FOSM)

The constitution of FOSM was promulgated in 1986 after the arrival of the first EKM submarine from Russia and implemented in 1987 just prior to the arrival of the SSK submarines from Germany.

FOSM's Interface with the Navy's Command and Control Organisation

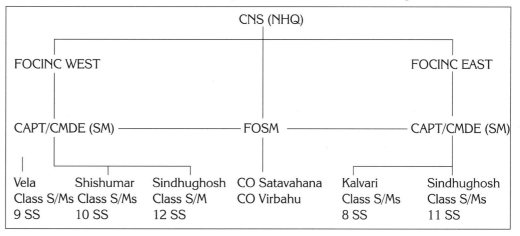

- FOSM responsible to NHQ for all Class Authority and training functions in regard to submarines.
- FOSM under the administrative control of FOCINCEAST.
- FOSM to interact with both FOCs-in-C on all matters related to his charter of duties.
- Captain/Cmde (SM) on the East Coast and CO *Virbahu* to be separate entities.

Submarine Rescue

Submarine Rescue Vessel (SRV) *Nistar* was acquired from Russia, commissioned in 1971 and based at Vishakhapatnam. She conducted the diving operation on the Pakistan Navy submarine, Ghazi, which sank outside Vishakhapatnam harbour in December 1971. From 1972 onwards, *Nistar* helped train the Navy's Deep Divers and Clearance Divers.

In 1975, a full-fledged medical organisation was sanctioned to provide cover for submarine rescue operations. In 1977, a safe 'Submarine Bottoming Area' was established off Vishakhapatnam to exercise mating trials between *Nistar* and submarines.

Between 1982 and 1987, contemporary European SRVs were evaluated for their suitability. A study was carried out of the utilisation, on payment, of the US Navy's air-portable Deep Submergence Rescue Vessel (DSRV) rescue system. Each of these had pros and cons in Indian conditions.

The drought of the late 1980s and the ensuing shortage of resources led to the acquisition of a new SRV being postponed and the search for an interim solution.

In 1988, a vessel, which Mazagon Docks had built as a Diving Support Vessel for offshore oil exploration work became available for acquisition. It had a dynamic thruster facility and a recompression chamber. It was taken on dry charter and fitted with the diving bell and other essential rescue equipment removed from Nistar. After trials, she was commissioned as *INS Nireekshak* on 8 June 1989. Even though she was not a perfect SRV, she was better than the *Nistar*, which had become due for decommissioning. The roles envisaged for *Nireekshak* were:

- Facilitate rescue from a submarine in distress.
- Facilitate training of saturation divers.

Transformation of *INS Satavahana* into the School for Submarine Warfare

When *INS Satavahana* commissioned in 1974, the Submarine Training Wing and the Submarine Escape Training Facility formed part of the Integrated Type Training Establishment for the Russian acquisitions.

In 1986, when Southern Naval Command was assigned the task of 'Training', NHQ decided that submarine training would remain under Flag Officer Submarines.

To concentrate surface ship training in Cochin and to make space available in *Satavahana* for the training equipment of the newly inducted 877 EKM submarines, all the training equipment in the Surface Training Wing of *Satavahana* was carefully disconnected, bodily lifted into

a landing ship and transported to Cochin where it was reinstalled and reconnected.

In 1989, *Satavahana* was designated as the School for Submarine Warfare.

By 1990, the EKM training equipment and the EKM command and control / attack simulator had been installed.

Nuclear Propulsion for Submarines

"Nuclear propulsion in India was first mooted in 1967 when a naval officer and a BARC scientist prepared a feasibility report. A more detailed report was prepared in 1971 as the Committee of Secretaries felt that R&D on nuclear propulsion technology was inescapable if India was not to be left too far behind by the end of the century, when atomic energy would be a major source for both propulsion and energy requirements. A small nucleus of engineers was located in BARC as early as 1978."[14]

"Seeing the advent of nuclear propulsion in submarines of other navies, a study was undertaken by BARC to study a nuclear propulsion package for naval ships and submarines. A stage arose when it became necessary to train serving personnel in this very important area of propulsion technology."[15]

"The offer by the Soviet authorities of a 'nuclear-powered submarine fleet' for the Indian Navy was made by Marshal Ogarkov during his visit to India in April 1981. The Soviets offered to arrange a two-year training programme for Indian naval personnel, lease one nuclear submarine for five years for practical training and to render technical assistance for creating maintenance facilities in India for nuclear powered submarines. He added that the sale, as also assistance for designing and constructing nuclear-powered submarines, could be taken up later."[16]

"An agreement was concluded with the Soviet Union and a team of officers under the supervision of Vice Admiral MK Roy was formed to steer the project. After a rigorous selection procedure, the first batch of the nuclear submarine crews, under the command of Captain S Daniel commenced their training in the USSR. The training was, perhaps, the most thorough and taxing course that any of the Indian submariners, most of whom had over a decade of submarining behind them, had ever undergone.

---

14. *War in the Indian Ocean* by Vice Admiral MK Roy, Pages 114 et seq.

15. Excerpt from *The Pictorial History of the Submarine Arm* published by Naval Headquarters 1992.

16. *War in the Indian Ocean,* by Vice Admiral MK Roy, pages 114 et seq.

They absorbed the new technology with professional aplomb."[17]

Between 1982 and 1986, the crew was trained. The base facilities were set up by 1987.

"On September 14, (1987) Admiral Roy, Vice Chief of the Eastern Naval Command, conveyed to me the pleasant news that the Government had finally decided to take the first nuclear-propelled submarine from the Soviet Union on lease, as purchase would entail acceptance of NPT conditions.

"The idea of acquiring a nuclear-propelled submarine was floated by me as Defence Minister and after months of bargaining the Soviets agreed. A training programme was arranged for Indian sailors. I had visited the trainees in Leningrad and Riga. I was also happy that the lease amount charged by the Soviet Union was fairly reasonable. The nuclear propelled submarine had the advantage of remaining under water, which was not possible for the conventional submarines. It was also proposed at that time that a second nuclear-propelled submarine would be built in India. The Atomic Energy Commission experts were confident of producing an atomic power pack for the submarine."[18]

The Lease of Nuclear Submarine *Chakra*

On completion of the sea training commitment, the submarine was taken in hand to prepare her for the three-year period of lease.

The Utilisation of Chakra

Chakra commissioned on 5 January 1988 and sailed for India on 15 January 1988. Except when transiting through shallow waters in the South China Sea, the Singapore Straits and the Strait of Malacca, her passage was submerged. Throughout her passage, she was tracked by Australian and American MRASW aircraft. The frigate, *Dunagiri* rendezvous'd her in the South China Sea to escort her homeward. On arrival at Vishakhapatnam, she was received by Prime Minister, Rajiv Gandhi, the Defence Minister KC Pant and the CNS Admiral Nadkarni. After embarking, they were taken to sea for an outing.

During the three years of her lease, *Chakra* worked with both the Fleets off the east and west coasts of India.

Developments After 1990

Kalvari / Vela Class Submarines

The four submarines of the Kalvari class decommissioned between 1989 and 2003 (giving an average in-service life of 28 years). Of the four Vela class, two underwent 6-yearly refits between 1995 and 1999 and are still in service. The other two decommissioned between 1997 and 2001.[19]

Chakra

On completion of the lease, *Chakra* sailed for Russia on 16 December 1990 and was thereafter decommissioned in January 1991.

Submarine Propulsion Batteries

The programme for the indigenisation of propulsion batteries for the 877 EKM submarines that had been initiated in 1987 had not completed when the Soviet Union dissolved in 1991. By 1992, however, part supply of the first battery set for both EKM and SSK submarines started being received from Standard Batteries and Chloride India respectively. It took some years for indigenous batteries to completely replace those coming from Ukraine.

German HDW 1500 Shishumar Class (SSK) Submarines

SSK 3, *Shalki*, commissioned on 7 February 1992 and SSK 4, *Shankul*, commissioned on 28 May 1994. After *Shankul's* commissioning, the indigenous submarine construction programme at Mazagon Docks came to an end.

---

17. Excerpt from *The Pictorial History of the Submarine Arm* published by Naval Headquarters 1992.

18. Former President, R Venkataraman, in his book *My Presidential Years*, pages 74, 75.

19. For details, see Historical Reference Data section titled "Commissionings and Decommissionings", page 376.

Overview of the Submarine Arm 1976-1990

Year	RUSSIAN KALVARI & VELA CLASS	GERMAN HDW CLASS	RUSSIAN EKM CLASS	RUSSIAN NUCLEAR CHAKRA	INFRASTRUCTURE
1975	KALVARI under refit in Russia Jan75-Jul 76 KURSURA continued torpedo firings for NSTL 58	Under evaluation	–	–	Escape Training Tower commissioned
1976	KHANDERI commenced refit in Visakhapatnam	Under evaluation	–	–	Indigenous production established of batteries for KALVARI and VELA class
1977	KALVARI-NISTAR submarine escape trials	Under evaluation			
1978	KARANJ under refit in Russia Feb 78-Oct 79	Under evaluation	Russian side mentions EKM	–	–
1979	–	Under evaluation	–	–	Refit facilities established in Visakhapatnam First submarine docked in ND(V) for repairs
1980	KHANDERI completed refit in Visakhapatnam KURSURA under refit in Russia Sep 80-Apr 82 VELA under refit in Russia Sep 80-Apr 82	Under evaluation	Russian side offers EKM		
1981	VAGIR under refit in Visakhapatnam Jul 81-Oct 84	Contract signed in Dec 1981	Russian side repeats offer	–	–
1982	VAGLI under refit in Russia Sep 82-Mar 84	–	–	Agreement signed Crew selected	
1983	–	SSKs 1 and 2 construction commenced in Germany	Indian side visits EKM	Crew commenced training in Russia	
1984	KALVARI under refit in Visakhapatnam Nov 84-Oct 88	SSKs 3 and 4 construction commenced in India	–	–	
1985	–	–	–	–	–
1986	–	SSKs 1 and 2 commissioned in Germany	EKM 1 commissioned	Crew completed training and returned to India	
1987	–	–	EKMs 2 & 3 commissioned	Crew standing by	Construction of VLF station commenced
1988	KARANJ under refit in Visakhapatnam Sep 88-Dec 90	Indigenous production established of batteries for SSK and EKM submarines	EKMs 4, 5 & 6 commissioned	CHAKRA commissioned	–
1989	KARANJ under refit in in Visakhapatnam	–	EKM 7 commissioned	–	Diving Support Vessel NIREEKSHAK chartered as interim Rescue Vessel

Year					
1990	KARANJ under refit in Visakhapatnam	–	EKM 8 commissioned	–	- VLF Station commissioned - Battery Commissioning Facility established in Bombay
1990	–	–	–	CHAKRA returned to Russia	–
1992	–	SSK 3 commissioned in India	–	–	–
1993	–	–	–	–	–
1994	–	SSK 4 commissioned in India	–	–	–

Retrospect

By any yardstick, the achievements of the Submarine Arm were remarkable. In the thirty years from 1962 when, starting from scratch, the very first submariners underwent training in the British Navy, until 1991, the Navy inducted eighteen of the latest conventional submarines of their time, sixteen from Russia and two from Germany (with two more German submarines under construction in Bombay) and also manned, operated and maintained a missile-firing nuclear propelled submarine for three years, apart from setting up submarine infrastructure facilities at Bombay and Vishakhapatnam.

The difficulties encountered in attracting into, and retaining in, the submarine cadre sufficient technical personnel (officers, artificers and non-artificers), the difficulties in refitting submarines and the difficulties in coping with the ripple effects of inadequate air conditioning in tropical conditions were tackled with the typically Indian tenacity to keep things going until solutions were found.

The best features of four distinct traditions (three pertaining to conventional submarines – the British tradition in the early 1960s, the Russian tradition in the 1970s and 1980s, the German tradition in the 1980s and the fourth tradition in the 1980s pertaining to Russian nuclear submarines) were adapted and synthesised into a tradition uniquely appropriate to Indian conditions and climate.

As in the case of warships, Admirals Gorshkov and Chernavin of the Soviet Navy did their utmost to help the Submarine Arm. The assistance of the Soviet and German governments and their navies was very valuable. Most valuable of all was the understanding of the Indian Government of the future potential of the Navy's Submarine Arm.

Submariners have always been an elite fraternity. The unique characteristic of submariners in every Navy, and one which India's submariners have nurtured with the utmost care, is the awareness that when dived, the safety of their submarine depends on every member of the crew doing everything right. Each one of the crew knows that the lives of all depend upon each one doing the right thing. Mishaps have been manageable and non-catastrophic.

Submariners also have unique customs. Writing in the Navy Foundation's annual magazine *Quarterdeck 1987*, Commodore (later Rear Admiral) KR Menon said:

> "Submarines may change, but customs and traditions don't. Submarines still leave homeport for change of base with a band on the jetty, and come back to be received by the Captain SM and the traditional cake."

16

The Russian Acquisitions 1976 To 1990

Preamble

The naval acquisitions from Russia (then known as the Soviet Union) started in 1965 when the Navy's traditional supplier, the British Navy, because of its own resource constraints, was unable to meet the Indian Navy's requirements for modern destroyers and submarines. The initial acquisitions from Russia were mainly for deployment in the Bay of Bengal to deter misadventure by a bellicose Indonesia laying claim to the island of Great Nicobar, which was separated from Aceh, the historically turbulent, northern tip of Sumatra by a mere 90 miles.

The Constraints During Initial Interaction between 1966 and 1976

At the working level, the first decade of Indo-Russian naval interaction was afflicted by the Navy's suspicions of the 'secretiveness' of the Russian specialists who came to India to provide guarantee cover for each acquisition. In the Cold War propaganda of the time, Western literature about the Soviet Union was in the English language and portrayed the negative Western view of Communism and of the Soviet Union. Many Indian naval minds became susceptible to this bias.

Decades later, the memoirs of Anatoly Dobrynin,[1] the Soviet ambassador in Washington from the 1950s till the 1980s, shed light on this secretiveness that perplexed the Navy in those days:

"Characteristics of Russian Official Dealing

– Strict sense of secrecy/mania for secrecy.

– Inappropriate to talk with foreigners unless witnesses were present.

– Ideological bias against everything foreign.

"Virtually no Soviet citizen was permitted to travel abroad on anything except officially sanctioned business or cultural exchanges.

"All Soviet citizens going abroad, either on a short trip or a long term assignment to embassies or trade delegations, were thoroughly checked by various authorities. The final decision was made by a special department of the Communist Party Special Committee. Every individual leaving the country was called to this department for an interview on his or her public position and private life, as well as on 'Rules of Conduct for Soviet Citizens Abroad'. These rules had been approved by the Central Committee; they consisted of written instructions and anyone going abroad had to sit through an explanation and sign a statement saying he had received and understood them.

"Most of the rules listed things that were prohibited or not recommended for Soviet citizens in foreign countries. They were supposed to prevent us from 'being probed and recruited by foreign intelligence' on the street and in stores, at the movies and theaters, at receptions and other events to which invited. Breaking the rules meant either being sent home immediately or refused permission to travel abroad again."

In those early years, three main factors were at work. The Indian Navy strictly enforced the policy of 'Need to Know' to comply with its assurance to the Soviet side that the security of their naval equipment would be assured. Secondly, there was a near total paucity of naval personnel who knew the Russian language. And lastly, there was the secretiveness of the Russian specialists who came to India. These factors combined to constrict the interaction that was so essential for coping with the new Russian technologies and procedures. Interaction improved slowly as the two sides got to know each other. It was after the 1971 war that interaction rose exponentially.

The Flowering of Mutual Understanding

The Indian Navy's innovative use of Russian missile boats in the attacks on Karachi during the 1971 Indo-Pakistan War led to two significant developments.

Within India, the Government and the nation became

---

1. *In Confidence* by Anatoly Dobrynin, Times Books, Random House, New York, 1995.

aware, for the first time since Independence in 1947, of the contribution that naval operations could make to national policy objectives and how the Navy's swift achievement of regional maritime supremacy had hastened the end of the war. This led, during the 1973 and 1975 Defence Reviews, to the Government's ready acceptance of the Navy's requirements for the acquisition, from Russia, of ships, submarines and aircraft to fulfill long deferred requirements.

Within the Russian Navy, respect had developed for the way the Indian Navy had used what Russia had supplied. The Russian side responded positively to the Navy's requests for progressively better equipment in future acquisitions.

The initial acquisitions of ships and submarines had been designed for the Russian Navy, which operated in a cold and dry temperate climate and in cold, low salinity seas. They had not been designed to operate in the hot and humid climate and the warm, high salinity, corrosive seas typical of the tropics. As the Indian Navy gained experience of operating Russian vessels in tropical conditions, it was able to identify, and project to the Russian side, the essential alterations and additions required to 'Indianise' the Russian designs.

Each vessel was covered by a twelve-month guarantee period during which the Russian 'guarantee specialists', deputed to India by the 'zavods'[2] of the respective 'Original Equipment Manufacturers' (OEMs), rectified all shortcomings and replenished all the spare parts consumed. The feedback by these specialists to their respective zavods in the Soviet Union reinforced the Navy's official projections to the Russian side regarding the improvements considered essential for operation in the tropics. As a result, the Russian side tried its best that each successor series of Russian acquisitions became better than their predecessors.

The agreement for each ship / submarine catered also for the supply of the onboard spares required for routine maintenance up to the annual refit of the ship's equipment and the initial training of its crew. Separate agreements had to be signed for shore facilities like the storage, maintenance and preparation of weapons, for setting up of facilities for major refits, for the supply of repair spares and repair technical documentation, for training in deep repair training, for crew training facilities having identical equipment as was fitted on board and for simulators on which the crews could practice operating procedures and tactics, etc. The implementation of each of these

individual agreements had its own gestation time and resulted in delays that affected operational availability. The effort to synchronise all such facets of each 'acquisition' began in 1975 with the Indian side's proposal for a 'Model Contract'.

Acquisitions Between 1966 and 1976

Vessels	Delivered	Class
• Two 730 tonne Landing Ships Tank (Medium) LST(M)s	1966	Gharial
• Five 80 tonne patrol boats	1967	P class
• Four 2,000 tonne ocean going submarines	1967-69	Kalvari
• A 6,000 tonne Submarine Depot Ship	1968	
• Five 1,000 tonne anti submarine vessels.	1968-69	Kamorta
• Eight 180 tonne missile boats	1971	205
• A 800 tonne Submarine Rescue Vessel	1971	
• Five improved 1,000 tonne anti submarine vessels	1972-74	Arnala
• Four improved 2,000 tonne ocean going submarines	1973-74	Vela
• Four improved 1,120 tone LST (M)s	1975-76	Ghorpad

Russian Acquisitions Between 1976 and 1990

Overview

Surface Vessels

- Eight missile boats in 1976.
- Three rocket boats between 1976 and 1978.
- Six coastal minesweepers between 1977 and 1980.
- Three guided missile destroyers between 1980 and 1983.
- Six inshore minesweepers between 1983 and 1984.
- Four landing ships between 1984 and 1986.
- Two guided missile destroyers between 1986 and 1987.
- Six coastal minesweepers between 1986 and 1988.
- Five gas turbine propelled missile boats between 1987 and 1989.
- Four anti submarine boats between 1989 and 1990.

Submarines

- Eight submarines between 1986 and 1990.
- Lease of nuclear propelled submarine 1988 to 1991.

---

2. *"zavod"* is the Russian word for factory, industrial enterprise, etc.

Aircraft

- Three MRASW IL 38s in 1977.
- Kamov 25 and Kamov 28 ASW helicopters from 1980 onwards.
- Two MRASW IL 38s in 1983.
- Eight LRMP TU 142s in 1988.

Infrastructure at Vishakhapatnam

- Construction continued of the new Naval Dockyard.
- South Dry Dock was completed in 1978.
- Missile Technical Position established in 1985.
- North Dry Dock Complex commissioned in 1990.

Infrastructure at Bombay

- Missile Boat Engine Repair Facility was completed in 1980.
- Mobile missile coast batteries.
- Moored sonobuoys and monitoring systems.

Technical and Design Assistance

- Fitment of Russian weapons, fire control systems, sensors and associated equipment in the indigenous frigates and corvettes.
- Licensed production of Project 1241 RE missile boats in Bombay and Goa.

Major Issues

Several issues animated the naval interaction between the Indian and Soviet sides during the period 1976 to 1990.

The Indian Navy's projections for progressively better sensors, weapons and systems, suitably modified for Indian conditions, to be fitted in the ships, submarines and aircraft being acquired from Russia, and in the Indian-built ships being fitted with a mix of Russian, European and Indian equipment.

The maximum headway was made in this regard. By 1990, better missile boats, minesweepers, guided missile frigates, submarines, helicopters and maritime reconnaissance aircraft had been acquired from Russia. The latest available equipment and weapons were fitted in the frigates of the Godavari class, the corvettes of the Khukri class and were being negotiated for the follow-on Project 16 A frigates of the Brahmaputra class, the follow-on corvettes of Project 25 A and the Project 15 guided missile destroyers of the Delhi class.

There were some critical requirements that the Russian side could not meet by 1990 like longer range surface to surface missiles, air-to-surface anti ship missiles fired from Russian aircraft, sub-surface launched anti ship missiles from submarine torpedo tubes, Airborne Early Warning helicopters etc. The Soviet side promised to offer these requirements as soon as they had been developed.

How best to keep Russian ships, submarines, aircraft and equipment properly maintained, repaired and refitted until the requisite refit facilities ashore had been fully erected and equipped at the respective home-ports.

Some headway was made on this issue. In the end 1960s, for security reasons of segregating them from the Western origin ships based in Bombay, all the Russian acquisitions had been based in Visakhapatnam on the East coast. Operational considerations gradually compelled critical facilities to be replicated in Bombay on the West coast. By 1990, essential repair and maintenance facilities had been set up on both coasts at most of the naval ports and air stations from where the ships, submarines and aircraft actually operated.

The time over-runs that plagued the completion of facilities in the new Naval Dockyard at Visakhapatnam have been discussed in the chapter on Maintenance, Repair and Refit Facilities, as has the adverse effect of these delays on the seaworthiness of ships and submarines. As far as submarines were concerned, where 'safety when dived' was paramount, the Russian side helped by undertaking their 6-yearly Medium Repairs in Russia, whenever this became inescapable.

The Procedural Inability of the Soviet Side to Supply 'Yard Materials' like Hull Plates, Pipes and Cables Critically Required for Refits.

The Soviet State Committee for Foreign Economic Relations (GKES) had under it two Departments – the General Engineering Department (GED) and the General Technical Department (GTD). The GED was responsible for the delivery of ships, submarines and aircraft complete with exploitation documentation, on-board spares and five years exploitation spares, the training of commissioning crews, training courses, etc. The GTD was responsible for dealing with all aspects of shore support (maintenance, repair, refit, refit spares, repair documentation, workshop equipment and machinery, etc). As ships and submarines started being taken in hand for major 3-yearly and 6-yearly refits, the problem arose of the supply of items like hull plating, pipes and electric cables, known as 'Yard Materials'. When demands for these items were raised on the GTD, the GTD advised that these be demanded from the Ministry of Foreign Trade. The Ministry of Foreign Trade declined to accept these demands because the order quantity was too small. The following excerpts reflect the nature of the procedural deadlocks:

"The supply of Yard Materials – hull plates, sections and pipes – for Soviet origin ships has been taken up time and again but without result. The GTD stand has been that these should be supplied by the Trade Agencies of the Ministry of Foreign Trade. The Ministry of Foreign Trade has not accepted our requirement on the grounds that the quantities required by the Indian side are uneconomical and should be supplied by GED/GTD. In July 1978, requirements of hull plates, sections and pipes for the next five years were given to the Ministry of Foreign Trade. They refused to accept and stated that the supply of yard materials by the Ministry of Foreign Trade was not possible in the foreseeable future.

"In view of this difficulty, it was suggested that GTD may obtain the material from the Trade Agencies and supplied on 'cash and carry' basis. GTD indicated that it did not deal with the supply of such materials, which are to be indented directly on Trade Agencies. The GTD suggested that the minimum quantity that the trade agency could supply should be ascertained and orders placed accordingly. It was also suggested that Indian Navy should explore the possibility of getting these materials through Indian firms dealing with Soviet trade agencies.

"The Indian side pointed out that some of the items supplied in the Remont spares for submarines, like plating and cables, were not sufficient to carry out refits. The Soviet side stated that the Soviet Navy also faced similar problems and that the Indian side should not attempt making wholesale replacement, but do so only if the equipment could not be repaired easily. The Indian side pointed out that in the context of our submarines undergoing refit, the Soviet side had advised it would be quicker and advantageous for us to replace full units and carry out repairs of machinery and equipment removed from ships / submarines before return to stock. The Indian side reiterated that the delay in supply of adequate quantities of cables, piping and plating was seriously holding up the progress of refits in India. The Soviet side stated that these were repair materials and had to be ordered on Soviet Industry through the Foreign Trade Agencies. The Indian side pointed out that the materials could be procured through the Trade Agencies only if we were able to calculate our total requirement and for this purpose, we had to depend entirely on the information being provided by Soviet Design agencies. If we were provided with design and repair technology, it would be of considerable help to the Indian side in speeding up refits."

Problems of the kind took years to unravel.

Indian Participation in Russian State Committee Acceptance Trials and Training in Deep Repair.

The Russian side was in complete agreement that the Indian Navy should be self reliant in 'repair expertise' to the maximum extent possible. The difficulty was how to 'transfer' this expertise.

Acceptance of a new Russian vessel was conducted in two phases. In the first phase, the Russian Navy's representatives participated in the Russian Government's 'State Committee Acceptance Trials'. Before accepting the Indian ship / submarine from a Russian shipbuilding yard, they checked that 'performance was as per contract'. A Russian Navy crew then sailed the ship to the port at which the ship would be handed over. The vessel would then be handed to the Indian commissioning crew to carry out 'Delivery Acceptance Trials'. During these trials, the Indian side would systematically verify that the performance specified in the contract for each system was satisfactorily demonstrated. Whenever the performance parameters stipulated in the contract were not met, there would be dissension. The Indian side, therefore, suggested that the Indian Navy's representatives should participate in the State Committee trials. This would not only help to avoid dissension during the Delivery Acceptance Trials, it would also enable the Indian specialists to learn how to achieve / restore peak performance in subsequent years after equipment had been overhauled during refits.

No headway could be made on this suggestion. Under the constitution law of the Soviet Union, it was not permissible for foreigners to be allowed into shipbuilding yards where warships were being constructed for the Soviet Navy. Similar considerations affected the Indian side's requests for Dockyard civilians to be allowed access into equipment factories for on-job-training in the deep repair of complex equipment.

To overcome this problem, the Soviet side did permit Indian Naval personnel and Dockyard civilians to learn how the first Indian submarine underwent Medium Repairs in Russia at their Vladivostok yard. Arrangements were also made, whenever asked for, for Indian personnel to be trained in the deep repair / overhaul of major equipment like gas turbines in special training centres set up for this purpose. In the case of the Rajput class guided missile destroyers, the Russian side specially arranged a location, away from their usual ship repair yard, for Indian personnel to learn, hands-on-the-job, how a Soviet Navy destroyer of the same class underwent Medium (i.e. 6-yearly) Repairs.

The crux of the problem lay elsewhere. In the Russian system, a specialist 'specialised' in one system or an aspect of it. By continuous association, each specialist mastered all there was to know about his system. In the Indian system, however, not only were Dockyard civilians not so vertically specialised, but also uniformed officers and sailors were regularly transferred out of the Dockyards to be assessed for performance in other assignments. Whenever the Navy suffered a major problem that it could not tackle, it would seek Russian assistance. The Russian side would suggest sending a large team of vertical specialists. The Indian side would demur and suggest fewer specialists. The Russian side would then send a general specialist. The problem would linger on until the Indian side agreed to accept the appropriate number of deep specialists.

As a long-term solution, the Russian side repeatedly suggested that the Indian side should ask for civilian experts from their Russian factories to come to India to train our Dockyard civilians. This never fructified. In the first place, our Dockyard civilians were not so vertically specialised as to learn deep repairs on a one to one basis. Secondly, apart from the financial aspect of accepting so many specialists, dozens of vertical Soviet specialists could not possibly teach highly technical, deep repair training, in the Russian language, via an interpreter, to a handful of Dockyard civilians whose knowledge of English was limited. Thirdly, six officers and fifty Dockyard civilians had been deputed to the Soviet Union in 1967 for training in Soviet yards; a team of 25 officers and Dockyard supervisors had been deputed to Vladivostok in 1975 for a full year to learn submarine repairs on-the-job; and a special Training Centre had been set up in the Kronstadt Dockyard in Leningrad to train Dockyard civilians; all these teams had absorbed very little. Fourthly, the Indian side somehow could not get rid of the suspicion that Russian specialists sought every opportunity for foreign travel, particularly to warm and hospitable India. And last but not least, there was the fear that the Western world would say that the Russians were running India's Navy. Cumulatively, the Navy was severely disadvantaged by its inability to overcome its reservations and resolve this *contretemps*.[3]

It took years of perseverance and innovation for our specialists to acquire deep repair expertise. Whenever determined technical officers tackled this problem by personal involvement, the results were extremely successful.

Grappling with the Russian procedures for the supply of the various categories of spares and repair technical documentation to sustain the combat readiness of the Russian acquisitions.

Very little headway could be made on this issue. On the one hand, the Indian side's inadequate knowledge of the Russian language and of the codification system of Russian stores resulted in indents being prepared incorrectly and their rejection by the Russian side as being incomprehensible. On the other hand, the time taken for the mandatory Indian procedure for financial scrutiny of the costing of each item in each indent was unable to mesh with the Russian side's stringent procedures for signing agreements in good time so as to dovetail with the annual production plans of Russian factories. The enormous, unsuccessful, efforts made by both sides to overcome these problems have been discussed in the chapter on Logistics.

Model Contract

As mentioned earlier, separate contracts had to be processed with the GED and the GTD for ships and for each of the different elements of their associated infrastructure like training, training facilities, repair documentation, repair facilities, repair spares, etc. The Indian side felt it essential to formulate a 'Model Contract' which, in a comprehensive document for each acquisition, would dovetail the delivery of refit spares with the operating and refit cycle, with the installation of refit facilities, with the completion of the repair training, with the delivery of repair documentation in English and so on. Only thus would it be possible to eliminate the serious difficulties that were being experienced as a result of these items being processed in separate un-synchronised contracts.

No headway could be made on this issue. Whilst the Russian side agreed that there might be scope for amalgamating some of the separate contracts thereby reducing the total number, detailed consideration of the Indian side's suggestion had shown that it was not possible to attempt a single contract to cover all aspects. The insurmountable problem was that too many ministries and factories were involved and under Russian procedure, each factory under each different ministry had to draw up its own contract in terms of financial clauses, delivery dates, documentation, guarantee specialists etc.

'Hybridisation'

The first decade of Indo-Russian naval interaction, 1966 onwards, had focused primarily on the induction of Russian ships and submarines and the creation of their support infrastructure. From 1974 onwards, the scope of interaction widened. In addition to acquiring better ships, submarines, aircraft, helicopters and weapons from Russia, interaction involved the installation of Russian weapons

---

3. This entire problem has also been dealt with in the chapter on the Naval Expert Committee, page 158.

and systems in Indian built hulls, interfaced with a mix of Western and indigenous equipment.

This 'hybridisation' began with the fitment in the 1960 vintage, British anti submarine frigate *Talwar* of surface to surface missile systems removed *en bloc* from a non-operational Russian missile boat. *Talwar's* installation was completed and successfully test-fired in 1976. The confidence so gained clarified the grey areas in synthesising European and Russian ship borne systems.

The next step came when deciding the weapon package for the three ships that were to follow the six Leander class frigates being built in Mazagon Docks. In 1974, particulars became available of the 5,000 tonne destroyers of the Rajput class and the 800 tonne ocean going rocket boat of the Durg class, the contracts for which had been signed in 1975. In consultation with specialists from the Russian Design Bureau, consideration began of the installation of the Rajput's radar and the Durg's surface to surface and surface to air missile systems in a new hull design. The outcome was the Godavari class missile frigates of Project 16. This project has been discussed in the chapter on Warship Design and Construction.

The next step, again in consultation with specialists from the Russian Design Bureau, was the installation of even more modern Russian weapon systems in the new Corvettes of Project 25 and the new Destroyers of Project 15.[4] These Projects too have been discussed in the chapter on Warship Design and Construction.

Licensed Production

Concurrently with this hybridisation, the licensed production commenced of the new, fast, 400 tonne, gas turbine propelled missile boats of Project 1241 RE. The first five boats of this class were acquired from Russia. The production of the remainder was shared between Mazagon Docks and Goa Shipyard. This Project has been discussed in the chapter on Warship Design and Construction.

JISWOG

By 1987, both the Russian and the Indian sides realised that the widening cooperation in surface warship building and design required regular overseeing and monitoring at high levels to ensure that:

• Agreements were signed and orders placed at the right time so that Russian equipment and material was delivered to Indian warship building yards at the right

time to avoid delays in their construction schedules.

• Soviet factory specialists arrived at the right time for equipment trials etc.

A high-level Joint Indo-Soviet Working Group on Shipbuilding (JISWOG), chaired jointly by the Deputy Minister of Shipbuilding of the USSR and India's Secretary of Defence Production, was constituted to meet twice a year, alternately in Delhi and in Moscow, to foresee and resolve problems. The Indian participants included the Chairmen of the three shipyards, representatives from Naval Headquarters' professional directorates and the Ministry of Defence. The Russian participants were from the concerned Soviet Ministries, the Heads of the relevant Design Bureaux, the designers associated with the specific Indian Navy Project, representatives of the GED, the GTD, the factories etc.

JISWOG held its first meeting in New Delhi in Mar 1988, the second meeting in Moscow in Sep 1988 and so on. In due course, the terms of reference of JISWOG were expanded to resolve problems of product support for Russian ships and equipment that had been supplied in earlier years. Moreover, with the interaction at JISWOG meetings yielding better foreknowledge of the equipment and weapons for future supply, it became possible to augment existing maintenance and repair facilities instead of setting up new facilities.

Indigenisation

In the Indo-Russian naval context, indigenisation had two phases:

• In the first phase, the 1970s and early 1980s, the focus was on resolving the logjam in the supply of spares.[5] The Russian side repeatedly stated that Indian industry was quite capable of making many of the items of spares and equipment that were being indented from Russia. The procedural requirements of licensed production of such items were discussed over the years but the quantities involved were never large enough to justify the investment.

• By the next phase, in the late 1980s, two things had happened. Firstly, considerable indigenisation had begun to be achieved in the equipment for the destroyers (Delhi class), frigates (Godavari and Brahmaputra classes), corvettes (Khukri class) and gas-turbined missile boats (1241 REs). Secondly, the economic restructuring taking place in the Soviet Union had led to the Soviet side

---

4. In the 1990s, similar action was taken for the follow on Corvettes of Project 25 A, the follow on Brahmaputra class frigates of Project 16 A – the successors of the earlier Godavari class and the follow on Bangalore class destroyers of Project 15 A.

5. See chapter on Logistics, page 166.

insisting on payment for equipment and spares only in hard currency or on 'cash and carry' basis, particularly for those items that were required urgently or where we were advised to deal directly with the manufacturing units. The combination of these developments spurred interest in widening indigenisation.

To make indigenisation cost effective, the Indian side initiated discussions in the JISWOG that:

- A large number of equipments for Soviet supplied ships and submarines had been indigenously developed, like submarine batteries, electric cables, welding materials and electrodes, converters, electric motors, control panels, pumps, generating sets, distilling plants, deck machinery etc.

- Indian industry was keen to export these items to Russia, if these were either in short supply or were being imported.

- Would the Soviet side consider entrusting to Indian PSUs like MDL or BEML the manufacture of items that were being obtained from other countries?

This interaction was to fructify, a decade later, in the co-development, co-production and co-marketing of projects like the Brahmos anti ship missile.

Acquisitions Between 1976 and 1990

Vessels/Aircraft	Delivered	Class
Eight 200 tonne Improved 205 ER Missile Boats	1976 to 1977	Prabal/Chapal
Three 800 tonne ocean-going Rocket Boats	1976 to 1977	Durg
Five IL 38 Maritime Recce Anti Submarine Aircraft	1977 to 1983	
Six 700 tonne Coastal Minesweepers	1977 to 1980	Pondicherry
Three 5000 tonne Guided Missile Destroyers	1980 to 1983	Rajput
Seven Kamov 25 Anti Submarine Helicopters	1980 to 1986	
Six 90 tonne Inshore Minesweepers	1983 to 1984	
Four 1,120 tonne Landing Ships Tank Medium	1984 to 1986	Cheetah
Two 5,000 tonne Improved Guided Missile Destroyers	1986 to 1987	Rajput
Thirteen Kamov 28 Anti Submarine Helicopters	1986 to 1988	
Six 700 tonne Coastal Minesweepers	1986 to 1988	Karwar
Six 2,000 tonne ocean-going 877 EKM submarines	1986 to 1988	Sindhughosh
Five 450 tonne gas- turbined 1241	1987 to 1989	Veer
Four 490 tonne gas-turbined 1241 PE A/S Craft	1989 to 1991	Abhay
Eight Long Range Maritime Patrol TU 142 LRMP aircraft	1988	
Two 2,000 tonne ocean-going 877 EKM submarines	1989 to 1990	Sindhughosh
A nuclear propelled submarine on a 3-year lease from 1988 to 1991		

Specific aspects relevant to these acquisitions have been discussed in the chapters on the Submarine Arm, the Air Arm, Refit Facilities, Logistics, Personnel and Indigenous Warship Construction.

Indo Russian Relations and Naval Acquisitions After 1990

Except for the serious dislocation caused in the availability of spares and equipment for the earlier acquisitions, Indo-Russian naval relations continued to flourish in depth and in width.

In 1994, India and Russia signed an agreement on long-term, bilateral, military-technical cooperation till the year 2000. In October 1997, this was extended till 2010.

In 1995, India acquired a second hand tanker from Russia.

From 1997 onwards, the Sindhughosh class 877 EKM submarines started being sent to Russia for modernisation.

In 1997, a contract were signed for three 3840 tonnes Krivak III guided missile destroyers of the Talwar class and two improved 877 EKM submarines.

In October 2000, India and Russia signed the Strategic Partnership Declaration pledging that the two nations would not join any political or military blocs and avoid treaties that would infringe on each other's national security interests. The declaration highlighted defence and military technical cooperation, service-to-service cooperation and joint R & D and training.

An Inter-Governmental Agreement signed in October 2000 agreed in principle for the following naval acquisitions, the final contracts for which would be negotiated separately:

- The acquisition, after refit, of the aircraft carrier *Admiral Gorshkov* with:

  - The naval version of the MIG 29 K Short Take Off Land (STOL) fighter aircraft, armed with air to air, air to surface, and television guided missiles, and capable of being refueled in-flight by tanker aircraft to extend strike range,

  - Kamov 28 anti submarine helicopters and,

  - Kamov 31 airborne early warning helicopters.

This contract was concluded in 2004.

An Indo-Russian Inter-Governmental Commission on Military-Technical Cooperation was set up, headed jointly by the Indian Defence Minister and the Russian Deputy Prime Minister. Two working groups of this Commission meet annually. The group headed by the Defence Secretary deals with military-technical cooperation. The group headed by the Secretary Defence Production deals with warship building.

Acquisitions After 1990

Surface Vessels

- A second-hand fleet tanker *Jyoti*.

- Three Krivak III, guided missile destroyers of the Talwar class.

Submarines

- Two conventionally propelled, missile firing, improved EKM submarines.

Aircraft

- Kamov 31 AEW helicopters.

Weapons & Systems

- For indigenously constructed warships of the Delhi, Brahmaputra and Khukri classes.

Facilities Established for Maintenance, Repair, Overhaul and Refit of Russian Acquisitions:

At Vishakhapatnam	For ships and submarines.
At Mumbai	For ships and submarines.
At Kochi	For inshore minesweepers.
At Goa	For MRASW aircraft and ASW helicopters.
At Arakkonam	For LRMP aircraft.

Retrospect

The Russian acquisition programme between 1976 and 1990 was qualitatively different from that of the period 1965 to 1975.

On the one hand, as in the previous decade, the Navy's technical side preferred to slow down the pace of acquisitions because the shortage of technical officers and artificers, the lag in setting up repair facilities and the backlog of refits combined to affect the seaworthiness of ships and submarines. On the other hand, there were other endemic causes that affected the Navy's ability to keep the acquisitions seaworthy and combat ready.

Until 1966, the Navy's ships were entirely of British origin. The machinery, weapons, sensors and other equipment were of almost the same technological vintage as ships in the British Navy, whose feedback kept the India Navy *au fait* with the problems encountered in the fields of operations, maintenance and logistics. Spares were readily available off the shelf, often through direct sourcing from the British Navy. Steam driven machinery permitted liberal usage. Rarely did anyone feel constricted by 'hours of usage'.

This changed after 1967. The vessels of various types procured from Russia were densely packed with equipment whose maintenance routines were governed rigidly by 'hours of usage'. The Russian operating – maintenance – refit – logistic system and procedures were designed to keep vessels at instant readiness for combat in the Cold War with the US Navy. This was achieved by strictly regulated usage between refits, backed up by an extensive maintenance and logistic infrastructure ashore. Repair and refit cycles were closely spaced and dovetailed with instant logistic support.

These Russian vessels arrived in India in an ambience of 'calendar based' maintenance, totally different from 'regulated hours of usage' they had been designed for. The Navy found that the procurement of spares from Russia required strict conformance with their inflexible, time-consuming process. The Navy was neither used to this process nor could it comprehend it for want of catalogues containing spare part reference numbers, difficulties in preparing indents in the Russian language, etc.

The submarines, inducted from 1968 onwards, required a very high level of technical monitoring and stronger logistic support. They had their own unique pressure hull and technical requirements to ensure safety when submerged. Soon thereafter, from 1971 onwards, the thin-skinned, high-speed missile boats arrived. They too had their unique support philosophy, involving special to type base support and training complexes for the boats and their missiles.

In a very short space of time, the Navy's entire refit, maintenance and logistic infrastructure, procedures and facilities came under pressure. The number of items handled by the Logistics Organisation multiplied and the rupee value of material used in the Naval Dockyard Bombay zoomed. Cumulatively, the induction of new types of ships and weapons, the new procedures requiring austere usage, hour-based maintenance and instant logistics, the inadequate facilities ashore for maintenance and refit and continually transferring personnel in and out of ships stressed the prevailing system to its limits.

These stresses and strains were compounded by the inability of the Navy to come to terms with the reality that the only way it could overcome the constraints of austere usage and closely spaced refits for which the equipment had been designed, was by indenting substantially more spares than what even the Russian side had recommended and by having efficient repair facilities. The chapters on Logistics and Refit Facilities have analysed why these could not be achieved.

There were other compulsions.

As has been discussed in the chapter on Personnel, an over-riding compulsion was the need to give equitable 'sea time' to every officer and sailor by rotating ships crews every one to two years.

From the very outset, the Navy, which was used to unrestricted usage of steam driven ships and auxiliary machinery, blithely ignored the repercussions of not adhering to the limitations laid down regarding the operating hours of critical machinery like diesel engines and diesel generators.

Vice Admiral A Britto, who retired as the Chief of Material, recalls:

"We had less success in coming to grips with management of technology in the acquisitions from Russia. Firstly, these inductions, significant in number, took place at short notice in the face of manpower constraints, as well as those that inhibited assimilation of technology as a whole. These platforms also necessitated radical changes in the philosophy of training, operation and maintenance and posed a major challenge to policy makers who were beset with traditional mindsets due to the Western experience. Executive officers, in particular, lacked understanding of the underlying principles of Soviet design, which were based on narrow design margins of equipment, restrictions in operating regimes and operational life of equipment, reduced manning / strong shore reliance and scrupulous demands on procedures for maintenance and upkeep. We were simply unable for many years to marry Soviet philosophy and practice into our scheme of things. Violations of technical philosophy, often insisted upon, had many an undesirable consequence."

There is substance in the Russian view, which was stated to every Indian delegation which complained about the non availability of critical operational spares, that the shortage derived more from what, by Russian norms, was 'excessive usage by the Indian side' and 'beyond what the equipment was designed to do'.

The Indian Navy's dilemma was that it just could not countenance not giving every officer and sailor equitable 'sea time'. It was a mandatory prerequisite for their next promotion. The perpetual compulsion of taking new crews to sea and the inability to accept that Russian equipment would break down as soon as its design limits were exceeded led directly to 'over exploitation'. Subsequently, rather ironically, the Navy had to turn a blind eye to the fact that time spent in ships that barely went to sea would still have to be treated as sea time.

From the technical angle, it was known that:

- The new Dockyard coming up at Vishakhapatnam specifically for the Russian acquisitions would take several years to be ready.

- Until the workshops of the new Dockyard were set up, the rudimentary Base Repair Organisation at Vishakhapatnam could never cope with the annual refit / docking, biennial refit and six yearly refit workload of submarines and ships.

- Even when, for operational reasons and also to ease the annual refit/docking load on Vishakhapatnam, the minimum essential facilities for annual refit were duplicated in Bombay for the Russian vessels based there, ships and submarines still had to return to Vishakhapatnam for their major three-yearly and six-yearly repairs.

The only way vessels could have been kept combat ready was to minimise the mal-operation of equipment. This was best done by conserving the experience of the officers and men trained in Russia, and avail of the expertise of the Russian guarantee specialists that came with each new acquisition. Neither of these resources was effectively harnessed. To save on the costs of training personnel in Russia, the experienced personnel of the first few vessels were sent back to Russia to commission the subsequent vessels, much to the detriment of vessels so deprived. As regards utilising the services of the Russian guarantee specialists, the difficulties of interacting in the Russian language and our fierce pride in 'not being technically dependent on the Russians' restrained productive interaction.

Despite all these vexatious problems, the Russian acquisition programme between 1976 and 1990 did manage to succeed, slowly to begin with and eventually beyond everybody's expectations. It was in these trying years that the solid foundations were laid for future Indo-Russian interaction.

After the initial resentment in the 1960s at the temerity of Indian crews to decline the weekly political lectures and the persistent questions of Indian officers and artificers seeking to master their equipment, the Russian Training Centres and their Academies accepted, with increasing respect over the next twenty years, that they were dealing with persons who were not only intelligent and professional but also diligent and innovative.

This professional respect over-arched the complex procedural constraints of each side. The Russians started feeling proud to see how the crews they had trained, meticulously carried out the Delivery Acceptance and Weapon Proving Trials before they confidently sailed their vessels back to India. On the Indian side, the moment the crews commissioned their ships and submarines, they realised how valuable the thoroughness of their Russian training had been.

As mutual respect increased at the local fleet level, it percolated upwards to Moscow and got reflected in the greater width and depth of interaction with Indian naval delegations to Moscow and Russian delegations to India.

A remarkable facet of the high level interactions in Moscow and in Delhi was that each successive acquisition was an improvement on its predecessor. The Vela class submarines were better than the Kalvari class and the Kilo class submarines were better than the Vela class. The second lot of Petyas was better than the Kamorta class. The second series of extended range missile boats was better than the earlier series and the 1241 REs were better than both. The Karwar class coastal minesweepers were better than the earlier Pondicherry class. The Cheetah class LSTs were better than the earlier Ghorpad class. The 4th and 5th guided missile frigates were better than the first three of the Rajput class. The TU 142 LRMP aircraft were better than the MRASW IL 38 aircraft. The KA 28 ASW helicopters were better than their predecessor KA 25s.

Much of the credit for this achievement must go to the tenacity and dexterity with which successive CNS', VCNS' and COMs pursued the briefs prepared for them by their young and eager staff in NHQ's professional directorates. The latter were keeping abreast of the latest developments in the Western navies and also of the latest developments in the Soviet Navy by avidly studying Western naval compendia. The Russians knew this and were good humoured enough to occasionally remark, in jest, regarding the Navy's persistence for 'something better

than what the West had' that 'India should purchase one from the West and give it to us and very soon we would give India something better!'

A substantial share of the credit for the success of Indo Russian naval cooperation must go to the then State Committee for Foreign Economic Relations and its much maligned departments – the General Engineering Department (GED) and the General Technical Department (GTD). Their enormous patience and tolerance was able to bridge the Indian side's inability to understand the inertia of the centrally planned, totally Government owned and controlled, Russian industrial system.

An equally great, if not greater, share of credit must go to the Indian Ministries of Defence and Finance (Defence). Their agility in negotiations and the painstaking discussions with their counterparts in the State Committee for Foreign Economic Relations belies the widespread naval belief that the Navy was treated like a stepchild. The Navy's incredible technological up-gradation in just twenty-five years after 1965 would not have been possible without the whole-hearted support of these two institutions.

A large share of the credit for laying a sound foundation for Indo-Russian naval cooperation belongs to Admiral Gorshkov until the mid 1980s and to his successor Admiral Chernavin thereafter. They intervened adroitly at every impasse. The calibrated release of larger, better and more modern ships, submarines and aircraft were not only in step with the larger objectives of Indo-Russian political, economic and defence cooperation but also a manifestation of their conviction that the Indian Navy would exploit to maximum effect whatever Russia gave. Admiral Gorshkov's confidence, and indeed that of the entire Russian naval establishment, first developed after the spectacular success of the missile boat attacks on Karachi harbour during the 1971 war. These attacks not only brought acclaim to the efficacy of Russian weapons when well exploited; they also validated Russian confidence in Indian naval competence. Over the years, whenever the Navy took Prime Ministers, Defence Ministers and high officials from the Defence Ministry to sea and they saw Russian missiles being shot down by Russian missiles, it must have gratified the Russians as much as it did everybody else.

It was this confidence and mutual respect which flowered in the years that followed to jointly design the sleek, elegant and powerful ships like the guided missile corvettes of the Khukri class, the guided missile destroyers of the Delhi class and the guided missiles frigates of the Brahmaputra class, fitted with the latest conventional weapons that the Russian Navy was fitting in its own ships.

None of the above would have been possible without the close rapport that prevailed between the Indian and the Soviet leadership at the highest political level in successive Governments, regardless of the party in power.

In retrospect, despite all the procedural limitations of each side, the induction and absorption of the Russian acquisitions has been as monumental an achievement as the Indigenous Warship and Submarine Projects.

17

Maintenance, Repair And Refit Facilities

Developments Till 1975

In 1947, when India became independent, the Bombay Dockyard provided all the maintenance, repair, docking and refit support that the ships of that time needed.

The Coastal Force Workshops at Cochin and Vishakhapatnam (then known in its short form as Vizag) had been established during World War II to support the coastal forces operating against the Japanese in Burma. They had a few machine tools, carpentry facilities for repairing wooden hulls, a small slipway and basic shops like foundry, electrical repairs etc.

Between 1947 and 1975, considerable progress was made in the expansion and modernisation of the facilities at Bombay, Vizag and Cochin and the creation of new facilities at Port Blair.

Bombay Dockyard[1]

After World War II ended in 1945, the Grace Committee was appointed in 1946 to make recommendations about the development of the Navy's only Dockyard at Bombay. It submitted its recommendations in 1947. Of the Committee's recommendations, two were far-reaching.

The first was that the Dockyard should dispense with the traditional British Navy Dockyard organisation, which bred departmental loyalties at lower levels. Instead it should adopt the 'industrial' system of management, pioneered and tested during World War II by the United States Navy, wherein all industrial activity was amalgamated under one technical head. This system ensured high level planning with meticulous details, coordination and progress at appropriate levels. It ensured economy and efficiency through the process of planning, estimating and progressing, by controlling material, labour and equipment, and above all pinpointing bottlenecks and manpower losses. It gave an example that could still, many decades later, be a model for today's Dockyards and Ship Repair Yards:

"When a ship comes in for repair in the United States Navy Yards, for approximately three or four days no work is done on board, and officers and men on board ship wonder what is happening. Behind the scene, careful planning is going on, along with the requirement of men and material to the last detail, as to how, when and where an item, for instance, is to be repaired. On the fourth day about a thousand men descend on board the ship like bees on a honeycomb, and the ship is ripped to bits, every individual knows exactly what is to be done, and in about three days the ship is completely repaired."

This recommendation was accepted. In 1948, the British Navy organisation was replaced. Under the Captain Superintendent, came the Industrial Manager, with four managers – Engineering, Electrical, Construction and Maintenance – in addition to a Gun Mounting Officer.

The second recommendation was that since buildings restricted the Dockyard's landward expansion, it should be shifted out from Bombay to Nhava Sheva across the harbour where there was deep water and vacant land for expansion. This recommendation was not accepted because Nhava Sheva had no electricity, no fresh water, no roads, no railway. Shifting the existing Dockyard would be prohibitively expensive. It would have to be expanded in situ without disrupting the existing repair and refit capability that was sustaining the Navy's ships.[2]

In 1948, in consultation with the British Admiralty, Sir Alexander Gibbs and Partners, a firm of internationally reputed technical consulting engineers, was appointed as consultants. Their terms of reference were:

● Creation of additional area by reclamation.

---

1. For details, please see *History of the Naval Dockyard Bombay* by Rear Admiral K Sridharan.

2. The same reasoning, twenty years later in the mid 1960s, compelled the choice of the present site of the Vizag Dockyard. It wasn't until the mid 1980s, when electricity, fresh water, road and rail infrastructure could be dovetailed, that it became possible to propose building a major dockyard from scratch at Karwar.

- Creation of additional berthing facilities by constructing new wharves.
- Creation of additional dry docking facilities.

At this point in time, the area enclosed by the Dockyard was about half a square mile, including the Wet Basin, the Old Bombay Dock and the Duncan Dock. There was little open space except near the docks. There was only one breakwater. The total alongside wharfage was 2,700 feet of the Wet Basin walls and the inner face of the Old Breakwater. A cruiser required 600 feet and each destroyer / frigate required 400 feet. At these berths, there was only restricted 220 volt DC supply and no permanent arrangements for the supply of compressed air or for sea water to supply the fire mains.

In their report submitted in 1950, the consultants recommended:

- Increase the existing land area of 39 acres to 120 acres by reclamation, including a portion of the Ballard Pier and by acquiring land surrounding the Royal Bombay Yacht Club premises.
- Construct 3,200 feet of breakwater to form a Tidal Basin and thus increase the protected water area from 24 acres to 150 acres.
- Construct new workshops, offices, stores and all necessary buildings on the extended land.
- Construct two graving docks of suitable size, and increase the total berthing within the area of the Tidal Basin for all classes of vessels by about two and a half miles.

The Master Plan envisaged a new main breakwater starting at the Apollo Bunder and enclosing a new outer basin. The dredging of this basin would result in the reclamation of an area to the south of the existing yard, which would accommodate two new large dry docks and their associated workshops. Other new wharves were to be constructed within the existing basin and the area behind them reclaimed by dredging the basin.

After discussion with the consultants, the Navy made one major modification. Of the two new docks, it moved the second smaller dock to a position inside and parallel to the existing Old Breakwater. This would enable the construction during the very first stage of the expansion scheme of a dock for the cruiser *Delhi*, already in service.[3]

The Alexander Gibbs report envisaged the Naval Dockyard Expansion Scheme in five stages over a period of twelve years. Approval in principle was accorded in 1952. This was modified subsequently to be undertaken in two stages. The Naval Dockyard Expansion Scheme started in 1954.

By 1975, nearly 5,000 feet of additional wharfage had been constructed to enable ships to berth alongside the new 'Barracks and Frigate Wharves' (completed 1956), 'Ballard Pier Extension' (completed 1966) 'Destroyer Wharf' (completed 1967), 'South Breakwater' (completed 1973). All the berths were being provided with appropriate power supplies, fresh water, sea water, compressed air, travelling cranes, etc. Acres of sea had been dredged and acres of land had been reclaimed. A new 'cruiser' graving dock had been built (completed 1962) on the reclaimed land and space had been earmarked for yet another and larger 'graving' dock. New workshops had been completed for repair of weapon systems, construction of boilers, testing of steam machinery, repairing of machinery spares, testing of generators and overhauling of diesel engines. Approval had been obtained for more new workshops as well as the modernisation of the old workshops.

Karanja Basin Bombay

Until the mid 1960s, ships used to anchor off Karanja and embark ammunition brought by barge from the Naval Armament Depot. This arrangement depended on the weather being fair. In the mid 1960s, after detailed studies by the Central Water and Power Research Station Poona, a breakwater-cum-jetty was constructed at Karanja, for ships to secure alongside and embark ammunition.

Since this created a siltation prone basin, the foot of the jetty was built as a piled-bridge structure to enable water to flow freely through the basin in both states of tide, thereby precluding stagnation of water and siltation.

Unfortunately, heavy siltation still occurred. It is not clear why this happened. One obvious reason was that the flow of water through the piled-bridge gap was obstructed by the material that the contractor did not fully clear. Water stagnated and the basin became a mud flat.

In the 1970s, the need increased for ships to embark missiles and torpedoes. This could only be done at alongside berths. To avoid these having to be brought by barges across the harbour, a scheme was considered that would solve this problem and also decongest the Dockyard of the smaller vessels by providing them alongside berths and a maintenance unit in an enclosed Wet Basin. Various ideas were considered to de-silt the basin and keep it free

---

3. This Cruiser Graving Dock, as it came to be called, was extended with great agility and initiative just before its completion to take the aircraft carrier *Vikrant*. In later years, necessity spurred the innovation of concurrent docking of 5,000 tonne destroyers, alongside 1,500 tonne submarines and other 400 tonne attack and patrol craft in the same dock.

of silt – reopening the piled-bridge structure, agitating the silt for the tide to flush it through, creating deep-water channels by capital dredging, etc. None of them was promising enough to follow through.

Vishakapatnam Dockyard

After the outbreak of World War II in Europe, the Royal Indian Navy set up a Boat Repair Workshop in Vizag to support the elements of the Indian Army deployed in Burma.

In December 1941, Japan entered the War that had started in Europe in 1939. Within months, Japan had occupied Southeast Asia and the Andaman and Nicobar Islands and was advancing through Burma towards northeast India and the oilfields of Assam.

The Navy instituted the 'Coastal Forces Eastern Theatre' in March 1942; initiated action to build coastal forces bases at Karachi, Trombay, Cochin, Mandapam, Madras and Vizag and laid the foundations for coastal force slipways and workshops at these ports. The Boat Repair Workshop at Vizag was augmented with machine tools and blacksmith and carpentry workshops, all of which were located inside the naval base, *INS Circars*. In 1943, the status of *INS Circars* was raised to that of a Forward Naval Base.

In 1947, this workshop was upgraded to a Centre for Care and Maintenance of Ships with a 200-tonne slipway.

In 1953, this Centre expanded into a Base Repair Organisation (BRO). An Electrical / Radio Shop, an ICE Shop and a Foundry / Welding Shop were created inside *Circars*. A new BRO Complex was constructed at the mouth of the Northwest Arm / Channel. Except for the slipway, the Woodwork Shop and the Blacksmith Shop, all the other shops were shifted to the new BRO Complex.

In 1958, the progress of Bombay Dockyard's expansion scheme was behind schedule. With the imminent arrival from Britain of the eight new frigates and the aircraft carrier, Bombay Dockyard would not be able to berth these ships alongside. It was proposed that a naval base be established at Vizag, starting with a new 1,120 foot jetty and a repair workshop. The Defence Committee of the Cabinet accepted in principle the establishment of a naval base and dockyard at Vizag.

In 1962, sanction was accorded for the construction of the new jetty and the workshop building. Sanction was also accorded for the acquisition of 550 acres of land from the Port Trust.

In 1963, survey ships were temporarily based in Vizag and the decision was taken to start setting up a naval base and a dockyard. Machinery and equipment was procured for augmenting the repair facilities to enable the normal refit and dry docking of one modern frigate and four small craft.

In 1965, two survey ships were permanently rebased at Vizag. For the first time, the annual refit of a survey ship was undertaken by the BRO Vizag.[4]

In 1965, the decision to acquire ships and submarines from the Soviet Union was accompanied by the decision to segregate, for security reasons, these acquisitions from the western origin ships based in Bombay and, with Russian assistance, to build a modern dockyard equipped to maintain, repair and refit Russian origin ships and submarines.

A basic choice that had to be made at that time was:

• Whether to build the new base and dockyard in the vicinity of the existing naval base, *Circars*, inside the existing harbour, the access to which was through a narrow channel which was susceptible to closure, or

• to opt for an altogether new 'greenfield' site (where the steel plant is now located) which, with its own, new, wide, entrance, would be less susceptible to closure and free of the delays caused by the movement of merchant ships inside a confined harbour.

In view of the high cost and the time delays inherent in the development of a completely new site that had neither rail nor road connections, Vizag harbour was preferred.

The 1965 Agreement for the Russian acquisitions included the preparation of a Project Report for the Vishakhapatnam Project that comprised facilities for a naval base and ship support facilities, a submarine base and submarine support facilities, a training complex for the Russian acquisitions and a Naval Dockyard to repair and refit ships and submarines.

As soon as the Project Report was received in 1967, the Directorate General of Naval Projects Vishakhapatnam, DGNP (V) was set up to execute the total works of the project.

In 1968, the Defence Committee of the Cabinet accepted the Soviet Project Report and financial approvals were accorded in 1969. Construction work commenced in 1970. In 1970, the Officer in Charge BRO was upgraded and re-designated Captain Superintendent Naval Dockyard Vishakhapatnam.

---

4. Until the new Dockyard's dry dock was ready in 1977, dry-docking of ships refitted in Vizag was done either in Hindustan Shipyard or in Vizag Port Trust, depending on dock availability and duration of docking.

Between 1970 and 1975:

- Since the new Dockyard would take years to come up, the facilities of the BRO Workshop were augmented and the BRO itself expanded.

- The BRO was re-named as Naval Dockyard on 29th March 1972.

- The 1,120-foot naval jetty, as well as the new wharves and jetties envisaged in the Project Report were completed and their approaches dredged.

- The Naval Base, the Training Complex, the Submarine Base and submarine facilities and the facilities for weapons were completed and commissioned.

Base Repair Organisation Cochin

After independence in 1947, the Coastal Force Workshop and its slipway located inside the naval base, *INS Venduruthy*, evolved into a Base Workshop, having 32 employees, a 178 metre long jetty and minimal facilities for engineering and electrical repair work. Its basic role was to help visiting ships seeking assistance to become seaworthy enough to proceed under their own steam to Bombay Dockyard.

Over the years, this workshop grew into a Base Repair Organisation (BRO) with additional facilities like a Machine Shop, Foundry Shop Blacksmith Shop, Battery Charging and Electro Plating Facilities, and a Weapon Mounting Repair Shop. By 1963, plans had crystallised to augment the BRO and build a new naval jetty on the Willingdon Island foreshore.

In 1963, the Ministry of Shipbuilding decided to set up the Cochin Shipyard, which would have an 1,800 foot jetty on the Ernakulam side of the channel. This made it necessary to shift the site of the proposed naval jetty closer to the Ernakulam Bridge.

In 1965, the three old Hunt class destroyers *Godavari, Gomati* and *Ganga* were rebased from Bombay to Cochin and proposals put up for additional workshop facilities. However, due to the large expenditure on the Bombay and Vishakhapatnam Dockyards between 1965 and 1975, substantial funds could not be allocated for augmenting BRO Cochin.

In 1972, the Training Squadron comprising the cruiser *Delhi* and the frigate *Kistna* was based at Cochin. In 1973, an Apprentice Training School was established inside the BRO and the yard craft in Cochin were placed under the BRO. In 1975, approval was accorded for the construction of the new naval jetty.

Base Repair Organisation Port Blair

After China's attacks in October-November 1962, the responsibility for the seaward defence of the Andaman and Nicobar Islands was transferred from the Army to the Navy. The first Resident Naval Officer arrived in Port Blair in November 1962. In mid 1963, the first Naval Garrison of five officers and one hundred and fifty six sailors arrived in Port Blair.

Until the Navy's Seaward Defence Boats arrived, sea patrols and inter-island transportation were supported by craft of the Central Board of Revenue. Soon, the need was felt for a maintenance and repair facility to sustain these small craft, which were operating so far away from the nearest BRO at Vizag.

In 1964, after *INS Jarawa* was commissioned as the parent establishment at Port Blair, the requirements of machinery, personnel, buildings and shore supply facilities for setting up a BRO were included in the overall plan for setting up an advance naval base. This plan envisaged the construction of a 1,200-foot wharf, half of which would be for naval use. In 1966, approval in principle was accorded for setting up a BRO and berthing facilities in three phases.

From 1966 onwards, as soon as the newly arrived Russian patrol boats and landing ships started operating in the islands, the need arose for a support-cum-repair facility at Port Blair to save the ships from having to go all the way across the Bay of Bengal to Vizag for repairs. From 1967 onwards, the old landing ship *Magar* was positioned in Port Blair to provide this support.

In 1967, approval was accorded to set up an advance base at Port Blair. Construction of the new wharf commenced in 1968.

In 1969, the old stores ship, *Dharini,* which had earlier been converted into a repair ship by equipping her with a workshop, machine tools and repair materials to support the coastal minesweepers, was positioned in Port Blair as an afloat maintenance facility. The arrangement did not prove satisfactory and *Dharini* returned to Bombay.

In 1972, a Base Maintenance Unit (BMU) was set up for the maintenance of the three Russian patrol boats then stationed at Port Blair. As naval activity increased between the mainland and the islands, the BMU expanded.

Gradually, intrusions increased in the southern group of the Nicobar Islands. These became easier to deal with if patrol boats did not keep returning to Port Blair... In 1973, a forward operating base, *INS Kardip*, was commissioned on Kamorta and patrol craft started operating from there. Soon, a small maintenance unit was set up in Kamorta.

In 1974, sanction was accorded for establishing a BRO having comprehensive facilities to repair the landing ships that were operating in the islands. Since its construction would take some years (it eventually commissioned in 1979), and the BMU was unable to meet the requirements of the landing ships, a Ship Maintenance Unit (SMU) was set up.

By 1975, the makeshift facilities at Port Blair and Kardip were managing to sustain the landing ships and patrol boats operating in the islands.

Developments After 1975

The Naval Dockyard At Bombay[5]

The Naval Dockyard Expansion Scheme (NDES)

The NDES commenced in 1954 and completed thirty years later in 1984. It was undertaken in two stages.

Expansion Works Undertaken in the First Stage	Commenced	Completed
Dredging of the Inner Tidal Basin	1954	1967 to 1970
Reclamation of 27 acres in front of Castle Barracks between the old breakwater and Ballard Pier	1954	1962 to 1970
Construction of 2,300 feet of wharfage on reclaimed land for the Barracks and Destroyer wharves	1954	1962 to 1970
Construction of the Cruiser Graving Dock on the reclaimed land	1954	1962
Extension of the Ballard Pier by 750 feet and incorporation into the Dockyard the extension of the inner face of Ballard Pier.	1963	1966
Provision of ship support services (electric power supplies, fresh water, sea water, compressed air, travelling cranes etc) for the Barracks, Destroyer and Ballard Pier wharves	1954	1966 to 1970
Expansion Works Undertaken in the Second Stage		
Construction of Rubble Mound Breakwater and South Breakwater (Deep Water Wharf)	1967	1974
Capital Dredging of the Outer Tidal Basin enclosed by the South Breakwater and reclamation of 39 acres of land in the area enclosed by this new break water, to provide space for a new Graving Dock and an additional 2,000 feet of wharfage	1972	1977
Enlarging the old breakwater into a Fitting Out Wharf	1975	1981
Provision of ship support services (electric power supplies, fresh water, sea water, fuel storage, compressed air, mobile rectifiers, steam supply, travelling cranes, capstans etc) at South Breakwater and Fitting Out Wharf	1981	1984

---

5. *The History of the Naval Dockyard Bombay* by Rear Admiral K Sridharan provides the full details of its development. The Naval Dockyard celebrated its 250th anniversary in 1986.

NAVAL DOCKYARD BOMBAY IN 1990

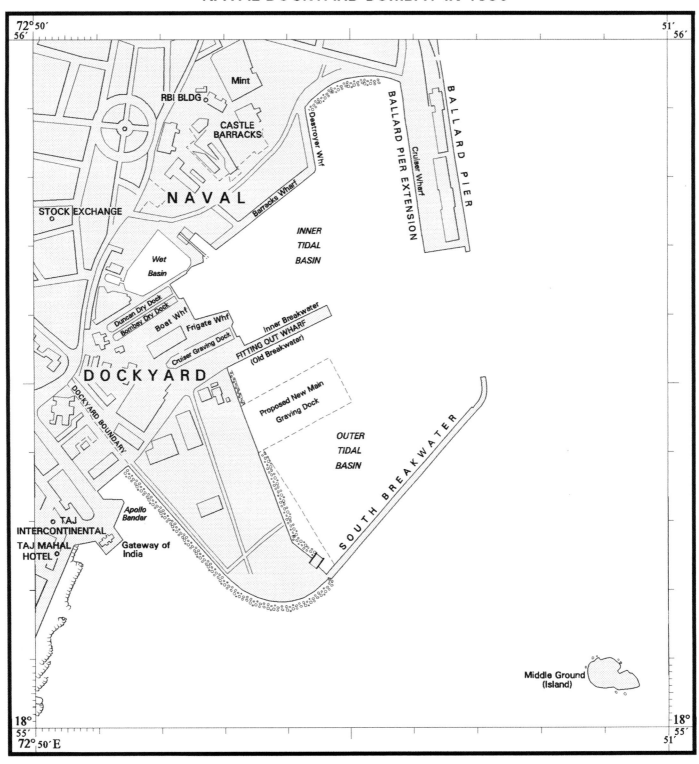

Subsequent Works

Modernisation of Bombay and Duncan Docks	1981	1985
New Main Graving Dock and additional wharves[6]	1995	Under construction

The Modernisation of the Dockyard

Certain works had commenced in 1965, sanctions for which had been obtained separately.

In 1969, the National Industrial Development Corporation (NIDC) was appointed as the official consultant to:

● Evaluate and analyse the Dockyard's present and future workload.

● Assess the Dockyard's existing and required capacity.

● Prepare a modernisation Master Plan indicating the location of each department, shop, road, storage area, canteen, toilet, office and shore facility for ships under maintenance.

The NIDC submitted two reports, 1971 and 1974. These recommended the modernisation of the Dockyard in three phases, catering for Immediate, Intermediate and Future requirements. Their report, approved in 1975, catered for ten workshops / facilities in two phases - four were to be implemented in Phase I and six in Phase II.

With expansion and modernisation being implemented concurrently, the Director General, Naval Dockyard Expansion Scheme, Bombay was re-designated in August 1978 as Director General Naval Projects Bombay - DGNP (B). As had been done in Vishakhapatnam, he was placed under the direct administrative control of Ministry of Defence. All the projects in Naval Dockyard, Bombay - the Expansion Scheme, NIDC modernisation, WECORS Phase III etc were placed under his purview to centrally coordinate their execution.

Modernisation/Augmentation Works Undertaken	Commenced	Completed
Weapon Control & Repair Shop (WECORS) Phase 1	1960	1966
Joiner Shop	1963	1965
Life Raft Repair Cell	1964	1965
Boiler Erection Shop for Leander boilers	1965	1969
Phased replacement of old machines/machine tools	1966	1968
Augmentation of workshop facilities	1967	1970
WECORS Phase 2	1967	1975
Test House for minesweeper Deltic diesel engines		1970
Interim Auto Control Bay for Leander equipment		1973
Light Internal Combustion Engine Workshop		1974
Light Diesel Engine Workshop		1974
Boat Repair Shop		1975
Steam Test House		1978
Submarine Battery Charging facilities		1978
Missile Boat/Durg/Minesweeper Engine Workshop	1972	1979
Auxiliary Machinery Workshop (NIDC Phase I)	1977	1981
Pipe Repair Shop (NIDC Phase I)	1977	1981
Auto Control Bay		1982
Galvanising Bay		1983
WECORS Phase III	1977	1987
Hull Assembly and Steel Preparation Workshop	1981	1986
Controls Engineering Workshop (NIDC Phase I)	1982	1984
Electrical Repair Shop (NIDC Phase I)	1982	1985

6. 75% of this 236 metre long, 37 metre wide, 8 metre deep dry dock was to be constructed under water using specialised precision equipment and 12,000 pre-cast blocks weighing 20 tonnes each. Bed concrete was to be laid at a depth of 10 metres, followed by placing of blocks and in situ concrete for creating a watertight structure. 1,000 metres of additional wharfage were to be created. During construction, a mishap occurred in 2000 when one wall of the dock collapsed. Work has been resumed.

	1985	1986
Air Conditioning/Refrigeration Shop (NIDC Phase II)	1985	1986
Submarine Base Complex		1988
Submarine Battery Commissioning Facility		1988
Heavy Diesel Engine Workshop (NIDC Phase II)	1985	1990
Epoxy Coating Shop (NIDC Phase II)	1986	1987
Electroplating Shop (NIDC Phase II)	1987	1989
Electrical Test Station (NIDC Phase II)	1988	1990

Dockyard Productivity

The availability of spares / machinery replacements is a basic determinant for completing repairs and refits on time. In the 1960s, refits started being delayed on this count.[7] It was decided to appoint consultants to recommend remedial measures.

The first study to be carried out was by the National Productivity Council (NPC) in 1963 to suggest ways and means for improving productivity and obtaining a higher degree of motivation and training for Dockyard personnel. The NPC studied the stores inventory system of the Naval Stores Organisation (NSO), of the Spare Parts Distribution Centre (SPDC) and of Naval Headquarters.

The second study pertaining to Quality Control was carried out by the Indian Standards Institute (ISI) in 1968.

The NPC and the ISI studies led to the establishment of the Planning & Production Control (PPC) and Quality Control (QC) Departments.[8]

The third study was carried out by the Administrative Staff College of India in 1971 to study the same problem that the NPC had studied in 1963 namely the vexed issue of non-availability of spares and stores delaying repair of equipment and refits of ships. . This study recommended that the Naval Stores Organisation and the Spare Parts Distribution Centre (SPDC) be merged. As a result, these organisations were merged into the Material Organisation, Bombay under a Material Superintendent under whom the four Controller Organisations, viz. the Controllerate of Material Planning (CMP), Controllerate of Procurement (CPRO), Controllerate of Warehousing (CWH) and Controllerate of Technical Services (CTS) came into being.

The Naval Dockyard At Vishakhapatnam

The Soil Conditions at the Site

The only area available of the size required for the Vizag Dockyard Project was a swampy, marshy estuary. It had been the bed of the Meghedrigedda River that had dried up several hundred years ago. The soil comprised soft, compressible, marine clay that was still consolidating under its own weight. The load bearing capacity was low – two tonnes per square metre – and, when subjected to load conditions, compressed endlessly. The top, weak layers of clay extended to twenty metres below ground level. A high water table that at places was just one metre below ground level aggravated these soil conditions. And, as was to become known later during construction, the deep streams under the rock layer caused lateral shifting of the soil leading to differential sinkage in buildings.

These complex geological and hydrological soil conditions compelled resort to time-consuming, expensive and special construction techniques:[9]

● Pile foundations down to rock level had to be sunk for every building.

● Workshops requiring specifically high floor loading had to be provided with suspended flooring at basement levels. The floor was supported on beams resting on end-bearing, bored cast-in-site piles. It was called 'suspended' because the load was directly transmitted to the bedrock via the end piles, thereby making it independent of the soil conditions beneath.

---

7. The causes of the malaise have been discussed in the chapters on "Logistics", "The 1979 Naval Expert Committee on Maintenance" and "The Russian Acquisitions".

8. The 1979 Report of the Naval Expert Committee on Maintenance was constrained to note that "————The consultants in each case have passed blunt, forthright and highly damaging strictures about the state of affairs and their management in the Dockyard. Even then, nothing seems to have happened. It appears to the Committee that only selected recommendations – those pertaining to up-gradation or additional manpower – are picked up and pursued. Little effort appears to be made to correct other aspects."

   The multitude of problems that the Dockyard had to cope with between the 1950s and the 1970s have been discussed in the chapter titled "The 1979-80 Naval Expert Committee Report on Maintenance," page 158.

9. The Soviet Project Report had stated that "Due to the unfavourable geological conditions of the site, expenditure on the development of water area, formation of territory and construction of dry docks, slipway, berths and other hydro-technical erections are very high, amounting to more than 60 % of the total cost of the Dockyard.":

The Soviet Project Report

The Soviet Project Report comprehensively delineated the role of the Dockyard for each of its envisaged tasks in ship repair:

- As a repair agency.
- As a manufacturing agency.
- As a testing centre.

These were accepted as guiding principles.

The Construction of the Dockyard

Construction commenced in 1968 as soon as the Report was accepted. In the draft contracts, it was agreed that:

- Sizeable designing effort would be undertaken in India.
- A large proportion of equipment and machinery would be of indigenous origin.
- Russian drawings, Russian equipment and Russian machinery for the Dockyard would arrive within six months of signing each contract.
- The development of the Naval Base and the Dockyard to provide full logistic support would be spread out over ten years.

From the outset, delays were experienced for a variety of reasons. These included civil engineering difficulties, escalations in cost and changes in the scope of some facilities.

The South Dry Dock (Varuna Dock)[10]

The location of this dock was finalised in 1968 with the help of the Soviet consultants. Design work started in 1969 and completed in 1971. Construction work commenced in 1972. Work had to stop to enable the dock floor to be redesigned because of poor soil conditions. In 1976, the head wall and entrance cofferdam were damaged. It was inaugurated in September 1978 after which it started being used as a single-chamber Dry Dock with a caisson gate at the entrance. In May 1979, a flap gate was installed at the entrance and the caisson gate shifted to the middle groove, thereby dividing the dock into two compartments. Problems cropped up. One was the flap gate itself. During the test operations of this 360-tonne gate, the steel wire parted due to excessive pull on the wires. This recurred during one of the docking and undocking operations. Compressed air had to be pumped under the gate to make the gate buoyant. The flap gate tilted over before it could be reinstalled. A second problem was that the Pump House, in which the de-watering pumps were installed, developed serious leaks. These had to be gnited underwater. The gates were handed over formally in December 1979. Overall, it took 10 years, from the commencement of design in June 1969 to final completion in December 1979, for the South Dry Dock to be fully operational. In its final configuration, it is a two-chamber dock, having three 'gate grooves' located 24 metres apart in which the caisson can be positioned as an intermediate gate, depending on the length of vessel being docked. Up to 9 ships of various sizes can be and have been docked.

The delay in the completion of the dock had two effects:

- The annual docking of ships became dependant on the availability of the Hindustan Shipyard and Port Trust dry docks, which had their own commitments to meet. Ships' hulls suffered.
- It aggravated the already dislocated crucial 6-yearly 'medium repairs' of submarines because neither of the above docks could be spared for the long duration that was essential for the detailed checking of a submarine hull and the dismantling and reinstallation of its heavy intricate machinery.[11]

The Steering Committee and the Phases

To overcome delays, a high level Steering Committee was constituted in 1973 to accord approvals and sanctions expeditiously.

Eventually, the Dockyard Project was executed in five phases (with approvals being sought and accorded phase-wise) and, except for ongoing augmentations for new acquisitions, was largely completed over the twenty year period between 1970 and 1990:

Phase I/IA: Setting up core Dockyard infrastructure and facilities for repairing and refitting:

- The first Russian acquisitions (submarines, Petyas, landing ships, submarine depot ship and patrol boats).
- Existing ships (wooden-hull minesweepers, frigates, seaward defence boats and survey vessels) so as to reduce the load on Bombay Dockyard.

Financial approval for Phase 1 was accorded in 1969 and construction of works commenced in 1970. In 1981,

---

10. The South Dry Dock is 272 metres long, 42 metres wide and 15 metres deep. Abutting the south wall of the dock is a 386 metre long, 25 metre wide Repair Berth for repairs and fitting out of ships.

11. The chapter on the "The Submarine Arm" discusses the chain reaction that occurred in Medium Repairs. See pages 115, 116.

the Steering Committee decided that work on Phase I should be closed by end 1982 and the creation of left over facilities be carried over to Phase II. The latter were referred to as Phase 1B, while those completed in Phase 1 itself were referred to Phase 1A. The South Dry Dock, completed in 1979, was part of Phase 1A.

Phase II/IB: Started in 1979, this phase was for completion of facilities carried forward from Phase 1 and augmentation of core facilities. This phase included progressive construction of married accommodation, which extended beyond 1990.

Phase III: Augmentation of existing repair facilities for undertaking 6-yearly medium refits of the Rajput class destroyers that had been contracted for in 1975.

Though the Soviet Project Report for this augmentation was received and defended in 1978, it took two years of deliberations to finalise its scope before seeking approvals in 1980. This two-year delay dislocated the commencement of the 6-yearly 'medium repairs' of the Rajput class destroyers.

Building	Additional/New Facilities in Phase III
15	Boiler Combustion Equipment & Cold-Pipe-Bending Facility. Machining of and bench work on propellers.
16-A	Main Propulsion Turbine and Turbo Alternator Turbine Repair Shop.
17 & 17B	Alternator (and its starter) Repair and Test Facility. Repair of generators and other electrical equipment. Repair of ships automatics, instrumentation of main engine auxiliaries, main steering system, testing facility for repaired gas turbines and for turbo-alternator turbines.
21	Test Stand for main propulsion turbines.
23	HP Compressor Station (provision of 400 kg/cum air).
25B & C	Armament Repair Facility.

Phase IV: Approval was accorded in 1984 for setting up a separately located and administered Marine Gas Turbine Overhaul Centre to overhaul Russian gas turbines and gas turbine generators. First called MGTOC, it commissioned eventually in 2000 as *INS Eksila*.

Phase V: This phase was taken in hand after 2000. It involved setting up facilities for undertaking the 6-yearly 'medium repair' refits of the Russian ships and submarines contracted for in the 1980s (877 EKM Sindhughosh class submarines, coastal minesweepers, gas-turbine-propelled missile craft of the Veer class and anti submarine patrol vessels of the Abhay class). This phase includes four new specialised facilities for Hull Repair of titanium and aluminium-magnesium alloy structures, Hull Cladding (removal and re-fixing submarine rubber tiles), HP testing of air bottles and a Test/Calibration Centre for control and instrumentation systems.

The North Dry Dock (Matsya and Surya Docks)

Sanctioned in 1980 and completed in 1990, the Dock has two, parallel, separate chambers, sharing the services in between.[12] The Surya Dock for surface ships is uncovered. The Matsya Dock for submarines is the longest covered dock in India. The Dock was scheduled for completion in 1986; however as a result of changes required by NHQ, the dock's completion was delayed till 1990.

The 1984 Master Plan

In 1982, a Board was constituted to identify the requirement of additional berthing facilities, augmentation of ship repair facilities, shore accommodation for complement of ships under refit, provision of zonal stores, provider stores section for the Dockyard and for fleet ships, an in-house training complex for the yard and pollution control facilities.

Taking into consideration the total land area of the Dockyard, the area of the co-located units and the area of the waterfront, the 1984 Master Plan:

- Identified the facilities originally envisaged in the Soviet Project Report but not created. Requirements of water supply, electrical supply, dredging of channel to maintain depths etc., were included.

- Re-examined the proposal to build ships in the Dockyard.

- Recommended facilities for a Commander of the Yard Complex.

- Analysed the details of manpower recommended in the Soviet Project Report.

---

12. Surya Surface Vessel Compartment: 272 metres long, 21metres wide and 14 metres deep. One flap gate and one caisson gate; the latter can be fitted in of three grooves. The advantage of having two adjustable chambers is that vessels requiring large duration of dry-docking are docked in the inner chamber. Those needing lesser duration of docking are docked in the outer chamber.

Matsya Submarine Compartment: 272 metres long, 16 metres wide and 14 metres deep. One flap gate and single position caisson gate. This enables two submarines to undergo 6-yearly 'medium repairs' concurrently.

The analysis of structures of the dock floor, floor piles and inter-compartmental wall was done by the IIT Delhi. The analysis and design of the dock gates was done by the IIT Kharagpur.

NAVAL DOCKYARD VISAKHAPATNAM IN 1990

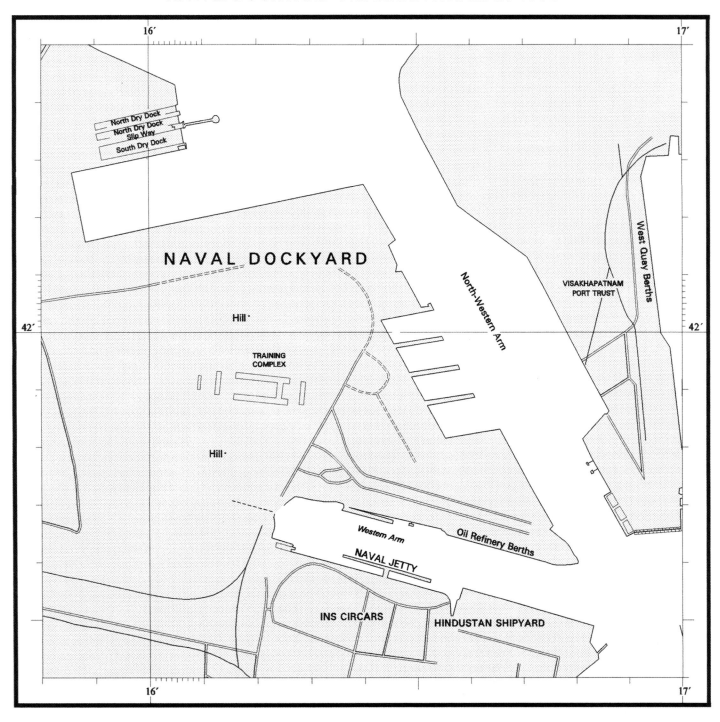

- Estimated up to 1992, the details of existing / sanctioned and proposed facilities.

The 1991 Master Plan

A Board was constituted again, in 1989, to prepare a Master Plan for 1991. This Board concluded that almost 90% of the Dockyard Project had been completed and that additional requirements would have to be met by additions / alterations or demolition of buildings. The 1991 Master Plan recommended:

- Additional berthing facilities.

- Augmentation of the Commander of the Yard Complex.
- Facilities for diesel engine repair and machinery control repair / calibration.
- A zoning plan for all facilities (Administrative Zone, Repair / Refit Zone, Services Zone, Training Zone etc).
- Facility to monitor the depths of channel.
- Long-term facilities like additional water reservoirs, sewage treatment facility, acquisition of land from the Port Trust for an additional parallel bridge, construction of a jetty between two existing jetties, etc.

Chronology of Commencement and Completion of the Works in the Vizag Dockyard

Works Undertaken	Commenced	Completed
Construction of wharves and jetties	1968	-
Energy Block for recharging submarine batteries	1968	1971
Dredging of Northwest Arm	1969	1969
Design of South Dry Dock	1969	1971
Weapon Repair Shop	1969	1973
Dockyard Apprentice School	1970	1973
Jetties No 3 &4 and Main Repair Berth	-	1976
Main Engineering Workshop (Building No.16)	1972	1976
Main Electrical Workshop (Building No.17)	1972	1976
Pipe Fitting Shop	1972	1976
Laboratory (Building No. 43)	1972	1976
Main Repair Berth	1972	1976
Jetty No 5 and other wharves/jetties	-	1977
Main Hull Shop (Building No.18)	1972	1977
Wharves 2 and 6	-	1978
New workshops for Hull, Engineering, Electrical and Submarine auxiliaries, and bays for Electroplating, Hydraulic Repair	1972	1978/80
Construction of South Dry Dock (Varuna Dock)	1972	1979
Periscope Repair and Armament Repair/Refit Captive power generation facilities	1976	1983
Capital dredging to create space for the new Armament Jetty and the Degaussing Basin	1979	1980
Degaussing Basin and Facility	1979	1989
Design of North Dry Dock	1980	1981
Construction of North Dry Dock (Surya & Matsya)	1980	1990
Augmentation of Weapon Repair Shop	1983	1986
Marine Gas Turbine Repair Workshop	1984	1990
New jetty on the eastern bank	1987	1991
Ammunition jetty	1987	1993

At the time of writing, the following major facilities were under execution:

- 600 tonne Slipway. Commenced in the mid 1990s, it will accommodate seven ships, two under cover and five in the open.
- Augmentation of facilities for undertaking the 6-yearly 'medium repair' refits of 877 EKM Sindhughosh class submarines, coastal minesweepers, gas-turbine-propelled missile craft of the Veer class and anti submarine patrol vessels of the Abhay class).
- Overhaul and test facilities at *INS Eksila* for main propulsion turbines of Delhi class destroyers
- Augmentation of training facilities in the Submarine Training School *INS Satavahana* for the 877 EKM Sindhughosh class submarines.

Today, the Dockyard has a ground area of 704 acres, a water area of 264 acres and, in round figures, 8,000 officers and men. Docking and undocking is not tide-dependent.

The Naval Ship Repair Yard at Cochin

Growth of the BRO into a Ship Repair Yard

From the mid 1970s onwards, the 1950s vintage, *Brahmaputra, Betwa* and *Beas* started being converted into cadet training frigates and based in Cochin to replace the 1940s vintage training frigates as they decommissioned.

In 1978, sanction was accorded for a new Internal Combustion Engines (ICE) Workshop and a new Electronics Workshop.

In 1981, the contract was signed for the acquisition of 90-tonne, Glass Reinforced Plastic (GRP) inshore minesweepers from Russia. It was decided to base them in Cochin. Contracts had already been signed for the acquisition of training equipment of the Rajput class destroyers, the Durg class rocket boats and the Pondicherry class minesweepers, some of which was to be fitted in the training schools in Cochin.

In 1983, approval was accorded for augmenting the BRO's facilities for undertaking the full scope of maintenance, repair and refits of the inshore minesweepers to avoid their becoming a burden on the Dockyards at Bombay or Vishakhapatnam. This augmentation was to be phased:

- **Interim to meet the immediate needs of the inshore minesweepers:** Large mobile cranes for the mine sweeping equipment, argon arc welding equipment, hydraulic self loader chocks, sling trolleys, high pressure water jet cleaning equipment and creation of GRP facilities.

- **Permanent facilities for undertaking 6-yearly 'Medium Repairs':** The Soviet Project Report recommended creation of a 100-tonne slipway. It was decided to modify the 40-year old 'coastal forces' slipway. This was commenced in the late 1980s and completed during the 1990s.

In 1985, four new survey craft were based in Cochin, followed by the new cadet training ship *Tir* in 1986. At the same time, as the number of ships based in Cochin was increasing, Russian weapon and sensor training equipment had started being installed in Dronacharya and the ASW, ND and Signal Schools in Cochin, all of which would need periodical maintenance and repair. It was time to review the role of the BRO.

New workshops, with special to type equipment were to be set up for the inshore minesweepers on the land adjacent to the old BRO. In the review of the BRO's role, it was decided to improve the layout and augment the equipment of the workshops to enable them to cope with:

- The refits of frigate sized ships, with docking being done in Cochin Shipyard.
- The maintenance of the Russian training equipment.

The resultant facilities were a Hull Fabrication Shop, a Machine Shop with modern machines, an Electrical Shop with electroplating facilities, a Weapon and Electronic Repair Shop, an Auxiliary Machinery and Shafting Shop, an ICE Engine Repair Bay with fuel injection calibration facilities and a Test House Complex to load-test engines and a Mine Sweep Repair Shop. Mobile equipment was provided to support the yard, the ships based at Cochin and visiting ships.

This 1,200 employee, 12-acre, upgraded BRO was re-designated as a Naval Ship Repair Yard (NSRY). It supports, repairs and refits the ships based at Cochin. It coordinates docking and associated repairs with Cochin Shipyard. And it provides technical support to the training schools and establishments in Cochin.

Alongside Berths

The South Jetty. The need for a new jetty had been accepted as early as 1975. Its construction could only commence in 1978 after sanction was accorded. It was scheduled to complete in 1981 but labour problems afflicted its completion. By 1985, considerable silting had occurred around the half completed piled structures.

Construction of the jetty was resumed in 1985. Since Cochin Shipyard was to undertake the periodic docking of the aircraft carrier *Viraat,* the 1,200 foot jetty was strengthened and dredged to berth *Viraat* alongside The jetty was commissioned in 1987, together with its allied shore facilities – the power house, the pump house and the de-mineralised water plant. It was named 'South Jetty' and earmarked for berthing operational ships.

The North Jetty. The old 'IN Jetty' was renamed 'North Jetty'. Being closer to the BRO, it berths ships under refit.

The Blossoming of Cochin into a Work Up Base

In 1972, a high-level Committee had been constituted in Bombay to recommend organisational changes in the light of lessons of the 1971 War.[13] One of the recommendations was that after refit in Bombay Dockyard, ships must:

- Get away from Bombay to decongest the Dockyard. This would enable ships companies to shake down, away from Bombay's 'home-port 9 to 5 routine'.

- Work up in Cochin where air and surface targets were available and where ships companies could learn to cope with defects instead of perpetually depending on Bombay Dockyard for assistance.

Apart from the reluctance to depart from home-port, the main argument advanced against this recommendation was that since Cochin did not have the workshops to assist in rectifying a defect that was beyond the capability of the ship's staff, the ship would have to return to Bombay Dockyard. It was therefore better that ships work up off Bombay. There was substance in this reasoning. Ships from Bombay continued to visit Cochin only for surface and anti aircraft firing practices rather than a full-scale work up.

In 1985, when the augmentation of the BRO was taking place to support the inshore minesweepers and work had to recommence on the new jetty, the opportunity was seized to give the BRO and the new jetty the kind of facilities that would attract ships to Cochin for workup – instant support from new, well equipped BRO workshops and all possible supplies (electrical, fresh water, fire main, chilled water, etc) when berthed alongside, to enable ships' systems to be conserved / maintained.[14]

The technical staffs of Headquarters Southern Naval Command were deputed to visit the Dockyards at Bombay and Vishakhapatnam, ascertain the particulars of the kind of workshop support and shore supplies required by the ships and submarines in service and about to enter service, and incorporate these in the design of the BRO and the new jetty to the extent feasible.

This was to prove valuable from 1993 onwards, when the Flag Officer Sea Training and his organisation were eventually established in Cochin.

Apart from the support extended to ships coming to Cochin for work up, the NSRY, in subsequent years, was able to support the increasing number of ships based in Cochin – six inshore minesweepers (from 1983 onwards), four survey craft (from 1985 onwards), two training ships (*Tir* from 1986 onwards and *Krishna* from 1995 onwards), two survey ships (*Jamuna* from 1991onwards and *Sutlej* from 1993 onwards), two OPVs (*Sharda* from 1992 onwards and *Sujata* from 1993 onwards), *Sagardhwani* from 1994 onwards and sail training ship *Tarangini* from 1997 onwards.

The Naval Ship Repair Yard At Port Blair

The proposals for the procurement of machinery / equipment and the construction of works that had been initiated in May 1968 and July 1972 were sanctioned in July 1975 and February 1976 respectively. The wharf was ready by 1977. The BRO started functioning from August 1980 to sustain the landing ships, SDBs and patrol boats that were progressively rebased from Vizag to Port Blair.

By 1983, the specific augmentation required to support the growing number of ships had been identified. And with the promulgation of the envisaged 1990 basing plan, it became possible to rationalise the requirements of repair and refit facilities for the A&N Islands.

At Port Blair, it was decided to:

- Procure a Floating Dock. A Floating Dock (FDN 1), having the capacity to dock ships of up to 11,500 tonnes was acquired from the Indian firm of Escorts and commissioned in 1987.[15] This saved ships from having to go back to Vishakhapatnam for their annual docking.

- Augment the BRO facilities.

- Extend the 600 foot naval jetty to 1,200 feet.

At Kamorta, it was decided to build a naval jetty adjacent to the naval establishment, *INS Kardip*.

---

13. The author was Western Fleet Operations Officer during the 1971 War and the member-secretary of this Committee.

14. The author directed and implemented this as Flag Officer Commanding in Chief Southern Naval Command in Cochin from February 1985 to December 1987.

15. Approval was accorded in August 1985 to acquire a Floating Dock for Port Blair. Tenders were floated. Offers were received from West Germany and Korea. Meanwhile Escorts who had acquired a Floating Dock from Japan and moored it in deep water in Nhava Sheva, across the harbour from Bombay, found that it was not cost effective; it was put up for sale and the Navy acquired it.

Except for the Floating Dock, the remaining three proposals had to be deferred due to the cutbacks in budget after the failure of the 1986 monsoon and the subsequent droughts. These proposals were revived in the 1990s after the financial position improved.

At Port Blair, the lack of trained manpower and inadequate BRO facilities made it difficult to fully utilise the FDN. This was overcome by docking as many ships as possible in the FDN and bringing them back to Vizag for the remainder of refit work. The alternative of sending trained manpower from Vizag Dockyard to assist the work at Port Blair was found to be unsatisfactory as it entailed wastage of time and manpower in transit. To overcome under-utilisation, commercial ships and craft started being docked in FDN.

On 10 November 1993, the BRO was re-designated as the Naval Ship Repair Yard, Port Blair.

At the time of writing, the NSRY has a complement of about 350 personnel and with the Floating Dock undertakes the complete refits of the LCUs, SDBs and LSTs based in the A&N Islands.

The Ship Maintenance Authority (SMA)

The 1980 Naval Expert Committee on Maintenance recommended the setting up of a Ship Maintenance Authority. Its report stated:

"There is a need to establish a Ship Maintenance Authority to perform maintenance support functions, both on and after introduction of equipment in service. A number of repetitive failures would have been avoided or better performance obtained from equipments.

"Some of the functions recommended to be performed by the SMA are:

- To standardise preventive maintenance data and point out discrepancies, errors and omissions.

- To collect, collate and process operating and usage data from all ships, Dockyards, special teams and Boards of Enquiry to optimise preventive maintenance.

- To promulgate amendments to existing maintenance schedules.

- To provide feedback on maintenance to Operational Commanders.

- To provide feedback affecting maintenance to training schools to help updating of training and to point out shortcomings and lacunae in training.

- To analyse reports of material shortcomings affecting reliability and to communicate collated information to

the design authorities.

- On the basis of feedback reports, to ensure remedial measures.

- To provide supporting data/evidence for alterations and additions and modifications to existing equipment.

- To finally vet, with the appropriate design authority, the contents and the format of technical documentation for ship-borne maintenance.

- To ensure that remedies, corrective measures and possible improvements in processes and procedures are published and communicated to all users, training schools, fleet and administrative authorities.

- To analyse and report shortcomings reported in the field of logistics, which affect maintenance. Excessive consumption of particular items should be analysed with a view to determine whether:

  – It is due to any defect.

  – It is due to faulty usage or operation.

  – It is due to incorrect ranging and scaling done at the initial stage.

  – There are any other causes, which need to be remedied.

- To monitor the achievements of Base Maintenance Units and Fleet Maintenance Units.

In 1981, Naval Headquarters sought sanction to establish the SMA. It took five years before the Government accepted the requirement in 1986 and sanctioned a 'nucleus unit' in Bombay and a 'satellite unit' in Vizag. NHQ promulgated SMA's charter in April 1987. It encompassed all aspects of upkeep of equipment / systems with the aim of improving the operational availability of ships, their machinery, weapons and sensors.

By 1990, the SMA had:

- Designed and established a Computerised Maintenance Reporting System.

- Designed an Integrated Support and Upkeep Maintenance System for ships – short title SUMS (Ships).

- Started on the creation of a computerised database (to provide an easily referable 'Single Point' repository of all upkeep data on ships) to be called Naval Upkeep Master Record Centre, short title NUMARC, a constituent of SUMS (Ships). NUMARC was to collate exploitation-related data through SRAR and DART returns.

- Started to collate the basic data in respect of equipment / systems – Ship Fit Definition short title SFD and to allot codes to all equipment / systems.

- Introduced computer-compatible returns titled:
  - Ship Running and Activity Return (SRAR) for rendition by all ships and submarines in service.
  - Routines Outstanding for Maintenance Periods (ROMP). ROMP reported, every quarter, the necessity to programme a Maintenance Period to give the ship's staff time to complete outstanding work.
  - Feedback of Upkeep Support Shortfall (FUSS). FUSS reported, on 31st December every year, the shortfall in support wherewithal by way of documentation, repair facilities, spares, shore facilities etc.
  - Defect and Repair Transaction (DART). DART replaced the existing Defect Return rendered by ships. It streamlined the defect reporting procedure and made defect data amenable to computerised processing.
- Introduced quarterly OPDEF analysis reports.

All these returns were to be analysed by SMA and the processed data was to be forwarded to Command and Naval Headquarters for follow up.

By 1990, Condition Based Maintenance had been introduced on selected ships. To enable the phased extension of this concept to all ships sanction had been sought for additional vibration measuring, recording and analysis equipment.

Commander VS Dixit served in the SMA in the late 1980s and early 1990s: He recalls:

"In the mid 1980s, the Indian Navy quantitatively consisted of 136 platforms fitted with a total of more than 42,000 equipment / systems. A need was felt to establish a central repository of all upkeep related activities of the entire Indian Navy with a view to evolve a modern, efficient, maintenance management system.

"In terms of diversity, the Navy consisted of 35 different types of platforms fitted with over 7,000 different types of systems obtained from Russian, Western countries and indigenous sources:

Item	No. of Types	Item	No. of Types
Main Engine Diesels	34	MF/DF Equipment	62
Prime Movers	68	V/UHF Equipment	33
Pumps	197	Echo Sounders	19
Steering Systems	44	Gun Mountings	11
Early Warning Radars	13	Logs	14
Navigational Radars	20	Motors	Over 600

"The problem areas that were identified at that point in time were:

- *Non-Standardised Maintenance Schedules.* The commissioning crew of the first ship of a class produced the maintenance schedules. Subsequent crews of sister ships made their own changes in these, based on their own experience. Different maintenance schedules existed for similar equipment fitted in different classes of ships. The Dockyards and the BROs followed maintenance practices, which were not necessarily standardised for similar equipment.

- *Absence of Systematic Refinement of Existing Maintenance Schedules.* Defects and experiences were analysed in isolation and hence did not always result in refinement of maintenance practices, thereby giving way to 'reinventing the wheel' situations.

- *Non-rationalisation of A & As / Minor modifications.* These were carried out in isolation squadron wise, command wise, fleet wise, without recourse in a systematic manner to either overall in-depth study or analysis based on overall experience gained / service operational needs.

- *Non-Standardised Dockyard Work Package for Refits of Ships.* Each ship raised its own version of Part I and Part II Defect Lists, based on their own maintenance schedules and experience and hence were not subject to proper scrutiny based on standards / technical audit system and hence accountability.

- *Absence of a Central Repository for Upkeep Related Activities.* There was no single line agency to coordinate information on upkeep related activities like:
  - Collection / preservation of all data in a systematic, easy to retrieve manner.
  - Policy on standardised maintenance and repair technology and practices.
  - Coordination of induction trials and defect analyses.
  - Spares consumption policy based on experience gained.
  - Coordinated indigenisation efforts etc with a single window approach.

"The tasks before the nucleus SMA established in 1987 were enormous. By 1995, the significance and role of the SMA became recognisable in the following areas:

- The basic database on "Ship Fit Definition (SFD)", created for all ships and submarines, was a gigantic task involving codification in logical manner for 7,000 different systems. By 1995, all ships, submarines and shore support organisations were provided with SFDs.

- Computerised maintenance schedules (MAINTOPS) had been designed and promulgated for most classes of ships.

- The DART, OPDEF and SRAR dynamic data banks formed the basis for evolving a more authentic and realistic Dockyard work package for ship refits. They also provided the basis for indent analysis.

- Based on the data bases created, a few important defect analyses were undertaken and computerised. "Acquaints" were promulgated which had a bearing on remedial measures in amendments to MAINTOPs, spares consumption and procurement policy, refit practices, A&As / minor modification, etc.

- The scope for future computerisation of upkeep related activities was well defined to include amendments to MAINTOPS, refinement of existing data bases, As&As, modifications, Acquaints, Part III defect lists, spares consumption / holdings in conjunction with logistic modules etc.

- The Material Organisations, Naval Dockyards, BROs and Command Headquarters started looking up information from the database for authentic defect and work packages for refits, defect acquaints for nature of recurring defects towards remedial measures, spares consumption pattern in relation to onboard holdings, etc."

Dockyard Manpower

Until the late 1940s, dockyard workers learnt 'on the job' by understudying their seniors and, over time, were graded as skilled workers. The Grace Committee Report of 1947 had stated:

"There has been no consistent and uniform policy followed in recruiting and training of apprentices. Recently, the education standard aimed at for recruitment has been matriculation, but insufficient candidates presented themselves to fill all the apprenticeships offered. No entrance examination was set; the candidate's own remarks on his educational attainments being accepted, and a statement by a person of standing as to his character being required. Selection was carried out by a panel representing the departments interested and the Personnel Officer. Previously, departments entered apprentices direct as and when required, there being no attempt to adopt a coordinated policy and a common standard for recruitment. At no time has a set examination been used as a method of placing the candidates in an order of precedence. Relatives of dockyard employees are given preference whenever possible."

The Committee recommended the opening of a Dockyard Apprentice School and recruitment to the 'apprentice cadre' by an open, competitive all-India examination. Bombay's Dockyard Apprentice School started in 1949. Initially the School provided apprentice manpower only for the Dockyard. In 1966, the School was brought under the ambit of the Central Government, Ministry of Labour's All India Apprentice Scheme. Thereafter, while the School primarily met the requirements of the Dockyard, it also provided skilled workmen to industry.

In Vizag, the Dockyard Apprentice School started in May 1971 and was formally inaugurated in 1973. In Cochin, the Apprentice Training School was established in 1973.

In their report,[16] the Naval Expert Committee on Maintenance commented on 'The Productivity of the Dockyard Work Force' and made recommendations for 'Improving Dockyard Productivity'.

By the 1990s, the Navy had introduced measures to increase the number of supervisors, to review the trade structures of workmen, to increase consciousness of Quality Control and Quality Assurance and to pre-plan annual programmes to upgrade worker skills. All these began gradually to improve the work culture in naval industrial establishments.

Reminiscences

Reminiscences of the Bombay Dockyard

Whilst there is no shortage of criticism of the quality of refits carried out by the Dockyard, there is unanimity that whenever the occasion demands, the Dockyard achieves amazing things, and it invariably does so before and during hostilities.

Vice Admiral Daya Shankar was the Industrial Manager of the Dockyard from 1952 to 1954 and Chief of Material from 1954 to 1957. In the book *"Memoirs and Memories"* he reminisced:

"The Dockyard workers respond very readily to challenges. This has been proved time and again, in 1965 and 1971, apart from other special cases. When challenged, they really sweat blood to get things done well and in quick time. They are also human and expect the management to look the other way when the load is light.

"In 1954, there was an unfortunate collision between two destroyers, *Ranjit* and *Rana*, while the Fleet was on its way to the Mediterranean. The damage to the ships

16. See chapter titled "The 1980 Report of the Naval Expert Committee on Maintenance", page 158.

was extensive and they were limping back to Bombay. It was assessed that repairs would take at least three weeks. We did not have that much time even assuming a high-speed voyage to Aden. The work had to be completed in ten days (to enable the ships to adhere to their prearranged programme). Mr Parmanandan (then Director of Naval Construction in NHQ) was deputed to Bombay to oversee repairs. There were men on board cutting away damaged plates as the ships entered the dry docks, long before they had settled down on the docks. In the plate shop, there was furious activity cutting and shaping plates for the structure, and, in short, the ships were on their way to Aden on the tenth day! The Dockyard met the challenge."

Commodore (then Lieutenant) Franklin recalls how the Dockyard repaired the submarine *Karanj* in 1970:

"*Karanj* had come in for repairs after a very serious collision with the destroyer *Ranjit*. (She had inadvertently surfaced directly under the *Ranjit's* bows). No drawings of the damaged portion of the submarine were available in the Dockyard or even in the Navy. (*Karanj* had but recently arrived from Russia).

"The Dockyard decided to make templates from the submarine *Kursura*, which happened to be in harbour at that time. Templates were made. Metal was bent and shaped and welded. Within months, *Karanj* was repaired and was on patrol during the 1971 War."

Reminiscences of the Vizag Dockyard

Rear Admiral CL Bhandari was the first Director General of Naval Projects Vizag from 1967 to 1971. He recalls:

"I was not involved in the site selection at all. The site was selected by Alexander Gibbs and Partners on a cursory visit there and they said, "Build this dockyard here." When I took over as DGNP, I found some distinct disadvantages in the site and I wrote to Naval Headquarters a one-page letter saying why this site was not suitable. The main reasons I gave were:

– The entrance channel was too narrow for all the ships to come in. *Vikrant* could not get through. *Mysore* could get through only with some difficulty.

– The site for the Dockyard was situated near the Vizag ore handling plant and the iron ore dust would certainly not be very friendly to the electronic equipment on board ships.

"I suggested that there should be a three-member team to investigate a new site and that Dr VKRV Rao, the eminent engineer should head the team, I would be

a member and would suggest a site 10 to 12 kilometres south of the present location.[17] The new site had a better entrance, better sea face, was not being exposed to iron ore dust and had plenty of land to back up various infrastructure projects. Naval Headquarters preferred the present site.

"We had a plot of 1,000 acres for the Dockyard. There was a Russian team consisting of 20 experts and I had a team of nine. We sat down for about 5 months to make out three alternative plans, Option I, II and III. At the end of that, we came to Naval Headquarters to give a presentation at which I had requested that Defence and Finance should also be invited, so that at the end of our presentation, we could get a clear directive as to which option we should go ahead with. Option II was selected. We went back to Vizag and got down to detailed planning.

"At the 1,000 acre plot it was planned to have submarine pens, dry docks, a slipway, repair workshops, sailors' accommodation, a diving tower for simulating escape from a sunken submarine, etc.

"To start with, I learnt that in the MES costing, five per cent of the project cost is allowed for arboriculture. So I asked my Chief Engineer, a Brigadier, 'How do you spend this five percent?' He said, 'Oh, we take it on as an extra contingency.' I said 'Nonsense, you take out five per cent and keep it for arboriculture and grow plants.' And we did grow lots of plants and trees in Vizag. In my first year there, I planted 1,000 trees, next year 3,000 trees, and in the third year 10,000 trees. Today, the Vizag Dockyard is full of trees.

"In a large project, the essence is to delegate authority. No one man, no matter how capable, can handle a project of that diversity and cost single-handed. It cannot be done. Something will slip up. My officers had the authority to issue letters without my seeing them. I would see them after they were issued. But signals and telexes had my approval. In my time in Vizag, I had an occasion to cancel only one letter.

"Another interesting aspect was when my Brigadier and I came up to Delhi and asked for funds for the year 1967-68. There was a large meeting. Rear Admiral Kohli was there, representing the Navy. Additional Secretary, Mr Sheth, was in the chair. The Financial Adviser and the Director General Works were there. Everybody said 'Oh give Vizag one crore for the balance of the year. That should be adequate because their record shows that Vizag has the capacity to spend up to one and half crore a year. Well, give two crores if you like.' I was listening to

---

17. This site is now the location of the Vizag Steel Plant.

all this talk without saying a word. So Rear Admiral Kohli turned to me and said 'Why are you not saying anything? Everybody is having their say and you are keeping quiet.' So I said, 'Normally one is told how to do one's job. This is the first meeting I have attended where I have been told how not to do my job.' Everybody laughed and Mr Sheth asked, 'How much money do you want for the first year?' I said 'Six crore, Sir. The following year ten crore, the year after that 15 crore and thereafter level out at 15 crore, because unless we do that, this yard will not be complete in time to receive the submarines.' So Mr Sheth said, 'Right, you have six crore.' The Financial Adviser asked him, 'Sir, from where would you be getting the extra four crore? You only allowed two crores for the Vishakhapatnam Project'. He said, 'Yes, I know. The Air Force never spends their money, so we will reallocate.'

"Having got six crore, the Defence Secretary asked me, 'Why are you insisting on six crore and followed by 10 crores and then 15 crores?' I told him, 'Sir, if you keep on giving 2 crore a year, it will take you 20 years to complete the project. By that time it will be no use, because our submarines would have arrived much earlier and there would be no way to refit them. I have got a young son in the Navy who is a Lieutenant. I do not think it is a good thing for people to point out to my young son and say, 'Rajan, was not your father the first DG for the Vizag Project. Look at the mess he has made!'

"So we went back to Vizag with six crore in our pockets and I started work. By the end of January we could spend only three crore. Three crore were left. So I told my engineers, 'We should spend these three crores on steel and cement. Make out a list of the steel required in various sizes for two crore and cement for one crore.' This list was produced and we placed an order for two crore of steel in various sections, 8mm, 10mm and 12mm and cement on ACC for one crore. The price we got was five per cent to seven percent less than the DGS&D price because we promised the supplier to make payment within two weeks of the stores being landed in our yard.

"Another interesting thing was that the Vishakhapatnam area did not have many contractors who could work. So we put an advertisement in the papers to all contractors in India to come and visit the Vishakhapatnam Project, where lots of projects were going to be taken up and come and bid for them. At one time, after mid 1968, we had five projects in hand going on at the same time.

"Very early in 1967, I had put a saying in the main hall of the project where the designers used to sit. On that wall was written, 'Any BF can do the work of two men.

What this project requires is each one of us should do the work of four.' When Admiral Gorshkov visited the project in 1968, he looked at this writing and told me his English was rather poor, he understood what was written but he did not know what 'BF' stood for. When I told him, he broke into hearty laughter. But that is a project that the Navy can really be proud of. It is the biggest, most complex and well fitted-out dockyard between Malta and Singapore. It has really got everything."

Vice Admiral (then Commodore) LR Mehta was associated with the construction of the South Dry Dock He recalls:

"The Naval Base Project at Vizag was conceived as a composite project, in the sense that there was a certain 'Fleet' element of the project and a certain 'Base' element of the project and a certain 'Dockyard' element of the project, besides the other 'store and logistics' elements.

"The Project Report was prepared by the Soviet Union and its implementation was to be done by the Government of India with the assistance of the Soviet specialists wherever necessary. And for this purpose, the Directorate General of Naval Project Vishakhapatnam was created.

"The Dry Dock element of the project was left out of the purview of the Director General at the behest of the Army Engineer in Chief. To construct a dry dock was much more technical than building store complexes or housing colonies. It needed a special kind of approach and a special kind of organisation to implement it. And the E in C put in a claim for this project. To strengthen his claim, he cited his past experience of participation in building the Dry Dock at Bombay under the guidance of Sir Alexander Gibbs and Partners and subsequently of participation in the construction of the Dry Dock at the Hindustan Shipyard in Vizag. The Government accepted this and agreed to a Dry Dock Project under a Chief Engineer. Naval Headquarters accepted this but felt the need for a naval member in the design team, who would project the naval requirements of operating services, etc, in the Dry Dock and I was appointed with the designation of Liaison Officer Navy. The Chief Engineer of the Dry Dock Project, a Brigadier, had his own team of designers. He also had a Garrison Engineer to provide administrative support.

"The preliminary design of the Dry Dock given in the Soviet Project Report was very massive, more or less sunk in the soil, at huge cost and time. The Chief Engineer Dry Dock was not happy with this design. He felt a better and cheaper design could be made and he evolved his own design, which was subjected to model testing and simulated testing. This was eventually accepted even by the Soviet team. The project was implemented under the direct supervision of the Chief Engineer. Equipment specifications were drawn up. The major equipments were the dewatering pumps. To empty out a complete Dry Dock of that size in about three hours required massive pumps of a size never made in the country before. Likewise, the design of a Dry Dock gate of that size had never been done before. There were many such areas, which were undertaken for the first time.

"It goes to the credit of the Chief Engineer Dry Dock, who showed great innovation and professional competence in tackling all these issues and in the end producing a very useful facility for the Navy."

Major General MK Paul, of the Engineer in Chief's organisation was the third Chief Engineer of the Vizag Dry Dock Project. He recalls:

"The organisation of the Chief Engineer Dry Dock and the East Coast Zone was created in June 1969 for the MES to construct its first and largest Dry Dock in India. The initial planning and design was done at Delhi and the formation moved to Vishakhapatnam in November 1969 to start its work.

"The Naval Dockyard area was developed by reclamation with dredged material during the deepening of the adjoining water areas. The typical soil profile consists of a top layer of high salinity sand deposited over a thick layer of marine clay. Under the clay layer the residual soil deposits were formed of in situ weathering of rocks. These deposits consisted of yellowish clay, then sand conglomerated weather rock and disjointed rock. Because of the soil conditions, bored piles resting on hard rock had to be used for the construction of the Naval Dockyard at Vizag.

"I arrived at a stage when the South Dry Dock was 80 per cent complete. It fell on me to hand it over. Several problems had to be tackled before handing over. One, was that the Pump House was half under water. It took three months of gniting under pressure to stop the leakage in the valves of the pump house. Another problem was the dry dock gate. The designed arrangement was to pull it up with a steel wire rope from one side. This gave trouble. It was rectified by putting an additional pulley. In fact there was an accident when the gate toppled over and had to be raised. Another problem was the flow of heavy silt towards the dock entrance and the gate support. There was also ingress of water through the dock walls, which had to be remedied by extensive gniting and by the use of chemicals. We learnt

a lot of lessons from South Dry dock. These lessons were implemented in the North Dry Dock, which started off in 1981.

"For the North Dry Dock, right from the planning and design stage, a liaison cell comprising a senior naval team and my design and structural engineers used to meet once a week. The shortcomings in the South Dry Dock were identified. We presented our 'lessons learnt' to the Steering Committee. They decided to send a combined team to Britain and Germany. We went and saw all the latest dry docks.

"At the design stage, we also interacted with whichever Russian specialists were available but not in a full scale because they were reluctant, not having been associated with the construction of the South Dry Dock. But they did give a lot of information on the pumping system and the valves that had given trouble in the South Dry dock.

"We did lot of improvement in the monoliths. South Dry Dock had two pocket monoliths – these have holes in the centre, with the cutting edge at the bottom – all the mud is taken out from inside and the monolith sinks slowly down. In the North Dry Dock, we designed four blocks so that the dock would not have lateral movement either way. Another improvement concerned the dirt that used to come between the two monoliths – we had a groove in each with rubber fittings so that there was no possibility of leakage."

Vice Admiral (then Commodore) NP Bhalla was the Commodore Superintendent of the Vizag Dockyard from 1976 to 1978. He recalls:

"A problem that I had in the Vizag Dockyard was that the equipment that had been provided by way of machine tools was partly in excess of what was required. The Soviets had drawn up this scheme thinking that the Dockyard would produce a lot of spares, as was done in the Soviet Union. But when Naval Headquarters asked for the drawings of these spares, they were never made available. The result was that a lot of the machines were left idle. I had suggested that we should make the surplus capacity available to the private sector – let them say what they want, we will produce it for them and cost it according to the norms laid down."

Captain (later Rear Admiral) SKK Krishnan was the Manager Quality Control in Vizag Dockyard from 1984 to 1986. He recalls:

"The interesting thing about the Vizag Dockyard, per se, is that officers of the current Navy brought up the Dockyard, unlike the Bombay Dockyard which has got

250 years of history. Even today, many things happen in Bombay Dockyard because they happened like that some 50 years ago. In some ways it might be a curse, but in some ways it is also a benefit. It depends on how we use the system.

"In Vizag, the local people were not used to the Navy's type of technology, which was quite different from the merchant ship technology of Hindustan Shipyard. That gap is closing now, but when I went there in 1984 it was still a big gap. Nevertheless they were trying to adopt Soviet technology in an orderly fashion.

"By the time it got ready, everybody believed that the Dockyard had become too big for our use. I believe even the Soviets said that it had become bigger than what they had imagined.

"Even in those days, there were a lot of Soviet specialists in the Dockyard. Most of them were fairly useful. But because many of us did not know their language and did not know their system, and they in any case were quite confused about their system, even the sincere ones, the actual work we got out of them was definitely not optimal.

"My first feeling when I went to Vizag was that the Dockyard did not respond as quickly to some situations as compared to Bombay. Later I came to realise that things actually got done in a much more reliable and in a much better and happier way. There was no unnecessary rancour in my time. That was one very good thing about the social system in Vizag. Living together in Naval Park, or going to work together or working together, developed a community way of life and people adapted to each other. A lot more was done harmoniously than it was in Bombay. For the same thing being done in Bombay, perhaps there would be a lot of arguments. So unit life was definitely good and that I think impinged on the working situation also."

Vice Admiral A Britto was the General Manager of the Dockyard in the late 1980s and retired after being Chief of Material from 1996 to 1997. He recalls:

"On the East Coast, a number of new workshops had to be set up to facilitate repairs of ships of Russian and East European origin. Large time frames were involved in generation of project reports, approvals / funding and project execution. It was generally experienced that the new facilities became functional, on average, almost 10 years after the induction of ships and submarines.

"Along with the creation of shore infrastructure, specialised training had to be given to uniformed and civilian technical personnel for all new acquisitions: elaborately more so for the Russian submarine acquisition programme. Large volumes of Repair Technical Documentation also remained to be translated from Russian to English, adding to the inertia of time frames. The position, however, started easing from the late eighties.

"A large number of Supplementary Agreements were signed for assistance by Russian personnel on know-how in setting up repair facilities, as also for specialised repairs. Although Indian repair specialists more easily achieved mastery of equipment repairs, those of hull structure and of complex systems (weapons and others), necessitated a lengthy and arduous 'learning curve'. The greatest difficulty was in the area of hull repairs of submarines during Medium Refits, where restoration of circularity of pressure hull and specialised structural repairs in the way of torpedo tubes proved major challenges. Time overruns in Medium Repairs of submarines were the order of the day.

"The availability of Russian specialists for specialised repair know-how during refits was helpful, though not without its drawbacks. Due to the demands of vertical specialisation, the composition of such repair teams was much larger than what one wished for. Moreover, the 'rigidity' of approach and 'mindset' of these specialists proved unhelpful on many an occasion, apart from rubbing off on their Indian counterparts who had been groomed in the Russian stream.

"A perfect example of such thinking was evident in the first major 6-yearly refit of *INS Rajput*, the new guided missile destroyer that had commissioned in 1981. This refit had been programmed at Vizag during 1987 for a duration of 11 months. A team of 54 Russian specialists was in position to assist the refit. On numerous occasions, the leader of the team advised the Dockyard against intended refit practices, stating that they were either 'prohibited' or 'inadvisable'. For instance, the lowering of four new propulsion gas turbines as per refit schedule was prohibited and advised to be kept in abeyance for five months till ship systems were buttoned up and the ship brought to standard loading condition as a pre-requisite for aligning propulsion systems. The overruling of this view by the General Manager[18] and the adoption of modified engineering practices saved a good five months to enable refit completion on schedule.

"Despite the assiduous and whole-hearted effort of the Dockyard, refit management was beset with a maze of other complexities that affected timely and

---

18. Commodore Britto was the General Manager at that time.

quality refits. Ageing Kamortas and Foxtrot submarines set up spiralling refit workloads in Medium Repairs, often accentuated by excessive wear and tear due to over-exploitation or inability to conserve systems during operational phases or in harbour, as adopted in Russian practice. The tenuous logistics system was simply unable to replenish material pipelines at the required pace, resulting in refit bottlenecks. Yard materials, fast moving consumables and spare parts were often in short supply – some typical items being hull and special steels, submarine electrical cables and welding electrodes. Intensive efforts to indigenise these resulted in some noticeable successes such as in the production of welding electrodes, hull steels including non-magnetic steels for mine-sweepers, bi-metallic joints for hull, friction pads for gas turbine propulsion clutches, etc. The Defence Materials Research Laboratory at Hyderabad was a major contributor to R&D and production efforts.

"Adapting to the maintenance and repair philosophies of Medium Repairs of Russian acquisitions proved most difficult in the Indian context. The concept of degutting ships and submarines to bare hull, whilst specified and insisted upon as per Russian practice, was simply not practicable given the material, support system within the Navy and prevailing industrial infrastructure.

"A number of hard lessons were learnt in the process and progressive revisions made to repair philosophy and practices. Certain major systems, equipment and assemblies like gas turbine propulsion units, generator units, electrical / electronic assemblies continued to be returned to the Original Equipment Manufacturers (OEMs) in the Soviet Union pending setting up of in-house facilities such as weapon workshops and the Marine Gas Turbine Overhaul Centre at Vishakhapatnam.

"A major factor bearing on lengthening refits appeared to be the high marine corrosion rates experienced in the Indian environment. It appeared that both sea-water and ambient air-corrosion levels were higher than experienced in Russian waters – the sulphur and ammonia laden atmosphere in Vishakhapatnam, due to the proximity of industries and cargo vessels handling toxic materials, also appeared to be major contributors in pushing up the quantum of hull repairs during refits."

Retrospect

The chapters on the 1979 Naval Expert Committee on Maintenance, on the Russian Acquisitions, on Logistics and on the Reorganisation of Naval Headquarters have depicted the diversity and severity of the difficulties that the Navy had to grapple with. That the Navy was able to

keep its ships and submarines operational, despite the delays in the completion of maintenance and refit facilities that were coming up in the Dockyards and the BROs is a lasting testimonial to the perseverance and innovation of the technical officers and sailors, afloat and ashore, and the civilian personnel ashore in the Dockyards, the BROs and the armament and store depots.

There was the view, usual in every expanding Navy, that slower induction would help the repair and refit facilities to catch up. It took time for the proponents of this view to come to terms with three realities:

- There will always be a time lag between the induction of vessels and the setting up of their special-to-type maintenance, repair, refit and logistic support and weapon facilities.

- When vessels are acquired from abroad, it is economical to acquire them in sufficient numbers, rather than one at a time. Inescapably, the bunching at the time of their acquisition leads, years later, to the bunching of their major refits. Since refit facilities always lag, the effects on operational availability have to be sagaciously managed as best as possible rather than bemoaned.

- As the experience between 1976 and 1990 showed, indigenously constructed ships, which were neither acquired from abroad nor inducted in batches, were afflicted with the same problems.

The unusual civil engineering difficulties that were encountered in the 1970s and 1980s, the sensible decision to augment facilities already under construction to cater for every new induction (rather than create a new facility every time), the delays in financial approvals caused by financial stringency from time to time, all contributed to the delay in the completion of facilities:

- In Bombay, the construction of the new workshops was linked to land reclamation and demolition of old structures.

- In Vizag, the soil conditions were unable to bear the weight of the heavy floors of critical priority workshops. Their floors sank, entailing extensive rework for 'suspended flooring'. The experienced gained in overcoming problems faced in the construction of the South Dry Dock helped in the construction of the more complex North Dry Dock. When completed, it emerged as the largest Dockyard in South Asia.

- In Port Blair, all construction machinery and material had to be ferried from the mainland across the Bay of Bengal. The preparation of a Master Plan, the zoning of areas, land acquisition, the funding for water supplies and electricity generation etc all had their own gestation times, because it entailed interaction between several ministries involved in the development of the A&N Islands.

Viewed in the context of the national priority of self reliance and maximum indigenisation, the expansion and modernisation of the Bombay Dockyard, the construction of the Vizag Dockyard, the construction of the Naval Ship Repair Yard at Cochin and the BRO at Port Blair, all by 1990, reflect the uniquely Indian synergy that was achieved between the Steering Committees in Delhi, the Engineer in Chief's personnel and the Navy in distant ports, and between the Indian, Russian and European suppliers of specialised machinery and equipment.

The experience gained in the creation of these facilities proved to be invaluable in planning the maintenance, repair and refit facilities for the new Naval Base at Karwar.[19]

19. See Section titled "The Third Naval Base at Karwar – Project Seabird", page 171.

18

1979-80 Naval Expert Committee
Report On Maintenance

Preamble

The year 1971 was a milestone in the Navy's history. In the first half of the year, the nation saw for the first time, the positive role that the Navy could so swiftly play in support of diplomacy when the Sri Lankan Government sought India's assistance to quell an insurgency. In the twelve-day Indo-Pakistan War of December 1971, the missile boat attacks on warships off West Pakistan's major port Karachi and the contraband control on shipping destined for East Pakistan's ports in the Bay of Bengal enabled the Navy to control the sea within the first four days of the war. For the second time in the same year, the nation saw the contribution that the Navy could make towards national military objectives.

In 1972, the Navy analysed the weaknesses revealed and the lessons learnt during this war and formulated its remedies.

The Defence Reviews of 1973 and 1975

In 1973, Government constituted an Apex Committee, headed by the Deputy Chairman of the Planning Commission. Its task was to examine the immediate requirements of the three services based on an assessment of the threat and to dovetail its recommendations with the resources likely to be available in the 5th Five Year Plan 1974-79.

This Apex I Committee recommended special consideration for naval development and cleared the Navy's proposals for replacing old ships and the development of support facilities. The Navy initiated discussions with the Soviet side for the next series of naval acquisitions within the framework of the Apex Committee's recommendations.

The Arab-Israel War of October 1973, led to a sharp rise in the international prices of oil. This seriously dislocated India's national budgeting and decelerated all defence projects.

By 1975, the debilitating impact of spiraling inflation on defence projects made it necessary to appoint another high-level Committee to review the recommendations of the earlier Committee.

The tasks of this Apex II Committee were to review in depth the needs of the three services in the light of:

- The compulsions of the economic situation and the rise in oil prices.

- The implications for the acquisition programmes of the three services of the latest weapon systems that had been fielded in the 1973 Arab-Israel War and the assessments made of their effectiveness by an inter-service delegation that visited the Arab countries.

- The need to improve fighting capacity as cost effectively as possible.

For the third task, 'Expert Committees' were to be constituted by each of the three Services to assist the Apex II Committee.

The Army Expert Committee

The Army was the first service to appoint its Expert Committee. It was headed by Major General (later Chief of Army Staff General Krishna Rao). In his book, *"Prepare or Perish"*, he has stated:

"The (Army) Expert Committee held extensive discussions with the Chairman of the Policy Planning Committee, the Deputy Chairman of the Planning Commission, Defence Secretary, Chief of Army Staff and Army Commanders, some past Defence Secretaries and Chiefs of Staff, Heads of Intelligence Organisations, Heads of Research and Development and Production, Directors of BARC and VSSC, a number of senior serving and retired officers with experience, and other important persons concerned with defence, such as Director, IDSA, apart from visiting the border areas, field formations, defence installations, and other civil establishments concerned with defence, and making in depth studies, before preparing its Report. Thus, for the first time, a long-term plan covering a period of 25 years (up to 2000 AD) was made for the defence of the country. The Reports of these Committees were accepted by the Government; and subsequent Five Year Plans were generally based on the long-term plans made by them. (Page 400)

"The recommendations covered strategic aspects, force levels over different time frames keeping in view likely accretion of strength by the adversaries, adoption of credible posture and maintenance of a deterrent capability, modernisation of the Army including re-structuring of organisations, acquisition / development of weapons systems and equipment, improvement of command and control, re-organisation of logistic set up, improvement of intelligence, organisation of training and improvement of teeth to tail ratio.

"Implementation of the recommendations so far carried out, has resulted in significant improvement of the defence posture. For instance, the armoured formations have been strengthened, the regiment of mechanised infantry has been brought into being, a mechanised division has been raised, infantry and mountain divisions have been strengthened, more powerful medium artillery has been acquired, assault engineers have been raised, communications set up improved and logistic efficiency enhanced. A number of weaknesses and imbalances have been set right. The border areas are being defended well forward. Indigenous production of some of the essential weaponry and equipment has been set up. By virtue of this comprehensive analysis carried out and recommendations made, the teeth to tail ratio has been further improved". (Page 406)

"The main thrust of the Expert Committee was towards developing adequate counter offensive capability." (Page 407)

The Naval Expert Committee

The Naval Expert Committee was not constituted until 1979. It was headed by a Commodore to start with and called a Study Group. In due course, it came to be headed by a Rear Admiral (X) and comprised a Captain (E), Captain (L), Commander (X) and Commander (S). By this time, the 1974-79 Defence Plan had come to an end and the 1979-84 Plan had already been formulated. The Expert Committee was headed by Rear Admiral (later Vice Admiral) S Mookerji.

The Introduction of the Naval Expert Committee's Report stated:

"Because of its serious implications in terms of cost and

Naval preparedness, the Expert Committee decided not only to give top priority to the study of the Navy's maintenance and logistics sectors, but also to allocate a major portion of the time available for the total study to maintenance, logistics and training. The Committee took a view that if sound findings and recommendations were identified to make these sectors most cost effective, the primary tasks of the Committee to safeguard naval preparedness at minimum cost would have been achieved.

"Due to various constraints and complexity of the issues involved, the Expert Committee decided to submit two separate reports on Maintenance and Logistics. Care has, however, been taken that these two reports intermesh and supplement one another."

Salient Excerpts From The Committee's Report

Adherence to Planned Preventive Maintenance (PPM) Routines

"Maintenance schedules lay down routines required to be carried out by ship's staff with or without assistance by Base Maintenance Unit / Staff and by Dockyards. During discussions in the field, there was overwhelming evidence that PPM routines are being treated with near total neglect by the ships' maintenance personnel.

"Documentation is near non-existent / unreliable.

"PPM returns are not faithful.

"Little or no analysis is made of PPM returns by Command / Naval Headquarters.

"Poor performance in planned preventive maintenance is due to several reasons. First is attitudinal i.e. absence of PPM consciousness amongst all levels of on-board maintenance personnel – officers, skilled and semi skilled sailors. Secondly, there is a total lack of organisation – both on board and ashore – for monitoring PPM activities, although personnel have been sanctioned. Thirdly, non-availability of serviceable test equipment rules out carrying out a number of routines. Fourthly, a lot of maintenance time in harbour is taken up – apart from attending to breakdown maintenance – by 'extra-curricular and external demands.'

"All these are happening in spite of the fact that all ships are grossly over borne in all categories of maintenance personnel. The conclusion is, therefore, inescapable that there is something radically wrong with training, appointment pattern, monitoring, controlling and directing in the maintenance organisation and personnel in ships."

Incidence of Operational Defects During Operational Period

"It has been universally acknowledged that the number of defects, which occur during the designated operation period, is too high. Besides curtailing the availability of ships, this creates chaotic situations in Dockyards, as scheduled refit work has to be shelved to undertake this 'fire fighting'. It must be appreciated that the magnitude of the disruption caused is far greater than the actual quantum of work involved."

Quality of Work Carried Out During Refits

"Two types of views have been expressed about the quality of work carried out during refits. The Dockyards have generally expressed satisfaction about the quality of work performed. They have also indicated that where the quality of refit had been below par, it was generally attributable to substandard material or spares or need to use the same / repaired part due to non-availability or absence of Repair Technical Documents (RTDs) etc rather than due to poor workmanship.

"The contrary view has been expressed by the ships, who have pointed out that besides the reasons adduced by the Dockyards / Base Maintenance Units / Base Repair Organisations, there have been many cases where defects or damage has occurred due to poor workmanship.

"There appears to be considerable validity in the opinion that continued non-availability of adequately trained manpower to undertake refit tasks is attributable, in large measure, to the organisations themselves, as they have failed to provide the necessary training. It also appears to the Committee that the onus of ensuring quality of materials used in refit rests with the Dockyards, at least to some extent."

Maintenance Concepts

"Our Navy decided to make unscheduled repairs during the operational cycle of the ship a responsibility of the Dockyards. In the British Navy concept, unscheduled repairs (as distinct from repairs due to accidents) are the responsibility of Fleet Maintenance Units. In the Soviet Navy concept, unscheduled repairs are the responsibility of the Base Complex. Both systems are very rigid about Dockyards not undertaking refits on unplanned basis or refit schedules being subjected to frequent changes – virtues that we lack. It takes time to build up expertise and set up facilities for vertical specialisation.

"There has been a considerable growth in the number and size of units carrying out material / maintenance 'functions' at all levels, Naval Headquarters downwards. The growth appears to have been on a piece-meal basis and there are no reasons to believe that this organisational growth has been based on a clear perception of long-term objectives / functions that should and can be carried out at various levels. Consequently, there has been overlapping of functions and diffusion of accountability and in many cases, has resulted in 'non-performance'. In the anxiety to justify existing and additional manpower, functions have been added on; many of which have remained on paper only.

"In so far as staffing pattern is concerned, levels of management – top, middle and low – have been manned almost exclusively by uniformed officers. Qualitative Requirements for even key managerial appointments do not exist. Officers with no previous experience in Dockyards / Base Maintenance Units (BMUs) have been appointed to hold key appointments both in the Dockyards and in the Directorate of Fleet Maintenance and Dockyards. To make matters worse, there has been, more often than not, quick rotation of officers at all levels with debilitating effects on the organisation."

Tenures in Dockyard Appointments

"It has been categorically asserted that the effect of shortages is aggravated by short tenures and lack of continuity. Though it has been accepted that it may take an incumbent as much as three to six months to perform effectively, the impact on quality of work, if short tenures of 18 to 24 months are given, has not been fully appreciated.

"There can be very little doubt that such frequent changes would lead to different tacks being taken in the policy of the directive or organisation, which would have an unsettling effect on lower echelons; lead to poor implementation of plans and make accountability difficult, if not impossible, to pinpoint.

"Non-functioning, malfunctioning and breakdowns of sensors and weapon systems / sub systems are the rule rather than an exception in ships at sea.

"The above state of affairs is a reflection, not merely on the qualitative and quantitative refit contents of our ships, lack of expertise in our Dockyards but, as importantly, lack of expertise in ships. A change in approach to our training and manning pattern needs serious examination. Expertise is not being built up, in most cases, to the level necessary. In cases where the necessary skill has been generated, it has been frittered away due to our training and manning pattern."

Excerpts From the Committee's Findings

On-Board Maintenance Workload *vis-à-vis* Maintenance Manpower

"The number of defects, which occur during operational period, is too high.

"Structured data regarding operational availability and combat effectiveness is not available. Neither monitoring nor analysis of the state takes place.

"The material state of ships is bad despite their being over-borne in number of maintenance personnel.

"The usage and deployment of our ships is less than designed and as such the maintenance load should also reduce.

"Our operational cycles and deployment are such that large amount of shore support would be available as well as personnel onboard could also be deployed on maintenance tasks.

"Normal notice for steam for our ships is much greater than for comparable ships in other navies and as such it should be possible for the ship's staff to undertake greater amount of maintenance tasks.

"The amount of manpower available onboard for maintenance purposes is at least equal to but in most cases greater than in comparable ships in the British Navy.

"There is an increasing reliance on repair by replacement for first and second echelons of maintenance onboard. The manpower requirements are lower if this concept is accepted."

Dockyards and the Quality of Refits

"Refit plans are not adhered to, both as regards spans of refits and refit cycles.

"A number of important defects are not undertaken during refits by Dockyards. Many defects and rework occur due to bad workmanship or poor quality of work done by the Dockyards.

"Dockyards do not have adequate control over their personnel and the powers are vested in Command or Naval Headquarters.

"The projected requirements of additional manpower, indiscriminate use of casual labour and overtime is indicative of management inefficiency. The management and planning at all levels is unsatisfactory. Generation of skills has been neglected due to lack of structured training and appointment pattern.

"The short tenures given to service officers, which lead to lack of continuity, are a major factor leading to ineffective supervision and poor management.

"Short tenures of naval officers have generated the following major drawbacks:

- Insufficient continuity, which is necessary in many skilled jobs.
- Experience, which has been gained, is not passed on for successive jobs.
- Instability has led to seeking short-term solutions sometimes at the cost of overall benefits."

The Productivity of the Dockyard Work Force

"The Navy is the service with the highest amount of civilianisation, particularly in the supporting arms. The Naval Repair Organisations and logistics infrastructure are primarily manned by civilians, in contrast to the situation in the other two services. The total number of civilians exceeds that of service personnel in the Indian Navy alone.

"Shop floor supervision is generally ineffective as the number of officers in production departments is inadequate in Bombay.

"Non-officer supervisors are ineffective due to lack of theoretical and practical knowledge. 60% of supervisors are not even SSC passed and 45% have no technical qualifications whatsoever. In general, the standard of both educational and technical qualifications of supervisory grades is poor. The quality of 'old timer' supervisors is poor.

"There is a total absence of supervisory training being accorded as a pre-requisite for promotion to that grade.

"A large number of tradesmen do not know how to read or write and an even larger number cannot read drawings.

"Workers have no incentive to undertake training courses, as it does not confer any additional benefit on them.

"Union rivalry is a major cause of industrial strife in Dockyards.

"Collective bargaining and militancy amongst workers have inhibited the management from taking legitimate and firm disciplinary actions.

"The disparity of wages between those paid in the Naval Dockyards and those paid in public and private sector undertakings for workers performing similar or less complex tasks is a major demotivating factor. This also causes problems in attracting and retaining the right kind of people.

"Till such time as the wage structure of workers and supervisors is brought at reasonable parity with their counterparts elsewhere and incentive schemes introduced, overtime will have to remain to pad up the wage bill.

"The problem of accommodation in Bombay and Vishakhapatnam, the recent boom in Gulf countries where workers can command large salaries and increased industrialisation in the country leading to better opportunities to skilled workers are contributory factors to poor retention.

"The material handling system in both Dockyards is archaic and has measurably reduced productivity.

"Non-availability of transport within Dockyards is a major factor leading to avoidable wastage of man-hours in both Bombay and Vishakhapatnam Dockyards.

"The inadequate and unreliable telephone system wastes a large number of man-hours and adds to coordination problems.

"The learning curve is likely to make a substantial impact on productivity, which would be a further cushion to the Dockyard. Automation of machinery and replacement of old equipment by new design is likely to either bring in more productive machines for the same manpower or ones which require fewer operators. This is likely to be true particularly for the Bombay Dockyard."

Excerpts From the Committee's Recommendations

Base Maintenance Units

"Ships should be supported by BMU only during operational cycles. Ships under refits are not required to be supported by BMU.

"Jobs should be off-loaded to BMU only if:

- The ship does not have the required equipment to repair the item.
- It is beyond the capacity of the ship's staff to complete within the specified time.

"Operational Defects be undertaken by BMU / Base Complex in the first instance (if beyond the ship's staff) and only those beyond their capacity should be off-loaded to the Dockyards.

"BMU's support should be extended to ships both for pre-refit trials and end of refit activities to cut down the time spent in completing these functions.

"Ships should be allowed to use equipment held in BMU to complete their jobs.

"A division of PPM routines between ships and BMU should be on the following basis:

- No routine should be done by BMU more than once in succession as far as possible.
- Routines of the same periodicity should be divided between ship and shore.
- All routines of longer periodicity should not be off loaded to the shore.

"The following functions should be performed by the BMU:

- To support ships by undertaking defined percentages of PPM routines.
- To undertake breakdown maintenance which is beyond the capacity of the ship staff due to lack of equipment or lack of time. This should be in the nature of exception. An item should be off-loaded to Dockyard by BMU only if BMU itself does not have the capacity.
- To provide workshop facilities and machining efforts as may be necessary to ships.
- To assist ships / other authorities when special investigation is required to be carried out on a particular defect to ascertain its cause as opposed to mere remedial action.
- To assist ships during Self Maintenance Period on an exceptional basis, if necessary.
- To assist ships during end of refit activity to cut down the time required to perform. Ships staff would be required to keep systems working within defined parameters during operational cycles.
- To assist ships in rectification of operational defects on an exception basis provided ships do not have either the equipment or the time to undertake these. Off-loading to Dockyard should be on an exception basis.
- To provide assistance to very small ships (SDBs and below), which may be required throughout their operational cycle.
- BMU would also be required to undertake the function to assist ships to survey their equipment. BMU would undertake the defective declaration of an item, which is considered Beyond Local Repair. It would, thereafter, assess the type of repair needed and the spare parts necessary to undertake the repairs.
- BMU is to undertake repair of those items of repairable stores as are within its capacity. Off-loading to Dockyard is to be done when BMU does not have the capacity or when so warranted by load.
- BMU would also assist ships in preservation, packing

and transportation of items, which are surveyed by it and are required to be sent to the Naval Stores.

Test Equipment

"There is a need to greatly improve the serviceability of test equipment.

"Test equipment needs to be calibrated at designed intervals even though a defect as such may not exist.

"Users need to be more familiar with the test equipment they are expected to use and must know the correct procedures of operation. Monitoring should also be done to ensure that this is actually being performed correctly.

Dockyards

"The objective of the Dockyards should be timely completion of refits, ensuring quality and at minimum cost.

"The planning function in the Dockyard needs revamping.

"There is a vital need to standardise refit content.

"The Dockyard should have the final say in deciding whether an item can be accepted or not. However, the Dockyard must accept the responsibility of the consequences of deferring routines due.

"Dockyards are recommended to be an autonomous organisation and be run by a Board of Directors with the (numerical) control vested in Naval Headquarters ensuring:

- Autonomy (of functioning).
- Effective naval control at the policy making level.

Improving Dockyard Productivity

Naval Officers Appointed to Dockyards

"It is essential to ensure at least 3 years' tenure for service officers in Naval Dockyards. It is desirable to extend it to 4 to 5 years at a later date. To enable these measures to be implemented, definition of sea time and its requirements for technical officers' promotion needs are to be reviewed. Greater civilianisation is likely to lead to reduced demand for service officers, thereby making it possible for longer tenures to the smaller number appointed to the Dockyards."

Civilian Personnel in the Dockyards

"There is a need to have increased civilianisation for the following reasons:

- It would enable longer tenures to be given to smaller

number of service officers in selected billets.

- It would enable greater continuity and build up of expertise in jobs requiring higher degree of skill.
- It would ensure that experience, which is gained, would be passed on for successive jobs.
- It would tend to lead to in-depth examination of the problems and seeking of permanent or long term solutions.
- It is likely to improve industrial relations in the maintenance field.
- It would firmly establish a customer-vendor relationship between the operational staff and the maintenance staff.
- It would enable corrections of certain imbalances regarding sea time etc, which have crept up in the technical cadres of the service.
- It may make it possible for a larger number of officers to be spared in areas of naval interest in R&D Organisation and PSUs.

"It is essential to achieve a reasonable parity in emoluments between workers of the Dockyard and those engaged in similar jobs elsewhere within the country. Monetary incentives and overtime could be used as management tools to this end.

"Civilianisation is not likely to effect more economy. Second class inducements are likely to attract second-class material. The emoluments and perks, which are to be provided to the civilians, must be comparable with what they would be able to get elsewhere in the public sector.

"Greater attention needs to be paid to the training function. Both tradesmen and supervisors need to be taught the theoretical and practical knowledge necessary to undertake the tasks expected of them. The latter also need to be given management training. To qualify in training courses, incentives should be provided to workers in the form of assurances of better records, small cash awards and generous publicity for those on the merit list.

"The supervisory training efforts as well as those necessary for other echelons need to be as much 'in house' as possible.

"Qualifying in a Leadership and General Management Courses of 4 to 6 weeks be made an essential pre-requisite for promotion to supervisor grade.

"Internal transportation system is essential to cut down wastage of man-hours and effort.

"Attention needs to be paid to internal communications

like telephones, which would help in reducing wastage of manpower, and achieve better inter-centre coordination.

"Arrangement be made for transport from station to Dockyard for Bombay and from city to Dockyard at Vishakhapatnam at nominal or 'at cost' payment.

"In adopting measures to improve productivity, the Committee strongly recommends that the Ministry of Defence and Defence / Finance view the overall package in the perspective as enlightened employers. The legalistic view is likely to be costlier in the long run.

"The Committee strongly recommends that its recommendations for increase in productivity be viewed as a package deal. Though it may be necessary to incur an additional expenditure on implementing the suggestions, the savings due to increased productivity and thereby doing away with the need for additional workers would more than offset the costs of improvements. It would also lead to better quality of work and hence greater reliability of weapons and propulsion systems to the ships. Operational availability of ships is also likely to go up substantially. The Committee, therefore, firmly believes that the proposals are both cost effective and necessary from the operational efficiency point of view and need to be implemented at the earliest."

Ship Maintenance Authority

"There is a need to establish a Ship Maintenance Authority to perform maintenance support functions, both on and after introduction of equipment in service. A number of repetitive failures would have been avoided or better performance obtained from equipments.

"Some of the functions recommended to be performed by the SMA are:

● To standardise preventive maintenance data and point out discrepancies, errors and omissions.

● To collect, collate and process operating and usage data from all ships, Dockyards, special teams and Boards of Enquiry to optimise preventive maintenance.

● To promulgate amendments to existing maintenance schedules.

● To provide feedback on maintenance to Operational Commanders.

● To provide feedback affecting maintenance to training schools to help updating of training and to point out shortcomings and lacunae in training.

● To analyse reports of material shortcomings affecting reliability and to communicate collated information to the design authorities.

● On the basis of feedback reports, to ensure remedial measures.

● To provide supporting data / evidence for alterations and additions and modifications to existing equipment.

● To finally vet, with the appropriate design authority, the contents and the format of technical documentation for ship-borne maintenance.

● To ensure that remedies, corrective measures and possible improvements in processes and procedures are published and communicated to all users, training schools, fleet and administrative authorities.

● To analyse and report shortcomings reported in the field of logistics, which affect maintenance. Excessive consumption of particular items should be analysed with a view to determine whether:

  – It is due to any defect.

  – It is due to faulty usage or operation.

  – It is due to incorrect ranging and scaling done at the initial stage.

  – There are any other causes, which need to be remedied.

● To monitor the achievements of Base Maintenance Units and Fleet Maintenance Units.

The Outcome of the Committee's Report

The Committee submitted its Report in two parts – Maintenance and Logistics:

The Report on Maintenance stirred a hornet's nest, particularly the finding that stated:

"The projected requirements of additional manpower, indiscriminate use of casual labour and overtime is indicative of management inefficiency. The management and planning at all levels is unsatisfactory. Generation of skills has been neglected due to lack of structured training and appointment pattern."

On the one hand, the 'brutal frankness and objectivity' of the Report raised hopes within the Fleets that the malaise that had been afflicting the material state of ships and submarines had at last been disclosed and that clear recommendations had been made, which if approved by the Government, would help the Fleets towards better operational readiness.

On the other hand, the maintenance fraternity took the 'Manpower' aspects of the report as an unjustified and over-critical exposure of systemic infirmities over which it had no control. This fraternity marshalled its energies to rebutting the Committee's findings from which the recommendations had been derived.

A major point of disagreement was the Committee's finding that the Dockyards had adequate manpower and that, if properly managed, no further increases in manpower were called for.

It took considerable time for the dust to settle. In due course, many of the Committee's seminal recommendations were implemented. However, many endemic facets of the malaise remained untended.

The Report on Logistics resulted in the shifting of the Material Organisations and Material Superintendents in Bombay and Vishakhapatnam from being under the control of the Dockyards to coming under the control of the Command Headquarters.

In view of the controversy on the manpower aspects of the Maintenance and Logistic Reports, the Committee's recommendations on Personnel & Training were summarised in an 'Executive Summary'. Since all aspects of Personnel & Training Policy came within the purview of NHQ, implementation was progressed to the extent possible.

Retrospect

The following points merit mention about the Naval Expert Committee's Report:

- The Navy's 'maintenance' infirmities were well known to every perceptive seagoing officer in Naval and Command Headquarters and in the Fleets. Remedies just could not be implemented for the simple reason that 'sanctions'

for any proposal had to be sought separately and, when scrutinised by the Ministry, inescapably got bogged down in the web of interconnected problems that the Report had so meticulously delineated.

- Only a Committee constituted by the Government and tasked with a broad mandate to 'Safeguard Naval Preparedness at Minimum Cost' could have had the freedom to carry out the kind of wide, in-depth analysis that the Committee did. The Findings and Recommendations of the Committee provided the Ministry with a detailed overview of the problem, within which framework, Naval Headquarters' individual cases for sanctions could be systematically progressed.

- Regrettably, the very frankness and courage with which the Committee analysed the infirmities, and the objectivity with which remedies were suggested, put the maintenance fraternity on the defensive. Instead of ignoring the Findings and whole-heartedly agreeing with the Recommendations, the aggrieved maintenance fraternity attacked the veracity of the Findings and the Recommendations. In the controversy that followed, the long awaited reforms got subsumed. The result was that it took years to get obviously logical proposals sanctioned. Many of the larger issues await resolution to this day.

In retrospect, perhaps a more gently phrased presentation of the same harsh realities may not have raised as many hackles within the Navy as it did and the reform process may have started earlier.

19

Logistics

"I don't know what this logistics is all about ... But I want some of it."

– Admiral Ernest J King, US Navy,
Chief of Naval Operations 1942-1945

Overview

In every Navy, timely logistic support has been imperative for operational readiness. It has been, also, for every modern Navy, an extremely complex and expensive problem.

In the case of the Indian Navy, logistic problems started becoming vexed from 1960 onwards, soon after the arrival of the eight new modern frigates from Britain. Within a few years, problems multiplied.

In the 1970s, the construction of the latest British Leander class frigates having British and Dutch equipment, the steady arrival of acquisitions from Russia of modern ships and submarines and the diversity of equipment in indigenously constructed ships strained the logistic system to its limits. The logistics of these new inductions had to be dovetailed, somehow, with the archaic logistic procedures that had sustained the second hand ships of World War II vintage acquired from Britain after 1947.

After 1976, when Russian and European sensors and weapons started being interfaced with indigenous equipment in the Godavari class frigates, logistic problems became even more complex.

It was not until the 1990s that the innovative New Management Strategy and Integrated Logistic Management System were able to reduce logistic problems to manageable levels.

The basic problem, however, has yet to be satisfactorily resolved. That is whether the maintenance and refit of ships and submarines would be more timely if the logistics function were to be controlled by the Chief of Material (single point accountability) or whether the Logistics function were better controlled by an independent Chief of Logistics (divided responsibility). There are pros and cons for both points of view. At present, a Controller of Logistic Support functions under the Chief of Material.

The ensuing chronology summarises the Navy's efforts, over the decades, to overcome its logistic problems.

Chronology of the Navy's Efforts to Cope with Logistics

1962: In Naval Headquarters (NHQ), the Director of Stores was placed under the Chief of Material (COM).

1967: A Central Equipment Depot (CED) was created at Vishakhapatnam to handle the avalanche of stores, spares and equipment arriving from the Soviet Union.

1969: The Public Accounts Committee commented adversely on the Navy's 'Accumulation of Repairable Stores.'

At NHQ, a Chief of Logistics (COL) was constituted as an independent Principal Staff Officer (PSO) to be responsible for logistics functions and expedite repairs of repairable stores through departmental and external repair agencies.

The Director of Stores was moved from under the COM and repositioned under the COL.

1970: The Administrative Staff College at Hyderabad was requested to study the Navy's Organisation and System of Materials Management, both at NHQ and in Bombay. Its major recommendations were:

- Amalgamate the Naval Stores Organisation (NSO) and Spare Parts Distribution Centre (SPDC) under a Materials Superintendent (MS) Bombay who would be directly responsible to the FOCINC Western Naval Command and be functionally responsible to the COM at NHQ.

- NHQ would be responsible for policy and liaison with Government.

- The Materials Organisation (MO) in Bombay would have three departments – Procurement, Inventories and Technical Services – who between them would be totally responsible for all procurement action. The Inventories Department would maintain stocks, raise indents, etc. The Technical Services Department would carry out inspection and provide technical support like standardisation, ranging and scaling, identifying disposable stores, clearance for purchase of stores that did have a pattern number, etc.

1971: The Administrative Staff College recommendations were implemented.

At Bombay, SNSO (B) and the SPDC (B) were merged into the Material Organisation (MO) Bombay under a Material Superintendent (MS). Under the MS, four Controller organisations came into being – Planning (CMP), Procurement (CPRO), Warehousing (CWH) and Technical Services (CTS). The Material Organisation, however, was placed under the administrative and functional control of the Admiral Superintendent of the Naval Dockyard Bombay – ASD (B), instead of under the FOCINC as recommended.

At NHQ, the Directorate of Stores and the provisioning elements of the then Directorate of Marine Engineering and Directorate of Electrical Engineering were merged to form the Directorate of Logistic Support (DLS) under COL.

At Vizag, in due course, the CED and NSD (V) were also merged to form the Material Organisation Vizag, under a Material Superintendent. Like its Bombay counterpart, MO (V) was placed under ASD (V).

1974: Financial powers were enhanced and delegated.

Computerisation of naval stores commenced.

1975: Computerisation of air stores commenced.

Financial powers were further enhanced and delegated.

1976: Financial powers were further enhanced and delegated.

A modified procedure for accounting of stores was experimented on board one ship. In this procedure, consumable stores were divided into two groups depending on whether their turn over was high or low. In respect of 'high turn over' items, an annual quantitative allowance was prescribed while the low turn over items could be drawn on 'as required' basis.

The high turn over consumable stores were accounted for only up to the point of posting the receipt vouchers. The low-turn over consumable stores were, on the other hand, accounted for only up to the point of issue from the depot to the ship. No stores ledgers were required to be maintained for consumable stores.

The procedure for survey of stores was modified – surveys were permitted to be carried out on board ship by departmental / professional officers.

This experiment helped in controlling inventories and in cutting down the non-productive effort involved in detailed accounting. Approval was sought for the phased introduction of the modified procedure in all ships.

1978: The Supply and Secretariat Branch was abolished and the Supply Branch merged with Executive Branch.

Excerpt from the Ministry of Defence Annual Report 1977-78 – Merger of Supply and Secretariat Branch with the Executive Branch:

"Modern warships are packed with weapon systems necessitating utmost economy in the space allotted for personnel. Taking this aspect into account, as also others including the fact that officers of the Supply Branch have been performing a variety of diverse functions, it has been found undesirable to have separate Supply Officers on board ships. It has accordingly been decided to merge the Supply and Secretariat Branch with the Executive Branch of the Navy with effect from 1 January 1978.

"As a corollary to this, the post of the Chief of Logistics, one of the Principal Staff Officers in Naval Headquarters, which was being held by an officer of the Supply and Secretariat Branch, has been abolished. The Chief of Logistics had been responsible for procurement, holding and supply of spares and components, while the responsibility for maintenance and carrying out repair and fitments was that of the Chief of Material. This had resulted in a certain amount of divided responsibility. With the abolition of the post of Chief of Logistics, it has been decided to entrust to the Chief of Material the responsibility for the provisioning of spares and components in addition to repair and maintenance. For this purpose, the Directorates of Logistic Support and Armament Supply of the erstwhile Logistics Branch have been placed under the Chief of Material. Two other Directorates under the Chief of Logistics viz. Directorate of Clothing and Victualling and the Directorate of Supply have been placed under the Chief of Personnel and the third, the Directorate of Naval Armament and Inspection has been placed under the Vice Chief of Naval Staff."

With the entrusting to the Chief of Material of the overall responsibility for logistics and the provisioning of spares and components, in addition to repair and maintenance, technical personnel started carrying out these duties in the Material Organisations. The Material Superintendents at Bombay and Vizag remained under their respective ASDs. Inventory Management techniques and policies were promulgated for guidance and implementation. Redundant items of naval stores were identified and their disposal expedited. Stocking and accounting procedure for Soviet Stores were modified to yield a better and quick result. The Ranging and scaling procedure was streamlined. The review system of machinery and spares was modified on the base of ABC analysis.

1979: Excerpt from the 1979 Naval Expert Committee Report on Maintenance

In 1979, the Naval Expert Committee examined the pros and cons of Admiral Superintendent Dockyard (Bombay) exercising organisational control over Material Superintendent Bombay and the Naval Armament Depot at Bombay. Its report stated:

> *"Background.* Historically, the Naval Stores Depot was physically situated in the premises of the Bombay Dockyard till 1954. Since the Dockyard was not a full-fledged repair organisation at this time but a fledgling organisation required to extend all type of support to RN and RIN ships during the war, the functions of overseeing of stores and ammunition depots were necessary. Though the functions of the Dockyard have been considerably enlarged subsequently and it has grown into a full scale repair yard, organisational changes have failed to keep pace with the added responsibilities. Similarly, the small warehousing organisations of both MS' has been transformed into an All India procurement organisation with capabilities of repairs to inventory as well. With the result that ASD still continues to control MS.

> *"Situation Elsewhere.* It would be seen that CSD (V) does not control NSD (V). There is no dockyard in Cochin but the BRO does not have any such links with the Stores Organisation. In both these stations, the Stores Organisation reports directly to the Commanders-in-Chief.

> *"Functional Responsibility.* Functionally, MS is answerable to DLS at NHQ for his All India functions of procurement and supply. The warehousing functions for the Bombay Command are also undertaken by a subsidiary organisation under the MS. It would thus be seen that there is certain dichotomy in the functions, which are performed by the MS. Some of them pertain to the Navy, as a whole, while some are comparable to any local Stores Organisation.

> *"Advantages of MS Being under ASD.* One of the major advantages of having MS under ASD is that if he were not to be under ASD but under C-in-C, the span of control for C-in-C would become unduly large. Effective control of MS may not be feasible for the C-in-C.

> "The second major advantage of ASD controlling MS is the ability to coordinate repair requirements with the logistic organisation. In theory, it should be possible for ASD to project and ensure all his stores requirements integral to his organisation. Quicker response and closer coordination may also be possible within an organisation rather than between two distinct agencies.

> "The relationship between MS and ASD is that of Customer and Vendor. Most of the time, the ASD is the Customer. However, where Dockyards are required to manufacture items for stocks and for repairs to repairable inventory, MS is the Customer and as such is in a position to assert himself on the Vendor.

> "A somewhat more tenuous advantage lies in the fact that since there is a requirement of engineering skills in the Material Management, overseeing of MS functions is better entrusted to a technical officer.

> *"Disadvantages of MS Being under ASD.* The argument regarding span of control, which holds good for C-in-C is equally applicable to ASD. Particularly in the present organisation structure of Bombay Dockyard, more than a dozen officers report direct to the ASD. This can, at best, be termed unwieldy. It is a moot point whether the C-in-C or the ASD needs to be relieved of some of his overseeing functions.

> "The Committee's study has found that putting MS under ASD has given rise to certain unwelcome practices. The chief reason of that being that the Customer / Vendor relationship becomes blurred. The checks and balances, which exist when two independent agencies are required to carry out two distinct functions, have also been lost. There is a greater tendency to sweep under the carpet both failures in forecasting and provisioning. An in-house system has given rise to somehow getting a job done without blaming anybody. The quality of some stores, which are supplied for refits, is stated to be poor and one of the reasons is that MS is under ASD and as such, the Customer cannot complain against a fraternal organisation to an external authority.

> "The most harmful effect of the present organisation system can be seen in repairable inventory and manufacturing for stock. As it is, the Logistic Organisation is not able to assert itself even when it is a Customer, as can be seen in Vishakhapatnam. However, when it is an integral part of the organisation, the situation becomes far worse. The rapidly increasing repairable inventory in Bombay and the inadequate effort made by Dockyard to manufacture items for stocks are clear indications that the present system is not working well. The Committee also considers

essential that the checks and balances, which introduced certain measures of quality control in the supply of stores, are essential in our environment.

"Recommendations. In view of the foregoing, it is clear that there is a necessity to remove MS from the administrative control of the Admiral Superintendent Dockyard. There is a greater need for functional control to be exercised over this organisation by the ultimate Customer i.e. the ships. Such control would be best exercised by interaction of Staff Branch with the Material Branch. For association in inspection of Material Organisation, greater interaction is necessary between Staff and Material Branches on this aspect also. Though Maintenance Organisation is a large consumer of the materials, it is not the majority consumer. Even items, which are required by the maintenance function, are ultimately for the service of the ships. To this end, it would be correct to state that the ultimate Consumer is still the Staff Branch.

"While the details of the organisation proposed to oversee MS are given in the Logistic portion of the Committee's Report, broadly MS would function as an ex-officio Chief Staff Officer to C-in-C. Greater functional control would be exercised by DLS to ensure that the objectives, which are set for the organisation, are met."

1983: As a result of the recommendations of the 1981 Naval Expert Committee, the administrative and functional control of the Material Superintendents and Material Organisations at Bombay and Vizag were removed from under the ASDs and placed under the FOCs-in-C West and East.

1986: *Poor Quality of Indigenised General/Engineering Stores.* Complaints had increased that the quality of standard engineering stores, e.g., clips, bolts, nuts, locking wire, hoses, washers, seals, pipes, paints, etc, being supplied to ships were of very poor quality. Material failures of these basic items were leading to serious damage to ships machinery, resulting in their non-participation in exercises or being laid up for prolonged periods. A study revealed that the reasons were:

- Inadequate / incorrect specifications, use of non-standard items, purchasing from substandard firms, deficiency in inspection, acceptance under deviation, keeping of time expired stores in depots and inadequate planning / timely forecast.
- 'Local Purchase' orders were the main problem, particularly where delivery periods were also short. Over

the years, an increasing number of purchases were being done through Local Purchase and all such purchases were not inspected by statutory and other agencies like Dockyard, CTS/MS, users etc.

The measures taken to improve the quality of stores supplied to ships were:

- As far as possible, minimise local purchase.
- Improve purchases by ensuring that supply orders catered for adequate time and included technical data and specifications to enable the inspection agency to carry out proper testing.
- Institute procedures for reporting defects.
- Strengthen testing facilities at the various Naval Inspection Wings and make good their shortages of inspecting officers.

1987: The Indian Institute of Management (IIM), Bangalore was requested to carry out a study on the Rationalisation of Inventory Management in the Navy. This study indicted every possible facet of the logistics organisation – materials, armament supply, aviation spares and weapon equipment. After its report was presented to the Ministry, the impression gained ground that the Navy was over-provisioning and over-stocking. Being the largest segment, 'material logistics' took the brunt of the criticism As a result, the normal replenishment process was viewed with suspicion. There was a clampdown on sanctions and release of foreign exchange for naval procurement. Imports of stores and spares suffered, upsetting the regular and continuous replenishment needed to maintain stocks at the right level. It also affected the quick response mechanisms for operational and urgent requirements.

1988: After the severe national drought of 1986-87, resources became scarce and procurement of spares was further cut back.

1989: To 'professionalise' naval logistics, a 'Logistics Cadre' was created.

In NHQ, the Controller of Logistic Services (CLS) was created to function under the COM.

The Cadre was to have four sub-specialisations – 'Material Management' and 'Financial Management' was fairly close to what the Supply Branch had been doing earlier. The Management Information System / Electronic Data Processing (MIS/EDP) and Works Management functions were new. Two major duties of the old Supply Branch – Secretariat Duties and Naval Law – were not entrusted to the Cadre.

Development After 1990

Soon after 1990, the fragmentation of the Soviet Union disrupted the supply of spares and aggravated the cutback in spares procurement that had started in 1988. Russia's restructured factories started demanding payment for spares in hard currency. It took time to work out the new financial arrangements.

The mid 1990s saw the inauguration of the Navy's Integrated Logistic Management System (ILMS) and the New Management Strategy (NMS) introduced to improve the productivity of cost and budget centres, starting with Naval Dockyards and Material Organisations.

20

Third Naval Base At Karwar
Project Seabird

Background

When the 1939-1945 World War started, the Royal Indian Navy had only one base – Bombay. All workshops, dry docks and the six rating training schools – Gunnery, Seamanship, Signals, Anti submarine, Boys Training Establishment and Mechanical Training Establishment – were concentrated inside the Naval Dockyard. By 1945, when the war ended, the Naval Dockyard workshops had upgraded but there had not been any substantial increase in berthing space.

Before and during the war, new entry ratings used to be taken in ships from Bombay to Karwar as it was found to be the best site for seamanship training. In the early 1950s, it was suggested that Karwar be developed as a naval base. This would avoid the Navy having to be confined in a siltation-prone Dockyard area and a congested urban metropolis like Bombay. This suggestion could not be pursued because the amount of money involved in developing Karwar as an independent naval base/port without some commercial significance was not a viable proposition. Moreover, Karwar had no rail and road connections. Without these connections to back up this naval base, Karwar would be a 'white elephant'.

By the mid 1950s, despite the training schools having been moved out of Bombay to make way for the cruiser, the six destroyers, the landing ship and the light tanker that the Navy had acquired, the Dockyard remained congested. The Naval Dockyard Expansion Scheme was initiated to relieve this congestion and also cater for the maintenance and refits of the eight new frigates and the six new minesweepers that had been ordered from Britain. The expectation was that the new ships would replace the older ones and congestion could be kept at manageable levels until the new berths of the Expansion Scheme became available. This did not happen.

The rapid expansion of the Pakistan Navy in the end 1950s compelled the Navy to keep the existing ships in commission, despite the fact that this would increase the congestion at Bombay.

Since the Bombay Dockyard would not be able to cope either with the refits or the berthing of the size of the Fleet taking shape, the Navy proposed:

- Setting up of a major naval base at Vishakhapatnam and made plans for the immediate construction there of an 1,120-foot jetty and a workshop.
- Decongesting Bombay by basing of some ships at Cochin, Vishakhapatnam and Calcutta.

By 1961, the second cruiser, eight new frigates, six new minesweepers, the aircraft carrier, a repair and store ship and numerous SDBs had arrived in Bombay. The congestion, though relieved partly by the re-basing of ships and a few new berths of the Expansion Scheme, remained a cause for concern.

In December 1961, the possession of Goa was resumed from the Portuguese. The airfield at Dabolim and the small workshop at Vasco were taken over by the Navy, who immediately suggested that Goa be developed as an 'intermediate base' where ships could operate from and still not be too far from the Bombay Dockyard for repairs. In New Delhi, however, there was difference of opinion between the Ministries whether Goa should be developed solely as a mercantile port or whether the Navy's requirement to have an intermediate naval base, half way between Bombay and Cochin, could be accommodated. This discussion continued until 1963.

Immediately after China's intrusion in end 1962, Government accorded sanction for the construction of the new jetty at Vishakhapatnam.

During 1963, decisions were taken to set up at Vishakhapatnam, the Naval Base and Workshop that the Navy had proposed in 1957 and also to develop Goa as an intermediate naval base.

In 1965, developments occurred in rapid succession:

- In April, Pakistan intruded into Kutch.

- In June, there was an increase in Indonesian intrusions into the Nicobar Islands. The Navy recommended an immediate increase in naval presence in the Bay of Bengal to deter further intrusions.

- The need for increased naval presence in the A&N islands precipitated the decision to accept the Russian offer of vessels that had been pending since September 1964.

- In September 1965, an agreement was signed for the acquisition from Russia of four submarines, a submarine depot ship, five submarine chasers, two landing ships and five patrol boats, all for deployment in the Bay of Bengal and the A&N Islands. These acquisitions were to be based at Vishakhapatnam to segregate them from the Western origin ships in Bombay. They were to be supported by a new Dockyard to be built by Russia.

These decisions did little to ease the congestion in Bombay, which could only occur after the new berths and workshops of the Expansion Scheme came up.

During the 1970s, the new Leander class frigates built in Mazagon Docks, the new missile boats, the new Russian rocket boats and the new minesweepers started being based in Bombay. And to further add to all the congestion, the new guided missile frigates of the Rajput class would be arriving from 1980 onwards.

The fact that all the Navy's bases were situated in large port cities imposed both growth constraints and security risks. In Bombay particularly, extreme berthing congestion and encroachment problems were becoming difficult to manage. Moreover, the steady increase in the number of ships based in Bombay was adding to the load of an over-burdened Dockyard, to the detriment of the maintenance and operational availability of ships.

It was also imposing hardships on the crews of ships because of the difficulties of housing, schooling and transportation. The number of residential units, both for officers and sailors, was far below entitlement. The Navy had no land in Bombay to build any more housing or schools. Disciplinary and domestic problems as a consequence of two, or even three, families' sharing a tiny two-room space were having a negative impact on the morale of sailors.

All these reasons added to the urgency of decongesting Bombay.

Conceptual Requirements for the Third Naval Base

During the 1970s, the 'Conceptual Requirements' crystallised for the 'Third Naval Base' (TNB) on the West Coast, in addition to Bombay and Cochin. These were:

- Large waterfront.

- Sufficient depth of water.

- Tranquil anchorage.

- Sufficient contiguous backup area inland for operational, technical, administrative and logistic facilities.

- Integrated development.

- Security considerations.

- Exclusiveness.

- Defence in depth.

- Self contained.

- Rail, road and sea communications.

The Choice of Karwar for the Third Naval Base

The locations considered were Ratnagiri, Pawas Bay, Goa, Karwar, Tadri, Mangalore and Tuticorin. The short-listed options emerged as Mangalore, Tuticorin, and Karwar. Karwar emerged as the preferred location.

Karwar is located 65 km south of Goa and 320 km north of Mangalore. Its location gave it the benefit of being free from cyclonic devastation. Many small islands, including Anjadip, offered protection against natural elements from the north, west and southwest. It had deep waters. The four-fathom line (24 feet) ran extremely close to the shore all along the coast. The range of tide was 2.5 metres (7 feet) during springs and 1.2 metres (4.5 feet) during neaps.

Two perennial rivers, the Kalinadi River to the north of Karwar Head and the Gangavalli River to the south, would provide potable water, uninterrupted water supply and had hydel potential. The Kalinadi Hydel Power Project was expected to generate a total of 910+278+128 MW of power in its three phases.

The Karnataka State Government was developing Karwar commercial port in three stages to become an all weather port to handle ships of up to 60,000 tonne DWT for ore and other general cargo traffic. National Highway 17 was being widened and strengthened to take 20-tonne cargo trucks. The Konkan Railway to the north and south would connect Karwar.

It was decided to include the Third Naval Base in the 1980-85 Defence Plan.

NAVAL BASE UNDER CONSTRUCTION AT KARWAR

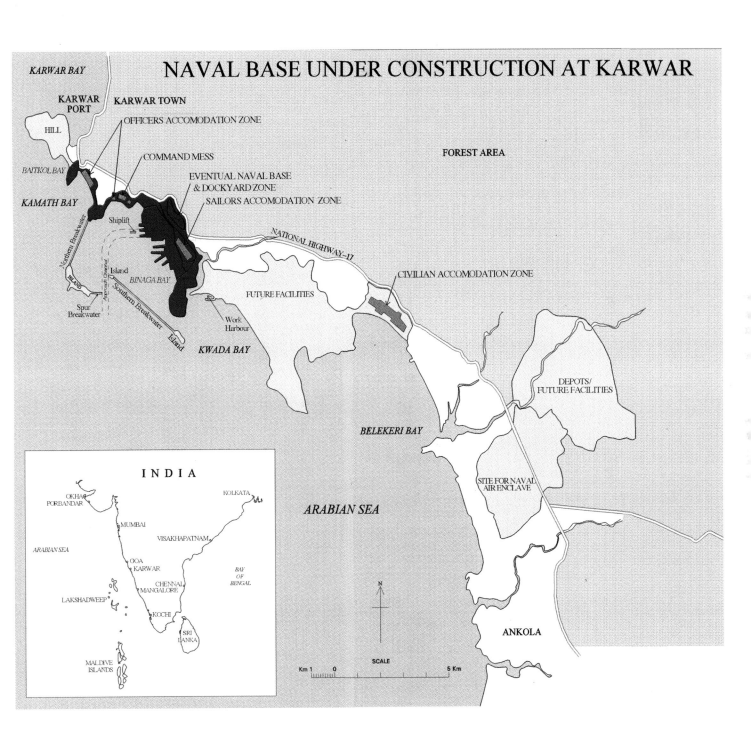

KARWAR BAY

KARWAR PORT   KARWAR TOWN

HILL

OFFICERS ACCOMODATION ZONE

BAITKOL BAY

COMMAND MESS

KAMATH BAY

EVENTUAL NAVAL BASE
& DOCKYARD ZONE

SAILORS ACCOMODATION ZONE

FOREST AREA

Shiplift

Northern Breakwater

Island

Approach Channel

Island

BINAGA BAY

Southern Breakwater

Spur
Breakwater

Island

NATIONAL HIGHWAY-17

CIVILIAN ACCOMODATION ZONE

FUTURE FACILITIES

Work
Harbour

KWADA BAY

DEPOTS/
FUTURE FACILITIES

BELEKERI BAY

ARABIAN SEA

SITE FOR NAVAL
AIR ENCLAVE

ANKOLA

INDIA

OKHA
PORBANDAR

KOLKATA

MUMBAI

VISAKHAPATNAM

ARABIAN SEA

GOA
KARWAR

CHENNAI
MANGALORE

BAY
OF
BENGAL

LAKSHADWEEP

KOCHI

SRI
LANKA

MALDIVE
ISLANDS

N

SCALE

Km 1   0   5 Km

Acquisition of Land

By 1983, the total land requirement had been ironed out.

Laying of Foundation Stone

In 1985, sanction was accorded for Phase I of the Third Naval Base at Karwar. Due to the enormity of the project and the fact that no Indian firm had undertaken planning and construction of such a major naval base, the Government approved inviting global tenders for consultancy. However, it was decided also to select a suitable Indian firm to be associated with this work.

For the management of the project, the Government approved the constitution an Apex Body headed by the Defence Minister, a Project Management Board headed by the Defence Secretary and a Project Management Authority headed by a Director General, who would be a Rear Admiral.

On 24 October 1986, Prime Minister Rajiv Gandhi, laid the foundation stone for the Third Naval Base and christened it as 'Project Seabird'.

From 1986 onwards, DG Seabird started liasing with the Ministry of Railways for connecting Karwar by rail to their network and with the Ministry of Surface Transport for diversion of the National Highway 17 for meeting security requirements.

Selection of Consultants

The first step was to select a suitable Indian consultant to prepare the broad requirements for inviting global tenders and draw up the Detailed Project Definition.

A Committee of Secretaries was constituted to select an Indian firm as consultants. From amongst the various firms that were pre-qualified, the Committee recommended Engineers India as the prime consultants for Project Seabird. This was approved by the Government.

Along with Engineers India, a global tender was floated for inviting consultants for planning and designing Phase I of the base. A total of forty-two firms and consortiums responded from all over the world, of which five were short-listed. In consultation with Engineers India, M/s Regional Engineering Development Consultants of Australia (Redecon) and M/s Netherlands Engineering Consultants of Netherlands (Nedeco) were selected as the foreign consultants.

The main tasks of the foreign consultants were to prepare a Master Plan along with a Detailed Project Report (DPR) for the marine works. The Indian consultants were to prepare a Detailed Project Report for the on-shore works.

Studies, Investigations and Model Tests

Prior to finalising the Master Plan and the Detailed Project Report, all the necessary geo-technical investigations, marine environment investigation, model testing of breakwaters etc had been carried out. The Central Water and Power Research Station, Pune conducted the wave and motion studies of the harbour and its configuration to evolve an optimal design / configuration of the breakwaters to ensure tranquillity conditions inside the harbour. The studies for model testing included investigations of prevailing wave, tide and wind conditions, sediment flow, soil testing etc.

The Master Plan was prepared by March 1990. The Detailed Project Report for the construction of breakwaters, dredging and reclamation was completed in June 1990. Engineers India submitted the Detailed Project Report for the on-shore facilities in August 1990.

Developments After 1990

The Financial Constraints of 1990-94 and the Revised Phase I

Due to the financial crisis in the early 1990s, there was a shortage of resources. Between 1990-94, the project could not progress further.

During this period, discussions were held on how best to prune down Phase I of the project in view of the financial constraints. In 1995, Government approved the Revised Phase I.

21

The Indigenous Panoramic Sonar
APSOH

Preamble

In the end 1960s, the Navy evaluated at sea the panoramic sonars fitted in the Russian Petya class submarine chasers. Concurrently, it was evaluating the European panoramic sonars being offered for the Leander class frigates to be built at Mazagon Docks. To achieve self-reliance in shipborne sonars, the Navy projected to the NPOL[1] its requirement for a state-of-the-art, medium range, panoramic sonar, designed specifically for Indian tropical and hydrological conditions.

The sinking of the frigate *Khukri* during the December 1971 Indo-Pakistan War led to intense efforts to remedy the inability of the subsequent Hunter-Killer operation to destroy the Pakistan Navy submarine.

The successful design, development, production and testing, between 1976 and 1983, of the Navy's first indigenous hull-mounted sonar, which in Indian waters performed better than all other sonars of that time, was the finale of a combination of unique circumstances. The derivatives of that outstanding sonar continue to be fitted in the Navy's latest ships.

Developments Prior to 1976

In the 1960s, the Navy had been experiencing difficulties in obtaining adequate performance of the Sonar 170B fitted in the new British frigates. The Bhabha Atomic Research Centre (BARC) had been requested to try and improve the signal processing.

In 1969, the Navy had nominated Lieutenant A Paulraj a gifted young electrical officer, for the M Tech course in the Indian Institute of Technology (IIT) Delhi.

In 1970, another young electrical officer, Lieutenant VK Jain, having just returned from a course in Britain, started working with the BARC Team on improving sonar signal

processing. During 1971, Lieutenant Jain tried out the BARC modification kit at sea. The trials were encouraging and he was working on further improving it when the war broke out in December 1971. Lieutenant Jain prevailed upon the Command Headquarters at Bombay to let him embark with his modification in *Khukri* when she was sailed for an anti submarine operation. During the next two days and until the *Khukri* was torpedoed and sunk, the modification kit was connected up. The submarine carried out its attack undetected.

The morning after the sinking of the *Khukri*, Lieutenant Paulraj was flown to Bombay from IIT Delhi. His assessment was that the BARC approach for modifying the sonar was not likely to be productive. He returned to Delhi and using IIT resources developed a different concept for modifying the Sonar 170B. His IIT-developed mod kit performed successfully during sea trials and was given to Bharat Dynamics (BDL) for production.

In 1972, Paulraj's innovative research at the IIT led to his becoming the first-ever naval recipient of a Ph D without having an M Tech degree.

In 1973, Britain's Loughborough University learnt of Paulraj's capabilities and invited him to Britain to work on their submarine sonar project for 18 months. Between January 1974 and September 1975, Paulraj was in Britain to work on this project. During this period, Naval Headquarters asked him to visit and assess the effectiveness of the designs of the latest panoramic sonars that manufacturers in Britain and Europe were offering to the Navy for fitment in the future Leanders.

Paulraj returned to India in 1975 and helped to install and set to work the mod kit that, during his stay in Britain, had been produced by BDL for the four British anti submarine frigates. This hands-on experience of the practical problems of modifying sonars on board ships was

---

1. The Naval Physical and Oceanography Laboratory, one of the three naval laboratories under the Defence Research and Development Organisation, specialised in the development of sonar.

to prove invaluable later when proving the new APSOH sonar at sea.

After installing the modification kit in *Talwar*, Paulraj was deputed to the NPOL to help in the development of the panoramic sonar project.

From 1975 onwards, Naval Headquarters commenced its detailed comparative evaluation of foreign sonars for fitment in future ships. Paulraj participated in these evaluations. With his unique theoretical and practical background, he concluded that the NPOL had the capability to produce a sonar more appropriate to the Navy's requirements.

NPOL gave a presentation of its sonar to NHQ and recommended that future ships be fitted with the NPOL sonar. The Navy accepted NPOL's recommendation. Sanctions were accorded; teams were assembled.

Developments From 1976 Onwards

In 1976, work started on what came to be called the APSOH (Advanced Panoramic Sonar Hull-mounted). In two and a half years, a wire-wrap prototype was ready. Sea trials were carried out in 1979 in which APSOH's basic concepts were proved.

After sea trials, the circuit design was transferred to Bharat Electronics Ltd (BEL). At BEL, Captain (L) Prabhala and Paulraj decided that to save development time and enable the APSOH to be fitted in the Project 16 Godavari class frigates, it was best to retain the same 'hull outfit' (for raising and lowering the sonar inside the dome), the same transducers as the Sonar 184 SS, the same standard cabinets as were fitted in the Leanders and to resolve shortcomings by adjustments in signal processing.

In view of the importance of this project, the Navy decided that:

- The first prototype APSOH sonar would be extensively tried out at sea, for one full year in a fully operational Leander class frigate, across the entire spectrum of hydrological conditions prevailing on the West and East coasts of India.

- During these sea trials, whatever modifications became necessary would be carried out in situ by BEL, the eventual producer of the sonar.

- On completion of trials, BEL would fit an updated sonar in whichever of the Godavari class frigates was nearing completion

In mid 1982, APSOH was installed in the Leander class frigate, *Himgiri* and problems were resolved in situ during 1983.

The first APSOH was not ready for installation till 1984. Since it was too late to fit APSOH in any of the Godavari class frigates, these three ships were fitted with the British 184 SS (solid state) sonar. Eventually, when APSOH was retrofitted in the Godavari class frigates, it proved to be a total success, particularly in detection and echo-classification.

The time taken to develop APSOH from concept to Sea Acceptance Trials was six and a half years; reportedly its closest foreign counterpart had taken ten years.

Commodore Paulraj's Reminiscences

"Early in 1969, I was nominated to attend a selection interview for the M Tech course at IIT (Delhi). I joined IIT in July 1969 for the M Tech course, overjoyed at a chance to pursue my interests in a real university.

"Soon Prof Indiresan became impressed with my work and asked the IIT and NHQ to allow me to transfer to a Ph D programme. I did not have a B Tech degree and therefore normally needed to complete a M Tech before starting on a Ph D. Prof Indiresan succeeded in persuading the IIT Senate to make a concession, but had much more difficulty with NHQ. Initially Vice Admiral Krishnan (the VCNS) gave a flat no, because, as he put it, he did not need scientists in the Navy. But Prof Indiresan persisted and wrote or visited NHQ. VCNS finally relented on the condition that I get back to the Navy in the two years allowed for the M Tech.

"I began my Ph D research in December 1969. After an initial start in more applied work, I was successful in developing many interesting results in filtering theory (extracting signals from noise). During early 1971, Prof Kailath from Stanford University visited the IIT. Kailath was already a legend. He encouraged my theoretical research interests. Prof Indiresan with his emphasis on 'practice' and Prof Kailath on 'theory' influenced my professional interests and they remain my principal heroes and mentors.

"In August 1971, my two years at IIT were completed, and I was posted to *Valsura* (the Navy's Electrical School). I still needed a mandatory additional year to submit my thesis. I did have interesting results, but it required more polishing and *Valsura*, lacking a research library, would have killed the Ph D. Once again, Prof Indiresan lobbied NHQ for a New Delhi posting and after a great deal of anxiety, I was assigned to the Directorate of Electrical Engineering at NHQ.

The Beginning

"One night in early December 1971, during the Indo-Pakistan War, we lost the frigate *INS Khukri* from submarine action. The next morning, the DEE (Director of Electrical Engineering, Commodore Chatterjee) asked me whether I knew anything about sonars. I don't remember what I told him, but later that afternoon, I accompanied him to Bombay. The next day, I became aware of Lieutenant Jain's association with the BARC experiments. I also examined some of the hardware developed by BARC. DEE then asked me if I would take over Jain's place and pursue the work to improve Sonar 170 B. I accepted and suggested that we do the project at IIT under Prof Indiresan. I was of course happy to get back to IIT to rescue my Ph.D.

The Sonar 170B Modification

"In March 1972, NHQ assigned me back to IIT Delhi to develop a modification kit to improve Sonar 170 B. NHQ allowed me to use any design approach. BARC was encouraged to continue its work. I had my misgivings about the BARC's approach, but kept quiet because of the sensitivity of the circumstances.

"By March 1972, IIT had a basic prototype and the team (Prof Indiresan, myself and three Ph.D. scholars) flew down to Bombay for trials on *INS Kuthar*. The first trial had problems in interface to the sonar. We were back again in June 1972, with an improved prototype and this time the trials went well. NHQ was enthusiastic. A final prototype was built during September 1972 to September 1973. It was cleared for production after extensive trials. BDL Hyderabad was nominated as the production agency. IIT handed over the design to BDL in December 1973. I left for the UK to work at Loughborough University in January 1974. The ex-BDL 170 B mod kits entered fleet service in 1976/77.

BARC vs IIT Technology

BARC Technology

"BARC used a technique called ping-to-ping integration (PI). Returned signals (after detection) from each ping are digitised and averaged together. This helped target detection since noise and reverberations are uncorrelated from ping-to-ping, but target echoes are more consistent. Over a number of pings, a weak target, not visible on a single ping, will begin to stand out on the PI output. The processing gain was between 5 to 8 db for 10 pings. The drawbacks with BARC's approach were:

- Sonar 170 B was a searchlight sonar. If we use several (say 10) pings in a given direction to extract gain from PI, the azimuth scan rate becomes too slow. Even a standard all-round search was too slow and a factor of 10 further reduction in search would have been unviable.

- The paper recorder in 170 B marked the signal as a raster on chemical paper. With a step-scan search, the echoes appear on several side-by-side traces and a similar ping integration gain is available through visual correlation. BARC's complex electronics added little additional gain to the paper recorder.

IIT Technology

"Three distinct techniques were used, each to be cut-in depending on operational conditions.

- Linear Frequency Modulation (LFM) pulse. An FM pulse de-correlated the reverberations and helped the target stand out. The idea of using LFM was borrowed from Sonar 184 M, which had used this to good effect.

- Noise Reduction using Digital Own Doppler Nullification (DODN). Sonar 170 B used a very wide band receiver to allow echoes that were Doppler shifted from own and target motion to enter the receiver. The inherent pulse bandwidth was only a few tens of Hz, but the receiver was about 2000 Hz wide. Most of this broadening was allowed for high own-ship Doppler. The target Doppler was smaller. In DODN, the mean frequency of the reverberations is estimated using a frequency lock loop (FLL) and then used to centre a narrow receiver band wide enough to pass the target Doppler variations. As a result, we narrowed the bandwidth by a factor of 10 and cut noise by 10 db.

- Notch Filtering (NF). Since we have (from DODN) the reverberation frequency, a NF can be used to reduce reverberations. As long the target was higher than 3 Knots Doppler, the NF passed the target echo without loss.

- Another improvement was the addition of an A-scan storage CRT display. This allowed the closer examination of echoes, to improve target recognition.

Performance Figures

- Close and low Doppler target: LFM mode improves target visibility in reverbs. Gain 5-7 db.

- Close and high Doppler target: NF mode removes reverbs and passes target echoes. Gain between 3 to 20 db.

- Far target (noise limited): NODN mode. Reduces noise by 10 db. NODN was also used in LFM and NF modes, but did not help close targets.

- The IIT system does not need multiple pings unlike the BARC technique. The single ping performance improved by an average of 7-12 db, resulting in near doubling in sonar range.

Comments on the BARC Project

"Lieutenant Jain had done a course in the UK at *HMS Collingwood* and had picked up sonar knowledge beyond his Valsura courses. In Bombay, Jain met Dr Phadnis of BARC who had returned from Italy where his professor had developed an instrument for nuclear scintillation logging. Phadnis had learnt in Italy that this technique can also improve sonars. So Jain and Phadnis, with Dr Dastidar's blessing, began adapting this instrument for use with Sonar 170 B. Jain was then at the Naval Dockyard Bombay's Weapon Workshop WECORS and Western Naval Command had clearly encouraged his association with BARC. I don't think NHQ was aware of the BARC project. Jain never visited or worked at IIT. I became aware of his involvement only after the loss of *Khukri* and his death. What I recollect hearing was that the BARC equipment was attached to Sonar 170 B which was operating when *Khukri* was hit and Jain was in the Sonar Control Room.

"I believe that the IIT system design is much superior to the BARC design. Once, during a meeting in Scientific Adviser, Dr Ramanna's office in 1973 to discuss the IIT vs BARC technology, I tried to explain why the PI approach of BARC had a problem and suggested alternate approaches. I am not sure if anyone understood. The BARC project went on for a few more years before being shut down. This was a high visibility project at BARC and it was politically hard for BARC to wind up the project on a negative note. However, BARC and Jain deserve the credit to have taken the initiative to start improving Sonar 170 B. Clearly, there would have been no IIT project (and the improvement of 170 B) and perhaps even APSOH if not for the BARC-Jain initiative.

UK and the Seeds of APSOH

"From January 1974, I spent 18 months at Loughborough University working on signal processing on an Admiralty Under-Water Establishment funded project. I used every chance to visit the sonar industry and learn whatever I could about the technology. Apart from my research into passive sonar signal processing, I had lots of fun building a minicomputer. At the end of my stay, I was given 2 months to visit sonar companies. This was a revealing experience:

- *Visit to Grasebys:* They were, at that point, building the Solid State version of 184 M for the Indian Navy. I discovered that the design team had only minimal grasp of sonar signal processing. During my brief stay, I helped them improve some of their designs.

- *Visit to Plessey:* I was told by Plessey that they had developed an improved Sonar 170 B. I found that they had not really improved the sonar, other than adding LFM. They had not figured how to do DODN.

- *Visit to Thompson CSF:* This was a strong team building the Diodon sonar for the Indian Navy. However, they did not know anything new.

"I arrived back in India in November 1975, confident that we could develop our own major sonar. Initially DEE assigned me for sea time. But then somebody intervened and I was assigned to NPOL. NPOL did not have a billet for me and I was finally posted on a transferred billet.

APSOH

"When I arrived in Cochin in February 1976, NPOL was already working on a sonar project. This had a budget of Rs 14 lakhs. Initially, NPOL's Director, Dr Srinivasan, did not involve me with this project. If I recall correctly, a computer system arrived from the US badly damaged and I managed to fix it. This impressed Dr Srinivasan and I was included in the project discussions. It soon became clear to Dr Srinivasan that I had the best grasp of system design and I slowly began to drive the project into high ground.

"Around this time, NHQ started looking for an advanced sonar. Dr Srinivasan and I managed to convince various people VCNS, DCPT (Captain Hiranandani) and others that we should build our own. It was a leap of faith for us all. NPOL had little track record to back up such an ambitious project. And I was a pretty green project leader. A CCPA paper was drawn up for Rs 280 lakhs. We had approval by end 1976 and APSOH was rolling.

"Our team grew from 10 in 1976 to about 60 by 1982. Captain Prabhala[2] headed the Engineering team at BEL. Relations between NPOL and BEL were initially good, but as deadlines appeared, there was much finger-pointing and our relations cooled. Looking back, I did a poor job in carrying BEL along and indeed also the DRDO brass. Too much of the technical leadership was centralised in me and my close relations with the Navy (innocent and indeed vital for the project) were unfortunately misread by many of my superiors in the DRDO and BEL.

"Serious problems cropped up in 1982 and VCNS and CNS had to intervene to keep NPOL - BEL fights in check. If not for these two senior officers, APSOH could have been stopped dead. Many heads soon rolled in the aftermath.

"After a 6-month installation on *Himgiri* commanded by Captain (later Admiral) Shekhawat, the APSOH

---

2. Captain S Prabhala, a talented electrical officer, later rose to be the Chairman and Managing Director of Bharat Electronics Ltd.

prototype took to sea in mid 1982. On the very first day, we saw 16 km ranges against a submarine target. It brought so many others and me great satisfaction. We had problems with the power amplifiers, which took a while to fix. But this aside, the system behaved superbly. The sonar screens were sometimes unreal in quality compared to anything known.

APSOH Credits (a personal list)

- The NPOL and BEL project teams.
- CNS Admiral Pereira and VCNS Vice Admiral Schunker for backing of the project, sometimes at personal risk to themselves.
- Dr Srinivasan for giving me near absolute freedom at NPOL to execute the project. This was not easy for him politically, but he stuck with it almost to the end.
- Key NHQ directors (Captain Hiranandani, Khandekar etc.) who backed APSOH. They believed in indigenous technology in a time when it was risky and unfashionable to do so.
- Commodore (later Vice Admiral) Ravi Kohli (DNRD) for his tremendous personal support.
- Captain Subbu Prabhala for managing the Bharat Electronics team with integrity and ability. He was unfortunately transferred in 1980.
- Captain (later Rear Admiral Pramod Datey) for doing a fine job of the installation.
- Many others in the Navy (Himgiri, Mazagon Docks, Naval Dockyard), DRDO and BEL who went out of their way to build a dream.

Thoughts on APSOH in Retrospect

"Now that I lead aspects of wireless technology at a worldwide level, I have a better understanding of the technology development process in the developed countries. I sometimes compare APSOH with other achievements I see in my new field. I am always amazed as to how such an inexperienced team, with such few resources, pulled off this major project in such a short period. APSOH was an impossible dream that came true for many of us.

The End

"One day in May 1983, as the APSOH trials were concluding, Dr Arunachalam, the Scientific Adviser to the Defence Minister, asked me to leave the country on sabbatical for two or three years and to do something completely different. He made it clear that my sonar career was over and I should find wider interests. Since I was not seconded to DRDO, the CNS's (Admiral Dawson's) clearance was needed, and went along with this. I was initially a little hesitant, but was willing to be persuaded. Thus, with some surprise, my sonar period ended almost as abruptly as it had begun, more than eleven years ago on the day after we lost the *Khukri*.

"In September 1983, I joined Stanford. It all worked out thanks to Prof Kailath who remembered my Ph D work and arranged the visiting faculty appointment. At Stanford, I returned to pure theoretical research in mostly applied mathematics, very far from sonars and mostly irrelevant to the DRDO or the Navy. However I came to enjoy Stanford a lot, and therefore in 1992, when I was at a loose end, I decided to return here to start a new activity in wireless communications for the University.

Acknowledgement

"I was fortunate to have played a role in the early development of the Indian Navy's sonar capability: Sonar 170 B Mod and later APSOH and its variants - I started the variants but was out of NPOL before these were completed.

"I acknowledge the support and encouragement of many people. Clearly the most important person was Prof Indiresan. His perseverance and faith launched me (an ex-NDA officer without a formal university degree or for that matter any real engineering training) into a world of high technology – IIT (Delhi), sonars, parallel computers, wireless networks, Stanford University and the rest.

"Recalling my sonar days, I was blessed with tremendous personal support from the highest levels in the Navy including every CNS and VCNS from 1972 to 1983. There are many others drawn from Navy, DRDO and BEL, too numerous to mention here."

For his achievement, Commodore (then Commander) Paulraj was awarded the Ati Vishist Seva Medal in 1984. The citation for his award stated:

"Commander Arogyaswami Joseph Paulraj, VSM, (50162 B) was commissioned in the Indian Navy on 1 July 1965. He stood first in the National Defence Academy and was awarded the President of India Gold Medal. He obtained a Ph D in Electrical Engineering in 1973 from the Indian Institute of Technology New Delhi.

"Commander Paulraj served onboard Indian Naval Ship Darshak *and in the Directorate of Electrical Engineering at Naval Headquarters before being nominated to the Research and Development Organisation. From the very beginning, he showed a great flair for research,*

tremendous ingenuity, ability for improvisation and hard work. He was awarded the Vishisht Seva Medal in 1974 for designing a new circuit in a record time of six months.

"Recently, Commander A Paulraj was nominated project leader of the project for development of APSOH – a hull mounted sonar designed for fitment in ASW frigates. From the initial conceptual stage to the installation and harbour/sea acceptance trials of the system, Commander Paulraj was totally involved in the project and brought it to a successful completion.

"APSOH is one of the most sophisticated sonar sets available in the world and ranks very favourably with those manufactured abroad, but not offered to this country. Through the successful development of the system, self reliance has been achieved in the field of surface ship sonars and a firm foundation laid for development of other sonars required by the Navy in the future. Such a tremendous achievement, which will greatly enhance the operational capability of our ships, was largely possible because of the selfless devotion to duty, high technical competence, result-oriented management and leadership provided by Commander Paulraj.

Commander Arogyaswami Joseph Paulraj has thus rendered distinguished service of an exceptional order"

The Hull-Mounted Variable Depth Sonar – HUMVAD

The Navy had also projected to the NPOL, the requirement for a panoramic, variable depth sonar. As soon as Commander Paulraj finished work on the APSOH, he started work on the HUMVAD. To save development time, HUMVAD retained the same towing winches, towing cable and tow cable fairing as in the British Variable Depth Sonar 199 fitted in the first Leander class frigate, the *Nilgiri*.

The towed body and the sonar inside it was a new design. The hull-mounted sonar was an upgraded version of the APSOH. In the 1990s, the HUMVAD was fitted in the Project 15 destroyers of the Delhi class.

22

Indian Naval Operations
1976 – 1990

Preamble

This chapter narrates the major operations that the Indian Navy was engaged in between 1976 and 1990. These were:

Year	Operation	Duration	Nature of Operation
1976	Godsal	March-April 1976	INS Godavari's salvage after grounding in the Maldives
1981	Starling	May 1981 to July 1982	Support of BSF personnel on New Moore Island
1986	Rajdoot	January-February 1986	Evacuation of embassy personnel from Aden
1987	Brass Tacks	January to March 1987	Major Tri Service Exercise
1987	Pawan	July 1987 to March 1990	Support of Army operations in Sri Lanka
1988	Cactus	November 1988	Suppression of coup against the Maldives Government
1990	Tasha	June 1990 to date	Anti militant patrols between India and Sri Lanka

The Salvage of *INS Godavari*

INS Godavari sailed from Cochin for the Maldives Islands on 19 March 1976. She was to rendezvous (R/V) off Male with *INS Delhi* and *INS Deepak* returning from a goodwill visit to Mauritius. On the night of 22/23 March, she ran aground on a coral reef north of Male before she could make the R/V.

Over the next three weeks, nine attempts were made to pull the ship off the reef. Eventually, after she had been pulled off, she had to be kept afloat, because her bottom plates had been badly damaged. She was towed back to Cochin, repaired, towed to Bombay and disposed off.

Captain (later Admiral and Chief of the Naval Staff) JG Nadkarni was in command of the cruiser *INS Delhi* and in charge of the salvage operation. He recalls:

"*Godavari's* salvage operation was quite a unique experience. It was one of those incidents where the famous poem 'for want of a nail, the shoe was lost' was very true. In February 1976, *Delhi, Deepak* and *Tir* had gone for a cruise to Mauritius. As it happened, *Deepak's* material state was extremely poor. We had the unique spectacle of the cruiser *Delhi* having to transfer by water

hose about 40 tonnes of water to the frigate *Tir* because the Fleet tanker *Deepak* couldn't give us water!

"On the way to Mauritius, one of *Deepak's* pumps, which was very crucial for her, packed up for the want of a small spindle. We immediately sent a signal for that spindle to be air-lifted to Mauritius. The spindle was located in Bombay and the Naval Stores Officer booked it by an Air India flight to Mauritius. Unfortunately, he forgot to mention that it was 'urgent defence cargo.' As luck would have it, something happened to the engine of the aircraft on which the spindle was loaded and another aircraft was nominated to go to Mauritius instead. The new aircraft that was nominated was a less powerful aircraft, which could not carry the entire cargo load. Therefore, only a limited amount of cargo from the first aircraft was loaded into the second aircraft, with the result that this particular spindle was left behind. When the aircraft arrived in Mauritius, we found that the spindle had not come and we had to sail without it.

"Our next port of call was Male in the Maldives and Naval Headquarters sent *INS Godavari* from Cochin with this spindle to meet us off Male. *Godavari* did not carry out her navigation properly. She was way off track. There are fairly strong currents off the Maldives. The next thing she knew, not having taken a proper fix of her position, was that she was aground. So you can see that the whole incident took place for want of that small spindle and a store officer not marking it properly!

"We were supposed to R/V *Godavari* off Male and take whatever she had brought for us. When we arrived at the R/V position, there was no sign of *Godavari*. We decided to enter Male harbour. Just as we were entering, there was a faint call from *Godavari* and a signal was received saying that she had run aground somewhere north of Male.

"We immediately went to that position and found *Godavari* high and dry. There was absolutely no hope of her being refloated on her own. She had run aground at a speed of about 10 to 12 knots. She was about nine-tenths on land and only the propellers were in the water. The ship was still having steam. They had tried to go astern to see if she could come off, but absolutely no hope.

"It took us 21 days to get that ship off the reef. The main reason for the delay was that we did not have tugs powerful enough to pull the ship off. Initially we had only our naval tug *Gaj*. We tried a lot with *Gaj* to pull *Godavari* off. But *Gaj* alone could not do it. Finally we managed to get a very powerful tug from Mangalore. We managed to pass a towrope to each of the tugs and one day, when both of them pulled with all their might, *Godavari* slid off her perch and entered the water.

"That, of course, was not all, because her bottom had been ripped open. She began to take in water and we had a terrible time to make sure that she remained afloat. Every available portable pump from the Fleet was commandeered. We found that only one or two of them worked!

"Fortunately for us, although everything else in *Godavari* was not working, one emergency diesel generator kept on working throughout. With the use of that emergency diesel electricity generator and one pump, we somehow managed to keep *Godavari* afloat over the next two days whilst she was towed to Cochin and berthed alongside.

"We learnt many things. Of course, it was the co-ordination by many ships and their equipment. But the one thing of particular note is that this was on a coral reef and, as you know, the water immediately next to a coral reef is about 2,000 fathoms deep. All the ships had to steam all the time for 21 days, without any respite to anchor. That was quite an achievement. There was a fairly strong current offshore. We had to keep the ships moving. And in spite of that, we took all the ammunition off from *Godavari*. We lightened her in many ways and finally, after much effort, we managed to pull her off the reef.

"We wrote a fairly extensive report on the whole operation. Our report concentrated on the absolute primitiveness of the salvage capability that the Indian Navy possessed. We recommended the creation of a salvage cell, where all the latest equipment would be stored. Things like inflatable 'camels', which when placed under a grounded ship can lift her using compressed air. We also recommended regular exercises to ensure that our salvage organisation remained on its toes.

"Frankly, I don't think that the Navy bothered to set up any salvage organisation. People said that where we have a ship running aground once in 25 years, why should we have an organisation for such things. So I don't think that to this day, any salvage organisation exists, either in the Indian Navy or in the Coast Guard.

"Recently a tanker went aground off Goa. I think they called in a Singapore company to do the salvage operation."

Operation Starling in the Bay of Bengal 1981-1982

In the early 1970s, a new low island emerged on a previously charted sandbank in estuary waters between India and Bangladesh. Surveys were carried out. It came to be called New Moore Island.

New Moore Island lies at a distance of 4,965 metres from the Indian coast and 7,040 metres from the coast of Bangladesh on a sandbank that is contiguous to the Indian coast. It is separated from the Bangladesh coast by a deep and continuous channel running north and south, leading into the estuary of the rivers Haribhanga, Jamuna and Raimangal. In conformity with international law, India claimed New Moore Island like all the other low elevation islands situated within 12 miles from its coast.

In June 1981, sentiments in Bangladesh were disturbed by what was considered to be a unilateral survey carried out by India and its inability to persuade India to undertake a joint survey. To forestall preemptive activity:

- The Navy ferried Border Security Force (BSF) personnel to the island and kept them supplied with food and water and periodically replaced them with fresh BSF personnel from the mainland.

- For the next twelve months, shallow draft ships patrolled around the island and beached whenever necessary to disembark and re-embark BSF personnel and stores.

The operation was terminated after sentiments had returned to normal.

Operation Rajdoot off Aden From 28 Jan to 3 Feb 1986

Following news of civil war in Aden in the aftermath of a coup, (the new) *Godavari*, along with the fleet tanker *Shakti*, were despatched for the evacuation of Indian nationals who might get stranded there. By the time the ships reached Aden, the situation was under control. Both ships patrolled off Aden for a few days before returning to Bombay.

Exercise Brass Tacks 1987

The Genesis of the Exercise

The annual 'Senior Officers' Conference' is attended by all the Commanders in Chief of a service to discuss matters with the Principal Staff Officers at the Service Headquarters. A 'Tri-Service Commanders Conference' would be attended by all the Commanders in Chief of the three services at which inter-service operational matters could be discussed.

In October 1985, Admiral Tahiliani was the Chief of the Naval Staff. He recalls:

> "In the month of October 1985, it was the Navy's Senior Officers' Conference where, for the first time, I had invited the Army and Air Chiefs. From what I had seen of past practice, for the Prime Minister's inaugural address, each service would invite the senior bureaucrats, the Cabinet Secretary, the Defence Secretary, the Financial Adviser Defence Services, but the other Service Chiefs were only included for social events like the dinner which the service chiefs traditionally had for the Commanders, where the Prime Minister was also an invitee. So I decided that it would be better if the Service Chiefs were also present at the inauguration of the Navy's Conference by the Prime Minister.

> "After my initial briefing, the Prime Minister in his remarks suggested that the services should plan a major exercise which would stretch the nation's resources to the full as would happen in time of war."

Several issues arose during the planning stage. Should the exercise test the entire sequence of procedures to be followed by every Ministry of the Government as laid down in the Union War Book? What would happen if we carried out a totally realistic exercise to test every single link of the civil-military chain in such a way as would highlight the shortcomings to be remedied? How long would it take to prepare for such an exercise? How long would it take to recover from the dislocation caused by such a large exercise? How much would it cost in money and in wear and tear? How long would it take to restore combat worthiness after this wear and tear? If the three services carried out a combined exercise on such a realistic scale, representative of what it would be if hostilities were to erupt on the western front with Pakistan, what precautions should be taken to avoid alarm and misinterpretation by Pakistan and China? And so on.

Over the next twelve months, the Navy held a number of major exercises, both naval and inter-service, in realistic scenarios.

The first Tri-Service Commanders' Conference convened in Delhi in October 1986. The three services discussed their plans. 1986-87 was also the year for the Army's triennial series of large-scale manoeuvres. The exercise that came to be called Brass Tacks was scheduled for the early months of 1987. It became the largest inter-service exercise that the Indian Armed Forces had staged since Independence in 1947.

The Unforeseen Escalation During the Exercise

The enormous expense incurred in a huge exercise like Brass Tacks makes it imperative that it has extremely realistic strategic and tactical objectives. It is imperative that it is held in terrain that is as realistic as possible, so that the lessons learnt are meaningful and justify the cost.

In end 1986, as part of the preliminaries of the exercise, the Army began moving formations towards the Rajasthan desert proximate to India's western border with Pakistan. Pakistan became suspicious and, by January, moved its strike corps to positions along the border to counter any misadventure by India. India reacted to the Pakistan Army's moves and the Armed Forces of both countries went on Red Alert. The situation was defused in time. Both countries pulled back from the brink of a war.

The Naval Aspects of Exercise Brass Tacks

The naval aspects of Brass Tacks created no controversy. The exercise was planned in phases from tactical games ashore to individual fleet exercises, followed by combined fleet exercises, culminating in an amphibious operation on the Saurashtra coast. Training for the amphibious phase, carried out on a beach near Mangalore, turned out to be extremely useful for both the Army and the Navy. During the amphibious landing phase, useful lessons were learnt by each of the three services, since it was the first time that they were exercising together for an integrated operation on this scale.

Operation Pawan – Naval Operations in Support of the Indian Peacekeeping Force in Sri Lanka 1987 – 1990

Overview

Operation Pawan started with the induction of the Indian Peacekeeping Force (IPKF) on 29 July 1987. The de-induction started in August 1989 and by October 1999, the bulk of the IPKF had withdrawn. The operation terminated on 24 March 1990, when the final contingent of the IPKF sailed out of Trincomalee on board ships of the

Eastern Fleet. When the last elements withdrew, there still had been no solution of the political problem.

In round figures, over 1,200 casualties and 3,500 wounded was the price that the gallant officers and men of the IPKF paid in life and limb to help a neighbour in distress.

From the point of view of the Navy's concern for the security of India's southern seaboard, Operation Pawan fulfilled the strategic objectives that had been listed by Prime Minister Rajiv Gandhi in his letter to President Jayawardene when the Indo-Sri Lankan Accord had been signed in July 1987:

> "You had, during the course of our discussions, agreed to meet some of India's concerns as follows:
>
> Your Excellency and myself will reach an early understanding about the relevance and employment of foreign military and intelligence personnel with a view to ensure that such presence will not prejudice Indo-Sri Lankan relations.
>
> Trincomalee or any other ports in Sri Lanka will not be made available for military use by any country in a manner prejudicial to India's interests.
>
> The work of restoring and operating the Trincomalee oil tank farm will be undertaken as a joint venture between India and Sri Lanka.
>
> Sri Lanka's agreement with foreign broadcasting organisations will be reviewed to ensure that any facilities set up by them in Sri Lanka are used solely as public broadcasting facilities and not for any military or intelligence purposes."

The wear and tear on naval ships was substantial. The exploitation of ships exceeded stipulated norms by 50%. The refits of all ships had to be deferred by months leading to their bunching beyond the capacity of the Naval Dockyards.

Personnel stood up well to the multifarious tasks of logistic and operational support for the IPKF, round the clock ship and air patrols and the transhipment of refugees. Many refugees were given medical attention at sea.

In the years after 1990, India has been quietly supportive of every peace-making move for reconciliation between the Sri Lankan Government and the LTTE.[1]

As soon as the last contingent of the IPKF had been de-inducted from Sri Lanka in March 1990, ships and aircraft of India's Navy and Coast Guard were deployed for Operation Tasha to patrol the Palk Straits to prevent the movement of militants and their material.

Operation Tasha started in June 1990 and continues, round the clock, to this day.

Sri Lanka's Strategic Significance

Ceylon is a comparatively modern name for the island, which at its northern point is separated from the south Indian state of Tamil Nadu by just eighteen miles of sea. The Ancient Indians knew it as Lanka, the Ancient Greeks knew it as Taprobane, the Arabs as Serendib, which the Portuguese changed, in the 16th century, to Ceilao, which in due course became Ceylon. In 1970, Ceylon was renamed as Sri Lanka.

Sri Lanka is located astride the main shipping route of the Indian Ocean. Colombo, on its west coast, lies on the main eastbound international shipping lines through the Red Sea. Trincomalee, on its east coast, with its fine deep natural harbour, was a major British naval and logistic base during World War II.

Sri Lanka is strategically significant because of its geographic proximity to the Indian mainland and to the sea lines of communication carrying Persian Gulf oil towards the Strait of Malacca and thence eastward. It is separated from the Indian peninsula by a string of islets known as Adam's Bridge. The Palk Strait, in which the Adam's Bridge is located, is an area of shallow seas, where only small craft can operate.

The Historical Background of the Ethnic Problem

According to Sri Lankan sources, colonists from the Ganges Valley led by Prince Vijaya, from southern Bengal or Orissa

---

1. A Sri Lankan point of view was stated by Lakshman Kadirgamar, a former Minister of Foreign Affairs and, at the time of writing, the Senior Adviser on Foreign Affairs to the President of Sri Lanka. The following excerpts are from his address to the 6th Asian Security Conference held by the Indian Institute of Defence Studies and Analysis in New Delhi in end January 2004:

   "It is probably correct that no other internal ethnic conflict has spawned a new (LTTE) Navy, replete with surface to surface missiles, fast attack craft and suicide boats laden with explosives which has fought a State (Sri Lankan) Navy for domination of certain parts of the ocean and poses indirectly, if not directly at the moment, a potentially serious threat to international shipping, the security of an adjoining State – India – and a renowned natural harbour – Trincomalee.

   "Ever since the mission of the Indian Peace Keeping Force ended unsatisfactorily in 1990, India has maintained a studied aloofness from any further involvement in the Sri Lankan problem. But it is becoming clear that this period of disengagement cannot go on indefinitely....a LTTE military build up especially around Trincomalee harbour on the East Coast of Sri Lanka has taken place over the last two years of the ceasefire and the build up of the LTTE's Navy in addition to the growth of its armoury of weapons poses a potential threat to the Southern flank of India."

came to Ceylon around 500 BC and overwhelmed the local population. His descendants married South Indian princesses and thus began the race of the Sinhalas. Over the centuries, they built roads and cities, felled forests, created irrigation works, and transplanted to Central and Southern Ceylon the culture of their Indian homeland, modified to suit local conditions.

The Tamil presence in northern Ceylon dates back to over 2,000 years. Ceylon became more and more vulnerable to the pressures of South Indian political expansion. Tamil incursions forced the Sinhalese to withdraw southwards into Central Ceylon.

The Sinhalese were converted to Buddhism in the third century BC through the missionary efforts of the monk Prince Mahindra, son of the Buddhist Emperor, Ashoka of India. Over the next two millennia, the majority of Sri Lanka's population became staunch followers of Hinayana Buddhism. Buddhism gave the Sinhalese a sense of identity and enriched their culture and literature.

By the12th century AD, the Tamils predominated in North and East Ceylon. The northern areas of Ceylon were, reportedly, part of various South Indian kingdoms. While Ceylon absorbed much of the Hindu culture and all of the Hindu people that Tamil intrusions left behind, it remained a Buddhist state under Buddhist rule.

Centuries of warfare between the Sinhalese and the Tamils and between feeble Sinhalese kings weakened the kingdom and brought about the downfall of the Ceylonese civilisation. For a brief period in the 15th century, a Chinese army invaded Ceylon and took the Sinhalese king prisoner to Peking. By the end of 1500, however, the Chinese occupation ended.

Till the arrival of the Portuguese and Dutch in the 16th and 17th centuries, a number of Sinhalese kingdoms co-existed with the Tamil kingdom in the north. The Portuguese arrived in 1505 AD and founded commercial settlements. A century and a half later the Dutch, who were establishing their colonies in the East Indies (now called Indonesia), drove out the Portuguese.

Arab traders brought Islam to Ceylon in the 16th century. Muslims settled all over the country, though the majority was concentrated in the East.

Jaffna was a small independent kingdom from the 17th to the 19th century. Ceylon remained under fragmented political rule until the British defeated the Sinhalese King of Kandy in the late 18th century. In 1785, Ceylon became a British possession and the island was unified.

In 1837, finding the Central Highlands of Ceylon ideal for tea plantations, the British brought in large numbers of Tamil labourers from India to work the tea gardens. These labourers were called Indian Tamils to differentiate them from the Ceylon Tamils of the North. In round numbers, the Ceylon Tamils constituted about 13% of the population and the Indian Tamils about 6%.

Under British rule, the Tamils availed of Christian missionary education. This provided avenues for more jobs, a higher standard of living and the development of political consciousness. A large middle class emerged with high aspirations.

The origins of the present antagonism between Sinhalese and Tamils lie in the prominence achieved by Tamils during the British colonial period. The British found that the Ceylon Tamils had a higher literacy rate and a greater capacity for economic performance. The result was that the Tamils, despite being a minority, became influential in the management of Sri Lankan political and economic affairs. The earlier historical, ethnic and religious tension was compounded by the Sinhalese feeling of being discriminated against and unfairly treated by the British with the support of the Tamils.

Ceylon became independent on 4 February 1948. After independence, the majority Sinhalese wanted the imbalance to be corrected. The ruling party re-defined citizenship in a manner that made the one million Indian Tamil plantation workers stateless. In effect, the Tamils were disenfranchised. This embittered the Tamils.[2] The resentment of the Tamil minority was exacerbated by the introduction of various majority-oriented legislative measures like declaring Sinhalese as the official language; requiring Tamils and other minority groups to secure higher merits than their Sinhalese counterparts for admission in universities; conferment of special constitutional protection for Buddhism; failure to grant local autonomy to Tamil majority district councils after promises to grant such autonomy had been made; creation of Sinhalese colonies in predominantly Tamil areas by resettling Sinhala families with a view, as perceived by Tamils, to altering the demographic pattern.

---

2. In 1964, India's Prime Minister Lal Bahadur Shastri and Ceylon's Prime Minister Sirimavo Bandaranayake signed an agreement to resolve the problem of Tamils of Indian origin under which over 5,00,000 disenfranchised Tamil labourers were to be repatriated to India and granted Indian citizenship. After the pact was signed, the Sinhalese suddenly realised that if this vast work force left, the tea industry would grind to a halt. The pact died a natural death.

From the time of its independence, Sri Lanka's security dilemma was 'fear of Big Brother India'.[3] The Sinhalese, despite constituting 80% of the population, viewed the Tamils not as a minority but as part of the demographic 'presence' of the millions of Indian Tamils of Tamil Nadu. They perceived Tamil Nadu as the natural support base of the Sri Lanka Tamils and were constantly apprehensive of India dismembering Sri Lanka under the pressure of Tamil Nadu. This underlay the reluctance of the Sinhalese-Buddhists to respond to Sri Lankan Tamil demands for devolution of power and for being acknowledged as a distinct ethnic group within the Sri Lankan polity.

The Sinhala complaint was that the Tamils never considered themselves as Sri Lankans and were, in fact, creating a situation where India would be forced to invade Sri Lanka militarily. The Tamils, while insisting on their indigenous pedigree, claimed that their growing dependence upon Tamil Nadu was a consequence of the Sinhala oppression and not its cause. The Muslims were ambivalent; some felt persecuted and alienated; others felt the community would benefit if it remained aligned with the majority.

Sinhala-Tamil antagonism increased during the 1960s. Agreements were signed by moderate Tamil leaders with successive Sri Lankan governments to obtain fair play for the Tamils; these were not implemented. The Tamils felt betrayed and alienated; frustration increased because of political discrimination and lack of opportunities for education and economic well-being.

The JVP (Janata Vimukti Peramuna), a radical political movement, was made up of those Sinhalese Buddhists who were both anti-Tamil and anti-Indian. Many of its members were political and social reformers drawn from the educated unemployed youth of southern Sri Lanka. In 1971, the JVP tried to topple the government to 'save their country from eastern imperialism and Indian expansionist designs'; it cut off all communications with the rest of the world.

In April 1971, Sri Lanka requested India's help to quell this uprising. The Indian Navy was tasked with preventing merchant ships (suspected to be North Korean) from ferrying arms to the insurgents.

Naval Operations in 1971

Ships of the Western Fleet patrolled Ceylon's west coast remaining out of sight. A frigate entered Colombo harbour to act as a communication link. Ships from Vishakhapatnam patrolled Ceylon's east coast, also remaining out of sight. After a few weeks, the crisis blew over and ships returned to their base ports. This was the Navy's first ever deployment in support of a foreign policy decision to respond to a neighbour's call for help. Its silent success marked the beginning of the awareness in the Indian Government of how useful the Navy could be in such sensitive situations.

In Sri Lanka, views were divided between gratitude for India's assistance and apprehension that India's role in Sri Lankan affairs would increase. The proposal by Sri Lanka in 1971 in the United Nations for the development of 'the Indian Ocean as a zone of peace was formulated with India in mind. In subsequent years, it came to be perceived as being central to Sri Lanka's security.

In 1972, Sri Lanka changed its constitution. It stressed the special position given to Buddhism, asserted Sinhala Buddhist culture and weakened protection for the minorities. These policies confirmed the Tamil feeling of being treated as second-class citizens and that their future lay in the creation of a separate state, to be carved out of northern and eastern Sri Lanka, where they could have Tamil as a language and Hinduism as a religion.

From 1972 onwards, the Tamils started resorting to violence. The failure of repeated efforts to meet Tamil aspirations was aggravated by economic problems and rising unemployment. It helped the rise of assertive and aggressive Tamil militancy spearheaded by the LTTE, the Liberation Tigers of Tamil Eelam, led by V Prabhakaran. The emergence of a militant Tamil separatist movement sharpened Sinhalese apprehensions of Indian intervention in support of Tamil militancy.

Things came to a head when the police broke into the 1973 World Tamil Conference being held at Jaffna. There was arson and looting of Tamil heritage and property. The Tamils saw it as an unforgivable act of cultural vandalism. Tamil militancy became more assertive.

Political options were tried out. The Tamils were unable to secure redress. With the failure of political initiatives, the Tamils converged into a single national movement in 1976 and formed the Tamil United Liberation Front (TULF). It demanded the formation of a separate state of Tamil Eelam in the areas that were considered the Tamil homelands in the north and the east. This demand paved the way for militants to attack Government targets and assassinate moderate Tamil leaders who were associated with the ruling party. Funds were collected by tax, a euphemism for ransom or protection money, and by looting banks.

---

3. Reportedly, after Sardar KM Pannikar pointed out that Ceylon had to be an integral part of India's Indian Ocean defence, Ceylon thought India was a hegemon and entered into a defence agreement with Britain ceding Trincomalee to the British Navy.

It was rumoured that the LTTE were engaged in drug trafficking.[4]

The Tamil Front fought the 1977 general election with its demand for secession. It was voted in as a major opposition party in the Assembly. The cry for the creation of Tamil Eelam stimulated the proliferation of militant groups.

Alarmed over these mushrooming militants and their growing popularity amongst the Tamil masses, the Sri Lankan Government rushed through legislation in 1978, banning the LTTE and the main militant organisations that were carrying out assassinations, ambushes and forcible collection of money.

For India, the political implications of Sri Lankan policies had, by 1980, become quite vexed.

On the one hand, the people of Tamil Nadu had a strong sense of Tamil political and cultural identity. As early as the mid 1960s, when attempts were made to impose Hindi as the compulsory national and official language of India, Tamil Nadu had been the first state in the Indian Republic to threaten secession and demand a separate state of Tamil Eelam based on Tamil ethnicity and Tamil language. During the 1970s, there were insistent demands by the political leaders of Tamil Nadu that India should intervene in Sri Lanka, militarily if necessary, to ensure the safety of the Sri Lankan Tamils and to compel the Government of Sri Lanka to modify its policies on the treatment of its Tamil minority. India's primary interest in the Tamil issue in Sri Lanka was to avoid the revival of secessionist tendencies in Tamil Nadu. Gestures had to be made to appease Tamil sentiments.

On the other hand, it was undesirable to interfere in the internal affairs of Sri Lanka and their legitimate reactions to Tamil militancy. India could not support the extremist Sri Lankan Tamil demand for a separate homeland because this would lead to incipient separatist demands within India itself.

Secondly, the cultivation by Sri Lanka of security and intelligence connections with Pakistan, Israel and the US began to be perceived by India as strategically disadvantageous.

India's fateful decision to be supportive of the cause of Sri Lankan Tamils was based on these political compulsions and strategic perceptions. There were absolutely no illusions that anything other than a political solution could meet both Sri Lankan and Indian concerns. From 1981 onwards, camps sprung up in southern India where training, weaponry and logistic support started being imparted to the Tamil militant groups.[5]

India's expectation was that the leverage gained by training the militant groups would help to moderate their extremist demands and thereby facilitate a political solution acceptable to both sides. There developed considerable two-way movement of men and material between Northern Sri Lanka and Southern Tamil Nadu. This tilt in Indian policy of extending support to Tamil militant activities in Sri Lanka was greatly resented by the Sri Lankan Government and India started being given the image of a supporter of Tamil militancy.

Developments Between 1983 and 1987

In mid 1983, Sri Lanka commenced intensive security operations against the Tamil militants. The latter reacted with ferocity. In July 1983, the LTTE ambushed a police patrol, killing 13 Sinhala policemen.

Sri Lankan retribution was swift; it took the form of widespread anti-Tamil riots throughout the length and breadth of Sri Lanka, particularly in Colombo. Over three thousand Tamils were slaughtered, thousands of Tamil homes were destroyed and nearly 150,000 Tamils fled to refugee camps. The Sri Lankan Government declared a state of emergency.

This large-scale massacre led to several developments. Over 100,000 Tamils sought refuge in Tamil Nadu. Tamil militant youth groups established bases in Tamil Nadu and selected militant cadres were armed and trained. The government in Tamil Nadu demanded immediate Indian involvement to stop the genocide of brother Tamils. It

---

4. The former Mossad (Israeli Secret Service) Officer, Victor Ostrovsky in his book *By Way of Deception* not only confirmed the LTTE drug connection, but also revealed that the Israelis had been training both Sri Lanka's anti-terrorist personnel, as also the LTTE.

5. General Depinder Singh's book *The IPKF in Sri Lanka* states, "In one of his many informal chats with me later on, Prabhakaran (the LTTE leader) was to confide that they received massive doses of financial and material assistance from India and were provided training facilities in Tamil Nadu. Interestingly, during 1983 and 1984 the Intelligence Bureau and the Research and Analysis Wing (two Indian intelligence agencies) got directly involved in training the militant Tamil groups and providing assistance to them. I might clarify here that, rumours to the contrary notwithstanding, the Indian Army was never privy nor party to the training imparted to Tamil militant groups. The LTTE resented this training and assistance to other Tamil militant groups perceiving it as an attempt either to divide and rule or tie them to Indian coat tails. Whatever be the scale and degree of assistance the LTTE procured from elsewhere, there can be no denying the fact that the main motivation factor that kept the LTTE going was the knowledge that moral, financial and material assistance from Tamil Nadu would always be forthcoming".

precipitated India's involvement in Sri Lanka's ethnic strife. India urged Sri Lanka to moderate its attitude to Tamil aspirations. Sri Lanka was well aware of the influence of Tamil Nadu politics on Indian policy and was not averse to Indian mediation. From 1983 onwards, India tried to bring the two sides together.

The Sinhalese-majority Government concluded that it could not contain Tamil militancy with its own resources. Nor could it look towards India for help because it would be politically impossible for India to disregard the sympathy of Tamil Nadu for fellow Tamils in Sri Lanka. The Sri Lanka Government had therefore started looking for external support and:

- Signed informal, confidential agreements with the Governments of the United States and Britain to bring their warships into Colombo, Trincomalee and the Gulf of Mannar. The frequency of visits by the warships of these navies increased between 1983 and 1987.

- Invited British mercenaries and Israeli intelligence agencies into its intelligence services.

- Sought assistance from Pakistan to train its Home Guards and its Navy.

In October 1983, the media reported that the USA had offered to assist in obtaining Israeli arms supplies and intelligence support for Sri Lanka and as a *quid pro quo,* Sri Lanka should provide strategic intelligence gathering facilities against India in Sri Lanka's Voice of America (VOA) broadcasting station.[6]

Sri Lanka also preferred the USA for the contract to repair and restore the 'Trincomalee Oil Tank Farms'. These were large oil storage facilities constructed by the Allies during the 1939-45 World War in the port of Trincomalee to support the naval operations of their South and Southeast Asia Command. The oil tanks had fallen into disuse and then into disrepair. India had bid for this project but despite being the most reasonable price offered, the Sri Lankan Government, taking political and other factors into consideration, preferred to give the contract to a consortium of companies led by the United States. India took the view that this provided the potential for an American strategic presence based in the sheltered deep-water harbour of Trincomalee, which for decades had been an important naval base of the British Navy.

Viewing all these developments with concern, India conveyed its disquiet to Sri Lanka.

In 1984, the Indian Navy started patrolling the Palk Bay to prevent violation of the International Boundary Line (IBL) by fishermen of either country and to prevent harassment of Indian fishermen by the Sri Lankan side. The demarcation, in 1976, of the maritime boundary in the Palk Strait and the Gulf of Mannar had helped to reduce tension but did not entirely remove it, partly because of the vexed problem of Katchativu.

Katchativu is a small island near Rameshwaram and Talaimannar. This island fell on the Sri Lankan side of the IBL after India ceded Katchativu to Sri Lanka.[7] Katchativu has only a small temple / church where the Rameshwaram fishermen and their families used to assemble once a year to take part in a festival. They also used to rest on the island in between fishing trips. The ceding agreement permitted Indian fishermen to 'dry their nets' on Katchativu. Indian fishermen, by habit, were attracted by the 'king prawns' available only near Talaimannar as the prawns hesitated to breed near Rameshwaram. The Sri Lankans disliked these 'intrusions by Indian fishermen' because they suspected infiltration by the LTTE masquerading as fishermen. Prior to the escalation of tension, the Sri Lankan Navy used to turn a blind eye to Indian fishermen visiting Katchativu. As tension escalated and suspicions increased of LTTE infiltration, the Sri Lankan Navy tightened their patrols and Indian fishermen felt harassed near Katchativu.

In October 1984, India's Prime Minister, Mrs Gandhi, was assassinated. Her son, Rajiv Gandhi, succeeded her as Prime Minister of India.

In 1985, India arranged a conference in Bhutan, attended by all the militant groups and Sri Lankan representatives, to discuss a document, jointly prepared by the Indian and Sri Lankan governments and the Tamil leaders, for meeting their political and constitutional aspirations. When its recommendations were about to be adopted, the Sri Lankan President backed out due to domestic political opposition.

From March to 19 May 1985, there was intense diplomatic activity by India on Sri Lankan issues to retrieve the situation created by the Sri Lankan President backing out from the recommendations of the All Party Conference. India's external intelligence agency, the Research and Analysis Wing (RAW) held extensive discussions with both the LTTE and the Sri Lankan Government.

In May 1985, Prime Minister Rajiv Gandhi told India's ambassador designate to Sri Lanka that while till 1985, India's

---

6. Reportedly, Sri Lanka authorised the VOA broadcasting against the Soviet Union and offered the USA naval facilities at Trincomalee.

7. In 1974, to defuse tensions, India had ceded the island of Katchativu to Ceylon.

Sri Lankan policy was influenced by Tamil Nadu politics and ethno-religious considerations, it would henceforth be "An Indian policy responsive to India's security and strategic interests and responsive to the principle of not disrupting the territorial integrity of a small neighbour". Within this overall framework, India's endeavour would be to ensure the maximum fulfilment of legitimate Tamil aspirations.[8]

In June 1985, Sri Lanka suggested joint Indo-Sri Lankan naval patrolling of the Palk Straits to prevent infiltration into Sri Lanka of Tamil militants from Tamil Nadu.

Meanwhile, the LTTE continued to grow in stature and strength, determined to become the predominant militant organisation. In May 1986, the LTTE went on a rampage and totally destroyed a rival militant group. Jaffna came under LTTE domination. With the civil administration totally paralysed and the Sri Lankan Armed Forces (SLAF) confined to camps along the coast, the LTTE virtually ran a state within a state. Following their successes, they felt emboldened to switch from the classic guerrilla tactics of 'hit and run' to those of small set piece battles.

Events Preceding the Accord of July 1987

Stung by their inability to operate effectively in the heart of the Jaffna peninsula, the SLAF decided to attempt a 'final solution'. Between January and May 1987, in preparation for a major offensive against the LTTE with the aim of retrieving control over Jaffna and denying entry of men and material assistance from outside, the SLAF placed the Jaffna peninsula under siege. It inducted additional troops, imposed an economic embargo and in May 1987, launched its offensive. Fierce fighting ensued in which most of the LTTE casualties were caused by artillery fire and aerial attacks by aircraft and helicopters. What began to hurt the LTTE, and even more the local population, was the economic blockade that snapped electricity supply and, with it, running water and denied entry of supplies and medicines. The mass exodus to India increased.

Diplomatic initiatives failed to ease the blockade for supply of essential medicines and food supplies. The Indian Government tried to send supplies and medicines by sea for distribution to the population of Jaffna. Ships of the Sri Lankan Navy stopped a convoy of fishing trawlers, flying white flags with a Red Cross, led by Coast Guard Ship *Vikram*. To avoid an incident, the convoy returned home without unloading its relief supplies.

On 4 June 1987, India sent a stronger message. Transport aircraft of the Indian Air Force airdropped supplies over Jaffna. The Sri Lanka Government called the air dropping a violation of international law. International concern for the people of Jaffna, and the low-key response to these objections and to Sri Lankan requests for assistance, induced Sri Lanka to halt the SLAF offensive.

The Indo-Sri Lanka Accord

Seeing the writing on the wall, the Sri Lanka Government sought discussions with the Indian Government. The outcome was the Indo-Sri Lanka Accord that was signed on 29 July 1987.

For Sri Lanka, the Accord sought to end the ethnic struggle that had claimed countless lives, damaged property and ruined its economy. Apart from the 150,000 refugees, mainly Indian Tamils, who fled their homes to seek shelter in refugee camps, there were over 100,000 Sri Lanka Tamils who had sought shelter in Tamil Nadu.

For India, whose armed forces were committed on its Western and the Northern borders, the Accord sought to safeguard the security of its southern seaboard, to subsume secessionist tendencies in Tamil Nadu and Punjab and to avoid the acquisition of footholds in Sri Lanka by foreign powers.

There was another aspect. In the negotiations between the LTTE representatives and the Indian interlocutors prior to the Accord, the LTTE sought for their 'Sea Tigers' the unfettered right to police the sea-lanes in the vicinity of India's coastline. They proposed the delineation of 'distinct naval boundaries' – each area being under the control of the LTTE and the Sri Lankan Navy respectively. India had categorically rejected the suggestion, not only because it would undermine Sri Lanka's authority but also because it would be tantamount to permitting a terrorist outfit to be treated as a legitimate force patrolling the seas adjacent to India's coastline.[9]

Relevant Excerpts From the Indo-Sri Lanka Accord

"2.9. The Emergency will be lifted in the Eastern and Northern provinces by August 15, 1987. A cessation of hostilities will come into effect all over the island within 48 hours of the signing of this agreement. All arms presently held by militant groups will be surrendered in accordance with an agreed procedure to authorities to be designated by the Government of Sri Lanka. Consequent to the cessation

---

8. *Assignment Colombo* by JN Dixit, (Page 4).

9. *Asian Age* of 5 May 2003 "Let not the Tigers coast to victory" by M K Narayanan, the Director of the Intelligence Bureau in 1987. The LTTE made the same proposal 16 years later in 2003.

of hostilities and the surrender of arms by militant groups, the Army and other security personnel will be confined to barracks in camps as on 25 May 1987. The process of surrendering of arms and the confining of security personnel moving back to barracks shall be completed within 72 hours of the cessation of hostilities coming into effect.

"2.16 (a). These proposals are also conditional to the Government of India taking the following action if any militant groups operating in Sri Lanka do not accept this framework of proposals for a settlement, namely, India will take all necessary steps to ensure that Indian territory is not used for activities prejudicial to the unity, integrity and security of Sri Lanka.

"2.16 (b). The Indian Navy / Coast Guard will cooperate with the Sri Lankan Navy in preventing Tamil militant activities from affecting Sri Lanka.

"2.16 (c). In the event that the Government of Sri Lanka requests the Government of India to afford military assistance to implement these proposals, the Government of India will cooperate by giving to the Government of Sri Lanka such military assistance as and when requested.

"2.16 (d). The Government of India will expedite repatriation from Sri Lanka of Indian citizens to India who are resident there, concurrently with the repatriation of Sri Lankan refugees from Tamil Nadu.

"2.16 (e). The Governments of India and Sri Lanka will cooperate in ensuring the physical security and safety of all communities inhabiting the Northern and Eastern Provinces."

In para 6 of the Annexure to the Agreement, it was stated that "the Prime Minister of India and the President of Sri Lanka also agree that in terms of paragraph 2.16 (c) of the Agreement, an Indian Peace Keeping contingent may be invited by the President of Sri Lanka to guarantee and enforce the cessation of hostilities, if so required."

Relevant Excerpts From the Letters Exchanged on Matters of Bilateral Interest when the Accord was Signed

In his letter to the President of Sri Lanka, the Prime Minister of India stated:

"2. In this spirit, you had, during the course of our discussions, agreed to meet some of India's concerns as follows:

- Your Excellency and myself will reach an early understanding about the relevance and employment of foreign military and intelligence personnel with a view to ensure that such presence will not prejudice Indo-Sri Lankan relations.

- Trincomalee or any other ports in Sri Lanka will not be made available for military use by any country in a manner prejudicial to India's interests.

- The work of restoring and operating the Trincomalee oil tank farm will be undertaken as a joint venture between India and Sri Lanka.

- Sri Lanka's agreement with foreign broadcasting organisations will be reviewed to ensure that any facilities set up by them in Sri Lanka are used solely as public broadcasting facilities and not for any military or intelligence purposes.

"3. In the same spirit, India will:

- Deport all Sri Lankan citizens who are found to be engaging in terrorist activities or advocating separatism or secessionism.

- Provide training facilities and military supplies for Sri Lankan security forces."

In his reply to the Prime Minister of India, the President of Sri Lanka stated:

"This is to confirm that the above correctly sets out the understanding reached between us."

Apart from inviting the IPKF, the Accord envisaged the following sequence of events:

- Cease fire within 24 hours and surrender of weapons by militants within the next 72 hours.

- Separate the SLAF and LTTE warring groups. The SLAF to withdraw to the positions they occupied prior to the offensive they launched in May.

- Immediate formation of an Interim Administrative Council to administer the Northern and Eastern provinces.

- The election, within 3 months, of an Administrative Council, which would take over from the Interim Council.

- The holding of a referendum, by end 1988, to decide whether the Eastern provinces would like to merge with the Northern provinces.

- Devolution by the Sri Lankan Government of more powers to the Administrative Council.

Indian Prime Minister, Rajiv Gandhi and Sri Lanka President, Jayawardene signed the Accord on 29 July 1987 at Colombo.

Ships of the Western Fleet in formation

Operation Cactus November 1988 - hijacked ship 'Progress Light', having Maldivian VIPs
as hostages, being persuaded to stop by small calibre naval gunfire

Landing ship exercising inter-service amphibious beaching

Marine Commandos infiltrating from seaward

Antarctic Expedition Research Vessel berthed alongside the 9-metre high Antarctic ice shelf. Naval Chetak helicopters carry out aerial and photo reconnaissance, ferry personnel and stores, provide medical support and evacuate casualties and assist scientific teams operating in hilly, rough and icy terrain

Admiral of the Fleet of the Soviet Union SG Gorshkov calling on Prime Minister Mrs Indira Gandhi in New Delhi

On board the first guided missile destroyer *RAJPUT* after her arrival from Russia in 1980. Sitting left to right: Mr Rajiv Gandhi, Commanding Officer Captain GM Hiranandani and Minister of State for Defence Mr Shivraj Patil

Floating Dock FDN 1 in Port Blair

INS *GODAVARI* entering New York harbour to participate in the International Fleet Review on the occasion of the Bicentennial Celebrations of the Statue of Liberty in July 1986

Sea Cadet Corps' Sail Training Ship *VARUNA*

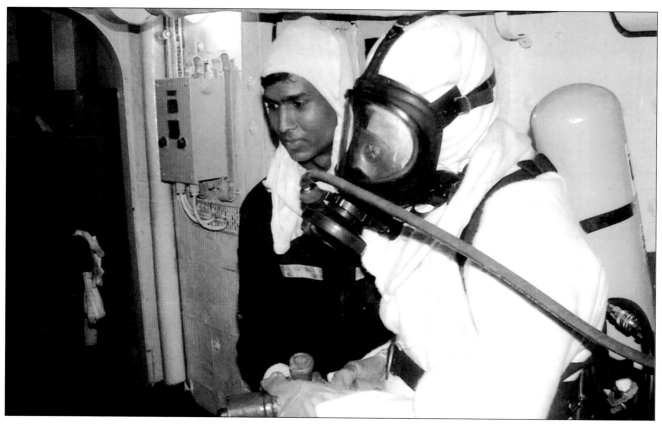

Nuclear-Biological-Chemical Warfare & Damage Control (NBCD) drill exercised on board warships

Project Seabird - aerial view of part of the Third Naval Base under construction at Karwar

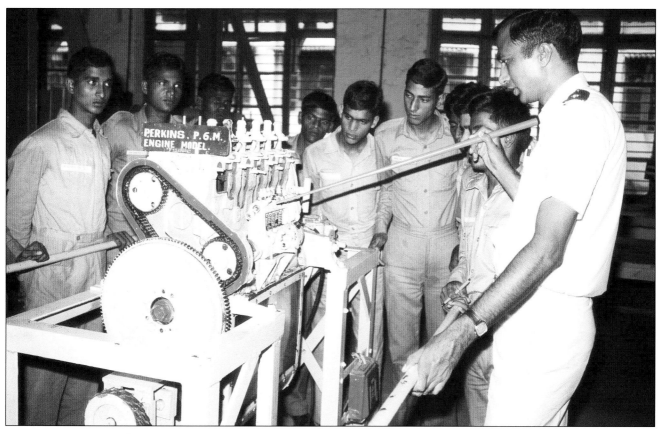

Engineering Branch sailors being trained on working models of warship machinery

'Beating Retreat' at the Gateway of India in Bombay after the 1989 Fleet Review

From 1985 onwards, there had been increased interaction between the US administration and the Indian government. American policy had started to become more understanding of Indian concerns. The US was quietly supportive of the Indo- Sri Lanka Accord of 1987.[10]

The Sequel to the Accord

The signing of the accord was followed by violent upheavals in Sri Lanka by the JVP. Sri Lanka immediately sought India's military assistance to stabilise the situation and safeguard Sri Lanka's unity and territorial integrity.

In the early hours of 30 July 1987, the Navy commenced the induction of the IPKF into Sri Lanka. The induction was by specific invitation. Its arrival was welcomed both by the SLAF and the Tamil population, but not by the Buddhist population.

During the next two months, the LTTE, which had initially been associated with the discussions that preceded the signing of the Accord, became increasingly reluctant to surrender all its arms. It felt that the Accord would not be honoured by the SLAF. The crisis peaked in the first week of October.

On 3 October 1987, the Sri Lankan Navy intercepted a boat carrying 17 LTTE personnel in Sri Lankan territorial waters. Among the 17, were the LTTE's regional military commanders of Jaffna and Trincomalee. The SLAF wanted to take the prisoners to Colombo for interrogation to ascertain where the LTTE personnel were returning from and what they had gone there to do. The LTTE argued that the Sri Lanka Government wanted to take the prisoners to Colombo where they intended to show them on television and compel them to make statements damaging to the LTTE cause; therefore, the IPKF should take over the prisoners and not allow them to be taken to Colombo. The SLAF counter argument was that these were SLAF prisoners caught outside the jurisdiction of the IPKF.

Indian intervention at the highest levels did not succeed in resolving the impasse.

On 5th October, when the SLAF started to escort the prisoners to waiting aircraft, all 17 swallowed cyanide capsules. LTTE reaction was swift and savage. Over 200 Sinhalese were massacred and over 10,000 rendered homeless. The 8 Sinhala prisoners held by the LTTE were executed on 6 October 1987. Bitter at the inability of the IPKF to protect its cadres, the LTTE decided to fight the IPKF.

In his book *The IPKF in Sri Lanka*, General Depinder Singh states:

"On 6 October 1987, the Chief of the Army Staff, General Sundarji flew into Palaly, where he was briefed about the situation. It was apparent that the political decision to employ force against the LTTE was already taken. However, he was en-route to Colombo where the Defence Minister, Mr KC Pant was proceeding the same evening for a meeting with the Sri Lanka President. Having met the latter on 4th October, I had no doubt about the riot act he would read out to compel the IPKF to use force. My recommendation to General Sundarji was that we must not go in for the hard option because, if we did, we would be stuck in an insurgency situation for the next 20 years. I was admonished not to adopt a defeatist attitude, to which my reply was that I was not being defeatist, merely realistic. The Chief then flew off to Colombo. I am not privy to what transpired there, but next day, HQ IPKF received direct instructions, in clear, from the Chief in Colombo to use force against the LTTE."

On 10th October, the LTTE ambushed an IPKF patrol. On 12th October the IPKF launched operations by helicopters to capture Jaffna. By 22nd October, Jaffna had been captured. In the ensuing months, the IPKF found itself bogged down in a guerrilla war in terrain in which the LTTE had the advantage. Overcoming suspicions and despite difficulties, the IPKF succeeded in establishing peaceful conditions in the Jaffna peninsula and the Eastern province.

The common perception amongst the Sinhalese was that the IPKF was a threat to the sovereignty of Sri Lanka.

---

10. An American perception is reflected in Dennis Kux's book *Estranged Democracies – India and the United States, 1941-1991*, Page 412 states:

"In policy terms, Rajiv continued the course Indira mapped out after returning to power in 1980. In addition to seeking better balance in India's non-alignment through better relations with Washington, Rajiv showed increasing willingness to assert India's primacy in the subcontinent based on its size and increasing military power. In 1987, India began a major initiative by sending several thousand troops against the insurgency mounted by Tamil separatists in the neighbouring island republic of Sri Lanka to India's south. Although the Sri Lankan government agreed to the intervention, the action – under which 50,000 troops were eventually deployed – provided a dramatic signal of greater Indian readiness to flex its muscles regionally. Uncertain how the United States would respond, New Delhi was relieved when Washington gave its blessing to the venture. Paradoxically, in the light of the accommodating US reaction, the Indo-Sri Lankan accords made gratuitous reference to 'outside powers' seeking to gain a foothold on the island and to foreign radio broadcasts from Sri Lanka. Since the Voice of America had been using a transmitter in Sri Lanka for many years, the criticism of the United States was thinly veiled."

In the Sinhala areas, the JVP triggered an insurrection that sought to "save the country from an unholy trinity of American imperialism, Indian imperialism and Tamil expansionism." The JVP movement nearly succeeded in destroying state institutions but was suppressed by Sri Lankan security forces.

The Buddhist clergy also resented the Accord. In their view, the Accord had betrayed the Sinhala people by conceding too much to the Tamils and allowing the Indians to enter the island as a peacekeeping force.

Elections were held in November 1988 and a moderate Tamil leader became Chief Minister of the Provincial Government. As required by the Accord, power was to be devolved to the province. Nothing happened. In January 1989, Sri Lanka elected a new President whose views were decidedly anti-Indian.

Between February and May 1989, the JVP again went on the rampage. Leading a coalition of Buddhist monks and students, the JVP launched a nationwide agitation against the IPKF and against the Government. Seizing the opportunity, the LTTE sought talks with the Sri Lankan government. The tables turned. The SLAF joined hands with the LTTE and transferred weapons and ammunition, which the LTTE desperately needed to fight the IPKF. Anti-Indian propaganda spread. The majority Sinhala community, the minority Sri Lanka Tamils and the Sri Lanka Government all developed an aversion for the IPKF. The new President confidently called for the withdrawal of the IPKF.

The IPKF started withdrawing in August 1989. In October 1999, the bulk of the IPKF withdrew. When the last elements withdrew on 24 March 1990, there still had been no devolution of power.

Operation Pawan – Naval Operations

Operation Pawan commenced as soon as the Accord was signed on 29 July 1987. The Navy was to induct Army units into Sri Lanka and sanitise the offshore sea areas. The first two Army battalions were landed in Kankesanturai (KKS) Harbour on 30 July 1987 – the day following the signing of the Accord.

Lieutenant Commander (now Rear Admiral) Shekhar Sinha (a Sea Harrier pilot) was in command of Coast Guard IPV *Rani Jindan* on patrol in the Palk Bay. He recalls:

"The Eastern Fleet anchored off KKS in the early hours and was greeted by *Rani Jindan*. The Fleet Commander called me up on radio and said 'You need to disembark troops and stores to Jaffna in the next 5 to 6 hours. As far as navigational information is concerned, there are no charts, winds are 30 knots on-shore, the sea is 3 knots

onshore, the pontoon is a broken down structure and a ship of 1.6 metres draught ran aground two days ago ahead of where we are going to berth – best of luck!'

"In adverse sea conditions, *Rani Jindan* made 13 entries into and exits out of the uncharted and unlit KKS harbour. She picked up troops and stores of No 1 Battalion Maratha Light Infantry from various ships and disembarked them ashore. The opposition of the Sri Lankan Navy was quite evident.

"My Coast Guard crew was extremely 'charged', this being the fist time that the Coast Guard was called upon to perform an operational task.

"Subsequently, post October 1987, we captured the first armed boat of the LTTE and escorted it to Indian shores. It was challenging chasing the LTTE and retrieving our injured troops from KKS by night in the face of heavy gunfire."

A rapid build-up followed after 30 July. A sea-borne logistic support chain was established with Madras. Merchant ships were chartered for troop and cargo transshipment. Amphibious Landing Ships ferried personnel and stores into the uncharted KKS Harbour and across uncharted beaches.

The Navy's Tasks

- Joint Indian-Sri Lankan naval patrols of Sri Lankan waters to prevent movement of arms and militants across the water in and out of Sri Lanka.

- Joint Army-Navy operations to combat militant activity.

- Logistic support for the build-up and maintenance of the IPKF in Sri Lanka.

- General operations to support the Accord, like 'transfer of refugees'.

Coast Guard Support

The Coast Guard's task was to support the Navy. Three shallow-draught Inshore Patrol Vessels (IPVs) were placed under the Navy's control for inshore patrolling in the Palk Bay. The Coast Guard's F-27 aircraft, operating from Madras, ensured air surveillance extending 100 miles to seaward of the east coast of Sri Lanka.

Initial Patrols

By 15 August 1987, the Joint Indian-Sri Lankan naval patrol had been instituted in the Palk Bay. It aimed at severing the LTTE conduit between Sri Lanka's northern Jaffna peninsula and the southern coast of Tamil Nadu by controlling the routes leading to Dhanushkodi, Rameshwaram, Vedaranyam and Nagapatnam, all of which were known settlements of Sri Lankan Tamils. The

OPERATION PAWAN (IPKF IN SRI LANKA) 1987 TO 1990

JOINT PATROLLING AREA BY ARMED TRAWLERS FROM NAVAL DETACHMENT RAMESHWARAM

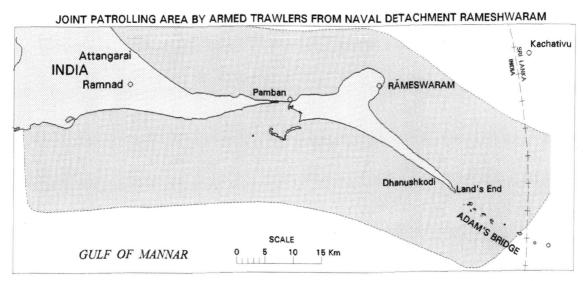

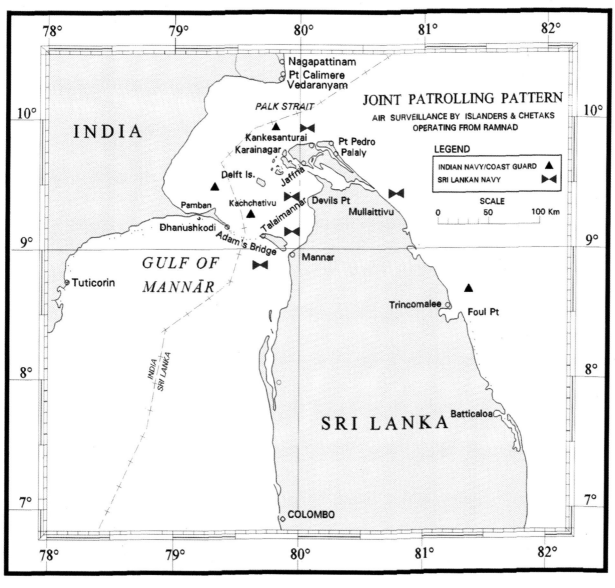

disused airfield at Ramnad was activated for air surveillance of the Palk Bay, using Naval Islander aircraft and Chetak helicopters for daylight surveillance. Indian Naval Liaison Teams (INLTs) were positioned at four locations in Sri Lanka – Trincomalee (Trinco), Pallaly, Kankesanturai (KKS) and Karainagar.

The LTTE's Reluctance to Abide by the Accord

The induction of troops and their supporting logistics by sea from Madras proceeded smoothly during August. By end August, problems started surfacing. Sceptical whether the Accord's commitment for devolution of power would be honoured by Sri Lanka, the LTTE became palpably reluctant to surrender its arms.

Cordon Militaire

On 7 October 1987, the IPKF received orders to 'Disarm the LTTE'. A *cordon militaire* was established across a 310-mile belt. It extended northwards from Talaimannar through the Palk Strait and along the east coast of Sri Lanka until its southern limit at Little Basses Island. Ships and aircraft on patrol were directed to use force, if required.

To prevent cross trafficking, a Line of Control (LOC) was established eastward of the international boundary in the Palk Strait. To curb militant activity on the eastern coast of Sri Lanka, fishing activity at night was banned.

Commodore Padmasankar was the Naval Officer-in-Charge Madras. He recalls:

> "The Line of Control (LOC), which was drawn to the east of Katchativu, was concurred by the Sri Lankan Navy at the Joint Patrol Meeting. This enabled Indian fishermen to use Katchativu as envisaged in the ceding clauses; it also reduced the area to be patrolled by the Sri Lankan Navy. In fact, the LOC enabled our fishermen to feel more secure in Indian waters and, to an extent, reduced the agitation of the fishermen of Rameshwaram. Both Navies respected this arrangement until the IPKF withdrew finally from Sri Lanka in 1990."

The *cordon militaire* effectively sanitised the offshore areas through intensive air and surface patrolling. On a daily average, the Navy and Coast Guard deployed four major warships and eight smaller patrol craft, whilst the Sri Lankan Navy provided five to six patrol craft. Naval air surveillance over the sea was mounted daily from various bases – Madras by F-27s, Madurai by armed Alizes, Ramnad by Islanders and armed Chetaks and Batticaloa by armed helicopters, which also functioned as a Quick Reaction Force (QRF). In January 1988, the Navy instituted a special force of 15 'armed trawlers', which operated from Rameshwaram. This helped to seal the LTTE's Dhanushkodi-Talaimannar conduit.

Special Operations

The Indian Marine Special Force (IMSF), a newly formed 'commando' arm of the Navy, made its debut in August 1987. A 40-strong group of 'marine commandos' (MARCOS) participated in 55 combat operations in its very first year. During their raids, they destroyed LTTE boats, ammunition warehouses and militant camps. They also proved to be a potent force in 'flushing out' operations in the islands, lagoons and inlets and were invariably in the van of amphibious raids.[11]

The Sri Lankan Scene

In November 1988, the Presidential elections in Sri Lanka posed a new contingency – the safety of President Jayawardene in case his party lost the election. As a precautionary measure, Operation Jupiter was planned to evacuate the President and his immediate family to safety. The Navy positioned at Tuticorin a Seaking-capable frigate, *INS Godavari* (and later *INS Taragiri*), with an IMSF team embarked. As it happened, the President's party was re-elected.

When Mr Jayawardene's term expired in January 1989, Mr Premadasa became the President of Sri Lanka He had been a staunch critic of the Indo-Sri Lanka Accord. He came to power on a political promise that he would "Send back the IPKF". Between March and July 1989, he initiated a dialogue with the LTTE, which is presumed to have resulted in a ceasefire between the LTTE and the SLAF. He then tried to buy peace with the JVP but to no avail – their subversive activities increased. He then served the Indian Government with an ultimatum to withdraw the IPKF by 29 July 1989, this being the second anniversary of the Indo-Sri Lanka Accord.

Special Contingency Plans

As the deadline approached, tension mounted. The JVP-incited violence intensified. Mr Premadasa announced his intention to bring out the Sri Lankan Army (from their barracks) on 29 July 1989, to patrol the Northern and Eastern Provinces. The led to planning for the contingency of misguided, unprovoked action against the IPKF by wayward units of SLAF.

Operation Roundup was planned to counter any backlash from the SLAF in the Northern and Eastern provinces. Operation Trojan was planned to evacuate Indian nationals from Colombo, in the face of opposition.

---

11. For details, see Section titled MARCOS, page 241.

The third operation, a modified version of the earlier Operation Jupiter of December 1988, was also planned in case the need arose to evacuate Indian nationals with the support of the SLAF.

Operation Jupiter

The aircraft carrier, *Viraat,* was at anchor in Bombay. On 18 July 1989, it was directed to embark all weapons and stores and arrive at Cochin on 20th July.

Captain (later Admiral and Chief of Naval Staff) Madhvendra Singh was the Commanding Officer of *Viraat* during Operation Jupiter. The following excerpts are from his recollections recorded in *The Magnificent Viraat – Decade and a Half of Glorious Flying*:

"Throughout that afternoon and early evening, ammunition barges, ration boats, aircraft launches, and fuelling barges continued to supply *Viraat* all that she had asked for and needed. It was a truly remarkable effort and the monsoon weather did not make it any easier. *Viraat* sailed at three o'clock that night in lashing rain.

"The ship picked up the first two Sea Harriers off Goa on the 19th morning and two more Sea Harriers off Mangalore on the 20th morning. She entered Cochin on the 21st morning to embark the support equipment of the Seaking Squadrons. Helicopters were assembled from all over the country. One Seaking 42 C and two Chetaks were embarked in Bombay; two Seakings Mk 42 and two Chetaks from Cochin and one Seaking Mk 42 C each from Coimbatore, Vishakhapatnam and Taragiri. A fifth Seaking Mk 42 C embarked later, as also 3 officers and 54 sailors of the Indian Marine Special Force (IMSF). With all 15 aircraft on board, *Viraat* sailed from Cochin to begin the work up of her air wing and IMSF detachment.

"While the *Viraat* was proceeding south, the 7th Battalion of the Garhwal Rifles which was at Pithoragarh in the Kumaon Hills[12] was ordered to get ready for the mission. On 24th July, they moved by road from Pithoragarh to Bareilly and on the morning of the 26th they were airlifted by IL-76 aircraft to Trivandrum, where they arrived in the dead of night. They were immediately put into state transport corporation buses and moved during the night *to INS Garuda* in Cochin where they arrived early morning of 27th July.

"On the 27th morning, *Viraat* was asked to embark the battalion with her helicopters. It was quite a task. When an Army battalion moves, it moves with everything to sustain itself. Besides the men and their equipment, arms and ammunition, this included rations, jeeps, chairs, tables, tents, and even cupboards! It was a wet and windy day. Regardless of the weather, the men of *Viraat* worked tirelessly for the next six hours to complete the combat embarkation of the battalion by the afternoon. With rotors running, 4 to 7 helicopters at a time were on deck being unloaded, refuelled when required and quickly launched for the next load. A total of 76 helo sorties of Seakings and Chetaks were carried out that day to embark 366 personnel, 36 tonnes of stores, 2 jeeps and a motorcycle with *Viraat* remaining 8 to 10 miles from the coast.

"Overnight, the *Viraat* had been transformed into a commando carrier. From a strength of about 1,000 in Bombay, her personnel strength rose to 1,800. Each man had a bunk, the Garhwalis were in their allotted messes and we still had 200 bunks kept vacant for evacuees and 60 bunks for any casualties in an improvised afloat hospital.

"The next morning, training began of working up the soldiers for an airborne assault operation. First dry runs were conducted with helos switched off on deck. These were repeated till the embarkation and disembarkation times were brought down to a bare minimum. With dry runs completed, they practiced embarkation and disembarkation with rotors whirring overhead and finally they rehearsed the actual assault phase at *INS Garuda* with echelons of one company strength repeatedly practicing airborne assault and evacuation. By the time they had completed their training, the 7th Battalion Garhwal Rifles had transformed from a footslogging infantry battalion into a formidable assault team, which had totally integrated itself with its base – *INS Viraat.*

"The *Viraat* and her task group continued to operate at / off Cochin for another two weeks, ready to execute the mission if ordered. On 12th August, we were ordered to disembark air squadrons, as the mission in Sri Lanka would no longer be required. The aircraft flew away as quickly as they had come and the ship returned to Bombay.

"For both the Garhwalis and the *Viraat,* it had been a very happy and educative association. Both were richer for the experience and both will, for a long time, look back with pride and nostalgia on a mission well executed. While Operation Jupiter was not launched, both units were fully prepared and both believe that in their own small way, they helped to make the operation unnecessary.

"In view of this operational association, the Garhwal Regiment was affiliated to *INS Viraat* on 2 February 1990 and this association remains to this day."

---

12. The Kumaon Hills are amongst the foothills of the Himalayas on India's northern border.

General VN Sharma was the Chief of Army Staff from 1989 to 1991. He recalls:

"As a result of a deal with the LTTE that he would call for the withdrawal of the IPKF, Mr Premadasa succeeded, in June 1989, in politically displacing Mr Jayawardene as the President of Sri Lanka. Immediately on assuming office, he asked that the IPKF withdraw. I was firm that under no circumstances would the Indian Army leave in circumstances that might, historically, sully its fair name. As and when it did leave, it would be with 'bands playing and flags flying high' as appropriate for a friendly army departing after rendering assistance.

"In Sri Lanka, the JVP and the LTTE fomented anti-India feelings. Political tension mounted. It became necessary to plan for the evacuation of our High Commission officials. I met Mr Premadasa in Sri Lanka and convinced him of the perilous situation he might be placed in if miscreants decided to displace him and how only the Indian Armed Forces could protect him from mishap. Mr Premadasa was duly 'persuaded'.

"As tension continued to rise, plans had to be made for the contingency that the Sri Lankan Armed Forces might oppose the evacuation from the High Commission. A battalion of troops was embarked in the aircraft carrier *Viraat*, which, along with an armada of naval ships, remained out of sight. When tension eased, the armada withdrew. In due course, the Army left Trincomalee with bands playing."

Political interaction between the two Governments had defused the crisis and the contingency plans were deactivated by mid August 1989. De-induction started in August 1989 and by October 1999, the bulk of the IPKF were withdrawn.

Operation Pawan terminated on 24 March 1990, when the final contingent of the IPKF sailed out of Trincomalee on board ships of the Eastern Fleet.

Statistical Overview of Operation PAWAN

Tactical Support	Jul 1987 to Jul 1988	Aug 1988 to Aug 1989
Militant boats destroyed	76	-
Suspicious boats apprehended	85	54
Militant casualties at sea	336	
Special operations conducted (IMSF)	55	09
Combat landings (LST/LCU)	35	13
Incidents/interceptions at sea	152	40-50 per day

Logistic Support

Troops transported (to and fro)	1,60,000	2,61,351
Army vehicles transported	7,000	807
Army stores transported	50,000 tonnes	54,000 tonnes
Detenus transferred	2,600	330
Refugees transferred	22,000	3,139 (520 by naval ships)

Naval Resources Deployed

IN/CG combat ship-days on patrol	3,676 days	1,994 days
Armed trawler days	2,690 days	5,226 days
IN/CG aircraft flying hours	5,115 hours	3,270 hours
Merchant ship sorties	220 sorties	285 sorties

Operation PAWAN in Retrospect

Lieutenant General Depinder Singh was the General Officer Commanding in Chief of the Army's Southern Command and the Overall Force Commander of the IPKF. In his book, *The IPKF in Sri Lanka*, he has recorded why things happened the way they did. The following excerpts refer to naval aspects. I have emphasised the lessons to be learnt in italics.

"This was the first time that an operation of this nature and magnitude was launched by our Armed Forces involving, as it did, the crossing of a sea obstacle. The only precedents were the annual Tri Service amphibious exercises carried out each year and we were to discover that there is an enormous difference between an exercise and the actual thing. For one, the exercise normally concludes 12-24 hours after the troops are landed and the problems of logistics like procurement over a longer time frame, storage and delivery never came to the fore. Neither did we bother to analyse the operational problems that would arise once the enemy has got over the shock of the attacker's arrival and commences the inevitable readjustment and move of reserves to separate the attacker's teeth from his tail. Additionally, in an exercise, loading of stores, equipment and vehicles is from locations where adequate preparation has been made. In war, such actions take place all over the country and you suddenly find all loading held up because a particular type of ramp is not available.

"In our system of managing defence, all three services have an equal say: I was very conscious of this and even though the functioning of the IPKF was primarily Army oriented, I tried to ensure that the other two services were kept constantly in the operational picture and received equal importance. *Despite this, service ego cannot be denied for long and, so, within a few days* of the arrival of IPKF in Sri Lanka, resources allotted from the other two services, the Navy and Air Force, started to be withdrawn; so also was the Naval and Air Force staff representation in HQ IPKF where the numbers were decreased and ranks reduced.

"When orders for creation of HQ Overall Force Commander (OFC), IPKF were first issued, certain naval and air force resources were allotted and I had the Chief of Staff, Eastern Naval Command and an IAF officer of the rank of Air Commodore as component commanders with their own staffs to deploy these resources. After the first flush of enthusiasm was over, the component commanders were the first to go; then went the resources and, finally, only skeleton staffs were left. So much for inter-services integration. We are still a far cry from achieving really effective inter-services integration and serious thought needs to be given to this aspect as, at the moment, there is too much of parochialism and possessiveness.

"We need proper sea craft to transport army units, so that the latter can reach the objective area in reasonably good shape. What was provided was generally primitive, with troops crammed on the top deck subjected to sun, wind and wave, sharing 4-5 toilets between 400-500 men; no wonder troops used to disembark at the destination looking pretty green. One suggestion is for the Shipping Corporation to acquire proper passenger ships so that, during emergencies, these can be utilised to ferry army units. Likewise, since we have created for ourselves an amphibious capability, we must acquire a floating dock to ensure maintenance of sea-landed forces at the earliest, in case suitable jetties are not available.

"In the matter of joint operations there is need to refine the provision of naval gun fire support. It was provided on one occasion during December 1987 north of Trincomalee and fire was off by over 2 kilometres. Commonality of maps needs to be introduced as the Navy operates off charts and the Army, maps.

"In Sri Lanka, port facilities were barely adequate to meet Sri Lankan needs; with the IPKF requirement added on they proved totally inadequate. Two ports were utilised by the IPKF – Trincomalee and KKS. The former was only intermittently available for IPKF use as it was a private jetty of Prima Flour Mills, used mainly for unloading imported flour. The Jetty at KKS was non-functional when induction first took place and it was some time before it became operational and, even then, it could take light loads only. In consequence, after 10 October 1987, we had situations where formations arrived by air in Palaly

and their transport and heavy luggage was landed from the sea in Trincomalee. It took weeks before the road communications could be opened to permit the two to marry up."

Field Marshal Manekshaw's foreword to General Depinder Singh's book states:

"Our troops have suffered heavy casualties in the operations in Sri Lanka. WHY? The operations of the IPKF had not been the success they ought to have been. WHY? The Indian Army is a professional army. It has served with great success in various theatres and in different kinds of operations in the past, including the insurgency operations in the Mizo Hills. Why then did it not have the same success in Sri Lanka?

"All these questions have remained unanswered, and I can only attribute these failures to the following:

– The political aim was uncertain, wavering and not firm.

– Troops were inducted into the theatre piece-meal, untrained, improperly equipped and without proper logistics.

– The Fighting Command had too many masters giving different orders and different assessments.

– Was it the Prime Minister issuing directions, was the Chief of Army Staff giving orders or was it the Director of Military Operations at Army Headquarters?

– Were the assessments of the General Officer Commanding in Chief at Headquarters Southern Command to be accepted, or the views of the Indian High Commissioner in Colombo?

– The Fighting Command and the troops were also cognisant of the fact that whereas they were operating against the Tamil insurgents, the insurgents were getting trained in India, were being supplied with large quantities of arms and equipment, money and moral support from Tamil Nadu. Surely, this could not but have had a deleterious effect on their morale.

– And finally, the Fighting Command, which includes the soldiery, had the feeling that the Government of India was not certain as to what it wanted the IPKF to achieve."

For the Army, the IPKF was not a happy experience. It served as an object lesson to India on the perilous political under-currents that afflict and endanger well-intentioned peacekeeping operations in neighbouring countries.

For the Navy, Pawan was a valuable experience of prolonged low intensity conflict and of the organisational

OPERATION CACTUS - NOVEMBER 1988

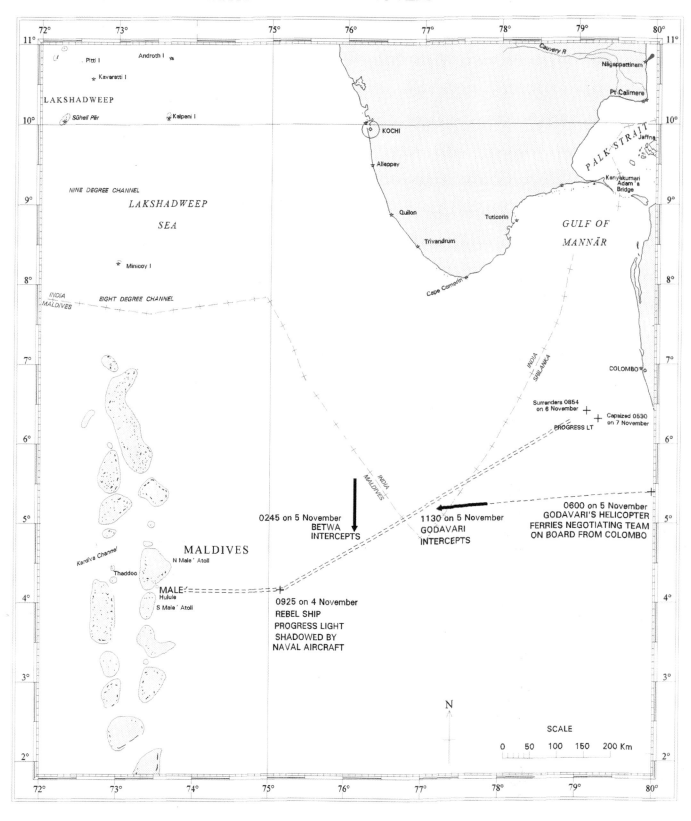

shortcomings to be remedied for future inter-service insurgency operations. Some of these shortcomings were:

- Of the naval ships, only the LSTs and LCUs were somewhat suitable as troop carriers.

- The merchant ships (cargo ships) were totally unsuitable for carrying soldiers overnight to and from Sri Lanka.

- The influx of troops after October 1987 was so large and so frequent that even elementary security checks could not be enforced by the Army at the boarding point.

- The inaccuracy of naval gunfire support by ships having large calibre guns against guerrilla targets in flat coastal terrain. Expectedly, the only ship that received the Army's appreciation for naval gunfire support was a Seaward Defence Boat fitted with a 40 mm anti-aircraft gun, because its shallow draught enabled it go close inshore. Her Commanding Officer was recommended by the Army for the award of a Vir Chakra!

Operation Cactus off the Maldive Islands From 3 to 7 November 1988

On the night of 2/3 November 1988, between 300 and 500 armed Tamil / Sinhala speaking mercenaries landed at the Male harbour by boats from a mother ship and captured key locations in Male. During this attempted coup, Maldivian President Gayoom went into hiding and, in the early hours of 3 November, sought India's help and immediate intervention.

Operation CACTUS

In response to this urgent request from the Maldivian Government, India launched Operation CACTUS. Its objective was to ensure the safety of President Gayoom and restore normalcy. The Army / Air Force concept of operations was to effect an air landing / para drop at Hulule airport, establish a bridgehead and thereafter secure control of the island of Male where the Maldivian Government was located. The Navy's task was to establish a *cordon sanitaire*

for which naval Maritime Reconnaissance (MR) aircraft and ships were deployed around the Maldive islands.

Naval Deployment

At sea, the nearest ships to the Maldives were the cadet training ship *Tir* and the frigate *Godavari*. They were diverted towards Male at maximum speed. *Betwa* was sailed from Cochin.

On 3rd morning, *Rajput, Ranjit, Gomati, Trishul, Nilgiri, Kumbhir, Cheetah* and the fleet tanker *Deepak* were directed to prepare to sail for the Maldives and MR aircraft were launched for air patrols.

Operation CACTUS was launched at 1300 hrs on the 3rd. Ships sailed from their base ports at best speed. By 1415 hrs, MR aircraft had established surveillance over the Maldives.

The Flight of the Mercenaries

Indian Air Force aircraft landed troops on the airport at Hulule Island on the night of 3/4 November. As soon as the mercenaries heard aircraft landing, they seized hostages and fled from Male in a merchant ship *MV Progress Light*. The hostages included the Maldivian Minister of Transport. Naval Headquarters received intelligence of the *Progress Light* having left Male harbour at midnight on 3/4 November.

Interception of MV Progress Light

Throughout the night, MR aircraft kept track on radar of all ships in the patrol area. At 0925 hrs on the morning of 4th November, the MR aircraft confirmed the detection of the *Progress Light* and homed *Betwa* (who was coming from Cochin) towards it. *Betwa* intercepted *Progress Light* on the night of the 4th /5th and followed it.[13]

In the meantime, a negotiating team had been flown from Male to Colombo. *Godavari's* Seaking helicopter embarked this team in Colombo and flew it on board *Godavari*. By midday on the 5th, *Godavari* made contact with the *Progress Light* and commenced negotiations for the release of the hostages.

---

13. An American perception is reflected in Dennis Kux's book *Estranged Democracies – India and the United States, 1941-1991*. Page 415 states

"To the south, in November 1988, India flexed its muscles once more as Rajiv ordered an Indian Army battalion flown to the Maldives, a thousand miles from India's southern tip to squelch a coup attempt. Although India was responding to a request from the small island republic, this striking projection of power far into the Indian Ocean – in some ways more dramatic than sending troops into Sri Lanka – underlined India's growing military capability and its willingness to use this power in a big brotherly fashion.

"The intervention won Washington's approval and was closely coordinated with the United States, from whom the Maldives first sought intervention before turning to New Delhi. A US Navy ship helped the Indians vector in on the escaping mercenaries and their hostages – a good example of US-Indian cooperation that did not infringe on US interests".

I was the Vice Chief of the Naval Staff in 1988. The American side in Delhi informed the Indian side that some US Navy ships were heading for Male to assist the Indian Navy. The American side was informed that the gesture was appreciated, that the Indian Navy had the situation under control and would not need any assistance. *INS Betwa* was homed on by the Navy's reconnaissance aircraft, made contact with the rebel ship at 0245 on 5th Nov and shadowed it until *INS Godavari* arrived later that forenoon with a negotiating team embarked. It was wise of the US Administration to advise the Maldives to seek India's assistance – it set a good precedent for Indo-US cooperation in such crises.

The Negotiations Phase

The leader of the mercenaries proved to be intractable. He insisted that the *Progress Light* would proceed only to Colombo and demanded intervention by an international team. After 15 hours of tension-packed dialogue between the negotiators and the mercenaries, during which the ship continued to head for Colombo, it became clear the rebels were not prepared to negotiate and change the destination of the *Progress Light*.

Meanwhile, the Sri Lankan Government had intimated that the rebel ship would not be allowed to enter Sri Lankan waters and that if it did, it would be attacked. The Maldivian Government had also made clear its desire that the *Progress Light* should not be allowed to proceed to Colombo.

Pressure Tactics

The safety of the hostages being the primary consideration, *Godavari* was directed to initiate graded pressure tactics and stop *Progress Light* from closing the Sri Lankan coast.

Vice Admiral SV Gopalachari (then Captain and Commanding Officer of the *Godavari*) recalls:

"Soon after midnight on 5/6 November, *Progress Light* was given the choice of returning to Male or heading for an Indian port - she refused. A firm warning was issued. This evoked no response. A warning shot was fired across the bows. It failed to persuade the hijackers. Close range gunfire was aimed at the forward goal post mast. It dislodged the swinging derrick which (fortuitously) fell on top of their fast speed escape craft.

After dawn on the 6th, pressure was increased. *Godavari's* Seaking dropped two depth charges ahead of the bows. *Progress Light* continued on her course. Close range gunfire was aimed at the aft mast and funnel. At 0825, a frantic report from the Master of the *Progress Light* indicated that the rebels had surrendered. The ship however continued to move ahead. *Betwa* opened fire - one of her shells hit *Progress Light* amidships and she stopped."

The hit started a fire on board *Progress Light*, frightened the mercenaries and caused the ship to stop. The mercenaries surrendered at 0854 hrs on 6th November. A Naval boarding party seized the ship, brought the hostages to *Godavari* and apprehended the mercenaries.

Evacuation of Injured Hostages

Eight injured hostages (including the Maldivian Minister of Shipping and Transport) were immediately evacuated by helicopter to the Military Hospital, Trivandrum for urgent hospitalisation. Hostages with minor injuries were treated on board *Godavari*.

Capsizing of MV Progress Light

Efforts by salvage parties from *Betwa* to extinguish the fire and control the flooding on board *Progress Light* were unsuccessful in the adverse weather conditions that prevailed. Its crew was transferred to *Betwa*. *Progress Light* capsized at 0530 hrs on 7th November, 56 miles southwest of Colombo.

Return to Male

Godavari and *Betwa* proceeded to Male with the captured mercenaries, the rescued hostages and the crew of *MV Progress Light*. At a formal ceremony on 8th November, the Commanding Officer of *Godavari* handed over the rescued hostages to Maldivian Government officials. President Gayoom was personally present at this ceremony.

The captured mercenaries were later taken by *Godavari* to an Indian Army detention camp located on Gamadoo Island on 9th November.

Lessons Learnt

The swift success of Operation Cactus was because the Maldives were within easy reach and also because an airfield was available for the air landing operation. This may not always be the case. The operation highlighted the need for the Navy to possess an integral helo-assault capability.

The prompt withdrawal of the Indian forces, at India's initiative, was well appreciated.

Operation TASHA in the Palk Strait

After the withdrawal of the IPKF from Sri Lanka in April 1990, the protection of the Tamil Nadu coast was entrusted to the Navy and the Coast Guard.

Operation Tasha commenced in June 1990 to continuously patrol the International Boundary Line in the Palk Strait to curb the smuggling of arms and ammunition, poaching, illegal immigration and activities of Sri Lankan Tamil militants.

From the outset, it was clear that Operation Tasha was going to be a 'low intensity conflict' commitment that was unlikely to end soon. The hiring of trawlers and arming them with MMGs for operating from the Naval Detachments at Rameshwaram and Nagapatnam was institutionalised. The earlier ad-hoc facilities for operating aircraft and helicopters from the Naval Air Detachment Ramnad were gradually improved. Logistic and maintenance infrastructure and maintenance personnel were established at Madras to sustain the SDBs and the other shallow draught ships patrolling the Palk Strait.

23

Assistance Rendered By The Navy In Peace Time
1976–1990

- Naval Assistance to Ships in Distress at Sea
- Search and Rescue
- Medical Assistance and Evacuation
- Cyclone, Flood and Earthquake Relief
- Maintenance of Essential Services
- Firefighting Assistance
- Naval Aid to Civil Authority
- Assistance by Naval Diving Teams
- Apprehension of Poaching and Smuggling Trawlers
- VVIP/VIP Transportation

Naval Assistance to Ships in Distress at Sea

Month & Year	Assistance Rendered to	Nature of Assistance	Location	by Naval Ships/ aircraft
Feb 76	Barge NANIAMMA	Repaired crack & towed to Mumbai	Oil Rig Sagar Samrat	UDAYGIRI
Apr 76	INS Godavari OPERATION GODSAL	Salvage of Godavari	off Male (Maldives)	BULSAR, DELHI, TIR, HIMGIRI, GAJ, KESARI & DEEPAK
May 76	ANDY THREE	Broken bottom. Search & Rescue. Survivors to Cochin	South of Sri Lanka	Super Constellation MR aircraft, PORBANDER and PONDICHERRY
Jun 76	Cypriot ship ILASIA	Medical assistance to crew members	Off Andaman & Nicobar Islands	INHS DHANVANTARI (Naval Hospital)
Jun 76	US Ship CAPODANNO	Diving assistance to clear choked inlets	Seychelles Port	NILGIRI & TRISHUL
Sep 76	MV Shant Kamal	Ran aground. Assisted in rescue operations	Veraval	NOIC Karanja
Sep 76	MV RAJSHREE	Crew abandoned ship – safely recovered	Havelock Island A&N	PULICAT
Dec 76	Trawler MV DURGA	Provided medical help to crew & towed to Mumbai	Off Bombay	DEEPAK
Jun 78	Fishing trawler BLUE BANANA	Salvage of grounded trawler	South of Daruva	SHARDUL
Aug 78	MV NAND MAYUR	Rescue of stranded crew	Vengurla Rocks	BETWA
Aug 78	CHITRA LEKHA & CASEW	Search & location of fishing boat & tug	Off Trivandrum	GARUDA Islander aircraft

Sep 78	Iranian Water Tanker KANGAN	Towed to Bombay	From southwest of Bombay	TRISHUL
Jun 79	MV AVILES	Medical assistance to survivors	Southwest of Bombay	DUNAGIRI
Jul 79	SEA SPIRIT	Rescue of 27 crew from ship aground	Off Kori Creek	Air Force helo assisted by Navy
Aug 79	MV RUKMAVATI	Crew of stranded ship evacuated	Gulf of Kutch	DUNAGIRI
Sep 79	BURMESE CARGO	Crew of stranded ship evacuated	Off Port Blair (A & N)	SHARDUL
Jun 80	VLCC ANGILIKI	Transferred stores and personnel to effect repairs	Off Bombay	UDAYGIRI
Jul 80	Panamanian Ship Eastern Liberty	Ship sank. IL 38 launched for search. Shakti effected rescue of ships crew	Off Pigeon Island	IL 38 & SHAKTI
Jul 80	MV JALADHIR	Location of ship in distress	West Coast	IL 38
Jul 80	CGV PURI	Located & escorted to Chennai	Off Madras	KAVARATTI, KESARI
Nov 80	MV MAHAJOK II	Rendered assistance	Off Kamorta (A&N)	KESARI
Nov 80	Russian merchant ship OSTRODONE	Medical assistance	Off Cochin	BETWA
Dec 80	Sea Cadet Ship VARUNA	Towed from Bhavnagar to Mumbai	Off Bhavnagar	HIMGIRI
Jun 81	CG Trawler	Towed to Bombay	Off Bombay	ALLEPPEY
Aug 81	MV PRIME ROSE	Ran aground. Crew rescued	Off North Sentinel Island (A & N)	Naval Ships/ Helo
Jun 82	UAE Ship MV NAJMA BEAUTY	Rescued & towed to Okha	Northwest of Okha	KUTHAR
Jun 82	MV SUBHASHINI	Fishing trawler adrift. Rescued & towed into port	Off Paradeep	KADMATT
Jul 82	ONGC oil rig SAGAR VIKAS	Blowout. Evacuation, medical assistance & surveillance	Off Bombay	DEEPAK, DUNAGIRI
Jul 82	Panama Vessel MV WINNO	Search and Rescue	Hut Bay (A&N)	SDB T-51
Oct 82	Fishing trawler	Rescued & towed	Off Vengurla	RAJPUT
Jan 83	Fishing Trawler	Rescue & towed	Off Vengurla	RAJPUT
Sep 83	Russian Ship MV MINSK	Medical aid to a heart patient	At Sea	GARUDA aircraft & helos
Aug 84	MV ORIENTAL PEARL	Investigation of wreck. Setting up Trisponder camps	At Sea	MITHUN & DARSHAK
Aug 84	MV DOVER	Crew rescued from burning ship & towed to Vizag	Off Visakhapatnam	KILTAN
Aug 84	MV MAGULI	Location and marking ship's wreck	Off Bombay	BHAVNAGAR, BEDI
Jan 85	MVF DIMPLE	Towed to Mumbai after drifting for 11 days	Off Bombay	MAKAR
Feb 85	MV CHIDAMBARAM	Firefighting Assistance	Off Madras	DUNAGIRI, ANJADIP & KADMATT
May 85	SAGAR PRAGATI	Towed to Dubai & personnel evacuated	Off Dubai	Naval Ships & helo
Jun 85	Singapore ship SAL VALOUR	Rescue& airlift of injured crew	Off Singapore	SHAKTI

Jul 86	Norwegian Tanker	Evacuation of sailor	Off Cochin	MULKI
Dec 86	MV JAGDOOT	Rescued from harassment by smugglers	Off Vishakhapatnam	MATANGA
Jun 87	Dredger MANDOVI	Assistance to Dredging Corpn	Goa	PONDICHERRY
Dec 88	Missing Whaler "Eklavya"	Search & Rescue	Lakshadweep	MITHUN, SHAKTI UDAYGIRI
Feb 89	MV SUBBALAXMI	Towed into Trincomalee	Off Trincomalee	MAHISH
Jul 89	MV VISHVA AMITABH	Grounded. Assistance rendered.	Lat 18 51 N, Long 72 53 E	DARSHAK

Search and Rescue

Month & Year	Assistance Rendered to	Nature of Assistance	Location	by IN Ships/ aircraft
Jun 76	Fishing vessels	Search & Rescue	Off Bombay High	ANDROTH
Nov 77	Fishing boats	Search & Rescue after cyclone	Off Calicut	GARUDA aircraft
Dec 77	Tug AJRAL	Search & Rescue. Towed back to harbour	A & N	KATCHALL
Nov 78	Marooned personnel	Search & Rescue	Off Trivandrum	Cochin Diving Team
Nov 78	Fishing boats	Search & Rescue	Off Madras	Islander aircraft
Feb 79	Burmese fisherman	Rescued after being adrift for 20 days	100 miles NE of Sembilian	KESARI
May 79	Fishing boats	Search & rescue after cyclone	Off Nizamapatnam	LCU L-31
Mar 80	Ferry boat St Xavier	Search and rescue	South of Cochin	GARUDA Helo
Jul 80	Fishermen	Search & Rescue	Off Bombay	SDB T-53
Jul 80	Fisherman	Search & Rescue	Off Goa	HANSA Helo
Jun 81	Sri Lankan fishermen	Search & Rescue	240 miles from Sri Lanka	HIMGIRI
Nov 81	Fishing boats	Search & Rescue after cyclone	Off Saurashtra And Gulf of Kutch	RAJPUT TARAGIRI DEEPAK BHAVNAGAR ALLEPPEY
Jul 82	Fishing boats	Rescue of five survivors from two capsized fishing boats	Near Ponnani	GARUDA helos
Oct 82	SAMUDRA JYOTI	Search & Rescue	Off Trincomalee	ANDAMAN
Sep 83	Fishermen	Search & Rescue	Off Kochi	GARUDA aircraft
Jul 84	Fishing craft	Search & Rescue	Off Dabhol	RATNAGIRI
Jun 85	MV RUSLI, (Honduras Cargo ship)	Crew Rescued	Off North Sentinel Island (A & N)	Naval helos
Jun 85	Fishermen	Search & Rescue	Off Bombay	KUNJALI helos
Oct 85	Fishermen	Search & Rescue after cyclone	Off Orissa Coast	MATANGA and Islander aircraft
Nov 85	Fishermen	Search & Rescue	Off Mumbai	KUNJALI helos
Mar 86	IAF AN 32 aircraft	Search for survivors/wreckage	North Arabian Sea	RANJIT
Jun 86	Fishermen	Search & rescue	Off Bhimunipatnam	MATANGA
Jun 86	Yacht YETI	Search & Rescue. Towed to port.	Off Port Blair	MATANGA, GULDAR
Aug 86	TRIPLEX TEXMACO	Search & Rescue of survivors	Off Madras	VIKRANT
Mar 87	Fishing boat	Search and rescue	Off Kakinada	NIRDESHAK
Jul 87	Fishermen	Search and rescue	Off Bombay	KUNJALI helos
Aug 87	Fishermen	Search & Rescue	Off Beypore	BETWA

Mar 88	Sailing boat Kanoji Angre	Search and Rescue	Off Porto Novo	LCU L-31
Jul 88	MV KONDUL	Search and Rescue	Off Barren Island (A & N)	SHARDUL, SDB T-60
Jul 88	Train accident	Salvage operations	Near Quilon	GARUDA helos
Aug 88	ONGC Helicopter	Search for wreckage & Rescue of survivors	Off Pondicherry	Naval ships & aircraft
Sep 88	Customs boat Algasia	Rescue of Customs personnel from sinking boat	Off Bombay	KUNJALI helo
Oct 88	Pawan Hans helicopter	Search and Rescue	Off Madras	SANDHAYAK
Dec 88	Burmese fishermen	Rescued after cyclone	Off Sacramento Lt (A & N)	KESARI
Jan 89	3 sailors missing from IN Detachment Rameshwaram	Search & Rescue. Boat located near Filadu Island after being adrift for 12 days	Off Male (Maldives)	BETWA
Mar 89	Lakshadweep Administration	Search & Rescue of survivors after collision between ISLAND STAR and MADAD ELAHI	Off Androth Island	TIR
Jul 89	Fishermen	Search & Rescue	Off Point Pedro (Palk Strait)	KESARI
Jul 89	Fishermen & marooned people	Search & Rescue after cyclone struck coastal Maharashtra	Malad, Raigad and Santha Ram lake Tarapore and Ratnagiri Coast	HAMLA, naval ships and aircraft from Bombay

Medical Assistance and Evacuation

Month & Year	Assistance Rendered to	Nature of Assistance	Location	By Ships/ aircraft
Jan 76	Civilian patient	Evacuated to Port Blair	From Neil Island (A & N)	PANVEL
Mar 76	Civilian patient	Evacuated from DARSHAK off Hut Bay to Port Blair	Off Hut Bay (A & N)	PULICAT
Mar 76	Civilian patient	Evacuated to Cochin	From Munnar	GARUDA helo
Dec 77	King Georges Hospital	Nursing assistance duties	Bombay	Medical personnel from INHS ASVINI
Sep 79	Civilian patient	Evacuated to Cochin	Kavaratti Island (Lakshadweep)	ABHAY
Jan 80	Civilian patient	Evacuation from merchant ship KEDARNATH	Off Alleppey	GARUDA helo
Aug 80	Civilian patient	Medical assistance	Amini island (Lakshadweep)	BEAS
Mar 81	Police patient	Evacuated to Port Blair	From Narcondum (A & N)	LCU L-34
Aug 81	Police patient	Evacuated to Port Blair	From Narcondum	LCU L-34
Mar 82	PWD Truck	Evacuation of injured personnel	Rangat Bay (A&N)	Naval helos
May 82	Civilian patient	Evacuation to Port Blair	From Hut Bay (A&N)	SDB T-51
Jun 82	Patient from Kuwait ship IMANJUBAVR	Evacuated to Cochin	Off Cochin	GARUDA helo
Jul 83	Railways	Medical assistance to derailed train near Raigarh	Raigarh-Jersiguda	INHS NIVARINI

Aug 83	Lakshwadweep Administration	Medical assistance to patients	Chetlat Island	INHS SANJIVANI
Jan/Feb/ Mar/Apr/ Jun 1985	Andamans Administration	Evacuation of patients to Port Blair from A & N villages Belliground, Dungong Creek, Kadmatalla, Diglipur, Mayabunder,		UTKROSH helos
Apr 87	MV GOLDEN ENDEAVOUR	Evacuation of casualty	Off Bombay	KUNJALI helo
Aug 87	Mine workers	Evacuated by helo and treated on board	Off Sri Lanka	NIRDESHAK
Nov 88	MV ALEXANDER ZAWABSZKI	Treatment of critically ill crew members	Off Port Blair	Naval medical team INHS DHANVANTARI
Dec 88	Injured Maldivian VIP hostages from hijacked MV PROGRESS LIGHT	Evacuated to MH Trivandrum (Operation Cactus)	Off Colombo	GODAVARI Helo
Jul 89	MV CHRISOLM	Evacuation of patient to Cochin	Off Cochin	MULKI
Jun 90	Indian Army Major of Bomb Squad	Evacuated to Bombay	From Tarapore	KUNJALI helo
Nov 90	Civilian patients	Evacuated to Port Blair	From Diglipur & Havelock (A&N)	UTKROSH helo

Cyclone, Flood and Earthquake Relief

Month & Year	Assistance Rendered to Govt of	Nature of Assistance	Location of District(s)	By
Nov 76	Tamil Nadu	Flood Relief operation. rendered assistance, rescued 46 persons	At Madras	Naval helos and Islander
Nov 77	Andhra Pradesh	Cyclone Rescue, food drop & first aid	Tiruchirapally Anakapalli, Kalpeni & Elamanchilli	Helos, diverse boats, Gemini dinghies & naval teams
Nov 77	Tamil Nadu	Cyclone Relief & Rescue	Tiruchirapally	Helos
Nov 77	Lakshadweep	Food drop	Kalpeni Island	Aircraft
Nov 77	Kerala	Search for missing fishing boats after cyclone	Off Calicut	Islander
Aug 78	Maharashtra	Tapi River Flood Relief	Jalgaon	Geminis & divers
Nov 79	Tamil Nadu	Flood Relief	Madurai & Ramnad	Boats
Sep 80	Orissa & Andhra Pradesh	Flood Rescue assistance to marooned train	Srikakulum Koraput	Helos, boats & Geminis
Jan/Feb 82	Andaman & Nicobar	Earthquake Relief operations. Carrying stores and personnel to tremor-affected inhabitants in Campbell Bay	Great Nicobar	DEEPAK, SHARDUL Naval aircraft & helos
Aug 82	Orissa	Flood Relief assistance with boats life saving equipment & medical kits	Khurda,	Naval teams
Sep 82	Orissa	230 tonnes of food grains & POL from Vizag to Paradip for flood affected people	Paradip	GHARIAL & ARNALA
Jun 83	Gujarat	Flood relief operations	Off Porbandar	NILGIRI
Oct 83	Andhra Pradesh	Flood relief operations & food drop	Visakhapatnam and Tuni	CIRCARS & helos

Nov 84	Tamil Nadu Andhra Pradesh	Cyclone Relief supplies of food, diesel & clothing to cyclone hit areas. Food drops, airlift of medical teams & diving assistance	Coastal Tamil Nadu & South Andhra, over Pulicat area	NIRDESHAK & SHARABH Helos & Naval Divers
Aug 86	Andhra Pradesh	Flood Rescue operations, food drops, evacuation and medical assistance	Godavari	CIRCARS Naval teams & helos
Jul 88	Andhra Pradesh	Flood Relief operations	Bhadrachalam	CIRCARS
Jul 89	Andhra Pradesh	Flood Relief assistance	Eluru &Warangal	CIRCARS
May 90	Andhra Pradesh	Cyclone Relief & rescue of marooned people	Tuni, Ankapalle Elamanchilli & Bhimunipatnam	CIRCARS helos & divers
Nov 90	Andamans	Cyclone relief	Rangat Island	LCU L-36

Maintenance of Essential Services

Oct/Nov 76	Bombay Port Trust	Merchant ship movements during a strike	Bombay	ANGRE
Dec 77	King Georges Hospital	Nursing assistance	Bombay	ASVINI
Dec 77- Feb 78	Maharashtra Govt	Running Bombay's milk supply schemes	Worli, Goregaon and Kurla Dairies	ANGRE
Aug/Sep79	Mazagon Docks	During a strike	Bombay	ANGRE
Oct 79	Andaman & Nicobars	To guard VAs & VPs during police agitation	Port Blair	JARAWA
Dec 79	Andaman & Nicobars	Transportation of personnel & stores from Port Blair	To Car Nicobar & Campbell Bay	Naval ships
Nov 81	ONGC A & N	Transportation of ONGC personnel & stores from Port Blair	To Teressa Island	SHARABH
Jan 82	Bharat Petroleum	Operate & maintain essential machinery during strike	Chembur Refinery	ANGRE
Nov 82	Goa	Ease tension between local & immigrant labour	New Vasem, Goa	GOMANTAK
Mar 84	Bombay Port Trust	Movement of merchant ships carrying vital cargo during port workers strike	Bombay	GODAVARI, CIRCARS, ANGRE
Mar 84	Madras Port Trust	Movement of merchant ships carrying vital cargo during port workers strike	Madras	ADYAR
May/Jun 84	Maharashtra Govt	Maintenance of peace during Bombay riots (Operation Suraksha)	Bombay	VIKRANT, NILGIRI, ANGRE
Apr 89	All Major Ports	Merchant ship movements during strike by Port Trust workers	All major ports	By local Naval establishments
Mar 90	Mauritius Govt	Restoration and manning of power supply in Mauritius after it was disrupted by a strike of workers of the electricity department	Mauritius	Teams from the Navy, Public Sector Units & Special Mobile Force
Oct/Nov 90	Govt of Maldives	Installation of communication equipment for the SAARC Conference	Male	Naval team

Firefighting Assistance

May 79	Bhangarwadi Village	Fire fighting assistances	Lonavla	SHIVAJI
Jun 79	Kurunda Village	Fire fighting assistance	Lonavla	SHIVAJI
Sep 79	M/s Bhandari Crossfield	Fire fighting assistance	Vadgaon	SHIVAJI
Feb 81	Binny's Godown	Fire fighting assistance	Cochin	VENDURUTHY
Oct 84	SCI Tanker MV Lala Lajpat Rai	Fire fighting assistance supplied 8000 litres of foam	Butcher Island jetty in Bombay	Naval Tug Balbir
Jun 87	Bombay Port Trust	Controlling the fire in a truck loaded with jute	Ballard Pier godowns	VIKRANT team
Apr 90	Bombay Fire Dept	Air-rescue from terrace after fire in multi-storey Hotel Oberoi Towers	Bombay	KUNJALI helos
Aug 90	Bombay Fire Dept	Air-rescue from terrace after fire in multi-storey Regent Chambers	Bombay	KUNJALI helos

Naval Aid to Civil Authority

Month & Year	Assistance Rendered to	Nature of Assistance	Location	By IN Ships/ aircraft
Mar 76	A & N Administration	Release of Burmese fishermen captured by police	Narcondum Island	PULICAT
Jun 76	Drilling ship Haakon Magnus	Spares were flown to drilling ship by ship's helo		UDAYGIRI
Jun 76	ONGC	Assisted in the location of a metal well head and carried out a bottom search around the last position of the well head by using its sonar		Himgiri
Mar 77	A & N Administration	Election commitments	Nancowry Group of Islands	PANVEL
Mar 77	A & N Administration	To dispel a bomb scare created by the discovery of aviation fuel drums left behind by the Japanese during the World War II	Andamans & Nicobar	Army Bomb disposal Unit under the aegis of the Indian Navy
May 78	Bombay Police	Recovery of dead body	From sea	TUNIR II
Mar - Apr 80	Customs Authority Cochin	To search a dhow abandoned	off Calicut	Ships
Feb 81	Forest Dept Port Blair	Transportation of a bulldozer	Port Blair to Little Andaman	GHORPAD
Feb 81	Andaman Police	Provision & rations transportation	For outpost at Narcondum	ANDAMAN
Apr 81	Yeoman service	Transporting 76 settlers & 142 cattle in two trips	Port Blair to Campbell Bay	GULDAR
Jun 81	Indian Railway	Rescue & Salvage work of train accident	Bagmati river near Samastipur	Aircrew divers of KUNJALI
Dec 81	Ex-servicemen settlers of Island	50 drums of kerosene oil Campbell Bay	Great Nicobar	LCU L-34
Jun 83	Scientists of CWPRS Pune	Surveying assistance for Seismic observations	Karanja	Survey Party & boats from DARSHAK
Dec 83	Scientists of CWPRS Pune	Laying, Monitoring, & Recording of data from Wave Rider Buoy	Karanja	Survey Party from DARSHAK

Apr 84	ONGC	Distance measurements	Bombay High	Survey party from DARSHAK
Jun 86	Customs	Seized smuggled items worth Rs150 lakhs	off Visakhapatnam	SDB T-53
Sep 87	Geological Survey of India	Two survey parties assisted survey project	Karwar	DARSHAK
Dec 88/ Jan 89	Scientists of CWPRS, Pune	For position fixing during the conduct of seismic survey	Ezhimala	MAKAR
Jan 88	Custom authorities	Rendered necessary assistance	Off Cochin	GAJ
Aug 88	Civil Adm	Rendered assistance to police post at Narcondum	Narcondum	SDB T-60
Apr 89	Ms Arti Pradhan (aged 16 Yrs)	Swimming from Dhanushkodi to Talaimannar	Palk Strait	Naval vessels

Assistance by Naval Diving Teams

Month & Year	Assistance Rendered to	Nature of Assistance	Location
Jan 76	Maharashtra Govt	Inspection of capsized dredger	Bombay
Jan 76	Coal India	Inspection of flooded coal mine	Dhanbad
Jan 76	Air Force	Recovery of bodies from crashed helicopter	Nasik
Feb to May 76	Pong Dam	Assistance during construction	Pong
May to Jun 76	PWD Goa	Inspection of Zuari River bridge foundations	Panjim
Jun 76	SS Capodanno	Clearing choked inlets of sea weeds	Seychelles
Jun 76	Kerala Constrn Corp	Inspection of bridge foundations	Ernakulam
Jul 76	Andhra Govt	Inspection of submerged idols	Rajamundry
Sep 76	Maharashtra Electricity	Underwater repairs at power station	Tarapur
Dec 76	Fisheries Project	Calibration of sonar transducers	Cochin
Jan 77	Eastern Railway	Inspection of damaged bridge piers	Daulatganj
Apr 77	Vizag Port Trust	Recovery of wire recorder	Visakhapatnam
May 77	Kerala Electricity	Lifting of Dam's emergency gates	Sengulam Dam
Sep 77	Kerala Constrn Corp	Salvage of pontoon from under bridge	Cochin
Sep 77	PWD Goa	Inspection of collapsed Zuari Bridge	Panjim
Oct 77	Cochin Shipyard	Fitting anodes on piles	Cochin
Jan 78	DGCA & Air India	Recovery of bodies, and salvage of engine, tail piece, digital flight & cockpit voice recorders from crashed Air India 747 Jumbo Jet 'Emperor Ashoka'	Off Bombay Airport
Jan 78	Kerala Engineering	Repair of slipway gate on water barrage	Tellicherry
Jan 78	Rajasthan Electricity	Underwater repairs at Rana Pratap Sagar Dam	Kota
Feb 78	Andhra Electricity	Inspection of Nagarjuna Sagar Dam gates	Nagarjuna
Mar 78	Kerala Electricity	Inspection of dam gates	Phozhassi
Apr 78	Kerala Police	Recovery of bodies from the sea	Trivandrum
Apr 78	Cochin Port Trust	Salvage & demolition of sunken dredger	Cochin
May 78	Bombay Police	Search and recovery of weapons dumped by criminals in Bassein Creek	Bombay
May to Jun 78	Rajasthan Electricity	Clearing obstructions in Rana Pratap Sagar Dam	Kota

Jun to Jul 78	PWD Bihar	Inspection of River Ganga bank near Patna for flood control	Narainpur/Rahimpur
Aug to Sep 78	National Thermal Power Corporation (NTPC)	Recovery of suction pump and inspection of sumps of Badarpur Thermal Power Station	Delhi
Aug 78	Andhra Electricity	Underwater inspection of Nagarjuna Sagar Dam	Nagarjuna
Dec 78 to Jan 79	Andhra Govt	Recovery of sunken car and body from canal near Rajamundary	Godavari Delta
Feb 79	Maharashtra Transport	Recovery of bus and tanker from Thana Creek	Bombay
Apr 79	PWD Madhya Pradesh	Inspection of Narmada River bed strata on National Highway No.3 near Indore	Indore
May to July 79	Bhakra-Beas Dam Management Board	Removal of eroded concrete from stilling basin of Bhakra Dam and repair	Nangal
Sep 79	Kerala Police	Recovery of police jeep from dam reservoir	Iddikki
Oct to Nov 79	Andhra Electricity	Inspection/repair of stilling basin of Nagarjuna Sagar Dam	Nagarjuna
Oct 79	Eastern Railway	Salvage of submerged bogie from River Falgu	Jangipur
Nov 79	Underwater Engineers Ltd	Therapeutic treatment of civilian divers	Goa
Nov 79	Andhra Govt	Recovery of bodies from bus fallen into river	Gudur
Dec 79	Shipping Corporation of India	Recovery of anchor and cable of Vishwa Apuva	Bombay
Jan 80	Cochin Shipyard	Fitting aluminum fenders on jetty	Cochin
Jan to Feb 80	Srisons Fisheries Karnataka	Recovery of fishing nets off Cochin	Cochin
Feb 80	Fortune Seiners, Ranjak & Java Durga	Re-floating of fishing trawlers hijacked by miscreants from fishing harbour and sunk off Fairway Buoy	Cochin
Mar 80	Bombay Customs	Seabed search for silver dumped by smugglers off Bombay	Bombay
Mar 80	Orissa Govt	Underwater inspection, photography and repair of cracks in up stream side of Dam	Hirakud Dam
Mar to Apr 80	Cochin Customs	Seabed search for dhow sunk after being chased for smuggling silver	Calicut
Apr 80	Mazagon Docks	Salvage of launch sunk off Bombay	Bombay
Jun 80	Central Bureau of Investigation	Search and recovery of arms and ammunition dumped into River Jamuna by assailants after committing murder	New Delhi
Aug 80	Goa Port Trust	Recovery of body in Goa harbour	Goa
Aug to Sep 80	Rajasthan Electricity	Inspection & repairs to the turbines at Rana Pratap Sagar Dam	Kota
Feb 81	Maharashtra Govt	Salvage of container from marshes	Tarapur
Mar 81	Bombay Port Trust	Unloading of limestone from sunken dhow	Bombay
Jun 81	Dredging Corporation	Salvage of sunken dredger	Visakhapatnam
Jun 81	Eastern Railway	Recovery of submerged bogies from the Bagmati River in Bihar	Samasthipur
Jul 81	Madras Port Trust	Salvage of sunken channel buoy	Madras
Nov 81	Madras Port Trust	Underwater repairs of hopper dredger doors	Madras

Nov 81	Cochin Shipyard	Underwater inspection of jetty piles	Cochin
Dec 81	Steel firm	Underwater demolition	Beypore (Calicut)
Apr 82	Bombay Port Trust	Salvage of dhow	Bombay
May 82	Kerala Forests	Underwater tree cutting	Periyar Lake
Jun 82	ONGC	Seabed search for metal/explosive detonating device in the vicinity of damaged undersea pipe line	Bombay
Jun to Jul 82	Paradip Port Trust	Salvage of trawlers sunk by cyclone	Paradip
Jul 82	Cochin Shipyard	Underwater Inspection of jetty piles	Cochin
Jul 82	Cochin Municipality	Recovery of body fallen from ferry boat	Cochin
Oct 82	Gujarat Fisheries Harbour Project	Underwater survey of breakwaters under construction at Veraval and Mangrol	Saurashtra
Oct 82	Punjab Govt	Recovery of bodies after boat sank in Nangal Reservoir	Nangal
Oct 82	Punjab Govt	Recovery of bodies from bus fallen into canal	Sirhind Nirvana Canal
Nov 82	ADE Bangalore	Recovery of pilotless target	River Kaveri
Jan to Mar 83	Calcutta Port Trust	Salvage of sunken trawlers and clearance of jammed caisson gate of basin	Haldia
Mar 83	Madras Customs	Salvage of fishing vessel	Off Madras
Apr 83	Indian Army	Recovery of submerged tank	Ramgarh
Apr 83	Bharat Petroleum	Isolating submerged jetty pump	Bombay
May/Jun 83	Indian Army	Underwater survey of canal bed	Suratgarh
May to Jun 83	PWD Madhya Pradesh Tawa Project	Underwater work on canal discharge pipes	Itarsi
Sep 83	MV MARTINI TORMS	Clearance of fouled propeller	Off Cochin
Sep 83	Kerala Govt	Recovery of bodies after ferry boat accident	Off Ernakulum
Sep 83	North Eastern Railway	Recovery of bodies from Girija Barrage	Gorakhpur
Oct 83	MP Government	Recovery of body from Narmada River	Hoshangabad
Nov 83	Central Fisheries Institute	Clearance of fouled propellers	Cochin
Dec 83 to Jan 84	Gujarat Fishery Harbour Project	Inspection of breakwaters under construction at Veraval and Mangrol ports	Saurashtra
Feb 84	Punjab Govt	Recovery of bodies from bus fallen into the Bhakra Canal	Nangal
Jan 84 to Feb 85	NTPC	Underwater inspection of Badarpur Power Station intake channel, cleaning of debris and installation of water screens	Delhi
Apr 84	Uttar Pradesh Govt	Underwater repairs to dam	
May 84	Rajasthan Electricity	Underwater repairs at Rana Pratap Sagar Dam	Kota
May 84	Sirvani Dam	Underwater inspection and repairs	Palghat
Jul 84	N E Railway	Recovery of sunken track	Kumedpur
Aug 84	Bharat Petroleum	Survey of seabed	Bombay
Sep 84	Air Force	Location of ditched trainer aircraft and recovery of body from Hussaini Sagar lake	Hyderabad
Dec 84	Cochin Customs	Recovery of sunken boat	Cochin
Jan 85	PWD Goa	Underwater inspection of bottom strata on which new pillars of Berim Road Bridge rested	Goa
Jan 85	Paradip Port Trust	Removal of sunken trawler	Paradip

Jan 85	NTPC	Underwater repairs at Badarpur Power Station	Delhi
Mar to Apr 85	Rajasthan Govt	Clearance of underwater concrete obstructions in the penstock gates of the main dam and clearance of grooves of emergency sluice gate in depths between 90 to 100 feet	Mahi Bajaj Hydel Project
Apr 85	Chakiat Agencies	Inspection of stern gland of MV Teckler Dosinia	Cochin
Apr 85	Central Fisheries Institute	Assistance to remove ropes from fouled shaft	Cochin
Jun 85	Kerala Electricity	Underwater recce of the Kakki dam site	Kakki
Jul to Aug 85	Cochin Port Trust	Underwater inspection of bottom strata on which first, third and fourth pillars of the Link Road Bridge rested	Cochin
Sep 85	Kerala Boat Association	Recovery of sunken boat	Kerala
Oct 85	Cochin Shipyard	Underwater inspection of jetty piles	Cochin
Feb 86	Cochin Port Trust	Underwater inspection of dredger	Cochin
Jun 86	Electricity Board	Underwater repairs of dam	Munnar
Jul 86	NTPC	Underwater repairs of Badarpur power station	Delhi
Jun-Jul 86	Orissa Govt	Underwater inspection and repairs of Dam	Hirakud dam
Sep 86	Air Force	Salvage of submerged MIG 21 aircraft	
Feb 87	UP Water Board	Inspection and sealing of underwater pipes	Lucknow
Jun 87	Orissa Govt	Rescue of survivors and recovery of bodies from ferry sunk in Brahmini River	Near Cuttack
Jul 87	Border Security Force	Recovery of bodies, arms and ammunition of BSF men after boat accident in Brahmaputra river	Teju (Assam)
Jul 87	Southern Railway	Rescue of passengers from bogies of derailed train	Kazipet (AP)
Jul to Nov 87	Karnataka Govt	Underwater repair of leaks in Dam	Talakalale Dam
Aug 87	Delhi Police	Recovery of body from Yamuna river	Delhi
Sep 87	Sikkim Govt	Recovery of bodies from sunken truck in Raman river	Sikkim
Dec 87	Kerala Electricity	Underwater inspection and repairs	Idamalayar Dam
Apr 88	Air Force	To locate the debris of a MIG aircraft that had crashed in Pong Dam reservoir near Talwara. Attempts by divers in Sep 86 were not successful Diving assistance was again requested in Apr 88 Diving team located and recovered half a tonne of debris (tail pipe, stabiliser etc)	Talwara (Punjab)
Apr to May 88	Madhya Pradesh Electricity Board	Under water inspection and clearance of under-water obstructions at a Hydroelectric Project	
Jun 88	Cochin Port Trust	Underwater inspection of sunken dredger	Cochin
Jul 88	Southern Railway	Rescue of passengers and recovery of bodies from, and salvage of, bogies submerged in Ashtamudi Lake after derailment	Quilon
Aug 88	Kerala Govt	Recovering of body from Meenarial river	Kottayam
Aug 88	Bihar Govt	Salvage of sunken motor launch	Manihari Ghat
May to Oct 88	Integrated Fisheries Project	Clearing fouled wire ropes from shafts and propellers of fishing vessels	Cochin
Feb 89	UP Govt	Rescue from boats that capsized during the Kumbh Mela	Allahabad

Mar 89	Rajasthan Govt	Recovery of bodies after boat capsized in in Jaisamund Lake	Udaipur
Apr 89	Karnataka Electricity	Survey, repair and plugging leaks upstream of the main wall of Talakalele Dam's balancing reservoir. (Saraswathi Valley Project)	Bangalore
Jun 89	Bombay Customs	Recovery of silver dumped into the sea	Bombay
Jul 89	Kerala Police	Recovery of bodies from submerged car	Pannikkode
Jul 89	Delhi Police	Recovery of body from river Yamuna	Jagarpur
Aug 89	Delhi Police	Recovery of body from river Yamuna	Delhi
Sep 89	Vayudoot Ltd	Recovery of bodies from wreckage of Vayudoot Dornier aircraft crashed in Ujani Lake	near Pune
Oct 89	Andhra Marine Archeological Department	Search and salvage of the Vishakheswara Temple	
Dec 89	ONGC	Recovery of bodies from, and salvage of, Pawan Hans Dauphin Helicopter sunk in the river Ganga	Patna
Mar 90	AP Govt	Recovery of bodies and submerged Buddha statue from Hussaini Sagar Lake	Hyderabad
Jul 90	DRDL	Recovery of weapon	Chandipur
Oct 90	Haryana Electricity	Underwater repairs to gate of Yamuna Nagar Power Station	Yamuna Nagar
Oct 90	Goa Govt	Recovery of bodies from under collapsed span of new Mandovi Bridge during construction	Goa
Dec 90	Kerala Govt	Recovery of bodies from capsized tourist boat	Pappara Dam

Apprehension of Poaching and Smuggling Trawlers

Month & Year	Number of Trawlers	Action Taken	Location	By Naval Ship(s)
Apr 76	Two Taiwanese trawlers	Apprehended & escorted to Madras	Off Krishnapatnam	ANDAMAN
Aug 78	Two Taiwanese trawlers	Apprehended & escorted to Cochin	Off Cochin	UDAYGIRI & TRISHUL
Oct 78	Two Taiwanese trawlers	Apprehended	Off Sandheads	AMINI, TRISHUL & ARNALA
Oct 78	Five Taiwanese trawlers	Apprehended & escorted to Cochin	Three off Trivandrum & two off Muttam Point	ABHAY with KRISHNA, GAJ
Nov 78	One Thai trawler	Apprehended	Off Sandheads	SDB T 53
Apr 79	One Taiwanese trawler	Apprehended & escorted to Porbandar	Off Porbandar	BULSAR
Apr 79	One Foreign trawler	Apprehended & escorted to Porbandar	Off Veraval	BHATKAL
Apr 79	Two foreign trawlers	Apprehended & escorted to Porbandar	Off Mangrol	SDB T52
May 79	Two Taiwanese trawlers	Apprehended & escorted to Cochin	Off Cochin	KUTHAR
Jun 79	Two Taiwanese trawlers	Apprehended & escorted to Cochin	Off Cochin	KRISHNA
Jul 79	One Taiwanese trawler	Apprehended & escorted to Cochin	Off Cape Comorin	DARSHAK
Aug 79	Two Taiwanese trawlers	Apprehended	Off Cochin	KRISHNA

Aug 79	Two Taiwanese trawlers	Apprehended	Off Muttam Point	ABHAY
Oct 79	Two Taiwanese trawlers	Apprehended	Off Cochin	KRISHNA
Jul 80	Three Taiwanese trawlers	Apprehended	Two off Beypore one off Cape Comorin	BEAS
Jul 80	One Taiwanese trawler	Apprehended	Off Tuticorin	SHAKTI
Aug 80	Two Taiwanese trawlers	Apprehended	Off Beypore	BEAS
Sep 80	Four Taiwanese trawlers	Apprehended	Off Quilon	BEAS
Nov 80	Four Thai trawlers	Apprehended	Off Sandheads	KAVARATTI
Feb 81	One Taiwanese trawler	Apprehended	Off Okha	TALWAR
Mar 81	Two Thai trawlers	Apprehended and escorted to Port Blair	Off Mayabandar	UDAYGIRI
Nov 81	One Taiwanese trawler	Apprehended & escorted to Cochin	Wedge Bank	BRAHMAPUTRA
Nov 81	Seven Thai trawlers	Apprehended & escorted to Haldia	Off Sandheads	KILTAN, NILGIRI KESARI
Nov 82	One Thai trawler	Apprehended & escorted to Port Blair	Off Narcondum	Islander & SANDHAYAK
Mar 83	Three Taiwanese trawlers	Apprehended & escorted to Port Blair	2 off Narcondum 1 off Kamorta	LCU L-32 LCU L-34
Jul 84	Two foreign trawlers	Apprehended	Off Campbell Bay	Islander & CGS vessels
Oct 85	MV LUCKY III PANAMIAN	Apprehended. Ship loaded with electronics & unregistered goods. Escorted to Port Blair	Off Barren Island	LCU L-34
Jul 86	MV JAGLADAKI	Apprehended – suspected to be involved in smuggling activities. Handed over to Customs	Off Vizag	KESARI
Sep 86	One Bangladesh fishing boat	Apprehended & escorted to Sandheads & handed over to CGS vessel	Off New Moore Island	AMINI
Mar 90	Three foreign boats	Apprehended – involved in illegal activities & crocodile hunting	Jackson Creek Bumila Creek Sunderbans	SDBs T-53 & T-55

VVIP/VIP Transportation

Month & Year	VVIP/VIPs	From - To	Transit/Island Territories	By Naval ships & helicopters
Dec 76	Defence Minister	Goa to Bombay	Transit	VIKRANT
Dec 76	Prime Minister Indira Gandhi	Bombay to Minicoy-Kavaratti- Androth	Lakshadweep	VIKRANT
Jan 79	Prime Minister Morarji Desai	Cochin-Kavaratti-Cochin	Lakshwadweep	SHAKTI & DUNAGIRI helos
Feb 81	Prime Minister Indira Gandhi	Cochin-Kavaratti-Cochin	Lakshwadweep	DEEPAK, DUNAGIRI UDAYGIRI, Seakings
Jan 82	A&N Chief Secy, Chief Commiss- ioner & MLAs of A&N	Car Nicobar to Great Nicobar & back for relief operations after Great Nicobar earthquake	A & N	DEEPAK & Chetak helos

Feb 82	Chief of Air Staff	Car Nicobar to Kamorta and back	A & N	DEEPAK
Mar 82	Defence Minister Dy Defence Minister Cabinet Secretary Scientific Adviser & 3 MPs	Car Nicobar-Little Andaman- Car Nicobar	A & N	DUNAGIRI
Apr 82	GOCinC East FOCinC East	Car Nicobar-Campbell Bay-INS KARDIP-	A & N Car Nicobar	DUNAGIRI
Oct 82	Chief of Army Staff GOCinC South DMO	Cochin-Minicoy- Kavaratti-Agatti- Androth	Lakshadweep	SHAKTI
Dec 82	Defence Minister -Kavaratti-Agatti -Androth	Cochin-Minicoy	Lakshadweep	SHAKTI
Feb 85	President Zail Singh	Port Blair-Car Nicobar	A & N	VIKRANT
Apr 85	Vice President R Venkataraman	Bombay to Goa	Transit	VIKRANT
Nov 85	Prime Minister Rajiv Gandhi	Cochin to Lakshadweep	Lakshadweep	GODAVARI
1986	President Zail Singh	Cochin-Minicoy- Kavaratti-Cochin	Lakshadweep	Western Fleet
1986	Prime Minister Rajiv Gandhi	Cochin-Kavaratti- Bingaram-Cochin	Lakshadweep	Western Fleet
Dec 86	Prime Minister Rajiv Gandhi	Port Blair to Nicobar Islands and back	A & N	Eastern Fleet
Nov 87	Governor General of Mauritius	Port Louis to Rodriguez (Mauritius)	Transit	TIR
Dec 87	Prime Minister Rajiv Gandhi	Trivandrum-Kavaratti- Agatti-Bingaram-Minicoy	Lakshadweep	VIRAAT
Dec 87	Defence Minister VCNS, FOCinC SOUTH	Goa to Karwar to view Project Seabird from seaward	Transit	VINDHYAGIRI
Jan 88	Prime Minister Rajiv Gandhi	Helo lifted from Bingaram to Kadmat and embarked on board for passage to Mangalore	Transit	Western Fleet
Dec 89	President Venkataraman	Cochin-Minicoy- Kavaratti-Bingaram- Cochin	Lakshadweep	TARAGIRI

24

Goodwill Visits To Foreign Ports 1976-90

The regard that is given to every nation by other countries is to an extent dependent on the impression its armed forces make in the matter of strength, equipment, efficiency, courtesy and discipline. Without exception, the Navy's ships and their ships companies have, during goodwill cruises and goodwill visits enhanced the regard in which India is held.

Fleet Ships and Submarines				
Ships		**Ports Visited**	**Year**	**Remarks**
Abhay (Old) Abhay (New)		Colombo Varna, Athens, Port Said, Djibouti	Apr 1977 Mar/Apr 1989	Homeward after Commissioning
Agray		Varna, Athens, Port Said, Djibouti	Feb 1991	Homeward after Commissioning
Ajay		Varna, Izmir, Port Said, Djibouti	Feb 1990	Homeward after Commissioning
Akshay		Varna, Istanbul, Port Said	Jan 1991	Homeward after Commissioning
Alleppey	a) b)	Gdynia, Le Havre, Lisbon, Bizerte, Aden Male	Jul-Aug 1980 Dec 1990	Homeward after Commissioning
Amba	a) b) c) d) e)	Colombo, Male Trincomalee Singapore Hongkong, Danang, Penang Penang	Sep-Oct 1981 May 1982 May 1983 Nov 1985 Jan 1986	
Amini	a) b) c)	Singapore, Ho Chi Minh City, Bangkok Singapore Port Kelang	Apr-May 1982 May 1983 Oct 1988	
Andaman	a) b) c) d)	Abu Dhabi, Bahrain Singapore, Bangkok Sabang, Belawan Penang, Kuching, Muara, Belawan, Lumut	Dec 1977 May 1983 May 1984 Sep-Oct 1987	
Androth		Port Kelang	Jun 1986	
Anjadip	a) b) c)	Singapore Singapore, Kota Kinabalu Surabaya, Martia, Singapore, Port Kelang	Apr-May 1982 Apr 1985 Jun 1986	Operation Octopus
Arnala		Port Kelang, Penang	May 1984	

Notes

* Seychelles Independence Day 29 June 1976
* Mauritius Independence Day 12 March 1968

Bedi	a)	Gdynia, Le Havre, Bizerte, Port Said, Port Sudan, Aden	May-Jul 1979	Homeward after Commissioning
	b)	Male	Dec 1983	
	c)	Male	Oct 1989	
Bhavnagar		Gdynia, Le Havre, Bizerte, Port Sudan, Aden	May-Jul 1979	Homeward after Commissioning
Cannanore (Old)		Colombo	Jan 1979	
Cannanore (New)		Gdynia, Kiel, Le Havre, Lisbon, Malta, Alexandria Massawa	Jan-Feb 1988	Homeward after Commissioning
Chakra		Singapore, Penang	Jan 1988	Homeward after Commissioning
Cheetah	a)	Le Havre, Tunis, Alexandria, Port Said, Aden	Dec 1984-Jan 85	Homeward after Commissioning
	b)	Chittagong	May 1990	
Cuddalore		Gdynia, Kiel, Le-Havre, Lisbon, Bizerte, Alexandria, Port Said, Massawa	Nov 1987-Jan 88	Homeward After Commissioning
Darshak		Penang	Apr 1976	
Deepak	a)	Port Louis	Mar 1976	Mauritius Independence Day
	b)	Doha & Kuwait	Dec 1977	
	c)	Port Victoria, Dar-Es-Salaam, Mombasa	Jun 1978	
	d)	Montara (Malagasy)	Jun 1979	
	e)	Port Victoria	Jun 1981	Seychelles Independence Day
	f)	Port Victoria	Jun 1982	Seychelles Independence Day
	g)	Port Victoria, Dar-Es-Salam, Mombasa, Diego Suarez	Jun 1987	Seychelles Independence Day
	h)	Male	Nov-Dec 1988	Operation CACTUS
	j)	Male	Feb-Mar 1989	Operation CACTUS
Dunagiril	a)	Bandar Abbas, Basra,	Dec 1977	
	b)	Colombo, Male	Sep-Oct 1981	
	c)	Singapore, Ho Chi Minih City, Bangkok	Apr-May 1982	
	d)	Port Kelang, Penang	May 1984	
	e)	Singapore, Bangkok, Jakarta	Apr-May 1985	Operation Octopus
	f)	Kuching, Muara, Belawan, Lumut	Sep-Oct 1987	
	g)	Singapore, Penang	Nov 1987	
	h)	Singapore, Penang	Jan 1988	RV & Escort CHAKRA
Gaj	a)	Colombo	Oct 1976	
	b)	Aden	Mar 1977	To tow VIJAYDURG to Bombay
	c)	Aden	Aug 1977	To tow SINDHUDURG to Bombay
	d)	Port Sudan, Aden	Apr 1978	To tow PORBANDAR and PONDICHERRY
	e)	Aden	Jan 1989	To tow NIPAT to Bombay
	f)	Djibouti	Nov 1989	To tow NISHANK to Bombay
	g)	Jeddah	Jan 1990	To tow NIRGHAT to Bombay
Ganga	a)	Massawa, Port Sudan, Jeddah	Oct-Nov 1986	
	b)	Belawan, Manila, Tokyo, Hong Kong, Port Kelang	Jul-Sep 1987	For EXPO in Tokyo
	c)	Penang	May 1990	For Royal Malaysian Navy's International Fleet Review
Ghorpad	a)	Belawan	Mar 1977	
	b)	Sabang, Belawan	Mar 1978	
	c)	Penang	Feb 1979	
	d)	Port Kelang, Penang	May 1984	

Godavari	a)	Port Victoria, Mombasa	Nov 1985	
	b)	Djibouti, Suez (Egypt), Sevastopol (USSR) Algiers (Algeria), Ponta Delgada (Azores Island Portugal), Norfolk (USA), Alexandria (USA), New York, Havana (Cuba), Kingston (Jamaica), Port of Spain (Trinidad), Georgetown (Guyana), Recife (Brazil), Accra (Ghana), Lagos (Nigeria), Luanda (Angola), Mocamedes (Angola), Maputo (Mozambique), Port Victoria (Seychelles)	May-Sep 1986	To America to participate in the International Fleet Review on the occasion of the Bicentennial Celebration of the Statue of Liberty in New York(USA). on 14 July 1986
	c)	Surabaya, Freemantle, Melbourne, Sydney, Port Moresby, Darwin, Port Kelang, Male	Sep-Nov 1988	For International Naval Review Bicentennial Naval Celebration at Sydney.
Gomati		Mina Qaboos, Ashuwyakh, Doha	Nov 1989	
Guldar	a)	Helsingborg, Le Havre, Malaga (Spain), Alexandria, Port Said, Aden	Jan-Feb 1986	Homeward after Commissioning
	b)	Padang	Sep-Oct 1989	
Himgiri	a)	Aden, Port Said, Odessa (USSR), Split (Yugoslavia), Athens, Sili (Turkey), Alexandria, Aden	Sep-Oct 1976	Paschim cruise
	b)	Singapore, Ho Chi Minh City, Jakarta	Apr 1978	
	c)	Trincomalee	Jul 1981	
	d)	Colombo	Jul-Aug 1987	Operation PAWAN
	e)	Port Victoria	Jun 1988	Seychelles Independence Day
	f)	Trincomalee	Nov 1988	Operation PAWAN
	g)	Male	Nov-Dec 1988	Operation CACTUS
	h)	Penang, Surabaya, Padang	Sep-Oct 1989	Exercise Arjun
Hosdurg		Gdynia, Le Havre, Algiers, Benghazi, Aden	Feb-Mar 1978	Homeward after Commissioning
Kadmatt	a)	Colombo	Jan-Feb 1976	
	b)	Penang	Mar 1977	
	c)	Penang	Mar 1978	
	d)	Singapore	May 1983	
	e)	Penang, Kuching, Muara, Belawan, Lumut	Sep-Oct 1987	
	f)	Singapore, Penang	Jan 1988	RV & Escort CHAKRA
Kakinada	a)	Gdynia, Kiel, Le Havre, Algiers, Alexandria, Port Said, Massawa	Apr-Jun 1987	Homeward after Commissioning
	b)	Chittagong	May 1990	
Kalvari	a)	Vladivostok	Jan 1975-Jun 1976	Refit
	b)	Manila, Port Swettenham	Aug-Sep 1976	
	c)	Penang	Feb 1979	Homeward after Refit
	d)	Port Kelang, Penang	May 1984	
Kamorta	a)	Colombo	Jan-Feb 1976	
	b)	Singapore	Apr 1978	
	c)	Belawan, Penang	Apr 1985	Operation Octopus
Karanj	a)	Colombo	Jan-Feb 1976	
	b)	Penang	Mar 1977	
	c)	Port Swettenham, Hong Kong, Kobe	Dec 77-Jan 1978	To Russia for Refit
	d)	Penang, Vladivostok	Mar 78-Oct 1979	Refit
	e)	Penang	Nov 1979	Homeward after Refit
	f)	Abu Dhabi, Dubai, Port Qaboos (Oman)	Mar 1983	
	g)	Belawan, Penang	Apr 1985	Operation Octopus
	h)	Kuching, Muara, Belawan, Lumut	Sep-Oct 1987	
Karwar (Old)		Colombo	Jan 1979	

Karwar (New)	a)	Gdynia, Le Havre, Cagliari, Port Said, Massawa, Port Sudan	Aug-Sep 1986	Homeward after Commissioning
	b)	Chittagong	May 1990	
Katchall	a)	Port Kelang	Mar 1979	
	b)	Singapore, Bangkok, Jakarta	Apr-May 1985	Operation Octopus
	c)	Port Kelang, Martia, Surabaya	Jun 1986	
Kavaratti	a)	Singapore	Apr 1978	
	b)	Singapore	Feb-Mar 1980	
Kesari	a)	Belawan	Mar 1977	
	b	Sabang, Belawan	Mar 1978	
	c)	Penang	Feb 1979	
	d)	Trincomalee	Oct-Nov 1979	
	e)	Port Kelang, Penang, Sabang, Belawan	May 1984	
	f)	Belawan, Penang	Apr 1985	Operation Octopus
Khanderi	a)	Ho Chi Minh City, Bangkok	May 1982	
	b)	Singapore	May 1983	
	c)	Singapore, Port Kelang, Martia, Surabaya	Jun 1986	
Khukri	a)	Penang, Labuan	May 1990	For Royal Malaysian Navy International Fleet Review
	b)	Kuantan (Malaysia)	Jun 1990	
Kiltan	a)	Colombo	Jan-Feb 1976	
	b)	Penang	Mar 1977	
	c)	Penang	Mar 1978	
	d)	Port Kelang	Mar 1979	
Konkan	a)	Gdynia, Kiel, Le Havre, Malaga, Alexendria, Port Said, Massawa	Oct-Dec 1988	Homeward after Commissioning
Kozhikode	a)	Gdynia, Kiel, Le Havre, Malaga, Alexendria, Port Said, Djibouti	Jan 1989	Homeward after Commissioning
Kumbhir	a)	Lisbon, Naples, Alexandria, Port Said, Aden	Oct-Nov 1986	Homeward after Commissioning
	b)	Port Kelang, Ho Chi Minh City	Oct 1988	
Kursura		Colombo	Jan-Feb 1976	
Magdala		Male	Oct 1989	
Mahe		Male	Dec 1990	
Mahish	a)	Le Havre, Palermo, Alexandria, Port Said, Aden	Jul-Aug 1985	Homeward after Commissioning
	b)	Jakarta	Nov 1990	
Malpe		Male	Oct 1989	
Matanga		Djibouti	May 1987	To tow VEER to Bombay
Mulki		Male	Dec 1990	
Mysore	a)	Penang	Mar 1977	
	b)	Penang	Mar 1978	
Nilgiri	a)	Port Victoria, Mombasa,	Jun-Jul 1976	Seychelles Independence Day
	b)	Bahrain, Abu Dhabi	Dec 1977	
	c)	Port Kelang	Mar 1979	
	d)	Port Victoria	Jun 1980	Seychelles Independence Day
	e)	Berbera, Djibouti, Hodeidah,	Feb-Mar 1982	
	f)	Port Victoria, Diego Suarez, Moroni	Jun 1983	Seychelles Independence Day
	g)	Port Kelang, Satahip, Ho Chi Minh City	Oct 1988	
	h)	Male	Dec 1988	Operation CACTUS
	j)	Jakarta, Singapore	Oct-Nov 1990	

HOMEWARD PASSAGE OF SHIPS AND SUBMARINES
FROM EUROPE TO INDIA - 1976 to 1990

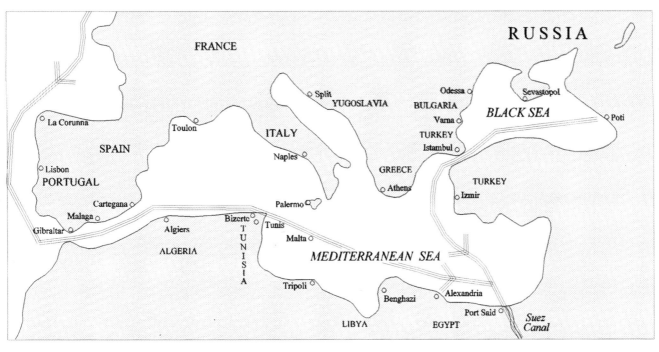

Nipat		Varna (Bulgaria), Athens, Port Said, Massawa, Aden	Dec 1988	Homeward after Commissioning
Nirbhik		Varna (Bulgaria), Athens, Port Said, Aden	Feb 1988	Homeward after Commissioning
Nirdeshak	a)	Port Louis	Jan 1985	
	b)	Port Kelang	Jun 1987	
Nirghat		Varna, Athens, Port Said, Jeddah	Dec 1989	Homeward after Commissioning
Nirupak	a)	Port Victoria	Jun 1988	Seychelles Independence Day
	b)	Male	Nov-Dec 1988	Operation CACTUS
Nishank		Varna, Athens, Port Said, Djibouti	Oct 1989	Homeward after Commissioning
Pondicherry	a)	Gdynia, Le Havre, Bizerte, Port Said, Port Sudan, Aden	Mar-May 1978	Homeward after Commissioning
	b)	Male	Sep 1985	
	c)	Male	Dec 1990	
Porbandar	a)	Gdynia, Le Havre, Bizerte, Port Said, Port Sudan, Aden	Mar-May 1978	Homeward after Commissioning
	b)	Male	Dec 1983	
	c)	Male	Sep 1985	
Rajput	a)	Athens, Aden	Sep 1980	Homeward after Commissioning
	b)	Aden, Jeddah	Feb 1982	
	c)	Abu Dhabi, Dubai, Port Qaboos	Mar 1983	
	d)	Port Victoria	Jun 1984	Seychelles Independence Day
	e)	Port Victoria	Jun 1985	Seychelles Independence Day
	f)	Penang, Surabaya, Padang	Sep-Oct 1989	Exercise Arjun
Rana	a)	Varna, Athens, Split, Aden	May-Jun 1982	Homeward after Commissioning
	b)	Port Victoria, Diego Suarez, Moronil	Jun 1983	Seychelles Independence Day
	c)	Port Victoria	Mar 1986	
	d)	Port Victoria, Dar-Es-Salaam, Mombasa, Diego Suarez	Jun 1987	Seychelles Independence Day
Ranjit	a)	Varna, Split, Alexandria, Aden	Nov-Dec 1983	Homeward after Commissioning
	b)	Massawa, Port Sudan, Jeddah	Oct-Nov 1986	
Ranvijay		Varna, Athens, Aden	Mar 1988	Homeward after Commissioning
Ranvir	a)	Varna, Athens, Port Said, Aden	Jul-Aug 1986	Homeward after Commissioning
	b)	Mina Salman, Mina Jebel Ali	Nov 1988	
Ratnagiri	a)	Gdynia, Le Havre, Lisbon, Bizerte, Port Said, Aden	Jul-Aug 1980	Homeward after Commissioning
Sandhayak	a)	Singapore, Bangkok	May 1983	
	b)	Singapore, Kota Kinabalu	Apr 1985	Operation Octopus
Shakti	a)	Port Victoria, Zanzibar	Jun-Jul 1976	Seychelles Independence Day
	b)	Hong Kong, Kobe, Vladivostok, Manila	Dec77-Feb 1978	Escorting KARANJ to Vladivostok
	c)	Port Victoria	Jun 1978	Seychelles Independence Day
	d)	Kelang	Mar 1979	
	e)	Port Victoria	Jun 1979	Seychelles Independence Day
	f)	Port Victoria	Jun 1980	Seychelles Independence Day
	g)	Aden, Jeddah	Feb 1982	
	h)	Massawa, Jeddah	Mar 1983	
	j)	Port Victoria, Diego Suarez, Moroni	Jun 1983	Seychelles Independence Day
	k)	Singapore, Bangkok, Jakarta	Apr-May 1985	Operation Octopus
	l)	Port Victoria	Jun 1985	Seychelles Independence Day
	m)	Port Victoria, Mombasa	Nov 1985	
	n)	Berbera, Port Sudan	Nov 1986	
	o)	Mina Salman, Mina Jebel Ali	Nov 1988	
	p)	Mina Qaboos, Ashshuwaykh, Doha	Nov 1989	

Shankush		Kiel, La Corunna, Tunis, Alexandria, Port Said, Djibouti	Dec 1986	Homeward after Commissioning
Sharabh	a)	Le Havre, Tunis, Alexandria, Aden	Feb-Apr 1976	Homeward after Commissioning
	b)	Singapore	Apr 1978	
	c)	Belawan, Penang	Apr 1985	Operation Octopus
Shardul	a)	Gdynia, Le Havre, Tunis, Alexandria, Aden	Jan 1976	Homeward after Commissioning
	b)	Singapore	Apr 1978	
	c)	Singapore	Feb-Mar 1980	
	d)	Singapore	Apr-May 1982	
	e)	Singapore, Bangkok	May 1983	
	f)	Port Kelang, Martia, Surabaya	Jun 1986	
Shishumar		Kiel, Le Havre, La Corunna, Algiers, Alexandria, Port Said, Djibouti	Dec 1986	Homeward after Commissioning
Sindhudurg		Gdynia, Le Havre, Bizerte	Aug-Sep 1977	Homeward after Commissioning
Sindhudhvaj		Kiel, Le Havre, Cartagena, Palermo, Port Said, Djibouti	Aug-Oct 1987	Homeward after Commissioning
Sindhughosh		Le Havre, Cartagena, Palermo, Port Said, Aden	Jul-Aug 1986	Homeward after Commissioning
Sindhukesari		Kiel, Cartagena, Naples, Port Said, Djibouti	Jan 1990	Homeward after Commissioning
Sindhukirti		Kiel, Le Havre, Malaga, Alexandria, Port Said, Djibouti	Dec 1989	Homeward after Commissioning
Sindhuraj		Kiel, Le Havre, Cartagena, Port Said, Djibouti	Dec 87-Jan 1988	Homeward after Commissioning
Sindhuratna		Cartagena, Naples, Port Said, Djibouti	Jan-Feb 1989	Homeward after Commissioning
Sindhuvir		Kiel, Le Havre, Cartegena, Port Said	Jul-Aug 1988	Homeward after Commissioning
Subhadra		Masan, Ho Chi Hi Minh City, Singapore	Feb 1990	Homeward after Commissioning
Sukanya	a)	Masan, Manila, Muara, Belawan	Sep 1989	Homeward after Commissioning
	b)	Djibouti	Feb 1990	To tow AJAY to Bombay
	c)	Mahe	Jun 1990	Seychelles Independence Day
Suvarna		Masan, Manila, Muara, Penang	Jun 1990	Homeward after Commissioning
T51,T52,T53		Colombo	Apr 1981	
Talwar	a)	Bandar Abbas, Basra		
	b)	Trincomalee	Jul 1981	
	c)	Berbera, Djibouti, Hodeidah	Feb-Mar 1982	
Taragiri	a)	Aden, Jeddah	Feb 1982	
	b)	Abu Dhabi, Dubai, Port Qaboos	Mar 1983	
	c)	Port Victoria, Mombasa, Dar-Es-Salaam	Nov 1985	
	d)	Port Victoria, Dar-Es Salaam, Mombasa, Diego Suarez	Jun 1987	Seychelles Independence Day
	e)	Male	Nov 1989	
Trishul	a)	Port Victoria, Mombasa	Jun-Jul 1976	Seychelles Independence Day
	b)	Port Victoria, Dar-Es Salaam, Mombasa	Jun 1978	Seychelles Independence Day
	c)	Port Victoria, Mombasa	Nov 1985	
	d)	Port Sudan, Berbera	Oct-Nov 1986	

Udaygiri	a)	Aden, Suez, Naples, Toulon, Lisbon, Gotesborg, Kiel, Portsmouth, London, Amsterdam, Liverpool, Algiers, Tripoli, Suez, Port Sudan	May-Aug 1977	To Britain to participate in the International Fleet Review on the occasion of the Silver Jubilee of the Queen of England's coronation. Seychelles Independence Day
	b)	Port Victoria, Dar-Es Salaam, Mombasa	Jun 1978	
	c)	Singapore	Feb-Mar 1980	
	d)	Port Kelang	Feb 1983	
	e	Port Kelang	May 1984	
	f)	Surabaya, Martia, Port Kelang	Jun 1986	
	g)	Penang, Kuching, Muara, Belawan, Lumut	Sep-Oct 1987	
	h)	Male	Jan 1989	
Vaghsheer	a)	Doha, Kuwait	Dec 1977	
	b)	Colombo	Oct 1978	
	c)	Singapore, Hong Kong, Kobe	Dec 82-Jan 1983	To Russia for Refit
	d)	Vladivostok	Feb 83-Sep 1985	Refit
	e)	Hong Kong, Danang, Penang	Nov 1985	Homeward after Refit
	f)	Port Victoria, Dar-Es Salaam, Mombasa, Diego Suarez	Jun 1987	Seychelles Independence Day
Vagir	a)	Colombo	Dec 1977	
	b)	Port Victoria	Nov 1985	
Vagli	a)	Penang, Hong Kong, Kobe,	Sep-Oct 1981	To Russia for Refit
	b)	Vladivostok	Nov 81-May 1984	Refit
	c)	Hong Kong, Singapore	Jun 1984	Homeward after Refit
	d)	Massawa, Berbera, Jeddah, Port Sudan	Oct-Nov 1986	
STS Varuna	a)	Colombo	Apr 1982	
	b)	Padang, Cilacap, Bali,	Oct 1987	To participate in Australian Bicentennial Celebrations
		Port Headland, Carnarvon, Geraldton, Lincoln, Melbourne, Sydney, Fremantle	Jan 1988	
Veer		Varna, Athens, Alexandria, Port Said	Apr-May 1987	Homeward after Commissioning
Vela	a)	Singapore, Manila, Kobe,	Jul-Aug 1980	To Russia for Refit
	b)	Vladivostok	Aug 80-Oct 1982	Refit
	c)	Danang, Port Kelang	Nov 1982	Homeward after Refit
Vijaydurg	a)	Gdynia, Le Havre, Bizerte, Port Sudan, Aden	Mar-Apr 1977	Homeward after Commissioning
Vindhyagiri	a)	Massawa, Jeddah, Port Louis	Mar 1983	
	b)	Port Victoria	Jun 1984	Seychelles Independence Day
	c)	Port Victoria	Jun 1986	Seychelles Independence Day
	d)	Port Victoria, Dar-Es-Salaam, Mombasa, Diego Suarez	Jun 1987	Seychelles Independence Day
	e)	Port Louis	Sep 1987	International Ocean Festival Mauritius
Viraat		Plymouth, Naples, Athens, Port Said	Jul-Aug 1987	Homeward after Commissioning

Training Ships				
Ship		**Ports Visited**	**Year**	**Remarks**
Betwa	a)	Singapore, Jakarta, Port Darwin, Suva (Fiji), Lautoka, Brisbane, Surabaya	May-Jul 1976	Spring Cruise
	b)	Port Victoria, Dar-Es-Salaam, Mombasa	Jun 1978	Seychelles Independence Day & Spring Cruise
	c)	Jakarta, Surabaya, Bangkok	Nov 1978	Autumn Cruise
	d)	Bangkok, Jakarta, Surabaya, Belawan	Oct-Nov 1979	Autumn Cruise
	e)	Male, Port Louis, Port Victoria	Apr 1980	Spring Cruise
	f)	Port Louis	Nov 1980	Autumn Cruise
	g)	Male	Oct 1982	Autumn Cruise
	h)	Port Louis, Colombo	Mar 1983	Spring Cruise
	i)	Port Kelang	Sep-Oct 1983	Autumn Cruise
	j)	Port Louis	Apr 1984	Spring Cruise
	k)	Singapore, Bangkok	Oct 1984	Autumn Cruise
	l)	Djibouti, Berbera, Port Qaboos	Apr-May 85	Spring Cruise
	m)	Diego Suarez, Port Louis, Moroni	Sep 1985	Autumn Cruise
	n)	Penang	Apr 1987	Spring Cruise
	o)	Male, Gan, Port Victoria, Port Louis, Rodrigues	Oct-Nov 1987	Autumn Cruise
Beas	a)	Port Victoria, Port Louis,	Apr 1978	Spring Cruise
	b)	Male, Port Louis, Port Victoria	Apr 1980	Spring Cruise
	c)	Port Louis	Nov-Dec 1980	Autumn Cruise
	d)	Benoa, Jakarta, Singapore	May 1981	Spring Cruise
	e)	Mombasa, Dar-Es-Salaam, Diego Suarez	Sep-Oct 1981	Autumn Cruise
	f)	Port Kelang	Apr 1982	Spring Cruise
	g)	Male	Oct 1982	Autumn Cruise
	h)	Colombo	Mar 1983	Spring Cruise
	j)	Port Kelang	Oct 1983	Autumn Cruise
	k)	Djibouti, Berbera, Port Qaboos	Apr-May 1985	Spring Cruise
	l)	Diego Suarez, Port Louis, Moroni	Sep 1985	Autumn Cruise
	m)	Port Victoria, Port Louis, Male	Sep-Oct 86	Autumn Cruise
	n)	Penang, Port Kelang	Apr 1987	Spring Cruise
	o)	Colombo, Male, Gan, Port Victoria Port Louis, Rodrigues	Oct-Nov 1987	Autumn Cruise
	p)	Djibouti	Apr 1989	To tow ABHAY to Bombay
	q)	Mombasa, Dar-Es-Salam, Port Louis	Oct-Nov 1989	Autumn Cruise
Brahmaputra	a)	Port Victoria, Port Louis	Apr 1978	Spring Cruise
	b)	Bangkok, Jakarta, Belawan	Oct-Nov 1979	Autumn Cruise
	c)	Benoa, Jakarta, Bali, Singapore	May 1981	Spring Cruise
	d)	Mombasa, Dar-Es-Salaam, Diego Suarez	Sep-Oct 1981	Autumn Cruise
	e)	Port Kelang	Apr 1982	Spring Cruise
	f)	Male	Oct 1982	Autumn Cruise
	g)	Massawa, Jeddah, Port Louis	Mar 1983	Mauritius Independence Day
	h)	Port Kelang	Sep-Oct 1983	Autumn Cruise
	j)	Port Louis	Apr 1984	Spring Cruise
	k)	Singapore, Bangkok	Oct 1984	Autumn Cruise
	l)	Port Louis, Djibouti, Berbera, Port Qaboos	Apr-May 1985	Spring Cruise
	m	Diego Suarez, Port Louis, Moroni (Comoros)	Sep 1985	Autumn Cruise
Cauvery		Colombo	Mar 1977	Spring cruise
Delhi	a)	Port Louis, Male	Mar 1976	Mauritius Independence Day
	b)	Colombo	Mar 1977	Spring Cruise

Kistna	a)	Male	May 1977	Spring Cruise
	b)	Colombo	Apr 1978	Spring Cruise
	c)	Colombo	Oct 1978	Autumn Cruise
	d)	Colombo	May 1980	Spring Cruise
Tir (Old)	a)	Port Louis, Male	Mar-Apr 1976	Spring Cruise
	b)	Singapore	Mar 1977	Spring Cruise
Tir (New)	a)	Port Victoria, Port Louis, Male	Sep-Oct 1986	Autumn Cruise
	b)	Penang	Apr 1987	Spring Cruise
	c)	Male, Gan, Port Victoria Port Louis, Rodrigues	Oct-Nov 1987	Autumn Cruise
	d)	Surabaya, Jakarta	May 1988	Spring Cruise
	e)	Port Kelang, Port Louis, Diego Suarez, Mogadishu, Male	Oct-Nov 1988	Autumn Cruise
	f)	Male, Port Victoria	Apr-Jun 1989	Spring Cruise
	g)	Mombasa, Dar-Es-Salaam, Port Louis	Oct-Nov 1989	Autumn Cruise
	h)	Fremantle	May 1990	Spring Cruise

25

The Navy's Participation In The Expeditions To Antarctica

The Continent of Antarctica

The continent of Antarctica comprises one tenth of the earth's land surface. The Antarctic seas comprise one tenth of the world's oceans. It is estimated that Antarctica's six million cubic miles of ice amount to 70% of the world's fresh water and more than 90% of the world's ice.

Antarctica is a desolate isolated plateau, the coldest and windiest blizzard affected region of the earth. It has 14 million square metres of ice-covered land (approximately 5 million square miles), with an average altitude of 8,000 feet. The lowest temperatures in the Antarctic winter are around –50 degrees Celsius in August and the highest temperatures in the Antarctic summer are around +5 degrees Celsius in January. It is the only continent with no inhabitants apart from animals like penguins. However, life has existed there from time immemorial in the form of the most primitive living beings, the microbes.

The Antarctic ice sheet is considered to be one of the important driving forces behind global atmospheric circulation. It is also a reference point for environmental and pollution studies because of its remoteness and the climatic conditions which restrict human activities.

The Antarctic Ocean is considered the most productive ocean in the world in terms of chlorophyll and organic compounds in the water that are of primary importance to maintain chemical and biological processes in the world's oceans. Millions of tonnes of 'krill'[1] (a valuable marine food product) can be harvested out of the ocean to combat protein deficiency in developing countries. There is an embargo on commercial exploitation of minerals from Antarctica till the year 2040.

Antarctic Research

The first recorded contacts with Antarctica date from the 1780s. Serious investigations of the continent began after the sixth International Geophysical Congress in 1895, which urged the promotion of Antarctic Research. Within 20 years, the South Pole had been reached and scientists began to explore the interior of the continent. At the conclusion of the International Geophysical Year (1957-58), the 12 nations that had participated in Antarctic work formally recognised the cooperative spirit of the venture by drafting the Antarctic Treaty in 1959. They agreed that "Antarctica shall be used for peaceful purposes only" and "banned any measure of a military nature".

India launched its first Antarctic Expedition in December 1981.[2] In August 1983, India was admitted to Consultative Status in the Antarctic Treaty system. A year later, in 1984, India was admitted to the Scientific Committee on Antarctic Research. Two years later, in 1986, India became a party to the Convention on the Conservation of Antarctic Marine Living Resources.

The broad objectives of India's Antarctic Research Programme have been to foster and promote scientific studies in atmospheric sciences, geology, geophysics, meteorology, biology, oceanography, geomagnetism and study of the ozone hole.

Specifically, Indian Antarctic Research covers the following long-term scientific programmes/activities:

- Ice-ocean atmosphere system in Antarctica and global environment.
- Antarctic lithosphere and Gondwanaland reconstruction, framework for delineating plate tectonic processes and assessment of mineral resources and hydrocarbons. The

---

1. 'Krill' is a Norwegian whaling term for small fish, which is the basic food of whales. It is estimated that Antarctica has a billion tons of krill, of which 50 million tons can be harvested annually without endangering the stock.

2. The first Indian to set foot on Antarctica was Lt Ram Charan, a Met Officer of the Indian Navy, who accompanied the 1960 Australian South Pole Expedition.

Global Positioning System (GPS) in Maitree has helped scientists to postulate that the Indian tectonic plate is moving annually 5 cms northward and northeastward.

- Antarctic ecosystems and environmental physiology.
- Solar terrestrial processes.
- Innovative technologies for support systems.
- Environmental impact assessment.
- Generation and structuring of databases (geological, topographic, thematic mapping and ecosystems changes, environmental parameters and health care.)

In addition to regular annual expeditions, India launched an expedition to the Weddell Sea in 1989 and an expedition for krill in 1995.

The Department of Ocean Development under the Ministry of Science and Technology plans India's Antarctica expeditions. Organisations participating in these expeditions include the Geological Survey of India, National Geographical Research Institute, India Meteorological Department, National Institute of Oceanography, Physical Research Laboratory, National Physical Laboratory, Indian Institute of Geomagnetism, National Remote Sensing Agency, Defence Research and Development Organisation, Oil and Natural Gas Commission, Indian Institutes of Technology, the Indian Navy, Army and Air Force and the Department of Ocean Development.

From 1992-93 onwards, an 'Antarctic Research Centre' has been functioning in Goa.

The other countries maintaining a presence in Antarctica are the USA, Russia, Britain, Australia, Japan, Germany, South Africa and China.

The Navy's Involvement in Antarctic Expeditions

The Navy's involvement commenced with the first expedition in 1981-82 and continued till 1994-95. During each expedition, the naval contingent comprised:

- A helicopter detachment of two Chetaks; the Navy's pilots were experienced in operating helicopters from ships and over the sea. Since Antarctica has no roads, most movements of personnel and stores between the ship and the camps have to be done by helicopter.
- Communication personnel to provide round the clock communication with India, during the expedition and for the 'wintering' team who stay behind in Antarctica during the Antarctic winter from March (when the research ship leaves for India) till December (when the research ship returns with the next expedition).
- Meteorological personnel for weather prediction, for briefing pilots on weather conditions and for research.
- Naval cooks, both for the voyage to and from Antarctica and for the wintering team.

In the initial years, the Navy also provided a medical team to deal with medical emergencies.

India's Antarctica Expeditions

The width of the ice belt around Antarctica ranges from 600 km to 3,000 km. Melting of the ice starts in November; rapid melting commences in December and continues till March. Freezing of the sea commences in end March and the area covered by pack ice increases, until by October it is more than double the area of Antarctica. It is during the period November to March each year that specially designed ships can reach the Antarctic coast. The mobility of the pack ice, under the pressure of the ships momentum, allows ships to penetrate it.

The expeditions were conveyed by 'special expedition vessels of the highest ice class' under the system of uniform time charter. An expedition vessel has a double skin, 25-tonne cranes, extremely large bunker capacity, a bow thruster, a heated hull, modern communication systems, a helicopter deck, air conditioned accommodation for 100 expedition members and box-shaped holds that are used as hangars or for cargo.

The stores carried by each expedition include fuel, food (from India's Food Technology Research Institute, Defence Food Research Laboratory, MAFCO and Modern Food Industries), construction material, spares for vehicles, clothing, camping equipment, hydrogen gas cylinders, medical supplies, LPG cylinders, scientific equipment, communication equipment, etc.

The expedition vessel departs from Goa in end November/ early December. After a few hours halt in Mauritius to stock up provisions, it reaches Antarctica in end December. It starts on the return journey in early March, spends a day in Mauritius and arrives at Goa in end March / early April.[3]

Of the 70 to 75 days that each expedition can stay in Antarctica, over half is afflicted by storms, blizzards and very strong winds. The effective working season is only 30 to 40 days. The pace of activity perforce has to be hectic.

After arrival at the pack ice, facsimile charts and route reconnaissance flights by helicopters help to navigate the ship through the pack ice (which is formed from the freezing of the sea surface) until the vessel reaches the 'fast ice' where

---

3. From the 20th (2000/01) Expedition onwards, expeditions departed from Cape Town in South Africa, instead of from Goa because it reduced the journey time to Antarctica from 25 days to 9 days.

INDIAN ANTARCTIC STATIONS

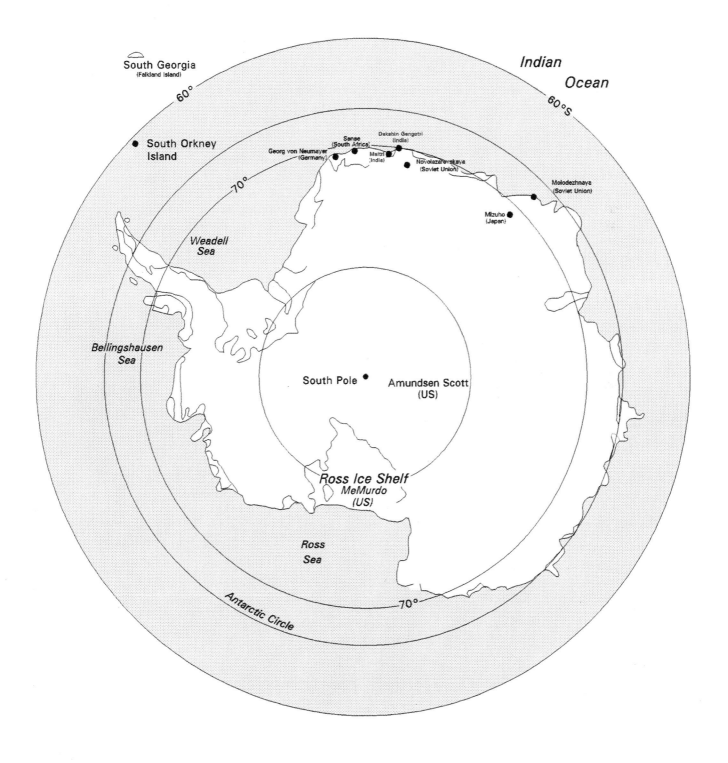

it berths alongside the approximately 9-metre high Antarctic ice shelf near Latitude 70° South and Longitude 12° East. Immediately after arrival, helicopters start ferrying personnel and stores to the camps in the interior.

Helicopters are used also for ferrying personnel and stores to the scientific teams in the various camps, for aerial and photo reconnaissance, for casualty evacuation and for medical support, for landing on icebergs and for assisting the teams operating in hilly, rough and icy terrain.

The 1st expedition started from Goa in December 1981. It set up a base camp near the ice shelf and carried out air surveys for a suitable site for constructing a permanent research station (later called Dakshin Gangotri) where a small team could spend the winter. The 2nd expedition ferried the materials and stores required to construct Dakshin Gangotri. The 3rd expedition commissioned Dakshin Gangotri. From the 3rd expedition onwards, the Navy established and maintained permanent wireless communication with New Delhi. The 8th expedition of 1988-89 commissioned India's second permanent station "Maitree" in an ice-free area.

There were other Antarctic Research Stations in the area where India set up its camps:

- *Soviet Union:* The Novolazerskaya camp was the nearest, 10 km from Dakshin Gangotri. Its runway, which could land Russian IL 14 aircraft, was 6 km away from Dakshin Gangotri.
- *East Germany:* Georg Forster camp was sited on the periphery of Novolazerskaya.
- *West Germany:* George von Neumayer camp.
- *Britain:* Halley camp.
- *South Africa:* SANE camp.

Chronology of Expeditions till 1990

Gist of Expedition Objectives and Naval Participation

- **First Expedition – 1981-82.** The 21-member expedition had a Naval contingent of 5 officers and 3 sailors.

    The objectives were to select a site on the ice shelf for a permanent station, which would in due course be called Dakshin Gangotri, establish an unmanned weather station, record geomagnetic intensity and measure magnetic storms.

    The Navy provided a detachment of two Chetak helicopters (specially modified for ice operations), a medical team and naval cooks. The helicopters recce'd a site for Dakshin Gangotri on a rock outcrop on the ice shelf, 100 kms inland in a flat area proximate to a fresh water lake.

The expedition landed in Antarctica in January 1982 and built a "refuge hut" at a rudimentary "base camp" on the ice shelf close to the ship not far from the Soviet station at Novolazerskaya.

- **Second Expedition – 1982-83.** The 28-member expedition had a Naval contingent of 6 officers and 3 sailors.

    The objectives were for the Army to assemble two huts at a permanent base camp and start setting up the equipment at the Dakshin Gangotri site.

    An ice runway was set up 5 miles from the base camp for helicopter operations. Close relations were established with the Soviet and East German camps.

    The Navy provided the same teams as in the 1st expedition.

    Problems were experienced in establishing communications between the base camp and the Dakshin Gangotri site and with New Delhi – the latter had to be maintained via the ship with the Navy at Bombay. The Russians at Novolazerskaya advised that a highly directional rhombic antenna would overcome the problems affecting communications with India.

    The Air Force sent a Wing Commander (fixed wing) and two Squadron Leaders (one rotary wing and one physician) to assess the extent to which the Air Force could assist the activity in Antarctica and to recce a site for a runway. On 18 February 1983, an Argentine Air Force C 130 aircraft, captained by the Argentine Air Force, and having a crew from the Indian Air Force, flew over the Indian base camp and para-dropped eight boxes containing provisions and newspapers brought from India. After circling the camp for 15 minutes, the aircraft flew back to Argentina.

    The expedition set up an automatic weather station and carried out land survey, mineralogy and petrography surveys and ozone layer observations.

- **Third Expedition – 1983-84.** The 82-member expedition had a naval contingent of 8 officers and 5 sailors.

    The objectives were to complete construction of the permanent station and leave behind the First Wintering Team of 12. The Navy provided similar teams as in the 1st and 2nd expeditions.

    The Air Force sent two MI 8 helicopters, of which one, unfortunately, crashed but whose crew was rescued by a Naval Chetak helicopter.

    On 13 January 1984, the first permanent station "Dakshin Gangotri" was established on the ice shelf in position 70° South, 12 ° East. A communication link was established with Naval Headquarters in New Delhi.

The First Wintering Team included naval cooks.

- **Fourth Expedition – 1984-85.** The 85-member expedition had a naval contingent comprising 9 officers and 8 sailors.

In addition to research activities, reconnaissance commenced for a second ice-free permanent station on firmer rocky ground and Maitree was identified as a possible site.

Since the efforts made by other agencies, including the Army, to establish a communication link had not succeeded during earlier expeditions, the Department of Ocean Development had requested the Navy to establish the HF communication link with New Delhi. The Navy established permanent round the clock communications with New Delhi on 18 January 1985. These have sustained thereafter without a break.

From the Second Wintering Team onwards, the Navy sent a communication team every year to man this HF link and the entire radio communication network in Antarctica, which included helicopters, ships, vehicles and mobile parties and also the mobile communication equipment for the reconnaissance mission to the South Pole.

- **Fifth Expedition – 1985-86.** The 88-member expedition had a naval contingent of 7 officers and 11 sailors.

Air Force helicopters conjoined for the first time with Naval helicopters. A series of incidents afflicted the operation of the Air Force MI 12 helicopters.

Scientific activities were extended into the interior areas of Antarctica. The expedition was tasked to probe aspects of the first Indian expedition to the South Pole.

Repair and maintenance was carried out of the permanent structures of Dakshin Gangotri.

- **Sixth Expedition – 1986-87.** The 90-member expedition had a naval contingent of 7 officers and 11 sailors.

Its scientific objectives were to study geology, geo-physics, meteorology, the upper atmosphere, geomagnetism and non-conventional sources of energy.

- **Seventh Expedition – 1987-88.** The 92-member delegation had a naval contingent of 6 officers and 12 sailors. Prefabricated structures and materials were brought from India for the construction of the second permanent station at Maitree.

The naval tasks were helicopter operations, maintaining uninterrupted communications with India, with the ship and between the station and the various camps, collection of meteorological and oceanographic research data and provision of domestic services.

The two naval Chetak helicopters were modified to carry under-slung Magnetic Anomaly Detection equipment to conduct aeromagnetic surveys.

- **Eighth Expedition – 1988-89.** The 100-member expedition had a naval contingent of 19 persons for the same tasks as the previous year. The expedition had two naval Chetak helicopters and three Army MI 8 helicopters.

Prefabricated structures and materials had continued to be brought from India for the construction of Maitree. Naval helicopters made a notable contribution through "under-slung operations" for the expeditious airlift of heavy machinery like boilers, generators, motors and the satellite communication dome from the ship to Maitree 100 kms away. Equipment for the water supply system was lowered from helicopters directly into the fresh water lake near Maitree.

A 5-member communication team shifted to Maitree, all the new communication equipment from the ship and the old equipment from Dakshin Gangotri and established communications with Delhi on 13 February 1989.

On 25 February 1989, the second, indigenously designed, pre-fabricated, permanent land station "MAITREE" was established at an altitude of 117 metres in the 7-km long and 2-km wide valley of the Schumacher Ranges, 70 kms from Dakshin Gangotri, at Latitude 70°46' South, Longitude 11°45' East.

Naval aircrews provided ferry flight facilities to the GSI and NGRI teams collecting rock samples from the Wolthat and Peterman mountain ranges.

Seven naval personnel were left behind to man Maitree and Dakshin Gangotri as the Sixth Wintering Team.

- **Ninth Expedition – 1989-90.** The final transfer of stores from Dakshin Gangotri to Maitree was completed by end January. On 25 February 1990, Dakshin Gangotri was decommissioned as a permanent base and converted into a supply base.

In January 1990, The India Meteorological Department discontinued meteorological observations from Dakshin Gangotri and established a full-fledged Meteorological Observatory at Maitree to study ozone depletion in the Antarctic spring and solar radiation.

The First Weddell Sea Expedition surveyed the area east of Berkner Island for a future station.

The hazards of operating single-engine Chetak helicopters in Antarctica's sub-zero conditions for exploratory missions that were increasingly distant from the base camp led to the decision that only twin-engine helicopters should be sent on future expeditions.

26

Naval Hydrography And Marine Cartography

Overview

The British East India Company first established the Marine Survey of India in 1770 to carry out its hydrographic surveys. Over a century later, in 1874, the British Government of India created the Marine Survey Department at Calcutta under a Surveyor-in-Charge. Seven years after Independence in 1947, this department shifted to Dehra Dun in 1954. In 1964, it was renamed as the Naval Hydrographic Office. In 1997, it was renamed as the National Hydrographic Office in keeping with the national responsibilities entrusted to it.

INS Investigator was the sole survey ship in 1947. By the mid 1970s, approval had been obtained for new survey ships and modern survey equipment began to enter service. Today the survey flotilla comprises eight ships, of which five have entered service after 1990.

Surveys were carried out of both coasts and of the island territories. Special surveys were undertaken for the new Naval Dockyard coming up in Vishakhapatnam, for underwater degaussing ranges and for submarine exercise areas. Survey ships were also employed for defence oceanographic surveys and marine resource surveys with the Naval Physical and Oceanographic Laboratory (NPOL), the National Institute of Oceanography (NIO) and the National Geographic Research Institute (NGRI).

In the early days, the originals of charts used to be engraved on copper plates. Later, charts were hand drawn in the Hydrographic Office. By the mid 1970s, the chart production facilities had been modernised. Today, charts are generated on computers and paper charts have been supplemented by paperless Electronic Navigation Charts for use with the latest Electronic Chart Display Information System (ECDIS).

To remedy the paucity of officers volunteering for the Hydrographic cadre, direct recruitment of Survey Officers had to be resorted to. Despite the upward revision in monetary allowances to compensate for the difficult nature of survey duties, personnel shortages persisted.

Hydrographic training started in Bombay in 1959. The school shifted first to Cochin in 1961 and later to its present location in Goa in 1978. Substantial UNDP assistance and the excellence of its training helped to make it the Regional Hydrographic Training Centre for uniformed and civilian personnel from Southeast Asia, South Asia, West Asia and Africa.

Developments Until 1975

When the Navy was partitioned at the time of Independence in 1947, the *Investigator*, was the only survey ship with the Indian Navy. Its very first tasks were to survey the approaches to the naval berths at Bombay and Cochin.

In those early years, because of the disruptive effect of the monsoon months, sea surveys were done in the 'survey season' between November and April. The 'drawing season' from May to September was spent in converting the surveys into drawings in the Drawing Office at Conoor in the Nilgiri Hills of South India. Until 1953, the results of the surveys used to be forwarded to Britain's Hydrographic Office for publication. The charts received from Britain were issued to ships from the Chart Depot located in the Naval Dockyard Bombay.

On 1 June 1954, a new Hydrographic Office was established at Dehra Dun in north India, proximate to the office of the Surveyor General of India; it started producing new charts, issuing Notices to Mariners[1] and publishing Sailing Directions, the Indian List of Lights, etc.

On 1 April 1956, India became a member of the International Hydrographic Bureau in Monaco.

By the mid 1960s, some progress had been made in charting Indian waters and streamlining the Navy's Hydrographic Department. In 1965, the survey flotilla comprised four ships[2] three converted from old frigates and

---

1. The first Indian Notice to Mariners was issued in 1958.

2. In 1949, Investigator was joined by the converted minesweeper, INS Rohilkhand, and two Seaward Defence Motor Launches (SDMLs 3110 and 3111). As the latter three decommissioned, *Investigator* was joined by *Sutlej* in 1953, *Jumna* in 1956 and *Darshak* in 1964.

INDIA'S EXCLUSIVE ECONOMIC ZONE

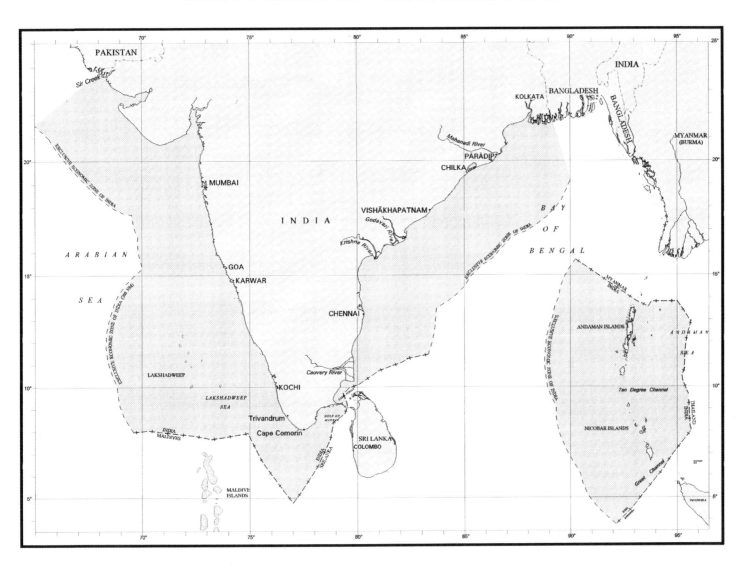

Exclusive Economic Zone Boundary

Maritime Boundary

Exclusive Economic Zone (200 NM)

one new indigenously constructed ship, *Darshak*, designed specifically for survey work. Steps had been initiated to overcome the shortage of survey officers, survey recorder sailors and civilian surveyors and hydrographic assistants but availability remained short of the requirements.

Surveys had been carried out in the approaches to ports on the east and west coasts, in the Gulfs of Kutch and Cambay, Bombay Harbour, the Mahanadi River entrance and the offshore island territories in the Andaman, Nicobar and Lakshadweep Islands. In 1964, the Chief Hydrographer was re-designated as the Chief Hydrographer to the Government of India.

The intake of officers into the Hydrographic Cadre used to be from General Service volunteers. Since surveying duties were arduous, far too many officers reverted to General Service after a short stint of surveying. From 1965 onwards, officers started being directly recruited for the Survey Cadre.

In 1971, the International Hydrographic Bureau (IHB) assigned to the Naval Hydrographic Office the responsibility of preparing nine bathymetric plotting sheets, based on source material received from data centres the world over. These were incorporated in the General Bathymetric Chart of the Oceans (GEBCO).

After the 1971 war, to assist the restoration of shipping traffic, surveys had been carried out of the entrances to the riverine ports of Bangladesh. Normal surveys continued on both coasts and in the island territories.

The Environment Data Unit was established at the Hydrographic Office in 1974. During 1975, this unit processed, analysed and interpreted the data received from:

- *Darshak's* Oceanographic Expedition of 1973-74.
- The USA's National Oceanographic Data Centre.
- The International Indian Ocean Expedition.

In 1975, the Naval Hydrographic Office was nominated by the Government of India as the National Centre for archiving and dissemination of Bathythermograph (BT) Data. BT data collected by all vessels of national agencies was required to be forwarded to the Hydrographic Office.

The fledgling Hydrographic School that had been started in Mumbai in 1959 shifted to Cochin in 1961 to overcome constraints of space. In 1965, approval was obtained for establishing a permanent school in Cochin. Cochin was not an ideal location and at one stage, it was decided that the school should be located in Vishakhapatnam. Eventually, in 1975, sanction was accorded to establish the permanent Hydrographic School in Goa. The School shifted from Cochin to Goa in 1978.

By the mid 1970s, approval had been accorded for three new survey vessels and four survey craft. Modern survey equipment had begun to enter service. The chart production facilities of the Naval Hydrographic Office had been modernised. Despite the upward revision in monetary allowances, personnel shortages persisted.

Developments 1976 to 1990

The 1982 UN Convention on the Law of the Sea

The deliberations of the Third Conference on the Law of the Sea spread over nine years. The Conference adopted the Convention on 30 April 1982. However, it formally came into effect twelve years later on 16 November 1994, only after all the countries had ratified it.

The essential features of the convention were:

- Twelve miles as the uniform width of territorial waters.
- An Exclusive Economic Zone (EEZ) of two hundred (200) miles within which the coastal state exercised sovereign rights and jurisdiction for specified economic activities. (India's EEZ of two million square kilometres is the twelfth largest in the world.)
- A continental shelf extending to the outer edge of the continental margin with reference either to three hundred and fifty (350) nautical miles from the baselines of territorial waters or to one hundred (100) nautical miles from the 2,500 metre isobath.
- Regimes for the abatement and control of marine pollution, for marine scientific research and for unimpeded transit passage through straits used for international navigation.

Passage of Foreign Warships Through Territorial Waters

From the naval point of view, the main issue left undecided was that of the passage of foreign warships through territorial waters. In 1958, India had proposed that the passage of foreign warships through the territorial sea of a coastal state should be subject to prior authorisation by, and notification to, the coastal state. This proposal was not accepted and therefore, not incorporated in the 1958 General Convention on the Territorial Sea and Contiguous Zone.

In protest, India declined to ratify any of the Geneva conventions. By 1973, India's stand mellowed. The requirement for prior authorisation was watered down to prior notification for the innocent passage of foreign warships through territorial waters.

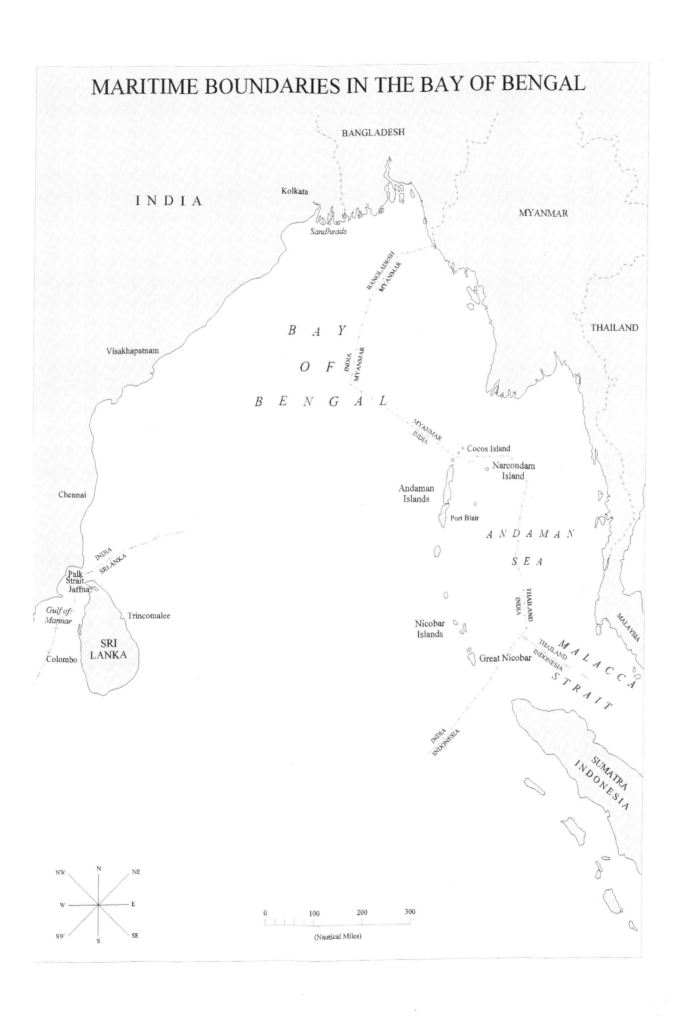

MARITIME BOUNDARIES IN THE BAY OF BENGAL

In the 1970s, the Cold War between the USA and the Soviet Union was at its peak. Both these super powers vehemently opposed every proposal that might jeopardise the secrecy of their warships' movements. There is, therefore, no provision in the 1982 Convention that requires foreign Navies to notify, in advance, the passage of their warships and submarines through the territorial waters of a coastal state. The operational implications of this problem have had to be dealt with in each Navy's 'Rules of Engagement'.

Meanwhile, between 1974 and 1977, India's neighbouring coastal nations – Pakistan, Bangladesh, Sri Lanka and Myanmar enacted maritime legislation requiring prior authorisation and notification for the passage of foreign warships through their respective territorial seas. India's Maritime Zones Act of 1976 required only prior notification (but not prior authorisation). It did, however, require submarines and other underwater vehicles to navigate on the surface and show their flag while passing through Indian territorial waters.

After the 1982 Convention, the Governments of the United States, Britain and West Germany lodged diplomatic protests, the gist of which was that two provisions of India's Maritime Act 1976 were against established International Law and not covered by the Law of the Seas, namely:

- Requirement of 'Prior Notification' by foreign war vessels, before passage through India's territorial waters.

- India's right to declare certain areas in the continental shelf and EEZ as 'Security Areas'.

To date, India has adhered to its stand.

Surveys of National Importance

The Deep Water Route in the Gulf of Kutch to the Salaya Oil Terminal

In 1974, surveys had commenced for a deep water channel to the off-shore oil terminal at Salaya for use by the 270,000 tonne Very Large Crude-oil Carriers (VLCCs) that brought crude oil from the Persian Gulf to the refineries in Gujarat. The channel was declared open in 1978.

Maritime Boundary Agreements

Maritime boundaries are based on charts prepared after detailed hydrographic surveys. After technical discussions and mutual consent on the boundary between the countries concerned, these charts are annexed to each Maritime Boundary Agreement.

The 1982 Conference was unable to reconcile the opposing viewpoints of whether the criteria for delimiting the boundaries of the EEZ and continental shelf between 'adjacent' and 'opposite' states should be based on 'equitable principles' or based on the 'equidistance' line.

Despite the ambiguity inherent in the word 'equitable', India concluded maritime boundary agreements with the five 'opposite' states:

- India and Sri Lanka signed their agreement on maritime boundaries in the Gulf of Mannar and the Bay of Bengal on 23 March 1976 and another agreement on 22 November 1976 extending their maritime boundaries in the Gulf of Mannar up to the tri-junction of India, Sri Lanka and Maldives.

- India and Maldives signed their maritime boundary agreement on 28 December 1976.

- India and Indonesia signed their agreement on maritime boundary in 1974 and another agreement in 1977 extending the boundary up to the tri-junction point with Thailand.

- India and Thailand signed their boundary agreement in 1977.

- India and Myanmar signed their boundary agreements in 1982 and 1984.

In these agreements, the 'equidistance' principle was used and minor modifications were negotiated amicably to meet the needs of equity or for other special reasons.

India has yet to delineate its maritime boundaries with Pakistan and Bangladesh. The reference in the 1982 UN Convention to 'equitable principles' appears likely to prolong settlement of maritime boundaries with these two 'adjacent' states.

The Naval Hydrographic School, Goa

The Hydrographic School moved from Cochin to Goa in 1978. Courses for Direct Entry officers and sailors and for Civilian Field Assistants, including some from foreign countries, continued to be conducted using facilities borrowed from other naval units at Cochin.

The new Hydrographic School was constructed within *INS Gomantak* and commissioned in three phases between 1978 and 1989 – Wing I in 1977, Wing II in 1983 and Wing III in 1989.

In 1980, the School received a UNDP grant of $ 3.5 million to acquire the modern survey training equipment that would equip it to become a Regional Training Centre. In 1982, the School received Category A certification from the International Hydrographic Organisation (IHO) for the conduct of the Long Hydrographic course, making it the third institution in the world to get this recognition (the other two being the Royal Naval Hydrographic School in Britain and the Ecole National Superiere des Ingenieurs des Etudes et Techniques d'Armament (ENSIETA) of the Service Hydrographique et Oceanographique de la Marine in France).

In 1984, the School was designated as the Regional Hydrographic Training Centre for South East Asia and African countries.

Hydrographic Surveys for Continental Shelf Claims

The 1982 United Nations Convention on the Law of the Sea (UNCLOS 82) had adopted:

- A 200 mile Exclusive Economic Zone (EEZ) within which every coastal state could exercise sovereign rights and jurisdiction for certain specified economic activities.

- A continental shelf extending to the outer edge of the continental margin, to be delimited with reference to either 350 nautical miles from the base line of territorial waters or 100 miles from the 2,500 metre isobath.

The latter clause entitled coastal states to claim a continental shelf over and above the 200 mile EEZ. Claims were to be submitted to the United Nations within ten years. This time limit has been extended from time to time (from 1994 to 1999 and presently to May 2009) to enable the coastal states to carry out the extensive surveys on which their claims could be assessed.

To substantiate claims, two types of surveys had to be carried out:

- Bathymetric surveys, which depicted the topography of the seabed.

  (The Navy's survey ships completed these surveys in 2001).

- Seismic surveys, which mapped the sedimentary thickness below the seabed to delineate the continental shelf. (These surveys, undertaken by the Department of Ocean Development, are still in progress).

To undertake these extensive surveys of the continental shelf, new naval survey ships were sanctioned to replace the ageing survey ships.[3]

The Survey Flotilla

Between 1976 and 1990, four new survey ships were commissioned of the six sanctioned. To the extent possible, every successive ship of the Sandhayak class was equipped with the latest available equipment and facilities for hydrographic work; the old survey ships were retrofitted with the same survey equipment that was being fitted in the new survey ships under construction. The older survey ships, *Sutlej*, *Jamuna* and *Darshak* continued on survey duties until they decommissioned.

Construction was also completed of four 185-tonne survey craft. These were to work in coastal waters in conjunction with survey ships and also independently carry out surveys of ports, harbours and their approaches. The hull design of these survey craft could not provide the stability required for survey work, except when the weather was calm. Despite the limitations of their craft, the perseverance of their young crews often succeeded in their completing offshore surveys, which were the task of the larger, more stable survey ships.

New Survey Ships and Craft	Commissioned on	Class	Shipbuilder
Sandhayak	26 Feb 1981	Sandhayak Class	Garden Reach
Nirdeshak	04 Oct 1983	Sandhayak Class	Garden each
Makar	31 Jan 1984	Survey Craft	Goa Shipyard
Mithun	31 Mar 1984	Survey Craft	Goa Shipyard
Meen	23 Jun 1984	Survey Craft	Goa Shipyard
Mesh	31 Oct 1984	Survey Craft	Goa Shipyard
Nirupak	14 Aug 1985	Sandhayak Class	Garden Reach
Investigator	11 Jan 1990	Improved Sandhayak	Garden Reach
Old Survey Ships	**Commissioned**	**Decommissioned**	**Years in Service**
SUTLEJ	23 Apr 1941	31 Dec 1978	37
JAMUNA	13 May 1941	31 Dec 1980	39
DARSHAK	28 Dec 1964	15 Jan 1990	26

Milestones & Major Inductions of Technology in Hydrographic Services

Year	Milestones	
	Hydrographic Office	Survey Ships
1981	Computer-assisted Plotting System	Geodetic Transit Satellite System
1982	West Coast of India Pilot	Electro-optical Distance Measuring Electronic Position Fixing[4]

---

3. In 1982, an Experts Group under the chairmanship of the Nautical Adviser to the Government of India recommended a plan to overcome the serious inadequacies and deficiencies of ship and other resources provided to the Hydrographic Department. The plan quantified the additional ship resources essential for undertaking the delineation of the Continental Shelf and the Exclusive Economic Zone, as required under the Convention on the Law of the Sea, within a period of 10 years. This would enable India to place its claims for these areas before the United Nations.

4. This Syledis system replaced the old Hifix system.

Rescheduling of the Survey Season

As a result of refit programmes and employment on other naval duties, it was found that survey ships and craft were not always available in the 'survey season'. Deployments, therefore, started being made in locations where survey work was feasible even during the monsoon season.

Developments After 1990

Surveys of National Importance

The Sethusamudaran Project

In 1985, an exploratory survey was carried out to find a suitable stretch of seabed between India and Sri Lanka that could be deepened sufficiently to enable medium draught vessels to transit between the west and east coasts of India, without having to go all the way around Sri Lanka. The project is still under consideration.

Continental Shelf Surveys

In view of the constraints in the naval budget in the 1990s, the Ministry of Shipping and Transport provided the funds for the construction of two ships to carry out the urgent surverys of the Continental Shelf.

India's Representation at International Hydrographic Fora

India's Chief Hydrographers have had the distinction of being elected to the International Hydrographic Bureau in Monte Carlo.

Commodore DC Kapoor was the first Chief Hydrographer to be elected to the Directing Committee in April 1972. He then served as a Director in the Bureau till 1982, having been re-elected for two successive terms.

Rear Admiral FL Fraser served from 1982 to 1987 as the President of the Directing Committee.

At present, the Chief Hydrographer represents India on the following:

- Committees of the International Hydrographic Organisation:
  - Strategic Planning Working Group;
  - Worldwide Electronic Navigation Chart Data Base;
  - Chart Standardisation Committee;
  - IHO-FIG International Advisory Board on Standards of Competence of Hydrographic Surveyors (Federation International des Geometres - FIG);
  - Commission on Promulgation of Radio Navigational Warnings.
- United Nations Commission on the Limits of the Continental Shelf (CLCS).[5]
- North Indian Ocean Hydrographic Commission (NIOHC).

The NIOHC was formed in 2000 by the initiatives of the Naval Hydrographic Department under the aegis of the International Hydrographic Organisation to encourage hydrographic cooperation among the countries of the Indian Ocean littoral region. India has retained the chairmanship of the Commission since its inception. It has been having annual meetings.

---

5. Chief Hydrographer Rear Admiral FL Fraser's role in ensuring the rights of the North Indian Ocean States was recognised at the time of formulating the UNCLOS.

    Chief Hydrographer Rear Admiral KR Srinivasan's role as Vice Chairman of the CLCS for five years was instrumental in formulating the technical and scientific guidelines of the CLCS.

27

Naval Oceanology & Meteorology

Overview

The Navy's involvement in oceanography sharpened after the 1971 war in which a frigate was sunk by a submarine that subsequently managed to escape the hunting force. 'Met' officers were sent to Britain and the USA to undergo training in oceanographic forecasting and sonar range prediction.

By the mid 1980s, Oceanographic Forecasting Cells had been established in the Command Headquarters, sonar atlases had been produced and a Directorate of Naval Oceanology and Meteorology created in NHQ.

By the end 1990s, data was being received from numerous national agencies, collated and disseminated to meet the needs of a variety of national users.

Developments Until 1975

In the early 1970s, a Met officer was sent to Britain's Royal Naval School of Meteorology and Oceanography (RNSOMO) for training in oceanography. On return, he was appointed to the Naval Hydrographic Office where he helped to produce a document on oceanography and sonar range prediction. Soon thereafter, a second officer was deputed to the US Naval Oceanographic Office in Washington DC for training in oceanography. On return, he was appointed to the naval air station at Cochin, *INS Garuda*, where the Seaking anti submarine helicopters were based.

In 1974, oceanography was introduced as a topic for study in Met sailors' specialist courses and in Observers' and Sub Lieutenants' courses. Oceanographic forecasting was made the responsibility of Met officers.

Developments 1976 to 1990

Monsoon Experiments

In the early 1970s, the World Meteorology Organisation (WMO) decided to study weather on a global scale. As part of this programme, a regional experiment called Monsoon Experiment (MONEX) was to be conducted in the Indian Ocean during 1979.

The objective of MONEX was stated as follows:

"A very important component of the fully developed summer monsoon circulation is the monsoon depression forming in the Bay of Bengal. It is not known whether monsoon depressions propagate from further east or form *in situ* over the Bay of Bengal and, if *in situ*, what role barotropic instability of the low level flow plays in such formation. In the presence of these disturbances, the low level flow over India and the Arabian Sea is strengthened. Once developed, these disturbances can bring major portions of the monsoon rainfall over northeastern / north central India. In this respect, the three-dimensional structure of the monsoon disturbance and the monsoon trough over the sea and over land needs to be ascertained."

As a forerunner of Monex 79, an experiment on a smaller scale called Monex 77 was conducted in 1977.

Monex 77

Monex 77 was aimed to collect meteorological and oceanographic data over the Arabian Sea, the Bay of Bengal and the equatorial Indian Ocean.

Indian Naval frigates *Beas* and *Betwa*, together with four Soviet research ships, were equipped with appropriate meteorological and oceanographic equipment. Scientists from the Bhabha Atomic Research Centre, the Tata Institute of Fundamental Research, the India Meteorological Department and the Naval Physical and Oceanographic Laboratory took part in this Monex.

The observation programme was divided in three phases - Phase I from 26 May to 19 June 1977, Phase II from 26 June to 15 July 1977 and Phase III from 4 to 19 August 1977. During the first two phases, ships operated in the Arabian Sea. In the last phase, *Beas* operated in the Bay of Bengal and *Betwa* in the Arabian Sea.

In the post Monex 77 meetings, it emerged that the results of the experiment could not be satisfactorily collated because not enough attention had been paid to organise the teams for the various research projects and the production of a report.

Monex 79

The aim of Monex 79 was to study aspects of the Southwest Monsoon like onset and withdrawal, dynamic and thermodynamic structure, and formations of depressions in the Bay of Bengal.

For Monex 79 between May and August 1979, the WMO used earth satellites, instrumented aircraft, dedicated ships, balloons and ocean buoys for collection of meteorological data. The Environmental Data Unit of the Naval Hydrographic Office arranged the fitment of Expendable Bathy Thermograph (XBT) equipment on board selected merchant ships plying in the Arabian Sea, to help acquire physical oceanographic data for subsequent dissemination to various national agencies.

Survey ship *Darshak*, frigate *Betwa* and tanker *Deepak* were fitted with the latest meteorological and oceanographic equipment and the Navaid Sounding System for accurately determining upper winds at sea. For the first time, a vast amount of upper air data over the Arabian Sea and the Bay of Bengal was collected.

The collation of meteorological and oceanographic data obtained during Monex 79 was better than that of Monex 77 and proved valuable in deriving:

- Monsoon dynamics and modelling experiments.
- Ocean currents and large scale aspects of monsoon circulation.
- Regional scale of monsoon circulation
- Variability of monsoon e.g. 'Break monsoon'.
- Monsoon disturbances.
- Heat source and energy calculations.

The severe tropical revolving storm (cyclone), which devastated the coast of Andhra Pradesh on 11 and 12 May 1979, was first reported by *Betwa* on 6 May 1979. *Betwa's* early warning helped the Government of Andhra Pradesh to evacuate over 200,000 coastal people in good time.

Oceanographic Data

The Environmental Data Unit and Forecasting Cell was first set up in the Naval Hydrographic Office in 1974 to provide oceanographic information to the fleet for anti submarine operations. The unit processed, analysed and interpreted the data received from:

- *Darshak's* Oceanographic Expedition of 1973-74.
- The USA's National Oceanographic Data Centre.

- The International Indian Ocean Expedition 1975.

In 1975, the Government nominated the Naval Hydrographic Office as the National Centre for archiving and dissemination of Bathy Thermograph (BT) data and directed that BT data collected by all vessels of national agencies be forwarded to this Centre. An Oceanographic Centre was set up in 1977. Data was received from:

- International agencies like the National Oceanographic Data Centre (NODC), USA and the Intergovernmental Oceanographic Commission (IOC).
- National agencies like the National Institute of Oceanography (NIO), the Central Marine Fisheries Institute (CMFRI), the Oil and Natural Gas Commission (ONGC), the Indian Meteorological Department (IMD), the Geological Survey of India (GSI), the Naval Physical and Oceanographic Laboratory (NPOL), survey ships and fleet ships.

On request from national agencies, the Centre collated and disseminated temperature, salinity, current, swell, wave and wind data. The Unit provided the Navy with Sonar Atlases and Oceanographic Charts containing information on Sea Surface Temperature, Mixed Layer Depth, Below Layer Gradient, Sonic Layer Depth, surface current, wind and wave data.

Bathymetric Charts

In 1966, the International Hydrographic Bureau assigned to the Naval Hydrographic Office the responsibility of preparing nine bathymetric plotting sheets, based on source material received from data centres the world over. These were incorporated in the General Bathymetric Chart of the Oceans (GEBCO), which were published in 1970-71. In the following year, responsibility was accepted for ten more sheets. At the time of writing, the National Hydrographic Office has published sixteen GEBCO charts.

In the 1980s, oceanographic data started being acquired by participation in the cruises of the Department of Ocean Development's Oceanographic Research Vessel (ORV) *Sagarkanya*.

In 1987, a facility was set up at NHQ and equipped to provide data for Meteorological and Oceanographic Briefings.

Oceanographic Forecasting At Naval Command Level

In January 1981, an Oceanographic Forecasting Cell (OFC) was established at Cochin under the operational control of the FOCINCSOUTH. This marked the beginning of oceanographic studies and forecasting in the Navy. The OFC was located in the premises of the Met School and headed by the officer who had been trained by the American Navy. The OFC's terms of reference were to liase with the National Physical and Oceanographic Laboratory (NPOL) located in Cochin and:

- Provide a general description of the major oceanographic and acoustic factors affecting a specified area of operation for a specified forecast period, the sea state at the beginning of the forecast period and significant changes expected during the forecast period.

- Collect and store processed oceanographic data in the form of atlases, charts and reports issued by the NPOL and the Chief Hydrographer.

- Collect oceanographic information, records and research outputs from agencies like the National Institute of Oceanography, OSTA and ONGC.

- Provide forecasts of thermal structure and salinity profiles based on the available past data and current oceanographic observations received from fleet ships during exercises.

- Devise and standardise codes for transmission of oceanic data and forecasts.

- Undertake selective studies in oceanography to update and validate the forecasting techniques developed by NPOL.

- Undertake studies on air-sea interaction in collaboration with NPOL and other agencies.

- Assist the Met Training School in the training of naval personnel in oceanography.

Although Met officers studied "introductory oceanography" as a topic during their Advanced Weather Forecaster's training, it was realised that they needed to be trained in oceanographic forecasting. The Cochin University conducted the first capsule course in Oceanography in April 1981. The Indian Institute of Technology Delhi conducted the second Oceanography capsule course in March 1982.

In 1981, sanction was received for three digital electronic systems to be installed at Naval Air Stations *Garuda* and *Hansa* to enhance safety during landing and take off. These were:

- The Ceilograph, which gave digital printouts of the heights of lowest cloud over an air station.

- The Skopograph which gave digital printouts of runway visibility; and

- The Current Weather Instrument System (CWIS) which gave digital printouts of weather parameters like humidity, temperature, wind direction and speed.

Formation of the Directorate of Naval Oceanology and Meteorology (DNOM) in 1982

By 1982, it became necessary to establish a dedicated directorate for 'Oceanology' in Naval Headquarters:

- Oceanographic forecasting was vitally important for anti submarine warfare.

- It was necessary to safeguard the security aspects arising out of the increased oceanographic activity in Indian waters.

- The Navy's existing arrangements to plan, coordinate and progress oceanographic tasks were inadequate.

- The Navy felt that it must be involved in 'ocean development'.[1]

The 'meteorology' component of the Directorate of Naval Education and Meteorology was transferred to a new Directorate and the disciplines of Meteorology, Oceanology and Oceanographic activity were re-grouped.

The new Directorate of Naval Oceanology and Meteorology (DNOM) was established in May 1982 under CNS' powers, concurrently with the creation of the Department of Ocean Development and the first expedition to Antarctica. Thereafter, DNOM became the single nodal agency dealing with all aspects of naval oceanology and meteorology.

DNOM's tasks were to:

- Coordinate all oceanology and meteorology activity.

- Systematise the collection of oceanographic data, its computerisation and its forecasting.

- Represent the Navy and liase for oceanographic research data, training, publications etc. with the Department of Ocean Development, National Institute of Oceanography, Geological Survey of India, Naval Physical and Oceanographic Laboratory, Department of Science and Technology and the Indian Institutes of Technology who were dealing with oceanography.

- Coordinate the naval component of the Indian Scientific Expeditions to Antarctica and help develop plans for a polar research ship and for airborne survey.

- Coordinate the security of oceanographic data. Scrutinise the security implications of requests for oceanographic data pertaining to Indian waters and the EEZ and for security clearance of oceanographic surveys by foreign ships.

- Monitor security of oceanographic data by ensuring that foreign agencies carrying out oceanic research / survey

---

1. As early as 1972, a Committee under the Scientific Adviser to the Raksha Mantri recommended the formation of a national body for oceanography. The proposal took shape by 1975 for the formation of an Ocean Science and Technology Agency. The Department of Ocean Development was established in 1981.

in collaboration with national agencies collect only that data which is cleared from the security angle.

- Coordinate atmospheric data collection and research with specific reference to predicting anomalous atmospheric conditions on naval radio, radar and EW systems (ANAPROP).
- Participate in oceanographic cruises.

Since its inception, the Directorate has contributed to and undertaken the following:

- Co-coordinated the Navy's help for Indian Scientific Antarctica Expeditions.
- Rendering consultancy for the design of polar research vessels for the Department of Ocean Development.
- Monitored the progress of oceanographic research undertaken by the DRDO and by CSIR's scientific organisations.
- Participation in UNESCO's Inter Governmental Oceanographic Commissions at Paris.
- Organised the oceanographic course in the Centre for Advanced Studies in Atmospheric and Fluid Sciences at IIT, New Delhi.
- Functioned as a think-tank for oceanographic data collection, its utilisation and application for naval activities.
- Interacted with the India Meteorological Department in Conferences of Forecasting Officers.

School of Naval Oceanology and Meteorology

Meteorological services for the Navy commenced in Cochin on 11 September 1952. A Meteorology Training Section was established in the Naval Air Station *INS Garuda* at Cochin on 3 June 1968 to impart training to 'Met' sailors in marine meteorology, aviation meteorology, and meteorological equipment.

On 18 October 1974, this Met Training Section was renamed as the Meteorology Training School and started imparting 'Met Training' to officers of the Naval Air Arm.

The Meteorological Training School was inaugurated at *INS Garuda* at Cochin on 25 April 1977. The School conducts Met courses for officers and sailors.

On 1 November 1985, the Met Training School was renamed as the School of Naval Oceanology and Meteorology (SNOM).

Developments After 1990

Monsoon Experiments

Experiments to study the vagaries of the monsoon were resumed under the aegis of the Indian Climate Research Programme:

Collection, Collation and Dissemination of Oceanographic Data

The Navy's need is for instant, accurate and reliable predictions of anomalous propagation above the sea surface and of acoustic propagation below the sea surface.

At the national and international level, considerable cooperation continued to take place to coordinate oceanographic and meteorological data from as wide a spectrum as possible.

28

The Marine Commandos

The Creation of the Indian Marine Special Force

The Navy had acquired Swimmer Delivery Vehicles (chariots) in 1975 for two basic purposes:

- To determine the measures to defend Bombay and offshore oil rigs / platforms from attack by such craft.
- To regularly exercise naval ships in harbour in defence against chariot attack.

In due course, selected qualified divers developed skills as charioteers.

In 1980, the "Interim Chariot Complex" at Bombay was commissioned as INS *Abhimanyu*.

In 1983, Naval Headquarters initiated the proposal for creating an Indian Marine Special Force (IMSF) as the "marine commando" arm of the Navy, comprising officers and sailors who were not only trained divers but also trained in other skills of Special Operations Forces.

Three developments took place whilst the IMSF proposal was still under consideration:

- The measures for the Defence of Bombay High against clandestine attack were finalised, one component of which was naval commandos to evict terrorists who might have already taken over an oil production platform.
- In 1985, sanction was formally accorded for raising the IMSF. Sanction was also accorded for specialised equipment and three Seaking Mk 42 C Commando version helicopters for the IMSF.
- The Navy liased with the other national agencies that were training Special Forces. It commenced deputing selected personnel in 1986 to undergo commando training with the Army's Special Frontier Force.

Marine commandos accompanied the IPKF to Sri Lanka in end July 1987 to deal with the LTTE elements operating in the lagoons.

In August 1987, sanction was formally accorded for a force of 38 officers and 373 sailors.

Meanwhile in 1986, INS *Abhimanyu* had been placed under the operational control of Flag Officer Maharashtra Area who was responsible for the defence of Bombay. When the IMSF was sanctioned for the defence of offshore assets, it was based in *Abhimanyu*.

Role and Training

Role

- To conduct clandestine operations, surveillance and reconnaissance missions combating maritime terrorism.
- To support amphibious operations and air and sea borne missions.

Training

The first eight batches of IMSF personnel underwent 10 weeks basic commando training followed by three weeks of Para Basic course. The course content was basically land warfare, handling of arms, ammunition and explosives. Kayaking, combat diving, airborne operations, photography, making of improvised explosive devices, charioteering, ship intervention drills and hijacking of oil rigs / platforms were conducted in-house at INS *Abhimanyu*.

The day-to-day training curriculum includes close quarter battle, jungle warfare tactics, making of Improvised Explosive Devices (IEDs).

Some of the skills that MARCOs specialise in are:

- Advanced weapon handling.
- Intervention / hostage rescue.
- Recapture of and destruction of offshore installations – i.e. to recapture own platforms and destroying enemy platforms.
- Counter Insurgency warfare – this is a war of brains and guerrilla warfare.
- Handling of the latest IEDs.
- Unarmed combat, Karate, Para Jumping and Sky Diving all of which are compulsory for all Special Forces personnel.
- Special Boat Section (SBS) operations.
- Chariot operations.

On completion of the above training, MARCOs join designated Prahars for 'on job' and advanced training. The advanced training is based on the principle of vertical specialisation in the following:

- Language and culture training of enemy areas so that MARCOs can operate and survive behind enemy lines.
- Sniper training and training on shoulder-launched missiles, MMGs etc.
- Sky diving with water-para jump capability.
- Counter insurgency.
- Making of IEDs with readily available items.

After 1990, all training was shifted to INS *Abhimanyu*. The Army's Para Training School at Agra has continued to conduct the para-drop segment of commando training.

Operations Between 1987 and 1990[1]

Operation Pawan

The IMSF made its debut in August 1987. A 40-strong group participated in 55 combat operations in its very first year. During amphibious raids, they destroyed the LTTE's boats, ammunition dumps and camps. They proved invaluable during 'flushing out' operations in the islets, lagoons and inlets and were invariably in the van of these raids. They were awarded a Maha Vir Chakra, two Vir Chakras and several Nao Sena Medals for gallantry during Operation Pawan.

Commander (then Lieutenant) Arvind Singh was awarded the Maha Vir Chakra. He recalls:

"On 19 October 1987, my team had to traverse through roads heavily mined with booby traps laid by the militants and in the face of militant fire from buildings and rooftops. The exemplary courage and valour of my team helped secure the area and the link up of 41 Brigade with 1 Maratha Light Infantry on 20 October 1987.

"On the night of 21/22 October, despite limited demolition equipment, our team destroyed the Guru Nagar Jetty and the militant speedboats in Jaffna Lagoon. Under cover of darkness, we swam underwater for a distance of two kilometres and destroyed eleven speedboats that were kept ready for hard-core militants to escape. During this operation, we came under heavy fire from the militants."

Commander (then Lieutenant) Anoop Verma was awarded a Vir Chakra. He recalls:

"Our group was embarked on board *Aditara* for water-borne operations to support Army operations off Jaffna Lagoon. On 21-22 night, we were tasked to destroy six speedboats, which the LTTE had been using to carry their personnel, arms and ammunition into the Jaffna Lagoon. These boats were secured at Guru Nagar Jetty, which was one of the LTTE's prominent possessions.

"We had very limited resources – two Gemini dinghies and some oxygen sets. We had no explosives. We took explosives on temporary loan from the Sri Lankan Navy. We managed to place explosives on all six speedboats and withdrew successfully. It was a well-coordinated operation as Army troops were closing in from the landward side and the destruction of the speedboats took the LTTE completely by surprise.

"Two days later, we were tasked to destroy another set of speedboats in the same location. We knew that this time the LTTE would not be taken by surprise. We went ahead, did a similar operation and managed to blow up about eight boats that night."

Commander (then Lieutenant) PS Chandavarkar was awarded the Vir Chakra. His citation read:

"On 17 November 1987 at about 0400 hours in pitch darkness, Lieutenant PS Chandavarkar led a boat patrol to intercept the militants in the Jaffna Lagoon in Sri Lanka. While traversing four miles in highly restricted and hostile waters, the boat patrol detected a high-speed boat dashing out of the lagoon. Lieutenant Chandavarkar and his team pursued the boat and opened fire to prevent its escape. Prior to sinking of the boat, the four militants in the boat were seen dumping objects into the Jaffna Channel.

After apprehending the militants, Lieutenant Chandavarkar carried out immediate diving operations and recovered a box of improvised detonators. The diving operations were conducted under extremely trying conditions and in very hostile waters.

He persevered for two days and was successful in locating a box of high explosives. He then proceeded to tow the box away to a safe area and neutralised it, thereby clearing the Channel for safe navigation."

Operation Cactus – December 1988

The hijacked merchant ship 'Progress Light' carrying the fleeing mercenaries and the hostages taken by them in Male had been forced to stop by naval gunfire. A Naval boarding party that included IMSF personnel seized the ship, apprehended the armed mercenaries and rescued the hostages.

Operation Jupiter – 1989

IMSF personnel and their Seaking Mk 42 C helicopter were embarked on board *Viraat* in case it became necessary to evacuate High Commission personnel from Colombo.

---

1. For details, see chapter titled 'Naval Operations', page 183.

29

The Foundering Of INS Andaman

Synopsis of the Incident

The 1,000-tonne Petya class submarine chasers acquired from Russia between 1968 and 1974 were among the most remarkable vessels of their time. They were propelled by gas turbines driving independent propellers to enable them to reach the reported position of an enemy submarine at very high speed. They had a diesel engine driving a centre shaft with a controllable pitch propeller (CPP) to provide the long endurance required for stalking and hunting a submarine. They were densely packed with electronics – sonars, radars and computer systems to control the fire of their anti submarine and anti aircraft weapons. To reconcile the need for speed with the need for maximum possible combat capability, the thickness of the steel plates of their hulls had been so minimised as to keep them seaworthy during the six-year period between major refits, provided the hulls were regularly inspected and properly maintained during the annual dockings.

Because of numerous unforeseen civil engineering difficulties, the new Naval Dockyard being constructed at Vishakhapatnam, specifically for refitting Russian ships, took much longer to get ready to commence the mandatory six-yearly refit programme of the Petyas. Due to the bunching caused by acquiring five Petyas at a time and the delays in starting their six-yearly refit programme, decisions had to be taken as early as 1979 to postpone and reschedule these important major refits. The effect of this postponement was particularly harmful for the hulls of the Petyas.

Andaman was the ninth ship of its type to be acquired from Russia in 1973. She joined the Eastern Fleet based at Vishakhapatnam and, like the other ships of her class, participated in Fleet exercises every year. During 1989 and early 1990, except for a short refit between September and December 1989, Andaman was deployed off the eastern coast of Sri Lanka during the winding down of Operation Pawan. After December, there had been repeated leaks in both port and starboard stabiliser fin housings, which had been cold-repaired and strengthened through cementing and shoring. From April onwards, the ship had participated in the Fleet's exercise programmes.

On 17 August 1990, the Eastern Fleet sailed from the Andaman Islands for Vishakhapatnam on the east coast of India. On the 20th, the Fleet ran into heavy weather. *Andaman* suffered flooding and breakdowns and foundered. Two frigates of the Eastern Fleet were standing by her when she sank on the 21st August, 140 miles east of Vishakhapatnam. Of the total of 132 officers, sailors and civilians, 117 persons were rescued. The bodies of two persons were recovered. The remaining 13 persons drowned.

The Commanding Officer was court martialled and found guilty of 'causing his ship to be lost at sea negligently or by default.' He forfeited six months seniority and was severely reprimanded. This lenient sentence undoubtedly took into account the operational, technical and administrative circumstances that had compelled the Navy to continue to operate its ships despite the considerable frailties that develop as ships age. He resigned from the Navy. In his view, instead of letting the Andaman incident herald the institution of remedies to prevent the neglect of ships' hulls, the Navy, by holding him culpable and not those sitting ashore, had sent the wrong message to Commanding Officers afloat.

Sequence of Events – August 1990

18th August, 1500 hrs

The Eastern Fleet comprising Dunagiri (FOCEF embarked), *Himgiri, Trishul, Anjadip* and *Andaman* sailed from Port Blair to rendezvous *Magar* (FOCINCEAST embarked) and *Arnala* 200 miles east of Vishakhapatnam. The FOCINCEAST's exercises on the 20th were to be followed by a simulated attack by Eastern Fleet on Vishakhapatnam port, in the face of submarine and air opposition, before entering harbour on the 21st.

---

* This chapter is based on information in the public domain, namely documents preceding and leading to the court martial, documents produced at the court martial, the verdict of the court martial, the recollections of personages involved and memoirs.

Andaman participated in the day's exercise programme without any breakdown.

19th August

Andaman continued to participate in the exercise programme without any breakdown.

Sea State 4 to 5. Wind Speed 20 to 25 knots. Long Swell.

20th August AM

A depression commenced to form in the Bay of Bengal and move in a north westerly/westerly direction towards India. It crossed the coast near Paradip on 21st August.

1000 hrs: The Fleet rendezvoused *Magar*. FOCINCEAST exercised the ships as planned and, at 1620 hrs, commenced his return to Vishakhapatnam in *Magar*.

Sequence of *Andaman's* Problems

20th August

0950 hrs   Main diesel fuel pipe burst.

1030 hrs   Defect rectified and rejoined Fleet

1545 hrs   Main steering gear failed. Resorted to manual steering from the Aft Steering Position (ASP). Water level in ASP found to be six inches above the floor plating. Pumping out commenced. Submersible pump got choked frequently with jute and rags. By 2000 hrs, water had risen to waist level.

1940 hrs   Level of bilge water in the Aft Engine Room (AER) rose to flywheel level. It was assumed that this was caused by the choking of the AER ejector. The main diesel was stopped to clear the ejector suction strainer and the bilges were pumped out. The possibility of water having ingressed into the AER was not visualised. On receipt of the ship's report regarding this flooding, FOCEF detached *Trishul* to remain in the vicinity of *Andaman*. FOCEF proceeded ahead in *Dunagiri*, with *Himgiri* and *Anjadip* to take up position for the next morning's attack on Vishakhapatnam.

2100 hrs   Bilge water in AER cleared. Efforts commenced to restart the main diesel.

Bilge water level in Stabiliser Compartment observed to be three feet above the bilges. Started pumping out using the fixed ejector in the Forward Engine Room (FER) and the portable submersible pump. Source of flooding was not established. The adjoining compartments – the Forward Engine Room and the Aft Engine Room were not shored.

2130 hrs   Water level in the ASP had risen to five feet above the floor plating (well above the waterline). ASP evacuated (without establishing the source of flooding, without appreciating that the flooding could be internal and without shoring the adjacent compartment). Flooding reported in Stabiliser Compartment.

2145 hrs   Stabiliser Compartment submersible pump failed. The submersible pump from the ASP was shifted to the Stabiliser Compartment. This also failed within half an hour due to short-circuiting of its motor winding. Since the third submersible pump was defective even before sailing from Port Blair, the ship now had no portable submersible pumps to pump out flooded compartments. This was reported to FOCEF four hours later at 0231 hrs.

2200 hrs   Depth Charge Compartment (above waterline) found flooded. It was evacuated (without assessing that the flooding could be internal or through an opening above the waterline).

2230 hrs   With all three portable submersible pumps non-operational, the fire pump located in the Stabiliser Compartment had been started to pump it out. It failed within minutes due to ingress of water short-circuiting its motor winding.

2300 hrs   Efforts to start the main diesel were unsuccessful and were attributed to contamination of the fuel tank in the Stabiliser Compartment. It was decided to lock the centre shaft and start the gas turbines (GTs). Centre shaft was locked by 2330 hrs.

21st August

0100 hrs   The 100 kw Diesel Alternator (DA) in AER switched off due to fluctuation in frequency. The 400 kw DA was started.

0112 hrs   Report made to FOCEF of non-starting of main diesel, of switching off of 100 kw DA, of water level in ASP at waistline and of intention to get underway on GTs by 0200 hrs.

0200 hrs   Water level in Stabiliser Compartment had risen up to the deck head level, on top of which was the Aft Switch Board (ASB). The source of flooding had still not been established. The port GT was started but it soon tripped due to interruption of power supply.

0230 hrs The Aft Switch Board became non-operational due to water level in the Stabiliser Compartment reaching the panel. The ASB was made dead. Thereafter, no attempt was made to take supply from the Forward Switchboard and start the GT again. By this time, water from the Stabiliser Compartment had entered the Machinery Control Room (MCR) from behind the MCR panels. The Duty ERA secured the MCR and secured all the compartments aft of the Forward Engine Room – namely the Stabiliser Compartment, the AER and the CPP post. He then left the MCR.

By making the ASB dead, three things happened:

- The 200 kw DA became inoperable. With the 100 kw DA having been switched off at 0100 hrs, the ship now had only the 400 kw DA to supply power.

- Number three and number four fire pumps became non-operable. Of the four fire pumps fitted, one had been non-operational before the ship had sailed for Port Blair, one had failed at 2230 hrs and the remaining two were now non-operable.

- The ejectors in the AER stopped working and flooding resumed in the AER.

Of the three salvage pumps fitted, one was fitted in the AER and had been non-operational before the ship sailed. The remaining two were not designed to take suction from the aft section of the ship.

From 0230 hrs onwards, the ship had no means of pumping water out from any of the compartments aft of the Forward Engine Room. All these compartments were left as they were, without posting any sentries or doing any shoring.

0335 hrs Report made to FOCEF regarding flooding of the Stabiliser Compartment stating that the cementing over the holes acquired in 1989 appeared to have given way.

0400 hrs On receiving the signal about flooding in the Stabiliser Compartment, FOCEF detached *Himgiri* to proceed to render assistance to *Andaman*.

0511 hrs *Trishul* took *Andaman* in tow using a nylon tow rope and built up to a speed of six knots.

0530 hrs The 400 kw DA tripped. The cause was suspected to be contamination of the tank that supplied fuel to the DA. The ship was now without power and could only communicate with FOCEF via *Trishul*.

0600 hrs During morning rounds:

- It was observed that the water level in the Aft Engine Room had again come up to the bottom end of the main diesel flywheel as it had the previous evening at 1940 hrs. It was not appreciated that after the ASB was made dead at 0230 hrs, the ejectors in the AER had stopped working and the ingress of water continued unabated.

- It was also observed that the water level in the CPP Compartment was two and a half feet above the keel.

0650 hrs Tow rope parted.

0820 hrs Tow rope passed – tow recommenced at speed five knots. To provide a catenary for the tow, *Andaman* started manually hauling cable up on to the foxle.

0930 hrs The water level in the AER rose to eight inches above the floor plating.

1000 hrs – The CPP Compartment was found fully flooded.

- Knee-deep flooding was observed in the aft mess.

- No effort was made to establish the likely cause of flooding in the AER, the CPP Compartment and the aft mess.

1030 hrs The Commanding Officer held a meeting with his Heads of Department. It was realised that the situation was deteriorating. The state of the flooded compartments was:

- ASP flooded up to five feet above the grating level.

- DC post flooded with one and a half feet of water at the aft end.

- Stabiliser Compartment and Aft Switch Board flooded up to the bottom edge of the MCR door.

- CPP compartment full and Aft Mess compartment knee deep.

- Aft Engine Room flooded up to eight inches above the floor plating.

1103 hrs Report was sent to FOCEF via *Trishul* that 50 tonnes of water had been shipped in the ASP and Stabiliser Compartment and the Aft Mess, and that there was water in the Aft Engine Room up to the grating level. (Subsequent analysis revealed that by this time 350 tonnes of water must have been shipped).

1215 hrs Towing stopped. Cable connected to tow rope. *Trishul* resumed tow – speed four knots.

1328 hrs *Andaman* started yawing whilst being towed. Speed reduced to zero.

1355 hrs The ship heeled over dangerously to port. Everybody on board suddenly realised that disaster was imminent. The Commanding Officer ordered 'Abandon Ship'.

1359 hrs *Trishul* saw that *Andaman* was about to sink and signalled *Himgiri* to immediately close her.

1401 hrs *Trishul* saw *Andaman* starting to go down and cut the tow rope.

1403 hrs *Andaman* sank stern first.

The Court Martial Findings

The Court Martial found the Commanding Officer guilty of causing his ship to be lost at sea, negligently or by default, for the following reasons:

- Failure to fight the initial flooding with all means at his disposal and failure to adopt all the damage control measures as laid down.

- Failure to ensure that all possible means and resources at his disposal were employed to establish the source of flooding in the Aft Engine Room and Controllable Pitch Propeller Compartment and subsequently to maintain vigilance in these compartments to prevent recurrence of flooding.

- Failure to exercise adequate vigilance in the Stabiliser Compartment which was a suspected area of weakness and failure to take timely action to contain flooding in this compartment, as a result of which the ship lost her propulsion and power generation capability.

- Failure to analyse and respond to a steadily deteriorating situation from 1600 hrs on 20th August onwards which resulted finally in the loss of the ship at about 1403 hrs on 21 August 1990.

Reactions to the Foundering of the *Andaman*

The Navy and the nation were aghast at the sinking of the *Andaman*, 140 miles from Vishakhapatnam, in broad daylight, before the eyes of two frigates standing by to assist her, just a day after the Commander in Chief and the Fleet Commander had been at sea exercising with these ships. There was adverse comment in the media and misinformed speculation that *Andaman* had been 'deserted' in her hour of need.

The fact was that when FOCINCEAST completed exercises and departed for Vishakhapatnam at 1620 hrs

on the 20th, *Andaman* had not reported any defect. He was to host a previously arranged seminar in Vishakhapatnam on 21st August being attended by the CNS and other dignitaries. Before FOCEF departed at 1940 hrs on the 20th to take up position for the next morning's exercise attack, he had detached *Trishul* to standby *Andaman*.

Invariably, whenever a catastrophe occurs, the first questions are usually based on gut reactions. How can a warship sink in peacetime? Was she sea-worthy? If not, had the ship reported it to superior authority? If not, why not? If the ship had reported that she was not sea-worthy, why did superior authority sail the ship? Concurrently, everybody concerned begins to ensure that no blame should be attributed to him. It takes time for the dust to settle and for a clear picture to emerge.

Andaman's material state and sea-worthiness were known. Concern had been recorded at all levels:

- As regards the Naval Headquarters and Command level, two significant letters were presented at the Court Martial as exhibits:

  – In October 1989, Naval Headquarters (NHQ) had written to Headquarters Eastern Naval Command (HQENC). Its gist was that *Andaman*'s six-yearly refit was scheduled to commence in October 1990, having been already delayed by nine years. Since her material state, particularly hull and fittings and systems, would have deteriorated beyond repair, this would enhance the work package extensively. It was therefore essential to review the desirability of giving the ship a six-yearly refit. HQENC was requested to assess the present material state of the ship and forward recommendations on the desirability or otherwise of giving the ship a six-yearly refit.

  – In November 1989, HQENC's reply to NHQ stated that compared to other Petyas of the same period, *Andaman*'s hull had required more attention as indicated in two successive Docking Reports. Whereas the machinery and equipment would not pose major problems to achieve a life of six years after the forthcoming two-year refit, the hull would have to be attended to. On balance, it was desirable that *Andaman* be refitted.

- *Andaman*'s Quarterly Letter of Proceedings dated July 1990 had stated that the hull state, by and large, did not cause anxiety, though age was evident. The holes of December 1989 in the stabiliser housing did have ingress of water at the rate of a bucket every four hours, but meticulous rounds were being ensured. Strengthening of the area was done under the direct supervision of HQENC. Doors, hatches and latches were in a bad state with watertight integrity being compromised constantly. What was constantly put as "Defer to Next Refit" now perforce would have to be taken up by the Naval Dockyard Vishakhapatnam during the three-month Short Refit scheduled to commence on 1 October 1990.

At the time of Andaman's foundering, Rear Admiral Vishnu Bhagwat was the Chief of Staff in Western Naval Command. He had earlier commanded a Petya. In later years, he had been FOCEF, FOCINCWEST and CNS. In his book "Betrayal of a Nation", Admiral Bhagwat has stated:

> "The Navy had lost Andaman, a Petya class patrol vessel, in August 1990. The Petyas were superbly designed, combined diesel and gas turbine driven ships with a design philosophy, stability and damage control features amongst the best in the world for a warship. Even if one third of the forward end and one third of the aft section of the ship suffered complete damage, the ship could still float. However, INS Andaman had been neglected for almost 10 years – essential refits and defect rectification work were deferred from refit to refit. These included underwater defects in the hull and sub-systems connected to the sea. The ship's officers and crew had given up the practice of preparing for Task I, Task II and Task III work-ups and inspections. The Commanding Officers were interested in clocking days at sea. "Staff-inspections", mandatory on completion of refit, and "Staff sea-checks" were shelved. Even the refit completion signal, which must be preceded by a joint certification by the Heads of Departments of the ship, the Captain and the Refitting Dockyard – at the General Manager's level – had become a mere formality. Hull surveys were carried out perfunctorily and the report itself did not reach the ship until months after the "completion" of the refit. The staffs in Command Headquarters were only too happy to defer rectification of serious defects, which directly affected the safety of the ship, till the next refit, thus taking unauthorised short cuts. (Page 47)

> "A document titled "Lessons learnt from INS Andaman" was formally promulgated by the Flag Officer Sea Training. (Page 48)"

In Retrospect

As can be seen from the other chapters in this volume, the Dockyard in Vishakhapatnam had serious limitations. The bunching of refits was being compounded by the requirements of Operation Pawan. It was not that the Navy did not know what Admiral Bhagwat has stated. The basic reality is that the Navy has to press on and depend on the professionalism of the ships' crews. Andaman had been operating in Sri Lankan waters for 283 days for Operation Pawan.

From one point of view, the foundering of the Andaman was an accident waiting to happen. For years, no meaningful solution has been found to the problems experienced in the maintenance of the hulls of the thin-skinned ships of Russian origin. Hull corrosion is known to be greater in the warmer and more saline seawater of the tropics than it is in the cooler and less saline seawater of the northern seas for which the Russian thin-skinned hulls have been designed. Unless full-scale refit facilities are available, which can remove and replace weakened hull plates and also, within the time frame of the ship's refit, cope with the removal and replacement of the dense wiring and electronic equipment on the inner side of the plates being replaced, there is no alternative to either 'adding doubler plates' or 'fixing cement boxes' to deal with leaks in the hull. When such improvised measures are resorted to, there have to be continuous and rigorous checks to see if they are holding. Andaman's signal sent at 0335 hrs on 21st August shows how she was overtaken by events.

From another point of view, like all other ships of the same vintage, Andaman was seaworthy but not perfectly so. Given the Navy's insufficient and overloaded refit facilities, its shortfalls in spare parts availability and its overstretched operational commitments, ships have learnt to live with the Dockyards' recommendation to "Defer To Next Refit" and Command Headquarters' "approval" thereof. Commanding Officers press on loyally with the operational tasks assigned to them and rely on the training, experience, seamanship and good judgment of their officers and sailors to cope with emergencies at sea.

The sequence of events and the findings of the court martial indicate how Andaman's officers and sailors were snowed under by the emergency. The speed at which crisis after crisis struck them overwhelmed them to such an extent that even the most elementary measures were forgotten:

- Like trying to pinpoint the source of flooding – was it internal from a burst fire main or external from a leak in the hull?

- Like positioning sentries to report the rate of flooding in each affected compartment and,

- Like shoring adjacent compartments to safeguard against their being flooded.

Some continue to believe that the fatal blow to Andaman came from an unusually high wave that fell with full force on to the ship's waist, which was awash, broke through the soft patch on top of the Aft Engine Room, flooded it instantly and eroded whatever little stability was left. They believe that but for this wave, *Andaman* might just have made it back to port. Such beliefs are speculative. Warships are designed to withstand very heavy weather. The essence of seamanship is never let a ship get into such a parlous situation that an unusual wave can sink it.

Apart from the technical aspects, the most basic of the lessons to be learnt from the foundering of the *Andaman* are:

- Never to take for granted that improvised repairs to the hull would withstand rough weather. In Andaman's case, the holes in the stabiliser fin housings were known to be an area of weakness. The conclusion that their cement boxes had failed came twelve hours too late.

- Never to take for granted that officers and sailors who have been trained "generically" or have the experience or even know how to cope with damage control or serious flooding will know how to apply that knowledge to the specific systems of the ships they happen to be serving in. The Regulations for the Navy make it explicitly mandatory for ships' officers and sailors to be rigorously trained, on board, for every possible eventuality in their ship. The very first of every warship's three priorities: To Float - To Move - To Fight - is To Float. The glamour of, and the over-emphasis on peacetime spit and polish, ship handling at high speed and the pressure to excel in weaponry must never be at the cost of the utterly unglamorous and backbreaking priority of seamanlike ship husbandry to ensure that the ship's floatability is intact.

- Always to check, again and again before leaving harbour, that all the ship's pumps are fully serviceable. Twelve hours before *Andaman* sank, not a single pump was operable to pump out water that was steadily flooding compartment after compartment.

30

Defence Of Offshore Assets

Preamble

The Oil and Natural Gas Commission's (ONGC) activity in the continental shelf off Bombay started in 1963 with an experimental seismic survey by the vessel *SS Mahindra*. Reconnaissance surveys by the Soviet ship *'Akademik Arkhangellskey* between 1964 and 1967 located promising oil and gas deposits in an area 75 to 100 miles northwest of Bombay. This area was named Bombay High.

In 1973, following the Arab-Israel War, the oil producing nations of West Asia raised the price of oil. This precipitated a worldwide financial crisis. It sharpened the urgency to develop Bombay High to minimise the outflow of foreign exchange to pay for oil imports.

Drilling in Bombay High commenced on 30 January 1974 using the Japanese built oil rig 'Sagar Samrat'. Oil was first struck on 18 February 1974. A year later, another oil-bearing reservoir was struck at a depth of 1,300 metres. ONGC intensified its surveys. These led over the years to the discovery of oil and gas fields that were named Heera, Panna, Ratna, Neelam, Mukta, Bassein and Daman. The installation of offshore platforms commenced in 1976.

At the time of writing, the offshore production facilities include nearly 30 'Process' and 'Well-cum-Process' platforms and over a hundred and twenty 'Well' platforms. Pipelines on the seabed carry oil and gas from the well platforms to the process platforms and from there to onshore terminals at Uran and Hazira.

The Defence of Offshore Assets

The magnitude of capital investment and the consequences of interruption in oil and gas production focused attention on protecting Bombay High from terrorist action during peacetime and enemy action during war.

The Coast Guard Act enacted in 1978 enjoined the Coast Guard to 'ensure the safety and protection of offshore terminals, installations and other structures and devices'. Discussions commenced on coordinating the responsibilities for the safety and protection of the offshore installations between the ONGC, the Coast Guard and the Navy.

An Offshore Security Coordination Committee was established in 1978. In 1983, an Offshore Defence Advisory Group (ODAG) was constituted under a Rear Admiral (FODAG) to plan and advise the Navy and the ONGC on the security and defence of Bombay offshore infrastructure.

In 1985, approval was accorded for the resources required to counter the peacetime threats to the installations in Bombay High, which, in view of the increasing number of oil and gas fields, came to be called the Western Offshore Region.

1982 UN Convention on the Law of the Sea - Safety Zones around Offshore Structures

After the first (1958) United Nations Conference on the Law of the Sea, the 1958 Geneva Convention on the Continental Shelf had provided for a safety zone of 500 metres around offshore structures and installations in which appropriate measures could be taken to ensure the safety, both of navigation and of the offshore structures and installations.

At the third (1972 to 1982) United Nations Conference on the Law of the Sea, India had stated that considering the size and speed of modern tankers and the time taken to stop or divert such huge vessels, a 500 metre safety zone was totally inadequate. India, therefore, advocated enlarged safety zones around oil installations and structures. This suggestion found place in the 1982 Convention on the Law of the Sea but in a modified form. The Convention incorporated an enabling provision 'allowing a coastal state to promulgate safety zones in excess of 500 metres around artificial islands, installations and structures, if authorised by generally accepted standards or as recommended by the competent international organisation.'

INDIA'S 0FFSHORE OIL BASINS

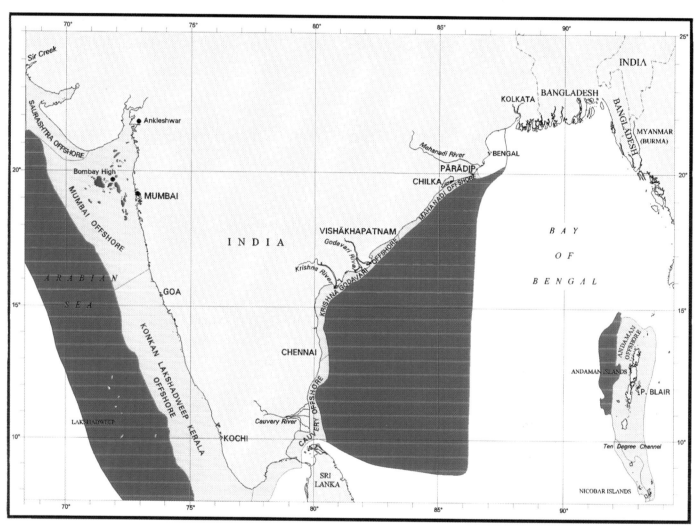

COLOUR CODE

: Offshore Oil Basins on the Continental Shelf.

: Deep Offshore beyond 200 metres depth (1.35 million Square Kilometres).

Traffic Regulatory Scheme

The Western Offshore Region straddles the customary route into Bombay Harbour. A Traffic Regulatory Scheme was promulgated in 1985. It required vessels destined for, or departing from, Bombay to follow 'recommended routes'. Since these were 'recommendatory' rather than mandatory, these routes were not always followed. A mandatory Vessel Traffic Separation Scheme is under consideration.

Resources for the Protection of Offshore Assets

After studying how other nations were dealing with the threats to their offshore installations and considering the nature of the threat in our environment, forces were built up for protecting the offshore installations. These included offshore patrol vessels (OPVs), Dornier maritime patrol aircraft, helicopters to fly in Marine Commandos of the Quick Reaction Force and radars.

Regular exercises are conducted with the Air Force, the Coast Guard and the ONGC to update contingency plans.

Developments in the 1990s

Surveys indicated that India's continental shelf had potentially rich oil and gas resources in the Palk Bay, Cauvery and Krishna-Godavari River Basins and gas reserves in the Andaman Offshore.

As part of the liberalisation reforms, private oil companies, both Indian and foreign, were permitted through joint ventures with the national oil companies to explore new oil and gas reserves, develop proven reserves, lay pipelines and establish refineries.

The extension of offshore activities to both coasts and into deeper waters increased ODAG's responsibilities.

31

Personnel

Preamble

Personnel management policy was driven by a wide range of considerations:

- To overcome shortages by constantly innovating the schemes of intake.

- To raise the educational standards of intake so that personnel could cope with the rising technological levels of naval equipment.

- To enhance allowances like flying bounty, submarine pay, diving money and survey allowance as incentives to attract talent into volunteering for these arduous specialisations.

- To juggle these considerations within the overarching constraint of avoiding disparity with the Army and the Air Force in educational, physical and medical recruitment standards, pay scales, length of colour service, pension benefits and equivalence with civilian trades at the time of resettlement.

- To reduce durations of courses, so as to increase the manpower available for manning new acquisitions.

- To induce personnel to remain in service and minimise the exodus of trained and experienced manpower to the better paid Merchant Navy / civil sector by offering longer careers, better emoluments, subsidised domestic accommodation, subsidised schooling for children, canteen facilities, Group Insurance Schemes and generous loans from the Indian Naval Benevolent Association to meet pressing domestic requirements.

- On board ships, to minimise disparities between departments and specialisations / trades in terms of workload and the less-relished duties like clean ship and ship husbandry.

All these considerations had to be harmonised:

- To keep officers and sailors ready for combat despite their having to be periodically rotated into and out of ships.

- To conserve expertise despite this endless movement of personnel.

- To rationalise trade structures to keep abreast of technological change.

- To optimise the utilisation of personnel and, in view of the costs involved, to minimise their movement across the subcontinent of India.

Even though Manning and Training are at the core of the Personnel function, they have been discussed in separate chapters to facilitate better understanding. This chapter discusses the issues that have not been discussed in those two chapters.

Officers

Increasing Officer Intake

The schemes of officer intake that had been initiated in earlier years continued to evolve:

- The Direct Entry Scheme that had started in 1965 was made more attractive in 1971 by offering Executive candidates 'permanent' commissions instead of 'short service' commissions. In 1975, this scheme started offering permanent commissions to Engineering and Electrical candidates also.

- In 1965, the University Entry Scheme, which till then was applicable only to commissions in the Electrical Branch, was extended to the Engineering Branch.

- The Revised Special Entry Scheme (RSES) had been introduced in 1968 for cadets who had reached the Intermediate standard in education. In 1969, a Naval Academy was temporarily established at Cochin to train 80 RSES cadets annually. In 1971, intake was increased through this scheme.

- In 1974, to maintain parity with the NDA graduate cadets, the educational level of the Naval Academy's intake was raised. Science graduates started being taken in for the Executive Branch under the Graduate Special Entry Scheme (GSES). The Union Public Service Commission's Combined Defence Services

(CDS) Examination was introduced in 1974 to replace the separate examinations, which used to be held for cadets to join the Naval Academy's GSES entry, the Indian Military Academy, and the Air Force Academy.

- In 1982, short service commissions were revived for University Entry Technical Graduate Scheme and the Direct Entry Scheme for the Engineering and Electrical Branches. Moreover, the disciplines of Aeronautical Engineering, Production Engineering, Metallurgical Engineering and Control Engineering were included in the eligibility for Direct Entry into the Engineering Branch.

- In 1983 and 1984, to further increase the induction of officers into the technical branches, new schemes of entry were introduced:

  - *Naval Sponsorship Scheme:* Up to 50 candidates could be selected from amongst 1st and 2nd year students in the Indian Institutes of Technology and selected Engineering Colleges and granted permanent commission on successful completion of their Engineering Course. Their tuition fees would be paid by the Government and they would also be paid a stipend of Rs.400/-per month whilst in college.

  - *10+2 Technical Cadet Entry Scheme:* 30 cadets per year could be inducted from amongst students, completing the 10+2 stage. These cadets would undergo a 4-year Basic Engineering Course at the Naval College of Engineering.

- In 1987, following on from the success of the 10+2 Technical Cadet Entry Scheme, the 10+2 Executive Cadet Entry Scheme was implemented for recruiting 80 Executive Branch cadets every year to undergo three years training at the Naval Academy.

Professionalism at Sea and its Linkage with Promotions

By the mid 1970s, new Leanders, Petyas and submarines had entered service. Helicopters were being embarked in ships. Attention turned to the linkage between promotions and professionalism performance at sea.

Several considerations had to be balanced:

- To be eligible for promotion, an officer was required to have gone to sea in the previous rank. There were not enough billets in ships to fulfil this requirement for each rank.

- How was 'sea time' to be interpreted? Appointment to a ship? Or appointments only to operational ships? Billets in operational ships were less than the number required for each rank.

- What should be the optimum duration of a sea tenure? Should it be long enough for expertise to develop? The longer this duration, the fewer the sea billets that would be available.

- What should be done if there were no seagoing billets at all in some specialisations and their ranks?

- How should parity be maintained between the officers in ships and those in the Air Arm and the Submarine Arm? For example, in the Air Arm, how was sea time to be counted for pilots and observers of flights embarked on board and not actually employed on watch keeping duties vis-à-vis pilots and observers performing operational duties in shore-based front-line squadrons?

- To overcome this problem of billets, should Executive branch officers in the rank of Commander and Captain be subdivided into Post List ('seagoing stream', colloquially known as the 'Wet List') and General List[1] ('non-seagoing stream', the 'Dry List')?

- Could tenures in specified shore billets be 'equated' to sea time?

- Was there a need to codify the weightage to be given to sea reports for promotion to higher ranks? The weightage, if given to sea-time as opposed to shore-time would work to the disadvantage of officers in high profile appointments ashore.

- Did the existing ACR appraisal form have enough inputs to enable the Initiating Officers to form a valid opinion regarding the suitability of the officer for sea-time / sea command?

Rationalising the 'Rules of Sea Time'

Each of the issues listed above was worked through to rationalise the rules for sea time:

- *Duration of Sea Tenure.* Officers of the rank of Lieutenant Commander would be given a minimum of 12 months sea time until such time as it became feasible for this duration to be increased to 18 months.

  All officers in command would be given 18 months' sea time.

- *Statutory Sea Time in the Rank of Lieutenant Commander.* This could be done either in the rank of Lieutenant Commander or after attaining six years

---

1. In naval parlance, the expression 'General List' has two different meanings depending upon the context:
   i. Those who joined as officers as opposed to the 'Special Duties List' comprised sailors promoted to officer rank..
   ii. The non-seagoing officers of the Executive Branch as opposed to the 'Post List' of seagoing officers of this Branch.

seniority in the rank of Lieutenant. For this purpose 'sea time' was defined as follows:

- *General List 'Executive', 'Engineering' & 'Electrical' Officers.*[2] Only billets on board ship / submarines, in fleet staff and in fleet support appointments would count as sea time.

- *Pilots / Observers.* Time in embarked squadrons / flights would count as sea time provided these officers carried out watch-keeping and other ship's duties. Commanding Officers were required to make specific mention in the ACRs of these officers of their performance as watch-keepers and in ship's duties. Officers of shore-based front-line squadrons would be appointed to afloat billets for sea time.

- *Air Technical Officers.* Air technical appointments afloat and appointments in all air squadrons, including appointments as flight engineers, would count as sea time.

• *Statutory Requirement for Sea Time in the Rank of Commander.* This was removed for both Executive and Technical officers. The guidelines promulgated for their career planning and promotion were:

- Promotion boards for Commanders and Captains would recommend executive branch officers for appointments afloat, including fitness for command afloat. Due weightage would be given to such officers for their subsequent promotion.

- For promotion to the next higher rank, Commanders and Captains of the Technical branches should have held one of the following appointments:

  * Appointment afloat.

  * Appointment in Dockyards, Base Maintenance Units (of ships and submarines), Base Maintenance Facilities (of aircraft), Afloat Support Teams (ASTs), Naval Aircraft Repair Organisation, Technical Position (TP) or a similar maintenance / repair organisation.

  * Staff appointment in Command Headquarters, air station / squadrons or squadron staff of ships.

  * Special naval projects as approved by the Chief of the Naval Staff.

'Wet' and 'Dry' Lists

The proposal for the formal classification of officers into Wet (Post) and Dry (General) Lists was not pursued because of the apprehension that would arise that the promotion prospects of officers in the Post and General Lists would vary widely and this would adversely affect the morale of the officer cadre. It was decided that Promotion Boards would recommend officers' suitability or otherwise for sea time / sea command. The Chief of Naval Staff would give due consideration to these recommendations when deciding afloat appointments.

Aircrew Officers in Embarked Flights

The problems faced by aircrew officers serving in helicopter flights that embarked only when ships went to sea continued to persist for several years. Due to the shortage of qualified aircrew and of operational aircraft, they were constantly transferred from ship to ship. Since these moves were classified as a 'temporary transfer', they disqualified flight crew from being reported upon whilst temporarily embarked unless they were able to serve the mandatory three months in a ship to ensure the initiation of an ACR. To avoid 'ACR injustice to aircrew', all flight / aircrew transfers started being promulgated by NHQ to give these inter-ship moves a semblance of 'permanence'. This did not work too well. In due course, it became possible to 'base' embarked helicopter flights in the proximate naval air station where the ships were based - *INS Kunjali* in Bombay, *INS Garuda* in Cochin and *INS Vega* in Vizag.

Improvements in Annual Confidential Report (ACR) Forms

ACR forms were reviewed to improve the inputs regarding the determination of suitability for sea-time / sea command.

Linking the Command Examination and the Staff Course

The 'Command Examination' had been instituted in 1974 to encourage Executive Branch officers to improve their professional knowledge. Subsequently, for the respective branches, the Technical Management and Logistic Management Examinations were instituted as equivalents of the Command Examination.

In 1977, qualifying in the Command / Technical Management / Logistics Management Examinations was made a prerequisite to selection for the Staff Course. To dovetail with the Staff Course annual programme, from 1978 onwards, these examinations started being held in February - March every year.

Career Prospects and Cadre Reviews[3]

From the mid 1970s onwards, the Defence Services found that they were no longer attracting candidates of

---

2. As opposed to Special Duties List.

3. The Navy's rationale and the after effects have been discussed in greater detail in the Historical Reference Data section titled "Cadre Reviews", page 299.

the requisite calibre. Despite lowering of intake standards, the services were, at times, forced to leave quotas unfilled. Service Headquarters started formulating proposals to make the Services more attractive. These proposals led to the Cadre Reviews.

A major proposal was to reduce the gap in career prospects between Defence personnel and those of other Central Government services. There were large differences in the percentage of officers promoted to the corresponding grades in the civil vis-à-vis service cadres. An equally wide gap existed in the number of years taken to attain these grades.

The First Cadre Review

The Navy's case for the First Cadre Review comprised proposals for better promotion prospects for officers and men and for improved perquisites like increase in sailors' Authorised Married Establishment (AME), facility to hire accommodation in places other than at duty station, higher percentage of jobs in the CPO/PO ranks, increase in the Special Duties (SD) Cadre (the Special Duties cadre comprises promotees from sailor rank to officer rank). Because of inter-service implications, the above proposals were deferred for further consideration.

Flag Rank Up-gradations

Discussions in 1979 centred on cadre review for Flag Rank. Approval was accorded for upgradation of three Rear Admirals to Vice Admirals[4] and eight Captains / Commodores to Rear Admirals[5], to be phased over a period of three years commencing 1980.

The Second Cadre Review

The aims of the Second Cadre Review were:

- Restoration of the post-Independence parity in the official status of Armed Forces personnel vis-à-vis the All India Civil Services.
- Recognition of the high risk career, personal hardships and sacrifices, strict code of discipline, devotion above and beyond the call of duty, and the qualifications of the Armed Forces personnel being commensurate with the technological advances.

- Offsetting the impact of the above through measures to enhance the official status and improve upon the economic condition of defence personnel.
- Project the eroding attractiveness of the Armed Forces and the immediate need for reversing this trend.

The proposals put up by the Navy for consideration in the Second Cadre Review were:

- Up-gradations in various ranks and pay promotions.
- Time scale promotion to the rank of Commander.
- De-linking of pay and pension from rank.
- Improvements in the Special Duties List Cadre.

There were misgivings in the Navy regarding the effect that the up-gradations would have on the traditional hierarchy on board ships. However, since the Army had decided to go for large-scale up-gradations and since the Air Force had fallen in line with the Army, the Navy subsumed its misgivings.

Officer Up-gradations in the Second Cadre Review

Approval was accorded for the creation / upgradation of the following to be phased over a period of two years commencing from the financial year 1984-85:

- Vice Admirals   –   2[6]
- Rear Admirals   –   5[7]
- Captains   –   45
- Commanders   –   100

Additional Concessions Approved as Part of the Second Cadre Review

- Promotion to the rank of Commander (Time Scale) on completion of 21 years commissioned service.
- Promotion from Lieutenant to Lieutenant Commander (Special Duties List) by time scale on completion of 11 years commissioned service.
- Ratio for promotion to the rank of Sub Lieutenant enhanced by 20%.

The Special Duties List

In 1976, the existing provision for the re-employment of retired officers of the General List up to the age of 56 years

---

4. These were Deputy Chief of the Naval Staff, Admiral Superintendent Naval Dockyard Bombay and Flag Officer Commanding Western Fleet.

5. These were Fortress Commander A&N, Chiefs of Staff of the Western and Eastern Naval Commands and in NHQ the Assistant Chief of Naval Staff (Operations), the Assistant Chief of Naval Staff (Air), the Assistant Chief of Personnel (Career Planning), the Assistant Chief of Material (Dockyards and Refits), the Assistant Chief of Material (Systems).

6. These were Chief of Logistics and Controller of Warship Production & Acquisition.

7. These were Chief of Staff, Southern Naval Command, Chief Instructor (Navy) DSSC, Chief Staff Officer (Technical) Western Naval Command, Flag Officer Bombay and in NHQ, Assistant Chief of Personnel (Civilians).

was extended to officers of the Special Duties List. Also, as a temporary measure for two years, approval was accorded for re-employed SD List officers to be appointed against vacancies in the General List.

In 1978, the promotion rules for SD List officers were liberalised:

- SD List officers could attain the rank of Lieutenant (SD) on completion of 3 years of commissioned service as against 5 years.
- The number of vacancies in the rank of Lieutenant Commander (SD) was increased from 10% to 20%. This would ensure that the rank of Lieutenant Commander (SD) would be available to 90% of eligible SD List officers as against 30% in the past.

To widen the promotion avenues, the age limits of sailors were lowered in 1982 from 30 years to 20 years for appearing in the Special Duty List examination for promotion to the officer cadre.

In 1983, eligibility for commission in the Special Duty List was extended to non-artificer technical sailors.

The Second Cadre Review enhanced by 20% the ratio for promotion to the rank of Sub Lieutenant and authorised promotion from Lieutenant to Lieutenant Commander (SD) by time scale on completion of 11 years commissioned service.

In 1984, approval was accorded for SD list Commanders with four years seniority to be be considered for promotion to the rank of Captain (SD).

The end position that emerged was:

- Sub Lt (SD) to Lt (SD)   – 3 years' commissioned service as Acting Sub Lt/ Sub Lt (SD).
- Lt (SD) to Lt Cdr (SD)   – 11 years' commissioned service.
- Lt Cdr (SD) to Cdr (SD)   – 3 years' seniority as Lt Cdr (SD).
- Cdr (SD) to Captain (SD) – 4 years' seniority as Cdr (SD).

Promotions up to the rank of Lieutenant Commander in the SD List Cadre were by time scale, subject to a satisfactory record of service, on completion of requisite number of years of service as indicated above.

Promotions to the rank of Commander SD and Captain (SD) were by selection. There was no separate sanctioned cadre of Commander (SD) and Captain (SD). Promotions to these ranks were made in exceptionally deserving cases only and against vacancies to the General List Cadre.

Honorary Commissions in the SD List

An Honorary Commission in the rank of Sub Lieutenant and Lieutenant in the Special Duties List was instituted as an award that deserving MCPO I/IIs could aspire for at the end of their service. The Honorary rank gave recipients some officer status and privileges and also certain monetary benefits[8] and was something that sailors who had served the Navy hard and long could look forward to at the end of their careers.

The awards are made on Republic Day and Independence Day each year at the discretion of the Chief of the Naval Staff. In selecting sailors for an award of Honorary Commission, some of the factors that are considered are length of service, sea service record, performance on instructional duties, annual 'superior' assessments, participation in extra curricular activities and recommendations. The award of an Honorary Commission is an expression of appreciation and its nature entails that it be given to the deserving sailors just prior to their retirement.

In 1984, the ratio for promotion for Honorary Sub Lieutenant was increased from 10 per thousand to 12 per thousand sailors sanctioned.

Naval Officers Computerised Management Information System

The computerisation of officers' personal records commenced in end 1980 and completed in mid 1983. The Naval Officers Computerised Management Information System (NOCMIS) contained confidential information like course grading, flying assessments and data from confidential reports. The Management Information System was designed to assist in deciding placements, selection for courses and key appointments, career and appointment planning, awards, retirements, post retirement placements.

Sailors

Increasing the Period of Engagement

Until 1965, a sailor's initial period of engagement had been ten years. On completion, he could re-engage for five years and for two years thereafter up to a total of seventeen years. The authority for re-engagement beyond seventeen years vested in Naval Headquarters. Normally, all sailors were re-engaged up to twenty years of service if recommended

---

8. In 1983, sailors granted Honorary Commission were admitted a fixed pay (Hon Sub Lt – Rs 1,000 and Hon Lt – Rs 1,100) along with Dearness and City Compensatory Allowance.

by their Commanding Officer. Re-engagement beyond twenty years was on a selective basis.

In 1966, to meet the increase in manpower for the Russian acquisitions, sailors were allowed to re-engage up to a total period of twenty five years or age of superannuation, whichever was earlier, subject to the Commanding Officers' recommendation. This helped to promote a greater sense of security of employment amongst sailors and ensure a longer career for those who volunteered for further service.

In 1973, re-engagement was permitted for five years at a time up to the compulsory age of retirement.

In 1976, the period of initial engagement was increased from 10 to 15 years to provide for a longer tenure of service and better utilisation of trained manpower resources. This also enabled all sailors to earn the minimum pension on completion of their initial engagement. Sailors wishing to continue their engagement could do so as per the rules in force.

In 1987, approval was accorded for the enrolment of sailors for an initial period of 20 years (instead of the earlier 15 years). This was particularly significant in the case of artificers because their employability now increased to 15 years after their initial training of 5 years.[9]

Changes in Sailors' Conditions of Service

In July 1976, in consonance with the recommendations of the Third Pay Commission, several changes were implemented in sailors' conditions of service:

- The educational qualification for entry was raised to Matriculation for Boy Entry sailors of all branches and for Direct Entry Seaman and Engineering branch sailors. As a result:

  - Direct Entry Seamen and Communication sailors, Engineering Mechanics, Electrical Mechanics, Writers, Stores Assistants and Medical Attendants all came on par, educationally and pay wise. All future entrants would receive the higher Group B scale of pay.[10]

  - Non-matriculate Direct Entry Stewards, Cooks, Musicians and Topasses could join on the lower Group C scale of pay.

  - Serving sailors who were already matriculates would re-muster into Group B and those who qualified subsequently would also re-muster into Group B.

  - The age of entry for Boys was revised to 16 - 18 years and that for Direct Entry sailors to 18 - 20 years.

- *Abolition of Boy Entry:* With the introduction of Matric Entry recruitment, it was decided to abolish the Boy Entry and have only one Sailors Training Establishment (STE).

- *Time Scale Promotion to Leading Rank:* To improve the career prospects of sailors, it was decided in 1977 that all sailors would be promoted to Leading Rank on completion of five years of service in man's rank, subject to having qualified in the prescribed examinations.

- *Increase in Retirement Ages:* Time Scale promotion to leading rank ensured that all sailors would be able to serve up to at least 45 years of age. The new retirement ages became 45 years for Leading Seaman and below, 50 years for Chief Petty Officers and Petty officers and 55 years for Master Chief Petty Officers.

Change in the Educational Qualification for Matric Entry Recruitment

In 1987, the educational qualification for Matric Entry Recruitment was revised in order to meet the challenge of operating and maintaining sophisticated equipment and machinery:

- General Candidates: Matric or equivalent with 55% or above marks.

- For sons and blood brothers of Naval Personnel: Matric or equivalent with 45% or above marks.

Policy for Transferring Sailors into and out of Ships

The driving wheel of the Navy's management of its sailor cadres was its 'transfer' policy. The Annual Training Programme for higher rank courses, the annual programme of Fleet Exercises during which sailors got 'sea time', the Annual Refit Programme and the closing of children's academic year were all dovetailed.

On the one hand, the promotion regulations required sailors to qualify in higher rate professional courses and to be given adequate sea time. On the other hand, this policy

---

9. Prior to 1976, artificers were required to serve for a period of 10 years on completion of initial Apprentice training of 4 years, i.e. after becoming Artificer 5th Class. The 1976 increase in the period of initial engagement to 15 years did not really achieve the desired objective of increasing the useful service of artificers appreciably and, in most cases, they were now required to serve only one or two years more than they were expected to serve prior to 1976.

10. The credit for this financially significant welfare measure belongs to Defence Minister Babu Jagjivan Ram. His rationale was that in the Indian milieu, every sailor, soldier and airman feeds at least five persons (himself, his wife and three children) and also looks after his parents. By raising this segment from Group C to Group B scales of pay, over five million families would benefit.

of continuously transferring sailors into and out of ships conflicted with the consolidation of expertise.

The Drafting Office (later named as the Bureau of Sailors) had the onerous task of balancing these conflicting requirements and of providing equal opportunity. It took several years to arrive at the right balance and evolve a system based on computerisation of sailors' records and systematising feedback from ships of individual sailor capabilities, limitations and expertise.

This issue has been dealt with in greater detail in the chapter on the Manning of Ships and the Conservation of Expertise.

The Master Chief Petty Officer (MCPO) Cadre

In 1968, as an inducement for sailors to re-engage for longer service, the MCPO cadre was created as the naval equivalent of Junior Commissioned Officers (JCOs) of the Army and Warrant / Master Warrant Officers of the Air Force. The MCPO Cadre was sanctioned as a percentage of the sanctioned cadre of CPOs:

	Technical	Non-Technical
MCPO Class I	15%	12 ½ %
MCPO Class II	25%	25%

Second Cadre Review Sailor Upgradations

Artificers	To Chief Artificers	59
Non-Artificers	To Master Chief / Chief Petty Officers	390[11]
	To Petty Officers	60

Additional Concessions Approved as part of the Second Cadre Review

- Increase in ratio for the award of Long Service and Good Conduct Medal and Meritorious Medal increased to 4 per 800 sailors.
- Authorised Married Establishment for the grant of Cash in Lieu of Quarters increased:

– For Leading Seamen / equivalents   From 80% to 90%

– For Seamen I/II / equivalents   From 35% to 50%

Artificers

With new technologies entering service with the Russian acquisitions and the Leander class frigates, the inability to make up the shortage of artificers remained a constant cause of concern. The better emoluments and perquisites offered by private industry and the Merchant Navy could not be matched by the Navy. Most experienced artificers left the Navy after having served minimum time.

Several schemes were initiated to remedy the shortage. One was to recruit holders of diplomas from polytechnics as 'direct entry artificers'. Whilst this helped to meet the immediate need by avoiding the long four-year initial training that artificer apprentices underwent, it had the disadvantage of insufficient naval indoctrination of an age group that would become Petty Officers on board ships within a few years of joining.

In 1966, recruitment commenced of diploma holders as artificers to be trained for 1½ years instead of the 4 years training given to regular entry artificer apprentices.

In 1967, Direct Entry Artificer intake was increased to 120.

In 1970, the shortage of artificers in the Submarine Cadre led to the induction of Direct Entry Artificers Acting 4th class of three / four year diplomas in mechanical, electrical and aeronautical engineering. Simultaneously, this entry was permitted for engineering and electrical artificers.

By 1971, the deficiency in the artificer cadre had been brought down from 30% to 10%. From 1972 onwards, the artificer shortage persisted at 10%. In 1983, approval was accorded for the recruitment, on a regular basis for a period of 5 years, of artificers from amongst candidates holding diplomas in the various engineering disciplines.

In 1987, the initial engagement for artificers was increased to 20 years. In 1988, shortages started reducing

---

11. Vice Admiral VL Koppikar served in the Personnel Branch from Deputy Director all the way up to Chief of Personnel, interspersed with appointments at sea. Writing in the Navy Foundation's annual publication 'Quarterdeck 2000', he stated:

   "Perhaps one of the most hastily implemented decisions of those years was the creation of two additional ranks, MCPO I and MCPO II in the Sailor Cadre. For a while, it threw the Navy completely off balance. There appeared to be no justification for these two ranks at the apex level without enhanced responsibilities or accountability. There were problems galore of manning and management, of accommodation and of detailing parties for various tasks. All of a sudden there were 'too many Chiefs and very few Indians'. Above all, it pushed the hitherto 'prestigious' ranks of CPO and PO into the shade. That, in my view was the saddest part."

   This is a classic example of the kind of dilemma that affects the management of naval personnel. On the one hand, it is unjust to deprive senior sailors of ranks that their Army and Air Force counterparts have. On the other hand, sailors' accommodation on board ships is graded rank-wise and in numbers according to functional combat requirements (and not 'equity' requirements). When ships have too many senior sailors, problems arise not only of habitability but also of their having to do work that was earlier being done by junior sailors. The result of the Second Cadre Review was that the ratio of senior sailors (Petty Officers and above) to junior sailors (Leading rank and below) halved from 1 : 4 to 1 : 2.

and the Direct Entry Scheme was discontinued. When shortages recurred, the scheme had to be revived.

The Navy-Entry Artificers Scheme

This scheme was started in 1987, as part of the measures to revitalise the Navy's manning and training systems. Its aim was to improve the career prospects for young, bright and technically oriented Matric Entry sailors of all branches and to reduce artificer shortages.

Non-artificer sailors from the Seaman, Communication, Engineering and Electrical branches including the Survey and Aviation cadres were made eligible to become artificers. To be eligible, a sailor had to secure 65% marks during initial training, be under 25 years of age, have three years service including one year at sea, have passed a written examination in English, General Knowledge, General Science and Mathematics. Selected sailors underwent conversion/professional courses, on successful completion of which they could be promoted to the rank of Acting Artificer Fourth Class.

432 MER sailors of all branches appeared in the first written examination held in January 1990 in which 53 sailors qualified, from which 27 were finally selected, based on merit and the vacancies available.

Changes in the Sailor Structure

After the arrival from Britain of the cruiser *Mysore* in 1957, the eight new frigates between 1958 and 1961 and the aircraft carrier *Vikrant* in 1961, it was clear that the increase in sophistication of ships and equipment called for a comprehensive re-look at the existing ranks, rates and trades of the Navy's sailors. A committee was appointed to review the sailor structure.

By the time this committee convened in 1966, the first of the Russian acquisitions arrived and sharpened the assessment that there was going to be a shortage of bunks on board. At this time, sailors were being selected to undergo training in Russia to man the submarines, the Petyas and the Submarine Depot Ship and problems had arisen on how to accommodate the Navy's numerous trades in the fewer bunks.

These and associated aspects have been dealt with in the chapter on the Manning of Ships and the Conservation of Expertise.

The Instructor Cadre

Up to 1979, the Navy had an Instructor Cadre in the Seaman Branch, namely Gunnery Instructor (GI), Torpedo Anti Submarine Instructor (TAS I) and Plotting and Radar Instructor (PR I). These 'Instructors' were a highly dedicated group of senior professional sailors backed up by specialised 'instructor' qualifying courses. Their major role was operational training on board ships and instructions at various professional schools. In addition, they were responsible through their respective departmental officers for the conduct of the sailors in their department and the overall efficiency of their department. In the course of their duties, these instructors shouldered extra responsibility and grew in stature. Although they did not get any monetary benefits, they had an edge over their counterparts and were looked up to with awe and respect.

In the 1970s, with the induction of the Leander class frigates and Soviet origin ships, weapon systems proliferated. Vertical specialisation and the Pre Commissioning Training were adopted to man and operate the complex new systems. These led to the conclusion that an Instructor could not possibly master the variety of systems in his specialisation and in 1979 led to the restructuring of the Instructor Cadre.

From 1980 onwards, sailors with aptitude for instructional duties and having the requisite professional knowledge were supposed to be selected to undergo a newly introduced instructors' course before appointment for training duties. The new scheme was not successful in attracting volunteers for instructional duties.

For the next ten years, very few instructors were trained. The previously trained Instructors continued to man key posts on board and ashore and their contribution continued to be found invaluable. With the passage of time, most of these sailors retired.

By the end 1980s, there was a growing consensus for the re-introduction of the Instructor Cadre in the Seaman Branch not only to rejuvenate training ashore but also consolidate and improve professional training afloat. In 1990, the Navy re-introduced the Instructors Cadre for all branches.

Computerisation of Sailors' Service Records

The computerisation of Sailors' Service Records commenced in 1979 and completed in 1982. This personnel management information system was designed to ensure effective management of sailors' appointments, training and promotions.

The Revised Commissions and Warrants Scheme

The number of sailors who became officers under the old Commissions and Warrants (CW) scheme was found to be very meagre. In 1978, a revised CW scheme was introduced for granting permanent commission to eligible sailors, both artificers and non-artificers, who had the minimum qualification of matriculation.

Distance Education Programme for Sailors' Educational Tests ET1/ET1 (M)

In 1990, Naval Headquarters launched the Distance Education Programme for sailors preparing for their ET1 & ET1 (M) examinations. Graded lessons in Language and General Knowledge and Mathematics were despatched to ships and establishments where sailors had registered for this programme.

The Navy's Civilian Personnel

The basic advantage of civilian personnel has been their greater continuity in shore assignments, as opposed to uniformed personnel whose assignments afloat and ashore change frequently. From the functional point of view, the Navy's dependence on civilian manpower lay principally in the following fields:

- In Naval Dockyards and Base Repair Organisations for the maintenance, repair and refit of ships and submarines, and for manning yard craft.

- In the Aircraft Repair Yard – for the maintenance, repair and refit of aircraft.

- In Naval technical functions like draftsmen, naval technical specialists in DRDO laboratories.

- In Naval Store Depots, Naval Armament Depots and Weapon Equipment Depots – for the storage, upkeep, accounting, repair and indenting of their respective stores.

- In shore offices for secretarial and clerical duties.

- In Naval shore establishments for motor transport driver and general conservancy duties.

In the case of the civilian personnel performing store-keeping duties, very little systematic career progression training had been attempted to enhance their productivity. The results of this neglect began to show from the 1960's onwards. The induction of new technologies in the Russian acquisitions and the Leander class frigates greatly increased the importance of the duties entrusted to civilian personnel. It did not take long for the infirmities in the civilian cadres to affect the operational availability of ships, particularly in the field of spare parts. This compelled the institution of the systematic training programmes that in subsequent years, helped to improve productivity in the shore depots.

As can be seen from the ensuing overview, the numbers of civilian naval personnel have remained more or less equal to the number of naval personnel in uniform from 1968 onwards.

Overview of the Navy's Borne Strength Between 1965 and 1990

In round figures, the comparative increase in the Navy's borne strength between 1965-1975 and 1976-1990 can be seen from this tabulation:

| As on 31 Dec | Naval Personnel | | | | Civilian Personnel | | | |
	Officers General List	Officers SD List	Sailors	Total in Uniform	Gazetted	Industrial	Non-Gazetted Non-Industrial	Total Civilians
Growth 1965 to 1975								
1965	1520	410	16,930	18,870	300	12,390	10,550	23,240
1966	1590	430	18,350	20,380	320	13,340	10,900	24,560
1967	1660	470	20,460	22,580	320	13,820	11,300	25,440
1968	1740	490	22,790	25,020	310	13,990	11,730	25,730
1969	1850	530	25,130	27,510	330	14,000	11,890	26,220
1970	1970	540	26,150	28,660	410	14,040	12,250	26,700
1971	2250	580	26,860	29,680	-	-	-	28,450
1972	2470	600	26,440	29,500	-	-	-	-
1973	2550	600	26,290	29,440	510	16,430	13,130	30,070
1974	2690	600	26,860	30,150	-	-	-	-
1975	2880	600	27,270	30,750	-	-	-	-

Growth 1976 to 1990

Year								
1976	2970	600	27,120	30,690	-	-	-	-
1977	3060	640	27,440	31,140	-	-	-	-
1978	3110	620	27,410	31,140	-	-	-	-
1979	3270	670	27,660	31,600	-	-	-	-
1980	3440	660	28,730	32,830	655	15,640	14,690	30,980
1981	3570	670	27,940	32,180	740	16,970	14,630	32,340
1982	3700	730	28,400	32,840	860	17,180	16,060	34,100
1983	3960	760	28,520	33,240	860	18,140	18,090	37,090
1984	4090	750	30,020	34,860	940	19,360	18,900	39,200
1985	4310	800	31,630	36,740	880	19,330	18,130	38,340
1986	4480	840	34,700	40,020	910	20,020	18,700	39,630
1987	4630	850	37,010	42,490	920	20,160	18,530	39,620
1988	4910	880	39,550	45,330	950	19,840	19,390	40,180
1989	5080	840	41,680	47,610	940	20,320	19,210	40,470
1990	5370	800	43,130	49,300	960	21,510	19,580	42,050

General

Controlling Manpower Costs From the Mid 1970s Onwards

In the 1950s and 1960s, manpower costs had not been a cause for concern. The emphasis had been on recruiting manpower as swiftly as possible to cope with acquisitions and their infrastructure. In the mid 1970s, these costs started spiralling as a result of:

- The recurring increases in Dearness Allowance to neutralise inflation after the global 1973 oil crisis.

- The cost of implementing the Third Pay Commission's recommendations.

To keep manpower costs under control and ensure the best utilisation of available manpower, every single proposal for increase in manpower had to be cleared by the concerned Principal Staff Officer in Naval Headquarters before it could go to the Ministry of Defence.[12]

Abolition of the Indian Naval Reserve and Indian Naval Volunteer Reserve

In 1976, consequent to the introduction of the 15-year initial engagement for sailors, transfers to the Fleet Reserve were discontinued. In 1977, it was decided to abolish the reserve cadre because training for a period of one month every alternate year was not serving any useful purpose. Under the new scheme, all sailors on release would be subject to recall to active service for a period their service fell short of 17 years for non-artificers and 18 years for artificers. During this period, released sailors would not be entitled to any monetary benefits nor would they undergo refresher training.

Discipline and Morale

The rapid expansion of personnel affected the quality of leadership, particularly at the Chief Petty Officer and Petty Officer level. Curtailed training programmes to cope with shortages eroded basic, time-tested traditional leadership practices. Both training and discipline suffered. This has been discussed in greater detail in the chapter titled 'Erosion of Leadership Values'.

The Merger of the Supply & Secretariat and Executive Branches

This topic has been discussed in the chapter titled 'The Merger of the Supply and Secretariat Branch with the Executive Branch in 1978 and the Creation of the Logistics Cadre in 1989'.

The Merger of the Engineering and Electrical Branches

In 1985, consideration commenced of the proposal to merge the Engineering and Electrical Branches. The rationale was:

---

12. The rationale for this draconian (and much resented at the middle officer level) requirement was that if a proposal could survive several layers of rigorous scrutiny then only would it be worth considering.

- The instrumentation in diesel electric propulsion in submarines and gas turbine propulsion in ships had increasingly becoming electrical and electronic in nature where sensors, amplifiers and digital displays had replaced the erstwhile mechanical and pneumatic instruments. With this incursion of electrics and electronics in the controlling elements of main propulsion machinery and auxiliaries, the division of responsibility between the two departments had overlapped and blurred.

- The functions of the technical cadres had diversified. No longer were the two branches concerned only with maintenance. Their functions had widened to include equipment evaluation and selection, design of installations and layouts, system interface, ship design, consultancy and guidance to equipment manufacturers and shipbuilding yards. A systems approach had to be applied to all facets of their functions, be they in the field of maintenance, system engineering or ship design. A new organisational structure was required in which all disciplines recognised their inter-dependence without jealousy, rivalry and competition.

- Future technological changes would require closely integrated functioning of the existing Engineering and Electrical Branches. This would best be achieved by amalgamating these Branches into a single composite cadre.

The proposal was discussed for several years. Technical officers' opinions were divided. Since no consensus could be found, the proposal was not pursued.

Naval Service Selection Boards

In 1982, the Navy initiated its proposal to set up an exclusively Naval Selection Board. In 1983, the proposal was modified to taking over two of the existing Services Selection Boards (SSBs) to be operated under the direct control of the Navy. In 1984, Number 12 SSB at Bangalore and Number 33 SSB at Bhopal were taken over for a trial period of one year. During the trial period, the Navy found that by focusing on naval requirements, it was able to increase the intake in the various branches of the officer cadre.

Thereafter, both these SSBs were made available for selection of naval candidates, whilst their administrative control continued to vest with the Army Headquarters. Both SSBs were to continue with the selection of candidates for the National Defence Academy and of the Combined Defence Services Examination.

Retrospect

Vice Admiral (then Captain) P S Das recalls:

"In 1984, just before taking over, the CNS designate Admiral Tahiliani constituted a three-member committee of Captain (E) (later Vice Admiral) MB Ghosh, Captain (L) (later Rear Admiral) PK Sinha and myself to take a dispassionate look at the Navy and suggest measures that could be implemented swiftly within NHQ's powers. On its recommendation, the following were implemented:

– More than 60 Lieutenant Commanders were removed from Naval Headquarters and sent to the Commands. They were replaced by 30 Commanders.

– Lieutenants of 6 years seniority were made eligible for promotion to Acting Lieutenant Commander.

– Commanders replaced Captains in command of the first four Leanders and the Trishul. The number of Lieutenant Commander/Lieutenant commands was increased.

– Operational activity was decentralised from Naval Headquarters to the Command Headquarters. Day to day reports like Birdstates, Birdefs, Opstates and Opdefs were kept at the Command level.

– Technical officers were informally 'streamed' so that only experienced people were appointed to the Dockyards and the Base Maintenance Units."

Given the ambit within which 'Personnel Policies' have to function, the achievements in the field of personnel management were impressive.

Many believed that with the Navy already fully stretched in inducting and coping with new acquisitions, personnel policies should not be tinkered with. Many believed that the reforms being recommended in manning and training required manpower in such numbers that the shortages would only be aggravated. Many believed that the reforms were filibustered by inter-branch tussles. There was truth in each of these points of view.

No perfect solution could be found. The very same issues arose whenever the complements had to be decided for the new ships being acquired from Russia. The same sub-optimal compromises had to be resorted to.

These issues were not unique to the Indian Navy. In one form or another they manifest themselves in every professional Navy. In his memoirs, German Grand Admiral Raeder stated:[13]

---

13. Grand Admiral Raeder was the Chief of Staff of the German High Seas Fleet in 1914-1918 World War II and the Chief of the German Navy during 1939-45 World War II .

On the 'Appointing of Officers':

"One of the most critical duties in the Navy is the assignment of officers to the particular duties for which their personal and professional qualifications best fit them.

"Not every officer is qualified for duties to which his age and previous training would normally entitle him. The responsibilities of the positions he has held, as well as his performance in those positions, must be carefully analysed.

"Considering the differences in character, intelligence, zeal and health of any half dozen officers, and the impossibility of knowing them all equally well personally, it is inevitable that errors of judgment in selection and assignment of officers will occur at times."

On 'Morale and Discipline':

"One reason for the deterioration in discipline in ships was that as the finer officers in the middle grade – Commanders and Lieutenant Commanders – were promoted to more responsible positions elsewhere, their less experienced replacements were not of the same high calibre.

"These occurrences impressed all responsible officers that for them, particularly in times of political upheaval, there was only one straight path – the path of complete abstinence from every type of party politics, and of unconditional loyalty to the State and to the government chosen by the people.

"Only through firm but friendly discipline can a crew be expected to achieve a high standard of efficiency. The prerequisite for such a state of discipline is a well-disciplined corps of officers and petty officers.

"A modest but definite feeling of pride and self-respect, commensurate with the officer's rank, must be instilled into the officer corps if it is to fulfil its duties."

32

Manning Of Ships And Conservation Of Expertise

Preamble

The Navy's procedures for manning ships had been inherited from the British Navy. In both navies, the specialisations of officers and the trade structures of sailors were analogous. The number of bunks in British origin ships was dovetailed with their 'Schemes of Complement'. No major manning problems were encountered either with the ships acquired from Britain or with the indigenously built ships.

These procedures experienced difficulties from 1966 onwards when deciding the complements of ships being acquired from the Soviet Union. The number of bunks in Russian ships had been dovetailed with the Russian Navy's officer specialisations and sailors' trade structure. The latter were different from those of the Indian Navy and the bunks fell far short of what the Indian Navy required.

The manning of ships has a direct bearing on combat readiness and on conservation of expertise. This chapter discusses how the Navy grappled with the problem of developing and conserving expertise.

The Sailors Trade Structure in 1947

The Navy inherited its sailors' 'trade structure', 'training programme' and 'career progression system' from the British Navy. A sailor could be promoted only after:

- He had qualified in a higher rank course in his trade, and;

- He had performed competently during his sea time in a seagoing ship.

To avoid disgruntlement due to delays in promotion, the Navy's Annual Training Programme was tailored to schedule sailor's higher ranks qualifying courses just before they were due for promotion. To avoid disgruntlement at delays in promotion due to lack of timely sea time, the Annual Block Transfer programme was tailored to sending sailors to ships as soon as possible after the higher rank course.

This system worked tolerably well until the end 1950s. This was because in the first series of acquisitions from Britain of second hand World War II ships (a cruiser and six destroyers) the mainly mechanical equipment was robust and simple.

Within a few years of the arrival from Britain of the second cruiser, *Mysore* in 1957, the eight new frigates between 1958 and 1961 and the aircraft carrier, *Vikrant* in 1961, it became clear that the existing sailors' trade structure could not cope with the increasing electronics in equipment.

The benefit of the promotion-based system was that it had minimised sailor discontent. But the cost of this benefit was the heavy wear and tear on electronic equipment caused by the unending annual flow of sailors into and out of ships, all striving to excel in manning sensitive, expensive, operational equipment. Improper use of equipment led to equipment breakdowns. Demands for spares and equipment replacement were of such high volume that they could not be met. Sub optimal performance of equipment defeated the very purpose that sea time was meant to serve. All these ill effects were widely recognised but no consensus could emerge on a better system.

The system came under further strain with the imminent arrival of the new Russian acquisitions from 1966 onwards when it became abundantly clear that there was going to be a severe shortage of bunks; these ships had been designed to accommodate crews of the Russian Navy's trade structure. The Indian Navy's trade structure compelled a larger crew. A committee was appointed to re-look at the existing ranks, rates and trades of the Navy's sailors.

The CROSS Committee of 1966

The Committee for the Reorganisation of the Sailors Structure (called the CROSS Committee) started its deliberations in 1966. It was headed by Commodore SS Sodhi. He recalls:

"The basic point that we made in our Report was that user and maintainer should be interlinked. It was no use saying that a maintainer was responsible for total maintenance from A to Z and the user was only to be an operator. The two had to be linked. That basically meant that the educational and the technical input into the user had to be enhanced and the maintainer had to have faith in the user's capability to handle the sophistication of the equipment. That was basically the recommendation that we made. The educational level of the seamen had to come up. Their training had to be modified to take on at least the first line maintenance of the equipment that they were operating.

"We also felt that the Topass trade could be abolished. Our experience showed that our own sailors, when they were operating with other navies, had no inhibitions about cleaning their toilets, and generally being responsible for the hygiene of the surroundings."

Commander VF Rebello was the Deputy Director of Personnel (Manpower Planning) in Naval Headquarters from 1967 to 1969 when the recommendations of the CROSS Committee were examined. He recalls:

"The Cross Committee went into the whole manning problem of the Navy with great thoroughness. They also examined the manning structure in the American and other Western navies and came up with very good suggestions on how to reorganise the manpower of our Navy. It was 'operator-maintainer' and 'vertical specialisation'. Unfortunately, the training requirements for such a scheme were so very expensive and extensive that it was beyond the scope of the Navy of that time to implement. We would require a large number of schools and a very big training schedule. It was estimated that at any one time about one-third of the sailors would be undergoing training and conversion and this the Government simply could not afford to have. Therefore, the recommendations of the Cross Committee were kept in abeyance.

"Abolition of Topasses was the only recommendation of the Cross Committee which was taken up."

Manning the Russian Acquisitions

From 1966 onwards, several committees were constituted to try and resolve the mismatch between the Indian Navy's sailor trade structure and the numbers required to efficiently man, operate and maintain the new ships being acquired from Russia, whose numbers of bunks were fewer than required:

- MAT I of 1966 (Manning and Training Committee No I) tackled the manning of the Russian LSTs and the Petyas.
- MAT II of 1975 was constituted after the implementation of the operator-maintainer concept for manning the

rocket boats (Durg class), minesweepers (Pondicherry class) and guided missile destroyers (Rajput class). It tackled the extension of the operator-maintainer concept to the other ships of the Navy.

- MAT III of 1976 led to the Operator-Maintainer Progress Committee Report.

There were two later committees – the 1985 Manpower Optimisation Committee and the 1986 Report on the Trade Structure of Seaman Sailors. These have been discussed in the chapter on Personnel.

MAT I

Manning and Training Committee No I (MAT I) was constituted in 1966 to decide how the Landing Ships and Petyas were to be manned so as to accommodate the Navy's numerous trades in the fewer bunks.

When the first two Petyas arrived in India in end 1968, the Navy was able to see, at first hand, the seriousness of the problem that the CROSS Committee had tried to solve:

- The Petyas were very densely packed with electronic equipment.
- The entrenched branch responsibilities inherited from the British Navy were that the seaman branch 'user' used the equipment and the electrical branch 'maintainer' maintained the equipment. Since a Petya had such a lot of electronic equipment, it needed more electronic maintainers. Since a Petya had so many more weapons, it also needed more users.
- Since a Petya had fewer bunks than were needed even for a normal Indian ships company, it could not accommodate the increased numbers of users and electrical maintainers.

Various options were considered - 'reduce the number of cooks and stewards', 'abolish topasses', 'adopt two watch steaming at sea instead of the usual three watches', 'convert all maintainers into users', 'teach seamen basic maintenance so as to reduce the number of non-artificer electrical sailors on board', 'transfer the less complicated power electric duties of the junior electrical sailors to the Engineering Department' and so on.

The abolition of topasses on board ships was attempted. It led to unrest. This option had to be revoked.

After arrival in India, each Petya was being manned by 120 sailors instead of the sanctioned complement of 95 sailors, despite the lack of bunks. It was decided to re-allocate branch responsibilities.

Re-Allocation of Branch Responsibilities and Duties in Petya Class Ships

The directives issued in 1969 stated:

"Taking a broad perspective, it is important that the various branches of the Navy develop with equitable distribution of workload and responsibility. With increasing sophistication of weapon systems, sensors and data processing, it is imperative that the Electrical Branch concentrates its energies to master these new fields.

"Other branches must be made capable of dealing with the diagnosis of faults and the maintenance of less complicated items of systems and equipment.

"This entails the Engineering Branch shouldering more responsibilities with regard to the generation, distribution of electric power and allied equipment, the Seaman Branch being entrusted with the non-artificer care and maintenance of the weapons, radar, and AIO equipment and the Communication Branch looking after the W/T, R/T and V/S equipment.

"In addition, the seaman and communication branches must substitute the lower levels of power and radio electrical sailors in assisting the artificers.

"The Electrical Officer will, however, continue to be the expert technical adviser to the Commanding Officer on electrical and electronic matters.

"In the initial stages, there may be no saving in manpower, but as experience is gained and personnel become more confident, the complement of modern ships will show a reducing trend, which will be an added advantage. Consequent on this review, detailed instructions will issue from time to time on the measures necessary for the revised training schemes and programme of assumption of new responsibilities.

"As a first step, the new measures will be applicable only in the "Petya cadre" and, based on the experience gained, will be extended in steps to cover the rest of the service. A start has been made by cross-training a number of engine room personnel of two Petya class ships in looking after certain electrical equipment of these ships.

"It cannot be over-emphasised that the success of this measure will depend largely on the spirit in which this change is undertaken, and the ready cooperation and willingness on the part of all concerned to work to the ultimate goal which will result in added efficiency and well being in the service.

"Commanding Officers are to ensure that every opportunity is taken by them and their heads of departments to explain the implications of these revised responsibilities to their ship's companies."

Branch Responsibilities

Transfer of Power Electrical Duties from Electrical to Engine Room Branch Sailors in "Petya" Class of Ships:

"It has been decided to cross-train all the Engineering Mechanic sailors of the Petya class of ships in power electrical duties up to the rate of LME. For the present, sailors of the rate of POEL (P) will be provided to the Engineering Branch in the above class of ships from the existing cadre of electrical sailors.

"It is not intended to cross-train POMEs in electrical duties. POMEs for power electrical duties will be found, in due course, from amongst the LMEs who have already been converted to power electrical duties.

"Electrical Equipment to be maintained by the Engineering Branch in the Petya class of ships:

"Power electrics will be transferred to the Engineering Branch, in two phases.

- Phase I: Lighting, ventilation motors and starters and sound powered telephones.

- Phase II: Pump motors and starters, except those directly associated with weapons, Compressor motors and starters, Cold Room and Air-conditioning machinery motors, Domestic Equipment, Capstans and Controllers, Motor Boat Equipment and Batteries, excepting those used with weapons, including charging sets and panels."

"The transfer of responsibilities for power electrics from the Electrical to the Engine Room branch will be implemented in stages:

- Pre Commissioning Training (PCT) (Engineering) – Eight Weeks.

  "On joining the Petya Training School, all Engine Room sailors of LME and ME rates are to undergo a PCT for engineering duties. The duration will be eight weeks.

- Harbour Training (Engineering) – Four Weeks.

  "After the PCT (Engineering) sailors will be given four weeks of harbour training to enable them to operate and maintain engineering equipment.

- Basic Training in Electrical Engineering – Sixteen Weeks.

  "On completion of the above training, sailors will be trained in the basic elements of electricity for a period of sixteen weeks.

- Familiarisation and Pre-Commissioning Training (Electrical) - Twenty Weeks.

"On completion of the basic training in electrical engineering, these sailors will undergo familiarisation training and PCT in electrical duties for a period of twenty weeks. During this period, they are to be instructed by the electrical department of the Petya Training School, to enable them to carry out the maintenance and operation of electrical machinery covered by Phase I and Phase II of the scheme, on board a Petya class of ship.

"At the end of this period, they are to be examined as to their competence to undertake the responsibilities to be entrusted to them. (emphasis added)

Task I and II Training (in harbour)

"The first two weeks of each phase will be devoted to Task I training and the next two weeks to Task 2 training pertaining to the equipment relating to the particular phase.

"At the end of this period, the Engineer Officer is to satisfy himself that the sailors are capable of undertaking the maintenance functions relating to the particular phase.

"Thereafter, the equipment is to be taken over by the Engine Room Branch.

Phase I

"During this phase, the equipment referred to in Phase I earlier will be taken over.

"During Phase I, sailors are to be given dog watch instructions in equipment for Phase II and may be utilised to assist the Electrical Branch sailors on maintenance of Phase II equipment, as mutually convenient to the two departments.

Phase II

"During this period, sailors will continue to be responsible for the Phase I equipment. On completion of Task I and Task II training, sailors are to take over the responsibilities in respect of the remaining equipment."

The Electrical Branch did not take kindly to these directives. They saw them as erosion of their domain. Views still differ on whether all the junior Engine Room sailors who underwent training in compliance with the above directives were deliberately failed in the examination conducted by the Electrical side after imparting twenty weeks familiarisation training or whether the non-matriculate Engine Room sailors lacked the mental ability to comprehend the prescribed syllabus for electrical training. (emphasis added).

To avoid disrupting the acquisition programme, it was decided to maintain status quo.

MAT II of 1975 and the Introduction of the Operator-Maintainer Concept

Soon after the contract was signed in early 1975 for the acquisition from Russia of ocean-going rocket boats (Durg class), minesweepers (Pondicherry class) and the guided missile destroyers (Rajput class), analysis indicated that there were not going to be enough bunks to accommodate the numbers that the Navy wanted. By end 1975, the complements of these three classes of ships were finalised on the basis of the Operator-Maintainer Concept.

Mid-level Electrical officers immediately expressed apprehensions regarding the loss of their departmental status on board these ships. To dispel these apprehensions, Naval Headquarters promulgated the rationale of the concept. It also constituted the MAT II Committee to carry out an in-depth study on how to consolidate the concept and extend it to other classes of ships and also to recommend measures to allay the apprehensions of Electrical officers.

Naval Headquarters' directive promulgating the Operator-Maintainer concept was issued under the signature of the Chief of the Naval Staff. It stated:

"Advance of technology and the basic and integral role that electrical engineering plays in all facets of naval warfare calls for a thorough review of our manning and training system. It will no longer suffice for a few to shoulder the burden of maintaining and repairing shipboard equipment for the many users, nor is there a place for the un-skilled or the pure operator type in the complex ships that comprise our fleets.

"It has been clear for some time that the existing system of manning and training in the Service by which ships are manned department-wise by the respective branches necessitates large complements on board, leading to conditions of overcrowding and all its attendant problems in life afloat. The present manning pattern by branches and cross-departmental employment also leads to a dilution of accountability and inter-branch stresses and strains.

"Naval Headquarters has therefore decided to adopt, as a permanent measure, the Operator-Maintainer concept for the Executive Branch and the transfer of power engineering to the Engineering Branch. The two schemes will be implemented in phases to minimise dislocation, maximise absorption of skills and ensure adequate protection of careers of officers and sailors of all branches. *It is emphasised that Naval Headquarters do not visualise abolition of any of the existing branches, though there will be a gradual change in the relative role and shape of branches and their employment pattern, as well as a shift of the higher echelons of maintenance from afloat to ashore.* (emphasis added)

"Naval Headquarters have had the problem examined in depth and the working parties appointed to find solutions to the problem have recommended that in order to provide for better operational efficiency, achieve greater economy in training and better conditions of habitability on board ships, department should be formed on a 'functional' basis. This implies officers and sailors of different branches working in functionally oriented composite departments. A degree of functional integration amongst the existing responsibilities of the various branches is, therefore, required to be introduced in the Service.

"A corollary of the above will be that erstwhile operators on board ships will have to acquire skills in maintenance functions and the erstwhile maintainers would also need to be trained in ship husbandry, seamanship and other operator tasks.

Manning & Control

"It is intended to commence this process of integration by manning the ships now proposed to be acquired from the USSR on the basis of the following functional departments:

- Gunnery
- Torpedo & Anti Submarine
- Navigation & Direction
- Communication
- Engineering
- Supply
- Medical

"Electrical personnel, who are a common factor in all the above mentioned functional departments except Supply and Medical, will be integrated with the respective functional departments and would be trained for all functions of operators, and become an integral part of the respective departments.

"In order to effectively exercise total system control, the head of the functional department will control, administer and supervise personnel of all branches that form his department.

"For example, Electrical personnel working on power generation, distribution and allied duties will be integrated into the Engine Room department and the Engineer Officer will exercise control over them. Similarly, the Electrical personnel maintaining or operating a fire-control system will be integrated into the Gunnery department and will function with the operator-maintainer sailors of that department, and be also employed on duties of ship husbandry and seamanship, under the Gunnery Officer.

Training in India

"The general pattern of training for the Seaman and Communication sailors, for the implementation of the above scheme of manning, will comprise the following:

- Training in basic technology and workshop practices in the Electrical School at Valsura followed by
- Professional training at the respective specialist school.

"The pattern of training of electrical sailors to be integrated into the Engineering, Gunnery, Communication, Torpedo and Anti Submarines, and Navigation and Direction departments will comprise the following:

- Training as maintainers at Valsura, Shivaji, Satavahana and Agnibahu.
- Operator and requisite seamanship training at the respective specialist school.

Programme of Integration

"Naval Headquarters considers that the implementation of the measures outlined in this letter is the first step in the process of integration. Further steps in this direction will be promulgated from time to time, as experience is gained and the pay structure of sailors is rationalised. It must necessarily be a process of evolution.

"I would like Flag and Commanding Officers to personally ensure that the purpose, purport and spirit of this policy directive and the programme of its evolution and implementation are understood by all officers and men under their command.

"I am confident that in this bold departure from our earlier manning and training pattern, the Service shall receive the dedication and loyalty from all ranks and all branches, which alone can make the scheme of integration a success. The cause is our Navy, which is higher than self."

The Introduction of Stream Training

In pursuance of the NHQ directive:

- "Stream Training" was introduced. 'A' stream for the new Leander class frigates and 'C' stream for the Soviet acquisitions. 'B' stream, the remaining Western origin ships, were to be gradually converted to 'C' or 'A'.
- Seaman sailors started being imparted maintainer training at the Basic Operator-Maintainer School (BOMS).

These measures were strengthened by the Government's acceptance of the Third Pay Commission recommendation that at the time of entry into the Navy, matriculation should be the minimum educational qualification for sailors of all branches, except cooks and stewards,

The first rocket boat (*Vijaydurg*), minesweeper (*Pondicherry*) and destroyer (*Rajput*) were manned on the above basis.

Apprehension arose again in middle rank Electrical Branch officers whether their status as a ship's Electrical Officer was being diminished. It began to be seen as a contest for 'turf' between the officers of the Executive and Electrical branches.[1]

The Electrical Officer Opposition to the Operator-Maintainer Concept

The apprehensions of Electrical officers about the Operator-Maintainer concept centred on three issues:

- Erosion of the traditional responsibilities of the Electrical Branch.

- When weapons failed to perform, the pinpointing of responsibility and accountability for failure between the Executive and the Electrical Weapon Maintenance Officer, and between seaman 'user' sailors and electrical 'maintainer' sailors.

- Fears of diminution in their career prospects.

MAT III of 1976 and the 1978 Operator-Maintainer Progress Committee Report

In 1976, Naval Headquarters appointed a Committee to report on the progress of the Operator-Maintainer concept that had been implemented in 1975.[2] The Committee's terms of reference were:

"To examine:

- Commander (L) nominated for the first destroyer is designated as Officer-in-Charge of Afloat Maintenance Team and is charged with the function of providing maintenance support. Would it be desirable for him to be based ashore with the maintenance team or should he be embarked on board himself and the bulk of his team continue to operate from ashore?

- If it is necessary to embark Commander (L) on board the first destroyer:

  – What should be his specific responsibilities, without eroding the working of functional departments and the Operator-Maintainer concept?

  – Should he act as an adviser to the Captain of the ship or should he be designated as head of department?

  – What should be the chain of command as regards the Electrical officers and sailors on board, taking into account that they would be all employed under the control of functional departments?

- What are the specific apprehensions of the Electrical Branch, if any, which may inhibit its involvement with the Operator-Maintainer concept and measures that the Committee recommend to allay the same?

- Whether feedback from the experience gained from the operation of functional departments in the first rocket boat (*Vijaydurg*) would be adequate to review the policy of extending the Operator-Maintainer concept to other ships of Soviet origin or should the review be carried out after the first destroyer (*Rajput*) has been commissioned, i.e. mid 1980 or so?

In its deliberations, the Committee is to bear in mind the same principle enunciated in MAT III also, namely that there is no dilution in the expertise of the Electrical Branch to meet our known commitments."

The Committee's Report started by restating the basic nature of the problem:

- As equipment becomes more automated, it needs fewer men to operate it. Cumulatively, the men required for operating the equipment in a ship are now much less than the number needed for its sustained maintenance. The number of equipments installed, their compactness, their complexity and the paucity of bunks make it more necessary than hitherto, that the maintenance and defect rectification workload be shared between the ship's crew and a support agency. The extent of this sharing will vary with equipment complexity. Simple equipment can be maintained / repaired by the ship's crew, complex equipment much less so, both being dependent on the man-hours available for maintenance.

- The men manning each item of equipment must know their equipment as intimately as possible to get the desired results from it. This entails 'action post manning and training', wherein each man is trained to operate and maintain the equipment in his action post. In so doing, a man's expertise gets deeper but his employability on equipment other than his own becomes less flexible. When he goes on long leave during a slack period, the ship may be able to do without his 'operator' function.

---

1. There is no evidence that the sailors of the Electrical Branch had any apprehensions about the NHQ directive.

2. The commissioning Commanding Officer of the *Vijaydurg*, the author as Commanding Officer (designate) of the *Rajput* and the Commander L (designate) of the *Rajput* were members of this Committee.

But the equipment has to continue to be maintained and, therefore, a relief who has been action post trained on the same equipment and knows it as well, must be provided 'on call' from a support agency. This requirement is particularly critical for the artificer type of maintainer who undertakes the skilled maintenance. It is much less so for the junior operator-maintainer who does the more elementary maintenance.

- In addition to being a platform whose equipment requires efficient maintenance, the ship is also the home of the ship's crew. This results in clean-ship, part of ship, watch-keeper and general ship's duties, which do not require equipment expertise, but do consume considerable junior sailor man-hours. A ship's company, whose numbers are restricted by the bunks on board, has perforce to divide its man-hours between continuation training for combat, maintaining equipment and general duties. Of these three activities, training and general duties have to be done by embarked crew; for the reasons described in the earlier two paragraphs, the maintenance workload has to be shared with the support agency.

- Where maintenance requiring artificer skills can only be done in harbour and these skills are not required at sea, it is more practical to position that artificer in the support agency than in the ship, and embark the junior operator-maintainer whose skills / training meet the operator requirement at sea and meet the requirements of general duties in harbour. When deciding a scheme of complement, a judicious balance has perforce to be struck on the above basis, together with the customary ones of ratio of senior sailors to junior sailors, senior sailors' accommodation, catering for domestic staff etc. The temptation to include the maximum number of maintainers to maximise on board maintenance capability has to be eschewed because the number of senior sailors that would be required would result in the ship having too few junior sailors for general duties.

As regards the working of the concept in the first rocket boat, *Vijaydurg*, in which the concept had first been implemented, the Committee found that:

- The non-technical sailors could carry out maintenance routines up to the monthly level without supervision and up to the quarterly level under the supervision and guidance of senior electrical sailors. They were, however, unlike junior 'L' sailors, not capable of any defect rectification. Since defect rectification in electronic equipment is almost invariably interlinked with maintenance routines (wherever readings, results and performances are found outside limits in the course of maintenance checks), this resulted in the senior electrical sailor being more heavily loaded; this would

not have arisen if it were feasible to have more junior electrical sailors on board, who, by their training and employment, are capable of normal non-complicated defect rectification e.g. changing components, testing valves, tracing earths, etc.

- Even though the operator-maintainer system was to apply up to the level of 'Leading' ranks, action-post manning made it necessary for all senior seaman and communication sailors to be trained and employed on maintenance on board these ships. These senior non-technical sailors assisted the senior electrical sailors in maintenance functions to the extent that their duties permitted.

- Under present conditions, the trainability and employability in even routine maintenance of the non-technical sailors of any rank was only up to the level equivalent to EMR or at most up to an LEMR.

- The ability of the non-technical sailor in maintenance was relatively more in the field of hydraulic and ordnance equipment than in electronic or electrical equipment.

- All senior electrical artificer and non-artificer sailors on board were employed on operator duties (action post functions) in addition to their maintenance responsibilities on their equipment. They had no difficulty in undertaking these functions competently.

- The ship's sophisticated missile, gunnery and ECM equipments were maintained by electrical personnel with the assistance of Seamen and Communication sailors, who also carried out operator functions on these equipments.

- After arrival in India, the availability of the non-technical sailors to assist in maintenance was limited, in view of 'part-of-ship' and other responsibilities that they had to perform.

The clear benefits and merits of the system were also discerned:

- The knowledge of the non-technical sailors about their equipment had improved, thus enhancing their involvement and efficiency in the operator activity. This would lead to fewer breakdowns on account of mal-operation.

- The ability and employment of the non-technical sailors in maintenance functions, even to the limited extent, added to their morale and gave them a sense of greater participation.

- The responsibilities and role of the maintainer as an operator had provided for greater interest and involvement on his part with the functions of the department whose equipment he was maintaining.

- The interaction and understanding between the user and maintainer sailors was also better, thus leading to smoother inter-personal functioning.

The Committee found that the apprehensions of Electrical branch personnel centred on:

- Aspects of morale of Electrical officers arising from the removal of the Electrical Department and the loss of 'head of the department' status on board.

- The adverse effects of restricting sea employment of Electrical officers in rigid functional departments on their growth and development and ultimately on the capabilities of the Electrical Branch in general and the shore support organisations in particular.

- The adverse effects, of non-centralised maintenance arrangements on board, on the material state of the ship's operational systems.

The Committee concluded that the system of on-board manning and maintenance that would fulfil the requirement could be achieved by:

- Implementation of the Operator-Maintainer and Maintainer-Operator concept for sailors to obtain the best utilisation of the personnel carried on board.

- Having electrical personal on board employed department-wise in G, ND, TAS, C and E departments, minimising across-the-department employment. This would ensure build-up and conservation of technical expertise.

- Making an electrical officer / senior sailor responsible to the head of the (functional) department to ensure that the equipment was defect-free and available when required. This would enable the head of the department to be fully responsible for the operational readiness and efficiency of his equipment.

- Continuing to have an Electrical Department with an Electrical officer on board the ship, to ensure correct standards of maintenance and provide for adequate flexibility in meeting the requirements of the ship as a whole and, as at present:

  - Making him responsible to the Commanding Officer for the total material state of all electrical (including power generation and distribution) and weapon equipment.

  - Assigning to him the responsibility to control, coordinate and provide guidance to the electrical personnel in the functional departments on all technical, material, personnel and logistic aspects pertaining to electrical and weapon equipment.

  - Making him responsible for dealings with outside authorities and organisations on the above matters.

  - Making the Electrical officer / senior sailor of the (functional) department responsible to the ship's Electrical officer for the material state of the equipment in the department.

In addition to the above suggestions, the Committee recommended that a detailed study should be carried out, as soon as possible, to recommend the steps necessary to create expertise and experience in personnel on board ships and across the service. Some of the essential areas, which needed to be covered in the study, were:

- The 'progression' of training of officers and sailors in service.

- The relative content of technology, equipment knowledge and technical management know-how in the training scheme to provide the correct mix of width of knowledge and depth of expertise required at the appropriate rank, for officers and sailors. This should include a revised narrower grouping of the equipment, which electrical personnel are required to maintain, based on the depth of expertise that each equipment requires for efficient maintenance and the numbers of such equipments that one man can efficiently maintain.

- Reassessment of the (Power, Control and Radar) trade grouping of electrical sailors and creation of additional trades, if necessary.

- Reappraisal of 'stream training' and creation of a system of 'pre-joining (equipment) training' (after identifying whether such training should be ship-oriented or system oriented), to provide the concentrated 'dose' of equipment knowledge required in the next appointment.

- A system of transfers, which ties up with the above training and minimises manpower turbulence on board.

- A system of career planning of personnel:

  - Where emphasis is on the needs of the ship and the service, without detriment to the career of the persons.

  - Where training, employment and grooming will provide the depth of expertise at the sailor and junior officer level, and the width of experience at the middle and higher management officer level.

The Outcome of the 'Operator-Maintainer' Scheme

In the first guided missile destroyer *INS Rajput* that commissioned in 1980[3], the Commander (L) was retained

---

3. The author was the commissioning Commanding Officer of *INS Rajput*.

as the Head of the Electrical Department. An Assistant Electrical Officer (ALO) was appointed to each functional department, and was responsible not to the head of the functional department but to the Commander (L).

This *via media* worked smoothly and until 1990 was adopted for all new guided missile destroyers, frigates and corvettes.

The Inability to Implement Fixed Commissions

In the British Navy, a ship commissioned for two years could be deployed to one of Britain's fleets anywhere in the world. On completion of two years, the ship returned to her homeport in Britain, decommissioned, underwent a thorough refit and then re-commissioned with another crew for the next fixed commission. The advantages of a fixed commission were that officers and men remained together for the full commission, got to know each others' strengths and weaknesses, got to know the capabilities and limitations of their ship's equipment and acquired expertise.

The Indian Navy neither had worldwide commitments, nor the number of ships, nor sufficient manpower to adopt Fixed Commissions. Ships remained permanently 'in commission' until they were finally 'decommissioned'. For the reasons already discussed, officers and men changed round every twelve to eighteen months for sea time.

Successive Fleet Commanders had repeatedly recommended the adoption of a Fixed Commission, at least for operational ships. The following excerpt is representative of the dilemma:

"FOCIF furnished statistics to show that a large number of transfers of officers and sailors from ships continued throughout the year. Transfer of key personnel after the work-up of the ships deprived them of the benefit of the work-up, which had virtually to start again with the arrival of new personnel.

"While the difficulties of the Fleet were appreciated, it was generally realised that so long as the present shortages continued, it was not possible to plan fixed commissions in ships. The appointment of a new ship's company after every refit presupposed the availability of a sufficient number of officers and sailors in the service, which, unfortunately, was not the case.

"Common agreement, however, was found to a suggestion that in spite of the present difficulties, a fixed commission for one of the ships of the Fleet be tried as an experiment. No change in the ship's company was thereafter to be made at least for a year."

Two basic issues were required if expertise was to be effectively 'conserved':

● The duration of sea tenure for expertise to develop.
● The compulsion of shuffling of sailors into and out of ships to give sailors sea time to qualify for promotion.

Since fixed commissions were not feasible and rotating personnel between ship and shore was inescapable, the gaining and conservation of expertise depended on random variables like whether the ship was operational or under maintenance, or whether the equipment was operational or defective or whether targets were available or not. This same aspect in regard to rotation of technical officers found mention in the Naval Expert Committee's Report.

The 1979-80 Naval Expert Committee Report on Maintenance – Excerpts

"Tenures

It has been categorically asserted that the effect of shortages (of technical officers) is aggravated by short tenures and lack of continuity. Though it has been accepted that it may take an incumbent as much as three to six months to perform effectively, the impact on quality of work, if short tenures of 18 to 24 months are given, has not been fully appreciated. Frequent transfers also bring in their wake problems of accommodation, schooling, etc, which do have an unsettling effect on the officers resulting in sub optimal performance. The problem is stated to be due to:

● Requirements of sea time for promotion.
● Promotion policy, which results in an officer becoming acting Commander with 12 to 13 years of service.
● Need to rotate officers between attractive and non-attractive stations.
● Shortage of billets at Vishakhapatnam / Cochin in the higher ranks.

Continuity in Key Billets

Non-functioning, malfunctioning and breakdowns of sensors and weapon systems / sub systems are the rule rather than an exception in ships at sea. This unsatisfactory material state was recently dramatised when a Fleet Commander had to abandon operational readiness inspection of a 5-year old Leander frigate. After a long refit lasting nearly one year, this ship spent the major part of the subsequent year in harbour for defect rectification. Yet, during the inspection, combat systems in the ship became non-operational within 2 hours of sailing. The story is not different with the first Leander, which after a 10-month refit is yet to complete Harbour Acceptance Trials and is being programmed for deployment without Sea Acceptance Trials.

"The above state of affairs is a reflection, not merely on the qualitative and quantitative refit contents of our ships, lack of expertise in our Dockyards but as importantly, lack of expertise in ships. A change in approach of our training and manning pattern – to be discussed in the appropriate volume of the Committee's Report – needs serious examination. Expertise is not being built up, in most cases, to the level necessary. In cases where the necessary skill has been generated, it has been frittered away due to our training and manning pattern."

The Advent of the Stabilised Operational and Maintenance Cycle (SOMC) to Build Up Expertise

The 'Trickle Drafting' that had been the practice for a number of years gave way eventually to the Stabilised Operational Manning Cycle (SOMC) for Fleet Ships that was promulgated by NHQ in 1979. SOMC was to apply to seven types of front-line ships and the period was to be between 18 to 22 months.

"There can be no doubt that a high level of operational efficiency and combat readiness in a ship are directly related to a stabilised crew, not subjected to changes after workup.

"After a detailed study, Naval Headquarters have decided to implement Stabilised Operational Manning Cycle for Fleet ships with effect from 7 September 1979. To start with, only the sailors complement will be stabilised. The scheme will eventually encompass officers. Since a certain amount of short term career planning will have to be done for individual sailors to implement the Stabilised Operational Manning Cycle, the concept is also expected to reap an improved employment pattern for sailors.

"Ships will be manned in accordance with Manning Plan 31 under issue. As this plan has been prepared after detailed dialogue between Naval Headquarters, Fleet Commanders, Commanding Officers and Drafting Office, it should be acceptable to all concerned.

"Since the concept is being deliberately implemented in the Navy, numerous queries on the execution of the scheme, modalities, its effect on future prospects, promotions and courses, are bound to arise. Commanding Officers of ships and establishments in your command may, therefore, be directed to educate their sailors about the details of the stabilised operational manning concept with a view to removing any doubts that may exist, particularly in respect of promotions, courses affecting promotion, safeguarding of seniority, transfers in relation to academic year, etc.

"Although preparatory work in implementing the Stabilised Operational Manning Cycle was completed sometime back, the introduction has been delayed in order to ensure that all concerned are made fully aware of the implications so that doubts may be cleared before this concept is implemented and later institutionalised.

"Since the Stabilised Operations Manning Cycle has to be linked with refit of ships, it is of the utmost importance that the Drafting Office is kept informed of the refit programme and the changes to it as and when they occur.

"With a view to assess the effectiveness of the programme and to improve on it, a review will be carried out after one cycle is over. Administrative Authorities are requested to forward their comments after 30 September 1980."

In the initial stages, the tendency was for ships to ask for key sailors to be retained despite SOMC. In some cases, a group of key technical sailors came into being who continued to be held on to by successive Commanding Officers.

By the late 1980s however, SOMC had taken root. The best that could be achieved was for 50% of officers and 33% of sailors to be changed every year.

The 1985 Report on Manpower Optimisation – Excerpts

In 1985, NHQ constituted a Committee to recommend measures to optimise the existing manpower of the service by assigning priorities for placement of manpower, critically analysing manpower requirement in various sectors for efficient functioning and examining subjects concerning training, manning, SOMC and courses.

In its introduction, the Committee's report stated:

"Early during the course of the study, the Committee appreciated that training was a very key area for two conflicting requirements. Firstly, it must be extensive and effective enough to permit skill development and secondly it must be done in the shortest possible time to permit optimum utilisation of manpower. It is also well known in the service that many transfers are necessitated by training requirements. The effects of this turbulence also need to be considered.

There are two distinct schemes of training. One for artificers and the other for non-artificers. In case of artificers, most of all inputs are given at the beginning of the service career. Thereafter, the Engine Room Artificers never need go back to *Shivaji*. However, Electrical Artificers return to *Valsura* for the EAP 3 / EAR 3 course as well as for the Chief Artificer attachment. Interestingly, the same pattern is repeated on the aviation side where only the Air Electrical /Air Radio sailors get inputs. There do not seem to be compelling reasons for this difference in basic pattern.

All non-artificers follow basically the same pattern. They have a relatively short initial course followed by repeated inputs to qualify for / immediately after qualifying for a higher rank. The occasions and durations vary from branch to branch. Seaman branch has another complication of specialist qualifications, which are in addition to qualifying for higher rate.

Skill Development

The Committee has all along given the highest priority for skill development. To re-state the obvious, skill development comes from two major factors. Training inputs and meaningful experience to consolidate that knowledge. Repeated courses, which teach the same thing do not achieve very much. The Committee does not feel confident that inputs given in the beginning of a service career will suffice till its end – twenty or more years after. A *via media* has been sought, which permits one course at Leading level after about 7 to 8 years of service experience for all non-artificers. It would also permit election of Mechanician candidates at a reasonably early stage. No further formal courses have been recommended till about the 13th or 14th year of service when those who sign on for another five years could be given a staff course conjoined with MCPO 'Qualifying' course.

Promotion Linked Courses

A major procedural hurdle to be overcome in restructuring the training of sailors is the fact that their promotions are linked with the passing of various examinations. In many cases, the place and in some cases, the duration is also specified. After a close and careful study of the Advancement Regulations, the Committee is of the view that most of the measures laid down therein are likely to have been at the instance of the Navy in the first place. The changes recommended are intended to reduce turbulence and increase effective time. Since the service and the State will be the gainer in the monetary aspect and the individual in effectiveness, not much difficulty is foreseen in getting the changes through the Government. There are many changes, which can be implemented without specific Government approval. For example, since course contents and durations are not statutory obligations, PCTs could well be equated to Specialist Qualification courses for Seamen sailors.

Substantial savings are likely to accrue, which would increase effective time by as much as 40 weeks for some categories of seamen sailors, 20 weeks for Communication and Electrical sailors and 10 weeks for Engineering sailors and Supply & Secretariat branch sailors. Greater benefit will accrue through better continuity and on the job effectiveness. This will not be immediately quantifiable.

Even though 'Savings' of a large magnitude shall accrue, the Committee reiterates that its primary concern is effective manpower and not savings per se."

The 1986 Committee to Review the Trade Structure of Seamen Sailors – Excerpts

In January 1986, whilst the revitalisation of training was in progress, NHQ constituted a Committee to review the trade structure of seamen sailors.

Excerpt from the NHQ letter constituting the Committee:

"The present training pattern is essentially promotion based, mainly to fulfil the requisites of NI 2/S/6I rather than need based. The time scale promotion of leading rank has further compounded the problem of giving the second rate courses to meet the promotion requisite.

This has resulted in some sailors going for the second rate course for only a short tenure on a ship in the previous professional rate. A time scale promotion denied on the date for want of not qualifying in the part II course also causes certain disgruntlement and affects morale. There is, therefore, a need to examine the de-linking of courses from promotion and other associated issues.

The present system of manning Soviet acquisition vessels, where a sailor is first trained in normal fashion in his parent school followed by PCT, poses tremendous constraints on the limited manpower resources. Further, the concept of vertical specialisation may be desirable when a sailor can remain on equipment throughout his career in the Navy and there are enough avenues for his promotion in this narrow confine. However, with the current shortages, considerable constraints are placed on manpower utilisation because of restricted usability of sailors in other fields due to his narrow training. There is, therefore, a requirement to evolve a suitable training pattern to meet the changing requirements of the Navy."

Terms of Reference

"There has been a large scale induction of sophisticated ships and equipment in our Navy during the last few years. As a consequence of this sophistication, it has become necessary to examine the trade structure, training and promotion pattern of seamen sailors.

Seamen sailors have been following the old trade structure inherited by us from the erstwhile Royal Indian Navy. The only two changes that have taken place are:

- Abolition of the GL rate.
- Abolition of the QM rate.

While these two rates have been abolished, no new rates have been introduced. It is also known that the abolition of QM rate met with growing dissent from the Commanding Officers as well as from the Fleet Commanders.

Based on the above and taking into account the requirements of the Service, it is necessary to carry out a detailed examination of the Trade Structure of seamen sailors (including Physical Training), and forward recommendations on changes that are necessary to meet the futuristic requirements of the Navy.

The examination is also to take into account the following:

- Whether there is a need to introduce specialised missile rates?
- Should the QM rate be re-introduced especially in view of the Action Post Manning?
- Is there a need to re-introduce instructor rates? If so, for which discipline and what incentives need to be given to these sailors?
- The need or otherwise to reorganise courses to cater to the manning requirements of ships.
- Should the courses be de-linked from promotion? If so, what are the ramifications?
- Is there a need to re-examine the contents of NHQ letter dated 7 September 1979 regarding the SOMC Concept?
- Whether PCT can be substituted for Higher Rank courses for purposes of promotion?"

Conclusions and Recommendations – Excerpts

"With the acquisition of Soviet origin ships, extensive thought was given to bringing in the Operator-Maintainer concept. After a lot of study and for reasons best known to the then naval hierarchy, a good concept did not find fruition and the Navy lapsed into another decade of *status quo*. Stream Training was the order of the day. The Navy missed the opportunity of bringing in the Operator-Maintainer concept as in the United States Navy and the limited 'maintainer to operater' philosophy as in the French, Soviet and British Navies.

The inevitable conclusion is that 'We must train for efficiency and manning / utilisation of equipment, and not train for promotion.' Albeit the man is important and accelerated promotions might lead to better morale, but efficiency will not necessarily follow.

Systems Training / PCT / OJT

The only efficacious form of training for seaman (operators) is a methodology, which culminates in 'hands on' training on the equipment that the sailor is required to man in his immediate next sea assignment.

The Soviet Navy has Task III & IV which is harbour and sea training respectively and was followed in our navy with the setting up of the Integrated Type Training Establishment at *INS Satavahana*. However, in the case of the new Durg and Rajput class ships, the concept changed to 'the old Commanding Officer and crew carrying out man-for-man training of the new crew.'

The period styled as 'On the Job Training' (OJT) was initially 4 weeks, and is currently 3 weeks. In the earlier stages, when the Rajput, Durg and missile boat training was at Bombay, the expert teams from *Agnibahu* consisting of officers and sailors, who had served on that class of ship and were subsequently appointed to that training establishment embarked, along with the old and new crews and actually carried out drills followed by system firings.

In the earlier Task III and Task IV concept, the number of drills, exercises and firings for each sensor, equipment, fire control, and finally system, were laid down and the Officer-in-Charge Submarine and Surface Training Schools, actually cleared the submarine and ship crew respectively for taking over from the old crew. It is believed that this is still followed by the submarine wing of *Satavahana*. This is the only way an efficient crew can be trained. If after this, results are not very satisfactory the fault can be traced to the training team.

In the present system of the old crew training and handing over to the new crew, the standards of sea training are variable and the level of knowledge is only as good as the keenness and zeal of the Commanding Officer, heads of departments and the old crew. If a ship has a bad track record, that gets perpetuated.

Further, miscellaneous sailors (who comprise lower quarters crews), engine room sailors, communication and RP sailors, cannot possibly get the advantage envisaged by getting together a crew, as at present, for eight weeks of PCT, followed by three weeks of OJT at each stage without an expert team guiding and testing them. The Royal Navy does this under Flag Officer Sea Training and his band of 'Sea Riders'. The US Navy has a similar system. Nowhere has the old crew the responsibility of training the new crew.

It was also gleaned that for purposes of administrative convenience, in a number of cases, sailors across all rates in a specialisation were grouped together for PCT instruction. A number of sailors, when interviewed, expressed frustration, particularly when the same things were being taught all over again, when they came round a second time to the PCT School, in the next commission. This has already been pointed out and the PCT School at Cochin which now houses all the course schemes for various classes of ships of Soviet origin has been asked to revert to separate courses of instruction for each rate. This is, however, to some extent wasteful of effort, because the strength of classes would be small and the number of instructors required has to be considerably increased. It would be, therefore, prudent to gang together at least two ships teams of the same class / system to make the training cost effective.

Stabilised Operational Manning Cycle (SOMC) Concept

Trickle drafting which had been the practice for a number of years gave way to the SOMC concept in 1977. The SOMC concept has been kept going by CABS, at great effort by providing additional manpower as and when asked for by the Commanding Officers of these ships, creating in some cases a pampered lot of key sailors who continued to be held on to by successive Commanding Officers, the situation being more acute in the case of technical sailors.

The current thinking is to retain sailors on SOMC ships for three years, changing one third of the sailors every year. This inhibits fixed commissions but is conducive to a Systems Training concept.

PCT/System Training For Communication/EW/Radar Sailors

Currently PCTs are in full cry. PCT / System type of training is given to all sailors. Whereas the necessity of consolidated systems training for gunnery and ASW systems is accepted, the necessity of PCT training in respect of RP and Communication / EW sailors is debatable, and wasteful of effort. Equally good, if not better, training can be given in the parent school in charge of an officer of the rank of Captain than in a PCT School particularly as by policy, equipment has been spread out to parent schools. Therefore, though a systems approach is called for generally, it does not appear to be beneficial for these two specialisations, particularly as PCT training is considerably wasteful of training effort without commensurate advantages. What the sensor schools require is simulator training on the type of audiovisual presentation they are likely to encounter on their consoles. In the case of console operators, training is individualistic and repetitious. And in the case of plotters, it is sheer plotting practice. This aspect may, therefore, be studied in depth.

Conclusion

It is considered that as a very workable *via media*, in SOMC ships, the concept of 'PCT training' should give way to 'Systems training' of users and maintainers, followed by OJT on board the ship, the sailors being appointed as before, for training en bloc. Application of Systems training to communication and RP sailors, however, is debatable and needs to be reviewed."

1989 Report on Economy Measures with Regard to Personnel Movement – Excerpts

Courses

"In a study carried out by DNT in April 1988, the requirement and duration of each of the courses, presently in existence, were analysed in great detail and recommendations were made to rationalise them with a view to reduce the movement of personnel. These recommendations have since been approved and are being implemented. However, the Committee is of the opinion that movements in respect of CO/XO Courses and PCTs have not been examined adequately and there exists scope for further reduction of movements in these areas. 468 officers have undergone CO/XO Courses and 559 officers have undergone PCTs. This amount of movement is exceedingly high. It not only results in financial burden to the State but also results in a loss of a large number of man-days for operations. The Committee recommends the following measures to reduce these movements:

- **CO/XO Courses**. It is the general opinion of the officers who have undergone CO/XO Courses that the curriculum covered during these courses is repetitive and is more to refresh the memory. In view of the current situation, it is recommended that these courses may be held in abeyance for LSTs / OPVs / SDBs / IPVs / Coast Guard ships / Tankers / Kamortas / Leanders. Further, officers who have done XO's time on a particular class of ship be exempted from the CO's course for the same class of ship.

- **PCTs**. Presently, in many cases, there is a wide gap between the conduct of PCTs and the officers taking up their appointments on board ships. This is because PCTs for various classes of ships are conducted only once a year and it is not possible, in most cases, to coincide the completion of PCTs with the officers' appointment dates. Therefore, the very purpose of PCTs is defeated. It is strongly recommended that the PCTs be done as a part of the Basic and Long Courses. DOP should inform the concerned Establishments / School as regards streaming of the officers in advance, so that the required PCTs may be conducted accordingly. The duration of the Long Course may be extended if necessary. Before joining the ship, 4 weeks of OJT be conducted in order to update the officer on the equipment of the ship.

- As far as possible, Officer PCTs should be done as part of Basic and Long courses. Four weeks of OJT be conducted before officers assume appointments.
- The number and duration of Sailor PCTs be reduced by conducting PCTs as part of the higher rank courses as far as possible."

The 1990 Study by the College of Defence Management to Rationalise the Sailors Trade Structure

Whereas the 1986 Committee had considered the 'Rationalisation of the Trade Structure of Seamen Sailors' from an 'efficiency' point of view, pressures built up a few years later to rationalise the entire sailor trade structure from an 'economy' point of view. The rationale was:

"We are currently faced with a severe resource crunch, necessitating optimisation of manpower as one of the measures of economy. It has now become essential, not just desirable, to resort to a lean and efficient manning policy, which would mean a breakaway from the narrow vertical specialisation resorted hitherto.

When hi-tech had suddenly hit us in the 1970s, vertical specialisation and dedicated equipment training was understandably essential in order to absorb and exploit the new equipment in the shortest time. It is now nearly two decades that we have been operating the new generation weapons, sensors and machinery. The need for vertical specialisation must therefore reduce in intensity.

Computer based technology in management information systems, weapons and sensors has helped to link and integrate various systems on board warships. This development lends itself to integration of existing fields of specialisation.

There is scope now to rationalise the trade structure of sailors with a view to reducing the number of specialisations and consequently the manning norms in ships.

Some apprehensions were expressed when the QM and RP were integrated into the RP specialisation or when GLs were merged with the RCs. The fears have subsided over the years, as these measures were well conceived. Similarly the Streaming concept, at one time a necessary measure, is no longer relevant to the same extent.

The present trade structure in the Navy is amenable to rationalisation and integration with a view to reducing the effective manning of ships. Some areas are highlighted as follows:

- Naval Air Photo and Naval Air Met trades could well form one combined trade.
- Naval Air Handlers could imbibe the same training as Naval Airmen Safety Equipment sailors.
- EMP and EMR functions could easily be combined into one.
- Mechanicians (Power) and Mechanicians (Weapons) can also be rationalised into one trade.
- Mechanicians Air Electrical and Air Radio can merge into one.

So far the reference has only been towards the merger of the various trades as existing today in the Navy so that we can rationalise and reduce the number of such trades. There are, however, certain areas therein there may be a requirement to introduce new trades – 'hull maintenance' is one such example. To improve the expertise in this area, we may have to introduce a new trade known as Hull Mechanics. There may also be other such areas, which require a detailed study.

Prima facie the existing trade structure in the Navy is amenable to rationalisation on a broader basis."

It was decided that a Committee should be appointed to study the problem covering all branches. As a first step, the study was entrusted to the College of Defence Management, Secunderabad as a project for a study team. Its Report was under consideration by Naval Headquarters in 1991.

Retrospect

Operator–Maintainer

Lieutenant Commander (later Commodore) IJ Sharma had undergone training in the Soviet Union in 1970 for commissioning and commanding the new missile boats, he commanded the missile boat that sank the Pakistan Navy destroyer *Khaibar* in the 1971 Indo Pakistan War and later, as Commander, underwent training in Russia and commissioned in the second Durg class rocket boat *Sindhudurg*. He recalls:

"Throughout my tenure on board *Sindhudurg*, we followed the Operator-Maintainer concept to the letter and the equipment remained very healthy. We did not find any difficulty between the technical and the executive staff; no one was trying to brow-beat the other. In fact, the Weapon Maintenance Officer depended very heavily on the s eaman Radar Control sailors and they really knew how to tune the system and how to carry out first line maintenance.

"I remember, Rear Admiral KR Menon who came as one of the Electrical Branch members of the Review Committee to interview us on board asking me 'What do you think of the Operator-Maintainer concept?' I said, 'You can examine any one of my sailors or officers from the Executive side and see for yourself how we are implementing it.' He questioned a number of sailors and officers of the Executive branch and they all came out with flying colours.

"When the concept was found successful, it started a controversy. Instead of trying to keep those crews together and build up on their expertise, there were objections from various quarters that this would mean that only some people were going to have knowledge of these latest systems, whereas the earlier policy was that each man gets an exposure to new systems. There were demands that vertical specialisation should not be allowed to take place. Whereas we, in the missile boat squadron and later on in *Sindhudurg* who had commissioned these ships after training in Russia, felt very strongly that there was a lot of merit in vertical specialisation. This was the feeling not only amongst the Executive officers, but also amongst the Electrical and the Technical officers who had undergone training with us.

"Electrical officers who had not been exposed to the rigorous Russian system of training felt that once the Executive officers knew their fire control systems and firing circuits thoroughly, they might ask searching questions from the Weapon Maintenance Officer as to why such and such had not been checked or why so and so had failed. This would impinge on their authority and their domain. That I think is the basic reason why they did not want operator-maintainer to succeed.

"Whilst the opposition was mainly from the Electrical Branch, I think there were some Seamen officers also, who were opposed to the concept because they had not had the opportunity to be rigorously trained in the Soviet systems as we had been.

"The Engineering Department, who traditionally have been operator-maintainers, always maintained their equipment much better. I remember when I was withdrawing from Karachi after the missile attack in 1971, I did 29 knots for several hours. By the time I reached the refuelling tanker off Saurashtra, I was practically sucking air from my fuel tanks and this was possible because the engineers really knew what they were doing on board."

Vice Admiral (then Commander) VL Koppikar had undergone missile boat training in the Soviet Union in 1970 and in subsequent years served in the Personnel Branch in almost all capacities from Deputy Director all the way up to Chief of Personnel. Writing in the Navy Foundation's annual publication, '*Quarterdeck 2000*', he stated:

"A change of considerable significance was the introduction of the "operator maintainer" concept in our ships. It aimed at more effective manning and utilisation of on-board manpower after a degree of cross-training to fulfil both these functions. We also hoped that the move would reduce, if not eliminate, over-crowding in our Soviet origin ships, which had extremely limited accommodation. However, while everyone talked glibly about the novel concept, its wholehearted acceptance was something else again. It not only threatened our age-old Branch structure, but also clashed with the 'spit and polish' culture we had inherited. It was an uphill task to make Commanding Officers of ships accept reduced complements. The scheme was eventually pushed through by providing some sops by way of additional floating manpower – just in case you landed up in the same ship as her next Commanding Officer!"

There is a view that the dilution of expertise ought to have been better tackled. As has been discussed, acceptance of concepts like vertical specialisation, SOMC and pre-commission training took time to gain acceptance and to implement.

At times, 'economy' was invoked as a reason for diluting / abolishing PCTs![4]

---

4. Report on Effecting Economies in the Movement of Personnel.

33

Training

Preamble

The concepts for manning of ships and the training of officers and sailors to exploit the combat potential of the ships they are to man in compliance with these concepts are inseparable faces of the same coin. To simplify for the lay reader what was attempted and how much was achieved in each of these inter-related areas, 'Manning and Training' have been discussed in separate chapters.

The chapter on 'Manning' discusses the changes that were attempted in the procedures for manning the ships acquired from Russia. Some changes like 'Transfer of Power Generation and Distribution from the Electrical Department to the Engineering Department' and Seaman-Electrical-Operator-Maintainer' could not gain wholehearted acceptance. Some changes like 'Functional Departments' succeeded. Some changes like 'Stabilised Operating and Manning Cycle' (SOMC) took time to settle at an achievable level.

This chapter on Training discusses the fundamental changes that the Navy's training organisation and policies underwent during the period 1976 to 1990.

Officers

The Naval Academy

The RSES Scheme

By 1968, the shortage of General List officers had become a cause of concern. The anticipated strength of 3,500 officers by 1975 required an annual intake of at least 150 cadets. Since the NDA could not take more than 65 naval cadets every year, it became necessary to start a 'Revised Special Entry Scheme' (RSES) and set up a separate Naval Academy.

To provide space for this academy, it was decided:

- To move the sailors' Basic & Divisional (B&D) Training School from Cochin to Goa.

- To set up a temporary Naval Academy at Cochin to meet immediate needs until a permanent location was chosen.

In 1969, approval was accorded for the institution of the Revised Special Entry Scheme. Under this scheme, naval cadets in the age group 17 to 20 years who had passed the Intermediate examination could be recruited in the Executive Branch. This scheme was identical to the NDA 'Special Entry Scheme' except that the initial training of one year would have to be conducted at Cochin in the Naval Academy.

RSES training commenced in January 1970 and the first batch of 36 executive cadets passed out of the Naval Academy on 14 December 1970. They joined the NDA's 39th batch of regular cadets for sea training on board the training ships *Tir* and *Cauvery*.

The GSES Scheme

In 1973, when the National Defence Academy got affiliated to the Jawaharlal Nehru University in Delhi, all NDA cadets, on successfully passing their final examinations, received a 'Bachelor's Degree'. As a result, the RSES candidate of the Naval Academy was out of step with his NDA counterpart. It was decided that instead of taking in pre-graduate candidates, it would be more cost effective to recruit Science graduates only and thereby reduce the duration of their training at the Naval Academy.

The Naval Academy discontinued the training of RSES Cadets after June 1974 and in July 1974, the first batch of GSES cadets entered the Naval Academy for an initial training period of 6 months. Whereas the original sanction was for a total of 80 cadets to be trained every twelve months, the Naval Academy now started training 80 cadets every 6 months.

As part of the 1974 reforms of Naval Training, it was decided that:

- The Naval Academy should undertake the training of all officer courses hitherto conducted by the B&D School.

- The B&D School in Cochin was to be closed down after the shift of Direct Entry Seamen training to Goa as soon as the new Seamen Training Establishment (STE) commissioned in 1976.

From 1974 onwards, the Naval Academy, in addition to training GSES cadets, started conducting the following officers' courses:

- *Initial Training* for Direct Entry officers of the Engineering and Electrical branches.

- *Naval Science Orientation Course* for officers of the Supply Branch and officers from foreign navies.

- *Special Duties (SD) List*[1] *Post Promotion Course* for sailors on initial promotion to Acting Sub Lieutenants (SD).

- *Divisional & Management (D&M) Course.* The B&D course done by all Executive Sub Lieutenants during their technical courses was re-designated as the D&M Course when it was transferred from the B&D School to the Naval Academy.

- *Lieutenants War Course.* The B&D School used to conduct a War Course of four weeks duration for Acting Sub Lieutenants of the Executive branch. In 1974, it was decided that this course was better suited to a Lieutenant. The course was re-designated as Lieutenants' War Course and conducted bi-annually at the Naval Academy.

- *Upper Yardmen Course.* Sailors who showed early promise at sea of being officer material used to be designated 'Upper Yardmen'[2] and given special assignments to test their potential. In end 1974, Upper Yardmen of all branches started being sent to the Naval Academy for their initial training.

- *Commanding Officers and Junior Commanders' Course.* In end 1974, two new courses were instituted – the Junior Commanders' Course and the Commanding Officers' Course. These courses were conducted at the Naval Academy in 1974, 1975 and 1976.

By 1976, the Naval Academy found that it was not cost effective to carry out, separately, the initial training of cadets and of Acting Sub Lieutenants of various branches. It was decided that all initial training for cadets of the Executive Branch and Acting Sub Lieutenants of all technical branches should be of the same duration, should have a common syllabus and should run concurrently. This was implemented from 1976 onwards.

With the steady increase in the number of trainees, the Naval Academy (set up in temporary buildings in 1970), found that it neither had the accommodation nor the

classrooms nor the infrastructure to cope with the increase in its training load.

After the acceptance in 1976 of the Third Pay Commission's recommendations regarding changes in sailors' conditions of service, the Boy Entry was discontinued and only Direct Entry matriculate sailors were recruited. Since training effort and costs could be minimised by having only one Sailors' Training Establishment (the new *INS Chilka* was expected to commission in 1980), it was decided to:

- Re-locate the temporary Naval Academy from Cochin to *INS Mandovi* in Goa as soon as possible after the STE moved from Goa to *INS Chilka*, and after the STE constructed for sailor-training at Goa had been re-modelled with cadets' cabins, a cadet's mess, etc to function as a Naval Academy for training cadets.

- Obtain sanction for a new permanent Naval Academy.[3]

By end 1985, when the Naval Academy shifted from Cochin to Goa, it had been entrusted with additional courses:

- Assistant Commandants of the Coast Guard from 1980 onwards.

- Short Service Commission Direct Entry Technical Officers from 1982 onwards.

- 10+2 Technical officers from 1984 onwards.

In the years after the Academy functioned from Goa starting January 1986, it commenced training:

- Medical officers from 1986 onwards.

- 10+2 Scheme Executive officers from 1987 onwards.

Sea Training of Junior Executive Officers

The increase in officer intake increased the requirement for ships to impart training at sea after passing out from the Naval Academy. The ageing cruiser, *Delhi* underwent a major refit from May 1971 to August 1972 for conversion to the training role. *Delhi, Kistna, Cauvery* and *Tir* comprised the Training Squadron till the late 1970s.

From the beginning of 1975, the Naval Academy started sending 80 cadets every six months to the Cadet Training Ships (CTS). To effectively train this number, there had to be a training squadron of three ships of which a minimum of two had to be operationally available every term. This led to the decision to convert the three diesel-engined

---

1. Sailors promoted to officer rank constituted the 'Special Duties (SD)' List / Cadre.

2. The expression 'Upper Yardmen' derives from the days of sailing ships when only the most competent, agile and fit sailors were entrusted with the hazardous task of furling and unfurling the highest sails in the ship in all weather conditions.

3. See Historical Reference Data section for the development of the new academy at Ezhimala in Kerala, page 323.

frigates, *Brahmaputra, Beas* and *Betwa* to the training role to take over from the older training ships as they decommissioned.

In 1975, the duration of initial training of Junior Executive Officers was reviewed and reductions were made:

Duration in/of	Until 1975	After 1975
Cadets Training Ship	6 months	6 months
Midshipmen Afloat Training	12 months	6 months
Sub Lts Courses	52 weeks	40 weeks
Sea Attachment for Watch keeping Certificate	3 to 6 months	6 months

Beas and *Betwa* commenced cadet training duties in 1976. *Cauvery* and *Tir* decommissioned in 1977. *Brahmaputra* commenced cadet training and *Delhi* decommissioned in 1978. *Kistna* decommissioned in 1981.

By 1981, deterioration was being reported in the standard of seamanship and watch keeping amongst junior executive officers. The complaints were that they were not conversant with fleet ship duties when they went to sea after their Sub Lieutenants courses for their watch keeping certificates. Their earlier sea time had been only in training ships. The sea time for midshipmen had been reduced from one year to 6 months. In short, inadequate sea time had resulted in the sea training of junior officers being insufficient in quantity and quality to give them a professionally sound base.

In 1983, a Fleet Commander was constrained to observe:

"In the context of junior officers, I am constrained to confess that there is marked decline in their professional standards. Professionalism and pride in self and service seem to be the prime casualties. It calls for a soul-searching look at our present day training concepts.

"There exists lackadaisical attitude with a total lack of keenness to keep abreast of events of professional interest. It is not incurable, but warrants consistent efforts by those concerned to nip it in the bud and to bring about a greater professional awareness and identity among the new entrants. May be we could take a leaf from the *inner führung* activities of West Germany and model our motivation classes in a like manner. Whatever be the means or methods we adopt, it should have the solitary aim of eradicating the present unconcerned attitude of the junior officers.

"One of the contributing factors to the attitude of junior officers could be the poor confidence reposed in them by their immediate seniors and Commanding Officers. There is too much of 'guidance' and 'looking over the shoulder' with the result that junior officers do not find scope for discharging their responsibilities independently.

"In short, somewhere along the line, the continued process of grooming an officer to function independently has been lost track of after the initial training at school. This could well be attributable to the 'play safe' tendency that has crept in at all levels which is bound to erode deeply into the offensive spirit of our Navy, an essential component of a fighting force. The solution needs to be corrected by delegating greater responsibility to junior officers and encouraging them to perform independently wherever possible."

There were no easy solutions:

- Fleet ships with their complex systems imposed restrictions on their usage at sea compared to their counterparts of the past, with the result that officers at sea, particularly the younger ones, suffered from lack of adequate sea time and experience.

- Cadets and Midshipmen had become insulated from operational ships until they arrived in Fleet ships to obtain their watch-keeping certificate as Sub Lieutenants.

- Increasing sea time for Midshipmen was not practicable because it would aggravate the already acute accommodation problem on board operational ships.

- The motoring hours of Soviet origin ships were restricted.

- Due to the shortage of training ships in 1981, NDA and NAVAC cadets were conjoining for 6 months sea training on board the non-seagoing cruiser *Mysore*. Batches of 70 to 80 cadets were being given short sea trips of a total of only 15 to 20 days in a fleet ship, a minesweeper and in the submarine depot ship *Amba*. The balance time was being spent in Bombay harbour alongside the breakwater.

In 1982, orders were placed on Mazagon Docks for two, quick-delivery, low-cost, diesel-engined Cadet Training Ships (CTS) to be built to commercial Lloyds standards (as opposed to warship standards), having accommodation and facilities for 120 cadets, having long endurance for prolonged sea training cruises and having a flight deck for operating a helicopter, but no hangar.

The first CTS, *Tir*, commissioned in 1986 and *Brahmaputra* decommissioned in the same year. The second CTS had to be shelved due to financial constraints. From 1986 onwards, the Training Squadron comprised *Tir, Beas* and *Betwa*.

Since *Betwa* and *Beas* were ageing, two alternatives were examined for their replacement. Convert the first Leander class frigate, *Nilgiri*, to the training role or utilise a recently acquired Offshore Patrol Vessel (OPV) for the 42-day seagoing commitment. Whilst the conversion of *Nilgiri* was still being examined, *Betwa* decommissioned in 1991 and *Beas* in 1992. The seagoing commitment started being met by *Tir* and an OPV.

In 1994, the opportunity arose of acquiring the 1968 vintage, British Leander class frigate *Andromeda* for cadet training. Its condition was better than that of *Nilgiri* and its cost was cheaper than converting *Nilgiri*. *Andromeda* was acquired and commissioned as *INS Krishna* in 1995. Thereafter the Training Squadron comprised *Tir* and *Krishna* with an OPV helping with the seagoing commitment whenever required.

Sea Training Requirements of Cochin Schools

One problem to which no lasting solution could be found was that there were never enough operational ships present at Cochin for providing practical sea experience to the Gunnery and ASW long courses whilst undergoing training. This lack was compounded by the diversity of new systems entering service in the new acquisitions.

It was only after PCTs, OJTs and closed-loop-manning were introduced in the 1980s that trainees were able to see the action posts that they would be manning and get the feel of what would be required of them at sea.

The Streaming and De-Streaming of Long Courses

Three streams had been introduced in the Training Reforms of 1975 - 'A' Stream for the Leander class ships fitted with West European systems, 'B' stream for the older ships fitted with West European systems and 'C' stream for systems fitted with Russian systems. All four Executive Branch long course specialisations were streamed – officers were required to learn their respective equipment in the greatest detail.

After a few years, the streaming of the long Navigation-Direction and Communications courses was discontinued in response to a plea that the diversity and complexity of systems in these specialisations did not justify streaming. The real reason was apprehension that narrow 'stream' specialisation might adversely affect career progression and the variety of appointments.

In 1981, the Gunnery and TAS Long Courses specialisations suggested that their streaming also be discontinued on the grounds that "streaming was leading to dilution of professional expertise and adverse effects on the professional career prospects of Gunnery and TAS officers. Streamed officers were not fully competent to carry out training, trials and staff duties of both streams because of their training and appointment patterns and this made it increasingly difficult to find suitably qualified specialist officers for Fleet, Command and NHQ duties". It was suggested that instead of streaming, the syllabi of long courses be modified to include a thorough study of one 'basic' system by all officers, to be followed by PCT and OJT to be introduced for those appointed to a Leander class ship or a Russian origin ship.

The acceptance of this suggestion would have entailed the formalisation of the PCT concept for all classes of ships. At that point in time, manpower shortage and resistance to change were against such formalisation.

Though the proposal for discontinuing the streaming of Long Gunnery and Long TAS courses was accepted in principle, NHQ directed that PCT courses were to be conducted in lieu and till such time these were instituted, the syllabi for the Long Gunnery and Long TAS courses were to be modified to include more time on Leander and Kamorta equipment. Whilst the de-streamed syllabus for the Long Gunnery course was implemented, that for the Long TAS course could not because in the absence of PCT for all classes of ships, it was found difficult to de-stream the syllabus.

Committee for the Review of Training of Officers of the Armed Forces

In 1986, the Chiefs of Staff Committee constituted an inter-service committee of the three Vice Chiefs to examine the training profile of officers consistent with the requirements of modern warfare and to devise new training syllabi starting from the NDA right up to the NDC with two aims:

- To increase the technical content of services' training.
- To increase inter-service interaction in training.

The Committee made several recommendations:

- The recommendations implemented right away were conjoining of segments of the Higher Command Courses of the three services – the Navy established the College of Naval Warfare in Bombay; naval officers started attending equivalent Army and Air Force Colleges of Warfare.
- The Long Defence Management Course was equated to the Higher Command Courses and accorded university recognition.

A recommendation on which a consensus could not be obtained was to raise the NDA's entry to B Tech level. The

Navy was keen to implement it in the new Naval Academy. The Army and the Air Force were reluctant to accept this recommendation. Another recommendation that could not find acceptance was the introduction of an Honours Course in the NDA and that cadets wishing to take the Honours Course should be allowed to do so and be awarded seniority in proportion.

The recommendation for the establishment of a National Defence University had to await an identical recommendation of the Group of Ministers on the 1999 Kargil Report and is now nearer to implementation.

In 1996, in an effort to reduce manpower costs, proposals were formulated to 'technicalise' all naval officers by their undergoing a four-year course to obtain a B Tech degree (two years basic training at the NDA / Naval Academy followed by two years technical training at the Naval Academy / the respective Army and the Air Force service academies). The proposal too did not find support and was not pursued.

Sailors

The Boys Training Establishment

The Navy's procedure for the intake and initial training of ratings had been adopted from the British Navy. Its basic premise was that ratings should be inducted when young and given long periods of initial training to indoctrinate naval discipline and to familiarise them with life at sea.

Accordingly, ratings were recruited as 'boys' and trained in a Boys Training Establishment (BTE) for two years before going to sea. Artificers were recruited as 'apprentices' and trained for four years before going to sea.

Surges in demand for sailors were met by resort to 'direct entry' recruitment, curtailing the duration of initial training and accepting the attendant consequence of reduced naval indoctrination.

Before the partition of the Navy in 1947, the only BTE of the Royal Indian Navy was located in Karachi. After partition, a temporary BTE was set up in Vishakhapatnam. Training was carried out in a New Entry Camp and a Main Camp, both of which were located in temporary barracks at *INS Circars*.

In 1962, the BTE started getting congested. In 1965, when the decision was taken to base the Russian acquisitions in Vishakhapatnam and build a major naval base with a new Dockyard, it was decided to shift the BTE out of Vishakhapatnam.

In 1969, the Navy chose a 1,600-acre site for the BTE on the bank of the Chilka Lake[4] in Orissa, where 1,200 boys could be trained at a time. The Prime Minister laid the foundation stone of the BTE. Construction commenced in 1973 and it was commissioned as *INS Chilka* in 1980.

The Sailors Training Establishment

In the 1950s, direct entry sailors started being trained at the Basic and Divisional School at Cochin. As the Navy expanded, the numbers increased and the search started for an alternative location. As in the case of the BTE, the primary requirement was proximity to a waterfront, where young sailors could be taught boat work, sailing and basic seamanship.

In 1968, the Navy's proposal was accepted to site the new Sailors Training Establishment (STE) at Goa. In 1969, approval was accorded for the construction of the STE on a 230-acre site on a hill at Reis Magos, five miles from Panaji, close to the northern bank of the River Mandovi. The STE was envisaged to train 500 direct entry sailors (including apprentices) at a time.

On 9 October 1969, the Prime Minister laid the foundation stone of the STE. In January 1976, the new STE commissioned as *INS Mandovi* and commenced training direct entry sailors and apprentices.

In consonance with the recommendations of the Third Pay Commission, the educational qualification for entry was raised to Matriculation for Boy Entry sailors of all branches as well as for Direct Entry Seaman and Engineering branch sailors. It was decided to:

- Abolish the Boy Entry and have only one STE.
- Move the STE from Goa to Chilka Lake as soon as construction there was completed.

The establishment at Chilka Lake was commissioned as *INS Chilka* on 21 February 1980. It commenced the initial training of all Direct Entry Matriculate Entry Recruits (MERs).

INS Mandovi continued to train direct entry apprentices till 1982, after which their training shifted to Chilka.

INS Circars continued to train Non Matriculate Entry Recruits (NMERs) until 1986 when, as part of the measures to rationalise training, their training also shifted to Chilka.

---

4. Chilka Lake is the largest brackish water lake in Asia and a well-established sanctuary for migratory birds. From its inception, *INS Chilka* has meticulously fulfilled the Navy's commitment to safeguard the ecology of the lake and the environment of that part the bird sanctuary falling under its jurisdiction.

From 1986 onwards, *INS Chilka* became the Navy's sole establishment for imparting initial training to sailors on entry.

The Abolition and Reintroduction of the Seaman and Communication Instructor Cadre

The Navy's Seaman Branch sailors' and communication sailors' structure always had an 'Instructor' specialisation at the apex. These Gunnery Instructors (GIs), Torpedo Anti Submarine Instructors (TASIs), Plotting & Radar Instructors (PRIs), Signal Instructors (SIs) and Wireless Instructors (WIs) were a specially selected, highly dedicated, dependable group of senior sailors, trained in all the systems of their specialisation. Their major role was operational training on board ships and imparting instructions in their professional schools ashore. On board ships, they were responsible through their respective departmental officers, for the conduct and specialist efficiency of the sailors of their department. In the course of their duties, these instructors invariably shouldered extra responsibility and grew in stature. They did not get any monetary benefits. They were looked up to by their sailors with respect and respected by their departmental officers.

By the late 1970s, the vintage and diversity of sensors and weapons in ships had led to the introduction of Stream Training and Pre Commissioning Training. The logical conclusion should have been that the more complex the system, the greater the need for an Instructor specialisation at its apex. However, the scarcity of senior sailors' bunks on board Soviet-built ships and the diversity of systems led to the conclusion that an Instructor could not possibly master the multiple systems in each discipline.

In 1979, a NHQ letter stated:

"With the introduction of new weapon systems and sensors in the Navy, the traditional concept of giving Instructor qualification only to sailors of Seamen and Communication branches is no longer valid. In order to meet present day and future requirements, it has been decided to discontinue the present system of training Instructor sailors and to restructure the Instructor Cadre with a view to introduce formalised training for sailors of all branches assigned for instructional duties. Selected sailors will be trained at NIETT and thereafter appointed as Instructors in training billets. As incentives, the new scheme was to award recommendations for accelerated promotion[5] on successfully completing the Instructor 'qualifying' course and grant of two years ante-dated seniority for promotion to MCPO II on satisfactorily carrying out Instructional duties for two years".

The scheme did not work too well due to a shortage of NIETT trained sailors and was modified in 1986. For the next few years, previously trained Instructors continued to man key posts on board and ashore. As the Instructors of yester-year started retiring, their absence started affecting training both ashore and afloat.

The proposal for the reintroduction of Instructors was first made in 1985. It took four years to accept that the abolition had been a mistake and that Instructors were necessary to rejuvenate training ashore and to consolidate and improve professional training afloat.

Eventually in 1990, a directive was issued to reintroduce Instructors. Their new nomenclature was GI (Weapons) and GI (Sensors), ASWI (Weapons) and ASWI (Sensors), SI and WI. These Instructor cadre sailors were to be selected during their 1st rate courses and would have to undergo an Instructors Course after a sea tenure. The Instructor Cadre Sailors would be posted to sea billets as well as to training establishments. They would also have better prospects for promotion in the form of seniority and additional weightage for promotion to CPO and MCPO ranks.

Revised Training Pattern for Logistic Cadre Sailors

With the introduction of the Logistic Cadre in 1987, the training pattern of logistic cadre sailors was revised to make it more responsive to job requirements and based on a three-tier training pattern of 'New Entry Courses', 'Leading Rank Qualifying Courses' and 'Petty Officer Rank Qualifying Courses'.

Promotion linked courses were discontinued. Promotion to the rank of Chief Petty Officer was to be on roster basis. For selected CPOs / MCPOs, specialised capsule courses were introduced like 'Office Management' for writers, 'Inventory Management' and 'Preservation of Stores' for Store sailors and 'Catering Management' for stewards.

The Training Reforms of 1974 - 1975

In the early 1950s, the Navy acquired from Britain second hand destroyers, followed in the late 1950s, by a second hand cruiser and new frigates, followed in 1961 by an aircraft carrier. Starting in the mid 1960s, the Navy acquired from Russia submarines, submarine chasers and landing ships, followed from the early 1970s onwards by more submarines, submarine chasers, missile boats, minesweepers, landing ships and destroyers. Added to this was the requirement from the early 1970s onwards to man the indigenously constructed Leander class frigates and their successors.

---

5. Known in naval parlance as 'Red Recommendations'.

To man these acquisitions, the Navy had to resort to measures like increasing the number of trainees per class, reduce the durations of courses and deny the training schools of good instructors because the best men were needed to man the newest ships. Over the years, this had tended to de-motivate the schools and training had settled into a rut.

Lessons were learnt in the 1971 war. In 1974, measures were taken to remedy the ennui that had enveloped naval training. The Director of Naval Training and the Director of Combat Policy and Tactics,[6] under the direct guidance of the Vice Chief of the Naval Staff and four flag officers formulated what, by 1975, became a major reform of the Navy's training practices.

Major Decisions

The major decisions were:

- Vertical specialisation to be achieved by the introduction of 'streams' and 'sub streams' for both officers and sailors.

- Institution of Professional Courses / Examinations for Executive and Supply Branch officers.

- Commencement of Seamanship courses for Leading Seaman (Qualifying) and Petty Officer (Qualifying) courses at the Technical Schools.

- Training Establishments to carry out improvisations to cope with the backlog in training created by the introduction of the 15-year engagement and the automatic advancement to Leading rank.

- Training aids to be produced indigenously by our officers and sailors.

- Training aids of entire systems to be fabricated ashore so as to make up for the limited sea training then available.

Stream Training

The aim was to usher in vertical specialisation and consolidate expertise, ensuring that career prospects were not adversely affected. Three 'streams' were instituted:

- 'A' stream for the equipment in the new Leander class frigates.

- 'B' stream for the equipment in the old Western origin ships.

- 'C' stream for the equipment in the Russian ships.

Officers and sailors would be assigned to one of the streams and be trained for selected equipment in that stream. Cross training was allowed at certain senior levels to safeguard career prospects.

The variations in streams and sub-streams as applicable to branches were:

- Engineering branch artificers were streamed into 'Steam' and 'Internal Combustion Engines (ICE)'. The latter was sub-streamed into Brahmaputra ICE or Petya ICE, since the diesel engines in these two types of ships were entirely different.

- Electrical branch artificers were streamed into 'Power', 'Radar' and 'Control' and sub-streamed into specific equipment systems.

In most cases sub-streamed syllabi led to reduction in duration of courses and economy in effort.

Organisational Changes in Training Schools in Cochin

- All officer training was taken away from the B&D School in preparation for its shift to STE Goa. The Naval Academy was re-organised into two wings: Cadets and Other Officers.

- To minimise bureaucratic delays in the 'chain of command', the parent schools were allowed, as a trial measure, to correspond directly with outside authorities on routine matters. Their responsibilities were specified in an updated charter of duties.

- A work-study of the Signal School and the TAS School was ordered to improve their internal management of training.

- As was being done for sailors, Naval Psychological Research Unit (NPRU) Aptitude Tests were instituted to select Executive Officers for the different specialisations.

- In the Gunnery specialisation, in view of the diminishing requirement for visual aiming, the Gun Layer (GL) and Radar Control (RC) trades were merged.

- To keep abreast with the latest developments in technology and to exercise quality control, intensive short courses were introduced at five-year intervals. For officers, these were the Lieutenants War Course and the Junior Commanders Course. For sailors, these were the revised PO and CPO Leadership Course and the MCPO (Qualifying) Course.

- The career and training pattern of Executive officers from midshipman to the rank of Captain was recast with:

  – A twelve-week, post-Long Course training period.

  – A five-week Junior Commanders course.

  – A five-week Commanding Officers Course.

---

6. The author was the Director of Combat Policy and Tactics.

- The gain and loss of seniority rules for all branches were standardised. In the case of cadets and midshipmen, the training period afloat was reduced from 18 months to 12 months. Midshipman's time was reduced to 6 months.

Introduction of the Operator-Maintainer Concept

Soon after the contract was signed in early 1975 for the acquisition from Russia of ocean-going rocket boats (Durg class), minesweepers (Pondicherry class) and the guided missile destroyers (Rajput class), analysis indicated that there were not going to be enough bunks to accommodate the numbers that the Navy wanted. By end 1975, the complements of these three classes of ships were finalised on the basis of the Operator Maintainer Concept. Naval Headquarters expectation was that it would lead to better training and rational utilisation of manpower.

The gist of the NHQ letter that promulgated this concept was:

"It has been clear for some time that the existing system of manning and training in the Service by which ships are manned department-wise by the respective branches necessitates large complements on board, leading to conditions of overcrowding and all its attendant problems in life afloat. The present manning pattern by branches and cross-departmental employment also leads to a dilution of accountability and inter-branch stresses and strains.

"Naval Headquarters has therefore decided to adopt, as a permanent measure, the Operator-Maintainer concept for the Executive Branch and the transfer of power engineering to the Engineering Branch. The two schemes will be implemented in phases to minimise dislocation, maximise absorption of skills and ensure adequate protection of careers of officers and sailors of all branches."

The apprehensions of mid-level Electrical officers regarding loss of status on board ships and the eventual *via media* that was found have been discussed in the chapter on Manning.

The Creation of the Training Command in 1985

The Rationale

In 1982, NHQ began considering the creation of a Training Command and the reorganisation of the Directorate of Naval Training. The pros and cons of whether it was better to strengthen this Directorate or whether it was better to create a Training Command were debated for the next few years.

This debate meshed, in 1985, with Naval Headquarters' larger proposal for having only two operational naval commands, Western and Eastern, whose Commanders in Chief would be relieved of the problems of the training establishments to enable them to devote their full attention to operational matters. The Southern Command would become the Navy's Training Command.

Views were divided on this concept:

- In one view, making 'Training', as a function, the primary responsibility of a Commander in Chief, and placing all the Navy's training establishments under him, would ensure that the training establishments' problems would get swifter attention. Training policy and procedures could be standardised and Naval Headquarters would receive well-considered suggestions to improve training.

- The opposite view was that it would be untidy for training establishments, which were physically located in the territorial jurisdiction of Western and Eastern Commands to be under the control of the distant Southern Command. Similarly, it would be untidy for the Naval Officers in Charge (NOICs) Goa, New Mangalore, Cochin and Tuticorin, who were administratively under Southern Command to be operationally under Western and Eastern Commands. Moreover, the Air and Submarine Arms felt that the problems and proposals of their respective training establishments would be better understood 'functionally' by Flag Officer Naval Aviation and their parent Submarine Directorate in NHQ than by Southern Naval Command. For the same reasons, the Engineering and Electrical Branches felt that their *alma mater* schools, *Shivaji* and *Valsura*, would receive better attention from their 'parent' professional directorates in Naval Headquarters than from Southern Naval Command. Last, but not least, was the view that it was unwise to create two grades of Commander in Chief, namely 'operational' and 'training', because it would lead to invidious distinctions in the highest ranks of the Navy.

In October 1985, Naval Headquarters sought approval to streamline the Navy's Command and Control structure.[7] The features of that restructuring, relevant to this chapter, were to:

- Reduce the Operational Control Authorities from three to two and make them accountable for all operational activity in their areas:
  - FOCINCWEST for the Western seaboard and the Arabian Sea.
  - FOCINCEAST for the Eastern seaboard and the Bay of Bengal.

---

7. See Historical Reference Data for section titled 'Changes in Command and Control Structure', page 362.

- Place the control of all Training Establishments hitherto under FOCINC WEST and EAST under FOCINCSOUTH and place the accountability for all training policy formulation and implementation under one authority, leaving the Directorate of Training in Naval Headquarters with the responsibility for interacting with the Ministry of Defence and the other services.

Naval Headquarters' proposals were approved and the revised Command Structure was implemented from 1 July 1986.

Delegation for Studying the US Navy's Training System

As a prelude to this restructuring, a delegation headed by the FOCINCSOUTH and comprising the Commanding Officers of *Shivaji* (the Marine Engineering training school), *Valsura* (the Electrical Engineering training school) and an Executive branch Commander representing the seaman and communication training schools was deputed to the USA to study the United States Navy's training system and, on return, to put up recommendations for reorganising the Indian Navy's training system.[8]

After visiting all the US Navy's relevant officer, petty officer and sailor training establishments and after detailed discussions on their basic concepts of training, the delegation made several basic recommendations, the most important of which were:

- Each officer and sailor must be trained ashore specifically for his next job at sea.

- In view of the hi-tech diversity in the Navy's ship systems, broad-brush courses were counterproductive. During his career, every sailor should acquire expertise in one system / systems fitted in one type of ship. During an officer's career, he should progress from expertise in one system to broader knowledge of ship systems.

- Personnel trained on the above principles should stay long enough on board to acquire expertise and, to enable them to develop and deepen expertise, their next sea tenure should be to a ship having the same or similar systems.

- To foster and nurture the esprit d'corps of officers serving in ships, they should wear the 'Surface Warfare Officer' insignia, analogous to the 'wings' worn by naval pilots and observers and the 'dolphins' worn by submariners.[9]

Naval Headquarters directed the delegation to make presentations of its recommendations in the three Naval Commands to prepare the Navy for the intended revitalisation of training. All officers of Commander's rank and above were to be present at these presentations and clarify their queries.

Despite these presentations and the clarification of all queries, there was resistance to change. It took some months for the scepticism to abate about the untidiness of 'a Command in the South exercising administrative control over training establishments in the West and the East', which for decades had been under their respective Commanders-in-Chief.

The 1986-1989 Revitalisation of Training

The measures implemented between 1986 and 1989 laid the foundation for the revitalisation of training that yielded results in the 1990s. These measures took into account the best features of the British, Russian and American systems of training and adapted them for the Indian context, keeping in mind all the difficulties that had been experienced in the past and the manning and training of foreseeable acquisitions. The erstwhile system of training 'jacks of all trades' and therefore 'appointable' to any class of ship was finally dispensed with.

Over-riding Principles

The three over-riding principles of the revitalisation were:

- Every officer and sailor was to be trained for his next job at sea.

- Officers were to acquire 'width' of knowledge and sailors were to acquire 'in-depth' knowledge and vertical expertise. Sailors were to specialise in one system / systems fitted in a class of ship.

- Officers and sailors in ships under Stabilised Operational Manning Cycle / Pre Commissioning Training (PCT) were to be recycled for the same system in successive sea tenures.

Specific Measures

In conformance with these principles, NHQ promulgated the following directives from 1986 onwards:

General

- Ships be divided into PCT / non PCT category. PCT ships to follow a closed-loop manning so as to recycle personnel on the same system. Non PCT ships to be manned on trickle transfer basis.

---

8. The author, as FOCINCSOUTH, led this delegation and subsequently implemented the revitalisation of training during 1986 and 1987.

9. It took twenty years for this recommendation to be eventually implemented on the 26 January 2004.

- Theoretical training to be reduced and greater emphasis laid on practical training.
- Surface Wing of *INS Satavahana* at Vishakhapatnam to be shifted to the specialist schools at Cochin and equipment reinstalled to the extent feasible.
- Russian 'C' Stream training to be discontinued.
- Western 'A' Stream to be redesignated 'Giri' (Leander frigate) Stream.
- Coast Wing School to be shifted from *INS Trata* in Bombay to *INS Dronacharya* at Cochin.
- Missile Boat Training Centre (MBTC) to be shifted from Karanja in Bombay to *INS Dronacharya* in Cochin and equipment reinstalled to the maximum extent possible.

SOMC for Ships Having Pre Commissioning Training

- Tenure of officers on Per Commissioning Training (PCT) ships to be increased to 2 years with 50 per cent changing every year.
- Tenure of sailors on PCT ships to be 3 years with 33 per cent changing every year.
- On completion of PCT, a composite module of 2-week On Job Training (OJT) followed by 2-week Task I to be introduced instead of only OJT as hithertofore.
- Rajput class destroyer PCT to be conducted from July to mid November every year followed by OJT / Workup till mid December.
- Godavari class frigate Durg class rocket boat / Minesweeper / Veer class PCT to be conducted from December to early April every year followed by OJT / Work Up till early May.
- The duration of PCT for Commanding Officer (CO) / Executive Officer (XO) to be revised as follows:

  – Rajput class destroyers   8 weeks

  – Godavari/Durg class /Minesweeper /   6 weeks
    Veer class

- Missile Boats / Trishul (SSM crew) PCT to be conducted in July and December followed by OJT / Workup from mid November to mid December and early April to early May.

Officers

- *Basic Training-Executive Officers.* 10+2 (Executive) scheme to be introduced at Naval Academy w.e.f. August 1987 if possible, but not later than January 1988. Intake per term to be examined by NHQ (COP). Action to be initiated by FOC-in-C South to process affiliation to a University for the award of a Bachelor of Science Degree with a curriculum structure towards Naval Technology inputs. Duration of 10+2 (Executive) Scheme to be of 3 years. The curriculum to be pitched somewhere between B Sc and B Tech syllabus in keeping with the futuristic requirements of the Service.
- *Sub Lieutenant Courses*

  – The Executive Sub Lieutenant courses to be modified to train officers for effectively performing as OOW/ OOD for carrying out duties in ships where no specialist officers were authorised;

  – Greater emphasis to be laid on service writing for officers of the Executive and Technical Branches.
- *Long Courses.* Duration of the Long Courses to be reduced and syllabi modified to ensure greater emphasis on tactics, operational analysis and computer application. Officers to be given an exposure on representative equipment of all systems concerning their specialisation.
- *CO/XO Course Non PCT Ships.* A 6-week duration CO/XO Refresher Course to be introduced for officers appointed to non PCT ships.
- *Basic Training-Technical Officers.* Present training pattern to be restructured in accordance with the decisions taken at the Senior Officers' Conference.
- *Mid-Career Naval Command Course.* FOC-in-C South to examine the introduction of a mid-career Naval Command Course for junior Captains / senior Commanders.
- *Long EDP Course.* FOC-in-C South to evolve a long EDP Course syllabus to be conducted at *INS Hamla*.
- Education Officers initial training to be revised and duration to be reduced to 50 weeks. Eight-week sea training syllabus to include Navigation and Meteorology.
- *Midshipmen's Board.* In order to have uniformity in standards, the Midshipmen's Examination / Board to be conducted by FOC-in-C South.

Sailors

- *Training at Chilka.* The following changes to be introduced:

  – Basic Training of MERs to be reduced to 16 weeks;

  – Sea training on completion to be reduced to 8 weeks;

  – Recruitment of sailors to be made every four months to coincide with the revised training pattern as stipulated above;

  – B&D training of Non Matric Entry Recruits (NMERs) to be shifted from *INS Circars* to *INS Chilka*.

- *Seamanship Training.* Seamanship training for Seaman MER, DE Artificers and NCC personnel to be undertaken at Seamanship School Cochin. Seamanship training for MERs to be reduced to 4 weeks.

- *PT III Course.* FOC-in-C South to introduce PT III Course at *INS Hamla* (PT School).

- *Medical Assistant (MA) Courses*

  - Specialist Qualification and Higher Rank Courses for MAs to be conducted at the same time;

  - Syllabi for MA courses to be reduced and revised by DMS (N) by end 1986.

- *CPO Management Courses.* A CPO Management Course for all CPOs of a suitable seniority to be introduced. MCPO Pre-Promotion Course to cease thereafter.

- *Higher Rank Courses.* Periods on 'Management Techniques' to be included for all higher rank courses.

- *Abolition of Courses.* The following courses / schemes to be discontinued with immediate effect:

  - Paint Application Course;

  - Navigator Yeoman's Course;

  - SSME Scheme;

  - EA 3 'Q' Course;

  - POEL 'Q' Courses.

- *Introduction of New Courses/Stream/Board.* The following new Courses/Stream/Boards to be introduced:

  - Ch EL and EA 'Q' Courses at *INS Valsura*;

  - Ch ME/ERA/Mech 'Q' Courses at *INS Shivaji*;

  - Gas Turbine Stream for Engine Room sailors;

  - EA 3 'Q' Board at Command level;

  - POEL Board at Command level.

- *Artificers.*

  - An open examination to be conducted at *INS Chilka* for selection of Artificers from amongst the MERs;

  - Standardisation of Artificer / Mechanician training as recommended by FOC-in-C South, approved 'in principle';

  - Revised trade structure of Electrical Artificers as recommended by FOC-in-C South, approved 'in principle';

  - FOC-in-C South to forward comprehensive proposals for selection of Mechanicians and Weapon Mechanicians through an open examination and introduction of Seaman Artificers.

- *Training of Seamen.* The need to avoid infructuous training was accepted in principle.

- *Introduction of Seamen Master Operator.* For optimum exploitation of modern sensors and weapon systems, a Master Operator Cadre with Special Grade Pay was to be introduced in the Seaman Branch.

- *PO Leadership Course.* The aim of making qualification in PO Leadership Course at *Agrani* a mandatory requirement for confirmation in the rank of Petty Officers for non-artificer sailors and a pre-requisite for Artificer sailors for promotion to Artificer 3rd Class was accepted. To minimise turbulence, the conjoining of PO Leadership Course with PO (Q) Courses to be examined.

- *Standard Swimming Test.* Southern Naval Command proposed that passing of the Standard Swimming Test (SST) be made mandatory for the promotion to the rank of Petty Officer. The aim of encouraging qualification in the Standard Swimming Test (SST) before promotion to Petty Officer rank was accepted but making it mandatory for promotion was not accepted. It was, however, agreed that certain incentives could be given for passing this test. FOC-in-C South was to forward suitable recommendations for incentives.

- *Increasing the Employability of Topass Sailors on Board Ships.* Topasses on board ships were under-utilised and they could be usefully employed for ship maintenance after a small capsule course on ship husbandry. Topass sailors, on completion of their initial training in *Chilka* to be given four weeks of training at the Shipwright School on ship husbandry, plumbing, painting, fire fighting and damage control.

- *Damage Control Training.* In the context of the foundering of the *Andaman* in August 1990 and the weaknesses identified of inadequate knowledge of damage control, there was an immediate need to enhance NBCD training in *INS Shivaji*. Additional instructors to be positioned at *INS Shivaji* to overcome the present shortages.

- *Training of Seamen.* In 1988, FOC-in-C South proposed that Part II qualification should not be made a mandatory requirement for promotion for seamen sailors. The issue was examined and NHQ decided to maintain status quo.

The national drought of 1986 was followed in the end 1980s by a serious shortage of resources. A Committee was appointed to recommend economy measures with regard to the movement of personnel. Some of this Committee's recommendations tried to reduce Pre Commissioning Training to minimise the cost of travel.

Extent of Revitalisation Achieved by End 1989

– Division of ships into PCT/ Non PCT Category	Action completed.
– Reduce theoretical training	Implemented
– Shift Surface Wing of *Satavahana* from Vizag to Cochin	Action completed
– Discontinue 'C' Stream training	Action completed
– Re-designate 'A' Stream training as 'Giri' Stream	Action completed
– Shift Coast Wing School from *Trata* to *Dronacharya*	Action completed
– Shift Missile Boat Training Centre from Karanja to Cochin	Action completed
– Revise tenure of officers and sailors on PCT Ships	Action completed
– Introduce composite module of 2-week OJT	Module proposed to FOCWF and 2-week Task I
– Conduct of PCT	Action completed
– Commence 10+2 (Executive) Scheme at *INS Mandovi*	Scheme introduced
– Revise syllabi of Sub Lieutenants Courses	Syllabi modified and War Course introduced for Sub Lieutenant (X) Courses
– Revise and reduce Long Course syllabi	All Long Course durations reduced to 40 weeks
– CO/XO Course for non PCT ships	FOC-in-C South recommended CO/XO course for PCT as well as non PCT ships. Details being finalised at NHQ.
– Revise Basic Training of Technical Officers	Revision of Electrical officers training pattern approved. Proposal to combine VI and VII term BEC and VIII term NEC with MESC was scrutinised at NHQ. Combining the training was not possible
– Revise Education Officers' Training	Initial training of 50 weeks duration implemented. Revised syllabus includes Navigation and Meteorology subjects during sea training
– Midshipmen's Board	Common board being conducted by FOC-in-C South
– Mid-Career Naval Command Course	The first Naval Higher Command Course of 24 weeks duration commenced in Bombay in September 1988
– Long EDP Course Syllabus	Implemented
– Seamanship Training	Action completed
– PT III Course	Action completed
– Medical Assistant (MA) Courses	Combining of Higher Rank & Specialist Qualifying courses not feasible in view of constraints of manpower and instructors
– CPO Management Courses	Implemented
– Higher Rank Courses – Management Techniques	Implemented
– PO Leadership Course	Conjoining of PO Leadership course with PO 'Qualifying' courses can only be considered for implementation after backlog is cleared of 2,100 POs and equivalents, waiting on the roster for the PO Leadership course
– Abolition of courses	Implemented
– Introduction of New Courses/Boards	Boards being introduced in a phased manner
– Introduction of Gas Turbine Stream	Implemented
– Artificers – Selection, Training, Revised Trade structure	Proposals in respect of standardisation of Artificer/Mechanician training, revision of trade structure of Electrical Artificers, selection of Mechanician and Weapon Mechanicians as also the introduction of Seaman Artificers have been received by NHQ from HQ SNC. Under scrutiny at NHQ. Follow up action will be initiated.

– Selection of Artificers from MERs

– Training of Seamen

Navy Entry Artificers Scheme' introduced.

To facilitate sailors to be recycled in ships for successive sea tenures to enhance operational capabilities and also to avoid infructuous training, sailors have been grouped for higher rank courses, depending on the equipment fit of ships for which they are being trained.

– Standard Swimming Test

No consensus between the Commands and NHQ on the incentives to be given for passing of Standard Swimming Test. The three Commands were, however, in favour of awarding a red recommendation and three months ante-dated seniority for passing this test. NHQ directed that the concept of Duty Sea Swimmer should be followed and exercised frequently as this would encourage sailors in qualifying SST.

– Introduction of 'Seaman Master Operator'

Held in abeyance by NHQ for three years

– Increasing the Employability of Topass sailors in Ship Husbandry on board ships

Implemented

– Damage Control Training

Additional instructors appointed to *Shivaji*

Training Equipment

Leander Training Equipment

The British radar and weapon systems of the first Leander, *Nilgiri,* were not replicated from the second frigate *Himgiri* onwards, which had Dutch equivalents. The Leander Training equipment installed in the schools conformed to that fitted in *Himgiri.*

- Radars, sonars, weapon control systems and electronic systems were installed in the respective parent training schools in Cochin for imparting user training. Installation was completed by 1979.

- Radars, sonars, electronics, weapon control and/ electrical systems were installed in the Electrical School *INS Valsura* for imparting maintenance training. Installation was completed by 1979.

- Steam Demonstration Room and Controls Training Building were set up in the Engineering School *INS Shivaji.*

Later *Taragiri* and *Vindhyagiri* also had changes in some of their systems and minimum essential training equipment was installed in the respective schools.

Type Training

In 1977, it was decided that *INS Shivaji* should extend engineering 'type training' of ships, which was hitherto restricted to a limited category of ships, to the Durgs and the new minesweepers in the field of machinery controls and systems. This would enable 'On Job Training' (OJT) to be conducted ashore prior to change over of ships' crew.

Project VAJRA

Vajra was the name of the project to install training equipment for the weapon, sensor, electrical and engineering equipment of the Rajput class destroyers, the Durg class rocket boats and the Pondicherry class minesweepers contracted for in 1975.

Three considerations limited the extent to which there could be duplication of equipment between the parent 'user' schools in Cochin and the 'maintainer' Electrical School *INS Valsura* as had happened in the case of the Leander training equipment:

- The prohibitively high cost of live radar, sonar, missile and weapon control systems.

- The implementation of Operator-Maintainer and Functional Department concepts in the manning and training of Russian built ships.[10]

- The cost of new buildings and civil works.

Eventually, the Vajra Project at Cochin was sanctioned at a cost of Rs 36 crore for providing training facilities in the parent 'user' schools in Cochin.[11] This did not include either the cost of the minimum essential duplication at the Electrical School or the cost of the propulsion gas turbines, the power generation gas turbine generators and other engineering equipment installed in the Engineering School *INS Shivaji.* Installation was complex. When completed in 1990, it was ten years after the first ships had arrived in India.

---

10. These have been discussed in the chapter on 'Manning of Ships and Conservation of Expertise', page 264.

11. Ministry of Defence Annual Report 1987-88.

Training Schools

The New Schools

Some schools were relocated, some new schools were established and one school has yet to come up:

- *The Shipwright School.* Located in the Naval Dockyard, Bombay since 1947, it moved to its new premises in Vishakhapatnam in 1981 and commenced training shipwright apprentices.

- *The Pre Commissioning Training School.* This new school was established as one of the core measures to revitalise training. It started functioning at Cochin from 25 April 1986.

- *The Navy's Physical Training School.* Established in *INS Angre* in Bombay since 1951, it shifted to *INS Hamla* in 1978. However, the sports infrastructure planned to be created on the land that had been acquired for the purpose could not be progressed due to environmental litigation. In 1987, the school shifted from Bombay to *INS Venduruthy* in Cochin where the required sports fields and infrastructure were readily available.

- *The College of Naval Warfare.* As part of the approved recommendations of the inter-service Vice Chiefs CORTOS Committee to institute mid-career professional courses, this new College was set up in Karanja in 1987.

In 1988, it commenced its first 24-week Naval Higher Command Course for Executive and Technical officers of the rank of Captain / Commander.*

- *The EDP School.* In 1987, a rudimentary EDP School started functioning in *INS Hamla.* The first 24-week Long EDP course commenced in 1987 and completed in February 1988. The full-fledged EDP School was inaugurated on 27 December 1989 to:

  - Impart computer literacy programmes on Personal Computers with their associated languages for officers, sailors and civilians.

  - Conduct system-manager-oriented EDP training for officers who would man key positions in logistic organisations, which had their own EDP system.

  - Conduct short duration modules of 'language / package'-oriented courses for updating the knowledge of personnel already working in EDP environments.

- *The Amphibious Warfare School.* In 1984, approval in principle was accorded for setting up an Amphibious Warfare School in the Andaman & Nicobar Islands. The Siting Board concluded that it would be better for the School to be located on the east coast of India. Waterfront land was identified at Kakinada. The Siting Board found the site unsuitable. A suitable site has yet to be identified.

The Training Schools in 1990

Branch	Specialisation	Name & Location	Parent School for:
Seamen	Gunnery	*INS Dronacharya* Fort Cochin, facing the sea for firing practices	Gunnery officers & sailors. PCTs of seamen missile gun & weapon system operator and electrical maintainer action post
	Torpedo & Anti Submarine	*ASW School* Within *INS Venduruthy* Willingdon Island Cochin	ASW officers & sailors. PCTs of seamen sonar and weapon operator and electrical maintainer action posts
	Communication & Electronic Warfare	*Signal School* Within *INS Venduruthy,* Willingdon Island Cochin	Communication officers & sailors. PCTs of communication and electronic warfare operator and electrical maintainer action posts
	Navigation, Direction	*ND School* Within *INS Venduruthy,* Willingdon Island Cochin	Navigation & Direction officers, radar plotters, quartermasters. PCTs of seaman operator and electrical maintainer Ops Room & AIO action posts
	Diving Cadre	*Diving School* Within *INS Venduruthy* Willingdon Island, Cochin	Divers and marine commandos
	Physical Training Cadre	*PT School* Within *INS Venduruthy* Willingdon Island, Cochin	Physical Training officers and sailors
Marine Engineering		*INS Shivaji* Lonavla in Maharashtra	Engineering officers, artificers, mechanics & basic training of all artificers. PCTs of Engineering and Damage Control action posts

Electrical Engineering		*INS Valsura* Jamnagar in Gujarat	Electrical officers, artificers & mechanics. Technical training for all electrical electronic & weapon systems
Logistics Cadre		*INS Hamla* Marve in Suburban Bombay	Logistic and EDP officers, writers, stores assistants, cooks and stewards
Air Arm	Observers	*Observer School* Willingdon Island, Cochin	
	Air Technical	*Naval Air Technical School* Within *INS Venduruthy* Willingdon Island, Cochin	Air Engineer & Air Electrical officers, Air Artificers and air technical sailors
	Airmen	*School for Naval Airmen* Within *INS Venduruthy* Willingdon Island, Cochin	Non-technical sailors of the Air Arm
Submarine Arm		School for Submarine Warfare *INS Satavahana* Vishakhapatnam	Submarine cadre officers and sailors, submarine PCTs and Escape training
Hydrographic Cadre		*Hydrographic School* Within *INS Gomantak* Vasco da Gama, Goa	Hydrographic officers and sailors
Education		*School of Naval Oceanology & Meteorology* Within *INS Garuda* Willingdon Island, Cochin	Meteorology and Oceanology
		Naval Institute of Educational Training Technology Within *INS Venduruthy* Willingdon Island, Cochin	Teaching Methods and & Training Technology
Shipwright Cadre		*Shipwright School* Visakhapatnam	Constructor and Shipwright officers, shipwrights, shipwright apprentices and shipwright mates (topasses)
Provost Cadre		*Regulating School* *INS Kunjali*, Bombay	Provost officers and sailors
Musicians Cadre		*School of Music* *INS Kunjali*, Bombay	Musician officers and sailors
All Petty Officers		Leadership School *INS Agrani*, Coimbatore	Petty Officers Leadership Course

Retrospect

It took two decades from the time of the CROSS Committee of 1966 to the Revitalisation of Training in 1986 for the Navy to adjust gradually to the new compulsions resulting from ships densely packed with a multitude of electronically interlinked sensors (radars, sonars, EW systems), weapons (missiles, rockets, guns) and weapon fire control systems.

By 1990, three over-riding principles were established:

- Every officer and sailor should be trained for his next job at sea.
- Officers should develop 'width' of knowledge and sailors should develop 'in-depth' knowledge and vertical expertise. Sailors were to specialise in one or more systems fitted in a class of ship.
- Officers and sailors in ships under Stabilised Operational Manning Cycle / Pre Commissioning Training (PCT) were to be recycled for the same systems in successive sea tenures.

For every new acquisition, a balance had to be struck between the cost of setting up new training facilities ashore or learning 'on the job'. The problem with the latter was that the wear and tear caused by 'learning on the job at sea' degraded the life of operational equipment. Eventually PCT came to be accepted as preferable to OJT.

Despite the high cost of live equipment for training personnel in schools ashore, each of the branch schools were provided with the minimum essential live equipment and simulators they needed to train personnel for their next job at sea.

As the following excerpts from *'My Life'*, the memoirs of German Grand Admiral Raeder[12] show, the German Navy experienced analogous (though not identical) problems as early as a hundred years ago. His reflections remain relevant today:

"Each training year began on 1st October, at which time that one third of the crews, which had completed its three-year enlistment, was replaced by new recruits. This date synchronised with the shift of officers and petty officers, who, however, were rotated on a two-year basis.

"Thorough and comprehensive battle training, including damage control, with wartime conditions closely simulated, began after Christmas. Rapid, efficient action was demanded of every one and, in the discussions held after the drills, each officer and man was required to present his ideas and back them up with logic. This intensive training, and the resulting critiques, made every man on board feel a joint responsibility and largely accounted for the reliability of our Navy in the First World War.

"The rigid programme of training, inspection and cruises, with no ship's captain permitted to deviate in the slightest, did speed up the men's purely mechanical actions, but just as inevitably destroyed any originality or independent thinking on the part of the commanding officers. Eventually a revaluation was made in an attempt to bring about more flexibility and variety in the training programme.

"The practice of all ships receiving their year's quota of recruits on board simultaneously on 1st October inevitably impaired the battle efficiency of the fleet as a whole for some time. Now it was proposed that one of the fleet's three squadrons was to receive all the recruits each October, while the other two squadrons, with relatively few changes in personnel, would be able to maintain a high state of readiness. In addition, the commanders of the individual ships were to be given much more independence in the matter of training."

---

12. Grand Admiral Raeder was the Chief of Staff of the German High Seas Fleet in the 1914-1918 World War and the Chief of the German Navy during the 1939-45 World War.

34

Merger Of Supply & Secretariat Branch With Executive Branch In 1978 & Creation Of Logistics Cadre In 1989

Preamble

The chapter on "Russian Acquisitions" has discussed the complex interaction with the Russian side on the timely supply of spares. The Historical Reference Data section titled "Changes in NHQ Organisation" has discussed what was attempted at the NHQ decision-making level. The chapters on "Maintenance, Repair and Refit Facilities" and on "Logistics" have discussed how the lack of spares delays refits.

This chapter discusses the events that led to the abolition of the Supply and Secretariat Branch by merging it with the Executive Branch and, when it was found that this aggravated the situation, recreating a Logistic Cadre.

The Events Leading to the Merger

From the mid 1960s onwards, the Navy constantly wrestled with the problem of Logistics. By 1968, it had become clear that placing the Directorate of Stores directly under the Chief of Material was unable to cope either with the management and replenishment of Russian spares or the delays in the indigenisation of spares.

In the 1969 'Reorganisation of NHQ', a new PSO was constituted, the Chief of Logistics, in the rank of Rear Admiral in charge of the Logistics Branch. In this new Branch were placed all the Directorates that could, in semantic terms, be considered "logistics" namely the Directorates of Stores, Armament Supply, Clothing and Victualling, Supply Branch, Civilian Personnel and Civil Engineering.

In the late 1960s, the Harbour Acceptance Trials and Sea Acceptance Trials that each ship had to undergo after refit started revealing the unreliability of equipment performance despite prolonged refit. These were substantiated by reports from the Fleet Commanders of the unreliability of ship performance during exercises.

Since the causes of this state of affairs were many and varied, the refitting authority blamed the provisioning agency that the spares required for the thorough refit of equipment were not available at the right time. The provisioning agency blamed the Dockyards for not forecasting their requirements more thoroughly and in good time. The refitting authority countered by suggesting that only "single branch responsibility for Repair / Refit and Logistics" could yield better results. Many had no hesitation in stating that the Supply Branch was structured for Secretarial functions rather than for modern logistics.

The 1972 Reorganisation of NHQ made a few changes in the Chief of Logistics' responsibilities. The Directorate of Civilian Personnel and Civil Engineering were shifted to other PSOs and the Directorate of Naval Armament Inspection was shifted to COL. The Directorate of Stores was renamed as the Directorate of Logistic Support. From 1972 onwards, the Chief of Logistics was in charge of the Directorates of Logistic Support, Armament Supply, Armament Inspection, Clothing and Victualling and Supply Branch.

None of these changes resolved the basic malaise. The Navy's repair, refit and logistic structure continued to remain stressed.

In the mid 1970s, rising manpower costs compelled a re-look at the Navy's organisational structure. There was avoidable duplication in some areas. Other areas remained understaffed. There was constant pressure for more manpower. A study was initiated whether the organisation could be rationalised and, to the extent possible, not only enable staffing requirements to be met within existing manpower resources but also provide for better accountability.

This study resulted in two major conclusions:

- The Supply and Executive Branches should be merged. Junior officers of the Supply Branch could volunteer to convert to the Executive Branch and those found fit would undergo conversion courses.[1] During the transition, officers of the Supply Branch in ships and establishments would be withdrawn without any relief. As regards Supply Branch sailors, the adoption of 'Operator-Maintainer' and 'action post' manning on the new rocket boats (Durg class), minesweepers (Pondicherry class) and guided missile destroyers (Rajput class) restricted the number that could be accommodated in the limited number of bunks.

- The 'Logistics' function, which had been set up under a different PSO, would be more functional if amalgamated with the Material and Personnel branches. This would result in a more streamlined organisation at NHQ. And, with the logistic functions coming under the Chief of Material, establish tighter material control of refits.

Merger of the Supply and Secretariat Branch with the Executive Branch

The rationale for the merger was:[2]

"Modern warships are packed with weapon systems necessitating utmost economy in the space allotted for personnel. Taking this aspect into account, as also others including the fact that officers of the Supply Branch have been performing a variety of diverse functions, it has been found undesirable to have separate Supply Officers on board ships. It has accordingly been decided to merge the Supply and Secretariat Branch with the Executive Branch of the Navy with effect from 1 January 1978.

"The existing officers of the Supply and Secretariat Branch with up to four years seniority as Lieutenant would be given an option to undergo an Executive conversion course. The remaining officers would be eligible for non-operational appointments currently held by the Executive Branch, in addition to the Supply appointments tenable by them.

"The proposed reorganisation, besides ensuring better utilisation of the erstwhile Supply and Secretariat Officers, would also ensure reasonable promotional avenues to them.

"As a corollary to this, the post of the Chief of Logistics, one of the Principal Staff Officers in Naval Headquarters, which was being held by an officer of the Supply and Secretariat Branch, has been abolished. The Chief of Logistics had been responsible for procurement, holding and supply of spares and components, while the responsibility for maintenance and carrying out repair and refits was that of the Chief of Material. This had resulted in a certain amount of divided responsibility.

"With the abolition of the post of Chief of Logistics, it has been decided to entrust to the Chief of Material the responsibility for the provisioning of spares and components, in addition to repair and maintenance. For this purpose, the Directorates of Logistic Support and Armament Supply of the erstwhile Logistics Branch have been placed under the Chief of Material. Two other Directorates under the Chief of Logistics viz. Directorate of Clothing and Victualling and the Directorate of Supply have been placed under the Chief of Personnel and the third, the Directorate of Naval Armament Inspection has been placed under the Vice Chief of Naval Staff".

The Intervening Years

By 1981, it had become clear that there was no significant improvement in the basic problem of timely availability of spares.

In 1982, the ACOM (Logistics), who functioned under the Chief of Material, recommended the immediate formation of a Logistic Cadre to revitalise the Logistics Organisation.

In October 1984, a new 'Logistics Branch' was created. At NHQ, a new PSO was created, Chief of Logistics & Administration (COLA)[3], and assisted by the erstwhile ACOM Logistics, now re-designated as ACOL. The Directorates placed under the new Logistic Branch were the Directorate of Logistic Support (DLS), the Directorate of Supply (DOS), the Directorate of Administration (DOA), the Directorate of Management Services (DOMS), the Directorate of Works (DW), the Directorate of Armament Supply (DAS) and the Directorate of Transport (DOT) when formed.

The Creation of the Logistics Cadre in 1989

From 1984 till 1989, discussions continued regarding the creation of a Logistic Cadre. The two basic issues were:

---

1. In the mid 1970s, Britain's Royal Navy attempted to amalgamate its Supply Branch with its Executive Branch. After the Indian Navy had merged these branches in 1977, it came to light that the Royal Navy had abandoned its attempt because of difficulties in the *modus operandi* to be adopted for a smooth changeover.

2. Ministry of Defence Annual Report 1977-78.

3. COLA was created as a PSO in the rank of Vice Admiral in the Second Cadre Review.

- How best to utilise the existing "erstwhile Supply Officers" – senior ones in the new Cadre and the junior ones who were surplus to the requirements of the new cadre.
- The career profile of officers in the new Logistic Cadre.

In July 1986, as part of the restructuring of the Navy and NHQ organisation, the logistic function was restored to the Material Branch. The Chief of Logistics was re-designated as Controller of Logistic Support under the COM.

In 1989, sanction was accorded for the formation of the Logistics Cadre as part of the Executive Branch and the first list of officers forming part of the Cadre was promulgated.

Reminiscences

Writing in *INS Hamla's* Golden Jubilee 2004 Logistics Journal, Commodore SK Sinha recalls:

"In 1976-77, a brain-wave in certain quarters caused the S&S Branch to merge with the Executive Branch and further entry to the S&S Branch was stopped. Although the aim behind the merger was apparently to afford better / higher career prospects to deserving S&S officers, the ground reality remained as before - not that there were no deserving S&S officers to claim higher Executive billets!!

"The only change that S&S officers saw was that they came into the Executive Cadre in the new Navy List with their seniority fitted in the appropriate level but they continued in their old career placements".

Writing in *INS Hamla's* Golden Jubilee 2004 Logistics Journal, Commodore V Janardan recalls:

"Discontent and unhappiness among the General List of Supply Officers had been simmering ever since I remember, as their job opportunities and promotion prospects (apart from the glamour) were considerably less than their Executive Branch counterparts. Often these officers were required to serve under their Executive Branch counterparts.

"I was appointed Commanding Officer *INS Hamla* in 1973. During the visit of the C-in-C, Vice Admiral Cursetjee to *Hamla* in 1975, I submitted to him the need for doing something for the revitalisation of the Branch or merger with the Executive Branch to improve the prospects and morale of General List Supply Officers.

"In early 1976, Admiral Cursetjee took over as CNS and I was appointed Director of the Supply Branch. After one of the meetings in the CNS' office, I reminded him of my submission to him in *INS Hamla*. He smiled and said, 'We will ask the Personnel Branch to examine it'. I met the DOP and apprised him of what had happened.

"Along with DOP, I proposed to pursue the subject with the Commands and carry the whole Navy with us. But the Chief of Logistics, Rear Admiral K Sridharan, preferred to move fast, hit the nail on the head while it was hot and in hindsight, I think he was right. The COL toured the three Commands and addressed the S&S officers and declared at the next PSO's meeting that 90% of the officers of the Supply & Secretariat Branch were in favour of the merger.

"The CNS discussed the case again at a meeting with the Cs-in-C of the three Commands and the Senior Officers at NHQ and the merger was finally decided upon. Subsequently getting Government approval for the merger was a mere formality."

Rear Admiral K Sridharan was the Chief of Logistics at the time. He recalls:

"I was appointed Chief of Logistics on 1 March 1975. Now during that period, there was a paper put up by Naval Headquarters that they wanted to re-organise Naval Headquarters. The idea was they wanted to introduce the Assistant Chief of Personnel, Assistant Chief of Naval Staff and Assistant Chief Material (Logistics). They felt that 'Logistics' should go under the Material Branch. They, therefore, wanted to abolish the Chief of Logistics and that had a lot of implications. I happened to be the incumbent. They of course reassured me that it would not be done until I completed my tenure.

"I was unhappy that if the Supply and Secretariat Branch cannot aspire to have the commanding heights of logistics then they have no star to aim for. I felt that it would not be fair for the Branch to be told that you can aspire to become Assistant Chief of Material (Logistics), be an Assistant PSO.

"So I felt that if that was the position, lets have a look at the entire branch and its organisation and its responsibilities and let us re-examine whether the branch if at all should exist. There were lots of discussions between the PSOs. Finally it was conceded that if the Chief of Logistics is abolished, the Supply and Secretariat Branch itself should not exist as it stands. I was given the task of re-organising the Branch.

"I had a difficult time trying to decide which was the right path, because I would be held responsible by posterity for having taken a decision which was not in favour with the majority of my Branch. So I volunteered to the Chief of the Naval Staff that I should go around and talk to all the Commands and explain to them what was really on the cards as proposed by Naval Headquarters.

"I went round talking to the Supply Officers in each Command. I called all the Supply Officers for the meetings. All who were not involved on duty were to attend. I repeated, like a parrot, the proposal and the pros and cons of the proposal. And I clearly told them, finally, 'Please raise your hands, for or against'. My secretary and various others in the team counted the hands. So if there was an under-current and they did not want to lift the hand but they have lifted, or if some people have lifted two hands, I can't say.

"Some people did get up and say 'Well this Branch was introduced during World War II for a reason. That reason still stands. Why should it be abolished now?' It is true that such a requirement still stands. I am not saying that the Logistics Branch should not be there but it should be there with some amount of opportunity for officers to grow. Whatever you say, in any service, personal advancement is nearest to your heart. So the personal aspects and their ambitions should not be forgotten. That is one of the main reasons why our sea time was being curtailed. The decrease in our number of jobs afloat was because of Supply Officers not going to sea.

"I then suggested a Logistics Branch comprising engineer, electrical and executive branch officers with special inclination for logistics, to be brought together and given specialist training in logistics. The Logistics branch could then be a conglomerate of all three branches because each branch had logistics problems of their own. They agreed with that suggestion. It was then put to the Government. On 1 January 1978, the Chief of Logistics was abolished, the Logistics specialisation as such was introduced and specialist training was started.

"What NHQ's intentions were for proposing to abolish the Logistics Branch within the short period of six to seven years of its institution I cannot tell.

"After I left the service, people started accusing me. Well I don't know whether posterity will support me or curse me. People from the Supply branch have proved their worth.

"The late Admiral Pereira even said in his introduction to my book on the "History of the Supply and Secretariat Branch" that 'one day an ex Supply Officer may even command the Fleet at sea'."

Writing in *INS Hamla's* Logistics Journal of January 2003, Vice Admiral Barin Ghose, Controller of Logistics, recalled:

"Prior to 1978, at NHQ the Chief of Logistics (COL) was directly responsible to the CNS for all Logistics and Supply matters. In addition, the Director of the Supply Branch was statutorily responsible for all accounting matters of cash and material to the Financial Adviser Defence Services and to the CNS for personnel administration and discipline of personnel of the Supply Branch. The Naval Store Depots, the Naval Pay Office, the Base Victualling Yards were functionally accountable and responsible to the COL.

"The then Fleet Commander had a Fleet Supply Officer who oversaw all supply functions of the Fleet and was the professional adviser to the Fleet Commander. On board ships, the Supply Officers were Heads of Department, reporting to the Commanding Officer. The Supply Officer was in fact the principal adviser for general administration, welfare of the ships' company, law and discipline, besides normal supply duties and responsibilities. The presence of the Supply Officer for Captain's Requestmen and Defaulters Table was mandatory.

"The revamping of the Supply functions culminated in 1978 with the abolition of the Supply and Secretariat Branch. Unfortunately, whilst we did away with the expertise to undertake the supply and logistics functions, and not the functions themselves, in a matter of three short years, it was realised that a reverse swing would be essential.

"By 1981, the Long Logistics Management Course was introduced to restore some degree of specialisation amongst junior officers in supply and logistics functions.

"By the mid 1980s, enormous problems of adequat e / effective Material Logistic and Financial Management were faced.

"In 1986, these problems were examined by the Indian Institute of Management, Bangalore at the behest of the Ministry of Defence. Its report to the Ministry revealed that the Material Support and Financial Administration in the Navy were in a 'virtual mess'.

"This led to the Navy proposing the revival of a specialised group of officers to undertake Materials and Financial Management, Transportation and Civil Works.

"To save face that there was to be no backtracking to the revival of the Supply and Secretariat Branch (we were not going to follow the British Navy), NHQ proposed that initially a Logistics Cadre within the Executive Branch be created, which after stabilising in two to three years, could convert to a full-fledged Logistics Branch. The Navy would thus 'recover from the enormous damage done by the overnight winding up of the erstwhile Supply and Secretariat Branch several years ago.'

"The proposal was approved in July 1989 and the Logistics Cadre came into being."

35

The Cadre Reviews

Preamble

In the 1970s, the Army, Navy and Air Force started experiencing difficulty in attracting volunteers of the desired calibre. For the Navy, three issues became a cause for concern:

- First, the promotion factor from the rank of Commander to Captain had become so low that large numbers of fine, experienced Commanders were leaving the Navy to join the Merchant Navy and elsewhere.

- Second, experienced artificers, who had reached the apex of the technical sailor structure after years of training and service at sea, were leaving the Navy for better prospects in the Merchant Navy and elsewhere.

- Third, agreements had been signed in 1975 for a major acquisition programme. The advanced technology of the ships and aircraft being acquired from the Soviet Union required to be manned by experienced personnel. With experienced Commanders and experienced artificers leaving the Navy for better prospects elsewhere, the Navy had to improve the incentives for retention.

Two thrust areas crystallised:

- *Pay Commissions.* The Navy's endeavours have been discussed in the section titled "The Fourth Pay Commission".

- *Cadre Reviews.* In March 1977, the Navy sought an inter-service consensus but without success. A year and a half later, in November 1978, the Navy tried again. Its reasoning is reflected in the ensuing paper on "The Cadre Review of the Defence Services". It was possible to obtain a measure of consensus. It led to the First Cadre Review of 1980 and was followed by the triennial Second Cadre Review in 1983.

The Navy's Paper on the 'Cadre Review of the Defence Services'

"Introduction

The vitality and verve of an organisation depends upon its ability to attract, motivate and retain quality manpower, particularly at managerial levels. The Navy and the Services in general have begun to experience serious difficulties in this regard. Witness our inability to fill officers' intake quotas without lowering selection standards and contrast it with the stampede to join the Civil Services. Similarly, if there were no curbs on premature retirements, there would be a mass exodus from the Navy today. This problem may not be so acute in the other two services because of the lesser market demand for the skills they possess, but that does not alter the basic fact that the service officer today is getting more and more disenchanted with his service conditions and would quit the service if given a chance.

In order to rectify this situation, which has long-term implications on National security, Naval Headquarters had put up a paper on 'Determination of Career-Factor / Ratio between Ranks – Defence Services Officers' Structure' for consideration of the PPOs Committee. This paper was discussed on 17 March 1977 by the PPOC but a consensus did not emerge. The underlying reason for this appeared to have been the feeling that large-scale proliferation of senior 'ranks' was not perhaps desirable. The Committee also appears to have been influenced by the possibility of career improvement as a result of the case for 'Deputation of Service officers to the Ministries of Government of India and State Governments and Public-Sector Undertakings' then pending with the Senior Selection Board. Nothing significant has emerged from that case even today.

That the Defence Services must offer career and remuneration prospects fully comparable to the highest civil services in the country is a fundamental fact of life which has been accepted in all countries, and there is little need to specially justify it in the Indian context. This being so, the argument that "Civil Services happen to have better career prospects than Defence Services because of differing job requirements" is untenable. The contention of differing job requirements is itself highly arguable, but if it were indeed so, then it is necessary to find an alternative approach to solve the problem.

Civil-Military Comparison

Promotion prospects stem from the interacting relationship between pay-grades. As far as promotion prospects prior to 1947, the Services were on par with Indian Administrative Service (IAS) / Indian Civil Service (ICS) in respect of both factors. Later the Services lost ground and came down to the level of the Indian Police Service (IPS) with regards to pay grades. As far as promotion is concerned, the Services have over the years plummeted so far down that not only IAS and IPS, but also nearly every Class I Civil Service and even a Class II Service like the Central Secretariat Service (CSS) has an edge over them. Since remuneration is a function of promotion prospects, this has led to the Services becoming disadvantaged economically and status wise in relation to the civil services with which they are on par pay scale wise. The higher leadership of the country appears to be quite unaware this state of affairs, which has come about because of the differing yardsticks that have been and are being adopted in the creation of senior posts in the civil and defence services.

Promotion prospects are essentially a function of vacancies in higher ranks including deputations. The despairingly bleak situation of the Services in this respect is clear from the following statistics:

	Services	IPS	IAS
Rear Admiral and above	202	85	805
Captain	1,260	420	175
Commander & below	42,500	1,650	2,558

The same figures, when converted into percentage basis, with Commander and below as 100, are:

	Services	IPS	IAS
Rear Admiral and above	0.48	5.15	31.47
Captain	2.96	25.45	6.84

Some of the manifestations of the unfavourable grade structure of the forces vis-à-vis the civil services can be seen from the following which compares the prospects of the 'regular entry' officers of defence and civil services:

- While about 1.5% and 4% of service officers make Captain and flag rank, 95% and 50% of IPS officers and 100% and 98% of IAS officers make equivalent grades.

- While service officers take about 21 and 27 years to reach those ranks, IPS officers take 14 and 21 years and IAS officers 17 years.

- While service officers spend on an average about 5 years in flag ranks, IPS officers spend about 15 years and IAS officers 19 years.

Career Factor

Career factor is a crucial ingredient in the personnel structure of any organisation. This has been accepted in all the civil services down to Class IV level. Unfortunately, in the Armed Forces, no career factor has been laid down to date and whatever factor exists *de facto* has evolved in a haphazard manner from post-by-post sanctions.

In India, the entrants to the defence services, the civil services, the public sector undertakings and the private industry come from the same manpower pool. In such a situation, if the career factor of one of the competing groups falls far behind the rest, it cannot but have the gravest repercussions on the quality and motivational level of its personnel.

The top and middle levels of the defence services today are manned by officers who joined when the serviceman's career prospects were roughly at par with his civil service counterparts. That is why there is as yet no deterioration in the quality of defence leadership. But if the present position where the Services are not able to attract calibre personnel continues, it cannot but affect national security in the long run. To quote General Omar Bradley, "Inferior inducements attract second rate men. Second-rate men at best provide second best security. In war, there is no prize for the runner-up."

The need for an adequate career factor has already been recognised in the case of the medical officers in the Defence Services. Non-practicing allowance to the tune of Rs. 600 per month, time-scale promotion to Commander after 16½ years of service, one to two rank higher staff appointments when compared to other branches, career based flag rank vacancies for specialists, have all been granted in recognition of the need to attract scarce manpower. Is it correct to say that the same considerations are not applicable to other branches merely because second-rate men are available and willing to fill the jobs spurned by first-rate men?

Job-Grade-Pay Nexus

In any organisation there is a trilateral nexus between jobs, grades and pay levels. The problem facing the defence services today is that while the civil services have been able to raise the grade levels of their jobs, the services have been held back because of certain cultural constraints. There were only a handful of Secretaries to the Government of India in 1947; today there are over 60 of that grade. There were only 5 officers of the rank of Inspector General of Police (IGP) in 1947; today there are nearly 200. All this has been done basically by dividing and upgrading jobs and creating new ones.

The Services have not been able to match the civil services in this regard because of the interposition of a unique fourth factor called 'rank' and certain constraints of tradition. The ranks of certain basic jobs in the Services, like the Officer Commanding a battalion being a Lieutenant Colonel or the Commanding Officer of a frigate being a Commander, have come to be fixed over the years. Since these act as bench marks, the Services find themselves unable to upgrade appointments in terms of rank to the extent required for obtaining an adequate career factor.

The nexus between grades and job is not strong in the civil services. The nature of jobs that are being done by officers of the Joint Secretary / Inspector General's grade today and those done by such officers 30 years ago bears testimony to this. In the Defence Services, however, because of the interposition of the additional factor called rank, we have a problem. Our internal culture would not accept the creation of several thousand additional posts of Generals and Brigadiers, which is what would be necessary if we were to attain career parity with the Civil Services through upgradation of ranks. But then, while we may not want to break the nexus between rank and job, there is no reason why we cannot snap the link between rank and pay grade.

The crux of the problem is that on the one hand, the Services require officers of a calibre and motivational level at least as high as the top civil services and, therefore, must offer career prospects fully at par with the latter. On the other hand, we have an organisational structure, which makes large-scale rank upgradations difficult. In the present circumstances, the best way to get round the problem would, therefore, be to enhance the career prospects in terms of pay grades of ranks, instead of ranks themselves. Thereafter, on the basis of career factor requirements, the Government may be requested to lay down the ratios between the various pay grades. This would enable us to grant pay to officers on the basis of the number of vacancies in each pay grade, without having to confer the rank that goes with it. For example, the ratio among pay grades laid down by the Government may entitle the Navy to have 1,200 vacancies in the Commander's pay grade while the billets for Commanders may be only 500. In such a situation, while only 500 officers will hold the rank of Commander, 700 Lieutenant Commanders will be able to draw the pay of Commander.

An argument that may be advanced against the proposed concept could be that 'pay' is based on 'function' and, therefore, it would be incorrect to grant the pay of a rank to a person who is not performing the job of that rank. A moment's thought would, however, show that this is a specious, syllogistic objection. First, nobody has determined the worth of each job in the Defence Services or for that matter in the civil services. There can be no conceptual objection, therefore, to the OC of a battalion drawing a Brigadier's pay if that is what is required to be offered to attract the requisite calibre of personnel. Second, the Government has accepted career factor as a personnel structure consideration quite independent of job requirements in regulating promotions. IAS and several other civil cadres have been, and continue to be, the beneficiaries of such career factor based upgradations.

Another objection could be that laying down of pay grade percentages for the defence services could lead to similar demands from other sectors. This again is untenable because:

- Provision for the cadre review of civil services is already in existence.
- All civil services, unlike the Armed Forces, have their 'associations' to project the career interests of their members.
- Defence Services are unique in having a 'rank' structure.
- Defence Services can improve their retention rate and reduce turn over rate by bettering the career prospects of its members. The resultant savings in training costs would be more than the financial cost of career betterment.

A Suggested Approach

The problem of improving the personnel structure of the Services has to be tackled in three planes. First, there is the functional need to upgrade a large number of jobs from their present ranks. Defence Services over the years have grown in functional complexity and their horizons have greatly widened. The planning for acquisition and utilisation of contemporary weapon systems and their supporting infrastructure requires the highest standards of management. Also, the middle level and senior level Service executive no longer functions in a sheltered environment, but has to interact constantly with civil services and the mainstream of public life. All this calls for considerable strengthening of the decision-making levels in the armed forces. At present, the cases for upgradations put up by individual services are stymied by the Ministries on the grounds of inter-service repercussions. Once it is established that inter-service comparison amounts to quibbling over trifles, and the valid comparison in so far as the career factor is concerned is between the Civil Services on the one hand and the Defence Services on the other, then the cases for these functionally necessary upgradations cannot be stalled.

Second, there is the question of giving the Services their due share of non-cadreised vacancies in the Ministries of the Central and State Governments as well as in the Public Sector Undertakings (PSUs). The basic rationale for the non-cadreisation of the senior posts in Ministries and PSUs is that they should be filled by the best available talent in the country. This being so, it should be a matter of national concern that only an infinitesimally small fraction of the nearly 60,000 highly trained officers (in disciplines ranging from specialised engineering fields like micro-electronics and high speed turbines to general management fields like personnel, material and finance) are currently employed on non-cadreised jobs. The door to jobs in the Ministries and PSUs, which at present has been opened only a crack for the Services, has to be opened wider in the interests of national development as well as the legitimate career aspirations of Defence officers.

However, it is important to realise that even when the functionally necessary upgradations and increased deputations to Ministries and PSUs visualised earlier above are carried out, it still will not be possible for the Services to achieve a career factor comparable to the Civil Services. Towards this end we should, as brought out earlier, request the Government to determine on the basis of civil / military career-factor equivalence, the number of officers who should hold each of the pay-grades in the Services. Each officer thereafter should have both a rank and a pay grade. The numbers, which can be held against each will be limited by what has been separately authorised by the Government. To give a concrete example, an officer may be holding Commander's rank but may at the same time hold the pay grade of a Captain.

A collateral advantage of this scheme would be that the Services would be able to promote its bright officers to positions of responsibility much earlier and there would be greater zest and youthfulness in the middle and senior levels of the services hierarchy. The basic concept would be that the low intensity jobs will be filled by officers who go up only in pay-grades and not in ranks while the key jobs requiring dynamism and vision will be filled by a smaller group of officers who will be promoted rapidly through the ranks.

Benefits from the Proposal

The above proposal will result in the following benefits:

- Although many officers may not be promoted beyond the rank of Commander / Time-Scale Commander, there will be a steady rise in the pay-grades of every officer.
- Every officer will be able to reach the pay grade of at least Captain Indian Navy by the time of his retirement.

- Consequently, every officer will be entitled for the pension of a Captain Indian Navy. This is of critical importance because very few realise how the Defence Services have been overtaken in the pension field by the Civil Services during the last 3 years. An IAS officer with 20 years service can retire today with a pension of at least Rs. 781 while a Service officer can hope to get Rs. 685 at best.
- Since Civil-Military equivalence in status is predicated on pay scales, this would enable many more service officers to be eligible for non-cadreised posts in the civil sectors which their ranks do not entitle them today.
- Once the above proposal is accepted, there will be no financial implications to upgradation in / of appointments and a major objection currently raised against upgradation proposals will be removed.
- With the improvement of the career factor, it would be easier to raise retirement ages, as the pressure on 'creating vacancies' would be reduced.

Mechanics of the Scheme

The number of posts in various ranks would continue to be determined on the basis of functional needs. The number of vacancies in each pay-grade will, however, be determined by the Cadre Review Committee on the basis of career equivalence with the Civil Services. Each officer will have a rank as well as a pay-grade. The audit authorities shall monitor the number of officers in each pay-grade and not the number of officers holding each rank.

Promotion Committees will clear officers in two categories as follows:

- A small group of officers for both rank and pay. Their numbers would depend upon the vacancies in ranks.
- A larger group of officers for pay only. Their numbers would be dependent upon vacancies in pay-grades. The elimination rate for this group would be something like that of civilian Departmental Promotion Committees (DPCs).

Officers will move from one pay group to the next higher pay group on the basis of rank and service in the rank. There will be no question, therefore, of a junior officer drawing more pay than a senior officer because of greater length of service.

Financial Implications

It has been estimated on the basis of rank-wise capitation rates, that the proposal to delink pay and rank would cost the exchequer about Rupees three crore. This amount pales into insignificance when viewed in the context of a total Defence Budget of nearly Rupees 3,000 crore. Further, by cutting down on premature retirements and increasing the retirement ages, which should be possible under the present proposal, we should be able to reduce the turnover in the Defence Services considerably and thus effect annual savings in training costs of much more than Rupees three crore a year.

Cadre Review

The approach outlined above needs to be converted into a detailed implementation plan. Also, the percentages of officers in each pay grade on the basis of career equivalence with the civil service should be worked out. This task can best be entrusted to an inter-service Cadre Review Committee with representatives of the Ministries of Defence and Finance and the Department of Personnel. There is already a provision for the cadre review of civil services, and the Department of Personnel Cabinet Secretariat Office Memo No. 5/1/71/PP/Vol VI dated 6 May 1972 stipulates that cadre reviews are to be carried out every three years. This has been amplified by the Ministry of Finance resolution F.II/35/75-IC (Published in the Government of India Extraordinary Gazette Notification No. 105 dated 1 May 1974), which states that, 'The Cadre Review Committee shall review on a priority basis the cadre strengths of Central Class One Services in order to improve, where necessary, the promotion prospects of these services.' The mechanism for cadre reviews is already in existence in the case of civil services and the proposal merely mounts to its extension to the Defence Services.

As a first step towards cadre review, it is proposed that the PPOC appoint a small Inter-Services Sub-Committee to prepare a joint Paper on the lines proposed above. After the Paper has been approved by the PPOs, it may be formally presented to the Chiefs of Staff Committee and thereafter to the Government for the initiation of a cadre review.

Conclusion

In a country of vast unemployment like ours, some aspirants can always be found regardless of the career prospects offered by an organisation. This fact should not, however, blind us to the steadily deteriorating quality of our officer entrants, the declining motivational level and the impact of these two on national security. The national leadership cannot fail to see the logic of comparative career prospects, and the need to remedy the lopsided situation today. This is particularly so when it can be shown that the proposed changes can be effected not at just no cost, but with net savings to the national exchequer."

The First Cadre Review

The Navy's case for the First Cadre Review comprised proposals for better promotion prospects for officers and men and for improved perquisites such as increase in Authorised Married Establishment (AME), facility to hire accommodation in places other than at duty station, higher percentage of jobs in the CPO / PO rates, increase in the Special Duties Cadre (SD) cadre etc.

The discussions in 1979 centred on a cadre review for Flag Rank. The Committee of Secretaries agreed to nine additional Rear Admirals and three additional Vice Admirals.

These upgradations of three Rear Admirals to Vice Admirals and nine Captains / Commodores to Rear Admirals were to be phased over a period of three years commencing 1980.

The remaining proposals were postponed for further discussion.

The Second Cadre Review

The aims of the Second Cadre Review were:

- The restoration of the post-Independence parity in the official status of Armed Forces personnel vis-à-vis the All India Civil Services.

- Recognition of the high risk career, personal hardships and sacrifices, strict code of discipline, devotion above and beyond the call of duty, and the qualifications of the Armed Forces personnel being commensurate with the technological advances.

- Seek to offset the impact of the above through measures to enhance the official status and improve upon the economic condition of the personnel.

- Project the eroding attractiveness of the Armed Forces and the immediate need for reversing this trend.

The proposals put up by the Navy for consideration in the Second Cadre Review were:

- Upgradations in various ranks and pay promotions.
- Time scale promotion to Commander.
- De-linking of pay and pensions from rank.
- Improvements in the SD List Cadre.

There were misgivings in the Navy of the effect of upgradations on the traditional hierarchy on board ships. However, since the Army had decided to go for large-scale up-gradations and the Air Force had decided to fall in line with the Army, the Navy decided to subsume its misgivings.

Officer Upgradations in the Second Cadre Review

Approval was accorded for the creation / upgradation of the following to be phased over a period of two years commencing from the financial year 1984-85:

- Vice Admirals   –   2
- Rear Admirals   –   5
- Captains   –   45
- Commanders   –   100

Sailor Upgradations in the Second Cadre Review

Artificers	To Chief Artificers	59
Non-Artificers	To Master Chief / Chief Petty Officers	390
	To Petty Officers	60

Additional Concessions Approved as part of the Second Cadre Review

- Promotion to Commander (Time Scale) on completion of 21 years commissioned service.
- Promotion from Lieutenant to Lieutenant Commander (Special Duties) by time scale completion of 11 yeaers commissioned service.
- Ratio for promotion to the rank of Sub Lieutenant enhanced by 20%.
- Increase in ratio for the award of Long Service and Good Conduct Medal and Meritorious Medal increased to 4 per 800 sailors.
- Authorised Married Establishment for the grant of Cash in Lieu of Quarters increased:

For Leading Seamen	From 80% to 90%
For Seamen I / II	From 35% to 50%

Developments After 1984

In 1984, NHQ put up proposals to create additional Naval 'Area Commanders', (analogous to Flag Officer Goa Area – FOGA), for the Saurashtra Area (FOSA), the Maharashtra Area (FOMA), the Tamil Nadu Area (FOTNA) and the Bengal Area (FOBA). These proposals were pended during the 1986 changes in the Navy's Command and Control organisation.

In 1988, proposals were put up for the creation of Area Commanders at Cochin, Madras and Vishakhapatnam on the same lines as FOMA, particularly for Madras in view of increased naval activity during Operation Pawan in support of the IPKF in Sri Lanka. NHQ was advised to include these in the proposals for the next Triennial Cadre Review.

Since an inter-service consensus was not in favour of another Cadre Review, these proposals remain pending. There have been no further Cadre Reviews after 1983.

Retrospect

Writing in the Navy Foundation's annual journal 'Quarterdeck 2000', Vice Admiral Koppikar, who had served in the Personnel Branch in almost all capacities from Deputy Director to Chief of Personnel, stated:

> "Rank up-gradation was another controversial measure which made people happy or heated depending on how it affected them. The Cadre Review bonanza was achieved after a tough fight with the Government in order to overcome serious promotion bottlenecks in the three services.

> "The downside was that the large-scale up-gradation had in fact resulted in a serious rank devaluation. Some even advocated going back to the *status quo ante*. Perhaps there was some substance in their argument because a number of upgraded billets did not merit such favourable treatment.

> "Also, a big chunk of the up-gradation went to the shore sector because of the inherent limitations and rigidity of rank and structure in ships.

> "Basically it was a question of 'too much too soon', and, therefore, we took steps to spread the bonanza over a period of time."

36

The Fourth Pay Commission

Preamble

The parameters under which the Third Pay Commission had structured its recommendations envisaged that they would be valid for the next ten years. The oil crisis of the mid seventies and the high inflation thereafter neutralised these parameters. The Government therefore introduced a series of ad hoc measures. These did not alleviate matters, especially for officers. The economic position of officers worsened, affecting morale and the quality of intake. By the late seventies, remedial measures became essential.

In 1982, the Chiefs of Staff Committee (COSC) forwarded to Government their paper on 'Quality and Morale' whose major recommendation was the extension of free rations to peace areas for officers up to the naval rank of Captain. The Government was inclined to grant this in cash. Admiral RL Periera, the Chairman COSC, was able to persuade Government to sanction free rations in kind.

Re-mustering of Seamen and Engineering Mechanics

In 1977, the Ministry of Defence accepted Naval Headquarters recommendation that to keep abreast with the growth of technology in the Navy, the educational qualification for recruitment of Seamen and Engineering Mechanics be raised to matriculation. The Government not only approved this up gradation in educational qualification, but also directed that they be paid matriculate rates of pay. Seamen and Engineering Mechanics were remustered from Group 'C' to Group 'B'. This linkage between pay scales and educational qualification eventually became the keystone for the rationalisation of the sailor's 'trade and pay group structure' after the Fifth Pay Commission.

The Fourth Pay Commission

The Fourth Central Pay Commission was set up in 1983. It submitted its Report in 1986. The Government accepted its recommendations, effective from 1 January 1986.

Excerpts from the Report pertaining the Armed Forces are reproduced as an Annexure. These excerpts reflect, accurately, the perceptions of the mid 1980s.

The gist of the Commission's outcome, as applicable to the Navy, is summarised below.

Officers

For the first time, an integrated pay scale (also known as 'the running pay band') was introduced, starting from the rank of Acting Sub Lieutenant up to the rank of Commodore. This ensured that officers in these ranks would be eligible for annual increments and could reach the maximum of the scale, irrespective of whether they were promoted to the next rank. The rationale was that an officer's domestic financial commitments (for example the cost of children's education, marriage etc) were, by and large, the same and not linked with rank.

In addition, to the running pay band, 'rank pay' was made admissible from the rank of Lieutenant to Captain. Increases were made, also, in all the allowances like Flying Pay, Submarine Pay, Technical Pay, Hard Lying Money, Dip Money, Diving Allowance, City Compensatory Allowance, Qualification Grants, Outfit Allowance, Submarine Allowance and Test Pilot Allowance.

Sailors

The pay scales of sailors were increased. The rates of Flying Pay, Submarine Pay, Survey Pay, Good Conduct Badge Pay and other allowances were also enhanced.

The New Pension Structure

Officers. The earlier system of 'standard pension', based on rank at the time of retirement, was abolished. Instead, retiring pension was based on 50% of average basic pay plus rank pay drawn during the ten months preceding retirement, the actual qualifying service rendered plus the weightage in years of service.

Sailors. The prevailing system of standard rate of pension for each rank with the existing weightage of 5 years remained unchanged.

Officers and Sailors:

- The rates of Disability pension, Special Family pension,

Ordinary Family pension, Liberalised Family pension for battle casualties and War Injury Pay were enhanced.

- The upper limit of Death-cum-Retirement Gratuity was raised.

Pensioners Who Retired On or Before 1 January 1986

- The improvements made in their pensions fell far short of their expectations. This issue became politically and financially contentious because of the demand of these pensioners for 'one rank, one pension'. After sustained efforts by the Ex Servicemen Associations over the next decade, the Fifth Pay Commission eventually conceded this demand.

Developments After 1990

The Fifth Pay Commission was appointed in 1994. Its terms of reference were wider in their ambit and scope than those of its predecessors. For the first time, the Commission was asked to examine the terms and conditions of service of Armed Forces personnel and to recommend the reforms necessary to bring about desirable changes in work methods, environment and attitudes, aimed at promoting efficiency in administration, reducing redundant paperwork and optimising the size of Government machinery.

In its deliberations, the Commission considered the following major issues that were specific to the Armed Forces:

- What steps could be taken to make entry into the Defence Services more attractive, so as to maintain the morale of personnel and to ensure their continued retention?

- Keeping in view the changed geo-political and strategic environment and the lessons of recent wars, was there a scope for restructuring of the Armed Forces with greater emphasis on technology than on manpower?

- Could changes in pay structure and promotion policies help to keep the Armed Forces young and meet aspirations for faster and assured promotions?

- Was it feasible to have one-rank-one-pension?

ANNEXURE

Excerpts From the Fourth Pay Commission's Report Pertaining to the Armed Forces

Officers

Page 284 Para 28.11 to 28.15 of Fourth Pay Commission Report Part I June 1986

28.11. It has been urged that the pay scales of service officers should be determined with reference to the requirements of the services. It has been pointed out that the nature of the cadre structure in services is different as the number selected for advancement in every rank is limited in view of the command and control structure of the services. As a result, officers who cannot be promoted are entrusted with other assignments requiring skill and experience. It has been suggested that it will be desirable to provide necessary incentives to such officers also. In a rank oriented organisation like the Armed Forces, Cadre Reviews, which result in upgradation of posts, cannot always achieve the desired effect. It has been pointed out that although the Cadre Reviews carried out in the past brought about some improvement in career progression of service officers, they created problems in the organisational structure. It has been emphasised that it is not possible to undertake any further large-scale Cadre Reviews without unacceptable aberrations in the functional hierarchical structure. It has therefore been suggested that the pay structure for defence services should be such that a fair share of the talent is attracted and kept motivated throughout their service. In the joint proposals, the Services have proposed a 'running pay band' for all officers covering a time span of 33 years. Separate 'rank pays' have been proposed for each successive rank on a cumulative basis. It has also been suggested that separate pay scales in respect of specialised cadres, Flying Branch in the case of Air Force and Aviators and Submariners in the case of Navy, may be dispensed with.

28.12. We have given careful consideration to the joint proposals of the Services Headquarters. We appreciate that the organisation structure and requirements of services are different. We also think that the pay structure should be such that it makes armed forces attractive as a career and provides a reasonable pay progression to the officers of the services. Taking all factors into account, we recommend the following integrated pay scale for all officers up to the rank of Brigadier and equivalent in the three services:

- Rs 2,300- l00-4,200EB-100-5,000

28.13. We also recommend that, in addition to pay in the above integrated scale, the following rank pays may be given to officers in the Army and their equivalent in the other services:

Rank	Amount of rank pay (Rs/pm)
– Lieutenant (Captain and equivalent)	200
– Lieutenant Commander (Major and equivalent)	400
– Commander [Lt Colonel (Selection) and equivalent]	600
– Captain (Colonel and equivalent)	800
– Commodore (Brigadier and equivalent)	1,200

In the Navy, a Captain, on completion of three years' service in that rank, will draw the rank pay of Rs 1,200 p.m. recommended for Brigadier.

28.14. With the adoption of the integrated pay scale recommended above, the existing selection grades in the ranks of Major and equivalent and Lt Colonel and equivalent should be abolished. The integrated pay scale will be applicable to all officers in the three services including officers in the specialised cadres of AMC, ADC and RVC. For officers of MNS, we have recommended separate pay scales.

28.15. The integrated pay scale recommended by us covers a span of 28 years. It is necessary to ensure that the selection process for promotion at all levels is effectively objective. There should be periodic reviews for those constituting the non-select stream so that such of them who can no longer be useful are not allowed to continue in the integrated pay scale up to the prescribed ages of retirement. There has to be selectivity, and we have suggested an efficiency bar after 20 years of service. We recommend that Government should review the existing rules relating to selection procedure and premature retirement of officers so that, at this stage, officers who do not make the grade are not continued in service.

Page 286, 287, 288 Paras 28.22 to 28.37 of Fourth Central Pay Commission Report Part I June 1986

28.22. It has been suggested that in the services training institutions, the trainees should be given the pay of an officer during the last 12 months of training. Keeping in view the existing facilities available to the trainees at the service institutions, we do not recommend that the pay of an officer should be paid prior to commissioning. However, on the analogy of the midshipman in the Navy, we recommend that during last 6 months of training at the respective service institutions, the trainees may be paid a fixed amount of Rs.1,500/- p.m. This will also be admissible to midshipman in the Navy in place of the existing rate of Rs. 560/-.

28.23. It has been brought to notice that the number of officers for the combat arms like infantry, artillery and armoured corps is gradually decreasing. It has been suggested that by way of incentive, qualification grant may be given to officers on passing the specified courses for infantry, artillery and armoured corps. We accept the suggestion and recommend that Government may identify the courses for artillery, infantry and armoured corps, which would qualify for sanction of qualification grant.

28.24. In the joint proposals, it has been suggested that military service pay at the rate of 25% of basic pay should be given to service officers for their arduous duties. We have kept all relevant aspects in view while formulating our recommendations regarding the pay and allowances, etc.

of service officers. We are not therefore recommending a separate military service pay.

Personnel Below Officer Rank

25.25. The Personnel Below Officer Rank (PBOR) in the armed forces belonging to different trades are grouped together and a separate pay structure is prescribed for different ranks in each group. There is, however, no uniformity in regard to the number of trades and the pay groups into which these are categorised in the three services:

- In the Army, there are 197 trades, excluding 9 trades held by Junior Commissioned Officers (JCO) only, which are distributed in five pay groups.
- In the Air Force, there are 45 trades, which have been allocated to four pay groups.
- In the Navy, there are three pay groups, which cover 68 trades.

There are special groups like those of 'flight engineer' and 'flight signaller' in the Air Force and Navy and of sailors belonging to the Naval Aviation and Submarine Arms in the Navy. There are differences in the entry qualifications, the prescribed training periods, terms of engagement, qualifying service for promotions and the rank and appointment structure, etc., for personnel below officer rank in the three services.

28.26. We have been informed that it has not been possible for the services to achieve a consensus in regard to the pay structure for personnel below officer rank. Separate proposals have therefore been received from the three services headquarters.

28.27. Army Headquarters have suggested that JCOs may be taken out of the group structure and given a separate pay scale. It has also been proposed by them that the existing five pay groups for other ranks should be reduced to three by abolition of the existing lowest Groups 'D' and 'F'. The proposals involve reclassification of about 130 trades from one group to another. The reclassification of trades has been suggested on the basis of a study undertaken by the Institute of Defence Management, Hyderabad. Similar studies were undertaken at the same institute for some of the trades in the Air Force and Navy, but no proposals have been made by Naval and Air Headquarters for reclassification of any trades based on these studies. In a subsequent proposal received from the Army Headquarters in May 1986, a special pay group has been proposed in addition to the three pay groups suggested earlier for certain high profile army trades. A revised distribution of trades within the proposed four pay groups has also been suggested.

28.28. We have been informed by Air Headquarters that a high level committee was appointed by Government in 1982 to examine the various aspects relating to flight safety in the Air Force. Based on the recommendations of the Committee, it has been proposed to upgrade five trades from the existing pay group II to pay group I of Air Force. Air Headquarters have also informed that in respect of four trades included in the existing group IV, the entry qualification has been modified for three of the trades. It has therefore been suggested that all these four trades may be included in Group III of Air Force.

28.29. We have given careful consideration to the suggestions of the Army Headquarters and Air Headquarters for reclassification of the existing trades. We find that there is a standing arrangement in the Army Headquarters for review of trade structure of other ranks. There is an Army Trade Qualification Committee (ATQC), which is mainly entrusted with the responsibility of examining the various proposals and making recommendations regarding introduction of new trades, abolition of existing trades and grouping and re-grouping of various trades. Such recommendations of the Committee, which have inter-service repercussions are referred to a Joint Special Committee. We have been informed that based on the recommendations of ATQC, some trades were deleted, merged or regrouped in the past. We find that in addition, a Manpower Evaluation Committee was constituted by Government in August 1983 comprising officers of the Ministry of Defence and Services Headquarters to, inter alia, assess the need for reclassification of certain trades of fighting arms to higher groups because of the requirement of higher skills due to modernisation of weapon systems. It was also required to analyse the need for and feasibility of building into the present system of 'rating of skills' and their consequent placement in various pay groups, the additional factor based on risk or hazard of trades in fighting arms, which have to bear the maximum brunt in any war. It appears that this Committee did not even start functioning and, apparently, it was decided to entrust the study for 'Reclassification of Trades' to the Institute of Defence Management, Hyderabad.

28.30. Modernisation of technology and upgradation of skills is a continuous process in the armed forces and Government have been taking appropriate decisions whenever necessary in the past. For example, in 1976, the trades of Radio Operator (Group II) and Flight Plotter (Group III) in Air Force were merged into a single trade of Air Defence System Operator and placed in Group II. Similarly, three new missile trades were created in Group I. In the Navy, the entry qualification for the Seaman Branch was modified to matriculation in 1976 and the seaman trade

was moved from Group 'C' to Group 'B'. The necessity of a change in the skill requirement due to application of improved technology to arms and weapons exists in each of the three services. As technology development and consequent changes shall continue to take place in the services, there is need for a suitable mechanism, which should continuously monitor the technology changes taking place and take steps for updating of skills. Such an arrangement already exists, which should not only be continued but also strengthened so that remuneration is related to the skills applied at identified levels of functioning in the three services. We notice that trades, which prima facie appear to be similar in the three services, are grouped and remunerated differently. We recommend that such cases should be examined by the ATQC or any other expert body on an inter-service basis so as to bring about uniformity between the three services for comparable trades. Until then, the existing pay groups in the three services may continue with the present distribution of trades in these groups.

28.31. The Third Pay Commission had recommended that a fully trained infantry soldier with three years' service should be placed somewhere between the semi-skilled and skilled workman. This was an improvement over the approach of the Post War Pay Committee (1947), which had equated a fully trained infantry soldier with 3 years' service to a worker classified as semi-skilled. Following the approach of the Post War Pay Committee, the Third Pay Commission added an amount to the pay of a soldier on account of 'X' factor as a compensation for the hardships of service life but made a deduction from his pay for home saving element. The pay of an infantry soldier was determined by the Third Pay Commission as follows:

Pay of corresponding civilian	-		Rs 225.00
Add 5% for 'X' factor	-	+	Rs 11.25
		=	Rs 236. 25
Less 20% for 'home saving element'	-	–	Rs 47.25
		=	Rs 189.00

Based on the above, a pay of Rs 175 was recommended for an infantry soldier in the pay scale of Rs 175-2-195, which after 3 years service and on earning one classification pay of Rs 7.50 would bring an infantry soldier on par with a worker falling between semi-skilled and skilled. The Commission was in favour of a slight edge to an infantry soldier over a constable in central police organisation like Border Security Force (BSF).

32.32. Government modified the recommendation of the Third Pay Commission *ab initio* and prescribed the pay scale of Rs 200-5-260 for the infantry soldier. This scale gave the infantry soldier an edge of Rs 5 at the start over the pay of Rs 195 for a BSF constable (Rs 210 minus Rs 15 deducted for rations). We have been informed by the Defence Ministry that the starting salary of Rs 200 for an infantry soldier includes 'X' factor of 12½% as against 5% recommended by the Third Pay Commission.

28.33. As regards the deduction of 'home saving element' from the pay of a soldier, it has been stated by the services headquarters that provision of free rations, accommodation and clothing is a service requirement and it will not be proper to make any deduction on account of savings resulting from the provision of these facilities. It has also been pointed out that on account of this deduction, the entitlement of dearness allowance over the years, of an infantry soldier has also gone down thereby nullifying the differential, which the infantry soldier had over the constable in the BSF. We have examined this matter. We find that the concession of free rations has since been extended to officers up to the rank of Brigadier in peace areas without any deduction for home saving element. We therefore recommend that there should be no deduction on account of the home saving element in determining the pay of an infantry soldier.

28.34. An infantry soldier is required to possess skills for handling modern weaponry, performing duties like laying mines, erection and destruction of the various types of obstacles and handling of electrical equipment and high degree of combat skill. It has also been brought to notice that the minimum qualification for enrolment of infantry soldier has been raised to Class 10. It has been urged by Army Headquarters that an infantry soldier is in no way less than a skilled worker.

28.35. In our view, the duties and responsibilities of an infantry soldier are such that he cannot really be compared with any other category of employees. After taking all the factors into consideration, we recommend that starting salary of an infantry soldier should be fixed at Rs 900.

28.36. The Third Pay Commission had observed that the fully trained infantry soldier should be viewed as equivalent to the Leading Aircraftsman of Group IV of the Air Force, with a small differential in favour of Able Bodied Seaman of Group 'C' of the Navy considering the relatively greater hardships inherent in sea life. The Commission was of the view that adoption of the above broad equation would lead to greater uniformity in pay scales among the three services.

28.37. Some changes have occurred since the report of the Third Pay Commission. In 1976, Government decided to change the entry qualification for Seaman Branch from pre-matriculation to matriculation and simultaneously the Seaman trade was upgraded from pay Group 'C' to pay Group 'B'. Similarly, in 1977 the then existing two classes of aircraftsman viz., Aircraftsman II and Aircraftsman I were merged into one rank of aircraftsman. We have been informed by Air Headquarters that merger of Aircraftsman II and I did not make any change in the qualification, method of recruitment, training and time taken for promotion to the Leading Aircraftsman.

Group D Civilian Personnel

Page 309 Para 29.12 to 29.15 of Fourth Pay Commission Report

12.12. Group D posts in the scale of Rs 196-232 consist largely of peons, messengers, helpers, orderlies, etc. As their promotional avenues are limited, we have recommended a longer pay scale for them in place of the existing ordinary and selection grades. These employees are at present eligible for promotion to 10% of the clerical posts if they are matriculates. Since the recruitment qualifications vary from 4th to 8th standard, many of them are not eligible for promotion. In the Railways and P&T, they are eligible for promotion to some specified cadres. In Railways, the percentage of promotion ranges from 25 to 33⅓ and it is much the same in P&T. We think it desirable that the utility and career progression of these employees should be improved so that they may have something to look forward to. They may be entrusted not only with the duty of running errands, opening mail and distribution of dak, etc., but also with operating minor office machines and clerical work of a routine nature. Training facilities may be provided to upgrade their knowledge and skill and, wherever possible, they may be sent to vocational training institutions where they may develop necessary skill in operating some simple office machines. Arrangements may also be made to provide in-house training facilities so that they may acquire multi-functional skills suited to the requirements of their office or organisation. They may be allowed to compete for departmental examinations if they otherwise become eligible for higher posts, and the question of relaxing the age limit may also be examined where necessary.

Integrity in Government Employees

29.13. There is a general feeling in the country that there is lack of integrity in some spheres of public service. Concern has been expressed in this respect both in Parliament and the press. The Service Rules, including Government Servant's Conduct Rules, may therefore be examined with care and tightened up. A sense of self-respect, integrity and patriotism should be generated and developed in government employees, and one way of doing so is to recognise integrity as an important factor for career progression and to give it very high weightage while selecting officers for promotion. Lack of integrity should be considered a serious defect and treated as such. So also, if there are instances of indiscipline, the defaulting employee may be passed over for promotion or even for grant of increments in his pay scale.

29.14. We have tried to improve the pay structure to enable a government employee to lead a clean, honest and respectable life at a standard compatible with what his likes attain or accept as reasonable at his level of living. It may be that the pay scales recommended by us may not enable a government employee to lead an ostentatious life, but we have attempted to give him what we consider reasonable and to protect his real income within certain practical norms, which should go a long way in giving him satisfaction. It has to be appreciated by every government employee that he has undertaken to discharge a duty in the service of his country to the best of his capacity and with a high sense of integrity and discipline. He has in fact undertaken to serve his fellowmen, and it should be his effort to do so with a sense of respect and consideration for them.

29.15. If we may venture to say so, the work of a Pay Commission is laborious and takes time. Moreover, Pay Commissions come at intervals of 10 years or so. A great many changes take place in the meantime, both in regard to the system of pay determination and the promotion policies, etc. Such changes take place quite fast in the case of compensatory allowance and other similar payments. An allowance that is considered sufficient today may not be reasonable if changes take place quickly. It is, therefore, necessary that there should be a permanent machinery to undertake periodical review of the pay, allowances and conditions of service of the central government employees. That will also enable government to oversee the implementation of its pay policy in an effective, systematic and coordinated manner. In their joint proposals, the Service Headquarters have suggested that a permanent review body should be set up to monitor the implementation of pay proposals and to review and update entitlements for pay, allowances and pension within the framework laid down by the Pay Commission and the Government. In the United Kingdom, pay review bodies undertake review of pay of both civilian and defence officers. We suggest that Government may set up such a body which should be responsible for maintaining and updating the basic data on pay and allowances of government employees and to review the pay scales and rates of allowances and other related matters.

Summary of Main Recommendations and Conclusions

Page 322 Paras 127 to 154 of Fourth Central Pay Commission Report

127. We recommend that all industrial employees should have the same leave entitlement and encashment as admissible to industrial employees of railways. All other kinds of leave available to industrial employees at present but not available to non-industrial employees may be discontinued. (26.61)

128. Government may consider whether the present scheme of Joint Consultative Meetings (JCM) and compulsory arbitration should be modified as to require that reasons for the recommendations of the Board of Arbitration should be given as far as possible. (20.68)

135. To provide pay progression to all commissioned officers in Army, Navy and Air Force, an integrated pay scale (Rs 2,300-5,000) has been recommended for all officers up to the rank of Brigadier and equivalent in place of existing separate scales of pay. (28.12)

136. In addition to pay in the integrated scale, service officers up to the rank of Brigadier and equivalent may be given a rank of pay ranging from Rs 200 to Rs. 1,200. (28.13)

137. Separate pay scales have been recommended for officers of the rank of Major General and above and equivalent. (28.16)

138. Army Commanders and equivalent and Vice Chiefs in the three services may be given pay of Rs 8,000 (fixed). (28.17)

139. Officers of the AMC, ADC and RVC may be given higher start in the integrated scale of pay. (28.19)

140. For officers of MNS, a separate pay structure has been suggested. (28.20)

141. The officers passing the specified courses for Infantry, Artillery and Armoured Corps may be given qualification grant. (28.23)

142. The starting pay of an infantry soldier may be Rs 900 per month. (28.35)

143. The rates of classification pay admissible to servicemen in Army may be doubled. (28.41)

144. The rates of appointment pay admissible to servicemen in Army may be doubled. (28.42)

145. The service officers posted to field areas may be paid an amount at prescribed rates if their families are not occupying government owned / hired accommodation. (28.61)

146. The rates of Compensation In Lieu of Quarters (CILQ) for personnel below officer rank have been rationalised and composite rates, including compensation for furniture, water and electricity / kerosene, have been suggested. (28.71)

147. The rates of outfit allowance admissible to service officers may be increased. (28.72)

148. The facility of free rations in peace areas may be extended to officers of the rank of Major General and above and equivalent. (28.85)

149. The existing separation allowance (peace) of Rs 200 per month admissible to officers of the rank of Major General and above and equivalent may be discontinued. (28.28)

150. The rates of specialist pay for the AMC / ADC / RVC may be improved. (28.92)

151. The rates of Non Practicing Allowance for medical officers of the AMC, ADC and RVC may be revised. (28.93)

152. The rates of good service / good conduct pay / good conduct badge pay for personnel below officer rank in three services may be improved.

153. The rates of flying pay may be revised.

154. The rates of submarine pay for officers and sailors may be improved.

Page 324 of Fourth Central Pay Commission Report Part I June 1986

Concluding Observations

In our country, 'public service' functions in a social setting where traditions, physical factors, geography, etc play an important role. We should not be very much concerned with management of pay systems and public service abroad, as conditions are not only different but often incomparable. We have felt that our problems are peculiar to our socio-economic system and solutions have to be found by us within our own confines.

Those who work in public office must realise that government office is a public trust where good performance and honesty will be rewarded and inefficiency, dishonesty and indiscipline will not be tolerated.

What is important is the need for a positive approach to public service with a feeling that working in government is a profession of the highest order. In fact, there should be an unwritten but well-recognised code of conduct to be affirmed and observed by every employee that:

- Primary duty of a public servant is to serve the public.
- Pay is to be earned on full day's work.
- Endeavour should be to get work done in most economic way.
- No special favour or privilege is dispensed to anyone.
- Public office is treated as public trust.

Acknowledgements

We have been able to complete this part of our report with the help and assistance of all concerned. We are grateful to the former Governor of Rajasthan, Air Chief Marshal OP Mehra (Retd) for giving us the benefit of his views. We are obliged to the Chief Ministers and Ministers of State Governments who were kind enough to respond to our invitation for discussion with us on various issues. We are grateful to the former Cabinet Secretary, Shri CR Krishnaswamy Rao Sahib, the present Cabinet Secretary, Comptroller and Auditor-General, Secretaries of Ministries and Departments, heads of various organisations and other officers for their suggestions. The three Service Chiefs and other officers of the armed forces favoured us with their views on different issues and we are grateful to them. We would like to express our thanks to the officers of ministries, departments, state governments, union territories and public sector undertakings who gave us all the necessary assistance in the completion of our work. We are also thankful to representatives' of the unions and associations of central government employees and others who gave us their views both in writing and during discussions on various matters. We thank the Director, National Informatics Centre, for processing our basic staff statistics. Our advisers and consultants, Shri CM Malik and Shri Shiva Nath and Lieutenant General Dr ML Chibber (Retd) gave useful suggestions and advice and we are thankful to them. We also thank Shri SP Gugnani and Prof BB Bhattacharya for some special studies.

37
Gallantry Awards 1976 – 1990

During the period 1976 to 1990 Gallantry Awards were given for individual acts in three areas:

- Saving the lives of others in hazardous conditions.
- The Antarctica Expeditions, which started in 1981/82.
- Operation Pawan, which started in 1987.

Antarctica Expeditions

Naval Chetak helicopters were used to transport personnel, stores fuel and construction material. Of the average of 70 to 75 days that a research ship stays in Antarctica, there are storms, blizzards, very strong winds and zero visibility conditions for 35 to 40 days, leaving only 30 to 40 days for the helicopters to ferry men and material to the permanent station miles inland. For details, please see section on Expeditions to Antarctica.

Operation Pawan

The Navy's Operation Pawan in support of the Indian Peace Keeping Force (IPKF) in Sri Lanka commenced in July 1987 and terminated in March 1990. Due to the shallow depths in the Palk Strait, the induction and de-induction of troops, vehicles and stores was done in LSTs. Operational Patrols were carried out by shallow draught, minor war vessels like SDBs, LCUs and Coast Guard patrol craft placed under operational control of the Navy. Naval and Coast Guard aircraft and naval helicopters carried out air patrols. For details, please see the chapter titled "Operation Pawan".

Abbreviations used in the table

LST:	Landing Ship Tank
Div:	Diver
SDB:	Seaward Defence Boat
SD:	Ships Diver
LCU:	Landing Craft Utility
PTI:	Physical Training Instructor
CGV:	Coast Guard Vessel
SAR:	Search and Rescue
CD:	Clearance Diver
O i/c:	Officer-in-Charge
ACD:	Air Crew Diver
i/c:	In-Charge

Rank, Name, Personal No	Appointment / Function /Activity / Event	Action performed under hazardous conditions and risk to life	Gallantry Award
1976			
Cdr SK Bhalla (40044 H)	O i/c Firefighting Team	Extinguishing fire in a merchant ship in Bombay Harbour	Nau Sena Medal
CH Mech PD Kholia (66736)	i/c Firefighting Team	-do-	Nau Sena Medal
Cdr Gulab Israni (00364 A)	Vampire Pilot	Safe landing after engine failure during test flight	Nau Sena Medal
Cdr SC Issacs (00414 R)	O i/c Diving Team	Diving operations Badarpur Thermal Power Station New Delhi	Nau Sena Medal
CPO (Div II) AD Mehta (48894)	i/c Diving Team	-do-	Nau Sena Medal

Cdr PA Debras (00417 Y)	Seahawk Pilot	Successful ejection from underwater after aircraft sank immediately after launch from Vikrant	Nau Sena Medal
LACD Majharul Hasan (91982)	Aircrew Diver	Rescue of ditched naval pilot after successful ejection from underwater	Nau Sena Medal
Cdr Sushil Issacs (00449 W)	Commanding Officer INS Ghorpad (LST)	Removal of sunken wreck obstructing jetty at Kamorta Island	Nau Sena Medal
Lt Cdr GAD Duke, NM (00621 K)	Executive Officer INS Ghorpad and O i/c Diving Team	-do-	Bar to Nau Sena Medal
Lt VP Kapil, VrC (00667 R)	O i/c Diving Team	Demolition of sunken wreck in Bhavnagar Port	Nau Sena Medal
POCD I Diwan Singh (63814)	Diving Team	-do-	Nau Sena Medal
Cdr RC Jagota (40066 H)	O i/c Oil Salvage Team	Salvage of oil from oil tanker stranded on Kiltan Island	Nau Sena Medal
Lt Cdr George Martis, VrC, NM (00445 K)	O i/c Diving Team	Refloating of oiler Purak grounded whilst savaging oil from tanker Kiltan Island	Bar to Nau Sena Medal
CPO Mahesh Kumar (65127)	INS Magar	Rescue of sailors trapped in fire on board INS Magar (LST)	Nau Sena Medal
LS CD 2 AC Singh (93112)	Diving Team	Diving operations beyond permissible depths. Ramganga Project Kalagarh Dam	Nau Sena Medal
1977			
Cdr N Radhakrishnan (Retd)	Cabinet Secretariat	Successful completion of a national security operation	Shaurya Chakra
Capt JG Nadkarni, VSM (00086 W)	Commanding Officer INS Delhi (Cruiser)	Salvage of INS Godavari stranded in the Maldive Islands. 1976	Nau Sena Medal
Cdr Gupteshwar Rai (00528 Z)	Commanding Officer INS Kesari (LST)	-do-	Nau Sena Medal
Lt Cdr Lokendra Kumar (00270 N)	Commanding Officer INS Gaj (Tug)	-do-	Nau Sena Medal
Lt Cdr (SDME) M Lal, VSM (85029 Y)	Salvage Team	-do-	Nau Sena Medal
Lt (SDB) Mewa Singh (83181 Y)	-do-	-do-	Nau Sena Medal
LS BD Chaudhary (85810)	-do-	-do-	Nau Sena Medal
SEA I VP Patil (83067)	-do-	-do-	Nau Sena Medal
Lt SS Kahlon (00826 A)	INS Vikrant SAR Flight Commander	Rescue of two Air Force pilots off Bombay after their helicopter ditched	Nau Sena Medal
1978			
Cdr MS Narayanan (00415 T)	O i/c Beaching Operations INS Shardul (LST)	Saving the life of a drowning jawan during amphibious beaching operation	Nau Sena Medal
PO (CD I) Shyam Singh (91064)	Beaching Party	-do-	Nau Sena Medal
Lt Sarvottam Handa (00887 R)	Seahawk Pilot	Safe forced landing after engine flameout	Nau Sena Medal

Lt KS Aulakh (01070 F)	INS Vikrant SAR Helicopter Flight	Rescue of ditched pilot in stormy weather	Nau Sena Medal
CPO JC Xavier (47205)	Rescue Team	Rescue of marooned villagers after floods in Tamil Nadu. Nov 1976	Nau Sena Medal
CPO CK Nair (65543)	-do-	-do-	Nau Sena Medal
LMA (ORT) MM Ameen (68141)	-do-	-do-	Nau Sena Medal
Sea I APJ Solomon (92159)	-do-	-do-	Nau Sena Medal
1979			
Cdr HDM Gori, NM (00452 A)	Helicopter Pilot	Medical evacuation by helicopter in stormy weather from a ship in distress. Jun 1978	Shaurya Chakra
Lt Cdr PB Chaudhary (00575 T)	Helicopter Pilot	Rescue by helicopter of villagers stranded after Andhra Pradesh Cyclone. Nov 1977	Shaurya Chakra
Lt Cdr SS Deodhar (00626-Y)	O i/c Rescue Team	-do-	Nau Sena Medal
SWA3 RB Singh (51528)	Rescue Team	-do-	Nau Sena Medal
Lt Cdr RK Sharma (0094 7-A)	O i/c Diving Team	Diving operations Nagarjuna Sagar Hydel Complex. 1978	Nau Sena Medal
Sea I (CD2) GD Khuspe (54944)	Diving Team	-do-	Nau Sena Medal
Lt Cdr KM Thomas (00999-W)	Seaking Pilot	Safe landing on Vikrant despite major gearbox oil leak during night	Nau Sena Medal
Lt PD Upponi (01152 T)	O i/c Diving Team	Prolonged diving amidst hazardous wreckage of Air India Boeing crashed off Bombay Jan 1978. Successfully located Digital Flight Recorder	Shaurya Chakra
Sea I CD 3 AS Sawant (95957)	Diving Team	Prolonged diving amidst hazardous wreckage of Air India Boeing crashed off Bombay Jan 1978. Successfully located Cockpit Voice Recorder	Shaurya Chakra
MCPO II (CD) AD Mehta, NM (48894)	Diving Team	Diving operations in wreckage of Air India Boeing crashed off Bombay. Jan 1978	Nau Sena Medal
CPO(CD1) Dewan Singh, NM (63814)	-do-	-do-	Nau Sena Medal
Sea I (CD3) Sardul Singh (95432)	-do-	-do-	Nau Sena Medal
Sea I (CD2) Jagmal Singh (94485)	Diving Team	Demolition of sunken wreck in Cochin Port	Nau Sena Medal
SEA I D Singh (202393)	INS Betwa	Passing of heavy tow wires to stranded merchant ship in rough seas	Nau Sena Medal
1980			
Lt DS Dalal (01625 T)	O i/c Diving Team	Diving operations to extricate bodies from bus fallen into Thane Creek. Feb 1979	Nau Sena Medal
PO (SR I) Rattan Singh (84135)	Detached Survey Party	Rescue of drowning sailor in the Sunderbans. Feb 1979	Nau Sena Medal

1981			
Lt SV Purohit (01066 Y)	Seaking Pilot	Safe and skilful ditching 120 miles from Cochin after total engine failure and disintegration of tail section 1981	Shaurya Chakra
L/S ACD ML Kathat (054925 F)	Aircrew Diver	Rescue in rough weather of drowning fisherman off Goa Jul 1980	Shaurya Chakra
Lt AV Vaidya (01462 Y)	SAR Helicopter Pilot	-do-	Nau Sena Medal
L/S CD 3 DS Sidhu (96898 Z)	Clearance Diver	Rescuing an elderly civilian lady, whohad accidentally slipped into the water whilst boarding a boat, from being crushed between the boat and the pontoon	Shaurya Chakra
Lt Cdr PB Chowdhury (00575 F)	Helicopter Flight Commander	Flying operations in stormy weather	Nau Sena Medal
Lt Cdr RS Kanwar (00995 K)	Helicopter Flight Commander	Medical evacuation from merchant ship in rough seas. Jul 1979	Nau Sena Medal
Lt Cdr SK Chandna (01060 H)	Helicopter Flight Commander	Rescue of ditched pilot and medical evacuation from merchant ship in stormy weather	Nau Sena Medal
LS Puran Chand (084369 Z)	Salvage Team	Recovery of heavy naval hardware from deep depth. Mar 1980	Nau Sena Medal
ME I NN Roy (057098 W)	-do-	-do-	Nau Sena Medal
1982			
Lt Cdr PD Upponi, SC (01152 T)	O i/c Diving Team	Extricating bodies from the sunken wreckage of the passenger train that fell into the Bagmati River in Jun 1981	Nau Sena Medal
Lt OP Sindhu (01591 R)	Diving Team	-do-	Shaurya Chakra
LS (CD1) Balbir Singh (085252-F)	-do-	-do-	Nau Sena Medal
LS (CD1) Jagmal Singh (094485-R)	-do-	-do-	Nau Sena Medal
LS (CD1) Rameshwar Jha (096338-A)	-do-	-do-	Nau Sena Medal
LS (CD2) SK Vayangankar (096952-Y)	-do-	-do-	Nau Sena Medal
LS (CD2) Puran Mal (054161 –W)	-do-	-do-	Nau Sena Medal
SEA I (SD) JJ Chelath (200856-T)	-do-	-do-	Nau Sena Medal
NA 1 AH 3 GS Chauhan (107377 R)	Ships Diver	Rescue of crew who had abandoned their boat after it caught fire. Bombay Harbour Sep 1981	Shaurya Chakra
Lt Cdr RLR Kshirsagar (00939-H)	Salvage Team	Salvage and recovery of stranded whaler in stormy weather. May 1981	Nau Sena Medal
Lt Cdr KDS Sandhu (01067-Z)	Helicopter Flight Commander	Numerous occasions of rescue of ditched pilots and medical evacuations in stormy weather	Nau Sena Medal

Lt Pradeep Roy (01824 W)	Flag Lt to FOCWEF	Rescue of sailors from Himgiri's boiler room after massive leak of superheated steam. Mar 1981	Nau Sena Medal
NAM I MS Bali (142324 R)	INS Dunagiri (Frigate)	-do-	Nau Sena Medal
POME GS Jat (055566 N)	-do-	Timely shutting down of Himgiri's boilers to control leak of superheated steam	Nau Sena Medal
PO JN Murthy (088359-T)	INS Sandhayak (Survey Ship)	Saving survey boats whilst hoisting during sudden storm	Nau Sena Medal
LS KK Bajpai (097736-B)	-do-	-do-	Nau Sena Medal
Sea I (CD2) Rati Ram (103669 N)	Rescue Team	Rescue of passengers from train stranded by flash floods in Andhra Pradesh. 1981	Nau Sena Medal
PO RS Chauhan (085140 A)	Rescue Team	Rescue of villagers after flash floods in Andhra Pradesh. 1981	Nau Sena Medal
1983			
Lt Cdr MAR Subhan (01115 H)	Fire in Missile Boat after missile explosion during practice firing	As Commanding Officer, personally ensuring safe survival of his boat and crew. 1982	Shaurya Chakra
SLt HD Motiwala (02015 B)	-do-	Personally directing fire fighting operations	Shaurya Chakra
EAP Jai Prakash (052484 H)	-do-	Personally assisting fire fighting operations	Shaurya Chakra
Lt Cdr AH Chitnis (01208 W)	Kamov Flight Commander INS Rajput	Location of fishermen in cyclonic weather leading to their rescue. Nov 1981	Nau Sena Medal
Lt Cdr KS Sandhu, NM (01067 Z)	1st AntarcticaExpedition 1981/82	As Flight Commander, flying in harsh weather conditions to establish base camp	Shaurya Chakra
Lt Cdr KS Samra (01219 W)	-do-	As Flight Pilot, reconnaissance for base camp in harsh weather conditions	Nau Sena Medal
Lt Cdr DK Chandani (01269 H)	-do-	-do-	Nau Sena Medal
CHEAAR M Mahapatra (051957 K)	-do-	As Flight Maintenance Team, defect rectification in harsh weather conditions despite limited resources	Nau Sena Medal
CHAA GVR Shirsat (094983 Y)	-do-	-do-	Nau Sena Medal
Cdr DS Brar (60090 T)	-do-	As O i/c Naval Contingent, ensuring safety of vital stores and helicopters that were breaking loose during sudden cyclone on passage to Antarctica	Nau Sena Medal
Surg Lt Cdr Salim J Thomas (75142 A)	-do-	As Surgical Specialist and O i/c Medical Team, providing medical emergency and surgical operating facilities for the Expedition	Nau Sena Medal
POMA JS Saini (059233 Y)	-do-	As Medical Team, Operating Room Technician, setting up medical and operation facilities for the Expedition	Nau Sena Medal
Lt Shekhar Sinha (01480 N)	Kiran Pilot	Safe forced landing despite engine and control failure in flight. Sep 1982	Nau Sena Medal

Lt Jiban Mahapatra (01960 B)	O i/c Rescue Team	Rescue of personnel marooned on an island during cyclonic weather	Nau Sena Medal
1984			
Lt Cdr AH Chitnis, NM (01208 W)	Kamov Flight Commander INS Rajput	Safe landing onboard after engine failure in stormy weather and low visibility	Shaurya Chakra
Lt Ravinder Kakar (01835 W)	Clearance Diving Officer	Removal of sunken trawler wrecks in Paradip Port after Orissa Cyclone. June 1982	Shaurya Chakra
Lt Rajan Gupt (01836 Y)	-do-	-do-	Nau Sena Medal
Cdr AN Karve (00593 Y)	Coast Guard HQ Madras	Interception of smugglers and salvage of contraband from sunken sabotaged craft	Nau Sena Medal
Lt Cdr RS Gill (01120 W)	2nd Antarctica Expedition. 1982/83	As Flight Commander, flying in harsh weather conditions and rescue of stranded members of the Expedition during blizzard	Shaurya Chakra
Lt Cdr KS Randhawa, NM (01189 A)	-do-	As Flight Pilot, flying in harsh weather conditions and saving helicopter from blizzard damage	Shaurya Chakra
Lt Cdr KS Samra, NM (01219 W)	-do-	As Flight Pilot, flying in harsh weather conditions and rescue operations	Shaurya Chakra
Lt Cdr R Sethi (01232 Z)	-do-	As Flight Pilot, flying in harsh weather conditions and ensuring safe recovery of stranded helicopter	Shaurya Chakra
Surg Lt Cdr DB Rao (75157 K)	-do-	As leader of the Naval Contingent, O i/c Medical Team and anesthetic specialist providing emergency medical services to the Expedition	Nau Sena Medal
CHEAA I Khan (094344 W)	-do-	As Flight Maintenance Team, defect rectification during blizzard despite limited resources	Nau Sena Medal
Air Mech III BS Thakur (093474 T)	-do-	-do-	Nau Sena Medal
POEAR (EL) RK Kapoor (097141 A)	-do-	-do-	Nau Sena Medal
Lt AR Vardhan (01498 B)	OOD, INS Taragiri (Frigate)	Rescue of drowning sailor and recovery of swamped boat in rough weather, Goa. Apr 1983	Nau Sena Medal
LS (CD II) Jagdish Chand (094801 H)	Diving Team	Diving operations in Periyar Lake to remove submerged stumps using explosives	Nau Sena Medal
LS (PTI) VS Rajput (103518 W)	Rescue Team	Rescue of drowning old man after flash floods in Orissa. Sep 1982	Nau Sena Medal
Sea I (CD3) M Sarkar (201882 Z)	Diving Team	Locating source of flooding, repairing leaks in INS Guldar aground in Car Nicobar to help refloat the ship. Jul 1982	Nau Sena Medal
1985			
Cdr Kesho Ram (00669 W)	INS Dunagiri (Frigate)	Emergency assistance to shut the bow doors of LST Gharial in rough seas. Apr 1984	Nau Sena Medal

MCPO I D Chand (046109-W)	INS Dunagiri (Frigate)	Emergency assistance to shut the bow doors of LST Gharial in rough seas. Apr 1984	Nau Sena Medal
CHSWA BR Choudhary (052389)	-do-	-do-	Nau Sena Medal
Surg Lt Cdr A Banerjee (75248 T)	3rd Antarctica Expedition 1983/84	Rescue and resuscitation of crashed MI 8 helicopter pilot and, as medical specialist, coping with medical emergencies of the First Wintering Team	Shaurya Chakra
Cdr VP Sathiamoorthy (00977-W)	-do-	As Leader of the Naval Contingent, timely setting up of permanent station at Dakshin Gangotri	Nau Sena Medal
Cdr SR Chandna, NM (01060 H)	-do-	As Flight Commander, flying in adverse weather conditions for transportation of heavy stores	Bar to Nau Sena Medal
Lt Cdr MS Khela (01380-K)	-do-	As Flight Pilot, flying in adverse weather conditions for transportation of heavy stores	Nau Sena Medal
Lt Cdr AS Chouhan (01440 –Y)	-do-	-do-	Nau Sena Medal
Lt AA Khan (40581-B)	-do-	As Flight Maintenance Team, maintenance and defect rectification in adverse weather conditions despite limited resources	Nau Sena Medal
CHEAA HP Kunchibuduka (052351)	-do-	-do-	Nau Sena Medal(
Mech (AAL) III H Singh (097109 B)	-do-	-do-	Nau Sena Medal
POEAR RK Kapoor, NM (097141 A)	-do-	-do-	Bar to Nau Sena Medal
Lt Cdr NP Singh (70114-Z)	-do-	As Met Officer, timely setting up of Met facilities at Dakshin Gangotri	Nau Sena Medal
CK (O) I C Venugopal (I107958 K)	-do-	Cooking for the Expedition in adverse weather conditions	Nau Sena Medal
CK (O) I Devassy Sebastine (107755 Z)	-do-	-do-	Nau Sena Medal
Cdr SK Dutt (00993 F)	Seaking Pilot	Rescue of personnel and medical evacuation in stormy weather conditions	Nau Sena Medal
Cdr GP Chalakkal (40194 Z)	Command Engineer Officer, HQ Southern Naval Command	Firefighting operations in the devastating fire in Cochin Refinery. Mar 1984	Nau Sena Medal
MCPO (AH) II Dal Chand (048487-Z)	i/c Crash Tender, Naval Air Station Cochin	-do-	Nau Sena Medal
Lt Cdr Sunil Batra (01127-K)	Helicopter Pilot	Repeated rescue of personnel and medical evacuations in stormy weather	Nau Sena Medal
Lt Cdr US Ghura (01169-F)	Seaking Pilot	Rescue at sea in stormy weather of crew from merchant ship engulfed in fire. Aug 1984	Nau Sena Medal
Lt Satyendra Sharma (01664-F)	O i/c Rescue Team	-do-	Nau Sena Medal
Lt UK Gautam (01754-K)	Executive Officer INS Matanga (Tug)	-do-	Nau Sena Medal

POCD I Rameshwar Jha (096338 A)	Rescue Team	Rescue at sea in stormy weather of crew from merchant ship engulfed in fire. Aug 1984	Nau Sena Medal
POCK (S) G Paswan (080847 W)	-do-	-do-	Nau Sena Medal
SEA 1 (CD2) N Sahoo (106847 K)	-do-	-do-	Nau Sena Medal
SEAI (CD2) HS Rathore (203271 F)	-do-	-do-	Nau Sena Medal
Lt Cdr GS Gill (01211-A)	Seaking Pilot	Repeated rescue of ditched pilots and medical evacuations in stormy weather	Nau Sena Medal
CPO Jagdish Ram (090998 F)	NCC Cadets Ocean Sailing Expedition	Safe survival in stormy weather. after getting lost	Nau Sena Medal
LS (PTI) BS Sheoran (202542 Z)	INS Shivaji (Shore Establishment)	Rescue and successful resuscitation of drowned sailor. Apr 1984	Nau Sena Medal
SEA I Raj Singh (146515 R)	INS Alleppey (Coastal Minesweeper)	Successful rescue of drowning civilian in Madras Harbour. Feb 1984	Nau Sena Medal
SEA I AK Pradhan (110748 H)	-do-	-do-	Nau Sena Medal
1986			
Lt Cdr AS Manaise (01244 A)	4th Antarctica Expedition 1984/85	As Flight Pilot, flying in stormy weather conditions for transporting stores and personnel.	Nau Sena Medal
Lt Cdr AK Khanna (01439 W)	-do-	As Flight Pilot, flying in stormy weather conditions for transporting stores and safe landing on an iceberg in an emergency	Nau Sena Medal
Mech (AW) 3 SH Mohamed (097353 H)	-do-	As Flight Maintenance Team, defect rectification in harsh weather condition despite limited resources	Nau Sena Medal
Lt Cdr APA Robin (70132 R)	-do-	As Expedition Met Officer performance of Met tasks in harsh weather condition	Nau Sena Medal
Lt (SDC) Dharampal Prashar (81937 W)	-do-	As O i/c Communications of Second Wintering Team, installation of equipment for maintaining communications between Dakshin Gangotri and India throughout the winter	Nau Sena Medal
CPOELR Kamal Dev (200385 Y)	-do-	As i/c Wintering Communication Team, maintenance of communication equipment despite limited resources	Nau Sena Medal
POR (TEL) Chand Singh (096240 B)	-do-	As a member of the Communication Team, installation and maintenance of communication equipment in harsh weather conditions	Nau Sena Medal
LCK (O) Bisna Ram (106912 H)	-do-	Cooking Services for the 82 member Expedition in harsh weather conditions	Nau Sena Medal
Lt HK Sinha (02339 R)	Helicopter Pilot	Safe crash landing in Sunderbans after emergency during flight. Jan 1984	Nau Sena Medal
LSCD II Pratap Singh (140539)	Diving Team	First Deep Saturation Diving Experiment in INHS Asvini. 1985	Nau Sena Medal
SEA I CD II T Vinod Rao (201754)	Diving Team	-do-	Nau Sena Medal

1987			
Lt KS Chundwat (01997 N)	Special Action Group INS Hamla	Rescue and resuscitation of six drowning picnickers entangled in fishing nets off Marve. Bombay Mar 1986	Shaurya Chakra
Lt MS Chillar (02191 B)	Special Action Group INS Kunjali	-do-	Shaurya Chakra
Cdr Vishnu Singh (00682-Z)	Executive Officer, INS Taragiri (Frigate)	Safe retrieval of radar antenna dangling from foremast and emergency repairs on yardarm in rough seas	Nau Sena Medal
Lt Cdr HS Oberoi (01441 Z)	5th Antarctica Expedition 1985/86	As Flight Pilot, transporting scientists to distant sites in harsh weather conditions	Nau Sena Medal
Lt Kunhiraman Ravindran (4074 7 F)	-do-	As Flight Maintenance Team, defect rectification in harsh weather condition despite limited resources	Nau Sena Medal
Lt Cdr Surinderjit Singh (70138-B)	-do-	As Expedition Met Officer, Met experiments in distant sites in harsh weather conditions	Nau Sena Medal
POELR SR Malvade (202765 F)	-do-	As Third Winter Communications Team, maintenance and defect rectification of radio equipment in harsh weather condition despite limited resources	Nau Sena Medal
Lt Cdr VB Naik (01706 A)	Diving Team	Second Deep Saturation Diving Experiment in INHS Asvini. 1986	Nau Sena Medal
Lt Dilip Baijal (01943 R)	Kiran Pilot	Safe landing after serious damage caused by bird hit. Nov 1985	Nau Sena Medal
Sea I CD 3 RA Yadav (143206 W)	Clearance Diver INS Matanga (Tug)	During towing of missile boats, diving in rough seas to clear propellers fouled by parted tow ropes. Jan 1986	Nau Sena Medal
Sea I CD 3 G Kumar (148117 H)	-do-	-do-	Nau Sena Medal
1988			
Lt Arvind Singh (02283 N)	O i/c Marine Commando Team	Operation Pawan. Destruction of LTTE militant speed boats during flushing out operations	Maha Vir Chakra
Lt A Verma (02293 K)	2 i/c Marine Commando Team	-do-	Vir Chakra
Lt PS Chandavarkar (01928 F)	Marine Commando Team	Operation Pawan. Diving to retrieve and neutralise LTTE militant explosives during flushing out operations	Vir Chakra
Lt Cdr Deepak Agarwal (01527 W)	Commanding Officer SDB T 56	Operation Pawan. Landing of marine commandos in uncharted waters during flushing out operations	Vir Chakra
Cdr KC Kaushal, NM (01056 Z)	Diving Team	Operation Pawan. Salvage of sunken pontoon and removal from Kankesanturai jetty to enable to landing of urgent IPKF stores	Bar to Nau Sena Medal
PO (CD1) Y Pandey (096333 R)	-do-	-do-	Nau Sena Medal

Lt Cdr Shekhar Sinha, NM (01480 N)	Commanding Officer, CGS Rani Jindan	Operation Pawan. Anti militant patrols in uncharted waters & capture of arms and ammunition	Bar to Nau Sena Medal
Lt Cdr S Prakash (01696 B)	Commanding Officer, LCU 31	Operation Pawan. Destruction of militant boats during flushing out operations	Nau Sena Medal
Lt Cdr P Mehra (01809 K)	Commanding Officer, Guldar (LST)	Operation Pawan. Successful disembarkation of IPKF vehicles in uncharted waters despite militant fire	Nau Sena Medal INS
Lt Cdr KR Nair (01829 F)	Commanding Officer, LCU 36	Operation Pawan Patrol. Anti militant patrols in uncharted waters	Nau Sena Medal
Lt Cdr S Biswas (02377 A)	Commanding Officer, SDB T 57	-do-	Nau Sena Medal
Lt Cdr M Nair (02400 B)	Commanding Officer, CGS Avvayyar	-do-	Nau Sena Medal
Lt Cdr SS Moharir (02403 K)	Commanding Officer, CGS Kittur Chinnamma	-do-	Nau Sena Medal
Lt JS Gill (02198 W)	6th Antarctica Expedition 1986/87	As Flight Pilot, transportation of scientists to distant sites in harsh weather condition	Nau Sena Medal
Lt DK Jetly (02538 T)	-do-	-do-	Nau Sena Medal
Lt SK Ramesh (02560 T)	-do-	As Flight Pilot successful rescue of stranded Soviet expedition members in harsh weather conditions	Nau Sena Medal
Lt SM Yusuf (40863 W)	Engineer Officer, INS Porbandar (Coastal Minesweeper)	Swift damage control after ship entangled with an uncharted wreck. Dec 1986	Nau Sena Medal
LS (CD2) CD Yadav (143003 H)	Diving Team	Operation Pawan Diving to retrieve and neutralise LTTE militant explosives	Nau Sena Medal
Sea I (CD3) JS Shanmugam (148940 A)	-do-	-do-	Nau Sena Medal
1989			
Cdr DS Johal (00903 A)	O i/c Naval Detachment Rameshwaram	Operation Pawan. Seizure of LTTE militant explosives, documents and stores. Mar 1988	Nau Sena Medal
Cdr SS Rai (01010 W)	Commanding Officer CGS Vikram	Operation Pawan. Anti militant patrol and transportation of IPKF troops in uncharted waters	Nau Sena Medal
Cdr SD Sharma (01089 Z)	Commanding Officer INS Mahish (LST)	Operation Pawan. Transportation of IPKF troops and stores in uncharted waters	Nau Sena Medal
Cdr RK Singh (01125 F)	Alize Pilot	Operation Pawan. Anti militant Armed Air Patrols	Nau Sena Medal
Cdr Y Choudhary (01271 N)	Helicopter Detachment in Sri Lanka	-do-	Nau Sena Medal
S/Lt AK Vaideeswaran (03154 T)	-do-	-do-	Nau Sena Medal
Lt PS Dhillon (02530 Z)	7th Antarctica Expedition 87/88	As Flight Pilot, casualty evacuation and rescue missions in harsh weather conditions	Nau Sena Medal

1990			
Cdr Pradeep Dixit, NM (01442 A)	8th Antarctica Expedition 1988/89	As Flight Commander, emergency life saving medical evacuation in extremely hazardous conditions	Shaurya Chakra
Lt Cdr Sudhir Pillai (02140 N)	-do-	As Co-pilot, emergency life saving medical evacuation in extremely hazardous conditions	Nau Sena Medal
Lt Arvind Gupta (02453 Z)	-do-	-do-	Nau Sena Medal
Lt UK Sondhi (02897 H)	Ajeet pilot with IAF	After failure of controls, managed to avoid crashing his aircraft into a village. In saving innocent lives, suffered severe burns and loss of a leg	Shaurya Chakra
Cdr HA Gokhale (01075 T)	Commanding Officer INS Betwa (Frigate)	Operation Cactus Nov 1988	Nau Sena Medal
Cdr AH Chitnis, SC, NM (01270 K)	Flight Commander INS Godavari Flight	-do-	Bar to Nau Sena Medal
Lt Cdr R Gulati (01741 F)	Gunnery Officer INS Godavari	-do-	Nau Sena Medal
Cdr Nagasubramanian (01349 R)	O i/c Naval Detachment Rameshwaram	Operation Pawan. Capture of LTTE militants and stores. 1988	Nau Sena Medal
Cdr NK Bhardwaj (01388 B)	Commander of Helicopter Flight Detachments in Sri Lanka	Operation Pawan. Anti militant Armed Air Patrols	Nau Sena Medal
Lt Cdr Ashvini Kumar (01583 Y)	Alize Observer	-do-	Nau Sena Medal
Lt JJ Nijhawan (02137 F)	Alize Pilot	-do-	Nau Sena Medal
Lt S Kohli (02795 A)	Helicopter Detachment in Sri Lanka	-do-	Nau Sena Medal
PO SK Lonkar (105594 N)	Naval Detachment Rameshwaram	Operation Pawan. Survival for 14 days without food and water adrift at sea after failure of engine whilst attempting to capture militants	Nau Sena Medal
LS AM Lokhande (147055 T)	-do-	-do-	Nau Sena Medal
SEA I JP Urawn (162257 T)	-do-	-do-	Nau Sena Medal
CHME RK Mishra (091296 T)	i/c Control Room Hold INS Chakra (Submarine)	Swift damage control after sudden pipe burst	Nau Sena Medal

38

The New Naval Academy At Ezhimala

Developments Until 1975

Sailor Training Establishments

Traditionally, there used to be two streams of sailor entry into the Navy – a younger 'Boy' entry and an older 'Direct' entry. The 'Boy' entry underwent longer training and was better inculcated in naval discipline. 'Direct' entry was resorted to whenever there were surges in the demand for manpower and shortages had to be made good. Direct entry sailors always underwent shorter training.

Prior to Independence in 1947, the Navy's Boys Training Establishment (BTE) was at Karachi. After 1947, a temporary BTE was set up at Vishakhapatnam to train the 'Boy' entry sailors. The 'Direct' entry sailors started being trained in the Basic and Divisional (B&D) School in Cochin. In 1965, when it was decided to base the Russian acquisitions in Vishakhapatnam, it became necessary for the BTE to shift out. Chilka Lake in Orissa was chosen in 1969 as the site for the new BTE. Prime Minister (Mrs) Indira Gandhi laid the foundation stone. Construction commenced in 1973 and *INS Chilka* was commissioned in 1980.

In 1968, intake had to be stepped up to meet the requirements of the Russian acquisition programme. It was decided to move the 'Direct' entry sailors training from the B&D School in Cochin to a new Seamen Training Establishment (STE). The Government accepted the Navy's proposal to site the new STE at Goa. In October 1969, Prime Minister (Mrs) Indira Gandhi laid the foundation stone. Construction commenced on a 230-acre site on a hill at Reis Magos, five miles north of Panaji, close to the northern bank of the River Mandovi. The STE was designed to train 500 direct entry sailors at a time.

Officer Training Establishments

Before the National Defence Academy (NDA) was set up in the early 1950s, 'Regular' entry officer cadets underwent four years training with the British Navy and returned to India as Sub Lieutenants. 'Direct' entry Sub Lieutenants underwent basic training in the officer wing of the B&D School in Cochin.

By 1968, the shortage of officers became a cause of concern. And, as in the case of sailors, intake had to be stepped up to meet the requirements of the Russian acquisition programme. The required strength of 3,500 officers by 1975 necessitated an annual intake of at least 150 cadets. Since the NDA could not take more than 65 naval cadets every year, it became necessary to start a Revised Special Entry Scheme (RSES) and set up a Naval Academy, separate from the NDA. Until a location could be found for a permanent Naval Academy and until it could be constructed, a temporary Naval Academy needed to be set up for the RSES.

In 1969, approval was accorded for the commencement of the RSES. Under this scheme, naval cadets in the age group 17 to 20 years who had passed the Intermediate examination could be recruited in the Executive Branch. This scheme was identical to the NDA's 'Special Entry Scheme', except that the initial training of one year would be conducted at Cochin.

A temporary Naval Academy was set up in Cochin in May 1969. RSES training commenced in January 1970 and the first batch of executive cadets passed out of the Naval Academy in December 1970. The Naval Academy continued training RSES cadets until January 1974.

In 1973, the NDA got affiliated to the Jawaharlal Nehru University (JNU) in Delhi. Thereafter, all NDA cadets, on successfully passing their final examinations, received a Bachelor of Science degree of the JNU. The RSES cadet of the Naval Academy became out of step with his NDA counterpart. It was decided that instead of taking in pre-graduate candidates, it would be more cost effective to recruit only Science graduates and thereby further reduce the duration of their training at the Naval Academy.

In July 1974, the first batch of Graduate Special Entry Scheme (GSES) cadets entered the Naval Academy for an initial training period of only 6 months. Whereas the original sanction was for a total of 80 cadets to be trained every year, the Naval Academy now trained 80 cadets every 6 months.

As part of the 1974 reforms of Naval Training, it was decided that:

- All officer courses should be conducted by the Naval Academy and it take over all the courses being conducted by the B&D School.
- The B&D School in Cochin was to be closed down after the shift of Direct Entry Seamen Training to Goa as soon as the STE commissioned in 1976.

From 1974 onwards, the Naval Academy, in addition to running basic courses for cadets, commenced conducting the following officer courses:

- *Initial Training* for Direct Entry officers of the Engineering and Electrical branches.
- *Naval Science Orientation Course* for officers of the Supply Branch and officers from foreign navies.
- *Special Duties (SD) List Post Promotion Course* for sailors promoted to officers in the rank of Acting Sub Lieutenants in the SD Cadre.
- *Divisional & Management (D&M) Course.* The B&D course done by all Executive Sub Lieutenants during their technical courses was re-designated as the D&M Course when it was transferred from the B&D School to the Naval Academy.
- *Lieutenants War Course.* The B&D School used to conduct a War Course of four weeks duration for Acting Sub Lieutenants of the Executive branch. In 1974, it was decided that this course was better suited to a Lieutenant. The course was re-designated as a Lieutenants War Course and conducted bi-annually at the Naval Academy.
- *Upper Yardmen Course.* Sailors who showed early promise at sea of being officer material were designated 'Upper Yardmen' and given special assignments to test their potential. In end 1974, Upper Yardmen of all branches started being sent to the Naval Academy for their initial training.
- *Commanding Officers and Junior Commanders Course.* In end 1974, two new courses were instituted: the Junior Commanders' Course and the Commanding Officers' Course. These courses were conducted at the Naval Academy in 1974, 1975 and 1976.

Developments From 1976 to 1990

The Interim Naval Academy at Mandovi

By 1976, the Naval Academy found that it was not cost effective to carry out, separately, the initial training of cadets and of Acting Sub Lieutenants of various branches. It was decided that all initial training for cadets of the Executive Branch and Acting Sub Lieutenants of all technical branches should be of the same duration, should have a common syllabus and should run concurrently. This was implemented from 1976 onwards.

After 1976 and the acceptance of the Third Pay Commission's recommendations regarding changes in sailors' conditions of service, the Boy Entry was dispensed with and only Direct entry matriculate sailors were recruited. Training effort and costs could be minimised by having only one sailor training establishment (STE) at *INS Chilka*, which was expected to commission in 1980.

With the steady increase in the number of trainees in the 1970s, the Naval Academy found that it neither had the accommodation, nor the classrooms nor the infrastructure to cope with its training load. It was decided to:

- Obtain sanction for a new permanent Naval Academy.
- Re-locate the temporary Naval Academy from Cochin to *INS Mandovi* in Goa as soon as possible after the STE moved to *INS Chilka*, and after the 'sailor-training STE' at Goa had been re-modelled to function as an 'officer-training Naval Academy'. The Naval Academy eventually shifted to *INS Mandovi* in 1986.

Conceptual Requirements for the New Naval Academy

The 'essential' requirement was for a site of 100 acres, in the vicinity of the sea or a lake for seamanship and waterman ship training, near a railhead yet removed from the township. The 'desirable' requirements were that the location should be within a short distance of a naval port and have a bracing and moderate climate.

The Choice of Ezhimala

The sites considered for the new Naval Academy were Aruvankadu in the Nilgiri Hills near Wellington and the Pykara Dam Lake, the Lloyds Dam (Bhatgarh) situated off the Poona-Kolhapur road, Hassergate Lake near Bangalore, Porbandar on the Saurashtra coast, Chingleput near Madras and Ezhimala on the Kerala coast.

In 1979, the Government accepted the need for a permanent Naval Academy. The Kerala Government offered the Navy 960 hectares of land at Ezhimala, north of Kannur (Cannanore) in northern Kerala. All essential infrastructure facilities like drinking water, water for construction, electricity, approach roads and bridges, capital dredging of the Kavvayi backwaters (for basic waterman ship training), building of a seawall to prevent erosion, augmentation of the nearest railway station at Payyanur etc, would be provided by the Kerala Government at no cost to the Navy.

In 1982, the Government approved the site at Ezhimala[1] and gave the Kerala Government a soft, medium term loan for acquisition of land and rehabilitation of evacuees.

Selection of Design Architects

Naval Headquarters took the view that a Naval Academy is built by a nation only once. From this institution would come the Admirals of the future. Therefore, the nation's best private architects should be invited to compete for the design of the prestigious Naval Academy.

This led to a *contretemps* in 1985. The Navy insisted that the Army's Military Engineering Service (MES) not be associated with this project because of its mandatory, procedural constraints, which had evolved over the years for austere, economical, standardised, defence construction. These constraints conflicted with the Navy's vision for how the newest Naval Academy in the world should look. Even the Prime Minister desired that the new Naval Academy should be a national monument, which the entire nation should be proud of. The MES expressed its inability to be associated with the project on this basis or even to compete with the private architects. The MES' stand was that they would only undertake supervision of the project if they were associated right from the design stage.

Prime Minister Rajiv Gandhi laid the foundation stone on 17 January 1987 and in 1987 itself, Government approved the Navy's proposal that the Naval Academy be designed by private architects and constructed through consultants. In 1988, a Project Management Board was constituted under the Defence Secretary.

In 1988, a two-stage, all-India, architectural design competition was conducted without the involvement of the MES. It was however ensured that the adjudging jury, headed by the Vice Chief of the Naval Staff and comprising eminent private architects, had from the MES side, the Director General Works and the MES' Chief Architect. The winning firm was appointed as consultant to the project.

In 1989, the MES agreed to supervise the project provided it was done under 'Engineer in Command'. The Navy declined to agree to the MES' stipulation to exercise total control over the project and recommended that a Public Sector Undertaking (PSU) management consultant supervise the project. The Navy's recommendation was approved.

By 1991, the MES was persuaded to relent – it was too prestigious a project. The MES offered to supervise the construction, even though private architects had designed it. In the larger interest, the Navy agreed to associate the MES with the project but under the control of a Project Management Board. This was accepted.

Commencement of Training

At the time of writing, the Academy is planned to commence training in July 2005, with minimum essential training facilities completed.

---

1. Historical records indicate that Ezhimala had been a landfall for Arabian and Chinese seafarers since time immemorial. Vasco da Gama's pilot knew that the first land to be sighted on the Indian coast would be 'a great mountain which is on the coast of the Kingdom of Cannanore'.

   The topography of Ezhimala, with Mount Dilli abutting on the Arabian Sea has, since ancient times, inspired the local people to weave a number of legends. The most popular is the one connected with the Ramayana tradition. At one stage in the war between Rama and Ravana, many of Rama's forces, including his brother Lakshman, were killed. An anxious Rama consulted Jambavan, the senior most in the Vanara sena. It was decided to bring four medicinal herbs, shalya karani, vishalya karani, sandhana karani and mritha sanjivani from the Himalayas for removing the arrows, healing the wounds, stitching the cuts and finally bringing the dead to life. Hanuman was entrusted with the task of collecting these herbs and he at once set out for the Himalayas. On reaching the Himalayas, however, Hanuman realised that he was unable to recognise the ayurvedic herbs. So he did the next best thing - he plucked the entire Rishabadri Mountain itself and flew back. On his way southwards, a piece of the mountain fell down near the sea and that is Ezhimala. The local people believe that Ezhimala still possesses these rare ayurvedic herbs.

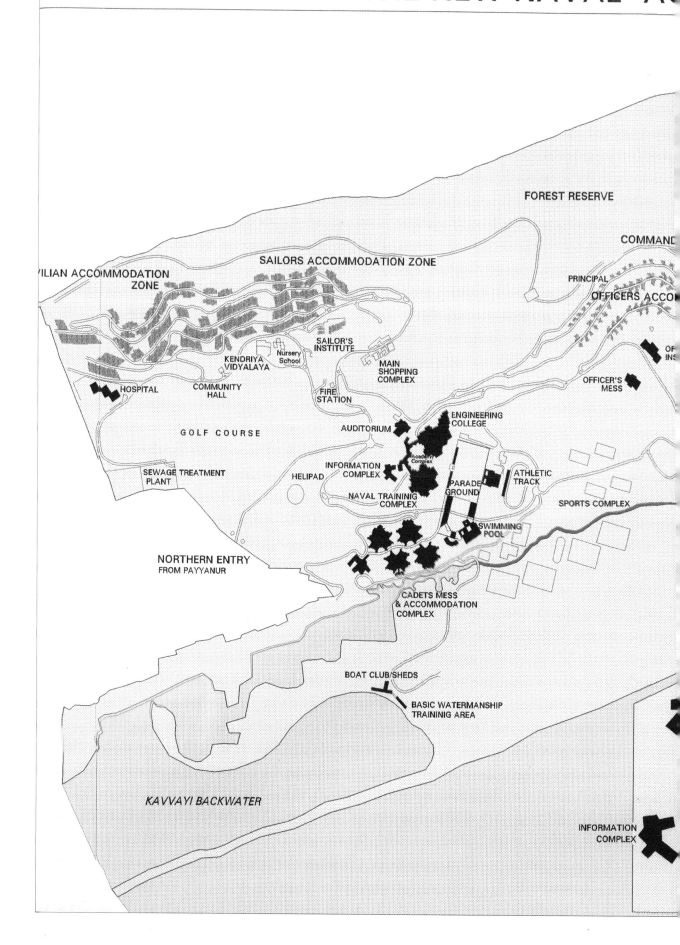

FOREST RESERVE

COMMAND

SAILORS ACCOMMODATION ZONE

PRINCIPAL

VILIAN ACCOMMODATION ZONE

OFFICERS ACCO

SAILOR'S INSTITUTE

Nursery School

OF INS

KENDRIYA VIDYALAYA

MAIN SHOPPING COMPLEX

OFFICER'S MESS

HOSPITAL

COMMUNITY HALL

FIRE STATION

ENGINEERING COLLEGE

GOLF COURSE

AUDITORIUM

Academy Complex

SEWAGE TREATMENT PLANT

INFORMATION COMPLEX

HELIPAD

PARADE GROUND

ATHLETIC TRACK

NAVAL TRAININIG COMPLEX

SPORTS COMPLEX

SWIMMING POOL

NORTHERN ENTRY
FROM PAYYANUR

CADETS MESS
& ACCOMMODATION
COMPLEX

BOAT CLUB/SHEDS

BASIC WATERMANSHIP TRAININIG AREA

KAVVAYI BACKWATER

INFORMATION COMPLEX

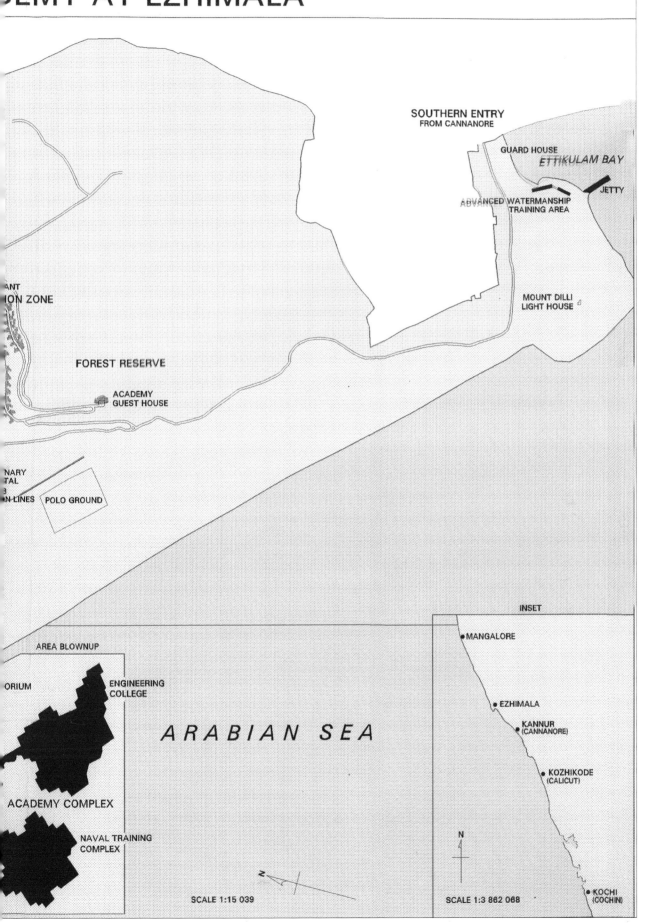

SOUTHERN ENTRY
FROM CANNANORE

GUARD HOUSE
ETTIKULAM BAY

JETTY

ADVANCED WATERMANSHIP
TRAINING AREA

MOUNT DILLI
LIGHT HOUSE

...ANT
...ION ZONE

FOREST RESERVE

ACADEMY
GUEST HOUSE

...NARY
...TAL
...3
...N-LINES   POLO GROUND

INSET

MANGALORE

AREA BLOWNUP

...ORIUM   ENGINEERING
COLLEGE

ARABIAN SEA

EZHIMALA

KANNUR
(CANNANORE)

ACADEMY COMPLEX

KOZHIKODE
(CALICUT)

NAVAL TRAINING
COMPLEX

N

SCALE 1:15 039

SCALE 1:3 862 068

KOCHI
(COCHIN)

39

Welfare

Preamble

The Navy's bases are located in large populated cities. The two major problems that affect morale in densely populated cities are housing and the education of children. These two aspects have received high priority in naval welfare activity.

On other welfare fronts, the Navy has set up welfare centres, family clinics, computer centres and children's parks and benefits from non-public funds have steadily improved.

Housing

The fundamental difference between the Navy and the sister services has been that the majority of the Navy's personnel perforce are stationed in major ports where the cost of living is high and hiring civil accommodation is beyond their means. Officers and sailors in Bombay or Cochin had to wait several months till they got some sort of accommodation. By the time they were allotted accommodation, it was time for them to be transferred.

Some headway could be made at Bombay and Cochin. Shortages at other ports had to be made up by hiring houses and using old, temporary, wartime hutments and buildings. Proposals for building new accommodation usually took time to resolve over where and how much was to be built.

After the 1965 War, a comprehensive review had been carried out of the shortages of family accommodation in the Army, Navy and Air Force. The deficiencies were found to be so large that it was decided that the aim should be to remove them over a period of 20 to 25 years.

By 1975, the shortages in Bombay, Goa, Cochin, Vishakhapatnam, Shivaji and Valsura had decreased. In mid 1975, differences in perception arose between the Ministry of Defence and the Service Headquarters regarding revision of the scales (i.e. square footage) of married accommodation. Until this issue could be resolved, no progress could be made on the construction of accommodation already sanctioned.

The Ministry's stand was that more accommodation could be built within available funds by reducing the square footage per dwelling unit. The Service Headquarters' stand was that the existing square footage was barely adequate and should not be scaled down, even as a temporary measure. Eventually, financial reality prevailed and construction on the reduced footage resumed in 1977.

Financial sanctions for new married accommodation increased from Rs 8 crore in 1980 to Rs 21 crore in 1981 to Rs 25 crore in 1983. It was anticipated that, by 1990, the percentage satisfaction would be 52% for officers and 72% for sailors.

Schooling

Prior to the commencement of the Kendra Vidyalaya Scheme, Naval Kindergarten (KG) Schools had been started in naval establishments where such schooling facilities were not available.

Kendriya Vidyalayas

The Second Pay Commission initiated the idea of having Secondary Schools with a common syllabus and medium of instruction to avoid disruption in the education of children of Central Government employees and defence personnel who were liable to frequent transfers and sudden transfers in the public interest.

Government approved the scheme in November 1962. The Central Schools Organisation started as a unit of the then Ministry of Education (now redesignated as the Ministry of Human Resources Development). In 1963, the Army's Regimental Schools were taken over as Central Schools.

In 1965, the Central Schools Organisation was redesignated as the Kendra Vidyalaya Sangathan and, as an autonomous body wholly financed by the Government, was tasked with opening and managing the Central Schools renamed as Kendra Vidyalayas (KVs).

KVs were set up, both at defence stations and at stations having a concentration of transferable Central Government civilian employees.

Until the end of academic year 1975-76, the children of defence personnel enjoyed first priority for admission to KVs throughout the country. In 1976, KVs were divided into two main sectors – the Defence Sector and the Civilian Sector. Children of defence / civilian personnel were accorded first priority for admission in their respective sectors. This division worked adversely for defence personnel in that they were given a lower priority for admission in schools other than those in defence sectors.

When the question was taken up to restore the original priorities, the difference in priority between defence and civilian personnel was done away with effect from academic year 1977. Thereafter, 'transferability', decided by the number of transfers during seven years preceding the admission, was made the sole criterion for admission to KVs.

Although naval personnel posted to stations not served by Defence Sector schools stood to benefit by this rule, the revised priority adversely affected naval personnel who were stationed mainly in large metropolitan cities having a considerable population of transferable Central Government civilian employees. It was clear that in these cities, a substantial number of admissions would be those of civilian personnel even though naval land had been made available for these KVs and all the initial facilities had been provided by the Navy.

Problems arose also for the admission of naval children in stations where the KVs were not sited within the campus of naval establishments.

To overcome these problems, the Navy decided to establish its own Naval Public Schools in its major naval bases at Bombay, Cochin and Vishakhapatnam as had earlier been successfully done in New Delhi. Since these schools had to be self-sustaining, personnel would be required to pay fees higher than those in the KVs. On the other hand, though KV tuition fees were less, admission was uncertain. In Naval Public Schools, admission policy would be under naval control and naval children would always be assured of admission.

KVs have four objectives:

- To provide a common programme of education to children of transferable Government employees including defence and para-military personnel.
- To set the pace of excellence in Secondary School education.

- To initiate and promote experimentation and innovation in collaboration with the Central Board of Secondary Education (CBSE) and the National Council of Education Research and Training (NCERT).
- To inculcate national integration and a sense of 'Indian-ness'.

In pursuance of these objectives, the KVs:

- Have common textbooks and bilingual English and Hindi medium of instruction.
- Give preferential admission based on highest number of transfers during the preceding seven years.
- Are affiliated to the CBSE.
- Are co-educational.
- Teach Sanskrit
- Maintain a judicious teacher to pupil ratio to ensure the quality of teaching.
- Waive tuition fees for boys up to Class VIII and waive tuition fees for girls and scheduled caste / schedule tribe children up to Class XII.

To date, 950 KVs have been set up, of which 29 are Naval KVs.

Naval Public Schools and Naval Kindergartens

As mentioned above, the Naval Public Schools were set up in the major naval stations. They function under the aegis of the Navy Education Society and are affiliated to the Central Board of Secondary Education. They are run on a self-sustaining basis. For infrastructure development, they are given grants from the IN Amenities Fund (INAF).

Statistics of Grants From INAF to Naval Public Schools and Naval Kindergartens

From 1988 to date, the Amenities Fund has made grants totalling Rs. 12.4 crore to Naval Kindergartens and Naval Public Schools:

Year	Amount in Lakhs	Year	Amount in Lakhs
1989-89	30.00	1989-90	17.11
1991-91	12.00	1991-92	41.25
1993-93	75.00	1993-94	74.70
1995-95	56.09	1995-96	67.30
1997-97	137.81	1997-98	186.22
1999-99	115.29	1999-2000	141.01
2001-01	56.76	2001-02	63.32
2003-03	61.82	2003-04	103.23

Total: Rs 1239 lakhs

At the time of writing, there are twenty-nine Naval Kindergarten Schools in naval establishments and nine Naval Public Schools located in Delhi, Mumbai, Kochi, Vishakhapatnam, Goa, Port Blair, Arrakonam and Lonavla.

Navy Education Society

The Navy Education Society was formed in October 1986. Its objective is to promote education, science, culture and fine arts amongst the children and families of naval personnel. The Society governs the Naval Public Schools and the KG Schools at naval stations. It is responsible for the formulation of broad policies, standardisation of curricula and administration / setting up of educational institutions at naval stations.

Welfare Funds

The Directorate of Non-Public Funds

In July 1985, a new Directorate of Financial Planning (Non Public Funds) was established under the Chief of Personnel. It was to be guided by an Investment Advisory Committee chaired by the Vice Chief of the Naval Staff and comprising the Chief of Personnel, the Assistant Chief of Logistics and the Director of Non-Public Funds for profitable investment of non-public funds namely the Naval Group Insurance Fund, the INBA, the IN Amenities Fund, the Naval Officers Contributory Education Fund, etc.[1]

Indian Naval Benevolent Association

The objective of the Indian Naval Benevolent Association (INBA) is to relieve hardship and distress among serving and retired naval personnel and their families. Requests for assistance received are examined every week by the Relief and Finance Committee chaired by the Director Non-Public Funds to decide cases as per approved norms.

The Evolution of the Family Assistance Scheme into the Naval Group Insurance Scheme

Concerned about the financial security of bereaved naval families, the Navy made a modest beginning with a self-help Family Assistance Scheme in 1969. In this scheme, an officer contributed Rs 10 per month and a sailor Rs 2 per month. The bereaved family received a modest sum that was clearly inadequate but nevertheless it was a beginning.

In December 1975, the Navy initiated its Naval Group Insurance Scheme 1975 under the aegis of the INBA in association with the Life Insurance Corporation of India (LIC). In 1976, on the advice of the then Controller of Insurance in the Ministry of Finance,[2] the three services proposed that they be permitted to run departmentally individual Group Insurance Schemes under Section 44 (f) of the LIC Act 1956. Approval was accorded. This approval provided the much-needed flexibility for the schemes to be improved as socio-economic conditions changed. The remarkable improvement over the years in the Group Insurance Scheme covering all naval personnel can be seen from the table below:

Improvements in the Naval Group Insurance Scheme

Scheme	Period	OFFICERS		SAILORS	
		Contribution (Rs)	Insurance Cover (Rs)	Contribution (Rs)	Insurance Cover (Rs)
GIS-76	Jan 1976 to Jun 1978	30	30,000	10	15,000
GIS-78	Jul 1978 to Jun 1980	60	60,000	25	30,000
GIS-80	Jul 1980 to Jun 1981	65	65,000	30	35,000
GIS-81	Jul 1981 to Feb 1985	100	1,00,000	45	50,000
GIS-85	Mar 1985 to Dec 1988	200	2,00,000	70	75,000
GIS-89	Jan 1989 to Mar 1991	225	2,50,000	120	1,50,000
GIS-91	Apr 1991 to Mar 1994	250	3,00,000	120	1,50,000
GIS-94	Apr 1994 to Oct 1996	250	3,50,000	120	1,75,000
GIS-96	Nov 1996 to Aug 1997	275	4,00,000	130	2,00,000
GIS-97	Sep 1997 to Nov 2003	500	7,00,000	250	3,50,000
GIS-03	Dec 2003 onwards	750	10,00,000	360	5,00,000

1. The Navy owes a great deal to the Investment Advisory Committee and to Commodore B Bhasin (Retired) for the astute management of the Navy's Non Public Funds from July 1985 to date. In recognition of his dedication, Commodore Bhasin was constituted Honorary Rear Admiral in 2004.

2. The Services have much to be grateful for to the Late Mr RK Mahajan, not only for this advice when he was in the Ministry of Finance but also for advice after he retired.

Being risk-cum-saving schemes, Group Insurance Schemes are intended to provide a meaningful amount to bereaved families and to those invalided out of service. To facilitate smooth rehabilitation in civil life, the avowed objective is also to give a reasonable amount to naval personnel on their retirement / discharge from service.

Apart from the increased insurance cover shown in the above table, there were other improvements:

- The disability cover was introduced for the first time in 1980.
- Additional group insurance schemes for Aviation, Submarine and IMSF personnel were introduced at the behest of the Government from 1 September 1981 to provide additional cover for these high risk groups.
- The Post-Retirement Death Insurance Scheme was introduced in 1982.

Major improvements in the scheme were effected after the first comprehensive actuarial review in 1988. The salient features of the revised scheme, introduced from January 1989, were:

- Higher insurance cover with a relatively smaller increase in monthly premium.
- Parity in insurance cover for death in peace and in war time.
- Payment of saving element in addition to the insurance cover for death and invalidment.

Since over 99.8% of naval officers and sailors retire hale and hearty, the thrust of the schemes has been to improve the saving element substantially.

After the award of the Fifth Pay Commission and taking into consideration the erosion in the purchasing power of the rupee:

- The insurance cover was increased as shown above.
- The Post Retirement Death Insurance Scheme, which provides insurance cover for death up to 15 years after retirement or 70 years of age, whichever is earlier, was enhanced to Rs 2.5 lakh for officers and Rs 1.5 lakh for sailors with a one-time term premium of Rs 8,000 and Rs 2,700 respectively. This has been improved w.e.f. 1 November 2003 to provide cover for 20 years after retirement or age 72 years, whichever is earlier. The sum assured is Rs 3 lakh for officers and Rs 1.5 lakh for sailors with a one-time, non-refundable term premium of Rs 19,650 and Rs 10,575 respectively.

NGIF Housing Loan Scheme

In 1987, Government expressed its inability to extend the benefit of a housing loan of Rs 2.5 lakhs to service personnel as was being given to civilian central government employees. To meet the essential requirement for a dwelling unit, a Housing Loan Scheme, directly financed from NGIF, was introduced in 1988.

In November 1997, the quantum of housing loan was increased to Rs 7 lakh for officers and Rs 3.5 lakh for sailors, subject to repayment capacity. The quantum of loan has been enhanced to Rs 10 lakh for officers and Rs 5 lakh for sailors w.e.f. 1 July 2002 due to the increased cost of construction.

INBA Subsidiary Fund

In 1988, a separate INBA Subsidiary Fund was instituted for the welfare of ex-naval personnel and their families. It started with an initial corpus of Rs 1 crore from the IN Amenities Fund and marked a watershed in the history of the INBA to alleviate financial distress and provide succour to naval pensioners in distress.

The fund is given an annual allocation from the IN Amenities Fund to augment its resources. Existing schemes have been improved and new schemes introduced:

- The enhancement in a phased manner of financial assistance for specialised medical treatment from Rs 10,000 to Rs 2 lakh each for member and spouse towards surgery and treatment for cardio-vascular diseases, cancer, renal transplant and complete hip / knee joint replacement.
- Enhancement in a phased manner of the ex-gratia grant on death to the next of kin to Rs 15,000 for officers and Rs 7,500 for sailors.
- Introduction of ex-gratia grant for the marriage of daughters of widows of naval personnel who die in service or as pensioners.
- Enhancement in the annual scholarship for higher education to the children of naval pensioners to Rs 3,000 for day scholars and Rs 6,000 for boarders.

Enhancement of INBA Benefits w.e.f. 1 July 2002

Reason for Loan @ 8% Interest	Officers (Rs)	Sailors (Rs)
Daughter's Marriage	40,000	30,000
Sister's Marriage	20,000	15,000
Self Marriage	20,000	15,000
Higher Education	100,000	100,000

Loans are recoverable in 25 instalments, except higher education in 36 instalments.

INBA Benefits to Retired Naval Personnel

- Scholarships for Post 10+2 Education.
- Scholarships for Handicapped Children.
- Lump Sum Grant on Death.
- Travel / Incidental Expenses of naval pensioners required to be transferred from one service hospital to another out station service hospital for medical treatment.
- Rehabilitation Grant to sailors invalided due to TB / Paraplegia / Leprosy etc.
- Assistance for Self Employment.
- Grant for Marriage of Daughters of Widows.
- Treatment for serious Diseases in Civil Hospitals. The INBA Medical Benefit Scheme considers reimbursement of balance of medical expenses incurred on serious diseases depending upon the financial status of the ex-naval personnel.
- Special scholarship for education of children of naval personnel who die in harness. The full cost of education is reimbursed under this scheme.

Indian Naval Amenities Fund (INAF)

The contribution rates have been progressively revised. The present rates of contribution effective September 1997 are Rs 60 per quarter by officers and Rs 18 per quarter by sailors.

Welfare Projects Financed From the INAF

- Augmentation of Kindergarten and Naval Public Schools.
- Modernisation of service hospitals.
- Augmentation of MI Rooms and Dental Centres for ex-servicemen and their families.
- Promotion of sports and adventure activities.
- Improvement of Officers and Sailors Institutes and Welfare Centres.
- Improvement in INCS Complexes and canteen facilities in ships and establishments.
- Loans for purchase of buses.
- Furniture and furnishings in messes.

Statistics of Disbursements for Welfare and Amenities (in Rupees Lakhs)
(Other than to Naval Kindergartens and Naval Public Schools)

Year	Western Naval Command	Eastern Naval Command	Southern Naval Command	NHQ	Sports & Adventure Activities	Modernisation of Hospitals & Medical Equipment
1977-78	6.61	3.24	7.10	0.73	2.44	–
1978-79	11.44	17.55	12.82	0.50	3.00	–
1979-80	19.85	25.89	20.70	–	5.44	–
1980-81	10.49	5.95	6.25	0.50	6.84	0.94
1981-82	22.85	18.86	11.73	2.58	10.55	0.80
1982-83	12.41	14.00	10.38	2.78	13.67	0.07
1983-84	13.10	20.10	10.00	12.07	11.39	0.05
1984-85	20.00	23.35	15.25	2.90	10.06	0.35
1985-86	9.60	9.00	4.55	3.00	13.67	–
1986-87	19.00	19.42	16.90	13.73	15.83	0.76
1987-88	26.85	18.48	24.00	53.82	23.97	0.15
1988-89	32.00	26.00	24.00	8.90	30.78	–
1989-90	28.00	20.00	37.33	8.50	60.21	–
1990-91	64.00	49.00	57.72	19.00	35.42	–
1991-92	62.00	62.00	62.00	41.42	52.18	1.45
1992-93	92.00	90.24	84.00	38.00	66.97	21.02
1993-94	70.00	72.50	72.00	32.00	57.26	74.84
1994-95	60.00	66.28	60.00	36.25	54.45	102.24

Year	Western Naval Command	Eastern Naval Command	Southern Naval Command	NHQ	Sports & Adventure Activities	Modernisation of Hospitals & Medical Equipment
1995-96	64.00	71.50	64.00	32.00	107.86	–
1996-97	137.00	125.23	86.00	39.00	90.05	–
1997-98	128.00	82.00	92.00	55.52	53.80*	
1998-99	147.83	82.72	80.70	54.53	30.03	24.61
1999-00	80.00	80.00	80.00	290.27	28.90	184.72
2000-01	75.00	70.00	70.00	123.74	37.05	112.53
2001-02	70.00	70.00	92.00	83.75	32.75	119.62
2002-03	90.00	87.00	66.00	65.00	40.00	145.84
2003-04	95.00	78.00	77.00	215.00	40.00	94.00
TOTAL	1467.03	1308.31	1244.43	1235.49	934.57	883.99

From 1997 - 98 onwards, most of the expenditure on Sports and Adventure activities is being met from public funds.

Resettlement

The Directorate of Ex-Servicemen Affairs

In June 1988, a new Directorate of Ex-Servicemen Affairs (DESA) was established under the Chief of Personnel to assist ex-servicemen and their families in making a smooth transition to civil life and expeditiously deal with their problems like settlement of pension and other dues, release of land and accommodation and finding suitable avenues for resettlement.

40

The Erosion Of Leadership Values

"Only an officer who has already proved his leadership abilities as a ship commander can succeed in fleet command, or in duty on the Admiralty Staff. For, important as is a knowledge of communications and the technique of giving commands, these are secondary to the great essential of proven character as a leader in practice."

– German Grand Admiral Raeder

The Malaise

The Navy was not, and could not be, immune to the 'careerism' that was prevalent in the other segments of society. The following depiction of the 'careerist' helps in understanding the malaise that afflicted the Navy during the period 1976 to 1990 and what followed in the 1990s:

"The careerist officer believes that he has a job to perform within a corporate bureaucracy, that the true measure of success is how far and how fast he can climb what he perceives as the ladder of success. His credo is risk avoidance and promotion of self, his loyalty is entirely personal, his ethics situational. If he manages to manoeuvre himself into a command position, he uses subordinates to advance his career with little understanding or appreciation of his role as a leader, a teacher and example to his subordinates. This tragedy of the careerist is that he is self replicating, for which he drives off many of the very type of officer needed in the armed forces."

Overview

At the time of independence in 1947, the highest rank held by the senior-most Indian officer was Acting Captain. Those who were 'Regular Entry' officers, and had undergone extended training with the British Navy and had imbibed, to a greater or lesser degree, the attitudes and value scales of their British counterparts. Those who had joined the Navy and participated in World War II as 'Reserve' officers had brought into the Navy the value scales of the civilian sectors from which they came. Overall, the qualities of leadership that prevailed at the end of the war were those that evolve during every long war – unquestioning obedience and survival.

The post-war demobilisation in 1945 and the partitioning of the Navy in 1947 created a serious shortage of officers. To meet this shortage, large batches of 'cadets' were sent to Britain to undergo training for four years. Concurrently, large batches of 'Direct Entry Sub Lieutenants' were inducted to undergo much shorter training in India. The social backgrounds of both types of entrants were diverse. The time available for them to develop high qualities of leadership was short of what it should have been. Nevertheless, it was possible to keep the system going by strict adherence to the Navy's Regulations and to the procedures that had been modelled on those that the British had evolved over the centuries for their Navy.

Viewed in retrospect, several factors that were not clearly visualised at the time began to erode the leadership system in the decades after 1947:

- **Increasing Technology of Naval Acquisitions.** Between 1948 and 1958, the Navy acquired second hand warships from Britain – two cruisers, six old destroyers and several minesweepers. Between 1958 and 1961, eight new frigates and an aircraft carrier entered service, whose equipment required higher skills than the older ships. The initial training of the large number of personnel required to man these acquisitions had to be minimised to cope with the surge in manpower requirements. These British acquisitions were followed by the acquisitions from Russia, starting in 1965, of ships and submarines densely packed with equipment, whose technology was more complex than that of the British. To this was added the induction in the 1970s of modern indigenous Leander class frigates and minor war vessels. Gradually, time-tested values of naval leadership were subordinated to technical proficiency.

- **The Compulsion of Sea Time.** The statutory promotion regulations required officers and sailors to have performed satisfactorily in seagoing ships before they could be considered for promotion. With the rapid growth of manpower, and despite the increase in the number of ships, it became increasingly difficult to give every officer and sailor 'equitable' sea time. Administrative measures like the adoption in the 1960s of 'Wet Lists' (those who would go to sea) and 'Dry Lists' (those who would not go to sea) were not well received. Nor did 'Deep Selection' (promoting a meritorious officer over the heads of his contemporaries) find acceptance because it was felt that seniority should receive respect. In what was essentially a peacetime Navy, it became a matter of professional survival for officers to 'prove' themselves during their appointments in seagoing ships, by adopting whatever shortcuts were necessary, to get a 'good report'. This attitude did not set a good example to either young officers or to sailors.

- **Favouritism.** Compounding these factors were delays in the availability of spares and the lags in setting up maintenance and training facilities for the new acquisitions. Those officers who, despite these difficulties, managed to do well at sea soon became *protégés*. In a short space of time, ambitious officers became 'mentors', 'networked' their clans, identified the *protégés* they could depend on, and carried them upward to the mutual benefit of their careers.

- **Master Chief Petty Officers.** On the one hand, the creation of MCPOs brought the Navy in line with the Army's JCOs and the Air Force's Master Warrant Officers. On the other hand, the traditional function of senior sailors as the 'vital link between officers and sailors' atrophied. On board ships, MCPOs were neither working hands nor effective supervisors. Their utilisation took time to work out. Leadership at the sailor level suffered.

Vice Admiral VL Koppikar served in the Personnel Branch at NHQ as Deputy Director of Personnel, Director of Personnel Services, Director of Personnel, Assistant Chief of Personnel and finally as Chief of Personnel from 1988 to 1990. In the Navy Foundation's annual journal, *Quarterdeck 2000*, he reminisced:

"Perhaps one of the most hastily implemented decisions of those years was the creation of two additional ranks, MCPO I and MCPO II in the Sailor Cadre. For a while it threw the Navy completely off balance. There appeared to be no justification for these two ranks at the apex level without enhanced responsibilities or accountability. There were problems galore of manning and management, of accommodation and of detailing parties for various tasks. All of a sudden there were 'too many Chiefs and very few Indians'. Above all, it pushed the hitherto 'prestigious' ranks of CPO and PO into the shade. That, in my view was the saddest part."

Two events in the early 1970s aggravated the malaise:

- With good intentions, the Navy started withdrawing topasses from ships. When confronted with the sailors' resentment and unrest, the Navy had to back off and abandon the attempt.

- The unrest in the flagship *Mysore* when the command implemented an unscheduled intensive work up programme at a time when sailors had already arranged domestic commitments. The sailors' unrest led to the replacement of the entire command and ship's company.

By 1975, erosion had occurred in the quality of leadership at all levels – between senior officers and junior officers, between officers and sailors and between senior sailors and junior sailors. Ostentation and showmanship began replacing competence and professionalism. Double-speak, clever-clever talk and physical, mental, and professional laziness began to creep in and replace exemplary conduct. Publicly, the Navy was lauded as an example for the rest of India to emulate because all castes and communities lived and worked on board ships as one family. Within the Navy, favouritism set in and factions formed based on caste, community, religion, language, cadre, department and specialisation.

Perceptive and upright officers, who could sense what was happening and resisted the deterioration that was becoming endemic, found themselves being sidelined. The alibi trotted out was that the Navy could not be immune from the erosion in values that was afflicting society as a whole.

The greatest damage was done by those officers who violated the basic tenet of desisting from involvement with the political establishment. Ambitious senior officers started going out of their way to cultivate bureaucrats in the Ministry and politicians of the party in power. Ostensibly, it was to obtain support and sanctions for naval projects. Not everyone could resist the opportunity it provided for personal advancement.

The events between 1976 and 1990 were the manifestation of this unfortunate malaise that had set in earlier and which culminated in the dismissal of a Chief of the Naval Staff in 1998.

The Deterioration From 1976 Onwards

All the excerpts that follow are from statements in the public domain:

Writing in the Navy Foundation's annual journal *'Quarterdeck 2000'*, Vice Admiral Awati, who was the Navy's Chief of Personnel in 1979 and 1980 stated:

"The management of our personnel, their recruitment, rank structure and training for war took a quantum jump during the 1970s. Looking back, there seems no doubt that in some areas at least, the change was too fast. It gave rise to distortions and the resultant disquiet, especially in the lower deck. The absence of an adequate feedback from the fleet caused complacency in the command. This led to a succession of unfortunate incidents in the fleet, which can only be termed 'mutinies' by future historians. Fortunately, these were handled with both firmness and imagination. The resultant pull-back from some unthinking changes, followed by reforms in rules governing advancement, pay and allowances, the quality of catering on board, in housing and even in the age-old pattern of sailors' uniform enabled the service to break out of a redundant mould of functioning.

"Unfortunately, the flip side of this welcome change was to become evident all too soon during the 1980s. The self-serving conduct of a few officers, both senior and middle rank, in seeking the intervention of the courts to obtain redressal of grievances was a slap to a disciplined service. Almost every one of these grievances pertained to promotions and appointments. The real cause of this malaise is yet to be analysed.

"The attitudinal change in some officers, miniscule though their number might be today, has become the cause of much disquiet in the service which it must do everything possible to dispel."

Vice Admiral Koppikar served in the Personnel Branch in almost all capacities from Deputy Director to Chief of Personnel. Writing in *Quarterdeck 2000*, he stated:

"Tried and tested over long years, the system does work well except when someone tries to tinker with it for whatever reasons. That can set you back by years and the process of confidence building has to start all over again. My general experience has been that an average officer is mature, understanding and disciplined. If he is truly unhappy, he will seek redressal of his grievance through established channels. Unfortunately, you do come across an odd case, when someone driven by overweening ambition or a vast sense of self-importance obstructs the process by going to court or approaching the court directly. The damage caused to the Navy is enormous and not easily retrievable."

The following excerpt is from a letter reproduced in the book, *Vishnu Bhagwat's Fiasco* by Thorat and Halbe. The letter was written by the Flag Officer Commanding in Chief Western Naval Command to the Chief of the Naval Staff in 1990:

"Of late, in the Service, a very insidious personality cult has been developed by encouraging loyalties of officers to an individual rather than the Service. This ethos has reached alarming proportions. Groupism, favouritism towards some and vindictiveness and victimisation towards others will be much in evidence in future. In this respect, it is quite easy to make a forecast of events and developments. Officers are being encouraged to spy and report on perceived rivals. This is unprecedented and a most un-officer-like behavioural pattern that has come to stay and will thoroughly vitiate the traditional camaraderie and esprit-de-corps in the Service to its great detriment.

"The culture of cultivating politicians, high officers, senior civil servants and other influential persons has, irretrievably, been established which will continue to plague the Service in future. It will do inestimable harm to the fighting efficiency of the Navy because senior officers will devote time and energy to such activities at the expense of their primary responsibilities.

"Press and influence peddlers have been cultivated and pampered."

Vice Admiral RB Suri was the Navy's Chief of Personnel from 1993 to 1995. His article in *Quarterdeck 2000* stated:

"The structure of the service... has inherent drawbacks. The very large base with a narrow top leads to a pyramidical structure where stagnation and supercession become inbuilt features. This results in unethical tendencies of a 'rat race' with its consequential adverse effects on values and discipline. Then comes the problem of equation with other services, most of which have a cylindrical structure. It is a question of 'izzat'. Many measures taken to cope with this situation have distorted the problem. Cadre Review exercises in the past have resulted in upsetting staff and line relationships. They also ended up 'degrading' ranks and it is not unusual to see Flag Officers doing the jobs done by erstwhile Captains. In the Indian ethos, everything is unfortunately linked to rank. Status, success, respect is equated to rank. Under these circumstances, the organisational goals were given a go-by. Increase of the retirement age and doing away with the 'tenure' by giving up the tenure system dislodged the inbuilt checks and balances. ...many bright officers get left out since no other profession has such a high degree of supercession. The best of the officers thus lose their motivation."

Excerpts from *"Betrayal of the Defence Forces – The Inside Truth"* by Admiral Vishnu Bhagwat, Chief of the Naval Staff 1997-98:

"Professional standards in the Indian Navy had been falling since the 1971 war with Pakistan. 'Bean count' of the number of operational ships on paper was what had mattered. In any case, in a non-professional environment, non-events like Navy Balls, extraneous social activities, golf, personal comforts, ships' anniversaries and all that is associated with a peacetime Navy took precedence. *INS Andaman* sinking in August 1990 and almost a repeat of it of a submarine in August 1996, again in the Eastern Command, were a chilling reminder, if a reminder was at all needed, that professionalism needed to be recognised and acknowledged as priority Number One, across the board in the service, if we were not to disgrace ourselves yet again. Far too long, had the 'smart ones' climbed the ladder adopting dubious means, generally at the cost of honest and committed professionals. A quarter century of peace had taken a heavy toll on the Navy. (Page 46)

"It takes a lifetime of professional preparation, thinking through of a strategic vision, concept and ideas to be able to really contribute in the senior ranks of the service. On the other hand, one can spend time on preserving the status-quo, not rock the boat, encouraging a 'Cozy Club' where the whole purpose is to make oneself as comfortable as possible, grab the privileges, strut around, globe-trot when you can, and be a part and parcel of the soft-state. (Page 49)

"Merit and substantive contribution are not always easy to reward, without ruffling feathers. Some people had only become just too smart to take only the advantages from the system. They had made an art of studying and then pandering to the wishes and desires of their seniors. The smart ones appeared always to edge out the 'good ones'. That 'bad money drives good money out of circulation' is not a new phenomenon but 25 years of a relatively easy life had bred a culture, which tended to negate the kind of professionalism innately required in a service like the Navy." (Page 51)

Developments After 1990

The malaise peaked in 1990 at the time of the change of the Chief of the Naval Staff. Allegations and counter allegations, published in the media, cast serious aspersions that shook the confidence of the Navy in its leadership. After the waves of disquiet had settled down, the Navy set up a Centre for Leadership and Behavioural Sciences to re-instil the leadership values that distinguish the Armed Forces from the civilian society around them.

41

Defence Procurement

"I recall that most revered public servant, Mr Dharmavira, telling me as to how as Cabinet Secretary, he had led a delegation abroad for the purchase of some essential defence equipment.

"After the negotiations had concluded, his counterpart on the other side of the table said, 'Mr Secretary how would you like to take the kickback? In whose name shall I make out the cheque for the discount?'

"Dharamvira promptly answered: 'Excellency, make it out in the name of the Government of India.' And he carried the cheque back to India and presented it to the Prime Minister, Pandit Jawaharlal Nehru.

"The Prime Minister was furious. 'What! You accepted a kickback - it is a disgrace.'

"Dharamvira kept his cool. He only said, 'Panditji, what did you expect me to do? Take it in my name, and put the money in a Swiss account?'

"The point was well made. Panditji was silent."[1]

An Overview of the Defence Procurement Process

In the early years after independence, in the end 1940s and early 1950s, the large acquisitions were second hand ships, aircraft and tanks from Britain. In the end 1950s, India embarked on the path of self-reliance. The 1960s saw the fruition of major indigenous projects with British assistance – the Navy's Leander frigate project at Mazagon Docks, the Army's tank project at Avadi and the Air Force's Avro project at Kanpur. All these were negotiated at Government-to-Government level.

For the acquisition of smaller defence equipment, the Service Headquarters scanned whatever was available worldwide and initiated enquiries through the attachés accredited to embassies abroad. The supplier firm would appoint a local representative who would act as the link to clarify queries. Since this representative was remunerated for his services, he came to be called a 'commission agent'. There was no ban on commission agents. They were an essential link with suppliers trying to sell the latest defence technologies that India wanted.

In the end 1970s, the Government promulgated precise instructions for commission agents – they were to provide their name, address, income tax particulars, bank account particulars etc so that it could be verified that they were paying income tax on the commissions they received.

From the 1960s to the 1980s, all defence acquisitions from the Soviet Union were solely through Government-to-Government interaction. Likewise, the large new acquisitions from Europe like tanks, aircraft and helicopters from France and Britain invariably involved Government-to-Government interaction. The less costly equipments like radars, sonars, torpedoes, ammunition, etc were usually negotiated with individual firms but always after clearances and assurances of the supplier government were incorporated in an Inter-Government Memorandum of Understanding (MOU).

Over the years, pragmatic procedures evolved to institutionalise defence procurement from abroad. Two of the basic procedures were:

First – Not to interfere in the Service Headquarters' process of short-listing the contenders, and to ensure, as far as possible, that there were always two contenders in the fray to facilitate competitive price negotiations.

Second – After the Service Headquarters had recommended their short-list, the Government would consider:

* The larger *'strategic' factors* like:
  – The likelihood of the supplier government imposing an embargo in a crisis.

---

1. Excerpt from a newspaper article by Mr Fali Nariman, ex Solicitor General of India.

- Obtaining safeguards, by an assurance at a Government-to-Government level, of spare parts support and updates / modifications to cover the life cycle of the acquisition.

- Whether the supplier was agreeable to transfer of technology, whether such transfer was cost effective in the context of the overall objective of self-reliance, etc.

● The larger *'financial' and 'economic' aspects* like:

- The availability from the supplier government of favourable financial terms (like soft / deferred credit, the initial moratorium before commencing repayment, the terms of repayment, long term loans at low rates of interest etc) in the context of the nation's overall debt burden.

- The possibilities for counter trade, whereby a portion of the payment for defence equipment could be paid in goods (like machine tools) and commodities (like tea).

- The possibilities for 'offsets', i.e. commercial arrangements that would obligate the seller to buy-back (e.g. spares / components manufactured indigenously) so as to counter the expenditure required for the sale. The percentage of offsets would depend on factors like:

  ＊The number being purchased. The larger the number, the larger the offset that could be demanded.

  ＊The capability of Indian industry to cope with the level of offsets.

  ＊Whether there were possibilities of Indian firms being given sub-contracts in the global market.

After considering the short list recommended by Service Headquarters, the Cabinet Committee on Political Affairs (CCPA) would accord approval in principle for the number to be acquired and the commencement of negotiations by a Price Negotiating Committee (PNC) comprising senior representatives of the Ministry of Defence, Ministry of Finance-Defence, Service Headquarters, the Defence Public Sector Undertaking concerned, DRDO and whoever else was concerned.

It was only after price negotiations commenced that each firm would make available the detailed documentation about their product that would enable detailed technical examination and comparison. During negotiations, grey areas would be clarified and costs calculated of spares, training, documentation, and delivery schedules. From these negotiations would emerge the cost-effective choice to be considered by the CCPA, whose final decision would be based on all the above strategic, political, economic and financial considerations.

PNCs were well aware that to win the contract, contending firms would reduce the basic cost of the main acquisition and make up for the reduction when supplying spares and other life cycle support.

The media and the public were not, and could not be, privy to these considerations. To win the contract, the contending firms would do their utmost to sway the choice in their favour. One way of achieving this was to disparage the competitor and allege kickbacks. This provided the basis for the suspicion of, and speculation in, the public mind regarding 'pecuniary malfeasance' in defence procurement. The faction that did not win the contract could allege that kickbacks had been the primary determinant of the choice.

Contending firms had to have a local representative (the 'commission agent') to be the link between the Service Headquarters and the parent company. At the short-listing stage, he would convey technical queries to his principals and they would send their replies to him to convey to the customer. At the negotiations stage, the agent's eagerness to earn commission was a double-edged weapon. The customer could leverage it to obtain better technology and lower cost. The parent company could use him as the conduit to decry the competitor. The media could be availed of to project the differing points of view in an effort to tilt the final decision. The primary aim was to win the contract. After a contract was signed, during 'after sales service', he would be the link for interaction regarding documentation, training, spares, modifications and improvements to equipment etc.

The Large Naval Procurements From Europe 1976-90

During the period 1976-90, there were three major naval procurements from Europe. The first two were from Britain – there was no controversy regarding the Sea Harriers – there was controversy regarding the Seakings Mk 42 B. The third procurement was the German SSK Submarine Project – there was considerable controversy.

In the case of the Sea Harriers there was no contender. Government-controlled British Aerospace and Rolls Royce were the only sources of supply. In the case of the helicopters, the contenders were the British Seakings made by Westland Helicopters and the French Super Pumas made by Aerospatiale. In the case of the SSKs, the contenders were HDW of Germany and Kockums of Sweden and, as emerged during the course of research, the majority shareholders of both these contenders were their respective Governments.

The Sea Harrier Aircraft Acquisition From Britain

In October 1977, the CCPA approved the acquisition of eight Sea Harrier aircraft, including two Trainers. A Memorandum of Understanding (MOU) was required to cover the British Government's support in training and maintenance, as well as quality assurance. The primary issues that required resolution prior to signing of the contract were the fixation of a base price and an escalation formula, waiver of the R&D levy, which amounted to about 10% of the total cost and a contractual clause to safeguard our interest in the event, however unlikely, of a cancellation of the Sea Harrier Programme by the British Government.

The clause about continued and uninterrupted supplies was the subject of considerable discussion. The best that could be achieved was that 'subject to overriding national interests, the British Government would not impose any restrictions on the continued supply of aircraft, equipment, information and other services.'

In 1998, twenty one years later, when the US imposed sanctions after India's nuclear tests, the supply of some of the US origin / patented parts were embargoed by the United States. At the time of writing in 2004, some items are still in the repair loop.

The Seaking Mk 42 B ASW/ASV Helicopter Acquisition From Britain

The Navy's staff requirements had stipulated both an anti submarine warfare (ASW) and an anti surface vessel (ASV) role. For the anti submarine role, the requirements were for a better dunking sonar and a system to monitor sonobuoys. For the ASV role, the requirement was for an anti ship missile.

International tenders were floated. Four proposals were received:

- The British Sea Lynx was not found suitable.
- An updated version of the British Seaking.
- The Italian Agosta. It transpired that this was the Italian version of the British Seaking; it was therefore excluded from further consideration.
- The French Super Puma.

The choice thus lay between the British Seaking and the French Super Puma. In March 1982, the CCPA accorded approval for the acquisition of 20 ASW/ASV helicopters.

The Comparative Evaluation of the British Seaking and the French Super Puma

The Super Puma's fuselage and rotor blades were made of the latest composite material. This was considered to be an advantage. Whilst the Super Puma was not yet operational in any Navy in the ASW role, the ASW equipment being offered for fitment met the Navy's staff requirements and was operational in the French Navy's MRASW aircraft and their Dauphine helicopters. However, the French could not offer their Exocet anti ship missile with the Super Puma because of a commitment they had given to the Pakistan Navy, when supplying them Exocet anti ship missiles for their Seaking helicopters. Nor were the British agreeable to let their Sea Eagle anti ship missile be released for fitment in the French Super Puma.

The updated version of the Seaking, named 42B, was still on the drawing board and none of the avionic systems being offered had yet been proven. On the other hand, the Indian Navy had acquired ten years experience in operating the Seakings and both infrastructure and expertise had been built up. The Sea Eagle anti ship missile was under development and yet to be proven in test firings.

Sonars

The Navy decided to carry out, in Indian waters, simultaneous evaluations of the dunking sonars being offered.

Commander (later Commodore) S Purohit, an experienced Seaking test pilot, participated in these trials. He recalls:

> "We evaluated, very systematically, three dunking sonars. These were the American Bendix, Plessey's modification of their British sonar 195 and the French Thomson CSF HS 12. NPOL was extensively involved in these trials, which were conducted off Cochin in the early 1980s.

> "By this time, we had considerably improved upon the procedures of the early 1970s for evaluating and testing helicopter sonars and had learnt the technique of making the manufacturers accept our demands that their sonar be tested in our own waters. We had realised that the hydrological conditions in their waters and overall sonar performance in their temperature were different from those in India. Equipment often gave problems because of heat and humidity and did not perform as well because of our peculiar hydrological conditions.

> "For the first time, we had three Seakings fitted with these three different sonars and pinging against the same submarine in the same hydrological conditions. This enabled their performance in identical conditions to be scientifically compared."

The American Bendix performed better than the French HS 12, which performed better than the British 195.

Radars

There were two competing radars – the French and the British. The British were not agreeable to put the French radar on the Seaking nor were the French willing to fit the British radar in the Super Puma.

Sonobuoys

The competing French and British sonobuoy systems were flying in their respective MRASW aircraft but both would require to be miniaturised for fitment in a helicopter.

The Decision in Favour of the Seaking Mk 42 B

In the light of the pros and cons of these options, views became divided, both in the Air Arm and in the Navy, for and against the Seaking and the Super Puma. Eventually, when the choice was made in favour of the Seaking Mk 42B, there was speculation that the choice had been made on extraneous considerations.

Reportedly, one of these considerations was that the British firm of Westland Helicopters, which made the Seakings, was in danger of having to close down for want of orders. This would have meant loss of jobs in that constituency. The British, therefore, tried their best for the contract to be awarded to Westland.

In retrospect, it seems likely that what determined the choice in favour of Westland was the advantage of standardising on Seakings to minimise the cost of additional infrastructure and capitalise on the ten years experience of operating Seakings in India's tropical conditions. It is also likely that the Seaking AEW helicopter, then under development, appeared a promising option to meet the Navy's pressing need for an AEW platform for anti missile defence.

In July 1983, agreements were signed with:

- British Westland for the helicopters;
- British Rolls Royce for the engines;[2]
- British Marconi for the Hermes Electronic Warfare ESM systems;
- French Thompson CSF for the HS 12 sonars;
- Italian Whitehead Motofides for the A 244 S torpedo installations;

In making these choices, the Navy had opted for the latest systems that were available at that time, some of which were still under development and had yet to be de-bugged and integrated into a coherent system.

Commodore Purohit recalls:

"The big problem was of developing the software for the Tactical Mission System. The Navy sent a multi disciplinary team to the UK consisting of air engineers, air electricals and experienced Seaking aircrew. This team actually did the work of defining and developing the parameters and algorithms for the entire software for this helicopter and we should be proud of it. In the process, we acquired the confidence to interface air weapons with air platforms. We have today a helicopter whose punch and capability is the best in the world. We could not have had it if we had not taken the bold step of contracting for something which nobody had and which was still in the concept stage."

The SSK Submarine Project Collaboration with Germany

The technical evaluations which led to the short-listing of the Swedish Kockums and German HDW submarines have been discussed in the chapter on the SSK project.

As per standard procedure, the governments of both contenders had been informed that in the event of being selected for collaboration, the Indian side would like the following points to be included in an Inter Government Memorandum of Understanding (MOU):

- Their shipyard had the necessary authorisation of its Government to sell submarines to India.
- Their shipyard was authorised to collaborate with India for constructing submarines in India under license and with provision for incorporation of subsequent improvements and modifications.
- Assurance of the supplier's Government for continued product support in all its aspects for the life cycle of the submarines or for 25 years.
- Similar assurances that no prohibitions or restrictions would be imposed by the supplier Government on the supply and services and continued flow of product support for that period.
- Authorising the shipyard for transfer of the full range of technology for the construction of submarines in India.
- Transferring from the supplier's navy the full range of design technology for the development of submarine design capability in India.
- Government clearance for sale to India of connected weapons, armament, sensors, machinery and systems.

---

2. The Seaking gearboxes were of American patent. In 1998, when the US imposed sanctions after India's nuclear tests, some of these gearboxes were in Britain for major overhaul. Their return to India was embargoed by the United States. At the time of writing in 2004, partial deliveries have been made. However, some items are still under repair.

- Support by the supplier's navy for the training of:
  - Indian Naval and Dockyard personnel for the operation, maintenance, repair and overhaul of submarines and the related systems.
  - Indian Naval crew in all aspects of submarine warfare including tactical doctrines, ESM, ECM consistent with national commitments,
  - Indian personnel for the logistic support for the submarine and its systems.
- Quality control, certification, trials and acceptance of the submarine and its related systems by the supplier's navy and supply of necessary documentation.
- Assurance by both sides regarding security of information and equipment.
- Consultations between the two Governments to resolve problems, if any, arising out of the implementation of the collaboration project.

The German side had made it known that it could not export weapon platforms or weapons to areas of tension. After the 1971 Indo-Pakistan War, the Indian subcontinent had been declared an area of tension. Moreover, Germany was reluctant to supply defence equipment to non-NATO countries because it felt that such equipment might be eventually used against their own allies.

The Swedish side had no such reservations.

The Choice

Within the Indian side, views were divided:

- The evaluations and 'matrix analyses' had placed Kockums marginally ahead of HDW. The Chief of Naval Staff preferred Kockums because its technology was superior to HDW and Kockums had no reservations on transfer of submarine design technology to India.
- A segment of the Navy's submariners preferred HDW. They felt that the Kockums technology was too advanced, many aspects of which had not been proven. HDW had built and exported a number of submarines designed by Dr Gabler, the highly reputed and experienced designer of German submarines during World War II.
- Mazagon Docks, already selected as the yard that would build submarines in India, had already invested resources in establishing the infrastructure for submarine construction, preferred HDW. The Kockums design was still on the drawing board and it would take Kockums a much longer time than HDW to deliver to Mazagon Docks the production drawings that would enable Mazagon Docks to commence construction.

Operationally, even though both Kockums and HDW were more or less on par, the Chief of the Naval Staff preferred Kockums. He felt that the Navy should start its submarine construction programme with the best available technology. Desk-top evaluations had shown, unanimously, that Kockums technology was more advanced than that of HDW. His preference was supported by his feeling that the Germans were less candid than the Swedes when answering queries on sensitive operational parameters like self-noise and indiscretion rate.

Years later in the end 1980s, when enquiries were instituted into the HDW contracts, the following excerpt appeared in the public domain, reportedly from a letter from the then Chief of Naval Staff, Admiral Pereira to the Public Accounts Committee of Parliament:

"West Germany, in my personal view, was half as open and they gave a very definite impression that they were doing us a favour. They also left me with an impression that they always tried to cloud the transfer of technology in legal wording. In fact, I remember that the evaluation team and the Naval Headquarters were not often very sure of what West Germany was exactly trying to give us. As far as technical evaluation of both was concerned, there was not a great deal of difference. I still preferred Sweden as I was most concerned with the transfer of technology which was the hub of the whole problem and (their) offer was loud and clear on the transfer of technology."

In end 1979, Naval Headquarters informed the Government that Kockums was higher in the matrix and was preferred. If, however, the Government preferred HDW for other reasons, HDW was acceptable to NHQ.

NHQ's reasoning was that having spent so many years in getting the project so near to finalisation, it would be not be in the Navy's interest to say that if Kockums was not acceptable to the Government, then the Navy was willing to forego the present SSK project and start evaluations all over again.

In April 1980, the CCPA approved the commencement of price negotiations with HDW and Kockums. Throughout this period, the media was full of claims and counter claims regarding the operational, technical, logistic and life-cycle-cost advantages / disadvantages and assessments of the HDW and Kockums options.

In June 1980, the CCPA approved the selection of the German HDW option.

In view of the German side's reservations, India considered it essential that before any contracts were signed, there should be some agreement at the Government-to-Government level to safeguard Indian interests. It took over a year of discussions to arrive at an agreement that met India's requirements. Between April 1980, when the CCPA approved the collaboration with HDW for the SSK Project and December 1981 when the contracts were signed, there were detailed discussions to formulate the 'Agreement on Technical Assistance' that was signed in July 1981 between the German and Indian Ministries of Defence. The agreement covered the following points:

- Designing and preparing planning documents for construction of submarines.

- Evaluation of trials data and support in torpedo trials.

- Execution of associated contracts.

- Release of classified military information.

- Quality Assurance for submarines and torpedos by the German Government's Quality Assurance Department.

- Training.

    Four contracts were signed on 11 December 1981:

- Construction by HDW of the first two submarines in Germany as per the German Submarine Construction Rules of 1979.

- Supply of Material Packages to MDL for the construction of two submarines.

- Gave India the option to order/buy two more material packages for SSKs 5 & 6 within 12 months i.e. 11 December 1982.

- With AEG Telefunken for the supply of torpedos.

Events Between 1982 and 1987

Construction in Germany of the first SSK began in March 1982. 54 months later, she commissioned as *Shishumar* on 22 September 1986. The second SSK, *Shankush* commissioned two months later on 20 November 1986. Both submarines were evaluated after arrival in Bombay and were found to be entirely satisfactory. Meanwhile, the construction of the 3rd and 4th submarines was progressing in Mazagon Docks.

The contract signed in December 1981 had an option clause for two more submarines to be exercised by December 1982. Extensions were sought whilst evaluations progressed on the extent to which better and more modern equipment could be fitted in the 5th and 6th submarines.

Eventually, in 1986 when price negotiations commenced, it was found that the cost of improvements that the Navy sought and the adverse deterioration in the Rupee-Deutsche Mark exchange rate resulted in a seven-fold increase in price. Discussions commenced in India on an item-wise analysis of the escalation. Many improvements were dropped from consideration to stay within the budget. Gradually the differences narrowed.

When HDW were unable to reduce the price any further, the Indian Ambassador in Germany was asked to take up the matter officially and make a final effort to bridge the gap, since failure to sign the contract would result in the loss of the skills and expertise that Mazagon Docks was building up in submarine construction.

In end 1986, serious political differences had developed between the Finance Minister, Mr VP Singh and the Prime Minister, Mr Rajiv Gandhi. To defuse the tension during Exercise Brass Tacks, the Prime Minister shifted Mr VP Singh from the Finance Ministry to the Defence Ministry in January 1987.

On 24 February 1987, the Indian Ambassador in Germany sent a cable to the Defence Secretary to the effect that the German side had expressed the hope that the final price for the SSK submarines could be negotiated satisfactorily but regretted that seven per cent commission payable to the Indian Agents of HDW under the terms of an open ended agreement had caused a great financial liability.

The sequence of events that can be speculated from what has appeared in the public domain appears to be:

- On 27 February 1987, three days after the Ambassador's cable arrived, German officials arrived in Delhi for a meeting after which the Indian side took the official line that no commissions had been paid.

- On learning of this, the Indian ambassador in Germany sent a telegram in March 1987 recommending that HDW be punished for falsely declaring that there was no agent in the deal.

- This came to the Defence Minister's notice on 9 April 1987. On seeing this cable:
  - He asked the Defence Secretary to conduct a full investigation of the HDW case;
  - He sent the file to the Prime Minister's office;
  - Issued a press release about it;

- The file arrived on the Prime Minister's desk after the newspapers had already published the Defence Minister's press release, disclosing the payment of commissions in the HDW deal of December 1981.

- There was a political furore.

- On 12 April 1987, the Defence Minister resigned from the cabinet.

Enquiries were commenced by the Public Accounts Committee of Parliament and by the Comptroller and Auditor General of India. Neither of them commented adversely on the Navy's rationale for recommending HDW. Both passed strictures on the negotiating process but could not pinpoint culpability.

The enquiry ordered by the Ministry of Defence in 1987 went on till 1990, awaiting responses from the German side to the information sought by the Indian side. After Mr VP Singh became the Prime Minister in 1989, he enquired about the progress of the HDW investigation.

In March 1990, the Criminal Bureau of Investigation registered a case against the members of the Price Negotiating Committee, the representatives of the German supplier companies and their commission agents in India.

The case alleged that Ministry of Defence and Naval officials had accepted gratifications for manipulating figures to sway the award of the SSK contract to HDW in 1981.

According to a press report in October 2002, the CBI had decided to drop the case because the German Government had declined to give any further information. This has yet to be officially confirmed.

It was not until the end 1990s that it became possible to consider resumption of submarine construction in India.

From the Navy's point of view, the SSK Project met all the objectives of transfer of technology for construction in India of submarines having the latest silent design and fitted with the latest proven equipment that could be obtained from Western sources.

42

Checks And Balances In The
NHQ-Defence Ministry Relationship

Preamble

One of the facets in the evolution of systems of governance, whether imperial, colonial, totalitarian or parliamentary, has been the method and degree of control to be exercised over the 'Armed Forces' by the 'civil side' – 'civil' being interpreted sometimes as 'the political component of Government' and sometimes as 'the civil service-bureaucrat component of Government'.

The Armed Forces have always been the 'ultimate power' of the state. During war, the state expects the Armed Forces to win. During peace, the state expects the 'power' of the Armed Forces to be credible enough to deter war. Understandably, there has always been apprehension in the 'civilian' mind that if the Armed Forces are permitted too much power, they might be tempted to take over the state, as indeed has happened in the countries neighbouring India. All systems of governance, therefore, have devised checks and balances to manage this inherent tension between the military and civilian arms of the state. The antiquity of this tension is reflected in innumerable clichés and aphorisms:

"War is too serious a matter to be left to the Generals and the Admirals."

"War is too serious a matter to be left to the politicians and the bureaucrats."

"The resources of the state must be *judiciously* apportioned between 'development' and 'defence'."

"A developing country like India must give priority to the basic needs of the people like drinking water, health care, education etc, even if it be at the cost of defence."

"The Armed Forces should be told how much money they will get and they in turn will tell the Government how much 'defence' that money will buy."

"Defence planning is a long term process. Resources have to be given now to prepare for threats that are anticipated several years in the future."

"Defence planning is based on the capabilities that likely adversaries are developing and not on their intentions. Intentions may change but capabilities do not."

"The security of the state does not depend on military strength alone. It must be inter-laced into a larger perspective of diplomatic, commercial and economic inter-relationships."

The list is endless. Each reflects a facet of the truth. Many reflect serious dilemmas.

In the Indian context, tension has been markedly vexed in two areas:

- *Financial Control.* In the Indian system, the Ministry of Defence and the Service Headquarters operate separately. Plans are made by the Service Headquarters and the Ministry controls the budgets. The view of Service Headquarters has been that Financial 'Advisors' to the Ministry of Defence tend to perform the role of 'Treasury Control'. This results in considerable delays in the sanctioning of vital projects due to endless queries on technical and professional aspects of case projections. In some cases, the very need of projects, already approved, are questioned by Finance (Defence). This is not cost effective as far as defence spending is concerned. Service Headquarters should be 'departments' of the Ministry of Defence, so that decisions are taken jointly and the implementation of approved projects speeded up.

- *Approval of 'Promotions and Appointments' Above a Certain Rank.* The system is that all promotions to the rank of Major General, Rear Admiral, Air Vice Marshal, and above require to be approved by the Ministry. Their appointments can be made only after approval by the Appointments Committee of the Cabinet. Due to manipulative pressures and pulls, this system has led to an increase in the number of senior officers seeking 'Redressal of Grievance', recourse to the courts and consequent adverse publicity.

This chapter discusses the evolution till today of the system of checks and balances that Britain had established to control, from London, the Armed Forces of colonial India and which India inherited at the time of independence. It examines the effect that these checks and balances have had on the Navy.

Financial Control

In the Navy, it is widely lamented that the interminable queries of Finance (Defence) on Naval Headquarters' proposals result in inordinate delays. It is true that in many cases, these delays have been deleterious to naval development – particularly because naval development is of long gestation. However, it is not widely known that this constricting role of Finance was not meant to be malevolent. Its genesis goes back to the rigorous British system of controls on the 'spending of public money'.

The British Legacy

In India, the Finance Division of Defence came into being in 1906. It became part of the Finance Ministry and was known as the Finance (Defence) Division. The Financial Adviser Defence Services (FADS) was one of the most important functionaries of the Finance Ministry. Even though the Commander in Chief India was, after the Viceroy, the second senior most official in India, and even though his mandate came from the War Office in London, defence expenditure in India came firmly under the control of the Ministry of Finance. This control was exercised by the Finance (Defence Division).

The British had laid down certain 'basic canons of financial propriety' and the 'duties of the Financial Adviser' appointed in every Ministry of the Government of India.

The Canons of Financial Propriety

- Every public officer should exercise the same vigilance in respect of expenditure incurred from Government revenue, as a person of ordinary prudence would exercise in respect of the expenditure of his own money.

- No authority should exercise its power of sanctioning expenditure to pass an order, which will be, indirectly or directly, to its own advantage.

- The amount of allowances, such as travelling allowances, granted to meet expenditure of a particular type, should be so regulated that an allowance is not, on the whole, a source of profit to the recipient.

- Government revenues should not be utilised for the benefit of a particular person or section of the community unless:

– The amount of expenditure involved is insignificant; or

– A claim for the amount could be enforced in a court of law; or

– The expenditure is in pursuance of a recognised policy or custom.

Another overarching canon of financial propriety laid down in the Financial Regulations Defence Services 1983 (which derive from the Government of India's General Financial Regulations – GFR) states the "The expenditure should not be more than the occasion demands".

These canons in the GFR were amended in 1989 by the addition of a sixth canon, which brought in the concept of accountability by the person who spends.

The Duty of the Financial Adviser

The financial control exercised by a Financial Adviser and his officers is basically a careful and intelligent scrutiny of all proposals involving expenditure from public funds. The objectives are the safeguarding of the economy, efficiency and propriety in public finance.

Before according financial concurrence to any proposal involving fresh expenditure, it is the duty of a Finance Officer to seek justification of the proposal. *He may even challenge the necessity for spending so much money or on such a scale to secure a given object.* (emphasis added). He asks:

- Whether the proposal is really necessary?

- Whether the same results could not be obtained in some other way with greater economy?

- Whether the expenditure involved is justified in the circumstances?

- Whether individual items are in furtherance of the general Government policy?

- Whether the canons of financial propriety have been observed?

In fact, he asks every question that might be expected from an intelligent taxpayer bent on getting the best value for his money.[1]

Developments 1965-1975

The decade 1965-1975 witnessed substantial naval expansion. At the macro level, the new Leander project and the new Russian acquisitions requiring new production, maintenance, repair, refit and logistic infrastructure involving large expenditure over several years were overseeable by

---

1. This became incongruous with the implementation of the Integrated Finance Concept introduced in 1983 when Finance (Defence) became Defence (Finance), totally integrated with the Defence Ministry and lost the role of 'Treasury Control'.

financially empowered Steering Committees chaired at Secretary level and assisted by the Additional Finance Adviser.

Problems were mainly at the micro level. Sanctions sought for personnel to man critically important small new units like Testing and Tuning Teams, Acceptance Trials Teams, Work Up Teams, Weapon Analysis Teams, Base Maintenance Units, Ship Maintenance Authority etc invariably got so entangled in protracted discussions with Finance (Defence) that the adverse effects of the delays in sanctions began to snowball.

The Government's consistent view was that the Navy should have a 'manpower ceiling' and until this was arrived at, proposals for additional manpower should either 'be met from within sanctioned manpower' or 'by matching savings elsewhere'. The Navy's consistent view was that an expanding service could neither have a manpower ceiling nor find 'matching savings elsewhere.' This *contretemps* was compounded by the financial crisis caused by the sharp rise in oil prices in 1974.

It became Government policy to control spiralling manpower costs by strict control on every proposal for additional manpower. The impact of absorbing the costs of the Pay Commission recommendations and the costs of recurring instalments of 'Additional Dearness Allowance' from 'within existing budget', together with the Government's strict control and the mushrooming requirements generated by the new acquisitions, placed Naval Headquarters in a cleft stick.

In the case of the large projects, the disadvantages of delaying manpower sanctions soon became evident in non-productive cost and time over-runs and Government constituted Steering Committees to monitor these projects and ensure timely sanctions for men and material. The sterling work done by the Leander Project Steering Committee and the Vishakhapatnam Project Steering Committee contributed immeasurably to the eventual success of these projects, albeit delayed by several years. Their deliberations, when seen in retrospect, reveal how harmoniously the Ministry of Defence, the Finance (Defence) Division and Naval Headquarters worked to overcome the complex and conflicting issues involved in large projects spanning decades.

It was at the small project and small manpower sanction level that naval resentments were greatest. Cynicism began to spread about the role of Finance (Defence). Many came to believe that Finance (Defence) could only justify its existence by pruning proposals, that the only reliable statistic that could prove their worth was the quantum of savings effected by their scrutiny and that the only way to obtain a sanction was to deliberately inflate the proposal to allow for the cut that Finance (Defence) would invariably make.

Reminiscence

The new Vishakhapatnam Dockyard was one of the Navy's largest projects that spanned the decades between 1967 and 1990. Rear Admiral CL Bhandari was the first Director General Naval Projects Vishakhapatnam. He recalls:

"From the inception, I felt that the Vizag Project had to be handled in a way different from the normal projects that we pursue on a file. So I approached the Defence Secretary and said, 'This is not the way to progress the Vizag Project – put up a file to the Defence Ministry, then get a sanction from the Finance Ministry and send a file up and down between Vishakhapatnam and Delhi.' He agreed with me and he said, 'All right you go and talk to the Finance Minister, Mr Morarji Desai.' So I went to Mr Seth who was the Additional Secretary. He said, 'Right, go up to the Finance Minister and get it sanctioned.' I said, 'No, he is your *jaatwala*[2], you go.' So ultimately, both of us went and saw the Finance Minister. We explained to Mr Morarji Desai that this was one project, which would neither materialise nor function if we were going to pursue every case on file. Mr Morarji Desai was a very patient listener. He listened to us for five minutes without interruption and in the end he said to me, 'All right Admiral, you have made your case. Push the project there. What financial powers do you want?' I said, 'Sir, I want the normal financial powers of a Chief Engineer of a military project, but I will have a Financial Adviser whose advice I shall abide by, just as is done in the Army. You appoint whoever you like for that.' So he said, 'Right, I will appoint a Financial Adviser and I will go one step further in that you will have the power to over-rule his financial advice if you wish to or if you have to.'

"In my four years there in the Vishakhapatnam Project, I had only one occasion to disagree with the Financial Adviser because the Engineers, the Brigadier and his team and the FA, Mr Sablok, they could not agree on a certain payment to the dredging firm. So I told Mr Sablok, 'Take the file home and come back on Monday and tell me whether you still disagree with the Engineers.' He brought the file back on Monday and said he had no disagreement.

"To my way of thinking, no project worth its salt, if it is viable, will be turned down by the Government, either by Defence or by Finance.

---

2. *Jaatwala* is the Indian expression for 'community'.

"I remember one particular incident when we set up DSP (Navy). I had made a list of the officers and other staff that I needed both for headquarters at Delhi and the staff at Calcutta and Bombay. The file went up and down three times without sanction. In the end I got fed up. I went to the Chief of Material, Rear Admiral Daya Shankar and said, 'I spent two weeks on preparing a case and the Finance Ministry at the level of Assistant Financial Adviser turned it down.' He replied, 'Right, go and talk with the Additional Financial Adviser.' I rang up the Additional FA and asked him for a suitable time when he could give me half an hour without interruption. He said, 'Six o' clock in the evening.' I said, 'Mr Krishnan, have you seen my case?' He replied, 'Yes.' I continued, 'But you have not signed on file.' He responded, 'We never sign.' I asked, 'Do you find anything wrong with my case?' He replied, 'Well, I have been informed that you have asked for too much staff. Can you reduce some?' I said, 'Mr Krishnan, I spent two weeks on this case. Please do not think that the prerogative of saving money lies only with the Ministry of Finance. We too are interested in having viable projects, in saving money for the Government, for the country. You tell me where to reduce and I will reduce. Convince me.' He said, 'Please reduce one peon.' So I reduced one peon and the file went through, without any problem. In my opinion, if you develop a personal rapport with the concerned officers at a high level, all your cases will go through.

"There was another Financial Adviser, Mr Jai Shankar. He was the only officer in the Ministry of Finance (Defence) who had the personal power of sanctioning projects of 10 lakh each. Rupees 10 lakhs was a lot of money in those days and any time we had difficulty, we would go to Mr Jai Shankar and after a chat, the case would be approved.

"I do not contribute to this theory that the Ministry was trying to starve the Navy. If the Navy had got a good case and had done its homework and worked out all the pros and cons, then the case would go through."

Developments 1976 - 1990

In October 1975, the Government introduced the concept of 'Integrated Financial Adviser' to help bring about closer association between the Administrative Ministries and their Financial Advisers and to enable the latter to play a more effective and constructive role. Under this scheme, the Financial Advisers became a part and parcel of the Administrative Ministry concerned and thereby became closely associated with the formulation and implementation of proposals.

This policy was not introduced in the main Ministry of Defence. In May 1976, the Integrated Financial Adviser was introduced in the Department of Defence Supplies and Defence Production, the Defence Research & Development Organisation and the Director General of Quality Assurance. The question of introducing the Integrated Finance System in the Department of Defence continued to be under discussion, presumably on the grounds that it should continue its mandate of examining the necessity aspects of proposals involving the largest expenditure.

In August 1983, it was ultimately decided to introduce the Integrated Finance System. Thereafter, there was complete integration of the former Defence Division of the Finance Ministry with the Defence Ministry.

Whereas earlier, the designation Financial Adviser connoted the restrictive function of 'Treasury Control', the new connotation emphasised the 'Advisory' function by his participation in all high-level committees whenever proposals having a financial bearing were discussed.

The Points of View

A Naval Point of View

Admiral Tahiliani had been Deputy Chief of the Naval Staff (1980-81), Vice Chief of the Naval Staff (1984-85) and, finally, the Chief of the Naval Staff (1984-87). In his article, "In Choppy Waters" in the *Times of India* in January 1999, he wrote:

"Because the Service Headquarters are treated as subordinate formations outside the Ministry of Defence, the Ministry maintains separate files on which the bureaucrats record their recommendations before Service Headquarters proposals are put up to the political leadership for final approval.[3]

---

3. In discussions with Financial Advisers, it emerged that the practice of maintaining separate files was established by the British and has been continued for many reasons, two of which are quite weighty:

- Particularly on large projects involving substantial resources over many years, there would invariably be more than one point of view within the Ministry of Finance. The pros and cons of such internal debates rightly take place on the Finance side's file for subsequent reference; there is no need for this internal debate to be disclosed. It is for this reason that the Finance side's note is usually quite succinct - it states that the proposal has been 'cleared' from the Finance aspect.

- It usually happens that when a major proposal has not been cleared by the Finance side and senior incumbents change, Service Headquarters 'start a new file'. On receiving this 'new file', the Finance side refers to its internal file in which the pros and cons had been recorded that led to the original proposal not being cleared. Parallel files help the Finance side to keep track of gambits.

"Therefore, there is a total and deliberate lack of communication in an institutionalised manner between the uniformed fraternity and the bureaucracy. If the Service Chief happens to enjoy a good equation with the political leadership, his proposals are accepted and this results in a smooth working relationship. If, however, this is not the case, the Service Headquarters concerned has to live with the Ministry's decisions.

"One can cite instances without number where the country's defence preparedness has been seriously and adversely affected because of the complex system which obtains in higher defence management.

"The uniformed fraternity over the years has been pleading that the Service Headquarters become an integral part of the Ministry of Defence. This has been stalled time and again because the politician does not have the time to come to grips with such organisational changes and the bureaucrats are dead against it since they would lose a great deal of their authority and also become accountable, along with their uniformed colleagues, for any failure of defence preparedness in an Integrated Ministry of Defence.

"If we continue to put such serious matters on the backburner, then the country will continue to get sub-optimal defence preparedness out of the investments it makes and reduce the attractiveness of the armed services as a career still further.

"With a total sense of responsibility, I can say that our poor country has not got the optimum in defence preparedness because of our defective higher defence organisation."

A Finance Defence Point of View

Mr AK Ghosh was the Financial Adviser in the Ministry of Defence in the 1990s. His views give some insights into the problem.

"The relevant Appendix in the Defence Services Estimates, brought out every year, clearly states the role of Defence Finance. The following points need to be noted:

– The Finance Division's mandate is to examine scrupulously the need aspect for every proposal sent to it for examination. The necessity aspect has to be examined not only from the point whether it is required or not, but also whether so much is required as proposed or a lesser amount would do.

– The tradition of having parallel files was, to some extent, a corollary of being part of the Finance Ministry and also for allowing adequate scope for proper examination of the proposals at all levels. It should be remembered that the structure of Defence Finance (or Finance Division as it was known before), parallels the structure of the Defence Department to allow examination and clearance at various levels depending on the nature of the case and the amounts involved.

– The Comptroller and Auditor General can always call for files. A convention is followed that Defence Finance files are not called for by administrative departments. One good reason for that is that the Finance Minister's approval is obtained on the parallel file maintained by the Finance Division and the comments of the Finance Ministry are recorded in the files of the Finance Division."

A Ministry of Defence Point of View

Though not necessarily involved in the financial sense, the Ministry of Defence can and does play a role, particularly where contentious issues remain unresolved, even at the level of the Chiefs of Staff Committee. The Navy's proposal for command and control of Maritime Reconnaissance is a case in point.[4]

Mr Govind Narain was the Defence Secretary in 1976. He recalls:

"The control of the air reconnaissance system over the sea was in the hands of the Air Force. The Navy wanted this control to be transferred to itself. This matter had been pending with the Government for nearly 10 years and it could not get resolved. In the 1971 war, all the three wings of the defence Forces played a very significant part and all concerned could observe their respective roles. The performance of the Navy in Karachi was brilliant and the whole country was very impressed.

"Pressure continued to mount from the naval side that they would do even better if their operators felt more confident, if the air recce system was also within their own control. On the other hand, the Air Force pleaded that they had all the airfield arrangements, they had all the know-how, they knew which aircraft from which country could be best for what purpose, and they had the maintenance facilities. All these were very strong points.

"When this matter came repeatedly to the Defence Ministry, what we did was to send the whole problem to the Committee of the three Chiefs of Staff and told them to deliberate afresh on these problems. We gave them two months time to come back to the Defence Ministry with an agreed solution. Whatever agreed solution was found would be acceptable to the Defence Ministry.

---

4. The Maritime Reconnaissance section of the chapter on the Naval Air Arm provides the background for this excerpt, page 100.

"At the end of the two months, no solution was forthcoming. In individual discussions, the three Chiefs expressed their helplessness that no agreement could be reached. We gave them another two months time to reconsider this matter as it was very urgent, very important and required their considered views. But again the matter remained with them for two more months and there was no solution forthcoming. Then we discussed with the three Chiefs that if they could not reach any conclusion, would they like the Defence Ministry to consider the whole matter objectively and find a solution. All the three Chiefs agreed that this should be done.

"Thus the matter came to be considered in the Defence Ministry. We collected the necessary information from the various countries of the world, which had developed a system of maritime reconnaissance. Then we analysed our own position. We went into great details of the points of view of the Navy. We went into great details of the points of view of the Air Force. Then we in the Defence Ministry prepared an elaborate note of 20 or 25 pages, putting down all points of view and reached the conclusion that it would be more prudent if maritime reconnaissance was put under the control of the Navy but the maintenance of the aircraft could be left with the Air Force. Naturally the Navy was jubilant and the Air Force was unhappy, but this solution was accepted by the Defence Minister, by the Political Affairs Committee of the Cabinet and finally by the Prime Minister and was enforced as a Government order."

Promotions and Appointments

The other cause of tension between the Service Headquarters and the Ministry of Defence was senior officers' promotions and appointments. The procedure inherited from the British was that, above a certain rank, the recommendations of every Promotion Board had to be approved by the Ministry of Defence and, as a further 'safeguard', senior appointments had to be approved by the Appointments Committee of the Cabinet. The Service Headquarters' view was that they knew best who should be promoted and, for career progression, where a senior officer was best posted.

In the normal course, the system worked well. Problems arose either when the Ministry found that the recommendation of a Promotion Board was not supportable by the Confidential Reports of a particular officer or when an officer had put up a statutory petition for 'Redressal of Grievance' or when the 'civil' authority, political or bureaucratic, sought to promote another officer, or deny promotion to the aggrieved officer.

In the 1980s, there was a marked increase in the number of cases where senior service officers started seeking the intervention of the courts to redress the injustice that they felt had been done to them. These court cases attracted adverse media attention. In some cases, the judicial process redressed the grievance. In some cases, the judicial process passed strictures on the system.

One outcome of this trend was the appearance in the media of articles by knowledgeable people of how the system actually worked.

The Points of View

A Ministry of Defence Point of View

Excerpt from an article titled "Does Bureaucracy Shackle the Services?" by NN Vohra in the *Sunday Times* of January 1998.

(NN Vohra held high office in the Ministry of Defence as Additional Secretary Defence (1987-89), Secretary Defence Production and Supplies (1989-90) and Defence Secretary (1990-92). He went on to become Home Secretary 1992-94 and then Principal Secretary to the Prime Minister.)

"Among the varied reactions to the Government's decision to remove the Naval Chief is the demand for the urgent 'liberation' of the defence services from the 'bureaucratic control' of the MoD and for the Chiefs to deal directly with the Raksha Mantri (RM) and the Prime Minister (PM). Some of the comments create the impression that the services have been under siege till now. The Defence Minister plans to reorganise the Ministry within a month, keeping in view the recommendations of the Chiefs.

"The Services' Headquarters are large organisations, especially Army Headquarters. They have extensive interface with the MoD, which comprises the Departments of Defence, Defence Production and Defence Research.

"The two major areas of intensive relations concern promotions and appointments above a certain rank, and financial approvals for incurring expenditures beyond prescribed limits. All appointments of Major General, Air Vice Marshal and Rear Admiral rank require the approval of the Appointments Committee of the Cabinet.

"Each service has laid down procedures for the redressal of complaints of its personnel. Those dissatisfied with the outcome of their petitions can move the MoD through a statutory complaint.

"Till about two decades ago, very few personnel filed complaints and fewer still sought relief through the courts which, in most cases, declined to interfere. All this has changed.

"The number of complaints and court cases has increased manifold; the courts are no longer unwilling to intercede; and those moving the courts today include the highest ranking defence officers. Quite obviously, the services have been shedding their centuries-old traditions and honour codes. These trends, reflecting on internal discipline, are beginning to affect the command and control of the Chiefs.

"As regards appointments, the Chiefs have been demanding enhanced authority. While, understandably, they object to their recommendations being modified unilaterally, it is altogether incorrect to suggest that they do not accept the Appointment Committee's authority.

"Our defence services are apolitical and have made vital contributions to maintaining the country's integrity. The functioning of the services is based on high discipline. This vital ingredient must not be eroded at any cost, and indiscipline must be harshly put down irrespective of the rank at which it occurs.

"While considering restructuring, the Defence Minister would need to take a frontal view about the Ministry's future role and responsibility.

"The services are extremely rank conscious. If, in the revised set up, the Defence Secretary is still required to play a role, it would be necessary to upgrade his position to resolve the unwillingness of the Chiefs to deal with a functionary junior to them. The working of the defence apparatus, so vital to national security, must not be subjected to frequent changes."

Excerpt from NN Vohra's article 'Between the Lines' in the *Indian Express* of 24 December 1998.

"In the Navy, and in the Air Force and Army, the claims for promotion of all officers in a given zone of seniority are examined by authorised Selection Boards (SBs). As per the laid down procedure, lists of officers to be appointed to General rank and above, in each service are evolved by SBs chaired by the Service Chiefs. Such lists, along with the dossiers of the officers considered by the SB, are forwarded to the Ministry of Defence (MoD). The Defence Secretary examines the recommendations and submits them to the Raksha Mantri (RM) for approval, where after the case is forwarded to the Appointments Committee of the Cabinet (ACC) for final approval.

"In the event of the Defence Secretary being unable to endorse one or more of the officers recommended for rejection / promotion, the matter is discussed by him with the Chief and resolved.

"In case this does not happen, the case is put up to the RM who takes a view after hearing both sides.

"After the ACC has accorded approval, the list of officers found fit or unfit to be elevated to the higher rank is notified.

"Based on the number of vacancies arising in the ensuing 6 to 12 months, the Chief forwards his recommendations to the MoD, suggesting specific appointments for each of the officers proposed to be promoted. While evolving his proposals, the Chief considers the seniority of the select officers under view, their career profiles and professional and personal qualities. After examination at Defence Secretary's level and clearance by RM, the proposals are forwarded for ACC approval.

"In case the Defence Secretary / RM finds difficulty in endorsing a particular proposal, the same procedure is followed as earlier described in regard to the approval of select lists recommended by the Chiefs.

"It is also relevant to note that as per the Transfer of Business Rules of the Government of India 1964, all appointments of Major Generals, Air Vice Marshals and Rear Admirals (equivalent to Joint Secretary on the civil side) and above can be made only with the ACC's approval. The Cabinet Secretary is responsible for submitting cases to the ACC.

"For years, the aforesaid procedure has been followed for seeking approval to senior appointments in the three services. It is relevant to record that the process followed has been essentially founded in not tinkering with the judgment of the concerned Chief and in cases of disagreement, resolving the issue through discussions with the Chief or over-ruling his view.

"The Chief's recommendations in regard to senior appointments in the services are invariably sustained. Situations have, however, arisen from time to time, when the MoD is compelled to disagree with a particular recommendation.

"Disciplined thought and conduct is what distinguishes the Defence Services from all others. If this most vital element of the national security apparatus is to continue to enjoy the most honoured position in the entire hierarchy of government, it would be necessary that any deviation from the norm is dealt with severely, irrespective of rank."

A Presidential Point of View

Excerpt from *My Presidential Years* by R Venkataraman (Finance Minister 1980-82, Defence Minister 1982-84,

Vice President 1984-87, and President of India 1987-92, Pages 452 et seq).

"The choice of the Chiefs of the Army, Navy and Air Force Staff is made by the government after assessment of their service records by the Defence Minister and the Prime Minister. Admiral Nadkarni, Chief of the Naval Staff, was to retire on November 30, 1990. Earlier, Nadkarni had extended the services of Vice Admiral Jain who was retiring before the CNS so that he would be eligible for consideration for the post of Admiral when time for choice came. This was nothing new. Similar action had been taken in the case of Air Marshal Katre and Vice Admiral Tahiliani. The natural expectation was that Vice Admiral Jain might be promoted as CNS over the next senior, Vice Admiral Ramdas.

"Prime Minister VP Singh had discussed the matter with me and said that he preferred Vice Admiral Ramdas for the post of Chief. I had told VP Singh that I had no personal preferences and that he could communicate his proposal for my approval. On receipt of the file, I perused the records and approved it.

"After Chandra Shekhar became Prime Minister, he asked me whether the appointment of Ramdas could be reconsidered. He also sent Defence Secretary Vohra to explain the reasons to me. I told the Defence Secretary that orders for the appointment of Ramdas had already been issued and gazetted and any attempt to overturn the decision, except on very serious charges of fraud, misrepresentation or suppression of material facts, would seriously damage the morale of the services. I also expressed doubt whether an order already passed could be revoked. Vohra enquired if Nadkarni could be given an extension for one month and the matter reviewed. I replied that it would set a bad precedent and every Chief of Staff would try to wrangle an extension in future. I also felt that a Chief on extension would suffer a serious loss of prestige as the officers and men would look upon him as a lame duck chief.

"On 27th November two Cabinet ministers called on me and discussed this issue. I explained to them the need to maintain high standards of discipline in the Armed Forces and also the sanctity of a decision. I cautioned them that there would be public suspicion of political interference if the appointment were changed with a change in government.

"On 28th November I hosted a dinner for the retiring Chief. As usual, I invited the CNS-designate, all Chiefs of Staff and retired Chiefs resident in Delhi. When my staff asked whether there would be any embarrassment in inviting Ramdas, I said that as long as his appointment

remained in force, he was entitled to attend. Ramdas took over as Chief of the Naval Staff on 30th November and except for stray references in the Press, the matter died out."

Civil Service Points of View

These views are of Senior Civil Servants who have held high office in the Ministry of Defence and who did not wish to be quoted.

- "The sad truth is that far too many Senior Officers have their eyes fixed on how to promote their own prospects for the next higher job, by prejudicing the chances of their contenders. It is astonishing how many allegations are received by MoD to queer the pitch of peer groups for criteria appointments. Inputs from the intelligence agencies are primarily negative feedback. The Defence Secretary does not do the empanelling of names for Service Chief. Only the RM, if he considers it necessary and then only informally, depending on the personalities involved and their inter-personal equations, seeks the views of the Chiefs regarding their successors."

- "The civil servants of the MoD are essentially a buffer between the 'political deciders' and the 'service proposers'. By training and by experience, civil servants take an overall, national view of each proposal.

  "As regards keeping a watchful eye on the activities of the Armed Forces, it is a matter of abundant caution to forestall anything untoward rather than forestall a coup.

  "The expectation that 'integrating' Service Headquarters with the MoD will improve their leverage in swifter decision-making or obtaining higher budget allocations is, by and large, wishful thinking. Those elements of Service Headquarters that do integrate with the MoD as a result of the post Kargil reforms will either become 'buffers' themselves or become an 'additional input'.

- "MoD's role is to help the Services, to the extent possible, to get what they seek, in terms of budget and in terms of inductions, on the best possible financial terms and to intermediate with other ministries, state governments and governments of other countries.

  "*There is a feeling that Senior Reviewing Officers, who may not have seen an officer at close quarters in that particular assignment, can write off an officer's career by downgrading Initiating Officer's and Reviewing Officer's gradings or penning remarks of faint praise. The MoD's role in such cases is vital and essential for balancing out, particularly in the case of very senior officers. (emphasis added)*

  "I fear that rank and file in services and junior officers come to see MoD as an adversary, the Babus of little understanding and lot of clout, slow, indifferent, corrupt and ignorant. In Finance terms, they often feel that funds for security take precedence over all else. At higher levels, the services refer to integration (as elsewhere). The down side is that people are people. The Babu and the service officer are prone to be as honest / dishonest, efficient / inefficient as the other. The Babu is trained to battle rules / politics / files. By integrating officers of the Army, Navy and Air Headquarters with MoD, the service officer will also turn into a Babu."

Views of Chiefs of the Naval Staff

Admiral Nadkarni was the Chief of Personnel (1983-85), Vice Chief of the Naval Staff (1986-87) and Chief of the Naval Staff (1987-90). In his article 'Armed Forces and Civil Service' in the *Hindustan Times* in January 1999, he stated:

"Over the years, India's Armed Forces have created an aura about themselves. It is generally believed that some of the ills which pervade the civilian administration have not penetrated the services, that everything is efficient, fair and square. This is a myth. Servicemen are as susceptible to being persuaded by a bit of sycophancy as civilians.

"Understandably, every officer has ambitions to reach the highest rung in the promotion ladder of his service. In that quest, he expects justice and fairness from his seniors. A fair and just system of promotions and appointments has to be built around well-publicised rules and guidelines.

"The present system in Service Headquarters lacks both transparency and a rigid adherence to rules. For many years now, the Government has tried to persuade Service Headquarters to frame a set of rules for promotion and appointments at the senior level. The Services have always resisted this on the grounds that rigid rules will erode the flexibility, which is necessary for making suitable placements for the benefit of the Service. Inevitably, flexibility has also resulted in arbitrariness and cronyism.

"Every senior officer who is cleared for promotion to the higher rank should be considered fit for each and every appointment in that rank. If certain appointments in the same rank such as Principal Staff Officers (in Service Headquarters) Corps Commanders (in the field) etc. are considered superior to others, then well-publicised rules and guidelines must be laid down for those.

"Above all, the Defence Ministry must acknowledge the right of the Chief to recommend appointments.

"A Chief's right to have his own team has to be tempered with equity and justice. The Ministry or the Government should have the right to approve or reject the Service recommendations.

"In the past, the Defence Ministry has got into the habit of asking for a panel of names for certain appointments. The Service Headquarters normally overcome this obstruction by forwarding the names of two or three obviously unsuitable candidates along with their main choice. The practice of asking for a panel of names should be avoided as it then makes the Defence Ministry the selector, a task, which by law, belongs to the Service Headquarters.

"If the Government, for any reason, decides not to approve the recommendations of the Chief, it should ask for another name to be submitted until finally a recommendation of the Chief is accepted. Neither the Appointments Committee of the Cabinet nor the Defence Ministry can take upon itself the task of making service appointments or promotions."

In a *Times of India* article on 24 May 1999 'For an Open Enquiry', Admiral Tahiliani wrote:

"The biggest area of political interference arises in the area of promotions and appointments of senior officers. We have seen polite arm-twisting where the Service Headquarters have acquiesced to the wishes of their political masters, even when these were at variance with their professional judgment. These led to many aggrieved officers resorting to legal action for redressal of grievances."

The Services Viewpoint

From what has been articulated in the public domain, the gist of the Services Headquarters viewpoint could be summarised as follows:

- Include the services in the security-related decision making loop.
- Greater authority in financial matters.
- Remedy the tremendous imbalance in the accountability and responsibility of the Chiefs.
- Autonomy in personnel matters.
- Regulate its revenue expenditure without interference from the MoD

Developments After 1990

The severe drought after 1986 was followed by a prolonged period of financial stringency. This led in early 1990 to the constitution of the Committee on Defence Expenditure (CDE) headed by Mr Arun Singh who had been the Minister of State for Defence under Prime Minister Rajiv Gandhi from 1985 to 1987. The Committee forwarded its report in 1992. One of its many recommendations concerned delegation and decentralisation of financial powers so that approval for buying spares did not have to run through a succession of hurdles. It was not logical that the accountability for procurement of equipment for execution of tasks should rest with one person whilst financial control rested with somebody else. It recommended that the Chiefs of the three services should be empowered to procure the equipment required for the execution of their tasks, whilst remaining within their overall budgetary allocations.

Meanwhile, in 1989, Naval Headquarters had forwarded to the Controller General of Defence Accounts a proposal suggesting a model to decentralise the management of Revenue Expenditure, which comprised more than seventy per cent of the budget. This led to the appointment of a Task Force.[5] Based on the report of this Task Force on Budgetary Centres, submitted to the Government in April 1992, the Government approved the concept of Authority and Responsibility Centres with clear-cut budgetary allocation (Budget Centres) for achieving laid down targets.

Having initiated the suggestion, the Navy took the lead. The Navy introduced the 'New Management Strategy' (NMS) in the field of Maintenance on 4 October 1993 and in the field of Logistics on 23 November 1994. Its aim was to enhance 'value for money' in revenue expenditure by establishing a clear linkage between resources utilised and outputs achieved.

---

5. The Task Force was headed by AK Ghosh as Officer on Special Duty. He later became Financial Adviser Defence Services and participated in the structuring of the New Management Strategy (NMS).

43

Changes In NHQ Organisation

Preamble

Soon after independence in 1947, the staff at Naval Head-quarters (NHQ), under the Chief of Naval Staff (CNS), was grouped into five 'Branches' under five Principal Staff Officers (PSOs). These were the Chief of Staff/Deputy C-in-C, Chief of Personnel (COP), Chief of Material (COM), Chief of Administration and Chief of Naval Aviation (CONA).

The 1955 Reorganisation

The first major re-organisation of NHQ after independence took place in 1955. The Chief of Staff/Deputy C-in-C was re-designated Deputy Chief of Naval Staff (DCNS). The Chief of Administration was abolished and its Directorates redistributed between the Staff, Personnel and Material Branches.

In 1959, DCNS was upgraded to Rear Admiral. This functioned satisfactorily until 1961, when the combined impact began to be felt of growth, modernisation and self-sufficiency.

NHQ After the 1962 Reorganisation

PSO	Directorates under PSO
DCNS (Rear Adm)	Operations, Intelligence, Signals, Plans, Weapons Policy & Tactics, Chief Hydrographer, Civil Engineering (Works).
CONA (Commodore)	Air Staff, Air Material.
COP (Commodore)	Personnel Services, Training, Education, Medical Services, Legal (JAG), Supply Branch, Clothing & Victualling, Civilian Personnel.
COM (Commodore)	Marine Engineering, Electrical Engineering, Weapons & Equipment, Fleet Maintenance, Stores, Armament Supply, Armament Inspection, Naval Construction, Scientific Research,
Naval Secretary (Captain)	Administration.

Changes Between 1965 and 1968

In 1965, the Chief of Personnel and the Chief of Material were upgraded in rank to Rear Admiral.

The Defence Plan 1966-71 had accepted the Navy's expansion programme and increase in manpower. With greater emphasis on self-sufficiency in the indigenous production of ships, weapons and ammunition, the nature and scope of the workload in NHQ began to increase.

In 1966, the Director of the Submarine Arm was sanctioned and placed under the Deputy Chief of the Naval Staff.

In 1967, the Deputy Chief of Naval Staff was re-designated as Vice Chief of the Naval Staff (VCNS), and the Chief of Naval Aviation was re-designated as Assistant Chief of the Naval Staff (ACNS).

In 1968, concurrently with the arrival of the first submarine in India, the CNS was upgraded in rank to Admiral. Also in 1968, two new Directorates were sanctioned. The Director of Acquisition Project, dealing with the acquisitions from the Soviet Union and elsewhere, was placed under the VCNS. The Director of Leander Project dealing with the indigenous construction of the Leander class frigates was placed under the COM.

In 1969, the Frigate Cell of Directorate of Naval Construction became Directorate of Leander Project.

By 1969, it became clear that the division of responsibilities and the workload needed to be rationalised. The objectives were:

- To remedy the imbalance in distribution of responsibilities between the VCNS, COP, COM and the ACNS, and the increasing overload on all of them as a result of the Navy's development.

- To make the appointment of VCNS tenable by a Vice Admiral so as to better supervise and coordinate work in NHQ and to enable a choice between two Vice Admirals (FOCINCWEST and VCNS) when considering a successor to a retiring CNS.

- To create a new Logistics Branch under a Chief of Logistics (COL) in the rank of Rear Admiral to deal with all matters concerning Stores, Clothing, Victualling, Supply and Civilian Personnel.

- To re-designate the ACNS as DCNS in the rank of Rear Admiral.
- To relieve the overload of the Directorate of Personnel Services, by splitting it into two directorates – 'Personnel' and 'Personal Services'.

Except for the re-designation of the ACNS as DCNS, the other objectives were met in the 1969 Reorganisation.

NHQ After the 1969 Reorganisation

PSO	Directorates Under PSO
VCNS (Vice Adm)	Operations, Plans, Weapons Policy & Tactics, Intelligence, Signals, Chief Hydrographer, Scientific Advisor (R&D), Naval Secretary.
ACNS (Commodore)	Air Staff, Air Material, Submarines, Acquisition Project, Meteorology.
COP (Rear Adm)	Personnel, Personal Services, Training, Education, Medical Services, Legal (JAG).
COM (Rear Adm)	Fleet Maintenance, Marine Engineering, Electrical Engineering, Weapons & Equipment, Armament Inspection, Naval Design, Naval Construction, Leander Project.
COL (Rear Adm)	Supply Branch, Stores, Clothing & Victualling, Armament Supply, Civilian Personnel, Civil Engineering (Works).

Changes Between 1970 and 1972

In 1970, a study was carried out to reorganise NHQ on functional lines:

- Whether the Staff Branch should comprise of Executive officers only or should Technical officers also participate in taking staff decisions?
- Should the Air and Submarine Arms be separate branches?
- Should Engineering and other specialist directorates look after 'Training' in their respective fields or should these branches be represented in the Directorate of Naval Training?

The factors taken into account in the 1972 Reorganisation were:

- The need to strengthen the policy-making apparatus to respond quickly to situations and also allow larger initiative to the Commands.
- The organisational lessons learnt during the conflict with Pakistan in December 1971.

- The growth and diversification of sea going forces and the doubling of manpower since 1962.
- The expansion and modernisation of maintenance facilities.
- The updating and enlarging of training complexes.
- The establishment of the Submarine Arm.
- The large variety of weapons and missiles, computerised fire control systems, communication and electronic warfare systems.
- The acquisition of sophisticated naval aircraft.
- The induction of gas turbine propulsion.
- The acquisition of ships from Russia with their new philosophies and practices in the fields of maintenance, logistics and training, all of which were substantially different, distinct and irreconcilable with extant practices.
- The march towards self sufficiency and the indigenous construction programme ranging from 200 tonne Seaward Defence Boats and Landing Craft to 2,000 tonne Survey Vessels and the 3,000 tonne Leander class frigates.

The salient features of the 1972 Reorganisation were:

- The creation of the Deputy Chief of the Naval Staff (DCNS) in the rank of Rear Admiral, responsible for 'Operations' and the associated disciplines of intelligence and signals, leaving VCNS to concentrate on the policy and planning functions of the Staff Branch.
- The upgradation in rank of Chief of Personnel and Chief of Material to Vice Admiral.
- The creation of three Assistant Principal Staff Officers (APSOs) in the rank of Rear Admiral namely Assistant Chief of the Naval Staff (Policy and Plans) (ACNS P&P), Assistant Chief of Personnel (ACOP) and Assistant Chief of Material (ACOM).
- The distribution and organisation of Directorates was rationalised, separating wherever necessary the problems of Russian and Western acquisitions. In 1970, the Design Cell of Directorate of Naval Construction became Directorate of Naval Design under COM. The 'Acquisition' functions of the Directorate of Naval Construction were entrusted to the Directorate of Acquisition Projects. The Director of Stores was renamed Director of Logistic Support.

NHQ After the 1972 Reorganisation			
PSO	Directorates under PSO	APSO	Directorates under APSO
VCNS (Vice Adm)	Combat Policy & Tactics Chief Hydrographer Staff Duties Scientific Advisor	ACNS(P&P) (Rear Adm)	Plans Civil Engineering (Works) Acquisition Projects
DCNS (Rear Adm)	Operations, Intelligence, Signals Air Staff, Air Material Submarines		
COP (Vice Adm)	Training, Medical, Legal Education & Meteorology	ACOP (Rear Adm)	Personnel, Personal Services Civilian Personnel
COM (Vice Adm)	Naval Design Leander Project Dockyards & Fleet Maintenance	ACOM (Rear Adm)	Marine Engineering Electrical Engineering Weapons & Equipment Naval Construction
COL (Rear Adm)	Supply Branch Logistic Support, Clothing & Victualling Armament Supply, Armament Inspection		

Changes Between 1972 and 1978

The Directorate of Management Services (DOMS) was created in 1974 and placed under ACNS (P&P). A year later, in 1975, it was placed directly under the VCNS.

By the mid 1970s, the Navy's organisation was experiencing problems in coping with the tempo of acquisitions. There was avoidable duplication in some areas, while other areas remained understaffed. There was constant pressure for more manpower. A study was initiated whether the organisation could be rationalised and, to the extent possible, not only enable staffing requirements to be met within existing manpower resources but also provide for better accountability.

This study resulted in two major conclusions:

- The Supply and Executive Branches should be merged. Junior officers of the Supply Branch could volunteer to convert to the Executive Branch and those found fit would undergo conversion courses. During the transition, officers of the Supply Branch in ships and establishments would be withdrawn without any relief. As regards Supply Branch sailors, the adoption of 'combat post manning' on board ships compelled reorganisation for economy in manpower to be achieved.

- The 'Logistics' function, which had been set up under a different PSO, would be more functional if amalgamated with the Material and Personnel branches. This would result in a more streamlined organisation at NHQ. And,

with the logistic functions coming under the Chief of Material, establish tighter material control of refits.

NHQ's recommendations were approved in 1977 and these formed the basis for the next major reorganisation of NHQ in 1978.

The salient features of the 1978 Reorganisation were:

- On the merger of the Supply Branch with the General List officer cadres of the Executive Branch on 1 January 1978, the support and maintenance functions of the Navy were placed under the COM. All 'Personnel' functions were regrouped under the COP. With the abolition of the COL, the number of Principal Staff Officers (PSOs) reduced from 5 to 4 – VCNS, DCNS, COP and COM under whom there were the three APSOs – ACNS, ACOP and ACOM. With the reduction of one PSO at NHQ (the COL), Southern Naval Area was upgraded to Southern Naval Command under a Vice Admiral.

- The Directorates of Logistic Support and Armament Supply under an ACOM (Logsitics) were placed under the COM for better coordination of all aspects of stores and machinery under one branch.

- The Directorates of Clothing and Victualling were merged into the Director of Supplies and placed under the COP as both functions were related to personnel.

- The Director of Naval Armament Inspection was placed under the VCNS for closer supervision of munitions.

- The Director of Staff Duties was redesignated as Director of Administration.

NHQ After the 1978 Reorganisation

PSO	Directorates under PSO	APSO	Directorates under APSO
VCNS (Vice Adm)	Combat Policy & Tactics Chief Hydrographer Administration Armament Inspection Management Services Scientific Research	ACNS(P&P) (Rear Adm)	Plans Civil Engineering (Works) Acquisitions
DCNS (Rear Adm)	Operations, Intelligence, Signals Air Staff, Air Material Submarines		
COP (Vice Adm)	Training, Medical, Legal Education, Meteorology Supplies	ACOP (Rear Adm)	Personnel Personal Services Civilian Personnel
COM (Vice Adm)	Dockyards Fleet Maintenance Leander Project Naval Design	ACOM (Rear Adm)	Marine Engineering Electrical Engineering Weapons & Equipment Naval Construction
		ACOM (Logistics) (Rear Adm)	Logistic Support Armament Supply

Changes Between 1979 and 1984

The salient features of the 1984 Reorganisation were:

- Implementation of the First Cadre Review. The rank up-gradations were of DCNS from Rear Admiral to Vice Admiral, and four NHQ Directors to the rank of Rear Admiral – DNO to ACNS (Operations), DNAS to ACNS (Air), DME to ACOM (Dockyards & Refits) (D&R), DEE to ACOM (Systems). The new Directorate was Directorate of Value Engineering (DVE).

- DLP renamed DNSP in 1980.

- Directorate of Harrier Project (DHP) established in November 1980 to deal with the induction of the new Sea Harriers. This directorate was renamed as Directorate of Aircraft Acquisition (DAA) in 1983 to deal also with the induction of the new Seaking Mk 42 B ASW helicopters.

- Directorate of the SSK Submarine construction project was established in 1982 under a Project Director of the rank of Rear Admiral.

- Directorate of Naval Oceanology and Meteorology (DNOM) established in June 1982 to deal with Oceanography, Meteorology, Antarctica expeditions and associated subjects.

- Directorate of Diving and Under Sea Activities (DOD) established in May 1983.

- In October 1983, the Controllerate of Warship Production and Acquisition was established under VCNS to integrate and coordinate the various activities of shipbuilding and ship acquisition at NHQ. The Director of Acquisition Project and the Director of Naval Ship Production were grouped under a Rear Admiral ACWPA.

- In October 1984, a new 'Logistics Branch' was created. At NHQ, the Chief of Logistics & Administration (COLA), created as a PSO in Phase 1 of the Second Cadre Review in the rank of Vice Admiral, was assisted by the erstwhile ACOM Logistics, now redesignated as ACOL. The Directorates placed under the new Logistic Branch were the Directorate of Logistic Support (DLS), the Directorate of Supply (DOS), the Directorate of Administration (DOA), the Directorate of Management Services (DOMS), the Directorate of Works (DW), the Directorate of Armament Supply (DAS) and the Directorate of Transport (DOT) when formed.

NHQ After the 1984 Reorganisation

PSO	Directorates Under PSO	APSO	Directorates Under APSO
VCNS (Vice Adm)	Combat Policy & Tactics Chief Hydrographer(R Adm) Dir SSK Project (R Adm) Armament Inspection Scientific Research	ACNS(P&P) (Rear Adm) ACWPA (Rear Adm)	Plans Acquisitions Ship Production
DCNS (Vice Adm)	Intelligence, Signals Submarines, Diving Oceanology & Meteorology	ACNS (Ops) (Rear Adm)	Operations

PSO		APSO	
		ACNS (Air) (Rear Adm)	Air Staff, Air Material Air Acquisitions
COP (Vice Adm)	Training, Medical, Legal Education,	ACOP (Rear Adm)	Personnel Personal Services Civilian Personnel
COM (Vice Adm)		ACOM (Systems) (Rear Adm)	Marine Engineering Electrical Engineering Weapons & Equipment Naval Construction
		ACOM (D&R) (Rear Adm)	Dockyards Fleet Maintenance Value Engineering
		DGND (Rear Adm)	Naval Design
COLA (Vice Adm)	Supply Branch Administration Civil Engineering (Works) Transport Management Services	ACOL (Rear Adm)	Logistic Support Armament Supply

Changes Between 1984 and 1986

- In February 1985, the Directorate of Ship Systems Development (DSSD) was created under the VCNS to deal with the training of personnel for, and the lease of a nuclear propelled submarine from Russia. In May 1985, he was placed under the ACWPA.

- On 1 April 1985, in accordance with Phase II of the Second Cadre Review:

  – The Controller of Warship Production & Acquisitions (CWPA) was created in the rank of Vice Admiral and placed under VCNS.

  – The Director of Civilian Personnel was upgraded to ACOP (Civilians) in the rank of Rear Admiral.

- In May 1985, the Directorate of the SSK Project and the Directorate General of Naval Design were placed under CWPA.

- In July 1985, Directorate of Financial Planning (Non Public Funds) – DFP (NPF) was created under COP for profitable investment of non-public funds.

- In September 1985, the Directorate of Naval Construction was renamed as the Directorate of Naval Architecture.

- In October 1985, sanction was accorded for Project Seabird (the Third Naval Base at Karwar) to be headed by a Rear Admiral; he was placed under VCNS.

  In November 1985, the Directorate of Combat Policy and Tactics was split. The renamed Directorate of Staff Requirements (DSR) was placed under ACNS (P&P). A new Directorate of Tactics was created in April 1986 and placed under DCNS.

- In July 1986, as part of the restructuring of the Navy and NHQ organisation, the logistics function was restored to the Material Branch. The Chief of Logistics was re-designated as Controller of Logistic Support under the COM.

NHQ After the 1986 Reorganisation

PSO	Controllerates/Directorates	APSO	Directorates
VCNS (Vice Adm) Administration	Chief Hydrographer (R Adm) Project Seabird (R Adm)	ACNS(P&P) (Rear Adm) Works	Plans Staff Requirements
	Armament Inspection SA to CNS		
	CWPA (Controller Of Warship Production & Acquisition) (Vice Adm)		

	Contracts Ship Production Equipment	ACWPA/SSK (Rear Adm)	Ship Acquisition Submarine Acquisition Ship Systems Dev (SSD)
		DGND (Rear Adm)	Naval Design
DCNS (Vice Adm)	Intelligence Signals	ACNS (Ops) (Rear Adm)	Operations Submarine Operations Tactics Diving Oceanology & Meteorology
		ACNS (Air) (Rear Adm)	Air Staff Air Material Air Acquisitions
COP (Vice Adm)	DMS Navy (Surg Rear Adm) NSEC Judge Advocate General	ACOP (CP) (Career Planning) (Rear Adm)	Personnel Manpower Planning Training Education
		ACOP (PC) (Personnel & Conditions) (Rear Adm)	Personal Services Pay & Allowances Non Public Funds
		ACOP (Civ) (Rear Adm)	Civilian Personnel
COM (Vice Adm)		ACOM (Systems) (Rear Adm)	Marine Engineering Electrical Engineering Weapons & Equipment Management Services Value Engineering
		ACOM (D&R) (Rear Adm)	Dockyards & Tech Services Refits & Maintenance Naval Architecture
CLS Controller of Logistic Support (Vice Adm)		ACLS (Rear Adm)	Logistic Support Armament Supply Transport Clothing & Victualling

Changes Between 1986 and 1990

- In May 1986, the Submarine Design Group was formed under the DGND.

- In November 1986, the CAIO Rule Writing Group was shifted from DSR to DOT.

- In January 1987, the concept of Branch 'Parent Directorates' was dispensed with in NHQ's Charters of Duties.

- In February 1987, the Director of Medical Services (Navy) was upgraded to Director General of Medical Services (Navy) in the rank of Surgeon Vice Admiral.

- From March 1987 onwards, the dormant Directorate of Equipment under CWPA was merged with the Directorate of Contracts also under CWPA.

- In April 1987, the Directorate of Systems Applications was established under DCNS for all work on satellite and space applications.

- On 14 July 1987, the Director of Armament Supply was upgraded to APSO status as Director General of Armament Supply.

- In June 1989, the Directorate of Naval Signals was shifted from being under DCNS to being under ACNS (Ops).

NHQ Organisation in 1990

PSO	Controllerates/Directorates	APSO	Directorates
VCNS (Vice Adm)	Chief Hydrographer (R Adm) Project Seabird (R Adm)	ACNS(P&P) (Rear Adm)	Plans Staff Requirements
	Administration Armament Inspection SA to CNS		Works Naval Academy
	CWPA (Controller of Warship Production & Acquisition) (Vice Adm)		
	Contracts & Equipment Ship Production	ACWPA/SSK (Rear Adm)	Ship Acquisition Submarine Acquisition Ship Systems Dev (SSD)
		DGND (Rear Adm)	Naval Design (Construction) Naval Design (Engineering) Naval Design (Electrical) Submarine Design Group
DCNS (Vice Adm)	Submarine Arm Intelligence	ACNS (Ops) (Rear Adm)	Operations Submarine Operations
	Systems Applications		Signals Tactics Diving Oceanology & Meteorology
		ACNS (Air) (Rear Adm)	Air Staff Air Material Air Acquisitions
COP (Vice Adm)	DGMS Navy (Surg Vice Adm) NSEC Judge Advocate General	ACOP (CP) (Career Planning) (Rear Adm)	Personnel Manpower Planning Training Education
		ACOP (PC) (Personnel & Conditions) (Rear Adm)	Personal Services Pay & Allowances Non Public Funds
		ACOP (Civ) (Rear Adm)	Civilian Personnel
COM (Vice Adm)		ACOM(Systems) (Rear Adm)	Marine Engineering Electrical Engineering Weapon & Equipment Management Services Value Engineering
		ACOM (D & R) (Rear Adm)	Dockyards & Tech Services Fleet Refits & Maintenance Naval Architecture
	CLS Controller of Logistic Support (Vice Adm)		
		ACLS (Rear Adm)	Logistic Support Clothing & Victualling Transport
		DGAS (Rear Adm equiv)	Armament Supply

44

Changes In Command And Control Structure

Preamble

Prior to and during the 1965 Indo-Pakistan War, the four Naval Operational and Administrative Authorities were Flag Officer Commanding Indian Fleet (FOCIF), Flag Officer Bombay (FOB), Commodore Cochin (COMCHIN) and Commodore East (COMEAST).

FOCIF was senior to FOB and was responsible directly to Naval Headquarters (NHQ) for the Fleet's activities and its operations during war.

Lessons were learnt during the 1965 war. It had been decided also to base the new acquisitions from Russia at Vishakhapatnam.

Accordingly, proposals were initiated in January 1966 to re-designate the nomenclature and responsibilities of the four authorities, so that, in war, as operational authorities, they would be directly responsible for the conduct of maritime operations and the operational control of maritime forces in their respective sea areas.

In 1967, NHQ's plans envisaged:

- For FOCIF:
  - Additional destroyers as part of the Fleet.
- For Bombay:
  - Phase II of the Naval Dockyard Expansion Plan.
  - Improvement of Port Defence Facilities.
  - Expansion of the Barracks and basing of additional ships.
  - Setting up NOIC Kathiawar and defences on that coast.
- For Cochin:
  - Expansion of the Base Repair Organisation (BRO).
  - Construction of a new wharf and additional berthing facilities.
  - Basing of minesweepers and patrol craft.
  - Establishment of Commodore Sea Training.

- Increase in training commitments and expansion of training facilities Inclusion of the NOIC Goa area under COMCHIN.
- For Vizag:
  - Establishment of a submarine base and basing of submarines, basing of Petyas, submarine depot ship, LSTs, LCUs, minesweepers, patrol boats, etc.
  - Establishment of a new major Dockyard.
  - Establishment of a Type Training School for the Russian ships and submarines.
  - Expansion of Vizag W/T for submarine communications.
- For the A&N:
  - Advance Base at Port Blair.
  - Training Base for the Andaman garrison.
- For Paradip:
  - Expanded Boys Training Establishment.
- For Haldia:
  - Base Facilities.

The Reoganisation of 1968

After dovetailing with other concurrent proposals for rationalisation and upgradation, the following re-organisation came into effect on 1 March 1968:

- The Flag Officer Bombay (FOB) who had hitherto been junior to the Flag Officer Commanding Indian Fleet (FOCIF) was re-designated as Flag Officer Commanding in Chief Western Naval Command (FOCINCWEST) and upgraded in rank to Vice Admiral.

- The Flag Officer Commanding Indian Fleet (FOCIF) was subordinated to the Flag Officer Commanding in Chief Western Naval Command (FOCINCWEST). Instead of 'all front line ships', including those undergoing refit being under FOCIF, 'only operational ships' as allotted by FOCINCWEST would be under the Flag Officer Commanding Western Fleet (FOCWEF).

The non-operational Fleet ships undergoing refit in Bombay Dockyard would be administered directly by FOCINCWEST.

- In anticipation of the formation of the Eastern Fleet under the Flag Officer Commanding Eastern Fleet (FOCEF) after the arrival of the ships and submarines from Russia, the Commodore East Coast (COMEAST) at Vishakhapatnam was re-designated as Flag Officer Commanding in Chief Eastern Naval Command (FOCINCEAST) in the rank of Rear Admiral.

- Commodore in Charge Cochin (COMCHIN) was re-designated as Commodore Commanding Southern Naval Area (COMSOUTH).

- All ships, aircraft, dockyard and logistics support facilities were placed directly under the respective administrative and operational control of FOCINCWEST, FOCINCEAST and COMSOUTH.

In 1970, COMSOUTH was upgraded to the rank of Rear Admiral and re-designated as Flag Officer Commanding Southern Naval Area (FOCSOUTH).

In 1971, the Eastern Fleet was constituted under FOCEF.

The Command and Control Structure in 1975

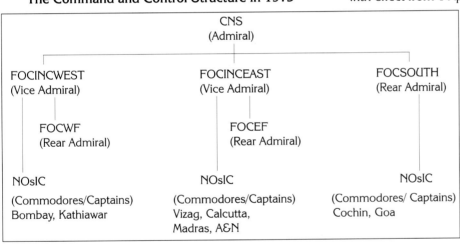

Changes in Command and Control After 1975

In 1977:

- FOCSOUTH was upgraded to the rank of Vice Admiral and re-designated as Flag Officer Commanding in Chief Southern Naval Command (FOCINCSOUTH).

- In Goa, there was a substantial increase in the Air Arm assets resulting from the basing there of:

  – Super Constellation maritime patrol aircraft taken over from the Air Force; and

– The IL 38 Maritime Patrol and Anti Submarine Warfare (MRASW) aircraft acquired from Russia.

The Naval Officer in Charge, Goa (NOIC GOA) was upgraded to the rank of Rear Admiral and re-designated as Flag Officer Commanding Goa Area (FOGA).

In the First Cadre Review of 1980, appointments were upgraded, phased over a period of three years 1981 to 1983:

- Flag Officer Commanding Western Fleet and Admiral Superintendent Naval Dockyard Bombay were upgraded from Rear Admiral to Vice Admiral

- Fortress Commander Andaman and Nicobar and the Chiefs of Staff of Headquarters Western and Eastern Naval Commands were upgraded from Commodores to Rear Admirals.

In the Second Cadre Review of 1983, appointments were upgraded, phased over two years 1984 and 1985:

- The Chief of Staff Headquarters Southern Naval Command, the Chief Instructor Navy at the Defence Services Staff College and the Chief Staff Officer (Technical) Headquarters Western Naval Command were upgraded from Commodores to Rear Admirals with effect from 1 April 1984.

- With effect from 1 April 1985, approval was accorded for upgrading the Naval Officer in Charge Bombay from the rank of Commodore to the rank of Rear Admiral in the redesignated appointment of Flag Officer Bombay. (This was kept in abeyance and implemented when Flag Officer Maharashtra was appointed on 1 July 1986.)

By 1984:

- *Ex-officio* NOICs Karwar and Lakshadweep were functioning under FOCINCSOUTH.

- The two Material Superintendents at Bombay and Vishakhapatnam, earlier under the Dockyards, were placed under their Command Headquarters.

- Naval Store Depots had been created at Port Blair, Goa and Cochin.

- Captains 8th and 9th Submarine Squadrons had been appointed under FOCsINC EAST and WEST respectively.

- A new Base Maintenance Facility (BMF) had been set up in Goa for Russian IL 38 aircraft and Kamov helicopters.

The Naval Aircraft Repair Organisation (NARO) in Cochin had been upgraded to a Naval Aircraft Yard (NAY).

Until 1984, the respective FOCsINC or their Chiefs of Staff used to be on the Boards of Trustees of the major ports in India. In 1984, the NOICs were appointed as the Naval members on these Boards and charged with the defence of the ships and other national assets located in their port area and also for providing aid to civil power under the overall directions of their FOCsINC.

The Reogranisation of 1986

The changes that took place in the Command and Control structure in 1986 were the cumulative result of:

- The rank up-gradations of the two Cadre Reviews.

- The troubled situation in Sri Lanka from 1983 onwards which required the demarcation of the geographical areas between the Eastern and the Southern Naval Commands to be rationalised.

- The proposals of 1984 to create additional Naval 'Area Commanders', analogous to FOGA, for the Saurashtra Area (FOSA), the Maharashtra Area (FOMA), the Tamil Nadu Area (FOTNA) and the Bengal Area (FOBA).

- The proposals of 1984 to create additional Naval Officers-in-Charge (NOICs) for Porbandar, Paradip, Haldia, Tuticorin and New Mangalore, in addition to the existing NOICs at Kathiawar, Bombay, Goa, Karwar, Cochin, Lakshadweep, Madras, Vizag, Calcutta and A&N (Port Blair).

- The proposals of 1985 to have only two operational commands and change the role of Southern Naval Command to the Navy's Training Command. These 1985 proposals consolidated / revised / rationalised all the earlier proposals.

In 1985, NHQ sought approval to streamline the Navy's Command and Control structure. The main features were:

- To reduce the Operational Control Authorities from three to two and make them accountable for all operational activity in their areas:
  - FOCINCWEST for the Western seaboard and the Arabian Sea.
  - FOCINCEAST for the Eastern seaboard and the Bay of Bengal.

- To place the control of all Training Establishments hitherto under FOCsINC WEST and EAST under FOCINCSOUTH and place accountability for all training policy formulation and implementation under one authority, leaving the Director of Training in NHQ to interact with the Ministry of Defence and the other services.

- To rationalise Command and Control of the Air Arm by designating FOGA also as Flag Officer Naval Aviation (FONA) and make FONA responsible directly to NHQ for all aviation training and maintenance activity and act as the class authority for all aviation matters. Operational deployment of all aviation units to continue to be controlled and directed by FOCsINC WEST and EAST.

- To rationalise Command and Control of the Submarine Arm by creating Flag Officer Submarines (FOSM) as the single point class authority and responsible for all training and maintenance of submarines, analogous to FONA for naval aviation.

- In NHQ, to restore the Logistics function to the Material Branch, redesignate the Chief of Logistics (COL) as Controller of Logistic Support (CLS), make the Chief of Material (COM) the single point of accountability for maintenance and logistics and regroup/rename NHQ Directorates as necessary.

- To constitute Flag Officer Maharashtra (FOMA) to be responsible to FOCINCWEST for the:
  - Operational control of forces assigned for the local naval defence of all ports in the Maharashtra area.
  - Administration of the establishments/units located at Bombay.
  - Interaction with the State Government and other agencies.

This would leave FOCINCWEST free to concentrate on larger operational matters.

NHQ's proposals were approved. The revised Command Structure was implemented from 1 July 1986.

Flag Officer Submarines was created on 1 September 1986 after the first submarines of the two new classes had commissioned – the Russian 877 EKM (Kilo class) and the German HDW 1500 SSK.

In 1988, proposals were revived for the creation of Area Commanders at Cochin, Madras and Vishakhapatnam on the same lines as FOMA, particularly for Madras in view of increased naval activity in Operation Pawan's support of the IPKF in Sri Lanka. NHQ were advised by the Ministry of Defence to include these in the proposals for the next Triennial Cadre Review. Since an inter-service consensus was not in favour of another Cadre Review, these proposals remained pending.

In 1990, the two Commands forwarded a proposal to NHQ to revert to the earlier Command and Control structure namely have three Operational Control Authorities – West, East and South, disestablish the Training Command and relocate FONA and FOSM. This proposal was the result of:

- Operation Pawan in Sri Lanka and Operation Cactus in the Maldives, both of which had highlighted the need for Southern Naval Command to be charged with operational responsibilities for effective command, control and logistics.

- The administrative incongruities of Southern Naval Command controlling major naval training establishments in other coastal states with whom the other Command Headquarters were interacting.

- The class authorities, FONA and FOSM, being too removed from the major decision making that took place in NHQ pertaining to acquisitions, maintenance, plans, etc.

- Western Naval Command wanting FOGA to be placed under it for more effective utilisation of air assets.

The changes proposed were:

- Creation of FOCINCSOUTH as an operational authority with a maritime area of responsibility.

- Reversion of the control of training to NHQ.

- Shifting of the two Class Authorities, FONA and FOSM, to NHQ as ACNS (Air) and ACNS (Submarines) for better interaction with other branches in major policy decisions.

- Placing of FOGA under FOCINCWEST.

After consideration, it was decided to maintain status quo.

The Navy's Command and Control Structure in 1990

CNS (Chief of the Naval Staff)

FOCINCWEST (Flag Officer Commanding in Chief Western Naval Command

   ├─ FOCWF (Flag Officer Commanding Western Fleet)
   │   ├─ Western Fleet
   │   └─ Warship Workup Organisation
   ├─ FOMA (Flag Officer Maharashtra Area)
   │   └─ NOIC (B)
   │   ├─ Local Flotilla
   │   └─ Harbour Defences
   ├─ ASD (B) (Admiral Superintendent Naval Dockyard)
   │   └─ Naval Dockyard Bombay
   ├─ FODAG (Flag Officer Offshore Defence Advisory Group)
   ├─ NOIC Saurashtra
   ├─ Ships/Submarines under direct control
   ├─ Naval Air facilities
   ├─ MS (B) (Material Superintendent Bombay}
   │   └─ Material Organisation & Store Depots
   ├─ Weapon Preparation & Armament Depots
   ├─ Shore Establishments/Authorities/Units

FOCINCEAST (Flag Officer Commanding in Chief Eastern Naval Command)

   ├─ FOCEF (Flag Officer Commanding Eastern Fleet)
   │   └─ Eastern Fleet
   ├─ FOSM (Flag Officer Submarines)
                   ├─ Submarine Base
                   └─ Submarine Training School

```
├─ FORTAN (Fortress Commander A&N Islands)
│                        ├─ Allocated ships
│                        ├─ Naval air facilities
│                        ├─ Base Repair Organisation Port Blair
│                        └─ Shore Establishments/Authorities/Units
├─ ASD (V) (Admiral Superintendent Naval Dockyard)
│                        └─ Naval Dockyard Vishakhapatnam
├─ NOICs Calcutta, Vishakhapatnam, Madras, Paradip, Tuticorin
├─ Ships under direct control
├─ Naval Air facilities
├─ MS (V) (Material Superintendent Vishakhapatnam)
                         └─ Material Organisation & Store Depots
FOCINCSOUTH (Flag Officer Commanding in Chief Southern Naval Command)
   └─ FOGA (Flag Officer Commanding Goa Area)
                         ├─ NOIC Goa
                         ├─ Ships/aircraft for Local Naval Defence
                         └─ Shore Establishments/Authorities/Units
├─ Training Squadron and Local Naval Defence Forces
├─ Training Establishments and Schools
├─ Base Repair Organisation Cochin
├─ Naval Store Depot Cochin
├─ Weapon Preparation & Armament Depots
├─ Shore Establishments/Authorities/Units
├─ NOICs Cochin, Lakshadweep, New Mangalore
└─ Administrative support of naval air establishments/units
```

Developments After 1990

Naval Officers in Charge (NOsIC) of the Coastal Areas

After 1990, the NOIC function in coastal areas was made the collateral duty of the local naval authority that was actually interacting with the local civilian authority:

Under	Collateral Duty of
FOCINCWEST	
NOIC Maharashtra	CSO to FOMA at Mumbai
NOIC Goa	CSO to FOGA at Goa

Note: NOIC Gujarat is a separate entity at Porbandar

FOCINCSOUTH	
NOIC Karnataka	O i/c N D School at Kochi
NOIC Kerala	CO Venduruthy at Kochi
& Lakshadweep	

FOCINCEAST	
NOIC Tuticorin	CO Kattaboman at Tirunelvelli
NOIC Tamil Nadu	CO Adyar at Chennai
NOIC Orissa	CO Chilka at Chilka Lake
NOIC West Bengal	CO Netaji Subhas at Kolkata
NOIC Andaman Islands	CO Jarawa at Port Blair
NOIC Nicobar Islands	CO Kardip at Kamorta

Note: NOIC Andhra Pradesh is a separate entity at Vishakhapatnam

45

The Coast Guard

The Genesis of the Coast Guard

While the Third United Nations Conference on the Law of the Sea (UNCLOS 3) was still in the early phase of discussing the Exclusive Economic Zone (EEZ) and well before India had enacted the Maritime Zones Act of 1976, discussions had commenced in India on how the EEZ was going to be safeguarded. In 1974, Naval Headquarters suggested to the Government to have an armed force on the lines of the US Coast Guard and stressed the importance of inter-ministerial coordination while selecting Coast Guard vessels, recruiting experienced personnel, setting up communication networks, using naval repair facilities, indigenisation etc. Such integrated Navy-Coast Guard development would avoid duplication and economise effort.

On 25 August 1976, India passed the Maritime Zones Act which claimed a 12 mile territorial sea, a 24 mile contiguous zone, a 200 mile EEZ and a continental shelf up to 200 miles or the outer edge of the continental margin, whichever was greater.

Soon after this Act was passed, a committee was set up to consider the type of force that should be created to enforce compliance with its provisions. Three options emerged:

- To entrust this responsibility to the marine wing of the Ministry of Finance, which already had a number of Central Board of Revenue (CBR) anti-smuggling vessels. This option was not pursued, as the functions were too onerous.

- To set up a separate Coastal Command, as a part of the Navy, to oversee these functions. This option was seriously considered since it would avoid the expenditure of raising and maintaining a separate armed force. The Ministry of External Affairs, however, felt that patrolling of the EEZ and protection of national assets was a peacetime role for which defence assets should not be used.

- To set up a separate armed force of the Union, along the lines of the US Coast Guard. This option was finally chosen, as it avoided the Navy being distracted from its primary role of preparing for hostilities.

When, therefore, the Coast Guard was created in 1978, it was in the context of the following assessments:

- Naval Force Levels were inadequate for non-military tasks like the protection of life and property at sea and law enforcement in India's maritime zones.

- 'Hi-tech' naval ships and highly trained naval personnel should not be wasted in carrying out the non-military tasks listed in the Coast Guard Act.

- The Navy should only be utilised for its wartime and its traditional oceanic naval roles.

The interim Coast Guard was constituted on 1 February 1977 with two frigates *(Kuthar, Kirpan)* and five patrol boats *(Panvel, Pamban, Panaji, Pulicat and Puri)* for enforcing the laws of the country in the field of customs, immigration, poaching, and pollution at sea, etc. It functioned under the aegis of the Navy until 1 August 1978.

The permanent Coast Guard was constituted as an armed force of the Union on 19 August 1978, under the Coast Guard Act 1978, which came into force on that day. The Coast Guard is funded by the Revenue Department of the Finance Ministry.

The Coast Guard Act 1978

The Act specified the following duties and functions of the Coast Guard:

- It shall be the duty of the Coast Guard to protect by such measures, as it thinks fit, the maritime and other national interests of India in the maritime zones of India.

- Without prejudice to the generality of the provisions of sub-section above, the measures referred to therein may provide for:

  – Ensuring the safety and protection of artificial islands, offshore terminals, installations and other structures and devices in any maritime zone;

  – Taking such measures as are necessary to preserve and protect the maritime environment and to prevent and control marine pollution;

- Providing protection to fishermen, including assistance to them at sea while in distress;

- Assisting the customs and other authorities in anti-smuggling operations;

- Enforcing the provisions of such enhancements as are for the time being in force in the maritime zones; and

- Such other matters, including measures for the safety of life and property at sea and collection of scientific data, as may be prescribed.

- The Coast Guard shall perform its functions under this section in accordance with, and subject to such rules as may be prescribed and such rules may, in particular, make provisions for ensuring that the Coast Guard functions in close liaison with Union agencies, institutions and authorities so as to avoid duplication of effort.

The Maritime Zones of India (Regulation of Fishing by Foreign Vessels) Act 1981

This act came into force on 2 November 1981. It laid down the procedure to regulate fishing by foreign vessels in the India's EEZ. It provided for deterrent punishments for illegal fishing in the EEZ like levying fines, confiscation of craft, etc.

Concurrently, notifications were issued extending the provisions of the Criminal Procedure Code and the Indian Penal Code over the EEZ.

The Coast Guard thus became the principal agency for enforcing all national legislation in the Maritime Zones of India, policing, surveillance and patrolling 7,683 kilometres of coastline and over two million square kilometres of the sea within national jurisdiction, patrolling offshore installations off Mumbai and the Tamil Nadu coast to ensure their security, working in close liaison with other Government authorities to avoid duplication of work.

During hostilities, India's Coast Guard would function under the overall operational command of the Navy, as is done by other Coast Guards of the world.

Organisational Structure

The broad structure that has evolved over the years is:

- Coast Guard Headquarters at Delhi.

- Three 'Regional Headquarters' at Mumbai, Chennai and Port Blair as Headquarters respectively of the Western, Eastern and Andaman & Nicobar (A&N) Regions.

- Coast Guard 'District Headquarters' for the nine Maritime States: for Gujarat at Porbander, for Maharashtra at Mumbai, for Karnataka at New Mangalore, for Kerala at Kochi, for Tamil Nadu at Chennai, for Andhra Pradesh at Vishakhapatnam, for Orissa at Paradeep, for Bengal at Haldia, and two in the A&N region – at Campbell Bay in the Nicobar Islands and at Diglipur in the Andaman Islands.

- Four 'Coast Guard Stations' at Vadinar (Gujarat), Okha (Gujarat), Tuticorin and Mandapam (Tamil Nadu).

- Coast Guard Air Station (West) at Daman, Coast Guard Air Station (East) at Chennai, Coast Guard Air Enclaves at Mumbai, Goa, Kolkata and Port Blair.

- Coast Guard Berthing Jetty, Base Maintenance Unit and Stores Complex at Chennai, Berthing Jetty at Vishakhapatnam.

Force Levels

At its inception, the Coast Guard acquired the frigates *INS KUTHAR* and *KIRPAN* and five patrol boats from the Navy. From 1983 onwards, the Coast Guard commissioned Seaward Defence Boats (SDBs), Offshore Patrol Vessels (OPVs) with Chetak helicopters embarked, Fast Patrol Vessels (FPVs), Inshore Patrol Vessel (IPVs) and Interceptor Boats (IBs). It also operates and mans the Indian Oil Corporation's fast interceptor boats at Vadinar.

A helicopter squadron was commissioned in 1982 and a maritime surveillance squadron was commissioned in 1983.

Manning and Training

In the initial stages, the majority of officers and sailors were deputed from the Navy. Later, naval personnel were either re-employed or absorbed in the Coast Guard. In due course, Coast Guard officers (Assistant Commandants), non-technical sailors (Naviks) and technical sailors (Yantriks), trained by the Navy, started manning the Coast Guard.

Achievements

The evolution of the Coast Guard has been remarkably cost effective. Most of its ships and aircraft are indigenous. With the Navy's help, its manning and training have been extremely economical. Its anti-poaching operations, its anti-smuggling assistance to the Customs, its pollution-control operations, its protection to endangered marine species like the Olive Ridley turtles on the Orissa coast, its Search and Rescue Operations, its sustained round-the-clock surveillance in the shallow waters of the Palk Bay between Tamil Nadu and Sri Lanka, all have been invaluable. From the time of its inception in 1978, till end 2000, the Coast Guard has, in round figures:

- Seized contraband worth over 300 crores of rupees.
- Apprehended over 100 smuggling vessels, over 700 foreign poaching trawlers and over 7,000 of their crew.
- Responded to over 40 oil spill incidents.
- Prevented over 20,000 illegal immigrants / infiltrators.
- Flown over 900 Search & Rescue (SAR) sorties and, in over 600 missions, saved over 1,000 lives at sea.

Developments After 1990

Since 1990, regular Indo-Maldivian training exercises, of the 'Dosti' series, have been held between the Indian and Maldivian Coast Guards to help enhance confidence levels and understanding.

In addition to its statutory functions, the Coast Guard assisted cyclone, flood and earthquake relief operations.

In 2001, the Coast Guard reached out as far as Japan to participate in an Indo-Japan Coast Guard Exercise.

Coast Guard vessels continued to participate in the joint Navy-Coast Guard patrols in Palk Bay (Operation Tasha), off the Maharashtra and Gujarat coasts (in Operation Swan) and around the Andaman and Nicobar Islands.

46

Commissionings And Decommissionings

Commissionings

Ships Commissioned 1976 to 1990

Name	Date	Ship Type
SHARABH	27 Jan 1976	Landing Ship Tank(Medium)
PRALAYA	17 Feb 1976	Missile Boat
PRATAP	17 Feb 1976	Missile Boat
PRABAL	17 Feb 1976	Missile Boat
PRACHAND	17 Feb 1976	Missile Boat
UDAYGIRI	18 Feb 1976	Leander Class Frigate
SHAKTI	21 Feb 1976	Fleet Tanker
CHAMAK	4 Nov 1976	Missile Boat
CHAPAL	4 Nov 1976	Missile Boat
VIJAYDURG	25 Dec 1976	Ocean-going Rocket Boat
CHATAK	9 Feb 1977	Missile Boat
DUNAGIRI	5 May 1977	Leander Class Frigate
SINDHUDURG	29 May 1977	Ocean-going Rocket Boat
SDB T 52	3 Sep 1977	Seaward Defence Boat MK 2
CHARAG	17 Oct 1977	Missile Boat
PORBANDER	19 Dec 1977	Coastal Minesweeper
HOSDURG	15 Jan 1978	Ocean-going Rocket Boat
PONDICHERRY	2 Feb 1978	Coastal Minesweeper
SDB T 53	12 Apr 1978	Seaward Defence Boat MK 2
SDB T 51	17 Nov 1978	Seaward Defence Boat MK 2
LCU L 31	4 Dec 1978	Landing Craft Utility MK 1
BHAVNAGAR	27 Apr 1979	Coastal Minesweeper
BEDI	27 Apr 1979	Coastal Minesweeper
LCU L 34	28 Jan 1980	Landing Craft Utility MK 1
RAJPUT	4 May 1980	Guided Missile Destroyer
TARAGIRI	16 May 1980	Leander Class Frigate
ALLEPPEY	10 Jun 1980	Coastal Minesweeper
RATNAGIRI	10 Jun 1980	Coastal Minesweeper
LCU L 33	1 Dec 1980	Landing Craft Utility MK 1
SANDHAYAK	26 Feb 1981	Survey Ship
VINDHYAGIRI	8 Jul 1981	Leander Class Frigate
LCU L 32	6 Nov 1981	Landing Craft Utility MK 1

RANA	19 Feb 1982	Guided Missile Destroyer
SDB T 54	1 Sep 1982	Seaward Defence Boat MK 2
TRV A 71	15 Sep 1982	Torpedo Recovery Vessel
TRV A 72	23 Feb 1983	Torpedo Recovery Vessel
MATANGA	2 Apr 1983	Ocean Going Tug
MALVAN	16 May 1983	Inshore Minesweeper
MANGROL	16 May 1983	Inshore Minesweeper
MAHE	16 May 1983	Inshore Minesweeper
SDB T 55	20 Aug 1983	Seaward Defence Boat MK 2
RANJIT	15 Sep 1983	Guided Missile Destroyer
NIRDESHAK	4 Oct 1983	Survey Ship
GODAVARI	10 Dec 1983	GODAVARI Class Frigate(Project 16)FFG
LCU L 35	17 Dec 1983	Landing Craft Utility MK 1
MAKAR	31 Jan 1984	Survey Craft
MITHUN	31 Mar 1984	Survey Craft
MULKI	10 May 1984	Inshore Minesweeper
MAGDALA	10 May 1984	Inshore Minesweeper
MALPE	10 May 1984	Inshore Minesweeper
MEEN	23 Jun 1984	Survey Craft
MESH	31 Oct 1984	Survey Craft
SDB T 56	31 Oct 1984	Seaward Defence Boat MK 3
ASTRAVAHINI	5 Nov 1984	Torpedo Launch and Recovery Vessel
CHEETAH	30 Nov 1984	Landing Ship Tank (Medium)
SDB T 57	26 Feb 1985	Seaward Defence Boat MK 3
SDB T 58	26 Mar 1985	Seaward Defence Boat MK 3
MAHISH	4 JUN 1985	Landing Ship Tank (Medium)
SDB T 59	10 Jul 1985	Seaward Defence Boat MK 3
NIRUPAK	14 Aug 1985	Survey Ship
SDB T 60	24 Aug 1985	Seaward Defence Boat MK 3
GULDAR	30 Dec 1985	Landing Ship Tank (Medium)
GANGA	30 Dec 1985	GODAVARI Class Frigate (Project 16)
SDB T 61	15 Jan 1986	Seaward Defence Boat MK 3
TIR	21 Feb 1986	Cadet Training Frigate
RANVIR	21 Apr 1986	Guided Missile Destroyer
KARWAR	14 JulL 1986	Coastal Minesweeper
LCU L 36	18 Jul 1986	Landing Craft Utility MK 2
KUMBHIR	31 Aug 1986	Landing Ship Tank (Medium)
LCU L 37	18 Oct 1986	Landing Craft Utility MK 2
LCU L 38	10 Dec 1986	Landing Craft Utility MK 2
KAKINADA	23 Dec 1986	Coastal Minesweeper
LCU L 39	25 Mar 1987	Landing Craft Utility MK 2
VEER II	26 Mar 1987	Fast Missile Attack Craft
VIRAAT	12 May 1987	Aircraft Carrier
MAGAR	18 Jul 1987	Landing Ship Tank (Large)

CUDDALORE	29 Oct 1987	Coastal Minesweeper
CANNANORE	17 Dec 1987	Coastal Minesweeper
RANVIJAY	21 Dec 1987	Guided Missile Destroyer
NIRBHIK II	21 Dec 1987	Fast Missile Attack Craft
GOMATI	16 Apr 1988	GODAVARI Class Frigate (Project 16)
KONKAN	8 Oct 1988	Coastal Minesweeper
NIPAT II	5 Dec 1988	Fast Missile Attack Craft
KOZHIKODE	19 Dec 1988	Coastal Minesweeper
ABHAY	10 Mar 1989	Anti Submarine Patrol Vessel
NIREEKSHAK	8 Jun 1989	Diving Support Vessel
KHUKRI	23 Aug 1989	Missile Armed Corvette (Project 25)
SUKANYA	31 Aug 1989	Offshore Patrol Vessel (ex Korea)
NISHANK	12 Sep 1989	Fast Missile Attack Craft
NIRGHAT II	15 Dec 1989	Fast Missile Attack Craft
INVESTIGATOR	11 Jan 1990	Survey Ship
AJAY	24 Jan 1990	Anti Submarine Patrol Vessel
SUBHADRA	25 Jan 1990	Offshore Patrol Vessel (ex Korea)
SUVARNA	2 Jun 1990	Offshore Patrol Vessel (ex Korea)
SAVITRI	20 Nov 1990	Offshore Patrol Vessel (ex HSL)
KUTHAR	7 Jun 1990	Missile Armed Corvette (Project 25)
AKSHAY	10 Dec 1990	Anti Submarine Patrol Vessel

Ships Commissioned After 1990

KIRPAN	12 Jan 1991	Missile Armed Corvette (Project 25)
AGRAY	31 Jan 1991	Anti Submarine Patrol Vessel
VIBHUTI	3 Jun 1991	Fast Missile Attack Craft
JAMUNA	31 Aug 1991	Survey Ship
SARYU	8 Oct 1991	Offshore Patrol Vessel (ex HSL)
KHANJAR	22 Oct 1991	Missile Armed Corvette (Project 25)
VIPUL	16 Mar 1992	Fast Missile Attack Craft
SHARDA	20 Dec 1992	Offshore Patrol Vessel (ex HSL)
SUTLEJ	19 Feb 1993	Survey Ship
SUJATA	3 Nov 1993	Offshore Patrol Vessel
VINASH II	20 Nov 1993	Fast Missile Attack Craft
SAGARDHWANI	30 Jul 1994	Marine Acoustic Research Ship
NASHAK II	15 Dec 1994	Fast Missile Attack Craft
VIDYUT II	16 Jan 1995	Fast Missile Attack Craft
KRISHNA	22 Aug 1995	Cadet Training Ship (2nd Hand Leander)
NIREEKSHAK	15 Sep 1995	Diving Support Vessel
JYOTI	20 Jun 1996	Fleet Tanker
GHARIAL	14 Feb 1997	Landing Ship Tank (Large)
PRAHAR	1 Mar 1997	Fast Missile Attack Craft
TARANGINI	11 Nov 1997	Sail Training Ship
DELHI	15 Nov 1997	Guided Missile Destroyer (Project 15)

T 80	24 Jun 1998	Extra Fast Attack Craft
KORA	10 Aug 1998	Missile Armed Corvette (Project25A)
MYSORE	2 Jun 1999	Guided Missile Destroyer (Project 15)
T 81	5 Jun 1999	Extra Fast Attack Craft
ADITYA	3 Apr 2000	Fleet Tanker
BRAHMAPUTRA	14 Apr 2000	BRAHMAPUTRA Class Frigate (Project16A)
TRINKAT	28 Sep 2000	Fast Attack Craft
MUMBAI	22 Jan 2001	Guided Missile Destroyer (Project 15)
KIRCH	22 Jan 2001	Missile Armed Corvette (Project 25A)
TILLANCHANG	17 Mar 2001	Fast Attack Craft
DARSHAK	28 Apr 2001	Survey Ship
KULISH	20 Aug 2001	Missile Armed Corvette (Project 25A)
TARASA	24 Aug 2001	Fast Attack Craft
SARVEKSHAK	14 Jan 2002	Survey Ship
TARMUGLI	9 Mar 2002	Fast Attack Craft
PRABAL II	11 Apr 2002	Fast Missile Attack Craft
GAJ	10 Oct 2002	Ocean Going Tug
PRALAYA	18 Dec 2002	Fast Missile Attack Craft
TALWAR	18 Jun 2003	Guided Missile Frigate (Project 1135.6)
TRISHUL	25 Jun 2003	Guided Missile Frigate (Project 1135.6)
T 82	9 Oct 2003	Extra Fast Attack Craft
T 83	14 Jan 2004	Extra Fast Attack Craft
KARMUK	4 Feb 2004	Missile Armed Corvette (Project 25A)
TABAR	19 Apr 2004	Guided Missile Frigate (Project 1135.6)
T 84	19 Apr 2004	Extra Fast Attack Craft
BETWA (Project16A)	7 Jul 2004	BRAHMAPUTRA Class Frigate (ex GRSE)

Ships Awaiting Commissioning at the Time of Writing

BEAS (Project16A)

Submarines Commissioned 1976 to 1990

Name	Date	Type
SINDHUGHOSH	30 Apr 1986	EKM (ex Russia)
SHISHUMAR	22 Sep 1986	SSK (ex Germany)
SHANKUSH	20 Nov 1986	SSK (ex Germany)
SINDHUDHVAJ	12 Jun 1987	EKM (ex Russia)
SINDHURAJ	20 Oct 1987	EKM (ex Russia)
CHAKRA	5 Jan 1988	Nuclear (lease completed)
SINDHUVIR	11 Jun 1988	EKM (ex Russia)
SINDHURATNA	18 Nov 1988	EKM (ex Russia)
SINDHUKESARI	19 Dec 1988	EKM (ex Russia)
SINDHUKIRTI	8 Dec 1989	EKM (ex Russia)
SINDHUVIJAY	17 Dec 1990	EKM (ex Russia)

Submarines Commissioned After 1990

SHALKI	7 Feb 1992	SSK (ex MDL)
SHANKUL	28 May 1994	SSK (ex MDL)
SINDHURAKSHAK	24 Dec 1997	EKM (ex Russia)
SINDHUSHASTRA	19 Jul 2000	EKM (ex Russia)

Naval Air Squadrons Commissioned 1976 to 1990

Squadron	Date	Aircraft Type	Role
INAS 312	18 Nov 1976	Super Constellation (ex IAF) succeeded by	Long Range Maritime Patrol (LRMP)
	16 Apr 1988	TU 142 (ex Russia)	
INAS 315	7 Oct 1977	IL 38 (ex Russia)	Maritime Reconnaiss ance and Anti Submarine Warfare (MRASW)
INAS 333	11 Dec 1980	Kamov (ex Russia)	AntiSubmarine Helicopters
INAS 318	8 May 1984	Islander (ex Britain)	Coastal Reconnaissance and Observer Training

Aircraft Inducted After 1990

Type	Source
Sea Harriers (in 300 Squadron)	Britain
Dorniers (in 310 Squadron)	Germany and Hindustan Aircraft
Advance Light Helicopters (ALH) in the process of induction in Utility/Commando/ASW versions	Hindustan Aircraft

Shore Establishments Commissioned 1976 to 1990

Establishment	Date	Location	Role
INS MANDOVI	5 Jan 1976	Verem, Goa	1976 Sailors Training 1986 Cadets Training
INS DRONACHARYA	27 Nov 1978	Fort Cochin	Gunnery School
INS CHILKA	21 Feb 1980	Chilka Lake	Sailors Training
INHS KASTURI	2 Jun 1980	INS SHIVAJI (Lonavla)	Naval Hospital
INHS NIVARINI	3 Oct 1980	INS CHILKA	Naval Hospital
INS ABHIMANYU	1 May 1980	Karanja, Mumbai	Chariot & Marine Commando Training
INS UTKROSH	11 May 1985	Port Blair	Naval Air Station
INS KALINGA	21 Nov 1985	Visakhapatnam	Missile Preparation Facility
INS KATTABOMAN	20 Oct 1990	Tirunelvelli	Submarine Communication Facility

Shore Establishments Commissioned After 1990

INS DEGA	21 Oct 1991	Visakhapatnam	Naval Air Station
INS RAJALI	11 May 1992	Arakkonam	Naval Air Station
INS VAJRABAHU	1 Feb 1996	Mumbai	Submarine Headquarters
Naval Air Station	1999	Mumbai(Kunjali)	Helicopter Base
INS EKSILA	28 Aug 2000	Visakhapatnam	Gas Turbine Overhaul

Commissioning of Floating Dock

Floating Dry Dock FDN-I was towed from Mumbai to Port Blair, moored and then commissioned on 11 July 87.

Decommissionings

Ships Decommissioned 1976 to 1990

Sl.No.	Ship	Date	Ship Type	No. of Years Service in Indian Navy
1.	MAGAR	31 Mar 1976	Landing Ship Tank(Large)	27
2.	BASSEIN	31 Jul 1976	Inshore Minesweeper	21
3.	GODAVARI	31 Aug 1976	Escort Destroyer(Hunt class)	23
4.	CAUVERY	30 Sep 1977	Cadet Training Frigate	34
5.	TIR	30 Sep 1977	Cadet Training Frigate	29
6.	DELHI	30 Jun 1978	Cruiser	30
7.	KUTHAR,} KIRPAN,}	18 Aug 1978	Anti Submarine Frigates (Transferred to Coast Guard)	-
8.	PAMBAN, PANVEL,} PANAJI, PURI,} PULICAT,}	18 Aug 1978	Patrol Boats (Transferred to Coast Guard)	-
9.	SUTLEJ	31 Dec 1978	Survey Ship	37
10.	KAKINADA,} CUDDALORE,}	30 Jun 1979	Coastal Minesweepers	23
11.	ABHAY	30 Jun 1980	Seaward Defence Boat	19
12.	JUMNA	31 Dec 1980	Survey Ship	39
13.	KARWAR,} CANNANORE,}	31 Mar 1981	Coastal Minesweepers	25
14.	KISTNA	31 Dec 1981	Cadet Training Frigate	38
15.	VEER	31 Dec 1982	Missile Boat	11
16.	GULDAR	15 Oct 1984	Landing Ship Tank (Medium)	18
17.	BHATKAL,} BULSAR,}	30 Apr 1985	Inshore Minesweepers	16
18.	MYSORE	30 Aug 1985	Cruiser	28
19.	TALWAR	30 Oct 1985	Anti Submarine Frigate	25
20.	ATUL	31 Mar 1986	Seaward Defence Boat	16
21.	BRAHMAPUTRA	30 Jun 1986	Anti Aircraft Frigate	28
22.	KAVARATTI	31 Jul 1986	Anti Submarine Vessel	16
23.	NIRBHIK	31 Dec 1986	Missile Boat	15
24.	KILTAN	30 Jun 1987	Anti Submarine Vessel	18
25.	GHARIAL	30 Sep 1987	Landing Ship Tank (Medium)	21
26.	NIPAT	29 Feb 1988	Missile Boat	17
27.	KATCHALL	31 Dec 1988	Anti Submarine Vessel	19
28.	NIRGHAT	31 Jul 1989	Missile Boat	18
29.	NISTAR	3 Nov 1989	Submarine Rescue Vessel	18
30.	VINASH	15 Jan 1990	Missile Boat	19
31.	DARSHAK	15 Jan 1990	Survey Ship	25
32.	ANDAMAN	21 Aug 1990	Anti Submarine Vessel (Sank off Visakhapatnam)	17

33.	NASHAK	31 Dec 1990	Missile Boat	19

Ships Decommissioned After 1990

VIDYUT	31 Mar 1991	Missile Boat	20
KAMORTA	31 Oct 1991	Anti Submarine Vessel	23
T 51	30 Nov 1991	Seaward Defence Boat Mk II	13
BETWA	31 Dec 1991	Anti Aircraft Frigate	31
VIJETA	30 Jun 1992	Missile Boat	21
TRISHUL	31 Aug 1992	Anti Submarine Frigate	32
KADMATT	30 Nov 1992	Anti Submarine Vessel	24
BEAS	22 Dec 1992	Anti Aircraft Frigate	32
T 61	31 Mar 1993	Seaward Defence Boat Mk III	15
T 53	31 Aug 1993	Seaward Defence Boat Mk II	15
T 52	31 May 1994	Seaward Defence Boat Mk II	17
DEEPAK	30 Apr 1996	Fleet Tanker	29
PRATAP	17 May 1996	Missile Boat	20
CHARAG	17 May 1996	Missile Boat	21
NILGIRI	31 May 1996	Leander Class Frigate	24
GAJ	14 Aug 1996	Ocean Going Tug	23
VIKRANT	31 Jan 1997	Aircraft Carrier	36
SHARDUL	30 Jun 1997	Landing Ship Tank	22
L 31	1 Feb 1999	Landing Craft Utility	20
MESH	1 Feb 1999	Survey Craft	14
ARNALA	9 Apr 1999	Anti Submarine Vessel	27
ANDROTH	9 Apr 1999	Anti Submarine Vessel	27
KESARI	10 May 1999	Landing Ship Tank	24
HOSDURG	5 Jun 1999	Ocean-going Rocket Boat	21
PRABAL	29 Dec 1999	Missile Boat	23
PRACHAND	29 Dec 1999	Missile Boat	23
PRALAYA	8 Jun 2001	Missile Boat	25
MAGDALA	31 Oct 2001	Inshore Minesweeper	17
AMINI	16 Sep 2002	Anti Submarine Vessel	30
VIJAYDURG	30 Sep 2002	Ocean-going Rocket Boat	26
MALVAN	3 Jan 2003	Inshore Minesweeper	19
CHATAK	5 May 2003	Missile Boat	26
MULKI	16 May 2003	Inshore Minesweeper	19
ANJADIP	13 Dec 2003	Anti Submarine Vessel	31
MANGROL	7 Apr 2004	Inshore Minesweeper	20
SINDHU DURG	24 Sep 2004	Ocean-going Rocket Boat	28

Submarines Decommissioned 1976 to 1990

KHANDERI	18 Oct 1989	Foxtrot Class	21

Submarines Decommissioned After 1990

KALVARI	31 May 1996	Foxtrot Class	28
VAGHSHEER	30 Apr 1997	Foxtrot Class	22
VAGIR	7 Jun 2001	Foxtrot Class	27
KURSURA	27 Sep 2001	Foxtrot Class	30
KARANJ	1 Aug 2003	Foxtrot Class	34

47

Commissioning Commanding Officers Of Major Inductions

Major Warships

Aircraft Carrier *Viraat* Captain (later Vice Admiral) V Pasricha

Rajput Class Guided Missile Destroyers

Rajput	Captain (later Vice Admiral) GM Hiranandani
Rana	Captain (later Vice Admiral) B Guha
Ranjit	Captain (later Admiral) Vishnu Bhagwat
Ranvir	Captain (later Admiral) Madhvendra Singh
Ranvijay	Captain (later Vice Admiral) JC De-Silva

Godavari Class Guided Missile Frigates

Godavari	Captain (later Rear Admiral) K Pestonji
Ganga	Captain (later Vice Admiral) KK Kohli
Gomati	Captain (demised in harness) KMS Rajan

Leander Class Frigates

Nilgiri	Captain (later Rear Admiral) DS Paintal
Himgiri	Captain (later Rear Admiral) NN Anand
Udaygiri	Captain (later Commodore) KN Dubash
Dunagiri	Captain (later Vice Admiral) S Jain
Taragiri	Captain (later Vice Admiral) SM Gadihoke
Vindhyagiri	Captain (later Vice Admiral) H Johnson

Other Ships

Shakti (Fleet Tanker)	Captain (later Commodore) K Rishi
Magar (Landing Ship)	Commander DB Roy
Tir (Cadet Training Ship)	Cdr (later Commodore) S Nath

Submarines

Kalvari / Vela (Russian Foxtrot) Class

Kalvari	Cdr (later Commodore) KV Subra Manian
Khanderi	Cdr (later Rear Admiral) MN Vasudeva
Karanj	Cdr (later Captain) MN Samant
Kursura	Cdr (later Rear Admiral) A Auditto
Vela	Cdr (later Rear Admiral) JMS Sodhi
Vagir	Cdr (later Rear Admiral) KR Menon
Vagli	Cdr Lalit Talwar
Vaghsheer	Cdr (later Commodore) PS Bawa

Shishumar (German HDW 1500) Class

Shishumar	Cdr (later Captain) PM Bhate
Shankush	Cdr (later Captain) OP Sharma
Shalki	Cdr (presently Rear Admiral) KN Sushil
Shankul	Cdr (presently Commodore) PK Chatterjee

Sindhughosh (Russian 877 EKM / Kilo) Class

Sindhughosh	Cdr KC Verghese
Sindhudhvaj	Cdr (later Commodore) SP Singh
Sindhuraj	Cdr (later Commodore) V Kumar
Sindhuvir	Cdr (later Captain) KR Ajrekar
Sindhuratna	Cdr (later Captain) E Sebastian
Sindhukesari	Cdr (later Commodore) SP Singh
Sindhukirti	Lt Cdr (later Commander) K Ramdas
Sindhuvijay	Lt Cdr (later Captain) S Govind
Chakra Class (Russian Charlie)	Captain (later Vice Admiral) RN Ganesh

Air Squadrons

Squadron	Aircraft	Commissioning Commanding Officer
300	Sea Harriers	Cdr (presently Admiral) Arun Prakash
312	Connies	Cdr (later Captain) RD Dhir
312	TU 142 Ms	Cdr (later Captain) VC Pandey
315	IL 38s	Cdr (later Commodore) BK Malik
318	Islanders	Lt Cdr (later Commander) JS Dhillon
333	KA 25/28s	Cdr (later Commodore) P Jha
339	Skg Mk 42 Bs	Cdr (later Commodore) SV Purohit

48

Naval Ceremonial

Reviews of the Fleet by the President

Traditionally, the President of India reviews the Indian Fleet once during his tenure in office. To date, all reviews have been held in Bombay Harbour.[1]

The Presidential Review is an impressive ceremony, second only to the Republic Day Parade. Naval ships and ships from maritime organisations like the Coast Guard, the Merchant Navy, the National Institute of Oceanography, the Oil and Natural Gas Commission, Training Ship *Rajendra* and Naval Yard Craft are anchored precisely in neat lines and dressed overall.

The President embarks in a naval ship nominated as the Presidential Yacht, which flies the President's Colours. After receiving a 21-gun salute, the President reviews the Fleet by cruising past each line of ships. Each ship's side is manned by her ship's company in white ceremonial uniform. As the President passes by, each ship's company, in unison, take off their caps in salutation and give three resounding 'Jais'.

At sunset, all ships at the anchorage participate in a fireworks display. As darkness descends, all ships, in unison, switch on their garlands of lights, which accentuate their silhouettes.

No Fleet Review was held for President N Sanjiva Reddy during his tenure from 25 July 1977 to 24 July 1982.

Presentation of Colours by the President

It is an ancient tradition for armed forces (and elements thereof) that accomplish meritorious and outstanding service to be presented with "Colours" to engender pride and esprit de-corps. These Colours are proudly paraded by the recipients on special occasions to add dignity and stature to parades and guards of honour.

In countries that have the monarchical system of government, the Colours are presented by the monarch. In countries that have the presidential form of government, the colours are presented by the President.

In 1951, Colours were presented to the Navy by President Rajendra Prasad.

Between 1976 and 1990, "Colours," identical to those earlier presented to the Navy, were presented to the Naval Commands:

Formation	Date of Presentation	By
Southern Naval Command	26 November 1984	President Giani Zail Singh
Eastern Naval Command	25 March 1987	President Giani Zail Singh
Western Naval Command	22 February 1990	President R Venkataraman

Date	Naval Ships	Submarines	Aircraft/ Helos	Coast Guard	Yard Craft	Mercantile Marine & Other Ships	Reviewed By
11 Jan 76	43	5	5 Navy	–	–	6	President Fakhrudin Ali Ahmed
12 Feb 84	45	3	32 Navy, 5 CG	2	7	9	President Giani Zail Singh
15 Feb 89	48	8	29 Navy, 8 CG	2	4	10	President R Venkataraman

---

1. The escort vessel HMIS Indus represented the Royal Indian Navy in the Coronation Review in England in 1937. This was the first ever participation of an Indian naval ship at the Royal Reviews held at Spithead off Portsmouth.

Naval Bands

In ancient times, marching was sustained by the beat of drums. In later times, martial music enhanced the effect of drums.

Today each major training establishment has a band. In addition, bands are positioned in New Delhi and Port Blair to meet ceremonial commitments. Listed alphabetically, bands are located in:

- *INS Chilka* for the new entry sailor training establishment in Orissa.
- *INS Circars* for ceremonial and training requirements at Visakhapatnam.
- *INS Dronacharya* for the Gunnery Training School at Fort Cochin.
- *INS Hamla* for the Logistic, EDP and Cookery schools at Marve (Bombay).
- *INS India* for ceremonial requirements at Delhi.
- *INS Jarawa* for ceremonial requirements at Port Blair.
- *INS Kunjali* for ceremonial and training requirements at Bombay.
- *INS Mandovi* for the Naval Academy in Goa.
- *INS Shivaji* for the Engineering Training School at Lonavla.
- *INS Valsura* for the Electrical Training School at Jamnagar.
- *INS Venduruthy* for ceremonial and training requirements at Cochin.
- *INS Viraat*, the aircraft carrier, for ceremonial requirements.

Bands invariably embark on board ships going on goodwill visits abroad, like the annual Seychelles and Mauritius Independence Day celebrations and international and prestigious events like:

- The 1967 EXPO at Montreal, Canada (embarked in *Brahmaputra*).
- The 1970 EXPO at Tokyo, Japan (embarked in *Trishul*).
- The 1970 Captain Cook Centenary Celebrations in Australia (embarked in *Tir*).
- The 1971 Ethiopian Navy Day Celebrations at Massawa (embarked in *Talwar*).
- The 1972 Southeast Asia Sailing Regatta at Colombo (embarked in *Amba*).
- The 1973 Ethiopian Navy Day Celebrations at Massawa (embarked in *Mysore*).
- The 1977 International Fleet Review in Britain on the occasion of the Silver Jubilee of the Queen of England's Coronation (embarked in *Udaygiri*).
- The 1986 Bicentennial Celebrations of the Statue of Liberty and the President's Fleet Review in the USA (embarked in *Godavari*).
- The 1987 International Fleet Review and EXPO at Tokyo (embarked in *Ganga*).
- The 1987 International Ocean Festival in Mauritius (embarked in *Vindhyagiri*).
- The 1988 International Naval Review and Bicentennial celebrations in Australia (embarked in *Godavari*).
- The 1990 International Fleet Review in Malaysia (embarked in *Ganga*).

The Indian Navy's Central Band was commissioned in Bombay in 1945 with a complement of 50 musicians, most of who had earlier belonged to the bands of India's princely states. *INS Kunjali* in Bombay is home to this band and to the Navy's School of Music.

Over the years, in addition to its traditional parade and ceremonial commitments, this band widened its scope by:

- Performing with civilian choirs and orchestras.
- Developing into a symphonic concert band, introducing traditional Indian musical instruments and including string instruments like violins, violas, cellos and string basses.

Today, the Naval Central Band has grown to a 125-piece Symphonic Orchestra. From martial music, successive conductors of the band have increased the Band's repertoire to include overtures, solos, duets, concertos and other forms of contemporary music including Indian classical and Indian and Western pop music.

RICHODHARA
CDR JS BATHENA (Retd)

DHRUVAK
CDR HC TANEJA (Retd)

SHANKH
LCDR CV DAVID (Retd)

KAKINADA
LCDR JS KARPE

NIRGHAT
LCDR Y BHIDE

NASHAK
LCDR T L RATTAN

NIRBH
CDR S GOPALAN

KESARI
LCDR GUPTESHWAR RAI

GHORPAD
CDR S ISSACS

GULDAR
LCDR G EIPE

GODAVARI
CDR NP SINGH

KIRPAN
CDR HK NAG

KUTHAR
CAPT GT WADHWANI, NM

KARANJ
LCDR RN GANESH

KURSURA
LCDR SC ANAND

AMINI
CDR SR IYENGAR

ANDAMAN
CDR SP TANEJA

ANDROTH
CDR RK KHANNA

ARNALA
CAPT SS KUMAR, Vr. C

BETWA
CDR MS RAWAT

BRAHMAPUTRA
CAPT RR SOOD, Vr. C, NM

TALWAR
CDR AK SHARMA, NM

TS RAJENDRA
CAPT INDER SINGH

DEEPAK
Ag. CAPT R VIR

AMBA
CAPT KS SUBRA-MANIAN-VSM

JAWAHARLAL NEHRU
CAPT TS KHARA

VISHVA ANURAG
CAPT A A NAZARETH

SAGAR
CAPT AS

INAS 300 - CDR G ISRANI

INAS 330 - CDR AS RAWAT, NM

INAS 310 - LCDR M VARGHESE

ADMIRAL SN KOHLI, PB, PVSM, Chief of the Naval Staff.

VICE ADMIRAL J CURSETJI, PVSM, Flag Officer Commanding - in - Chief, Western Naval Command

VICE ADMIRAL KL KULKARNI, PVSM, Flag Officer Commanding - in - Chief, Eastern Naval Command

REVIEW

SHRI FAKHR
PRESIDENT OF T
11th J
B

Designed and Prepared by the Naval Hydrographic Office, Dehra Dun, 11 Jan 1976, under the

NIPAT
LCDR VK VOHRA

VEER
LCDR N KAPUR

VIDYUT
CDR AJ LOBO

VINASH
LCDR MJ SINGH

VERY
S BOSE

JAMUNA
CDR BS NEWAR

SUTLEJ
CDR BA RAO

VAGIR
LCDR BS UPPAL

VAGHSHEER
CDR JMS SODHI VSM

VAGLI
CDR L TALWAR

KILTAN
CDR P SWANI

KAMORTA
CDR PK GUPTA

KADMATT
CAPT CV PARTHASARATHY

VHNEY

UDAYGIRI
CDR KN DUBASH

HIMGIRI
CDR KN ZADU, Vr.C

NILGIRI
CAPT OS DAWSON, AVSM

DELHI
CAPT JG NADKARNI, VSM

MYSORE
CAPT SL SETHI N.M. AVSM

VIKRANT
CAPT MK ROY, AVSM

JALARATNA
CAPT AK MEHTA

INDIAN VALOUR
CAPT KD SINGH

FLEET

ALI AHMED
BLIC OF INDIA
976

REAR ADMIRAL RL PEREIRA, AVSM, Flag Officer Commanding, Southern Naval Area

REAR ADMIRAL RKS GHANDHI, Vr.C, Flag Officer Commanding, Western Fleet

REAR ADMIRAL VEC BARBOZA, AVSM (Bar), Flag Officer Commanding, Eastern Fleet

COMMODORE REVIEW - CMDE GM SHEA, AVSM (Bar)

PRESIDENT'S YACHT - CANNANORE - CDR S RAMSAGAR

STANDBY YACHT - KARWAR - LCDR BL SHARMA

Superintendence of Commodore F. L. Fraser, AVSM, FIS, Chief Hydrographer to the Government of India.

Review C
By The President Of

INAS-300
Cdr A Prakash, VrC

INAS-330
Cdr G Sharma

INAS-333
Cdr S S Kahlon, NM

INAS-315
Cdr V Pandey

CGAS-700
Cdr S Goel

R Adm S C Chopra,

APSARIKA
A H Pagarkar

SHANKH
V R Bhabal

GHORPAD
Lt Cdr K R Rao

KES
Lt Cdr A K M.

BHAVNAGAR
Lt Cdr A Puri

BEDI
Lt Cdr S Pradeep

RATNAGIRI
Lt Cdr Pritpal Singh

MANGROL
Lt K N Rao

GAJ
Lt Cdr M V Raghavan

SINDHUDURG
Cdr S C S Bangara

VIJAYDURG
Cdr L Shanker

BETWA
Cdr V Viswanathan

BRAHMAPUTRA
Capt A S Rawat, NM

TALWAR
Cdr S V Gopalachari

KADMATT
Cdr B K Gupta

KAMORTA
Cdr M L Yadav

AMINI
Cdr C Narayan

HIMGIRI
Capt R Sikka

NILGIRI
Capt I Wadhwani

DUNAGIRI
Capt R G Kumar

UDAYGIRI
Capt V K Malhotra

TS RAJENDRA
Capt T K Joseph

SHAKTI
Capt I Sharma, AVSM, VrC

DEEPAK
Capt P D Sharma, NM

SAVESHANI
Capt K P Gopal Rao, MVC, VSM (Retd)

SAGAR KANYA
Capt S K Oberoi

SAMUDRA SURAKSHA
Capt S Chand

JALA JAYA
Capt A M Misquitta

FLAGSHIPS

INS VIKRANT...ADMIRAL O S DAWSON, PVSM, AVSM, Chief of the Naval Staff
INS RANA ....VICE ADMIRAL M K ROY, PVSM, AVSM, Flag Officer Commanding - in - Chief, Eastern Naval Command
INS RANJIT....VICE ADMIRAL R H TAHILIANI, PVSM, AVSM, Flag Officer Commanding - in - Chief, Western Naval Command
INS RAJPUT.....VICE ADMIRAL K K NAYYAR, PVSM, AVSM, Flag Officer Commanding - in - Chief, Southern Naval Command

PRESIDENT'S YACHT............INS PONDICHERRY
Cdr R K Ahluwalia

STAND - BY YACHT...........INS PORBANDAR
Lt Cdr R Datta

Bomba

COMMODORE REVIEW · COMMODORE 8

Designed and Prepared by the Naval Hydrographic Office, Dehra Dun, Feb, 1984 under the

he Fleet

ia, Giani Zail Singh

INAS-310
Cdr G Jankiraman

INAS-551
Cdr U P Bapat

INAS-321
Lt Cdr R S Bhandari

INAS-550
Cdr S P Singh

CGAS-800
OMDT P B CHOWDHURY, SC, NM

LCU 33
Lt Cdr V D Nagar

LCU 32
Lt Cdr S R Chikodi

VARUNA
Lt Cdr G R Iyengar

MALVAN
Lt N Vijayssarthy

CHATAK
Lt Cdr A Shagra

CHARAG
Lt Cdr D Subramanian

PRATAP
Lt Cdr A K Mehra

CHAMAK
Lt Cdr S J Sarma

PRABAL
Lt Cdr L N M Krishnan

NIRBHIK
Lt Cdr S K Krishnan

VIKRAM
Capt P J Jacob, VSM

NIRDESHAK
Cdr K R Srinivasan

DARSHAK
Capt P P Nandi, VSM

TRISHUL
Capt R N Sharma

KHANDERI
Lt Cdr G Mathews

VELA
Lt Cdr O P Sharma

KALVARI
Cdr K S Brar

KATCHALL
Cdr B K Kumar

ANDAMAN
Capt S Padmasankar

TARAGIRI
Capt R S Vohra

VINDHYAGIRI
Capt R S Rai

GODAVARI
Capt K Pestonji, NM

RANJIT
Capt V Bhagwat

RANA
Capt P P I Sivamani, NM

VIKRANT
Capt K A S Z Raju, NM

INDIAN FAME
Capt D N Kalapesi

VISHVA AJAY
Capt D M Patwardhan

ZAKIR HUSSAIN
Capt R Tandon

FLAGSHIPS

VICE ADMIRAL M R SCHUNKER, PVSM, AVSM (Retd), Director General Coast Guard ....CGS VIKRAM
VICE ADMIRAL I J S KHURANA, Flag Officer Commanding Western Fleet ....INS GODAVARI
REAR ADMIRAL L RAM DAS, AVSM, Vr C, VSM, Flag Officer Commanding Eastern Fleet ....INS ANDAMAN

Feb 84

PRIME MINISTER'S YACHT..................INS ALLEPPEY
Lt Cdr M V Dhavale

M. Naval Officer-in-Charge, Bombay

ce of Commodore A. G. Morales, FIS, Chief Hydrographer to the Government of India

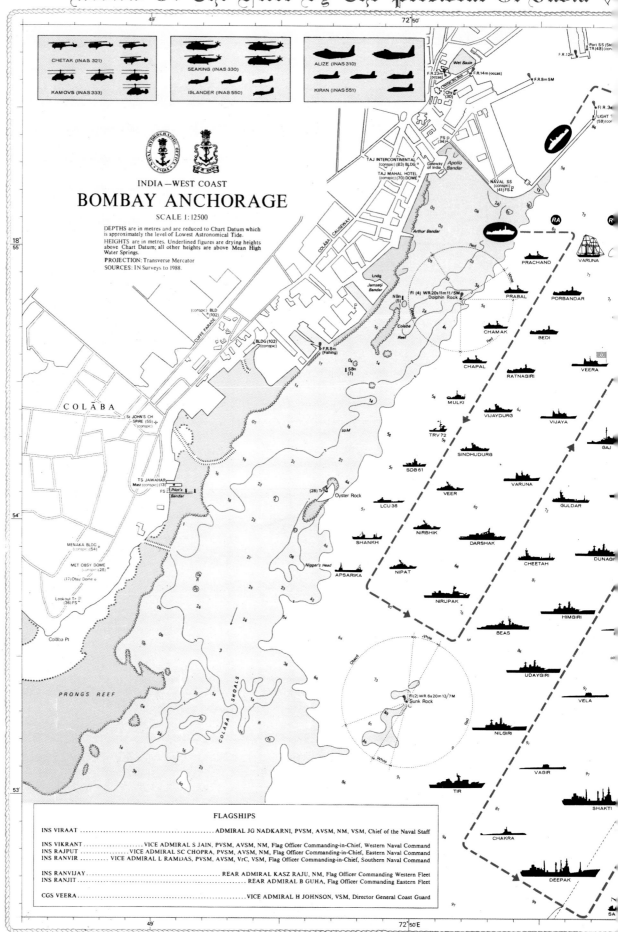

CHETAK (INAS 321)

KAMOVS (INAS 333)

SEAKING (INAS 330)

ISLANDER (INAS 550)

ALIZE (INAS 310)

KIRAN (INAS 551)

INDIA—WEST COAST
BOMBAY ANCHORAGE
SCALE 1:12500

DEPTHS are in metres and are reduced to Chart Datum which is approximately the level of Lowest Astronomical Tide.
HEIGHTS are in metres. Underlined figures are drying heights above Chart Datum; all other heights are above Mean High Water Springs.
PROJECTION: Transverse Mercator
SOURCES: IN Surveys to 1988.

COLĀBA

PRONGS REEF

COLĀBA SHOALS

Colāba Pt

Oyster Rock

Nigger's Head

Sunk Rock

Dolphin Rock

Fl (4) WR.20s 11m 11/5M Dolphin Rock

Fl (2) WR.6s 20m 13/7M Sunk Rock

TAJ INTERCONTINENTAL (conspc) (83) BLDG
TAJ MAHAL HOTEL (conspc) (70) DOME
Gateway of India
Apollo Bandar

Ships in review: PRACHAND, VARUNA, PRABAL, PORBANDAR, CHAMAK, BEDI, CHAPAL, VEERA, RATNAGIRI, MULKI, VIJAYDURG, VIJAYA, TRV 72, SINDHUDURG, GAJ, SDB 61, VARUNA, VEER, GULDAR, LCU 38, NIRBHIK, DARSHAK, CHEETAH, DUNAGIRI, SHANKH, NIPAT, APSARIKA, NIRUPAK, HIMGIRI, BEAS, UDAYGIRI, VELA, NILGIRI, VAGIR, TIR, SHAKTI, CHAKRA, DEEPAK

FLAGSHIPS

INS VIRAAT .... ADMIRAL JG NADKARNI, PVSM, AVSM, NM, VSM, Chief of the Naval Staff

INS VIKRANT .... VICE ADMIRAL S JAIN, PVSM, AVSM, NM, Flag Officer Commanding-in-Chief, Western Naval Command
INS RAJPUT .... VICE ADMIRAL SC CHOPRA, PVSM, AVSM, NM, Flag Officer Commanding-in-Chief, Eastern Naval Command
INS RANVIR .... VICE ADMIRAL L RAMDAS, PVSM, AVSM, VrC, VSM, Flag Officer Commanding-in-Chief, Southern Naval Command

INS RANVIJAY .... REAR ADMIRAL KASZ RAJU, NM, Flag Officer Commanding Western Fleet
INS RANJIT .... REAR ADMIRAL B GUHA, Flag Officer Commanding Eastern Fleet

CGS VEERA .... VICE ADMIRAL H JOHNSON, VSM, Director General Coast Guard

भारत सरकार के मुख्य जलसर्वेक्षक, रीयर एडमिरल बी.के. सिंह, बी.एस.एम. एफ.आई.ए
Designed and Published at the Naval Hydrographic Office, Dehra Dun, 15 Feb 1989 under the

बम्बई में 15 फरवरी 1989 को बेड़े का पुनरीक्षण
Shri R. Venkataraman At Bombay On 15 Feb 1989

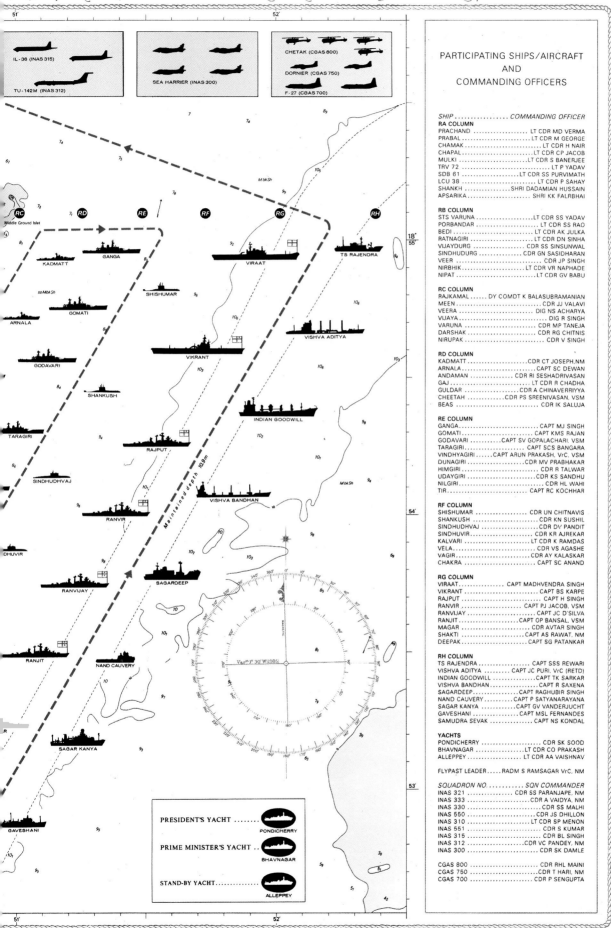

IL - 36 (INAS 315)

TU - 142M (INAS 312)

SEA HARRIER (INAS 300)

CHETAK (CGAS 800)

DORNIER (CGAS 750)

F - 27 (CGAS 700)

PARTICIPATING SHIPS/AIRCRAFT AND COMMANDING OFFICERS

SHIP	COMMANDING OFFICER
RA COLUMN	
PRACHAND	LT CDR MD VERMA
PRABAL	LT CDR M GEORGE
CHAMAK	LT CDR H NAIR
CHAPAL	LT CDR CP JACOB
MULKI	LT CDR S BANERJEE
TRV 72	LT P YADAV
SDB 61	LT CDR SS PURVIMATH
LCU 38	LT CDR P SAHAY
SHANKH	SHRI DADAMIAN HUSSAIN
APSARIKA	SHRI KK FALRBHAI
RB COLUMN	
STS VARUNA	LT CDR SS YADAV
PORBANDAR	LT CDR SS RAO
BEDI	LT CDR AK JULKA
RATNAGIRI	LT CDR DN SINHA
VIJAYDURG	CDR SS SINSUNWAL
SINDHUDURG	CDR GN SASIDHARAN
VEER	CDR JP SINGH
NIRBHIK	LT CDR VR NAPHADE
NIPAT	LT CDR GV BABU
RC COLUMN	
RAJKAMAL	DY COMDT K BALASUBRAMANIAN
MEEN	CDR JJ VALAVI
VEERA	DIG NS ACHARYA
VIJAYA	DIG R SINGH
VARUNA	CDR MP TANEJA
DARSHAK	CDR RG CHITNIS
NIRUPAK	CDR V SINGH
RD COLUMN	
KADMATT	CDR CT JOSEPH, NM
ARNALA	CAPT SC DEWAN
ANDAMAN	CDR RI SESHADRIVASAN
GAJ	LT CDR R CHADHA
GULDAR	CDR A CHINAVERRIYYA
CHEETAH	CDR PS SREENIVASAN, VSM
BEAS	CDR IK SALUJA
RE COLUMN	
GANGA	CAPT MJ SINGH
GOMATI	CAPT KMS RAJAN
GODAVARI	CAPT SV GOPALACHARI, VSM
TARAGIRI	CAPT SCS BANGARA
VINDHYAGIRI	CAPT ARUN PRAKASH, VrC, VSM
DUNAGIRI	CDR MV PRABHAKAR
HIMGIRI	CDR R TALWAR
UDAYGIRI	CDR KS SANDHU
NILGIRI	CDR HL WAHI
TIR	CAPT RC KOCHHAR
RF COLUMN	
SHISHUMAR	CDR UN CHITNAVIS
SHANKUSH	CDR KN SUSHIL
SINDHUDHVAJ	CDR DV PANDIT
SINDHUVIR	CDR KR AJREKAR
KALVARI	LT CDR K RAMDAS
VELA	CDR VS AGASHE
VAGIR	CDR AY KALASKAR
CHAKRA	CAPT SC ANAND
RG COLUMN	
VIRAAT	CAPT MADHVENDRA SINGH
VIKRANT	CAPT BS KARPE
RAJPUT	CAPT H SINGH
RANVIR	CAPT PJ JACOB, VSM
RANVIJAY	CAPT JC D'SILVA
RANJIT	CAPT OP BANSAL, VSM
MAGAR	CDR AVTAR SINGH
SHAKTI	CAPT AS RAWAT, NM
DEEPAK	CAPT SG PATANKAR
RH COLUMN	
TS RAJENDRA	CAPT SSS REWARI
VISHVA ADITYA	CAPT JC PURI, VrC (RETD)
INDIAN GOODWILL	CAPT TK SARKAR
VISHVA BANDHAN	CAPT R SAXENA
SAGARDEEP	CAPT RAGHUBIR SINGH
NAND CAUVERY	CAPT P SATYANARAYANA
SAGAR KANYA	CAPT GV VANDERJUCHT
GAVESHANI	CAPT MSL FERNANDES
SAMUDRA SEVAK	CAPT NS KONDAL
YACHTS	
PONDICHERRY	CDR SK SOOD
BHAVNAGAR	LT CDR CO PRAKASH
ALLEPPEY	LT CDR AA VAISHNAV
FLYPAST LEADER	RADM S RAMSAGAR VrC, NM

SQUADRON NO.	SQN COMMANDER
INAS 321	CDR SS PARANJAPE, NM
INAS 333	CDR A VAIDYA, NM
INAS 330	CDR SS MALHI
INAS 550	CDR JS DHILLON
INAS 310	LT CDR SP MENON
INAS 551	CDR S KUMAR
INAS 315	CDR BL SINGH
INAS 312	CDR VC PANDEY, NM
INAS 300	CDR SK DAMLE
CGAS 800	CDR RHL MAINI
CGAS 750	CDR T HARI, NM
CGAS 700	CDR P SENGUPTA

PRESIDENT'S YACHT .... PONDICHERRY

PRIME MINISTER'S YACHT .. BHAVNAGAR

STAND-BY YACHT .... ALLEPPEY

Middle Ground Islet

RC RD RE RF RG RH

KADMATT GANGA VIRAAT TS RAJENDRA

SHISHUMAR

ARNALA GOMATI

VISHVA ADITYA

GODAVARI VIKRANT

SHANKUSH

INDIAN GOODWILL

TARAGIRI

RAJPUT

SINDHUDHVAJ VISHVA BANDHAN

RANVIR

DHUVIR

RANVIJAY SAGARDEEP

RANJIT NAND CAUVERY

SAGAR KANYA

GAVESHANI

Maintained depth 109m

नौसेना जलसर्वेक्षण कार्यालय, देहरादून द्वारा आकल्पित एवम् प्रकाशित,15 फरवरी 1989
...nce of Rear Admiral V.K. Singh, VSM, FIS, Chief Hydrographer to the Government of India.

CEREMONIAL CHART 5083

49

Naval Philately

General

The first postage stamps in the world originated in Britain in 1840. In India, stamps were first introduced in Sind province in 1852 in what is now known in the philatelic world as the 'Scinde Dawk' (Dawk being the Anglicisation of the Indian word 'dak' meaning 'post').

Common daily use stamps, called 'Definitives', are issued as a series in various denominations and their design pertains to one theme. These are printed in large numbers. The Navy has never figured in 'definitives'.

'Commemorative' stamps are issued on a specific date to commemorate personalities or a significant national / international event. The Navy has figured in 'commemoratives'. Linked to the release of a commemorative stamp is the 'First Day Cover' (FDC) issued by the Department of Posts. This envelope bears, on the obverse, a 'Cachet Design' which is a written and pictorial / graphical representation of the event being commemorated. The stamp being released is affixed on the FDC and a 'First Day Cancellation' is made on the stamp. This cancellation is different to the regular cancellation and its design relates to the purpose of the stamp.

Owing to the limited number of such stamps issued every year, it is not feasible for every event to be commemorated through the release of a stamp. For events or occasions of lesser national significance, a 'Special Cover' with a 'Special Cancellation' can be sponsored and released by any organisation in association with the Department of Posts. This envelope, like the FDC, bears a cachet design and the special cancellation. Any stamp / stamps, of total denomination sufficient to meet postal rate for an ordinary cover, could be used. The Special Cancellation is affixed only on the day of the event.

Ships and establishments can arrange to release 'special covers' with 'special cancellations' after obtaining the approval of the Chief Post Master General of their concerned postal circle.

The Navy has figured in many philatelic releases. Prior to Independence in 1947, the only philatelic materials having a naval connection were:

- The nine pies Soldiers' and Seamen's Envelope and its one anna overprint version.

- The 1941 'Pigeon Mail' covers commemorating the naval mail being sent by pigeons from the naval establishment at Kalyan to the Naval Dockyard, Bombay. The sale of these covers helped to raise war funds for the Royal Indian Navy.

- A set of four World War II Victory stamps, of similar design, issued in 1946.

After Independence, the Navy's ships, submarines, aircraft and events have figured in stamps. Until 1979, there were only two stamps relating directly to the Navy. These were:

- The Armed Forces 'Jai Jawan' stamp issued in 1966 after the 1965 Indo-Pakistan conflict, which depicted the cruiser *INS Mysore*.

- The 20 paise *INS Nilgiri* stamp issued when the Prime Minister launched India's first indigenous frigate in October 1968.

In 1979, young naval enthusiasts[1] founded the Naval Philatelic Society (NPS) to increase public interest in the Navy. This society organised Naval Philatelic Exhibitions in 1979 and 1980. The NPS helps to design commemorative stamps, special covers and pictorial cancellations to mark naval events and activities. It has organised the release of the following stamps:

- Lord Mountbatten, 1980.

- *INS Taragiri,* 1981.

- The President's Review of the Fleet, 1984.

- The 250th Anniversary of the Naval Dockyard Bombay, 1985.

- National Maritime Day, 1999.

---

1. Among them are Commodore Anil Dhir and Commander UN Acharya (presently the Honorary Secretary of the Naval Philatelic Society, India) who to this day remain dedicated and enthusiastic naval philatelists.

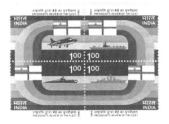

The releases thereafter have been:

- 400th Anniversary of Kunjali Marakkar.
- Martyrs of the 1971 War – the Navy stamp shows the old *INS Khukri* that was torpedoed and sank with her Commanding Officer, Captain MN Mulla.
- Special commemorative stamps on the occasion of the International Fleet Review 2001 in Mumbai.

Apart from the above, there are inter-service stamps. Though the Navy is not specifically represented, there are naval linkages like 'Greetings To Our Forces' (four stamps, of which one shows a stylised ship), Defence Research & Development Organisation commemoratives, the Rashtriya Indian Military College Dehra Dun (where some naval officers studied), the National Defence Academy, the Defence Services Staff College, the Antarctica expeditions (in which naval personnel have participated), the 1965 Mount Everest Expedition (in which a naval officer participated), the 1982 Asian Games (in which naval officers won medals in sailing), the round the world voyage of the sailing vessel *Trishna* (in which a naval officer participated), the Indian Peace Keeping Force (in Sri Lanka), and so on.

Chronology of Issues

S No	Date of Issue	Occasion / Event	Description	Depiction
1.	26 January 1964	Presentation of President's Colours to Southern Naval Command	–	Special Cover issued with cancellation
2.	26 January 1966	Republic Day after the 1965 Indo-Pakistan War	'Jai Jawan'. Silhouette of the cruiser *INS MYSORE* together with an Air Force Gnat aircraft and the bust of a soldier	Stamp 1
3.	15 December 1968	Navy Day	Commissioning of the first Leander frigate *INS NILGIRI* on 23 October 1968	Stamp 2
4.	15 August 1972	Independence Day after the 1971 Indo-Pakistan War	"Greetings to our Forces" Joint Services Crest with vertical colour bands of the Army, Navy and Air Force in the background	Stamp 3
5.	4 December 1972	Navy Day	Special cancellation	Cancellation
6.	30 June 1978	Decommissioning of the cruiser *INS DELHI*	–	Special cover issued with cancellation
7.	28 August 1980	Commemoration of British Admiral of the Fleet Lord Louis Mountbatten	–	Stamp 4
8.	4 December 1981	Navy Day	Fifth Leander frigate *INS TARAGIRI*	Stamp 5
9.	18 May 1982	15th anniversary of Submarine Headquarters in Vishakhapatnam	*INS VIRBAHU*	Special cover issued with cancellation
10.	8 December 1982	15th anniversary of the Submarine Arm		Cancellation
11.	4 December 1983	Navy Day	30th Anniversary of the Naval Air Arm	Special cover issued with cancellation

S No	Date of Issue	Occasion/Eventent	Description	Depiction
12.	12 February 1984	President's Review of the Fleet	Set of four stamps depicting the silhouettes of the aircraft carrier *VIKRANT*, the submarine *VELA*, the guided missile destroyer *RANA* and a naval Sea Harrier aircraft	Stamp 6
13.	7 July 1985	Silver Jubilee of the naval fighter aircraft squadron	INAS 300	Special cover
14.	29 August 1985	Decommissioning of the cruiser *INS MYSORE*	–	Special cover issued and cancellation
15.	11 January 1986	250th Anniversary of the Naval Dockyard Bombay	Bombay Dock, ships and the Dockyard Building	Stamp 7
16.	16 February 1986	Silver Jubilees of the aircraft carrier	*INS VIKRANT*	Stamp 8
17.	9 May 1986	Silver Jubilee of the naval anti submarine aircraft squadron	INAS 310	Special cover issued with cancellation
18.	17 September 1986	Arrival in India of the first EKM submarine from Russia	*INS SINDHUGHOSH*	Special cover issued and cancellation
19.	23 September 1986	Arrival in India of the first SSK submarine from Germany	*INS SHISHUMAR*	Special cover issued with cancellation
20.	5 April 1987	Presentation of President's Colours to Eastern Naval Command		Special cover issued with cancellation
21	18 May 1987	Silver Jubilee of Naval Hospital at Vishakhapatnam	*INHS KALYANI*	Special cover issued with cancellation
22.	31 July 1987	Commissioning of the first indigenous Landing Ship	*INS MAGAR*	Special cover issued with cancellation
23.	4 December 1987	Navy Day at Hyderabad and Secunderabad	–	Special cancellation
24.	21 December 1987	20th Anniversary of the Submarine Arm		Special cover issued with cancellation
25.	15 February 1989	President's Review of the Fleet	Fleet Ships in Line Abreast	Stamp 9

The author acknowledges with gratitude the inputs provided by Vice Admiral AS Krishnan who retired in 2002 as the Chief of Material and who, for many years has been the doyen of Indian Naval Philately.

50

The Navy And The Army's Military Engineering Service

Preamble

The Military Engineering Service (MES) functions under the Engineer-in-Chief of the Indian Army. It designs and oversees the construction of military buildings. It repairs and maintains all the buildings of the three services and other organisations under the Ministry of Defence.

All Naval civil construction work has been undertaken by the MES, except for two projects during the period 1976 to 1990 – the new Naval Academy at Ezhimala in Kerala[1] and the new Naval Base at Karwar in Karnataka. In their association with the Navy, the MES built up considerable expertise in the construction of Dockyards and special-to-type works.

The MES' Involvement with the Navy

The MES' involvement with the Bombay Naval Dockyard Expansion Scheme commenced in the late 1950s when the civilian contractor was unable to keep to the construction schedule of the Ballard Pier Extension and the Barracks and Destroyer wharfs. It has continued thereafter under the Director General Naval Projects Bombay.

In the case of the Vizag Dockyard, the organisation of the Chief Engineer Dry Dock and the East Coast Zone[2] was created in June 1969 for the MES to construct its first and largest Dry Dock in India. The initial planning and design was done in Delhi and the formation moved to Vishakhapatnam in November 1969 to start its work.[3]

Major General MK Paul was associated with the Bombay Naval Dockyard Expansion Scheme and with the construction of the Dry Docks in the Vishakhapatnam Dockyard. He recalls:

"Until 1941, the Royal Indian Navy was responsible for planning and executing its own civil works. After the Japanese Navy's attack on the US Navy in Pearl Harbour in December 1941, the scope and quantum of naval works increased rapidly and the Corps of Engineers – the Sappers - were made completely responsible for planning and execution of civil works. All wartime construction at the major Naval bases was made by the MES. At the time of partition in 1947, the buildings and roads assets apportioned to the Navy were only about Rs. 2 crore.

"After partition until 1962, the development of naval assets was not much, despite the works in Bombay and in Cochin. It is really after the Chinese aggression in 1962 and thereafter that the momentum of civil works started building up.

"The factors which the MES bears in mind when dealing with the Navy could be covered under several heads:

– The process of release of funds for the execution of naval works is invariably faster than that in the Army and the Air Force. The reaction time therefore for the MES is much shorter.

– Communications in the Navy are much faster than in the other two services and this affects the relations between the planner and the user.

– In the 1970s and 1980s, the Navy was the fastest expanding of the three services. It was inducting accelerating technology, which meant that in the civil works, which were planned, often there would be changes in the original design, which the MES would need to adjust to.

---

1   For this *contretemps*, see the section titled "The New Naval Academy at Ezhimala", page 323.

2. The civil works of the East Zone covered the construction of the Sailors Training Establishment at Chilka, the depots at Koraput and Bimlipatnam, all civil works in the North, Middle and South Andamans, in Little Andaman, at Car Nicobar and at Kardip and Campbell Bay in Great Nicobar.

3. The MES' notable contribution in the construction of the Vizag Dockyard has been covered in the Chapter on "Maintenance, Repair and Refit Facilities," page 152.

- The interaction between the MES and the Navy had to take into account that the seniority structures were somewhat different and the organisational structure was somewhat different and that these factors should not intrude in the way of professional interaction.

- As a rule, naval personnel, both officers and men, are better educated than their counterparts in the other two services. The MES had to take this into account when dealing with the user.

- The average naval person is more technologically aware and these technological awareness factors often get factored into civil works.

- Promotions in the Navy were generally faster than those in the Sappers. It often happened that officers who had earlier been part of the same pay group got segregated when MES officers became junior to their contemporaries.

"The most important facet of interaction between the MES and the Navy is the geographical factor. Unlike the Army and the Air Force, the Navy is generally on the coast. The number of naval establishments are limited. They are concentrated at a few points, all at urban conglomerations where there is paucity of space and much pressure of land. This means that the Navy has been forced to go in for multi-storeyed construction with its attendant services like water supply, electric supply and the consequent increase in the industrial establishments of the MES stations. In any case, the electric supply, water supply, civil services and most of the urban necessities on which the MES depends are hardly adequate to meet their own needs. Thus the MES is forced to provide its own independent systems and plan the requirements at least 20 years ahead.

"The climatic conditions along the coast are well established. Heavy rain is one of the major characteristics. Many naval stations are subjected to cyclonic influence. The MES has to take this into account since it affects the drainage and layout of waterproofing and area drainage systems.

"The other problem pertaining to location of major naval stations is the soil. In many cases, the territory is estuarine and as such there are heavy over layers of alluvium. Also in most cases, due to shortage of space, vast tracts of land are always being reclaimed. At these places, the soil is mostly marine clay with its peculiarly treacherous characteristics. Thus the expenditure on foundations is generally 40% to 60% of the expenditure of structure in most of the naval stations. The MES have invariably had to evolve the optimum for each station regarding the type and depth of foundation vis-à-vis the number of storeys to be constructed.

"Corrosion is another problem at most naval stations. The periodicity of painting stipulated in the MES regulation is quite inadequate to keep corrosion at bay. Similarly, the temperature and high humidity encountered in most naval stations makes air conditioning and refrigeration essential. This involves both heavy capital as well as maintenance expenditure compared to the Army and the Air Force. The Navy's air conditioning and refrigeration requirements are substantially higher and the magnitude, location and centralisation of these plants at these stations are a matter that requires the deepest possible study to arrive at cost effective solutions."

Proposals to Restructure the MES

By the end 1980s, the volume of the Navy's civil works had become so large, the need for them so urgent and the delays so frustrating that scepticism grew about the MES' capability to cope. The causes of disenchantment being articulated were:

- It takes unduly long to complete civil works. Shore infrastructure, therefore, lags far behind our urgent needs.

- The quality of finished work leaves much to be desired. As a result, we do not get full value for the money spent.

- Architectural designs have not kept pace with time and tend to be stereotyped, repetitive in nature and over-cautiously heavy.

- Modern construction techniques are not adopted.

It was felt that the situation would improve if the MES Chief Engineers in each Command were under the respective FOCs in C in Bombay, Vishakhapatnam and Cochin instead of under the E in C in Delhi.

These issues were examined at length. It was decided that Zonal Chief Engineers (Navy) would be positioned as follows:

Naval Command	Zonal Chief Engineer
Eastern Naval Command	Chief Engineer Navy Vizag
Fortress Commander A&N	Chief Engineer Navy Port Blair
Southern Naval Command	Chief Engineer Navy Cochin
Western Naval Command	Chief Engineer Navy Bombay

51

The Navy And The Sea Cadets

The Genesis of the Sea Cadet Corps

In the 1930s, Mr Gokaldas S Ahuja's Karachi-based business of exporting carpet-grade wool to Europe brought him into contact with the sailing fraternity in Karachi. Fond of the sea and of sailing, he acquired a converted fishing boat and along with a few young boys, who were equally fond of the sea, used to sail in Karachi harbour.

In May 1938, he and a few others set up the Karachi Sea Scouts (as a counterpart to the Boy Scouts) with the aim of teaching young boys swimming, sailing, knots and splices. The organisation grew and in due course a Sea Scout Council was formed.

In July 1942, a sailing dinghy of the then Royal Indian Navy capsised in Karachi's China Creek. Sea Scouts who happened to be in the vicinity, promptly assisted in the rescue of the three naval trainees. As a gesture of appreciation, the Commanding Officer of the Navy's Boys Training Establishment, *HMIS Dilawar*, obtained approval for the Sea Scouts to use his establishment for their training. In due course, Sea Scouts embarked ships of the Navy for training cruises and were given small arms training in the Navy's Gunnery School (*HMIS Himalaya*) in Karachi.

During the 1939-1945 World War, Mr Ahuja and some of his officers of the Sea Scouts were granted honorary commissions in the Royal Indian Navy Volunteer Reserve and they participated in the motorboat patrols of Karachi harbour. The young Sea Scouts learnt and imparted first aid training and did air raid precaution duties.

After the war, in recognition of their contribution to the war effort, the Sea Scouts were presented with two motorboats to facilitate their waterman-ship activities. During these war years, Mr Ahuja got to know the naval officers who later migrated to India after Partition.

By mid 1947, Mr Ahuja had raised Rs 2,50,000 from the public, the Karachi Port Trust, the Government of Sind and the Governor's War Purposes Fund and, on the foreshore of the China Creek, had built a "stone frigate" as the headquarters of the Karachi Sea Scouts.[1]

After the Partition of India in 1947, Mr Ahuja and many of his Sea Scouts migrated to Bombay. The Navy allowed the Sea Scouts to conduct their training in the Naval Dockyard and later in *INS Angre*.

In 1950, Mr Ahuja visited the United States and Britain to study their naval youth movements. In Britain, he found that the Sea Cadet Corps was closest to his objectives. In 1951, the Sea Scouts were renamed as the Sea Cadet Corps. As the number of cadets increased, training started being carried out both at *INS Kunjali* and *INS Angre*.

In the late 1950s, a suggestion was made to the Sea Cadet Corps that it should amalgamate with the naval wing of the National Cadet Corps. The suggestion did not find favour because bringing the Corps under government purview would require every decision to be approved by an outside authority and slow things down.

In 1956, the Sea Cadet Council was formed. Its objectives were:

- To create sea-mindedness in the citizens of India.

- To help in the formation of and running and controlling the Sea Cadet Corps Units in various ports and other places in India.

- To give technical training to and instill Naval Traditions in boys who intend to serve in the Indian Navy or the Merchant Navy, both in war and in peace and also to those sea-minded boys and girls who do not intend to follow a sea career but who, given this knowledge, would form a valuable reserve for the Indian Navy and the Merchant Service.

- To provide for the physical, mental, moral, spiritual, social, educational and cultural development of the Cadets.

- To develop character and good citizenship in their widest sense among boys and girls through sea training, discipline and love of adventure.

---

1. The 'stone frigate' was inaugurated by Mr Jamshed Nusserwanji, a renowned theosophist and philanthropist and Mayor of Karachi.

In 1957, the Sea Cadets presented a guard of honour to Prime Minister Jawaharlal Nehru at Raj Bhawan. The Prime Minister told the cadets:

"What I have seen today has pleased me immensely – that our boys and girls here in Bombay have voluntarily joined the Sea Cadet Corps and are learning the rudiments of seamanship and that they are doing this with very keen enthusiasm. Now that I have met you, I wish to be kept informed about you and your activities, so that I can continue to know what is happening and what you're doing."

At the Prime Minister's behest, the Bombay Port Trust gave the Sea Cadet Corps a plot of land on the south Bombay foreshore at Colaba, at a nominal rent, for building their "stone frigate" headquarters. The Bombay Port Trust also gave a grant of Rs 100,000 and a recurring annual grant of Rs 5,000.

At the invitation of the Prime Minister, the Sea Cadets started participating in the Republic Day Parade in Delhi from 1958 onwards. Participation ceased after 1991 due to objections raised by the National Cadet Corps (NCC). In their home states, Sea Cadets participate in the Republic Day, Independence Day, State Day and other parades.

In 1963, when laying the keel of the "stone frigate" headquarters, Prime Minister Nehru told the Sea Cadets:

"I wish that every boy and girl in this country should be able to undergo this kind of training in one form or the other, whether Navy, Army or Air Force. This time particularly it is essential on account of the emergency when our border has been violated.[2] But even without the emergency, our young men should become active and disciplined and the lethargy in us must be wiped out. For this reason, I am especially happy to be here to participate in the keel-laying ceremony of the national headquarters ship and I sincerely hope that the Sea Cadet Corps will flourish."

In 1973, the Sea Cadet Council registered as a Public Registered Charitable Trust with the Flag Officer Commanding-in-Chief Western Naval Command as Chairman Trustee and eminent persons in the fields of shipping, industry, administration and the Navy as its Trustees.

The tempo of sailing activities increased in the 1980s and fund raising commenced for the construction of a "boating station" and associated facilities. The Naoroji Pirojsha Godrej Memorial Building Boat Station was built adjacent to TS Jawahar on land leased from the Government of Maharashtra for 99 years at a nominal rent of Rs 1 per year. It was commissioned by the Chief of the Naval Staff in November 1991. It provides storage for the sailing boats with their masts rigged, dormitory accommodation for 100 cadets, boat building and boat repair facilities.

In 1994, the Chief of the Naval Staff became ex-officio President of the Sea Cadet Council with the Flag Officers Commanding-in-Chief of the Western, Eastern and Southern Naval Commands as Senior Vice Presidents.

At the time of writing, the Sea Cadet Corps remains a non-government, non-political, non-sectarian youth organisation having 15 units all over India. Most units are located in naval establishments and the Navy provides training facilities and officer and sailor instructors. Boys and girls in the age group 10 to 12 years are eligible to apply. Training lasts for four years.

Its 7,000 school/college-going boys and girls voluntarily come for an average of 5 hours theoretical and practical training every Sunday throughout the year and for training courses during vacations. They acquire smartness through parade training and physical training and learn about first aid and communications.

Sailing and water-based activities are carried out on Saturday afternoons and during school vacations. By learning to handle pulling boats at a young age, they acquire confidence and proficiency in watermanship, seamanship and sailing.

All Sea Cadet officers are honorary and voluntary and hold Sea Cadet Corps ranks. Officers and cadets provide themselves with uniforms and receive no honorarium or expense of any kind. Cadets pay an admission fee on joining and a nominal annual subscription. Many cadets are from non-privileged backgrounds, and at the end of their training, emerge better equipped for mainstream life.

Vice Admiral RKS Ghandhi, resides adjacent to TS Jawahar. He recalls:

"I often return from fishing very late at night. Whenever the day comes for young boys and girls to submit their applications to become Sea Cadets, I have seen their parents queuing up in the middle of the night to submit the forms the next morning. As for those who are already Sea Cadets, their enthusiasm to excel, both on board their 'stone frigate' and in watermanship activities has to be seen to be believed!"

Retrospect

From its inception in 1938 as the Sea Scouts and later as the Sea Cadets, the founder of the Corps, Mr Gokaldas

---

2. China had violated India's northern and north-eastern borders in October 1962.

Ahuja, had a symbiotic relationship with the Navy and with every single Admiral of his time. From 1947 onwards, the Navy gave the Sea Cadet Corps whatever it sought to impart parade, small arms and watermanship training, not only because of Mr Ahuja's irresistible enthusiasm but also because the Navy shared his vision of making children better acquainted with the sea around them.

On the recommendation of the Navy, the President honoured him by progressively granting him honorary naval rank, the last of which was Honorary Commodore. After his demise, the cause of the Sea Cadets has been continued by his son Commodore (Sea Cadet Corps) Rabi Ahuja, who has been associated with the Sea Cadets from a young age. Following in his father's footsteps, he was granted the rank of Honorary Captain Indian Navy in 2003.

The citation of Mr Gokaldas Ahuja's Padma Shri stated:

"Honorary Commodore Ahuja's achievements span half a century. His endeavours have been responsible for giving to this country not only responsible citizens but also yachtsmen of international repute, fine officers in the Indian and merchant navies and many of the leading citizens in our great cities.

"In recognition of his services to the Sea Cadet Corps, the maritime community of India, to the youth of the country and indeed to the country as a whole, the President is pleased to bestow the title of Padma Shri on Gokaldas Shivaldas Ahuja."

This citation reflects how much the vision and perseverance of a single individual in a worthy cause can benefit so many. Over 20,000 boys and girls have received Sea Cadet training; many of them have succeeded in the Navy, the Merchant Navy, the Army, the Air Force and in the corporate world.

The Sea Cadet Corps has excelled in fostering sailing. Its officers and cadets have won gold medals in Asian Regattas and World Championships. *TS Jawahar* and the Navy have jointly organised and conducted national and international sailing championships. Today, the co-located facilities of the Naval Sailing Club Mumbai and *TS Jawahar* are amongst the finest in the world for conducting international sailing regattas and championships.

The ensuing chronology records the development of the close relationship between the Navy and the Sea Cadet Corps.

Chronology

1951: Sea Scouts renamed as Sea Cadet Corps.

1954: Sea Cadet Band formed.

1955: The Sea Cadet Corps admitted the first batch of 24 girl cadets to its ranks and like the boy cadets, the girls were trained in squad drill, signaling, shooting and boat work.

1956: The Sea Cadet Council was formed as a controlling body of the Corps with the Governor of Bombay as its President. The Council comprised the Chief Minister, the Education Minister, the Army Area Commander, the Flag Officer Commanding the Indian Fleet, the Mayor of Bombay and the Commodore-in-Charge Bombay.

Sea Cadets were organised into three units: Bombay Unit No 1 at *INS Angre*, Bombay Unit No 2 at *INS Kunjali* and Bombay Unit No 3 of girl cadets at *INS Angre*.

To raise funds for the permanent headquarters to be housed in a 'stone frigate' on the foreshore in Bombay Harbour, Dr Homi Bhabha permitted the Sea Cadet Ball to be held on the lawns of the Tata Institute of Fundamental Research in December each year. The Sea Cadet Magazine started being published, timed for release during the Ball.

1957: Summer and Winter Camps started being held in the National Defence Academy in Poona. Four Sea Cadets proceeded to Britain at the invitation of their Sea Cadet Organisation in London to undergo training with the British Navy.

1958: At the invitation of the Prime Minister, the Sea Cadets started participating in the Republic Day Parade in Delhi.

1959: Sea Cadet Unit commissioned in Madras.

1961: The Chief of the Naval Staff authorised the Captain Superintendent of the Sea Cadet Corps to hoist the Indian Blue Ensign, having the badge of the Corps, on board ships of the Sea Cadet Corps as long as these vessels were exclusively in the service of the Sea Cadet Corps. This was ratified by an Act of Parliament.

1963: Prime Minister Jawaharlal Nehru laid the keel of the 'stone frigate' that was to become the National Headquarters of the Sea Cadet Corps.

Vice President Radhakrishnan inaugurated the Silver Jubilee Celebrations.

Sea Cadet Unit commissioned in Tiruchirapalli.

1964: Sea Cadet Unit commissioned in Calcutta in INS Hooghly, now named INS Netaji Subhash.

1966: President Radhakrishnan commissioned the 'stone frigate' as the National Headquarters of the Sea Cadet Corps and named it 'Training Ship Jawahar' in memory of late Prime Minister Jawaharlal Nehru. The Government of Maharashtra donated Rs 250,000, the Municipal Corporation of Greater Bombay donated Rs 100,000 and the Scindia Steam Navigation Company donated Rs 100,000. These moneys, together with the Rs 100,000 earlier granted by the Bombay Port Trust and the funds collected during the Sea Cadet Balls helped to defray the construction costs of *TS Jawahar*.

1969: Sea Cadet Sailing Association formed and affiliated to the YAI.

1970: Sea Cadet Unit commissioned in Visakhapatnam in INS Circars.

1971: Cadet class National Association formed on board *TS Jawahar*.[3]

1972: The Captain Superintendent of the Sea Cadet Corps, Mr Gokaldas Ahuja was promoted Honorary Commander in the Indian Navy.

1973: Sea Cadet Unit commissioned in Delhi in INS India.

1974: Honorary Commander Gokaldas Ahuja promoted Honorary Captain Indian Navy.

1975: Sea Cadet Unit commissioned in Cochin in *INS Venduruthy*.

1976: In the Cadet Class World Championships organised by *TS Jawahar*, Sea Cadets Farook Tarapore and Sanjiv Rawell won the Bronze Medal, the first ever medal won by an Indian in an International Individual sports event.

1979: Honorary Captain Gokaldas Ahuja promoted Honorary Commodore Indian Navy.

Keel of the Sea Cadet Corps' Sail Training Ship laid at Bhavnagar by the FOCinC West.

1980: Sea Cadet Unit commissioned in Ootacamund in the Good Shepherd Public School.

Sea Cadet Corps' Sail Training Ship launched by the Chief of the Naval Staff.

India's first square rig sail training ship commissioned by the Chief of the Naval Staff as *SCC STS Varuna*.

1982: TS Jawahar along with the Naval Sailing Club conducted the Asian Games Yachting Event in Bombay Harbour. Ex-Sea Cadet Farook Tarapore and Sea Cadet Midshipman Zarir Karanjia won a gold medal.

1986: Honorary Captain Gokaldas Ahuja awarded the Padma Shri.

1987: Sail Training Ship Varuna sailed for the Australian Bicentennial Celebrations and Tall Ships Race from Hobart to Sydney with a naval crew and two Sea Cadets in September 1987.

TS Jawahar along with the Naval Sailing Club conducted the First Commonwealth Regatta.

1988: *Varuna* returned to Bombay after her Australian voyage in April 1988.

TS Jawahar conducted the International 'Cadet Class' World Championship. For the first time in the history of Indian sailing, India won a Gold medal in a world sailing event. These gold medals were won by Sea Cadets Cyrus Cama and Amish Ved. In the same event, Sea Cadets Nikhil Ved and Vikas Kapil won Bronze Medals.

1989: Two Sea Cadet officers, Shakeel Kudrolli and Sumeet Patel won gold medals at the Asian Regatta held in China, the first gold medals won overseas.

1990: Sea Cadet Unit commissioned in Bombay at INS Hamla at Marve.

1991: *TS Jawahar* assisted the Naval Sailing Club in the conduct of the International Enterprise World Championship.

Pirojsha Godrej Memorial Boating Station commissioned to further develop *TS Jawahar's* sailing infrastructure.

1992: Sea Cadet Unit commissioned in Jamnagar in *INS Valsura*.

1993: Sea Cadet Units commissioned in Goa in the Hydrographic School in INS Gomantak and in Port Blair in *INS Jarawa*.

1994: Sea Cadet Unit commissioned in *INS Chilka*.

1995: Sea Cadet Unit commissioned in Lonavala in *INS Shivaji*.

1996: *TS Jawahar* conducted the International Cadet class World Championships.

2000: Sea Cadet Units commissioned in Pune in JN Petit Technical High School and the National Defence Academy's KV School.

2001: Sea Cadets participated in the Navy's International Fleet Review and had the honour of leading the City Parade carrying the flags of 33 participating navies.

TS Jawahar hosted the Sea Cadet Annual Conference and an International Muster for foreign Sea Cadets.

---

3. The two-hander Cadet has nurtured most of India's top class sailors.

Sea Cadet Unit commissioned in Okha in *INS Dwarka* and in Daman in the Coast Guard Air Station's Public School.

2003: Two Sea Cadets embarked in the Navy's *Sail Training Ship Tarangini* during the 42-day middle leg in the Great Lakes.

The Sea Cadet Corps conducted the International Optimist Dinghy Asian Sailing Championship with 58 participants from 12 Asian countries.

2004: Two Sea Cadets embarked in *Tarangini* for the final leg from Singapore to Kochi.

52

Sailing And Yachting

Preamble

In India, sailing is as ancient as its history. Sailing vessels carried India's merchandise as far east as China and as far west as the Red Sea and the east coast of Africa.

Sailing as a sport was introduced in India by the English in the 19th century and remained an exclusively English sport. The first Yacht Club was established in 1846.

A number of sailing clubs came into being wherever there was sufficient water and sailing enthusiasts. The prominent clubs were in Bombay, Poona, Calcutta, Barrackpore, Madras, Maithon[1] and Secunderabad. Clubs owned their own boats and also looked after the boats owned by their members.

From the naval point of view, sail training imparts first hand experience of wind, weather and the vagaries of the sea and fosters nicety of judgement and the quality of "sea sense". Its unique value lies in its ability to develop initiative, courage, comradeship, teamwork and endurance, particularly in rough weather. The Navy imparts sail training to cadets as soon as they embark on their naval career.

Naval Sailing in the 1950s

In the 1950s, frigate-sized ships and above used to have two-hander 14-foot sailing dinghies embarked on board for sail training. On Wednesday and Saturday afternoons and on Sundays, it was customary for ships to lower their dinghies, in whichever harbour or anchorage they happened to be in, and except when sailing races had been scheduled, leisurely sail around the harbour. Commanding Officers usually took one of their ships' officers to crew for them and the ships' officers usually took one of their younger officers or midshipmen to crew for them. This helped the younger officers to learn and acquire 'sea sense' from their elders.

Yachting[2] from 1960 Onwards

In 1960, the yachting enthusiasts of Bombay and Poona, led by the Army's College of Military Engineering (CME) in Poona, succeeded in launching the Yachting Association of India (YAI) and patterned it on the Royal Yachting Association of Britain.

Since the CME and its Sappers Sailing Club came under the Engineer in Chief (E in C) at Army Headquarters, the first President of the YAI was the E in C. The Commandant of the National Defence Academy, Rear Admiral BA Samson was the Vice President. Major KO Stiffle of the CME who had been the driving force in the creation of the YAI was the first Secretary. Today, there are 42 clubs affiliated to the YAI.

Commander (then Lt Cdr) RN Gulati was the Assistant Secretary of the YAI in 1960. He recalls:

"In a matter of two years after 1960, due to the untiring efforts of the YAI, the several sailing clubs located in different parts of India were brought under the YAI banner and All-India Regattas were held. The Navy took serious note of this development and naval officers began to feature prominently in such regattas - Lieutenant Commanders Mammen, Mongia, Contractor and Moghal were among them. It is significant that they were all products of the National Defence Academy,[3] barring Mammen who was in charge of the NDA's Naval Training Team.

"With the Navy's greater involvement in racing, the mantle of the Presidentship of the YAI shifted to the Chiefs of Naval Staff, which continues to this day.

"In February 1962, whilst at the NDA, I organised and skippered an off-shore sailing expedition from Bombay to Goa and back. Of course, once again the Sappers of the Army had beaten us in this regard as well, as in

---

1. The 80-square mile Maithon Lake is located in the Damodar Valley.

2. In contemporary sailing parlance, 'a yacht is a craft raced under sail measuring to a standard size.'

3. The National Defence Academy is located beside the 15-square mile Kharakvasla Lake.

the mid 50s, Major Stiffle had skippered a Seabird class yacht to visit Karachi and Bandar Abbas in Iran.

"In 1970, when I was the Deputy Director Naval Training at NHQ, I started the ball rolling for the acquisition of an ocean-going yacht. Unfortunately, it didn't materialise then. However the seed had been sown. It resulted in the acquisition of the square-rigged brig *Varuna* in 1987, which completed around the world voyage following in the footsteps of the Army *Trishna's* similar voyage a few years earlier."

The Sea Cadet Sail Training Ship *Varuna*

The Section titled, "The Navy and the Sea Cadet Corps" has dealt with the genesis of the Sea Cadets in Karachi in 1938, their re-naming as Sea Cadets in Bombay in 1951 and the subsequent development of the Corps in close association with the Navy. Its founder, Mr Gokaldas Ahuja, had two visionary dreams:

- The first was to raise the funds for the construction of a 'stone frigate', as the headquarters of the Sea Cadet Corps. In 1966, the President of India commissioned Training Ship *Jawahar,* on the eastern foreshore in Bombay harbour.

- The second was the construction of a Sail Training Ship in which his Sea Cadets could actually go to sea. This was fulfilled on 20 April 1981 when the Sail Training Ship *Varuna* was commissioned by the Chief of the Naval Staff, Admiral RL Pereira.[4]

The 110-tonne, 29-metre long *Varuna* was built by Alcock Ashdown in Bhavnagar, at a cost of Rs 32,50,000,[5] to the drawings of the "Royalist", a brig owned by the Sea Cadet Corps in Britain. The design had been chosen for its capacity to allow the maximum number of cadets to be trained, without their having to handle unduly heavy sails and having the facilities for acquiring skills in navigation, engineering and communication.

Varuna was the first square-rigger in Asia. She had 5,000 square feet of sail – six square sails and six fore and aft sails. She had a bunk each for 21 cadets, a modern galley and a chart house well-equipped with navigational aids. Her normal speed under sail was 6 to 7 knots though she could make up to 10 to 12 knots with all sails rigged. She was fitted with two diesel engines for manoeuvres in harbour and for use when wind conditions were unfavourable. She could sail for 8 to 10 days at a stretch.

The Navy undertook to man and maintain *Varuna* as a tender to the training cruiser *Mysore*. In return, the Navy used *Varuna* for three days a week for the sail training of *Mysore's* naval cadets.

Varuna's Voyage to Australia for the Bicentennial Celebrations

On 26 January 1988, Australia was to hold the bi-centennial celebrations to commemorate the landing of the first Australian settlers in and around the port of Sydney. As part of these celebrations, a "Tall Ship" race was scheduled from Hobart to Sydney in which 250 square-rigged ships would be taking part. It was decided that the Indian Naval Adventure Foundation would sponsor *Varuna* for the celebrations.

After being refitted in the Naval Dockyard Bombay, *Varuna* sailed on 14 September 1987 on her first oceanic voyage, manned by seven officers, five senior sailors, 16 naval cadets and two Sea Cadets. She carried 2½ tonnes of fuel and 2,700 litres of water, which limited their water consumption to five litres per head per day during the 29,600 km voyage.

On the outward journey, *Varuna* called at Goa, Cochin, the Indonesian ports of Padang, Cilacap and Bali, and the West Australian ports of Port Headland, Carnarvon, Geraldton and Fremantle.

After departure from the South Australian port of Adelaide, Varuna suffered a setback off Port Lincoln. She lost both her masts with sails at sea on 20 December 1987. At her next port of call, Melbourne, she was refitted with a new rig, (without square sails but only fore and aft sails) in which configuration she participated in the Tall Ships event with improvised 'jury masts' and arrived at Sydney on 14 January 1988, as planned, for the Tall Ships Parade.

Varuna departed from Sydney on 29 January 1988. After calling at Melbourne, Adelaide, Esperance, Fremantle, Carnarvon, Christmas Island, Jakarta, Singapore, Penang, Campbell Bay, Cochin and Goa, she arrived in Bombay on 15 April 1988, having completed a 15,000-mile voyage in seven months.

Indian Naval Sailing Vessel *Samudra*

Tri-Service Expedition 1988-89

In 1987, the Navy acquired the 13-metre sailing yacht *Samudra*. In 1988, it was decided to send *Samudra* on

---

4. Her keel had been laid in 1979 and she had been launched in 1980.

5. Apart from an interest free loan from the Navy, the Prime Minister contributed Rs 100,000 annually from the National Defence Fund for the maintenance of *Varuna*.

a Tri-Service expedition to circumnavigate the globe. The first leg of 7,590 miles was from Vizag on the east coast of India to Dakar on the northwest coast of Africa. The second leg of 9,735 miles was from Dakar to Hawaii in the middle of the Pacific Ocean. The final leg of 10,660 miles was from Hawaii back to Vizag.

Flying the Blue Ensign of an Indian Naval Fleet Auxiliary, *Samudra* set sail westbound from Cochin on 15 November 1988, manned by six officers – four from the Navy and one each from the Army and the Air Force.

On the first leg, *Samudra* called at Aden, Port Said, Malta, and Cartagena and arrived at Las Palmas on 2 February 1989.

She set sail from Las Palmas on 6th March and after calling at Cayenne, Georgetown, Trinidad and La Guaira arrived at Panama on 5th May where a new engine was fitted.

She sailed from Panama on 24th May for San Cristoba (Ecuador). To avoid the hurricane season off the west coast of Mexico, *Samudra* was re-routed via the South Pacific Ocean.

After calling at the Galapagos Islands, Nikuhiva and Tahiti, she arrived at Rorotonga on 26th July where she remained until 9th September when she sailed for Port Villa. After calling at Port Moresby, Darwin, Surabaya and Port Blair, she arrived at Vizag on 4 December 1989.

During her 52,000 km voyage round the world, *Samudra* visited 27 ports in 18 countries.

Bali Yatra 1992

In November 1992, the Navy in collaboration with the Government of Orissa sent *Samudra* on a sailing expedition to Bali in Indonesia to commemorate the trading links and the sailing route used by traders during the period of the Gupta Empire.

Chronology

1950: Naval Sailing Club Bombay started functioning with three boats owned by the Naval Officers 'Vasant Sagar' Mess and maintained by the Shipwright School in *INS Angre*.

1955: *INS Shivaji* Sailing Club started functioning on Shivaji Lake.

1960: The Yachting Association of India formed on 15 May 1960 at the CME Poona. Like other Commonwealth countries, it was affiliated to the Royal Yachting Association of Britain and was recognised as the National Yachting Authority for India.

August 1960: First YAI Regatta held under the auspices of the National Defence Academy on Kharakvasla Lake.

1961: Defence Services Sailing Club inaugurated at Delhi-Okhla on the river Yamuna.

Indian Naval Sailing Association (INSA) established.

Naval Sailing Club Vishakhapatnam inaugurated when *INS Circars* took over the local yacht club.

Second YAI Regatta held under the auspices of the Naini Tal Yacht Club on Naini Tal.[6]

1963: The International Yacht Racing Association (IYRU) granted India the sail letters "KI". (K was used by all Commonwealth countries and I was for India).

1964: Naval Sailing Club Cochin inaugurated in September.

1965: Naval Sailing Club Bombay shifted from *INS Angre* to its present location in Colaba after the Coast Wing Boat Pool was taken over from the Army.

1969: Sea Cadet Sailing Association formed and affiliated to the YAI.

1970: In the Asian Games Yachting in Bangkok, Lieutenant Commander S Contractor won the Bronze Medal in the Enterprise class event. He received the Arjuna Award.

1971: India became a full member of the International Yacht Racing Association and the letters "IND" replaced the letters "KI" on Indian sails.

1972: Lieutenant Commanders S Contractor and T Mogul participated in the 1972 Olympics sailing events in Kiel, Germany.

1973: National Enterprise Association formed in the Naval Base Cochin.

1977: The International Yachting Championship in the Enterprise class boats was held at Goa from 11 to 17 December 1977. This was the first time when such an event was held in an Afro-Asian country.

1978: In the Asian Games Yachting at Bangkok, Commanders SK Mongia and D Kumar won Silver Medals in the Enterprise class event. Commander SK Mongia received the Arjuna Award.

---

6. Subsequent YAI Regattas were held on a number of occasions at Maithon, Madras, Delhi, Bombay, Kirkee, Cochin, Secunderabad, Bangalore and Kharakvasla.

1980: The Navy inaugurated the annual Seabird Rally from Bombay to Goa.

1981: April 1981 – Sea Cadet Sail Training Ship *Varuna* commissioned.

In the Enterprise class World Championships held in Canada, Captain SK Mongia won the Bronze Medal.

The Headquarters of the YAI shifted from the Army Headquarters' Engineer-in-Chief to Naval Headquarters.

1982: In the Asian Games Yachting in Bombay, Sub Lieutenant F Tarapore won the Gold Medal in the Fire-Ball class event. He was awarded Rs 10,000 for his achievement by the Chief of the Naval Staff. He also received the Arjuna Award.

1984: Lieutenants F Tarapore and D Bhandari participated in the 1984 Olympic sailing events at Los Angeles.

1985: The Indian Army's 'Sappers' commenced their one and a half year 50,000-kilometre circumnavigating voyage round the world in their 37-foot fibre-glass yacht *Trishna*.

1986: In the Asian Games Yachting at Pusan, Lieutenants F Tarapore and D Bhandari won Silver Medals in the 470-class event. Lieutenant D Bhandari received the Arjuna Award.

Naval Sailing Club Port Blair inaugurated.

1987: September 1987 – Sail Training Ship *Varuna* sailed for the Australian Bicentennial Celebrations and Tall Ships Race from Hobart to Sydney.

1988: April 1988 – Varuna returned to Bombay after her Australian voyage.

Watermanship Training Centre Mandovi inaugurated in the Naval Academy.

November 1988 – *Samudra* sailed for the Tri-Service Sailing Expedition.

1989: December 1989 – *Samudra* returned to Vizag after circumnavigating the world.

1990: At Asian Games Yachting in Beijing, Lieutenant F Tarapore won the Bronze Medal in the 470-class event. Lieutenant Commander H Motivala and Lieutenant PK Garg won the Bronze Medal in the Enterprise event. Lieutenant PK Garg received the Arjuna Award.

INS Shivaji Sailing Club shifted to the new Shivsagar Lake.

Naval Sailing Club (Mandovi) constituted in November for the Naval Academy.

1991: In the Enterprise class World Championships held in Bombay, Lieutenants F Tarapore and KS Rao won the Gold Medal.

1992: November 1992 – *Samudra* sailed on the expedition to Bali to commemorate the sailing route used by traders during the period of the Gupta Empire.

The Naval Sailing Club Mumbai

The Naval Sailing Club Mumbai is the largest yachting complex in India. It houses the National Sailing Institute of the Sports Authority of India. It hosts national sailing championships and international sailing and yachting regattas and championships.

The Indian Naval Sailing Association

The Indian Naval Sailing Association (INSA) was established in 1961. Its aims were:

- To promote the sport of sailing and yachting amongst naval personnel.
- To encourage the growth of naval sailing clubs in ports and, where facilities exist, in naval bases and establishments.

INSA started off with four Naval Sailing Clubs – Bombay (*INS Angre*), Visakhapatnam (*INS Circars*), Cochin (*INS Venduruthy*) and Goa (Dona Paula). Since then Naval Sailing Clubs have been inaugurated in *INS Shivaji* (the Engineering School at Lonavala), *INS Valsura* (the Electrical School at Jamnagar), *INS Hamla* (the Logistics, Management, Computer and Catering School at Marve, Bombay), *INS Agnibahu* (the parent naval establishment at Karanja, Bombay), *INS Gomantak* (the parent establishment at Vasco da Gama, Goa), *INS Mandovi* (the Naval Academy at Panjim, Goa), *INS Chilka* (the Sailors Training Establishment on Chilka Lake in Orissa) and *INS Jarawa* (the parent naval establishment at Port Blair in the Andaman Islands).

INSA conducts annual intra Navy championships and fields individuals and teams for national championships.

Four Yearly Asian Games

Year	Venue	Class	Skipper & Crew	Medal
Up to 1970		No yachting events		
1970	Bangkok	Enterprise	Lt Cdr S Contractor	Bronze
1974	Teheran	No yachting events		
1978	Bangkok	Enterprise	Cdr SK Mongia	Silver
			Cdr D Kumar	Silver
1982	Bombay	Fireball	Sub Lt F Tarapore	Gold
1986	Pusan	470 470	Lt F Tarapore Lt D Bhandari	Silver Silver
1990	Beijing	470 Enterprise	Lt F Tarapore Lt Cdr H Motivala Lt PK Garg	Bronze Bronze Bronze

EARLY EUROPEAN TRADING POSTS AND BASES IN THE INDIAN OCEAN

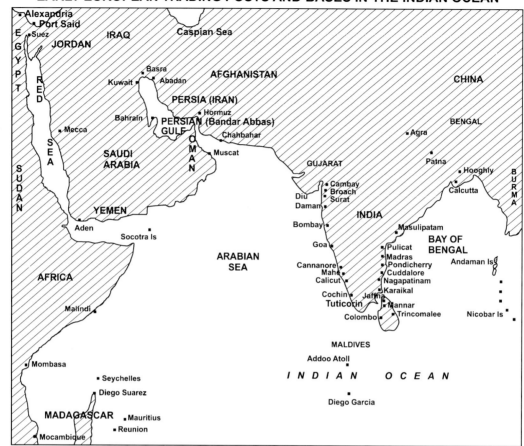

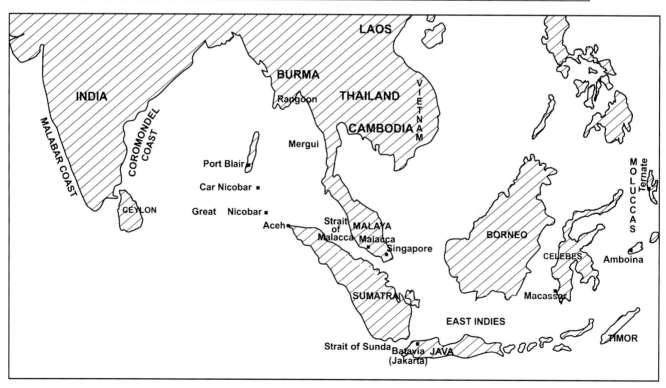

Reference Notes

1. Historical Overview of Naval Presence in the Indian Ocean - 15th to 18th Centuries

The Chinese

In the 14th century, rampant piracy off China's coast had led Chinese emperors to commence the construction of a long north-south inland canal through which merchandise-laden boats could ply between the southern and northern regions. Whilst this canal was being constructed over the decades, armed imperial Chinese ships kept the pirates at bay.

In 1402, the Ming emperor decided to extend his commercial influence westwards into Southeast Asia and the Indian Ocean. He selected Cheng Ho[1] to command these missions. Between 1405 and 1434, Cheng Ho led seven voyages of over sixty ships at a time, the largest and best equipped exploring fleets then known, laden with gold, silks, porcelain and other Chinese wares. During these voyages, unprecedented for that era, he visited Indochina, Java, Sumatra, Ceylon, Calicut on India's Malabar Coast, Hormuz at the entrance to the Persian Gulf, Aden at the entrance to the Red Sea and the coast of east Africa.

These voyages were intended to encourage Indian Ocean kingdoms to come and trade with China and at the same time to discipline private Chinese merchants who belonged to a pirate fringe. This policy was given up in the 1420s when the Chinese capital moved from Nanking to Peking to cope with the Mongol threat in the north.

After the inland canal was completed, water-borne traffic shifted from the sea to the canal route. The fleets built up during Cheng Ho's voyages were allowed to run down. This coincided with the imperial perception that China was self sufficient enough to be the centre of the world and that there was no need to interact vigorously beyond its maritime boundaries.

Piracy in the China seas, which had been one reason behind the Chinese voyages into the Indian Ocean, intensified with the northward withdrawal of the Imperial Navy. To counter pirate attacks, the later Mings (1435 to 1644) and the Manchus (1644-1911) tried to insulate China from the sea.

The next significant voyage of Chinese naval ships into the Indian Ocean took place 550 years later in 1985.

The Portuguese

In 1492 Columbus sailed westwards from Spain in search of the Indies. Five years later, Vasco da Gama sailed southwards from Portugal in 1497. After rounding the Cape of Good Hope, he went up the east coast of Africa and engaged an Indian Gujarati pilot who navigated him across the Arabian Sea to make landfall near Calicut on the Malabar Coast of India in 1498.[2]

---

1. The voyages of Cheng Ho (Zheng He, meaning Three Jewel Eunuch) helped to extend Chinese political, maritime and commercial influence in Southeast Asia and the Indian Ocean. His voyages reinforced the foundations laid from the 9th century onwards for the emigration of Chinese traders to Southeast Asia, who became the forbears of today's 'Overseas Chinese' of this region.

2. Vasco da Gama sailed from Lisbon with four ships on 8 July 1497. In November, he rounded the Cape of Good Hope. By the time he reached the port of Moçambique, he ran into Muslim hostility but at Malindi on the coast of what is now Kenya, he managed to secure a Gujarati pilot to guide him eastward. He set sail on 24th April with three ships and reached Calicut (now Kozhikode) on the Malabar Coast of India on 20/21 May 1498.

   When he offered the paltry gifts that he had brought with him (cloth, hats, coral etc) to the Hindu ruler known as the Zamorin, he was told that 'it was nothing to give a King and that the poorest merchant who came from Mecca would give him more than that'. Instead he was asked for gold. Vasco was unable to sign a trade agreement. With the winds against him, the voyage back to Malindi took three months and many of his crew died of scurvy before they arrived in Portugal in September 1499. On his return, he informed Portugal's King Manuel that the Indians were not interested in European trinkets and clothes. They made far better fabrics and trinkets themselves.

   To follow up Vasco da Gama's discoveries, Pedro Álvares Cabral was immediately dispatched to India with thirteen ships and a thousand men. He established a trading post in Calicut. When news reached Portugal that this trading post had been razed by the Zamorin and Cabral had to flee to Cochin, Vasco da Gama was sent to India again in February 1502 to avenge that act. On the way to India he attacked a number of Muslim ships killing more than 400 men, women, and children returning from a Haj pilgrimage to Mecca. Arriving in Calicut, he subdued the inhabitants with superior fire-power and forced the Zamorin to make peace. Bearing a rich cargo of spice, he started homeward, establishing en route Portuguese colonies at Moçambique and Sofala on the coast of what is now Mozambique, before arriving in Portugal in September 1503. Rewarded by the Portuguese monarch for supposedly 'breaking the Muslim monopoly on trade with India', Vasco da Gama settled down to profit from his ventures. For the next two decades, he saw no active sea duty. In 1524 he was named viceroy and sent to India to correct the mounting corruption among the Portuguese authorities there. He died in Cochin three months after his arrival.

   By pioneering the Portuguese sea route to India, Vasco da Gama had established Lisbon as the centre of the European spice trade, and laid the foundation for the Portuguese control of trade with the ports of eastern Africa, south-west India and the East Indies.

The Portuguese objectives were to monopolise the trade in spices, which the Arabs then controlled, and secondly to undermine the Ottoman-controlled monopoly by depriving it of its terrestrial spice trade.

The first two Portuguese viceroys, Francisco de Almeida from 1505 to 1509 and Afonso de Albuquerque from 1509 to 1515, evolved and implemented, with remarkable speed, the concept of naval power based on fortified posts and backed by settlements:[3]

- On the east African coast at Kilwa in 1505 and Mozambique Island in 1507.

- Near the entrance to the Red Sea in the island of Socotra in 1507.

- On the west coast of India at Cochin in 1502, Cannanore in 1506, Goa in 1510, Diu in 1535 and Daman in 1558.[4]

- On the Malay coast of the Malacca Strait at Malacca in 1511.

- At Timor in 1511.

- At Amboina in the Moluccas in 1512.

- At the entrance to the Persian Gulf at Hormuz in 1515.

Subsequent viceroys established posts in Ceylon at Colombo in 1518, in the Spice Islands – at Ternate in the Moluccas in 1521 and Macassar in the Celebes in 1545, at Bombay in 1534, at Macau in China in 1557 and at Mombassa in 1593 on the east coast of Africa.

For nearly a century, the Portuguese operated in the Indian Ocean without European competition. Whilst their network of trading posts and forts gave them a measure of maritime control, they never gained total control of the trade in pepper and fine spices. There were several reasons:

- Until the arrival of the Portuguese, much of the intra-Indian Ocean trade had been conducted by Arabs. At first, the Portuguese intended to oust the Arabs entirely.

They found it impossible to manage without them. The Arabs were soon trading again, with Portuguese concurrence.

- Even though Portuguese ships patrolled both the west coast of India and the Strait of Malacca, shippers were able to bypass Malacca and India. They brought spices from the Moluccas through the Strait of Sunda to Aceh in northern Sumatra for transhipment directly to the Red Sea. Albuquerque's inability to capture Aden at the Red Sea entrance allowed the resumption of Red Sea Arab traffic up to Alexandria from where Venetian ships carried the spices to Europe.

- Portugal's naval power could not fully dominate the Indian Ocean because resource constraints precluded having the number of ships necessary to control the vast water expanse. Indian Ocean footholds became expensive to maintain. Frequent mishaps to fleets, from shipwreck or enemies, reduced profits. The lack of a true monopoly prevented the Portuguese from charging the prices that they wished in European markets.

- With fewer than one million people and involved in similar forays in Africa and South America, Portugal was short of manpower. Soldiers from the home country could only be spared in limited numbers. This made the Portuguese rely on alliances with local states and enlist local troops.[5] To overcome the manpower limitation, the Portuguese turned their forts into settlements to provide a resident population for defence. Intermarriage was encouraged.[6] Christianity was encouraged through the church.[7] The new mixed population became firmly Roman Catholic and successfully resisted attacks and sieges.

- From viceroys to humble soldiers and seamen, the Portuguese succumbed to the temptation to line their own pockets.[8]

In 1580, the Portuguese crown passed to the Spanish Habsburgs until in 1640, a revolt restored independence.

---

3. Portuguese ships, sturdy enough to survive Atlantic gales and mounted with cannon, easily disposed of Arab, Indian and Malay vessels. Whenever they faced opposing fleets, they usually prevailed with their superior ships and cannon-fire.

4. The enclaves adjacent to Daman were established much later – Nagar Haveli in 1783 and Dadra in 1785.

5. This policy was continued throughout the Indian Ocean by the Dutch, the French and the British until 20th century.

6. In Goa, a Luso-Indian community resulted from Albuquerque's policy after 1510 of subsidising marriages between Portuguese residents and Hindu brides. Even though Malacca was the nerve centre for the spice-producing islands of the East Indies and the exchange mart for the trade with East Asia, the Portuguese preoccupation with the Ottoman fleet in the Red Sea, Goa became the capital of the Portuguese East in preference to Malacca.

7. Saint Ignatius Loyola had founded the Jesuit order in 1534. Soon thereafter, Goa was selected as their headquarters in the Indian Ocean. The See of Goa was established in 1537. In 1542, the great Jesuit saint, Francisco Xavier, selected by Ignatius Loyola and appointed Papal Nuncio, arrived in Goa. In 1557, Goa was made a Metropolitan See and in 1560 an Archbishopric.

8. This malady afflicted all the powers that followed the Portuguese.

It was during this period, 1580 to 1640 that Portuguese power declined in the Indian Ocean. The Portuguese ran short of skilled manpower to crew their vessels and the rising naval power of Holland and England challenged their position. Under Dutch blows in the East Indies and those of the English in India,[9] Portuguese dominance ceased, though they continued to retain colonies like Mozambique, Goa and Timor well into the 20th century.

The Indian Ocean region did gain a few things from the Portuguese presence. The tangible benefits were the introduction of products like tobacco, potatoes, pineapples, tomatoes, papayas, cashew nuts, and two varieties of chillies.

The Dutch

After the defeat of the Spanish Armada in 1588, the route to the east lay open to both the English and the Dutch. In the race to the Indian Ocean, the Dutch, having larger resources, were the first to arrive.

Since the 1590s, many Dutchmen had voyaged to India and the East Indies in the service of the Portuguese as gunners, traders and clerks. Representatives of Amsterdam merchants had been to Lisbon to collect information on the sea route and the Portuguese trade.[10]

In 1602, the Dutch parliament granted the Dutch East India Company, the VOC, a charter giving it a trading monopoly that extended from the Cape of Good Hope in South Africa eastwards to the Strait of Magellan in South America, with sovereign rights in whatever territory it might acquire to conclude treaties with local princes, to build forts, maintain armed forces, wage war and conclude peace. By so doing, the Dutch Government made the VOC its instrument of war and conquest. Administrative functions were to be carried out through officials who were required to take an oath of loyalty to the Dutch government.

In the initial stages after the formation of the VOC, the role of the Dutch Navy was limited to providing guns to VOC ships and for providing small warships to escort, and protect from English depredations in the North Sea, the convoys returning from the Indian Ocean. The large Dutch warships remained 'in being' to oppose the English fleet in the ongoing Anglo Dutch Wars.

The primary VOC objective was neither religion nor empire but the spice trade. Knowing that the Portuguese had no forts in the Moluccas, Java or Sumatra, they went directly to the main source of spices, the Spice Islands – the Celebes and the Moluccas – and secondarily to India's Malabar Coast for pepper and cardamom and to Ceylon[11] for cardamom and cinnamon. In 1619, they fixed their headquarters at Batavia (now Jakarta) in West Java.

Their strategy was to take control of the spice trade by isolating the East Indies from trading in spices by sinking all vessels found in the archipelago's waters, opening fortified trading posts, expanding its presence by direct force and through alliances with local rulers.

The English East India Company (EIC) had followed the VOC to the East Indies. It was no match for the VOC in resources. In 1632, the VOC killed all the English agents in Amboina, the main trading post for spices in the Moluccas. After this massacre, the EIC withdrew and made Surat the centre of their India system (based on friendly relations with the Mughal emperors) and obtained a footing at Goa by an amicable arrangement with the Portuguese.

The VOC broke down the Portuguese monopoly by the persistent use of force. With superior resources and better seamanship, the Dutch wrested Portugal's trade and bases. Malacca,[12] Ceylon, and Cochin fell to the Dutch in 1641, 1658, and 1662 respectively. In 1652, the VOC established the first European settlement in South Africa on the Cape of Good Hope. At the peak of its power in 1669, the VOC had 40 warships, 150 merchant ships, and 10,000 soldiers.

---

9. The Persians, with English help, ousted the Portuguese from Hormuz in 1622. Bombay passed to England by marriage treaty in 1661. Ousted from most strongholds, the Portuguese retained their capital at Goa, despite blockades and sieges.

10. In 1595, small companies of Amsterdam merchants had started their first voyages to the Indian Ocean. These voyages had followed the Portuguese route around the Cape and, expectedly, were opposed by the Portuguese. In Amsterdam, these small companies started competing for profits thereby spoiling the market. The leaders of the Dutch Republic commenced efforts to unite the small companies into one company, which in 1602 became the Vereenigde Oost-Indische Compagnie (VOC) - 'United East India Company' – the world's first 'joint stock company.'

11. Dutch ships first visited Ceylon in 1602 and found the local king eager to enlist Dutch help against the Portuguese. In 1610 and 1612, when the Sinhalese again sought help, the Dutch signed treaties. In 1638 and 1639, the Dutch captured Batticaloa and Trincomalee respectively. In 1642, the Dutch and the Portuguese signed a 10-year truce treaty, followed by a 1644 treaty for sharing the cinnamon producing areas. In 1656, a Dutch fleet blockaded and captured Ceylon, except for the Portuguese strongholds of Mannar and Jaffna in the north of Ceylon that were supported by their Indian strongholds of Nagapattinam and Tuticorin. In 1657, the Dutch evicted the Portuguese from Tuticorin and in 1658 from Mannar, Jaffna and Nagapattinam.

12. In 1641, the VOC captured Malacca, but this no longer ensured control of the spice trade to Europe. To impose a monopoly, the VOC restricted the cultivation of cloves to Amboina and of nutmeg and mace to the Banda Islands, destroying the spice trees elsewhere.

Much larger than the English EIC, the Dutch VOC had the character of a national concern. Dutch naval power, more efficient than that of the Portuguese, secured monopoly conditions in the islands and sea-lanes. It was only in land areas like Travancore (in Kerala) that resort had to be made to competition.

As regards the problem of payments for commodities, the VOC, like the EIC, (and the Portuguese before them) were short of exchange goods. Textiles were needed to buy spices and silver was needed to buy cotton and silk in India and China respectively. To work the spice monopoly, the VOC developed an elaborate system of trade extending from the Persian Gulf to Japan, the ultimate object of which was to secure the goods with which to secure the spices without recourse to scarce European resources. It was this trade that brought the VOC to northwest India at Surat,[13] to the southeast Coromandel Coast at Nagappattinam, to Bengal[14] in northeast India and up-country at Agra.

By the late 17th century, the VOC declined as a trading and naval power and became more involved in the internal affairs of Java. By the 18th century, the VOC had changed from a commercial-shipping enterprise to a loose territorial organisation interested in the agricultural produce of the East Indies archipelago. It established plantations for coffee and other new crops and instituted a system of forced deliveries. This relied on the cooperation of amenable Javanese aristocrats, and on intermediaries from the growing local Chinese population whose immigration the VOC promoted. In the Moluccas and much of the East Indies archipelago, VOC trading rights were converted into political control, with local rulers retaining their internal autonomy and collecting tribute for the VOC.

Gradually, internal disorders, the growth of British[15] and French power and the consequences of a harsh policy towards the inhabitants enfeebled the VOC. The corruption of VOC officials, financial mismanagement and a decline in trade eventually led to the VOC's bankruptcy. In 1799, the Dutch government revoked the VOC's charter, took over its debts and assumed direct control of what came to be called the Dutch East Indies (now Indonesia).

The English

The English venture to India was entrusted to the East India Company (EIC), formed for the exploitation of trade with East and Southeast Asia and India. It received its monopoly rights of trade by royal charter on 31 December 1600. It was not comparable to the 'national' character of the VOC. Its initial capital of £ 50,000 was less than one-tenth of the VOC's.

The EIC's first objective being the 'the spices of the East Indies', the first two voyages went there. On the third voyage, one of the ships came to Surat in 1608 to obtain cotton textiles for exchange with the spice growers in the East Indies.[16]

The EIC's naval victory off Surat in 1612 over the Portuguese, whose control of the Haj pilgrim sea route to Mecca was already being resented by the Mughals[17], brought about a dramatic change. The embassy of the Englishman Sir Thomas Roe (1615-18) to Emperor Jehangir's court secured an accord (in the form of a *firman*[18], or grant of privileges), by which the EIC secured the right to trade and

---

13. As early as 1604, the Dutch had tried, without success, to open trade in Surat, in the Gulf of Cambay on the northwest coast of India, to secure Gujarat cottons for the Moluccas, Sumatra and Europe. In 1616, the Surat merchants, fearful that the Dutch might attack their shipping, granted the Dutch 'provisional' permission to open a trading post. In 1618, despite English opposition, the Dutch succeeded in negotiating a treaty of commerce with Prince Khurram, the son of Mughal Emperor Jehangir. Thereafter trading posts for indigo and textiles were established at Broach, Cambay, Ahmedabad, Agra and Burhanpur.

14. In 1627, the Dutch established their first trading posts at Pippli and Balasore. After the Nawab of Bengal gave the Dutch the villages of Chinsura and Bernagore in 'perpetual fief', the Dutch set up trading posts at Chinsura and Qassimbazar up the Hooghly River and further upstream on the Ganges at Patna. Their exports were textiles and silk, saltpetre, rice and opium for Java and China.

15. It was powerless to resist a British attack on its possessions in 1780.

16. The captain had a letter from the king of England to Emperor Jehangir asking permission to trade. He went to Agra and presented this letter in person in 1609. Jehangir promised trading facilities but the Portuguese, whose trading posts were already well established in India, made it plain that they would resist any attempt by the EIC to encroach on their preserves. To continue the trade, the EIC, in 1611, established a trading post for cotton textiles on southeast India's Coromandel Coast at Masulipatam. The EIC's sixth and seventh voyages were unable to trade at Surat owing to the presence of a Portuguese fleet. In 1612, therefore, the EIC sent out a squadron of fighting ships. This squadron arrived in Surat in September and obtained a *firman* confirming Jehangir's permission to trade. In October, a Portuguese fleet arrived to dispute the matter. A running fight of several days followed, neither side securing any decisive advantage. In end November, the Portuguese drew off. The EIC ships returned to Surat, landed their goods and set up their first trading post.

17. The annual Haj pilgrimages to Mecca, whose route lay through Gujarat and Surat had for years been hassled by Portuguese extortion and dominance of the Arabian Sea. Indeed, the safe performance of Haj by the Muslim ladies of Emperor Akbar's household had to be arranged under passes issued by the Portuguese.

18. This *firman* from the Mughals, combined with the EIC's exclusion from the East Indies by the VOC in the same period, determined that India, and not the Far East, should be the chief theatre of English activity in Asia.

to establish trading posts in return for becoming the virtual naval auxiliaries of the Mughal Empire.[19]

The EIC's attempts to penetrate the East Indies had met with stout opposition from the VOC. After the Amboina massacre in 1632 (in which the VOC seized the EIC trading post and executed all the English, Japanese, and Portuguese traders), the EIC's trade for spices steered discreetly clear of the VOC's domain.

Shivaji, the founder of Maratha power in India, had perceived the need for ships to harry both the Mughals and the EIC and had built up a modest fleet of agile indigenous armed ships called *ghurabs* and *gallivats*.[20] In January 1664, Shivaji, assembled his fleet and attacked Surat by land. Six years later, in 1670, Shivaji attacked Surat again.

For the rest of the century, the EIC settled down to a trade in cotton and silk piece goods, indigo, and saltpetre, with spices from south India. From India, it extended its commercial activities to the Persian Gulf, Southeast Asia and East Asia.

On the Coromandel Coast, the trading post established at Masulipatam in 1611 was moved up to the site of Madras in 1639 to be nearer to the weaving centres from which the EIC obtained cotton textiles for export to Persia and the East Indies. In 1641, Madras became the EIC's headquarters in south India and became the first settlement to be fortified.

The only exception to the arrangement of trading posts operating under Mughal firman was the island of Bombay. In the First Anglo-Dutch War in Europe (1652-1654), England and Portugal had been allies. After the war, the Portuguese ceded Bombay to the king of England in 1661 as part of the dowry for his marriage to a Portuguese princess. Since there was no way that the king could administer Bombay from England, he transferred it to the EIC in 1668. The EIC had a precarious time for seventeen years until 1685, when it moved its headquarters from Surat to Bombay and fortified it.[21]

In 1690, political instability in south India made it necessary to acquire a second fortified trading post, besides that in Madras. The EIC purchased a fort, later named Fort St David, near the town of Cuddalore, about 100 miles (160 km) south of Madras.

The trade developed by the EIC differed substantially from that of the VOC. It was a trade in bulk instead of in highly priced luxury goods. The profits were a factor of volume rather than scarcity. It worked in competitive instead of monopolistic conditions. It depended upon political goodwill instead of intimidation.

The EIC's trade became more profitable than that of the VOC, because of the smaller area covered and because the absence of the armed forces for enforcing monopoly reduced overhead expenses. But it encountered the same difficulties of payment. Indians would take little other than silver in exchange for their goods, and the export of bullion was an offence to England's reigning mercantilist political economy.

To solve the silver problem, the EIC developed a system of country trade not unlike that of the VOC, the profits of which helped to pay for the annual dispatch of goods to England. Madras and Gujarat supplied cotton goods, and Gujarat also supplied indigo. Silk, sugar, and saltpetre (for gunpowder) came from Bengal. There was a spice trade along the Malabar Coast on a competitive basis with the VOC and the Portuguese. Opium was shipped to China and became the basis of the Anglo-Chinese tea trade.

Towards the close of the 17th century, when the VOC's financial crisis compelled its ships to decay and its relations with local rulers started depending on flattery and presents, the EIC concluded that its position in India had to depend on naval and military power. It tried to copy the VOC's policy of the use of force. It resorted to armed trade and attacked the Mughals. This 1686-90 venture ended in disaster. Out of this fiasco, however, came the foundation

---

19. There is an apocryphal story that the Mughal Empress, Noor Jehan, had the prescience to caution Emperor Jehangir against granting this *firman* to the English because they might infiltrate his empire from seaward. But the Emperor told her that women should not meddle in matters of statecraft.

20. The 'ghurabs' were beamy, shallow draught, square-rigged sailing ships of 300 to 400 tonnes with two or three masts and armed with sixteen to thirty nine-pounder and twelve-pounder guns.

    The 'gallivats' were smaller, shallow draught galleys of 70 to 120 tonnes, armed with four to ten two-pounder and four-pounder guns and propelled by a single bank of oars, with a triangular mainsail as 'auxiliary'.

    Their usual tactics were to lie in wait for a single ship and then attack with eight or ten ghurabs and forty and fifty gallivats carrying boarding parties. The ghurabs would lie off astern of the ship at long cannon-shot and fire at her masts. If they succeeded in dismasting her, the gallivats with their boarding parties would close her from all sides and board her.

21. The situation in Bombay was quite piquant. The EIC was on Bombay Island, the Portuguese on Salsette and at Mahim and Varsova, the Mughals at Mazagon, and the Marathas on Khanderi and Elephanta Islands. For the best part of twenty years, the EIC balanced in a precarious neutrality between the Marathas and the Mughals, taking no part in the fierce and bloody battle fought between their fleets off Thana (in which the Sidi, the Mughal admiral, secured an overwhelming victory), but trying, in pursuance of orders from England 'to keep out of wars and obtain trading rights from both sides'.

of Calcutta in 1690 – a mud flat that had the advantage of a deep anchorage.

At Madras, Fort St George was already fortified. A fort had been built in Bombay. Fort William in Calcutta followed in 1696. By the end of the 17th century, the EIC had three centres of power on the coasts of India, each sustainable by sea.

The EIC found that India produced the world's best cotton yarn and textiles. To this huge 'cottage industry', they provided the powerful stimulus of European demand. By the end of the 17th century, India had a sophisticated market and credit structure and controlled a quarter of the world trade in textiles.[22] It had twenty three percent share of the world's GDP (roughly the USA's share of the world's wealth today). Indian cottons had transformed the dress of Europe.[23]

The French

The French had shown an interest in the Indian Ocean from the early years of the 16th century but their voyages were few and far between.[24]

In the 17th century, French trading companies were established under different names to oversee French commerce with India, East Africa and other territories of the Indian Ocean, and the East Indies. French ships periodically visited the Spice Islands, Malacca, Japan and the coasts of Arabia and India. But the VOC's determination to monopolise the trade checked the French from establishing an effective naval presence in the Spice Islands.

In 1642, the French established a trading post on Madagascar's southeast coast at Fort Dauphine as it was easily reached by ships coming from or going to India.

In 1643, Île de Bourbon (now the island of Réunion) was settled as a layover station for ships rounding the Cape of Good Hope en route to India. The French established a settlement there in 1662.

In 1664, the French monarchy approved the formation of the Compagnie des Indes Orientales (CIO), granting it exclusive privilege of trade for 50 years from the Cape of Good Hope to India and the South Seas. The CIO was granted also the perpetual grant of Madagascar and the neighbouring islands on the condition of promoting Christianity there, the perpetual grant of all lands and places conquered from France's enemies and the ownership of all mines and slaves it might take.

The CIO first arrived at Surat in 1668. In pursuance of the *firman* given by Emperor Aurangzeb, the CIO established a trading post and began to trade westwards with Bandar Abbas and Basra in the Persian Gulf and eastwards up to the Spice Islands.[25]

The CIO flourished briefly until 1675. By 1680, little money had been made and many ships were in need of repair. Further progress of French settlements was interrupted by events in Europe. The VOC captured Pondicherry in 1693. When the CIO retrieved it in 1697, it had regained a fine fort but had lost the trade. By 1706, the CIO seemed moribund.

Other European Companies in the 17th Century

There were four other European enterprises in the Indian Ocean during this period:

- **Danish.** Initial attempts to gain a share of the East India trade were not very successful. Ships operated intermittently from 1616 onwards from Tranquebar on the Coromandel Coast. After the Danish East India Company was formally chartered in 1729, it acquired Serampore in Bengal in 1755 and prospered until the British advance of power there later in the 18th century. The company waned after Britain destroyed Danish naval power in its 1801 war in Europe. In 1845, Britain purchased Tranquebar and Serampore.

- **Belgian.** In 1723, the Ostend Company of Austrian Netherlands merchants appeared for a brief period as

---

22. Economic historians have done considerable research on the wealth of India between the 16th and 18th centuries. At the end of the 16th century, India's wealth sustained more than a hundred million people. With plenty of arable land, its agriculture was vibrant with productivity comparable to the best in the world. There was a large and vigorous skilled artisan work force that produced not only cottons but also luxurious products for the landowners and the courts. The economy produced a great financial surplus and the annual revenues of the Mughal Emperor Aurangzeb (1659-1701) were more than ten times those of his contemporary Louis XIV, the richest king of Europe.

23. The English steadily learned from India about cotton textiles. By the end of the 18th century, they began making textiles with machines generated by the Industrial Revolution.

24. 29 years after the Portuguese, the first French ship appeared at Diu. In 1530, two French ships reached the west coast of Sumatra. In 1601, two ships visited the Maldives and, via Ceylon and the Nicobar Islands reached Sumatra.

25. By 1671, trading posts were established in Malabar, in Masulipatam on the Coromandel Coast, Ceylon, Malacca and in Bantam in the Spice Islands. In 1671, a French fleet visited Surat, Daman, Bombay, Goa, Calicut, Crangannore and Cochin. After rounding Ceylon, it obtained from the king of Ceylon the grant of Trincomalee. In 1676, the CIO acquired Pondicherry on the Coromandel Coast, 85 miles south of Madras. In constant competition with the already-established VOC, the CIO's ships were often harassed and sometimes confiscated by the VOC. In 1690-92, the CIO obtained Chandarnagar, 16 miles north of Calcutta, from the Mughal governor.

a serious rival in Indian Ocean trade. In 1731, it was eliminated by diplomatic means.

- **Sweden** and **Prussia** tried to establish profitable companies – both were unsuccessful.

The 18th Century Anglo-French Contest

In the economic wisdom of the 18th century, colonies, trading companies and their settlements existed to provide the mother country with a favourable balance of trade, a profit held in gold and silver to pay for its army and navy in times of war. The wars of the 18th century therefore aimed to dispossess other European powers of their colonial sources of wealth.[26] After the demise of the Dutch East India Company (the VOC) in 1699, the trade contest was between the English East India Company (the EIC) and the French East India Company (the CIO).[27] Britain's Navy was, by this time, the largest force of its kind in the world.

For the first half of the 18th century, the EIC confined its relations with the Mughal emperors (who by then had spread into south India) to disputes over rights and terms of trade at local levels. Fresh privileges were obtained from the Mughal Emperor in Delhi, and these, the English were content to argue about, rather than fight for.

The CIO was reconstituted in 1720 and under the close supervision of the French government, underwent a dramatic change; over the next 20 years, it opened new trading posts as trade expanded.[28]

The Situation in the Middle of the 18th Century

In north India, the Mughal Emperor was sickly, in western India the Marathas were dominant and in peninsular India there was competition between the Marathas, the Mughals, and the local rulers for regional political primacy. The Marathas were both active and ambitious.

It was on this scene that the wars in Europe precipitated an Anglo-French naval contest in the Indian Ocean. In an internecine dispute in 1740, Prussia had seized Silesia. France supported Prussia. Britain supported Silesia. The British decided to contest France's Indian Ocean trade. The neutrality of previous years was abandoned. Both sides depended on naval power for success.[29]

By 1761, the French threat to British power in south India had been contained. In 1769, France suspended the operations of its CIO.

In 1778, war broke out in Europe again, this time between Britain and a coalition of France and Holland. The EIC seized the CIO trading posts on the Coromandel Coast. The Dutch naval force had confined itself to the East Indies. The French Navy was tasked to confront the

---

26. In 1534, the Sultan of Gujarat, in return for a promise of a contingent of 500 Portuguese soldiers to fight against Mughal Emperor Humayun, ceded to the Portuguese the islands of Bombay and Bassein.

27. In the 18th century, the EIC gradually prevailed over the VOC in the race to satisfy Europe's extraordinary appetite for the silks and cottons of Bengal and for the tea of China. The consumption of tea helped to fuel a new explosion of sugar production in Caribbean plantations worked by slaves bought in West Africa and paid for in such diverse imports as Brazilian sugar, Coromandel and Bengal cottons.

28. Mauritius (Île de France) was settled in 1721. Mahe on the Malabar Coast and Karaikal on the Coromandel Coast were acquired in 1725 and 1739 respectively. Chandarnagar in Bengal was revived.

    The CIO prospered between1735 to 1754. In 1742, Dupleix, the ablest leader of the CIO, was appointed the governor-general of French India. He directed the struggles of the CIO against the EIC. The capture of Arcot, however, in 1751 by the EIC's Lieutenant Colonel Robert Clive restricted CIO control to south India, where it remained dominant until 1761, when the British captured the CIO's capital, Pondicherry.

29. The French moved first into the Bay of Bengal. An improvised fleet from Mauritius relieved the British siege of Pondicherry, blockaded Madras by sea, defeated British ships in two naval actions and drove them up to Calcutta. Dupleix captured Madras in September 1746 but failed to take the neighbouring British fort of St David which, in the 18th century, had become a second centre of British power in south India. In 1747-48, aided by the presence of a British fleet, Fort St David withstood a French assault. In the treaty that ended the war, France returned Madras to the British.

    After the CIO's capture of Madras, the French had grown in prestige as skilful soldiers, and grown in power by troop detachments left behind by the French fleet. The CIO seized the opportunity for exploiting this increase in French reputation by involving itself in a dispute over the succession to the governorship of a large state in south India.

    Partisans of the rival families looked impartially to the Marathas, the Mughals, and the Europeans for help. The CIO assessed that the reward for the success of their protégé would be the undermining of the EIC's trade in southern India and greater influence over the affairs of peninsular India. The CIO allied itself with one group. In a battle that demonstrated convincingly the superiority of French arms and methods of warfare, fortune favoured the CIO. The EIC reacted by supporting the other claimant. There developed a private war between the two companies. In the next battle, the CIO was worsted, forced to surrender and make a settlement with the EIC.

    During the next war in Europe (the 1756-63 'Seven Years' War between France and England), both countries sent their fleets to the Indian Ocean. The first British force was diverted to Calcutta. This gave the French general the initial advantage; however, after taking Fort St David, he lost time, his attack on Madras miscarried and the EIC was able to defeat the CIO decisively.

    In 1758, Fort St David was retaken by the CIO but was abandoned when the French Pondicherry was attacked by the EIC. After a siege, Pondicherry, the capital of French India, was captured. The French surrendered in January 1761.

EIC and the British Fleet in the Bay of Bengal, retrieve the trading posts, assist the French troops besieged in Cuddalore and assist Hyder Ali, the ruler of the Carnatic who was fighting the British. This required the interruption of sea communications in the Bay of Bengal between the EIC settlements and especially between the British strongholds of Calcutta and Madras, despite the disadvantage of France having no naval bases to support its Fleet.

Between February 1782 and June 1783, a French Naval fleet under Admiral Suffren repeatedly got the better of the British fleet under Admiral Hughes in a series of naval actions. With no naval bases available to assist, Suffren doggedly repaired the damage suffered by his ships during each encounter, using locally available materials and his ships crews.

For want of adequate support from the French Government, Suffren did not succeed in his objective to decisively defeat British naval power in the Bay of Bengal. Nevertheless, his achievements were substantial. For two years, he operated hundreds of miles away from the nearest French naval base. And his threat against British naval domination forced a satisfactory peace, in spite of the other reverses to French arms.

Suffren believed that the proper work of a Navy was to crush the enemy in action and that the command of the sea could never be secured whilst a hostile fleet was undefeated. This ran counter to the principle of the French naval authorities of that time that the destruction of the enemy's fleet was to be subordinated to the furtherance of operations on land – a principle that Suffren boldly disregarded in his campaign.

On return to France, Suffren was promoted to Vice Admiral. The inscription on the medal struck in his honour succinctly stated his achievements – 'The Cape Protected', 'Trincomalee Taken', 'Cuddalore Delivered', 'India Defended', 'Six Glorious Combats'.

The principal factor for the French lack of success was the British command of the sea. The French could get no Indian allies for lack of money and no money for lack of supply from France. Because the French saw more profit from trade in the West Indies, the French CIO in the Indian Ocean lacked whole-hearted government support. The British could supply Madras from both Britain and from Calcutta.

Whilst this naval contest was going on in the Bay of Bengal, a body of opinion grew within the EIC that only British control of India could end the constant wars between the Indian states and provide really satisfactory conditions for trade. Full dominion would be economical as well as salutary.[30] The British government began to control EIC policy through a regulatory board responsible to Parliament.[31]

Until the end of the 18th century, Portugal, Holland, France, and Britain continued to engage in naval encounters in their respective regions to retain local control of the sea routes that linked their overseas colonies to the parent country. Britain emerged victorious from this struggle.

---

2. 19th Century British Hegemony in the Indian Ocean

The following excerpt from a book ('War and Diplomacy in Kashmir 1947-48') based on recent research by Ambassador C Dasgupta elaborates on this strategy:

"For two centuries, the Indian Empire was both the object and the instrument of British strategy in the Indian Ocean. The defence of India was secured by a twofold policy. In the first place, Britain controlled the entry points into the Indian Ocean through a ring of naval bases. Port Said and Aden guarded the entrance through the Red Sea, the Cape route was controlled through the base at Simonstown in South Africa, while bases in Singapore and Fremantle guarded the entrance from the Pacific.

The second element of Britain's imperial policy was to prevent any land-based great power from securing an outlet into the Indian Ocean. The object, in other words, was to prevent the outflanking of British sea-power. In the 19th century, Britain viewed the Turkish Empire in Arabia and the kingdoms of Iran and Afghanistan as a buffer against Russia's expansion to the shores of the Indian Ocean. Up to World War I, Britain sought to preserve the integrity of the Ottoman Empire in Asia in the belief that its collapse might advance Russian interests.

The defence of the Indian Empire was thus organised on a regional basis through a policy which effectively converted the Indian Ocean into a 'British lake'.

---

30. Many of the EIC's employees looked longingly at the territorial revenues that might assist their own enrichment.

31. The EIC's commercial monopoly started to break in 1813. From 1834 onwards, it was a 'managing agency' for the British Government of India. It was deprived of even this after the first Indian War of Independence in 1857 (which Western history books refer to as the Indian Mutiny). The events of 1857 compelled Britain to formally take over the governance of India from the EIC. Britain's Navy assumed strategic responsibility for the Indian Ocean. The EIC ceased to exist as a legal entity in 1873.

It is equally true that it was the Indian Empire which made it possible to implement this policy. With its central situation in the Indian Ocean, India was the focal point of sea and, later, air communications in the region. It was a great supply and storage centre. Above all, the Indian Army was the instrument of British control over the littoral countries.

Indian military units were permanently garrisoned at Aden, Singapore and Hong Kong. At various times, Indian troops were sent overseas to protect British imperial interests in East and North Africa, Sudan, the Gulf, Malaya and even China."

---

3. The Operations of the German Cruiser *Emden* in the Indian Ocean in 1914

Emden commenced its operations in the Bay of Bengal by bombarding Madras, capturing / sinking 25 steamers and sinking warships in Penang. Merchant shipping started being kept in port. British warships started searching for *Emden*.

After two months in the Bay of Bengal, *Emden* headed for the Arabian Sea to target the steamer traffic between Aden and India. Enroute, W / T intercepts alerted *Emden* that the search for her was intensifying.

The Captain decided to target the Cable and Wireless Station in the Cocos Islands and disrupt communications

between Britain and Australia. But before the Germans could land to cut the undersea cable and destroy the W / T mast, the Station sent out a warning which *Emden* jammed but too late.

Fortuitously, an Australian Navy force happened to be in the vicinity escorting a troop convoy to Egypt. The cruiser *Sydney* was dispatched to investigate. In the ensuing battle, Sydney's superior gunfire prevailed. *Emden* grounded herself and eventually surrendered.

---

4. The Japanese Navy's Foray into the Bay of Bengal in 1942

(Excerpt from 'White Ensign - The British Navy at War 1939-1945' by Captain S W Roskill Royal Navy, pages 186 to 189).

After the sinking of the two British battleships, the Prince of Wales and the Repulse and the surrender of the British naval base at Singapore ... "A new crisis suddenly blew up in the Indian Ocean. There by the end of March 1942, the Admiralty had managed to scrape together a new Eastern Fleet consisting of two large aircraft carriers and a small one, five battleships (four of which belonged to the old and slow R Class), seven cruisers, sixteen destroyers, and seven submarines. Its commander was Admiral Sir James Somerville, who had made his reputation while in command of Force H working from Gibraltar.

Although on paper the strength allocated to him appeared substantial, in reality he was very unenviably placed. Firstly, his air element was far too weak to enable him to oppose the main Japanese carrier striking force. Secondly, many of his ships were old and not in first-class condition; and thirdly, his bases were ill-equipped to supply his needs.

Thus there were very real grounds for anxiety over the outcome of an incursion into the Indian Ocean by the splendidly trained and so far consistently successful Japanese carrier force commanded by Admiral Nagumo; and Ceylon was the obvious place for him to strike at next.

Towards the end of March we received strong indications that such an attack was to be expected in the very near future, and Admiral Sir Geoffrey Layton, who had recently been appointed Commander-in-Chief, Ceylon, with full powers over all civil and military authorities, took energetic steps to meet the expected blow. Because Colombo and Trincomalee were ill defended and too far forward to provide security, Somerville's fleet was actually working from a secret base at Addoo Atoll in the Maldive Islands.

On the last day of March he moved from there to concentrate his forces to the south of Ceylon, while reconnaissance aircraft searched the waters to the east through which the enemy was almost certain to approach. By 2nd April, however, no sign of Japanese movements had reached Somerville; and he therefore decided to allow normal shipping movements to be resumed, and himself returned to Addoo Atoll to refuel. Just when he was approaching the base, the first sighting report of strong Japanese forces some 360 miles south-east of Ceylon reached him.

In fact, Admiral Nagumo, with five fleet carriers (having some 300 aircraft embarked), four battleships and three cruisers had sailed from a base in the Celebes on 26th March, passed south of Sumatra and entered the Indian Ocean on 3rd April. A smaller force under Admiral Ozawa (one light carrier and six cruisers) was moving across the Bay of

Bengal from Mergui in southern Burma, with the object of attacking our shipping off the east coast of India.

It was Nagumo's main force which was sighted on the afternoon of 4th April, and that report caused Admiral Layton to clear every possible ship out of the harbour of Colombo. He also sent the heavy cruisers *Dorsetshire* and *Cornwall*, which Somerville had detached from his main fleet on the 2nd, back to rejoin the Commander-in-Chief.

At 8 am, on 5th April, the expected attack on Colombo took place; but the defences were fully alert, and Admiral Layton's timely precautions resulted in the damage to shipping and port installations being comparatively light. The raid had nothing like the deadly effects of that on Port Darwin in the previous February; and although Japanese aircraft losses were far fewer than we believed at the time, they were high enough to constitute a check to Nagumo's heretofore uniformly successful carrier aircrews.

Unfortunately the good work done by the defenders of Colombo was partly offset that same afternoon, when the Japanese striking forces located the *Dorsetshire* and *Cornwall* on their way south to rejoin the fleet, and sank them both with a series of devastatingly accurate dive-bombing attacks. Meanwhile, Somerville was steaming towards Ceylon from Addoo Atoll; but his slow division was still far behind his faster ships. The C-in-C next anticipated an attack on his secret base; for Admiral Layton had signaled to him that a powerful enemy force was believed to be between Ceylon and the Maldives.

Throughout the 5th, reconnaissance aircraft from the carriers flew wide searches; but they failed to sight Nagumo, who had in fact withdrawn far to the south-east, and in the evening Somerville turned back to the north-west to safeguard his base. Meanwhile, Nagumo's aircraft were combing the waters to the south and east of Ceylon for the British Fleet, and we may be thankful that they never found it; for had they done so it is difficult to believe that Somerville's weak and motley force could have survived attack by the Japanese carrier planes.

On the 8th one of our shore-based reconnaissance aircraft resighted Nagumo's ships 400 miles to the east of Ceylon, towards which they were again steering. The harbour of Trincomalee was at once cleared of shipping, and the expected attack took place early next morning. Unfortunately some of the ships sent out from Trincomalee were found by the Japanese striking forces close to the coast, after they had reversed course to re-enter the harbour. The small carrier *Hermes*, a destroyer, a corvette and two tankers were at once completely overwhelmed and sunk.

Admiral Ozawa's force had meanwhile entered the Bay of Bengal; and from the 4th to 7th April he played havoc among the unescorted and unprotected merchantmen which had been sent south from Calcutta and other ports to avoid the danger of attack while they were lying helpless in harbour. The original order to clear Calcutta of shipping was probably wise; but for some unexplained reason it was kept in force until the 6th – by which time it should have been plain that the ships would be safer where they were lying.

In five days, twenty three merchantmen totaling over 112,000 tonnes were sunk by Ozawa's squadron off the east coast of India; and to that heavy toll, Japanese submarines working off the west coast added a further five ships of 32,400 tonnes.

British shipping movements along both coasts of the whole sub-continent were brought to a standstill; and the confidence of the men of the Merchant Navy in the protection which they had always relied on receiving from their comrades of the Royal Navy was severely shaken.

Happily the Japanese had not planned to make an extended foray in the Indian Ocean, or to penetrate west of Ceylon. By 12th April both Nagumo and Ozawa were returning to Singapore by way of the Malacca Straits, while the Admiralty had suggested to Somerville that his slower ships should withdraw to East Africa to guard the long and vulnerable WS convoy route (from England to support the Army in Egypt, since the Suez Canal was closed).

Comparative calm thus descended on the Indian Ocean, and we were afforded a breathing space in which to improve the defences of our bases and the protection of our shipping; and, very gradually, reinforcements sent out from home reached Admiral Somerville. None the less, the shock sustained by the blows struck by Nagumo and Ozawa had been very severe; for the vulnerability of our maritime control over a vast and important area of ocean had been ruthlessly exposed.

Looking back today, it is plain that the disasters of April 1942 derived partly from the error we had committed in the previous autumn when, under strong pressure from the Prime Minister (Winston Churchill), the Admiralty had reluctantly agreed to Admiral Phillips's weak and unbalanced force being sent to Singapore. Though it is, of course, impossible to say what proportion of the heavy losses which we suffered between December 1941 and April 1942 might have been averted had we adopted the Admiralty's strategic purpose of concentrating every ship that could be spared in Ceylon, it is none the less clear that the Naval Staff's views on strategy were much the sounder; for at the very least their policy would probably have resulted in Phillips's squadron surviving to play a part in the defence of the Indian Ocean.

That could not, of course, have saved Malaya or the Dutch East Indies; but it might well have discouraged the Japanese from sending Nagumo and Ozawa into those waters, it might have saved Rangoon, and it would surely have reduced the time needed for us to regain the initiative at sea".

5. The British Navy's Attack on Madagascar in 1942

On 4 May1942, the British aircraft carriers *Illustrious* and *Indomitable* attacked Diego Suarez in French Madagascar. The British stated at that time that they had acted to prevent the island from falling into the hands of the Japanese. In his memoirs, Winston Churchill stated that the operation took place at a time "when we sorely needed success". After the loss of Malaya and the loss of the battleships *Repulse* and the *Prince of Wales*, after the loss of Singapore and Hong Kong, Diego Suarez promised an easy victory. It took several months to capture the whole island of Madagascar. Later, British forces attacked the French island of Reunion.

6. The Recapture of the Andaman & Nicobar Islands

In April 1945, the French battleship Richelieu bombarded Car Nicobar. On 2nd May, Richelieu bombarded Port Blair. From 10th May onwards, two groups, one formed around the battleship *Queen Elizabeth* and the other around the battleship *Richelieu*, searched for the Japanese cruiser force reported to be near Port Blair. On the night of 16th May, British destroyers of the Richelieu group sank the Japanese cruiser *Haguro* by torpedo attack.

7. "Results to the British Commonwealth of the Transfer of Political Power in India"

(Excerpts from the 'The Transfer of Power' Volume 8 Pages 50 to 57 - Note of July 1946 i.e. one year after the end of the 1939-45 World War and one year before India's Independence forwarded to London by Field Marshal Wavell, Viceroy of India

I. "The transfer of political power in India to Indians will affect Great Britain and the British Commonwealth in three principle issues: Strategy, Economics and Prestige. This note is an attempt to assess very briefly our prospective gains and losses in each of these fields.

II. "The principle advantage that Britain and the Commonwealth derive from control of India is Strategic. The greatest asset is India's manpower. The War of 1939-45 could hardly have been won without India's contribution of two million soldiers, which strengthened the British Empire at its weakest point.

III. India was also, during this period, a very valuable base of war. Her contribution in material was very considerable; and the potential will increase as India's industrial capacity expands.

IV. The Naval bases in India and Ceylon have enabled the British Navy to dominate the whole of the Indian Ocean region, except for a short interlude in the last war; these bases are of importance for the protection of oil supplies from Persia and the Persian Gulf.

V. India will also be an indispensable link in the Commonwealth air communications both in peace and war.

VI. "The strategic consequences of independence for India are set out in the GHQ paper that follows.

(*Note:* The GHQ Paper/Appreciation has been inserted here for coherence. Para VI continues after the *End of Appreciation*.)

Beginning of Appreciation

Object

The object of this paper is to appreciate the value of India to the British Empire, and to set out the strategic advantages and disadvantages should India become an independent sovereign state outside the British Commonwealth of Nations.

Factors

Introduction

The strategy of the British Commonwealth is at present based on the ability to move troops and material by air and sea across the world without interference by any hostile power.

In order to be able to protect our merchant shipping, we have established Naval bases on the main lines of communication in order that the necessary warships may be maintained and repaired. We are now establishing air lines of communication and air bases from which both our maritime and air lines of communications (L of C) can be protected.

The increasing range of shore based aircraft and the development of guided missiles has already made it difficult to protect convoys in narrow waters, and there is little doubt that we shall have to rely less on narrow waters such as the Mediterranean, and more on the broad waters of the great oceans. In effect our L of C will gradually be pushed southwards and we shall come to rely on the Cape route to the East much more than on the Mediterranean.

Importance of the Indian Ocean

It is the openly expressed policy of His Majesty's Government that no potentially hostile power shall establish bases in the Indian Ocean area, and any attempt to do so would be regarded as a hostile act. (Emphasis added)

The oil from the Persian Gulf is essential to the British Commonwealth, and its safe passage must be assured.

Our normal sea communications with Australia and New Zealand pass across the Indian Ocean, but these could be deflected round the Cape or through the Pacific without undue dislocation. From a Naval point of view, a hostile India within the next five years would not seriously affect our position, but if India was dominated by Russia with powerful air forces, it is likely that we should have to abandon our command of the Persian Gulf and the Northern Indian Ocean routes.

Air Communications

The Imperial Air Communications between the UK and Australia and the Far East must of necessity pass through India. A subsidiary route for Long Range Aircraft could be established using routes such as:

– Arabia-Ceylon-Cocos Island-Australia.
– Ceylon-Andaman/Nicobar Islands-Burma/Malaya.
– East Africa-Seychelles-Diego Garcia-Ceylon/Cocos Island

These routes could be further developed by the use of floating bases and Aircraft Carriers.

Ceylon

Ceylon is of value only if it can be used as an effective substitute for the Naval and Air bases now located in India. It is considered that even if the island were converted into a fortress, it would be of limited use in the face of a hostile

India, and it would be untenable if India were dominated by a major power such as Russia.

India as a Base

Major operations of war must be based upon a land mass which is capable of containing all the necessary base installations, repair shops, hospitals which are necessary for the maintenance of modern Naval, Army and Air Forces. Furthermore such a base must have an indigenous industrial capacity, which can expand to meet the extra load placed upon it in war.

With the coming of Atomic Warfare there is increased necessity for space, which will allow of proper dispersion of base installations.

Should it be necessary for the Commonwealth to undertake military operations on a large scale in the Far East, India is the only suitable base from which such operations could be sustained.

Australia has the space and, to some extent, the industrial capacity, but has not the manpower from which to provide fighting forces and also to expand her industry.

Indian Manpower

From a military point of view, one of India's most important assets is an almost inexhaustible supply of manpower. India, including the Indian States and Nepal, can produce as many soldiers as the Commonwealth can maintain.

Without this help it would have been difficult to win the last two wars.

It must, however, be remembered that up to date all recruits have been volunteers, and by the end of the last war the limit of voluntary retirement had been reached.

British Manpower

This para concerns **British Manpower.** Its gist is 'Britain is at present experiencing great difficulty in finding sufficient armed forces to meet her worldwide commitments. A relief of 7000 officers (800 British Army, 1500 RAF, 300 RIN, 4,400 British Indian Army) and 33,900 men (16,400 British Army, 10,000 RAF and 7,500 British Indian Army) would be of very great importance. In addition, a large proportion of approximately 2,000 British officials and 30,000 non-officials would leave India and be available for service elsewhere in the Empire.'

Natural Resources

India is the sole producer of jute, and one of the largest producers of tea in the world. Both these commodities are of great value to the Commonwealth.

Thorium exists in Travancore and this mineral may become of increasing importance in connection with atomic warfare.

Industrial Capacity

India is at the beginning of an industrial revolution. Her cotton and steel industries are beginning to rival those of any country, and there is no doubt that her heavy industries are capable of enormous expansion. In twenty years, India may be a highly developed industrial country, and may be capable of producing herself all the equipment required by modern armed forces. If India is part of the Commonwealth, this constitutes a great and increasing asset. If India is hostile or dominated by a hostile power, the threat to the Commonwealth would be extremely serious.

Effect of British Withdrawal from India

Although potentially powerful, India is at present so divided within herself, that if the British should 'quit' India entirely, leaving the leaders of the various parties to work out their own salvation, the country would be left open to Russia.

It is not possible to estimate whether Russia would actually establish bases in India, but with her taste for power politics, it is considered likely that Russia would take advantage of an unprecedented opportunity to establish herself in a position from which she could threaten the whole fabric of the British Commonwealth. History has shown that Nature abhors a vacuum and if the British step out, we can expect the Russians to step in.

Effect of a Hostile India

If India were hostile, our naval position would not be seriously affected, but if she was dominated by a hostile power we cannot guarantee our sea communications in the Northern part of the Indian Ocean and our oil supplies from the Persian Gulf would probably be cut off.

Andaman and Nicobar Islands

We have already pointed out that Ceylon would be untenable in the face of an India dominated by Russia. It is however considered that the Andaman and Nicobar Islands are just far enough from India to allow a reasonable degree of security. If we 'quit' India, we shall presumably continue to hold Malaya, although it is doubtful whether we shall hold Burma permanently. Our communications to Burma and Malaya will then be from the East and Southeast and we shall be in a similar position to the Japanese in 1942-45.

In these circumstances it is considered that we should not give up the Andaman and Nicobar Islands, but should hold and develop them as an outpost to Burma and Malaya. (Emphasis added)

The harbours should be developed, and airfields should be built from which to defend Malaya against attack from India.

Summary

The disadvantages to the British Commonwealth of an independent India may be summarised as follows:

- The supply of oil from the Persian Gulf is dependent upon the maintenance of our sea communications in the Persian Gulf and Arabian Sea. These could not be assured if India was dominated by Russia, and we consider that Russia would not neglect her opportunities of influencing an Independent India.

- Air communications between Arabia and Africa on the one side and Burma, Malaya, Australia and New Zealand on the other could not at present be maintained without the use of bases in India.

- The value in use of Ceylon would be largely reduced if India was hostile, and the island would be untenable if India was dominated by Russia.

- India as a base is of the greatest importance to the successful prosecution of operations in Southeast Asia.

- Indian manpower is an enormous asset to the Commonwealth Armed Forces.

India's natural resources and industrial capacity are of increasing importance.

The only advantage we can see in an independent India is a relief for British Manpower commitments.

We consider that it is impossible to guarantee that an independent India would not be unfriendly or would not be influenced by a power such as Russia, China or Japan, hostile to the British Commonwealth. Should such a situation arise, we could not maintain our power to move freely by sea and air in the Northern part of the Indian Ocean area, which is of supreme importance to the British Commonwealth.

A reorientation of Commonwealth strategy, whereby we might make use of the Pacific in place of the Indian Ocean is a palliative which may be forced on us, but it will not adequately replace the value of the Indian Ocean to the British Commonwealth."

End of Appreciation

Para VI continued. "It is clear (from the above *Appreciation*) that a defensive alliance with India is of great importance to Britain. Such an alliance cannot be forced on a free India, but is likely to be sought by India itself, if we manage well. It should secure our naval position in the Indian Ocean and Persian Gulf, the maintenance of the link in air communications and so far as possible the use of Indian manpower. Without such an alliance, Britain stands to lose very heavily by abandoning India.

The greatest danger is that an independent India may come under the domination of Russia. It is very difficult to estimate how likely this is to happen. An independent Indian Government could hardly be unconscious of the length of its seaboard or of the fact that 90% of its trade is seaborne. The defences of the country are so much stronger by land than by sea that India would naturally look first for a naval alliance, especially at a time when a steady flow of imports is so vital to the development of the country. And it must surely be many years before Russia can become a formidable naval power in the Indian Ocean. Again communications by land with Russia are so bad that Russian help would be no substitute for British and American help in developing the country. It seems therefore that the future Government of India will not of its own choice go for Russian protection.

Russia might however try to employ her usual tactics of giving support to a revolutionary party. Conditions in India are not unfavourable – a few capitalists and Princes have enormous fortunes, while labour is still exploited, has genuine grievances, and has begun to feel its power. Maladministration can easily cause local scarcity and famine. The nucleus of a Communist organisation already exists and is making itself felt. It would not be difficult for Russia to gain a foothold in the country by its usual methods if the Government is weak and if the gateway of Afghanistan is not effectively barred.

Unfortunately there is every prospect of an Indian Government being ineffective. It is a tremendous task to take over control of a country as large and diverse as India. There is no evidence that either the political or the administrative capacity exists to do so. If the Indian Government does turn out to be weak and incompetent, the country is likely to lapse into chaos and disorder. If that condition occurs, the loss to Britain in strategic position, manpower resources, communications and trade, will be very serious even if Russia does not intervene. Indeed, any advantages to Britain that can be anticipated as a result of handing over political power are all conditional on there being a stable successor Government that can rule the country.

To sum up, it is vital to Britain that when she gives over political power in India, she may be able to hand over to a stable and friendly Government and contract with it a genuine defensive alliance. Fortunately, India's interests quite obviously point the same way. If this objective is achieved, the demission of political power may bring advantages and not loss. In all other circumstances the debit balance will be heavy".

8. Britain's Perception of the Russian Threat

It had taken Russia three centuries to recover from the Mongol and Tatar invasions that had begun in the 13th century. As early as 1552, conquering the khanates of Central Asia became a security priority for Russia. In the 17th century, Russia conquered Siberia.[32] By the mid 1800s, Tsarist Russia strove to build an empire to extend its might, spread orthodox Christianity and gain vast farmlands and cotton fields for its merchant class. In the 19th century, it conquered the Caucasus – the gateway to Persia, Turkey and the Middle East and pushed westward against Europe.

Tsarist Russia also started pushing southward from the frozen north towards China, Persia, India and Afghanistan. Britain viewed this Russian advance into Central Asia as a threat to its position in India which, in the 19th century, it was consolidating as the pivot of its empire in Asia. Fearing that the Russians wanted to advance as far as the warm water ports of India, Britain scrambled to check Tsarist expansion.

At the end of the 19th century, the relentless outward thrust of Russian expansion was blocked chiefly by five containing powers – Germany and Austria – Hungary in Europe, by the Ottoman Empire to the South and by Japan in the Far East. These powers managed to keep Russia a continental rather than a global power.

To prevent Russia from securing an outlet into the Indian Ocean that could outflank British sea-power:

- Britain's Navy was modernised and built up to cope with a combination of any two hostile navies. Bases were established at the Cape of Good Hope in 1806, Mauritius in 1810, Singapore in 1818, Aden in 1839 and Hong Kong in 1841.

- In the 'Great Game' with Russia in Central Asia, Britain converted Afghanistan, Persia, Tibet and Thailand into landward buffers against Russia's expansion to the shores of the Indian Ocean.

---

32. Russian fur traders and Cossacks gradually advanced eastward 2500 miles across the Siberian wilderness and reached the Pacific coast in 1639. In 1741, Russian settlements had been established in Alaska, across the Bering Strait. Until 1867, when the US bought it, Alaska was known as Russian America.

9. Iran

A wealthy Englishman started the search for oil in Iran in 1901. After much expense, his venture struck oil in 1908 in southwest Iran near Abadan and, in 1909 the Anglo-Persian Oil Company (APOC) was formed. APOC then needed capital to build its refinery.

At this point in time, Britain's Navy was debating changing over from coal to oil fuel. In 1911, Winston Churchill, then head of the British Admiralty, used £ 2 million of Government money to buy half of the APOC on behalf of the British Navy. Churchill also decided that new British battleships would be fueled by oil rather than coal. APOC had managed to find a new backer and a good customer. The Iranian oil supplies were to prove valuable to the British in the 1914-1918 World War.

In 1935, APOC was renamed Anglo-Iranian Oil Company (AIOC). AIOC had German engineers and technicians in their refinery. This became a problem when Britain and Germany became enemies in the Second World War (1939-1945). Britain asked that Iran expel German nationals. Iran's refusal to comply and growing pan-Arab support for Germany impelled Britain and the Soviet Union to occupy the southern and northern halves of Iran in 1941. This ensured Allied possession of the Iranian oil fields, forestalled any such German move and opened a southern route for delivering war supplies to Soviet armies in the north. Iran did not take kindly to this 'invasion'. The occupation by foreign powers fomented resentment in the Iranian people.

After the war ended, a dispute erupted in 1946 between Iran and the Soviet Union regarding Iran's northern border with the Soviet state of Azerbaijan. The Soviet Union's immediate proximity to the oilfields of the Persian Gulf worried the US. This led the US Administration to declare its Truman Doctrine[33] of assisting states against Soviet 'Communist' intrusion. After America and the Soviet Union arrived at an understanding that neither side would try to influence developments in Iran and would respect each other's sensitivities, the Soviet Union withdrew from the northern half of Iran. The American and other western oil companies continued with their activities in Iran.

In Iran, nationalist, anti-foreign sentiment continued to simmer. In 1951, the new nationalist government in Iran, led by Mr Mossadeq tried, in vain, to get Anglo-Iranian Oil Company and the other oil companies to agree to the same kind of profit-sharing that major American oil companies had negotiated with the Saudi and Venezuelan governments. Finally, the Iranians lost patience and, following massive demonstrations, nationalised all the oil companies in Iran.

In retaliation, the US embargoed Iran for nationalising its oil industry. The major oil companies, acting together, boycotted Iranian oil, refusing to handle any crude oil produced by the fields under the new regime. Their control over transport and refining was so thorough that Iran's oil exports dropped from $400 million in 1951 to $2 million in 1951 and 1952. The deficit to oil supplies could be made up easily because the Middle Eastern fields were being operated at much less than capacity. Additional pumping by their companies in Kuwait, Saudi Arabia, and Iraq not only made up the difference, but also delighted the three Arab nations concerned, who had no particular liking for the non-Arab Iranians.

Britain challenged the legality of Iran's action at the International Court of Justice. The Court ruled in Iran's favour.

In 1952, Britain planned to oust Prime Minister Mossadeq from power in a secret coup. The Truman Administration was against the idea. In 1953, the Shah of Iran tried to dismiss Mr Mossadeq. He failed and had to flee the country.

The Administration of the newly elected President Eisenhower became apprehensive that Iran's political chaos would inspire the Soviet Union to impose a communist dictatorship. It is believed to have approved a plan drafted by British and CIA intelligence officials for a CIA-assisted 'regime change' to overthrow Mr Mossadeq and institute a western-style government. The Mossadeq government did collapse and the Shah of Iran was restored to the throne. It laid the basis for the belief that the CIA could topple any regime in the world.

Obediently, the Shah agreed to let British and American oil companies take over oil production again. The real or suspected CIA involvement in the Shah's restoration sowed seeds of anti-Americanism that continued to afflict the Shah's regime. Over the next 26 years, Iran became

---

33. The gist of the 1946 Truman Doctrine was that 'the US must support free people who are resisting attempted subjugation by armed minorities or outside powers.' It declared the US commitment to preserve the pro-West orientation of states in the Persian Gulf bordering the Soviet Union. The US secured military facilities in Dhahran (Saudi Arabia) in 1947 and port facilities in Bahrain for US Navy ships in 1949. Today Bahrain is the base for the US Navy's Fifth Fleet.

one of the richest countries in the Persian Gulf accounting for nearly one tenth of the world's oil production.

From 1967 onwards and throughout the 1970s, America encouraged and funded the Shah of Iran's ambitious plans for the expansion of the Iranian armed forces.

The Shah's naval plan envisaged the development of new and modern naval bases at Bandar Abbas (near the Strait of Hormuz) and at Chahbahar (in the Gulf of Oman and the Arabian Sea). In the 1970s, the naval development of Chahbahar was funded by US loans and designed to support not only the warships which the US was supplying to the Iranian Navy, but also the US Navy's ships deployed in the Arabian Sea and the Persian Gulf.

When President Nixon assumed office the Nixon Doctrine was supplemented by its 'Twin Pillars' policy wherein the US sought to promote Saudi-Iranian cooperation in maintaining stability. This policy fitted neatly into the plans of the Shah of Iran to acquire the armed muscle necessary to protect the Iranian oil lifeline running the length of the Persian Gulf. It was strengthened by the Saudi decision to embark on a similar programme to arm itself. The US played the major role in helping Saudi Arabia to procure modern weaponry and training for its armed forces believing that cooperation between Iran and Saudi Arabia would ultimately protect US security interests.

In 1968, Britain announced the phased withdrawal of its remaining military forces from East of Suez. This was immediately followed by the first deployments of Soviet naval ships in the Indian Ocean. When Britain finally withdrew from East of Suez on 30 November 1971, the Shah of Iran announced that Iran would police the waters in and around the Persian Gulf.

During the 1973 Arab-Israel war, the Organisations of Arab Petroleum Exporting Countries clamped a complete embargo on oil exports to the US because it supported

Israel. To exert further pressure on the US, the Organisation instituted a series of cutbacks in oil production that reduced the availability of oil worldwide, created an acute shortage of oil and caused the price of oil to skyrocket. As a result of the quadrupling of oil revenues in 1973, the Shah of Iran embarked on a massive arms build up.

By the mid 1970s, the US realised that a permanent naval presence would be necessary for rapid deployment in the Gulf. It planned to further develop Diego Garcia as a basing facility for a US task force in the Indian Ocean. In 1976, the US Senate opposed this expansion until the President reported to Congress his Administration's efforts to negotiate with the Soviets on de-militarisation and naval arms limitations in the Indian Ocean. The Ford Administration turned down the suggestion on the grounds that negotiations on such matters were not in the US interest while the Soviet Union and its Cuban surrogate were actively engaged in support of revolution in Africa, especially in Angola.

One of the first actions by the Carter Administration in 1977 was to initiate negotiations with the Soviet Union leading toward a demilitarisation of the Indian Ocean. That effort was suspended as a result of Soviet and Cuban intervention in the Horn of Africa.

In 1978, the US increased the flow of arms and advisers to Iran to bolster the Shah's efforts to counter growing domestic dissidence against 'westernisation'. In response to Soviet concern over US attempts to influence developments in Iran, the US stated that whilst they would not interfere in Iran's internal affairs, the US firmly supported the Shah in his efforts to restore tranquility in Iran and would maintain relations with Iran in foreign policy, economics and security. In the end of 1978, a conservative Islamic revolution, inspired by Ayatollah Khomeini, took over and forced the Shah to abdicate.

10. British Indian Ocean Territory

In 1964, Britain announced its decision to withdraw gradually from the Indian Ocean. It became essential to find a location where facilities could be established for berthing naval ships, for refuelling maritime reconnaissance aircraft and for strategic communications where there would not be any local political opposition. Since the Chagos archipelago was strategically situated at the centre of the Indian Ocean and lay out of the path of cyclonic storms, it was found very suitable.

On 8 November 1965, before granting independence to Mauritius, Britain created a new colony called the British Indian Ocean Territory (BIOT), by amalgamating the Aldabra Islands and the Farquhar and Desroches Islands (all purchased from the Seychelles) with the Chagos Archipelago (formerly a dependency of Mauritius).

On 10 December 1965, the British Colonial Secretary announced in the House of Commons the decision to set up a new colony to be known as the British Indian Ocean

Territory to provide defence facilities for the British and US Governments in the Indian Ocean, the nucleus of which was to be the Chagos Archipelago. The other islands concerned were Aldabra, Farquhars and Desroches.[34]

In 1966, America and Britain signed an agreement for the construction on Diego Garcia of a major Anglo American, air and naval, refuelling and support station, along with a communications facility. Most of Diego Garcia's transient population was relocated to Mauritius and the Seychelles. Until the early 1970s, the production of copra from coconut palms was the only economic activity. Thereafter, the last of the plantation workers and their families were moved to Mauritius.

The littoral and island states of the ocean protested strongly against the development of Diego Garcia. They wanted to preserve the 'zone of peace', non-militarised status of the Indian Ocean as embodied in United Nations resolutions, but to no avail. From 1965 to 1976, the administrative headquarters of the BIOT were at Victoria in the Seychelles.

In June 1976, the islands purchased from the Seychelles were returned to the newly independent Republic of Seychelles. After that date, the BIOT comprised only the atolls of the Chagos Archipelago and its administrative offices moved to the Foreign and Commonwealth Office in London.

Although there is no permanent civilian population in the atolls, about 3,500 US and British military and contract civilian personnel were stationed there in the mid-1990s.

---

11. Iraq

In 1958, the Hashemite kingdom of Iraq was displaced by the socialist Ba'athist regime. It soon received Soviet economic and military assistance.

In 1961, Iraq nationalised all the oil concessions in Iraq that were not then being exploited. The US and Britain launched an embargo of Iraq in an attempt to persuade Mr Saddam Hussein to re-privatise oil. Mr Saddam Hussein simply found a new customer – the Soviet Union.

In 1972, Mr Saddam Hussein and his Ba'ath party nationalised the oil holdings of the Iraq Petroleum Company, which actually was owned by a group of western oil companies including Dutch, American and French firms. Prior to nationalisation, Mr Saddam Hussein made a peace offer to the dissident Kurds in Iraq, who were warring against his regime. Reportedly, the Kurds were about to accept his offer, but the Nixon Administration offered them $16 million in weapons as incentive to keep fighting – and they did (with additional help from the Shah of Iran). Eventually, Iraq set up its own national company and nationalised all the oil fields.

By 1980, with Soviet help, Iraq had built up its military strength to become the most powerful state in the Gulf. After its 1979 Revolution, Iran had become the new enemy. The US Administration started improving relations with Iraq – militarily, Iraq was the Gulf's most important state and, after Saudi Arabia, the Gulf's most important oil producing state.

Iraq seized the opportunity of the Revolution in Iran to settle old territorial disputes. It invaded Khuzistan, where Iran's oil fields were located. During this war, the US Administration facilitated arms sales to Iraq not so much to support Mr Saddam Hussein, but out of antipathy toward Iran's Ayatollah Khomeini, who had overthrown the Shah. The Iran-Iraq war lasted from 1980 to 1988. Iran recovered its territory at an enormous cost in lives. When Iraq resorted to chemical warfare, Iran sued for peace.

After Iraq won that devastating war, Mr Saddam Hussein continued to pursue independent economic development rather than letting transnational corporations reap profit from his country's oil resources. He worked to form the Arab Cooperation Council to join Iraq with Jordan, Egypt, and Yemen in a regional trading bloc.

In 1990, Iraq invaded Kuwait to settle several disputes – territorial and financial. It led to the US led Gulf War of 1991 that forced Iraq to withdraw from Kuwait. The Administration of President Bush (Senior) described the Persian Gulf region as a 'nerve centre' of the industrialised and developed Western economies. In the US view, it was 'a stark struggle against Iraq for domination and control of oil resources of the region – these oil resources were not only the life-blood of modern developed countries but also a vital element of military power.'

There was another view. Reportedly, just eight days before Iraq invaded Kuwait, the US ambassador Ms April Glaspie told Mr Saddam Hussein that the US Administration had 'no opinion' regarding Iraq's 'border dispute' with Kuwait. This gave Mr Saddam Hussein the impression that the US would turn a blind eye to his invasion of Kuwait. Reportedly,

---

34. *London Times* of 11 November 1965.

US intelligence learned of Iraq's invasion plans several days in advance, but no deterrence was attempted. In this view, the Gulf War of 1991 was engineered as an excuse to bring down Mr Saddam Hussein. For reasons not yet clear, US forces did not attempt to enter Iraq but ceased operations after Iraqi troops withdrew from Kuwait.

12. The Iran – Iraq War 1980-1988

The cause of Iraq's invasion of Iran on 22 September 1980 was that after deposing the Shah of Iran in 1979, the new Irani Shiite state established by Ayatollah Khomeini was messianic and wished to expand its influence throughout the Islamic world. In doing so, it began to interfere significantly in Iraqi affairs, attempting to influence Iraq's sizeable Shiite faction. (About 55% of Iraq's population was Shiite, 20% was Kurdish and the ruling Sunni secular minority was 25%.).

Iraq penetrated deeply into Khuzistan where the oil fields are located but failed to defeat Iran decisively.

After a year, Iranian forces went on the offensive, regained almost all of their lost territory and approached Basra. Here the offensives stalled and the war became a stationary battle of attrition.

Meanwhile, Iraq began to develop nuclear and chemical warfare capabilities. The nuclear capability was seen as such a danger by the Israelis that they conducted a preemptive air attack in and destroyed Iraq's primary nuclear facility.

Iraq used its chemical warfare capability against Iranian forces in 1984, 1985 and 1986 and on its own rebellious Kurdish population.

These capabilities alarmed the West. The US developed a policy that was intended to halt both the Iran-Iraq War and the development of the Iraqi chemical and nuclear warfare capabilities.

In January 1983, the US established a new unified Central Command, (CENTCOM), and assigned it the responsibility for a huge geographic area, including the Persian Gulf. The forces assigned to the Rapid Deployment Force were increased. As a result, CENTCOM had seven Air Force tactical fighter wings, two strategic bomber squadrons, five Army divisions, a Marine Corps Expeditionary Force, three carrier battle groups, a surface action group, and five maritime air patrol squadrons. US military positions throughout the Middle East were expanded to handle the deployment of large numbers of US troops, an airfield was built in southeastern Egypt, and supplies were pre-positioned in Oman and Diego Garcia.

13. The Iraqi Invasion of Kuwait 1990

The reasons for the Iraqi invasion of Kuwait go back to the creation of the present day Kuwait. In 1899, Britain and Kuwait signed a treaty in which Britain assumed control of Kuwait's foreign affairs. This was done to thwart German imperialist designs in the region, and after WW I began, Britain established a protectorate over Kuwait.

WW I led to the collapse of the Ottoman Empire and the creation by the European powers of Iraq and a number of other countries. The finding of oil, and later in the 1970s its greatly enhanced value, aggravated an already troubled tribal situation.

Kuwait was an artificial creation imposed by the West, and it both denied Iraq a considerable amount of oil and restricted its access to the sea. This arrangement was never accepted, and when Kuwait received its independence on 19 June 1961, Iraq almost immediately claimed it, basing this on the facts that Kuwait had been part of the Ottoman Empire, that it was an artificial British creation, and that it threatened Iraq's access to the sea.

Threatened by invasion, Kuwait appealed to Britain, whose military reaction was enough to thwart Iraq. Kuwait was admitted to the United Nations and the Arab League, but Iraq did not renounce its claim, would often resurrect it, and would cite it to justify the August 1990 invasion.

There were four reasons for Iraq's decision to invade Kuwait in August 1990:

- Iraq could not repay the $65 billion that it had borrowed from Kuwait and Saudi Arabia to finance the Iran-Iraq War. It could argue that this war was in Kuwaiti and Saudi interests since the enemy was Irani messianic Shiite fundamentalism, which potentially threatened both of them. Kuwait's decision to not forgive Iraq's debt provided economic and emotional justification for the Iraqi invasion.

- Second, the Kuwaitis were rich and had huge investments abroad. Access to this wealth would resolve Iraq's financial problems.

- The third reason was alleged Kuwaiti oil drilling in the Rumaila oil field, which lay in disputed border territory.

- The fourth reason was Kuwaiti overproduction of oil. Gulf revenues were depressed as a result of an oil glut on the spot market in the late 1980s. In July 1990, Iraq threatened to use force as retribution for Kuwaiti overproduction and under-pricing, claiming that Kuwait and the UAE had cost Iraq $14 billion in oil revenue. When Iraq suggested face-to-face peace talks, Kuwait preferred Arab League mediation.

On 2 August 1990, Iraq invaded Kuwait and by 4th August, Iraqi forces were amassed along the Kuwaiti-Saudi border for a possible invasion of Saudi Arabia. If Iraq occupied Saudi Arabia, it would not only establish itself as the secular leader of the Arab world, but also would control 45% of the world's oil. Moreover, if Iraq invaded Saudi Arabia, then an invasion of the UAE would soon follow. If these moves were successful, then Iraq would have a major influence on the world's oil supplies.

Immediately after the invasion, the US froze Iraqi assets in the United States. The first United Nations resolution demanded that Iraq withdraw from Kuwait. The second resolution imposed an oil embargo. Russia agreed to honour the sanctions. Twelve European states also froze Iraqi and Kuwaiti assets and embargoed Iraqi oil.

The embargo was not immediately effective. Sanctions and blockades have poor records of success, and as the embargoes effects were assessed in the ensuing months, it was concluded that if it were to succeed (and this was a question in itself), then it would take a long time, certainly at least a year, to force Iraq to withdraw.

The US and Britain believed that war was necessary, because if Iraq withdrew, then they would have to commit to a costly long-term peace-keeping force, and Iraq would be free to continue its nuclear, chemical and biological warfare programmes.

By November, it was obvious that sanctions were not enough to force a withdrawal from Kuwait. The US and Britain began actively advocating the use of force. France, China and Russia all opposed this, but US and British efforts culminated in a UN resolution which approved the use of force to expel Iraq if it did not leave Kuwait by 15 January 1991.

Meanwhile, Iraq attempted reconciliation with Iran to break the blockade. It offered to return virtually all the territory taken during the Iran-Iraq war – this included 164 square miles in the Elam region and the strategic Shatt-el-Arab waterway.

Iran was not persuaded for several reasons, including the costly Iran-Iraq War, the traditional enmity toward Iraq and the economic need to improve relations with the West. However, Iran did remain neutral in the 1991 War and provided humanitarian assistance.

Iraq had been an important client of Russia, one that offered a balance to Iranian theocracy. However, the implosion of the Soviet Union that followed the policies of *perestroika* (restructuring the economy) and *glasnost* (transparency in policy), constrained Russian foreign policy. Russia's immediate and urgent priorities were to preserve the integrity of as much of the USSR as possible; to transform the economy; to gain technological help from the West; and to recast its armed military into one that offered strategic defence and strong regional capability. Russian policy during the war was to try and persuade Iraq to withdraw from Kuwait while providing limited military assistance.

The air war started on 17 January 1991. By February, total air superiority had been achieved and severe damage inflicted on Iraqi forces in and around Kuwait. The land campaign started on 24th February and in a few weeks Kuwait had been recaptured and Iraqi troops pushed back into Iraq.

Select Bibliography

Title	By	Publisher
GENERAL		
Wings of Fire – An Autobiography	A P J Abdul Kalam	Universities Press, Hyderabad 1999
Defending India	Jaswant Singh	Macmillan India, 1999
Nuclear Weapons & Indian Security – The Realist Foundations of Strategy	Bharat Karnad	Macmillan 2000
Prepare or Perish – A Study of National Security	Gen KV Krishna Rao	Lancer 1991
Weapons of Peace – The Secret Story of India's Quest to be a Nuclear Power	Raj Chengappa	Harper Collins 2000
My Life	Grand Admiral Erich Raeder German Navy	US Naval Institute Annapolis USA 1960
U Boats - History, Development and Equipment 1914 - 1945	David Miller	Conway Maritime Press 2000
Admiral S M Nanda – The Man Who Bombed Karachi – A Memoir	Admiral S M Nanda	Harper Collins & India Today Group, New Delhi 2004
Betrayal of the Defence Forces – The Inside Truth	Admiral Vishnu Bhagwat	Manas Publications New Delhi 2001
The Magnificent Viraat – Decade and Half of Glorious Flying	Commemorative Publication	
IPKF-OPERATION PAWAN		
Assignment Colombo	J N Dixit	Konark Publishers
The IPKF in Sri Lanka	Lt Gen Depinder Singh	Trishul Publications, Noida
The Sri Lankan Crisis	Maj Gen Afsar Karim Major Shankar Bhaduri	Lancer International, New Delhi
CHECKS AND BALANCES		
My Presidential Years	R Venkataraman	Indus-Harper Collins India 1994
A Cabinet Secretary Looks Around	B G Deshmukh	Bharatiya Vidya Bhavan Mumbai 1998
A Cabinet Secretary Thinks Aloud	B G Deshmukh	Bharatiya Vidya Bhavan Mumbai
HDW SSK SUBMARINES		
The Dynasty-A Political Biography of the Premier Ruling Family of Modern India	S S Gill	Harper Collins India New Delhi 1996

The Lonely Prophet-V P Singh A Political Biography	Seema Mustafa	New Age International New Delhi 1995
Bofors – The Story Behind the News	Chitra Subramaniam	Viking, Penguin India 1993
Memoirs and Memories	Vice Admiral Daya Shankar	The Shankar Family A-1/23 Safdarjang Enclave New Delhi 2003

BRASSTACKS

The War That Never Was	Ravi Rikhye	Chanakya Publications 1988
Brasstacks and Beyond – Perception and Management of Crisis in South Asia	Kanti P Bajpai P R Chari Pervaiz Iqbal Cheema Stephen P Cohen Sumit Gangulyu	Manohar, New Delhi 1995

EXTERNAL NAVAL PRESENCE IN THE INDIAN OCEAN

Asia and Western Dominance	K M Pannikar	George Allen & Unwin London 1953
The Portuguese Empire in Asia, 1500-1700: A Political and Economic History	Sanjay Subrahmanyam	Longman Group UK 1993
The Portuguese in India 1498-1598	Denison Ross	Cambridge History of India Volume V
Jahangirnama Memoirs of Jahangir, Emperor of India	Wheeler M Thackston	Oxford University Press 1999
Indonesian Trade and Society	Jacob Van Leur	The Hague 1955
The Dutch East India Company Expansion and Decline of the VOC	Femme S Gaastra	Walburg Pers, Zutphen 2003
The Rise of Merchant Empires – Long Distance Trade in the Early World 1300 to 1570	James D Tracy (editor)	
Merchants of Maritime India 1500-1800	Ashin Das Gupta	Varorium Series 1994
The Origins of a Dispute – Kashmir 1947	Prem Shankar Jha	Oxford University Press New Delhi 2003
War and Diplomacy in Kashmir 1947-48	C Dasgupta	Sage Publications, 2002
The Transfer of Power 1942 to 1947		Her Majesty's Stationery Office 1980
White Ensign – The British Navy at War 1939-1945	Capt S W Roskill, RN	US Naval Institute, Annapolis, USA
The Royal Australian Navy	Commodore J Goldrick And Others– Edited by David Stevens	Oxford University Press Australia 2001
Estranged Democracies – India and the United States 1941-1994	Dennis Kux	

Index

GREENLAND

NORTH
AMERICA

BRITAIN
Le

La Corunna
SPAIN   To
Lisbon
Azores Is   Gibraltar
(Panta Delgada)
Tangier   Algiers B
Casablanca   ALGER

Canary Is
Las Palmas

USA   New York

Norfolk

ATLANTIC

Havana
CUBA   OCEAN
Jamaica

Dakar

Conakry   GHANA
Accra   La

Georgetown
GUYANA

PACIFIC

OCEAN

Point N
M

BRAZIL
Recife

SOUTH
AMERICA

Cape

ANTARC